A LATTER-DAY SAINT

COMMENTARY

ON THE

OLD TESTAMENT

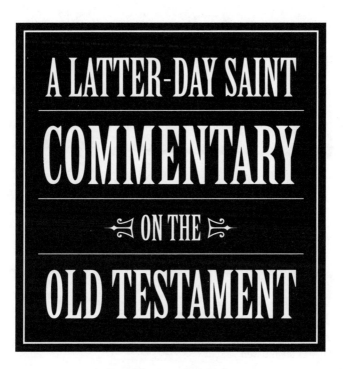

A LATTER-DAY SAINT

COMMENTARY

⊱ ON THE ⊰

OLD TESTAMENT

ELLIS T. RASMUSSEN

DESERET BOOK COMPANY
SALT LAKE CITY, UTAH

Library of Congress Cataloging-in-Publication Data

Rasmussen, Ellis T., 1915–
    Old Testament commentary / Ellis T. Rasmussen.
       p. cm.
    Includes index.
    ISBN 0-87579-712-1
    1. Bible. O.T.—Commentaries. I. Title.
    BX1151.2.R375 1993
    221.7—dc20   93-47675
                                                        CIP

Printed in the United States of America

10 9 8 7 6 5 4 3 2

CONTENTS

PREFACE

It is true, as the Preacher recorded in Ecclesiastes 12:12, that "of making many books there is no end." That has been true especially of books about the Bible.

So why do I produce yet another?

This one is intended to offer such help to readers of the Old Testament as that for which a certain Ethiopian visitor to Judea expressed a need (Acts 8:30–31). Philip found him in his chariot, reading from the scroll of Isaiah as he drove homeward from Jerusalem. Philip asked, "Understandest thou what thou readest"? The Ethiopian replied, "How can I, except some man should guide me?"

This book is an Old Testament reader's guide. The intent is to help beginners understand more as they read for the first time and to help more mature students discover here and there some added meaning, some deeper implication, or some broader application. This volume complements the footnotes, Bible Dictionary, Topical Guide, and other study aids in the edition of the King James Version of the Bible published by The Church of Jesus Christ of Latter-day Saints. More sophisticated aids are available in Bible dictionaries and in multivolume commentaries and exegeses; this interpretive guide is intended particularly for LDS readers of the Old Testament.

The individuals and the peoples of the Old Testament experienced hopes and fears, aspirations and disappointments, achievements and failings in all of which we can find examples of good or evil, to be emulated or avoided. Indeed, as we see Old Testament accounts of our spiritual forebears and sense their faith, reverence, hope and joy—or feel their doubt, infidelity, despair, and misery—we may find ways to avoid pitfalls ourselves, reach our ideals, and attain more joy. But it must here be declared that the most important aid to understanding the Old Testament, or any other book of scripture, is the inspiration from the Holy Spirit, which is promised to us in those scriptures (see 1 Cor. 2:10–12; 2 Ne. 25:1–4; Moro. 10:4–5; TG, "Discernment, Spiritual"; "Scriptures, Study of ").

May all of these resources be combined to enhance your enjoyment of the Old Testament and make it rewarding; and may your "weariness of the flesh" (Eccl. 12:12) in studying be minimal.

ACKNOWLEDGMENTS

This book has its roots in many origins and is the result of many forces that have influenced, instructed, and inspired me. The greatest of them are the scriptures, the gospel, the Church, and the guidance of the Holy Spirit.

Among the people who must be acknowledged for their help is the late Sidney B. Sperry, whose influence on me began in 1941. His passion for and devotion to scriptural studies drew me into the languages and literature of the Old Testament. His instruction and encouragement helped me as a student, and he gave me the opportunity to become a teacher in the field. It was he who pointed out a pearl of great price contained in the book of Abraham, which has been the keystone of all my Old Testament teaching (Abr. 1:18–19; 2:6–11).

Other leaders and colleagues at Brigham Young University and the Church Educational System have given encouragement through the years to my study and teaching of the Old Testament. They are many, including B. West Belnap, Daniel H. Ludlow, Robert J. Matthews, Truman and Anne Madsen, David B. Galbraith, and D. Kelly Ogden. Kelly still uses some of my syllabi materials, improved and embellished by him, in teaching BYU home-study students.

I appreciate BYU Press for first suggesting that I produce a commentary on the Old Testament and then, in 1982, for giving me the copyright release to do so.

My wife has always given me devotion and support and, in our retirement years, a little prodding to "get the book to press." My family have also given their support, interest, and encouragement.

I am indebted to leaders past and present at Deseret Book, including William James Mortimer and Eleanor Knowles, especially in our work on other projects since 1973. They and others unmentioned have made the present project possible. Suzanne Brady's keen insight, careful attention to detail, and patient persistence in editing have been vital. She has clarified abstruse sentences, sensed inconsistencies, corrected errors, and polished the final product. And the help of others at Deseret Book, including Richard Peterson and Emily Watts, is also much appreciated.

But in the end, as in the beginning and throughout all my work, the Spirit of the Lord has helped the most. For that I am grateful.

INTRODUCTION

WHY STUDY THE OLD TESTAMENT?

We study the Old Testament from time to time as individuals and as families, in Sunday School and elsewhere. Why do we do it? Why *should* we do it? Some Christian peoples make the amazing assumption that because Jesus our Savior "fulfilled the law" he abrogated the Old Testament—the Law, the Prophets, and the Writings. We know, of course, that he fulfilled the law of sacrifice; the supreme redemptive offering *by* the Father and *of* the Son did indeed fulfill and end the law of sacrifice by the shedding of blood.

But other laws, practices, and principles in the Old Testament endure. Jesus reiterated moral and spiritual *laws* taught by Moses and the other prophets—elucidating, defining, and applying them and urging our obedience to them. Many *prophecies* recorded in the Old Testament are now being fulfilled or shall yet be fulfilled. And certainly the poetic *writings* and wisdom literature of the Old Testament are full of good moral, spiritual, and theological truths, as valid today as they were in the past. We might well consider several uses of Old Testament scripture by Jesus and his apostles and also by Book of Mormon peoples, a few examples of verses in the Old Testament that are inspiring and vital to modern readers, and some other reasons why the Old Testament is still valuable to us today.

OLD TESTAMENT SCRIPTURE IN OTHER BOOKS OF SCRIPTURE

Luke recorded a parable by Jesus about a certain rich man and a poor beggar named Lazarus, both of whom were in the spirit world of the dead after departing from this life. Having asked several times for relief, the former rich man supplicated "father Abraham" that Lazarus be sent back to earth to warn five brethren about what they must do to avoid being sent also to the place of torment.

In response, Jesus taught a parable in which Abraham says, "They have Moses and the prophets; let them hear them." The erstwhile rich man argues, "Nay, father Abraham: but if one went unto them from the dead, they will repent." Abraham replies, "If they hear not Moses and the prophets, neither will they be persuaded, though one rose from the dead" (Luke 16:29–31). Jesus taught by means of this parable that people should hearken to the teachings of Moses and the other prophets: "Search the scriptures; for in them ye think ye have eternal life: and they are they which testify of me" (John 5:39). The scriptures, of course, were those that came through Moses and other prophets. We still may learn from them some of the ways to qualify for eternal life, especially from the multitude of scriptures that testify of Christ.

Jesus, after his resurrection, talked with two disciples on the road to Emmaus about prophecies written by "Moses and all the prophets" in the scriptures "concerning himself." Soon thereafter he reviewed for the apostles in the upper room details "written in the law of Moses, and in the prophets, and in the psalms" about himself (Luke 24:27, 44). Those Old Testament scriptures can still help us appreciate Jesus the Redeemer.

When Paul and Silas taught the gospel in the synagogue of the Jews at Berea, "they received the word with all readiness of mind, and searched the scriptures daily, whether those things were so. Therefore many of them believed" (Acts 17:11–12). The scriptures available to be searched in the synagogue were those of the Tanach, our Old Testament. We also can use them in our study and teaching to enhance the testimony that "those things were so."

In Acts, we read about a Jewish missionary named Apollos who, "knowing only the baptism of John," taught the people with enthusiasm but imperfectly. Aquila and Priscilla "took him unto them, and expounded unto him the way of God more perfectly." Thus instructed, Apollos "mightily convinced the Jews, and that publickly, shewing by the scriptures that Jesus was Christ" (Acts 18:24–28). The scriptures those early Christian missionaries used to teach people more perfectly and convince them mightily are still there for our missionaries to use for the same purposes (TG lists more than fifty topics with scriptures about Jesus Christ).

Paul wrote to the Christians in Rome that "whatsoever things were written aforetime were written for our learning, that we through patience and comfort of the scriptures might have hope" (Rom. 15:4). May we not also learn to exercise patience, receive comfort, and increase our hope through those and other such "things written aforetime" in the Old Testament?

Paul wrote to the young Timothy, "From a child thou hast known the holy scriptures, which are able to make thee wise unto salvation through faith which is in Christ Jesus" (2 Tim. 3:15). At the time Paul was writing, the New Testament books had not all been collected or even written, so the scriptures to which he referred were those of the Old Testament; they are still good for us who would like to be more wise in enjoying salvation through Jesus Christ. Paul gave Timothy a very meaningful evaluation of those Old Testament scriptures: "All scripture is given by inspiration of God, and is profitable for doctrine, for reproof, for correction, for instruction in righteousness: that the man of God may be perfect, throughly furnished unto all good works" (2 Tim. 3:16–17). That is still true of the Old Testament as well as of our other scriptures.

In the Book of Mormon, young Nephi exhorted his brothers by rehearsing unto them the words of Isaiah, by which his rebellious brothers "were pacified and did humble themselves before the Lord" (1 Ne. 15:20). Nephi taught his brothers about the "covenant which should be fulfilled in the latter days; which covenant the Lord had made to our father Abraham" and of "the restoration of the Jews, or of the house of Israel" (1 Ne. 15:18, 20).

Then he taught them the meaning of father Lehi's dream. The rod of iron "was the word of God; and whoso would hearken unto the word of God, and would hold fast unto it, they would never perish; neither could the temptations and the fiery darts of the adversary overpower them unto blindness, to lead them away to destruction" (v. 24). There are still good portions of the word of God and his commandments in the Old Testament for us to hold onto as a rod of iron that we too may be humbled, pacified, guided, and safeguarded thereby.

After Lehi's death Nephi wrote about the prophecies and blessings of his father: "I write the things of my soul, and many of the scriptures which are engraven upon the plates of brass. For my soul delighteth in the scriptures, and my heart pondereth them, and writeth them for the learning and the profit of my children" (2 Ne. 4:15). It was while he pondered these things that he wrote his own beautiful psalm of supplication and praise. Who knows what such scriptures might engender also in you or me?

King Benjamin taught his sons to read the language of their fathers, that they might "become men of understanding" and "know concerning the prophecies . . . delivered them by the hand of the Lord . . . on the plates of brass," that they might emulate Lehi who had been "taught in the language of the Egyptians; therefore he could read these engravings, and teach them to his children." Without knowing God's commandments and "his mysteries," the king said, the Nephites "would have dwindled in unbelief." With them available on the brass plates, his people could learn to "keep the commandments of God" and then "prosper in the land" (Mosiah 1:1–7). We have in the Old Testament now many of the teachings the people of Lehi had on those plates of brass.

SOME OLD TESTAMENT SCRIPTURES INSPIRING FOR OUR TIMES

Deuteronomy 8:3. Quoting from the Law to refute a temptation of the devil, Jesus said: "It is written, Man shall not live by bread alone, but by every word that proceedeth out of the mouth of God" (Matt. 4:4). Those words from a book of the Law may likewise admonish us, and there are many, many others like unto them throughout our scriptures.

Psalm 19:7–11. "The law of the Lord is perfect, converting the soul." This passage impressively affirms that the law of the Lord, with his testimonies, statutes, and commandments, can convert the soul, make wise the simple, cause the heart to rejoice, and enlighten the eyes; thus the scripture will engender reverence which is cleansing, and judgments which are true and righteous altogether. By them one is warned, and in keeping them there is great reward.

Isaiah 8:20. "To the law and to the testimony; if they speak not according to this word, it is because there is no light in them." This was Isaiah's advice to those who went to wizards and fortune tellers for enlightenment or guidance. It is still good advice, and "the law and the testimony" to which he referred are still there in the Old Testament.

Hosea 4:1–6. "Because there is no truth, nor mercy, nor knowledge of God in the land," said Hosea, his people were in controversy with the Lord; and they were in danger of destruction through their swearing, lying, killing, stealing, adultery, and violence. Why was Israel in such a state of deterioration? The prophet revealed the basic reason: "My people are destroyed for lack of knowledge; because thou hast rejected knowledge, I will also reject thee. . . . seeing thou hast forgotten the law of thy God, I will also forget thy children." Can such things happen to the Lord's people today, if they allow such behavior? Surely.

Micah 6:8. "He hath shewed thee, O man, what is good; and what doth the Lord require of thee, but to do justly, and to love mercy, and to walk humbly with thy God?" The justice, mercy, and humility recommended by Micah can still bring us peace, joy, and the blessings of the Lord.

Malachi 3:16–18; 4:1–2: "A book of remembrance was written before him for them that feared the Lord, and that thought upon his name. And they shall be mine, saith the Lord of hosts, in that day when I make up my jewels." Read the promises of the scriptures to those who revere the Lord and think upon his name through studying the scriptures and being obedient. Note the warnings, too. Both promises and warnings are good guides for us here and hereafter.

OTHER REASONS WHY THE OLD TESTAMENT SCRIPTURES ARE VALUABLE TO US

Scriptures began to be written, because "it was given unto as many as called upon God to write by the spirit of inspiration" in the days of Adam. "A book of remembrance was kept . . . in the language of Adam, . . . having a language which was pure and undefiled" (Moses 6:5–6). A book of remembrance was God's way of perpetuating divine culture. All such divinely inspired scriptures are authentic; therefore "we believe the Bible to be the word of God as far as it is translated correctly" (A of F 8).

Abraham contributed to ancient collections of scripture, for he could "delineate the chronology running back . . . to the beginning of the creation" (Abr. 1:28) because, said he, the "records of the fathers, even the patriarchs . . . the Lord my God preserved in mine own hands" (Abr. 1:31). So, even though Moses was the writer of the first book in our Bible, "The First Book of Moses Called Genesis" (as it is titled on the first page of Genesis), there were antecedents for his writings, which the Lord made known to Moses, and they are authentic.

The Lord revealed to Moses epochal facts "concerning this earth, and the inhabitants thereof, and also the heavens." He also explained the purpose of it all: "to bring to pass the immortality and eternal life of man." Even before he began to tell Moses of the beginnings of Creation, he commanded Moses to "write the words" he would speak (Moses 1:36, 39; 2:1). Those revelations are still available and valuable to us.

As his mission proceeded, "Moses wrote all the words of the Lord. . . . And he took the book of the covenant, and read in the audience of the people" (Ex. 24:4, 7; see also Deut. 31:9). Scholars of the scriptures in the literary posture called "higher criticism" proclaim that Moses did not write the books of Moses and that indeed they were not written until sometime near the Babylonian captivity (just before 600 B.C.). We believe the revealed book of

Moses of our dispensation, which supports internal evidences in the five biblical books that Moses not only wrote the revelations but also taught the children of Israel by reading those revelations to them (cf. TG, "Scriptures, Writing of").

Joshua wrote a copy of some of the law of Moses on stone and also "wrote . . . words in the book of the law of God." Thus Joshua, according to internal evidences in the Old Testament, continued writing in the "book of the law of God" after the time of Moses (Josh. 8:32; 24:22–27). Such internal evidences of authorship and authenticity are not lightly to be dismissed.

"Samuel told the people the manner of the kingdom, and wrote it in a book, and laid it up before the Lord" (1 Sam. 10:25). The established manner of writing and preserving scriptures as sacred treasures continued in the days of the prophet Samuel. He could not have been the author of both of the books called the "books of Samuel," because his death is recorded before the end of the first book (1 Sam. 25:1), but there are evidences that he and other such prophets and seers contributed to our Old Testament (1 Chr. 29:29).

"Now the rest of the acts of Uzziah, first and last, did Isaiah the prophet, the son of Amoz, write." Thus Isaiah served as a "church historian" as well as prophet in his times (2 Chr. 26:22). In Isaiah's book is written that which the Lord commanded him, "Take thee a great roll, and write in it" (Isa. 8:1). Later he recorded the Lord's command to write a prophecy "in a table, and note it in a book, that it may be for the time to come for ever and ever" (Isa. 30:8). Like Moses, he was divinely commissioned, and the literature of his book shows that he was a master writer.

The Book of Mormon quotes passages from throughout the book of Isaiah (see Book of Mormon index, "Isaiah"). Jesus himself quoted and commended Isaiah's writings (3 Ne. 22; 23:1).

"Baruch wrote from the mouth of Jeremiah all the words of the Lord, which he had spoken unto him, upon a roll of a book" (Jer. 36:4). Thus that prophet's teachings were recorded. Then Jeremiah's secretary went, as the prophet had commanded him, to read all those words "in the ears of the people in the Lord's house upon the fasting day . . . in the ears of all Judah that come out of their cities," because, said Jeremiah, "It may be they will present their supplication before the Lord, and will return every one from his evil way, for great is the anger and the fury that the Lord hath pronounced against this people" (Jer. 36:5–7). Similar indications of authorship and intent can be found in other books of the prophets in the Old Testament.

The apostle Peter testified, "Prophecy came not in old time by the will of man: but holy men of God spake as they were moved by the Holy Ghost" (2 Pet. 1:21). He thus commended the prophetic writings of the Old Testament.

Recall again that Jesus said through father Abraham in a parable, "They have Moses and the prophets; let them hear them" (Luke 16:29). We may well follow his admonition.

GENESIS

Moses was given revelations from God regarding the world, the patriarchs, and the peoples before him. Some time after his call at the "burning bush" (Moses 1:17; Ex. 3:4), Moses was given visions of the earth, its many lands and inhabitants, and its past and future (Moses 1:25–29). The visions prompted Moses to ask, "Tell me, I pray thee, why these things are so, and by what thou madest them?" (Moses 1:30). The Lord replied that although He would not show Moses all of His purposes and processes in creating "worlds without number," He would give him "an account of this earth, and the inhabitants thereof" and commanded Moses to write and preserve the information (Moses 1:33, 35, 40; 2:1).

Through these revelations, Moses was being prepared by the Lord to leave his refuge in Sinai and return to Egypt to lead the children of Israel out of bondage to the land promised long before. The Israelites were then to be prepared to serve the Lord as their forefather Abraham and his seed had been called of God to do (Gen. 12:1–3; Abr. 2:6–11).

The information given to Moses reveals the Lord's purposes in creating this earth, and in placing his children upon it (Moses 1:39; 2:26; 3:16–18, 23–24; 4:1–31). That and later information helped Moses understand the Lord's intent in calling Abraham's seed to their mission. Those revelations must have clarified the purposes of Moses' own mission.

Family histories were then given, listing Israel's ancestors from

1

Adam and Eve on through the antediluvian patriarchs and their wives and children. All of this information helped Moses know why the Israelites needed to be rescued from bondage and death in Egypt and be established in the land of promise. It also helped him (and it helps us) understand why the Lord would conduct that rescue operation in which the Egyptians and the Canaanites suffered and Israel was saved.

All who read these accounts can learn from those and later revelations. They reveal how earth life can best be used, how and why earth's early leaders were taught and called to teach God's ways, why the earth was cleansed in the time of Noah, what Abraham and his extended families were assigned to do to make the blessings of salvation available to all the families of all nations, how the Abrahamic family of Israel got into Egypt, and why the Israelites needed to be freed and established in the land promised to Abraham's seed. All of this information can help those who inherit or accept a part of Abraham's mission.

COMMENTARY

1:1 In the beginning God created the heaven and the earth

Of course the announcement "In the beginning" refers only to God's organizing, or creating, "this heaven, and this earth" (Moses 2:1; 1:35) and not to the beginning of God or his beginning to work with the elements of the universe, because both he and they are eternal (Abr. 3:22–25; D&C 20:17; 93:33). Many related scriptures may be considered on this matter (TG, "Creation"; "Earth, Purpose of"; "God, Creator"; "God, Works of"; "Jesus Christ, Creator"; "Spirit Creation").

The English word *God* is the usual biblical translation for the Hebrew title *Elohim*, which is a plural noun from the Semitic root word *el*, connoting "might," "power." In this plural form, *elohim* can bear the concept of "almighty," "all-powerful." It usually refers to God the Father, who was in charge of the creative processes and working through his Firstborn Son (as other revelations affirm; John 1:1–3, 14 and fn.).

Created is used to translate the Hebrew word *bara*, which

2

means "formed" or "organized" (Gen. 1:1*c;* Abr. 4:1); it allows the concept that this earth was organized and formed out of existing, eternal elements (D&C 93:33).

1:2 And the earth was without form, and void; and darkness was upon the face of the deep

After being organized and formed, the earth obviously would not still be "without form, and void"; the Hebrew words here could better be translated by the phrase "empty and desolate" (cf. Abr. 4:2).

"Darkness" prevailed upon the primeval material until the creative force, called "the light of Christ" (D&C 88:7), focused upon it. Each periodic return of this organizing "light" to the project is called a "day" in the Creation epoch.

The "deep" was doubtless the surface of the primeval ocean covering the earth; note the parallel phrase "face of the waters" at the end of the verse.

1:2 the Spirit of God moved upon the face of the waters

Moved here translates the Hebrew *merakhephet,* which connotes what a bird does in incubating and guarding her eggs and young (cf. Deut. 32:11). It symbolizes the light of Christ influencing, or moving upon, the elements in the creative process, as mentioned in the comment on "darkness" above. Some translations use *fluttered, brooded,* or *hovered* rather than *moved,* and in those words the action of the bird over the nest is thus retained.

1:3 And God said, Let there be light: and there was light

The Hebrew verb here translated *said* bears also the sense of "proclaimed" or "commanded." A single short word in Hebrew, translated by the English phrase "let there be," expresses God's will that the divine emanation of "light" be brought to bear directly upon the formative earth. The light bathing the incipient planet was probably not that of the sun but rather the activating power called the Light of Christ. See the commentary on Genesis 1:2 about the creative power beginning to act upon the primeval "deep" and the commentary on Genesis 1:14–19 about the transmission of the physical light rays of the sun, moon, and stars through space and atmosphere to the earth.

1:4 . . . it was good

In both Hebrew and English, words meaning "good" are used to describe that which functions properly, constructively, harmoniously; in contrast, words meaning "bad" or "evil" connote that which functions improperly, destructively, disharmoniously, or disruptively. "Good" is repeated in verses 10, 12, 18, 21, and 25, evaluating each phase of the Creation; then, in verse 31, "very good" describes the whole Creation.

1:4–5 and God divided the light from the darkness. And God called the light Day, and the darkness he called Night

Although the period of active light was called by God's word for "day" and the absence of it was called "night," there is no reason to assume that this "day" and "night" were measurements of periods of the same length as ours. Our days and nights are measured for us by our planet's revolutions in the sunlight; other periods are indicated for other of God's realms (Ps. 90:4; 2 Pet. 3:8; Abr. 5:13; Fac. 2, fig. 1–5). Indeed, even after they had placed Adam in the Garden, "the Gods had not appointed unto Adam his reckoning" (Abr. 5:13, 11–12).

1:6–7 And God said, Let there be a firmament. . . . And God made the firmament, and divided the waters which were under the firmament from the waters which were above the firmament

Firmament is used here to translate *raqiya'*, which means "expanse" (Gen. 1:6a; Abr. 4:6). This expanse is all or any part of space. From the surface of the earth outward, this expanse includes the atmosphere in which the birds fly and in which the clouds float as "waters . . . above" the earth, as well as all the space of the astral universe beyond (Gen. 1:7, 14–18, 20).

Evidently the Septuagint translation of *raqiya'* as *stereoma* (Gr., "that which has been made firm or solid") became the rationale for translating the Hebrew with the Latin-English word *firmament*. It implied that the sky was a "firm," or solid, dome. That is one of the items we believe only "as far as it is translated correctly" (A of F 8).

Our atmosphere includes water vapor and clouds floating a short space above the earth; but on parts of the surface of the earth is the fluid water of the oceans, rivers, lakes, and seas. Thus the atmosphere permits a division of waters "above" (in the air) from waters "below" (on the surface).

The marvelous evaporation-condensation cycle of water brings dew and rain to the land, making life possible on what would otherwise be a desolate planet.

1:8 God called the firmament Heaven

Several languages, including English, German, Hebrew, and Greek, use one word to designate either the vaulted "sky" or the "abode of the Gods." Only the context indicates which concept is intended. Here the firmament, or the expanse called "heaven," is evidently the "sky."

1:9–10 Let the waters . . . be gathered . . . , and let the dry land appear

The first creative actions of the third day perhaps entailed a wrinkling of the earth's solid crust to let some matter appear above the waters and become dry land. Evidence is given later (Gen. 10:25*a–b*) that for a time there was only one land mass. Other revelations indicate that this dry land was prepared by the Creators during the third day to support living things, which had been "spiritually" created before they were "naturally upon the face of the earth." They were "formed" later (Abr. 4:11–12; 5:4–5; cf. Moses 3:4–7).

1:11–13 Let the earth bring forth grass, . . . the herb . . . , and the fruit tree

A second project on the third day was the creation of varieties of plant life, each with power to reproduce itself according to its species or kind. The corresponding verses in Abraham's account (Abr. 4:11–13) state that the Creators "organized the earth" in this creative period, or prepared it, to bring forth grass, herbs, and trees from their seeds, but the establishment of plant life in the earth came later.

1:14–19 And God said, Let there be lights in the firmament . . . And God set them . . . to give light

On the fourth day of the Creation, "the Gods organized the lights in the expanse of the heaven" (Abr. 4:14), evidently placing the earth in an orbital relationship with our sun to allow transmission of a proper portion of sunlight through space and the atmosphere to the earth's surface so that life might flourish here. The earth's rotation upon its axis would provide the alternating periods of light and darkness we call days and nights. Starlight and moonlight would brighten the night, and the moon in its own orbit around the earth would mark seasonal sequences. The earth's orbital journey about the sun, with its axis at an optimum angle to its orbital plane, would provide annual growing seasons and promote the movement of essential moisture-laden air. Although in translation it appears that the sun, moon, and stars were created and "set" in the heavens *after* the earth was created, the Hebrew can be understood otherwise. *Set* here translates the Hebrew *natan*, but its basic meaning is "gave" or "provided." *Natan* is translated in the Bible hundreds of times with that meaning. Thus the sun, moon, and stars were "provided" as light sources for this earth; the stars and sun could have been associated with the "worlds without number" created earlier by God through his Son. Many worlds had been created, many had "passed away," and many "now stand" (Moses 1:33, 35; 7:30; D&C 76:24).

1:20–23 And God said, Let the waters bring forth . . . the moving creature . . . and fowl

The fifth creative period brought forth the living creatures of the waters and the fowls of the air that fly in "the open firmament of heaven." The waters were caused to "swarm with . . . living creatures," fowls, and "great sea-monsters" (Gen. 1:20*b*, 21*a*).

1:24–25 And God said, Let the earth bring forth . . . cattle, and creeping thing, and beast of the earth

In the sixth creative period came the *cattle,* the English word used to translate a Hebrew word that is often used for herbivorous and domesticated animals in contrast to the "beasts," or the carnivores and wild animals. Also in this period were created the "creeping" things, or insects and other little creatures.

1:26 Let us make man in our image

Genesis does not indicate who said to whom, "Let us make man in our image," but Moses 2:26 says it was God the Father speaking to the Son (cf. John 1:1–4, 14; Heb. 1:1–3). God had eternal purposes in making his earthly children in his image and giving them "dominion" on earth (Gen. 1:26*a–f*).

1:27 in the image of God . . . ; male and female

Eliza R. Snow wrote poetically in "O My Father":

> In the heav'ns are parents single?
> No, the thought makes reason stare!
> Truth is reason; truth eternal
> Tells me I've a mother there.
> (*Hymns* [Salt Lake City: The Church of
> Jesus Christ of Latter-day Saints, 1985],
> no. 292)

Reason indeed precludes the idea that a father could beget children without a mother to bear them. Thus the "male and female" children were "in the image" of their Heavenly Parents. Consider the potential of men and women eternally married to be like unto their Heavenly Parents (D&C 132:15–24; TG, "Family, Eternal"; "Marriage, Celestial").

1:28 multiply, and replenish the earth

The greatest opportunity of all, to learn eternal values and achieve heavenly potentials, resides in the responsibility and the privilege to create bodies for others of God's spirit children (TG, "Man, Potential to Become like Heavenly Father").

The very same Hebrew verb translated *fill* in verse 22 is here translated *replenish*. It means simply "fill," not "refill."

1:28 subdue it: and have dominion

The invitation to Adam and Eve and all their descendants to perform in the image of the eternal Father and Mother in bearing children and caring for them, making use of earth's resources and facilities, and employing creative and just powers of rulership ("dominion") are awesome and challenging. Recall the ultimate challenge issued by Jesus in the Sermon on the Mount: "Be ye therefore perfect, even as your Father which is in heaven is perfect" (Matt. 5:48); it directs all of us toward ideal "dominion."

1:29–30 to you it shall be for meat

Thus far only fruits, seeds, and other vegetable matter are mentioned as food (Gen. 1:29a, 30a). The whole gamut of food chains of the later, mortal world had not yet been inaugurated.

1:31 it was very good

When the Creators evaluated all living things and their potential support systems, they found that everything would function harmoniously (commentary on Gen. 1:4).

2:1–3 Thus the heavens and the earth were finished

Genesis 2 begins with a summary of the work of the six creative periods outlined in Genesis 1, followed by a poetic ("chiastic") introduction to the Sabbath and its purposes:

"Thus the heavens and the earth were finished, and all the host of them;

"[a] And on the seventh day God ended his work which he had made;

"[b] and he rested on the seventh day from all his work which he had made.

"[c] And God blessed the seventh day,

"[c] and sanctified it:

"[b] because that in it he had rested from all his work
"[a] which God created and made."

The Hebrew of that last phrase says that God then "rested from all his project which God created to do," implying that his activity and involvement continued after cessation, or "rest," from the primary creative work (Gen. 2:1–3 and fn.).

2:1, 4–5 *Thus the heavens and the earth were finished, . . . And every plant of the field before it was in the earth, . . . before it grew*

The creative processes in heaven and on earth had been completed (Gen. 2:1, 4); then it is indicated that living things had not been placed on earth, although earth had been "prepared" for them (Abr. 4:11–12, 20–21, 24–31). All things had been created "spiritually" before they were created "naturally" and "all the children of men" had been created; but "there was not yet flesh upon the earth, neither in the water, neither in the air," because, said the Lord God, "in heaven created I them" (Moses 3:5; Gen. 2:5). The revelation to Abraham affirms that the Gods then "came down and formed these" and performed "all that which they had said concerning every plant of the field before it was in the earth, and every herb of the field before it grew" (Abr. 5:4–5).

2:4ff. *The* LORD *God*

Thus far in Genesis, Deity is called "God" (Heb., *Elohim;* commentary on Gen. 1:1). From this point on through Genesis 2 and 3, two words are used together to designate Deity: LORD God (Heb., *Jehovah Elohim*). The meaning of this combination title may be "Jehovah of the Gods," for *elohim* can be used as a plural common noun and Hebrew permits a genitive relationship of two nouns thus placed together without a preposition between them. Alternatively, the meaning may be "the Lord Omnipotent," which is a divine title for Jehovah, or Jesus, that is used several times in the Book of Mormon (e.g., Mosiah 3:5, 17, 18; 5:2, 15). This argument is persuasive, because *elohim* can be translated with the phrase "all might" or "all power" (see commentary on Gen. 1:1; TG, "Jesus Christ, Creator"; "Jesus Christ, Jehovah"; "Jesus Christ, Lord").

Throughout the Old Testament, with very few exceptions, LORD is used in English translations in place of the Hebrew word *Jehovah;* however, *GOD* (occasionally) and *God* (frequently) may refer to the Son rather than to the Father (BD, "God"; "Jehovah"). In some cases it is difficult to determine which Deity is meant (Gen. 7:5, 9, 16); but that is not necessarily a problem for one who understands that the Son always works under the direction of the Father and that together they work as one. It is not uncommon for the Son to deliver a message to humankind in behalf of the Father, speaking the words of the Father (Moses 4:1–4; D&C 29:1–42; TG, "God the Father—Elohim"; "God the Father—Jehovah").

2:6 there went up a mist . . . and watered . . . the ground

The final step in the preparation of the inanimate matter of earth to sustain life was the evaporation, movement, and recondensation of moisture to provide dew and rain, the lack of which had been mentioned in Genesis 2:5. Watering the dry ground made of it a medium suitable to sustain living things as we know them.

2:7 man of the dust of the ground

The spiritual being who had previously been created was at this point put into a tabernacle of flesh constituted of elements of the earth, and this body was energized through breathing the atmosphere of this earth. This creative act is also described elsewhere (Abr. 5:7; TG, "Man, Physical Creation of").

Adam is identified in other scriptures as the archangel Michael (D&C 107:53–54; BD, "Adam"). His role in the premortal earth life included leading the forces of the Lord against Satan in the war in heaven before the world was created (Rev. 12:7–12). He is the patriarch of our earthly family and will again lead the forces of good against the forces of evil in the final strife at the end of the Millennium (Dan. 10:13, 21; 12:1; D&C 29:26; 78:15–16; 88:111–15). The priesthood and his position in it shall continue (Moses 6:7, 64–67; D&C 27:11; 84:16; 107:41–55; BD, "Michael").

*2:8–9, 15 the Lord God planted a garden eastward in Eden . . .
the tree of life . . . and the tree of knowledge of good and evil*

In an eastern part of the land of Eden (Heb., lit., "pleasantness"), the Lord God provided the first earthly home of our first
ancestors. There were trees both beautiful and useful, including
two that provided them the opportunity of choice—the "tree of
life" and the "tree of knowledge of good and evil." The first would
sustain life eternally (Gen. 2:9*c–d*); the second would permit them
to learn by experience to discern good from evil but would also
bring about the eventual separation of spirit and body, called
death. Lehi described those two trees as opposites, "even the forbidden fruit in opposition to the tree of life; the one being sweet
and the other bitter" (2 Ne. 2:15). In that garden of opportunities
Adam was given his first responsibility: "to dress it and to keep it"
(Gen. 2:15*c*; D&C 42:41–42).

2:10–14 a river went out of Eden . . . , and became into four heads

Four tributaries or "heads" of a river flowed eastward "out of
Eden" and *into* the garden to water it. In the land encompassed
by the first tributary there were precious stones and gold. The
names of all those rivers and lands in humankind's primeval home
have later been used for other lands and rivers not located in such
a single river drainage system (Gen. 2:13*b;* Moses 3:13*a;* BD,
"Eden, Garden of"; "Euphrates"; "Cush").

2:9, 16–17 thou mayest freely eat: . . . but

The opportunity for exercising choice, or agency, was then
presented: in the garden the first inhabitants could "freely eat" of
any of the foods produced except one, if they desired to remain
there. They could not eat of the "tree of the knowledge of good
and evil" if they wished to remain. In whatsoever day they would
eat of it, they would begin to learn by experience the distinction
between the good and the evil; but in that state they would eventually die. There would be two types of death: in a "spiritual
death," they would immediately be separated from the "tree of
life" and the presence of the Lord; later, in a "physical death," their

spirits would be separated from their bodies (D&C 29:41; BD, "Death"; TG, "Death, Spiritual, First"). After physical death, their bodies would return to the ground, whose elements had been used in their creation (Gen. 3:19).

It is reasonable that on earth as in the premortal Council in Heaven (Abr. 3:25–28; TG, "Agency") humankind was free to choose to live either in "a state of probation" or "in a state of innocence, having no joy, for they knew no misery; doing no good, for they knew no sin" (2 Ne. 2:23, 21–22). God's children thus would be proven as to whether they would live by divine direction in "all things" (Abr. 3:25) or whether they would seek to "be as gods, knowing good and evil," gaining wisdom through their own experiences (Moses 4:11–12, 28).

"That satan" (Heb., *ha-satan,* "the adversary"), during the Council in Heaven, had "sought to destroy the agency of man which I, the Lord God, had given him" (Moses 4:1, 3). In Eden, he "sought to destroy the world," "for he knew not the mind of God" (Moses 4:3, 6).

2:18 It is not good that the man should be alone; I will make him an help meet for him

Events seem to be in topical rather than chronological sequence in this chapter: the bringing of the female spiritual being into a body of earthly materials is related in one scripture before the naming of certain creatures (Abr. 5:14–19), whereas it is mentioned before but completed afterward, according to other scriptures (e.g., Gen. 2:18, 21–22; Moses 3:18, 21–22).

The words "an help meet for him" are from a composite word in Hebrew meaning a "helper like-the-opposite-of-him." The English adjective *meet* means "appropriate, fitting." Thus, husband and wife are to be complementary to each other's nature and needs.

2:19 Adam

The common noun *adam* in Hebrew is a collective noun meaning "man," "human," or "mankind"; as a common noun, it is used with "the"; but it may be used as a proper noun, *Adam,* without "the," and it appears as such for the first time in this verse. For its use as a collective noun, see Genesis 5:2.

2:19–20 whatsoever Adam called every living creature, that was the name thereof

The beginning of man's earthly language is represented in the naming of the beasts and fowls by Adam. More about the divine Adamic language is told elsewhere (Moses 6:5–6, 57; 7:13; Ether 1:33–37; 3:22–24; 12:24). A future restoration of the "pure language" on earth has been promised (Zeph. 3:9).

2:21–24 and they shall be one flesh

The details of just how the man was made of the dust of the earth and the woman made of the same bone and flesh as man have not been revealed. Indeed, the ongoing miracle of creation we see in our continuing procreation of life is still marvelous to us, from the genetic combination at conception on through the intricate organization and preparation of a body for independent existence, ready at the proper moment for separation of child from mother. It is prophetically promised, however, that marvelous information about creation and other matters will continue to be discovered and revealed (D&C 101:32–34; 121:26–33); thus we eventually will understand the mysteries of creation and procreation.

As a properly married couple, the man and the woman can be compatible, complementary "help meets" (as suggested in Gen. 2:18). They are made of the same material and ideally formed to become "one flesh" in begetting and bearing children. They can also be united in rearing them, unselfishly cooperating in purposes, goals, and programs—manifesting constant concern about the welfare of each other and their children.

2:25 not ashamed

What engenders shame? Is it not consciousness of some impropriety, evil, or guilt? Clearly, the first man and woman had no cause for shame up to that time.

3:1 the serpent was . . . subtil . . . And he said

Into that garden of pleasantness (Heb., *eden*) came the being sometimes called the serpent, the tempter of man, the adversary of God. He spoke "by the mouth of the serpent," according to Moses 4:7; but he is often called by that metaphoric term, *serpent* (Gen. 3:13; 2 Cor. 11:3; Rev. 12:9, 20:2; 2 Ne. 2:18; Mosiah 16:3; D&C 76:28; 88:110; Moses 4:20–21). He launched his first earthly attack by a question inviting a reassessment of God's instructions: "Yea, hath God said—Ye shall not eat of every tree of the garden?" (Moses 4:7).

3:2–5 Ye shall not surely die: . . . ye shall be as gods

As mentioned in the commentary on Genesis 2:9, 16–17, Satan had rebelled against God and had "sought to destroy the agency of man" in the premortal council (Moses 4:3; Isa. 14:12–15). In Eden, Satan "knew not the mind of God, wherefore he sought to destroy the world" (Moses 4:6) by frustrating God's plan here. Apparently he did not know the divine plan of redemption as we know it (2 Ne. 9:5–10). For his own purposes, therefore, Satan sought to persuade the ancestors of the family of humankind to do a deed that would separate them from the presence of God in spiritual death and later separate their spirits from their bodies in physical death; then they would be like his unembodied spirit followers and subject to him (2 Ne. 9:8).

Satan's combining a falsehood (that they would not die) with a half truth (that by simply partaking they would "be as gods") was persuasive. Satan's statement was intended for his own gain; but ironically, by their response Eve and Adam launched into the desirable process of learning good from evil by experience through the use of their own precious agency. Thanks to God and His Beloved Son, their choice did not relegate them and their descendants to a hopeless predicament. It initiated a program, already planned, whereby humankind could work toward eternal life (TG, "Devil"; "Earth, Purpose of"; "Man, Potential to Become like Heavenly Father"; "Redemption").

*3:6 she took . . . , and did eat, and gave also unto her husband
with her; and he did eat*

There has been much speculation, but no revelation, about
what the "fruit" was that the woman saw and perceived to be
"good for food," "pleasant to the eyes," and "a tree to be desired
to make one wise." She partook of it partly because of those per-
ceptions and partly because she was deceived (Gen. 3:13; 1 Tim.
2:14–15). Later, when she fully understood the potential of her
choice (made available through the plan of redemption), she rejoiced about it (Moses 5:4–11). It was good that she gave the fruit
also to her husband and that he did eat, so that procreation, with
all its positive potential, could proceed (Moses 5:11; 2 Ne.
2:22–27).

3:7–10 they knew that they were naked. . . . Adam and his wife hid

Adam and Eve had been "in a state of innocence, having no
joy, for they knew no misery; doing no good, for they knew no
sin" (2 Ne. 2:23). By an act done *in spite of* a warning, and, in
part, *because of* a satanic enticement, they had begun to learn
about actions and reactions, laws and consequences; they experienced fear and perhaps shame (Gen. 2:25). They tried to escape
by hiding from God but learned that that is impossible. Doubtless
these basic lessons were revealed to Moses and recorded by him
so that the descendants of Adam and Eve could learn such truths
by vicarious experience and be spared some more costly personal
experiences with all their consequences.

*3:9–13 Where . . . ? Who . . . ? Hast thou . . . ? What is this thou
hast done?*

Obviously, because God knows all things, he asked questions
about where his children were, who had told them about nakedness, whether they had of their own agency chosen to partake,
and what they had done so that he might give them their first
opportunity to evaluate, confess, and thus begin to repent. The
consequences of what they had done could then be plainly linked

to the deeds. Adam responded that Eve had influenced him, and Eve said that "the serpent" had "beguiled" her (Gen. 3:13*a*).

3:14–15 the Lord God said unto the serpent, . . . thou art cursed

The Lord began in reverse order to point out the consequences. First he addressed Satan, who had sinned in contradicting divine warnings and had imposed his own will and influence upon others for his own purposes. He had sought to destroy the proper purposes of the world-laboratory that God had created for his children's development (commentary on Gen. 3:1; 3:2–5). Therefore, the Lord told Satan, he would be cursed above all.

Being cursed is the very opposite of being blessed; God's blessing graciously invokes good, whereas his curse justly invokes evil upon one deserving it. Thus Satan was informed through symbolic terms that he would not have the privilege of earth life that even cattle and beasts have. He had persuaded humans through their appetites and ambitions to do what he thought would destroy them; and although he would be permitted to continue to tempt or test humankind through their visceral appetites and mental urges and would inflict some basic afflictions—"bruise his heel"—yet one Seed of the woman would come to nullify Satan's triumph—"bruise thy head" (Gen. 3:15*b–d;* Gal. 3:16). Many prophecies and accounts concern the suffering of that chosen Seed, the Savior, in overcoming Satan's gains (Isa. 53:10–12; final chapters of the four Gospels). The words metaphorically spoken to the "serpent" can reassure all of us, for though Satan has the power to tempt us, we have been given power to resist him. If we need help to resist, or if we are overwhelmed by him, we may be aided to stand firm, or to recover, through the administration of those who bear priesthood powers to cast out Satan in the name of Jesus Christ. Thus we see that both Satan's freedom to act and his power to overcome people are curbed by the curse he received (James 4:7; Matt. 10:1; Mark 3:15; D&C 24:13).

Significant antithetical parallels occur later, as in Moses' raising a bronze serpent on a pole to bring about the healing of deadly serpent bites (Num. 21:6–9). That in turn symbolized Jesus' being raised upon a cross, as he himself said (John 3:14–18; Hel.

8:13–18). The serpent was reminiscent of the tempter who had persuaded Eve and Adam to disbelieve part of God's warning and do something that brought about death, but looking upon the bronze serpent with faith in the prophet Moses, and in God's promise through him, could heal and preserve lives. Just so, we may look up with faith in Jesus Christ's atonement, which gives promise that his death and resurrection can bring about our resurrection, a cleansing forgiveness from sin, and eternal life—if we obey the laws of the gospel. Paul summed it up in concise parallelism: "For since by man came death, by man came also the resurrection of the dead" (1 Cor. 15:21). One serpent symbolized the bringer of death; another symbolized the Bringer of Life.

3:16 multiply thy sorrow . . . ; in sorrow thou shalt bring forth children

Sorrow is used in Genesis 3:16 and 17 to translate the Hebrew *'etzev*, which connotes "toil, pain, travail." Doubtless the burdens and pain of pregnancy and childbirth were thereby anticipated (Gen. 3:16*b*).

This is a great revelation to women. Eve and her daughters can become cocreators with God by preparing bodies for his spirit children to occupy on earth and later in eternity. Mothering would entail inconvenience, suffering, travail, and sorrow; these the Lord foretold as natural consequences and not as a curse. Satan had sinned and was justly cursed; but Eve had made a reasonable choice and was told some of the results of that choice. Later, she rejoiced when she learned about the ultimate results (Moses 5:11; 1 Tim. 2:15).

In mothering, nurturing, and caring for children, mothers (and women who adopt or otherwise give loving care to children) develop that most godlike virtue called mother love (Gen. 3:16*a–e*).

3:16 thy desire shall be to thy husband . . . rule over thee

In the Hebrew text there is often a depth of meaning not evident in the translated words. An intimate, loving, and righteous relationship is implied, but it must be fostered (Eph. 5:25–33; Col. 3:19–21; D&C 121:41–42).

3:17–19 cursed is the ground for thy sake; in sorrow shalt thou eat of it

As in Genesis 3:16, the Hebrew word translated *sorrow* connotes toil, pain, and travail (Gen. 3:17c). Woman would suffer one kind in her mothering functions, and man another—in sweat and toil, as provider and protector. The ground was cursed, but humankind was not; and the ground was cursed for their "sake," so that humankind might learn good from evil by experiencing both. Thus the ground was cursed to bring forth opposites of all sorts, including weeds (thorns and thistles) rather than only the plants of Eden, which were all "pleasant to the sight, and good for food" (Gen. 2:9 and fn.).

3:19 till thou return unto the ground . . . , and unto dust shalt thou return

The inevitable separation of the spirit body from the mortal body of "dust" is sometimes symbolized by related Hebrew words such as *adam* ("mankind"), *dam* ("blood"), and *adamah* ("ground" or "dust") in the scriptures (Gen. 3:19c–d).

3:20 Adam called his wife's name Eve . . . the mother of all living

The Hebrew form of her name is *Chavvah*, related to *chayyah*, "life"; thus her name prophetically signifies her giving and sustaining life.

3:21 clothed them

The Lord clothed Adam and Eve with garments of skins (Gen. 3:21a) as coverings for their naked bodies. The Hebrew word translated *coats* is really the name of a garment worn next to the skin. Their garments would impress them with the sanctity of the body and protect it from abuses. Profane exhibition is now commonly used to entice people to actions having little to do with the primary and proper purposes and potential of these beautifully formed and marvelous bodies.

3:22–24 the man is become as one of us, to know good and evil

The truth that Satan had enticingly mixed with a falsehood

18

was confirmed; by use of their agency, the man and woman did begin to "be as gods, knowing good and evil" (Gen. 3:5). But to prevent their choosing to return to the primeval "good" of an easy life in the Garden of Eden where perfect food was freely available, they were sent out of the garden, and the way to the "tree of life" was closed and guarded. As the Lord doubtless intended, humankind's challenge to find ways to satisfy needs and alleviate discomforts has resulted in the development of much pure and applied science and art, ever since humankind was launched into this world of experience and enterprise.

3:24 Cherubims, and a flaming sword

Ever since the supernatural guardians were placed at the gateway to Eden, the entrances to holy places in many ancient cultures have been guarded by some form of *cherubim* (already a plural, without adding *s*). The meaning of the word *cherub* (singular) is not precisely known, but the ancient statues representing cherubim were usually composite creatures with parts from the bull, lion, eagle, and so on to symbolize superior powers (BD and TG, "Cherubim").

The nature of the "flaming sword which turned every way" (Heb., lit., "gyrating flame of the sword") has also not been revealed. Compare the supernatural phenomenon described in Ezekiel 1:4.

3:24 tree of life

The symbolic tree (Gen. 2:9*c;* commentary on Gen. 2:8–9, 15) had functions at the beginning and will again at the end of the earth's program. References to it in the last book of the Bible are informative, and those in the Book of Mormon also broaden and deepen the meanings and concepts associated with that remarkable "tree."

4:1–2 Cain . . . Abel

Although only two children of Adam and Eve are mentioned here, the existence of others is implied later, when Cain and others took wives. A third son, Seth, and his descendants are reported in detail beginning in Genesis 5.

Restored scripture (JST Gen. 4:1–13; 5:1–3; Moses 5:1–15) reveals that much time had passed and many events had occurred before the birth of Cain and Abel. Adam and Eve had worked together for years and had had children who had grown up and in turn had children before Cain and Abel were born. Adam and Eve had received important revelations and commandments, through which they had learned about redemption and atonement and rejoiced in anticipation of it. They had learned ordinances and covenants to keep and to pass on, with all their meaning, to all their children. After all these items of family history, the account of Cain and Abel is presented.

Cain's name appears to be related to one Hebrew verb for "get, acquire" and another for "fit together, forge, fabricate"; thus his name was appropriate to his career—as names of biblical people often are. Abel's name is the Hebrew word for things evanescent or transitory, such as "vapor, a breath, a puff," and seems to have anticipated the brevity of his life.

The reasons for the preservation of an account of only these two children of our first parents are not explicit. It may be that they typify earthly tragedies that arise out of the conflicts between fair and unfair, proper and profane. Many of earth's sorrows have indeed arisen out of plots involving murder for gain by individuals or nations, practiced both covertly and overtly.

4:3–7 Cain brought of the fruit of the ground. . . . Abel . . . brought of the firstlings of his flock

Offerings of fruits, vegetables, and grains are later known and used in thanksgiving and supplication (TG, "Sacrifice"), but the only offerings thus far specified for Adam and Eve and their family (JST Gen. 4:5–9; Moses 5:5–9) were the firstlings of the flock. After Adam and Eve had been commanded to make such offerings and had obediently begun to do so, they were informed that they could thereby anticipate the redemptive offering of the Savior, the Only Begotten Son of God to come. Cain's substitute offerings of the fruit of the ground were not "a similitude" of that saving sacrifice and thus were not an acceptable innovation. He was corrected and assured by a personal revelation, "If thou doest well, thou shalt be accepted" (Moses 5:23). Both the right attitude and the right performance of covenant ordinances are important. Abel had performed his sacrifice in a way that was acceptable and effective. Evaluations of both sacrifices are recorded in later scripture (Heb. 11:3; 1 Jn. 3:8–12).

Cain was instructed by God also regarding consequences: if he did not master sin and its initiator, they would master him; and danger for him was imminent, "at the door" (Gen. 4:7; Moses 5:23). The restored account in Moses 5:18–33 (JST Gen. 5:6–18) provides the significant fact that it was Satan who had suggested the alternate sacrifice of crops because he desired to "have" Cain; hence he was pleased with the Lord's rejection of Cain's sacrifice and with Cain's anger. Note also that Cain "loved Satan more than God" and "rejected the greater counsel which was had from God" (Moses 5:18, 25). He actually made a covenant with Satan, receiving from him the "great secret" that it is possible to "murder and get gain"; that is, he could kill his brother and get his brother's flocks. How many horrible crimes and wars have been motivated by that "great secret"? (Moses 5:31).

4:8–18 I know not: Am I my brother's keeper?

The first murder was followed by the first cover-up lie. When confronted by the Lord, Cain denied knowing where his brother was and sarcastically asked whether he was responsible for his brother's welfare. *Keeper* is used to translate a word whose root meaning is "to watch and guard." The Lord declared that evidence of the evil deed arose from the very ground that had received Abel's blood; but He gave Cain one more opportunity to confess what he had done.

The ground (the same Hebrew word is used here as in Gen. 3:10, 17) which had given evidence against Cain would not thereafter give abundant yields of fruit and other crops to him. He would be cursed, or punished, by the very ground that had been cursed for man's sake (see commentary on Gen. 3:17–19); he would become a wanderer and a fugitive.

The phrase translated "My punishment is greater than I can bear" can also be translated ". . . too great to be forgiven," because the Hebrew verb can be rendered either *bear* or *forgive.* There is scriptural evidence that such a deed as Cain's, committed after personal communications by revelation from God, can bring one to "perdition," without hope of pardon or forgiveness (TG, "Sons of Perdition"; "Murder, Murderer").

Cain was to suffer poor crops, the danger of vengeance, and isolation from God and man. Feeling the weight of that estrangement, Cain did as many do: he sought some amelioration by placing blame elsewhere. He blamed Satan for tempting him and blamed God for rejecting his offerings while accepting those of Abel (Moses 5:38–41).

Translators and interpreters differ considerably on the rendition and meaning of the statement that "whosoever slayeth Cain, vengeance shall be taken on him sevenfold." Perhaps the most apt summation of the important point is in later revelations from the Lord: "To me belongeth vengeance and recompense," and "Vengeance is mine; I will repay, saith the Lord" (Deut. 32:35; Rom. 12:19; Heb. 10:30; 1 Jn. 3:11–12). Cain feared that "every one that findeth me shall slay me" (Gen. 4:14), but the Lord does not approve such anarchic "justice."

The stated purpose of the "mark" (Heb., lit., "sign," an identifier) set upon Cain by the Lord was to prevent others' assuming the prerogative to punish him. Many false assumptions have been generated over the centuries about the "mark of Cain." Other scriptures somewhat clarify the purpose of such an identification (Gen. 4:15*a*). There is a question about why the mark would be perpetuated upon the descendants of the one punished. "The sins of the parents cannot be answered upon the heads of the children" in God's justice (Moses 6:54; Deut. 24:16; TG, "Accountability"). Nevertheless, parents can and do pass on impairments and disadvantages, advantages and blessings, to their children; and it will be seen that refinements and extensions of Cain's evil "secret" were known and used by his descendants and others (Ether 8:11–19; TG, "Secret Combinations") and that they too suffered thereby.

Doubtless Cain's exclusion from "the presence of the Lord" (Gen. 4:16) had many effects upon his way of life and that of his family. Perhaps there is symbolism in the name of the land to which they migrated, the land of *Nod* (Heb., lit., "land of wandering"). Tents and cattle characterized their nomadic way of life (v. 20).

Do not confuse the names of Cain's descendants with the names of the descendants of Seth (Gen. 5), whose names are similar. Cain even had a son, with a city, whose name was Enoch (Gen. 4:17).

4:19–22 tents . . . cattle . . . harp and organ . . . brass and iron

Recorded here is the genesis of some positive developments fostered in agriculture, music, and metallurgy among Cain's family.

4:23–24 If Cain shall be avenged sevenfold

The song of the righteous gives thanks and praise to God (e.g., Eve's song, Moses 5:11), but the song of a sinner is boastful and cynical, like this stanza in three couplets of synonymous parallels by Lamech, a fifth-generation descendant of Cain (translation mine):

> Adah and Zillah, hear my voice,
> ye wives of Lamech, give ear to my speech;
> for I have slain a man for wounding me,
> even a young man for bruising me.
> If Cain shall be avenged sevenfold,
> then Lamech, seventy-sevenfold!

Lamech evidently misunderstood or misapplied the Lord's warning to anyone usurping His prerogative to punish Cain and cynically arrogated to himself a tenfold greater "protection" from vengeance.

The contrasting righteous and wicked developments in the two different cultures among the descendants of Adam and Eve are summarized in the restored account (Moses 5:49–59).

4:25–26 then began men to call upon the name of the Lord

Eve bore Adam another son, Seth (Heb., lit., "put, place, or appoint"), to replace Abel; and it was among Seth's descendants that righteous ways, doctrines, and ordinances were perpetuated (Moses 6:1–8; cf. D&C 84:16; 107:42–54). In the days of Seth and Enos, the righteous were instructed to supplicate God in the name of the Lord (Heb., *JHVH,* "Jehovah"; Moses 5:8; TG, "Jesus Christ, Jehovah").

5:1–32 the book of the generations of Adam

The phrase "the book of the generations of Adam," or a similar one ("These are the generations of—"), usually introduces a chapter of family history. Adam and his heirs were called "by the spirit of inspiration" to write this first "book of remembrance" in "a language which was pure and undefiled" (Moses 6:5–6). This was the real beginning of the writing of scripture.

In the last days, preparatory to the peaceful reign of the Lord on earth, "a pure language" will be restored to humankind (Zeph. 3:9). That should be one contribution to peace on earth.

Note that similar phrases compare Adam to God and Seth to Adam (Gen. 1:26–27; 5:3); thus the "anthropomorphic" concept of God was taught early in the scriptures.

As stated earlier (commentary on Gen. 2:19; 3:19), the Hebrew collective noun *adam* means human, and it is the same word as the proper noun *Adam;* thus the whole family of humankind can collectively be called *adam* (Gen. 5:2*a*). In Hebrew there was no capital letter to differentiate common from proper nouns.

Many theories have been proposed to rationalize or explain the long life span of these early forefathers, but, of course, none can be proven. Modern revelation confirms that Adam did live long enough to bless seven generations of his descendants (D&C 107:53; Moses 6:10ff). Life spans were reduced by about half after the flood of Noah (that is, from more than nine hundred years to around four hundred years), and half again after the Tower of Babel (to about two hundred years).

During the six hundred and twenty-two years during which were born the seven patriarchs who were preachers of righteousness, unrighteousness was also developing (Moses 6:11–29). The restored records (Moses 6:31–7:69; JST Gen. 6:28–7:78) tell of a remarkable preaching of repentance by Enoch, a patriarch who "walked with God" (Gen. 5:22; Moses 7:69). He taught vital doctrines concerning the Fall, sin, salvation, and Adam's baptism. He contrasted the wicked, called "sons of men," with the righteous, called "sons of God"; he built "Zion"; he foresaw the perfect "Son of Man" and the final Zion and New Jerusalem (Gen. 5:22–24 and fn.; BD, "Enoch"). Enoch's Zion was miraculously removed from earth when evil prevailed all around it (Moses 7:15–16, 19–21, 69).

Enoch's son Methuselah remained on earth and prophesied, as did Methusaleh's son Lamech, father of Noah (Moses 8:1–9). Lamech named his son Noah, meaning "rest" (Gen. 5:29*a*); and he did bring the troubled earth to rest and repose in the cleansing baptism of the Flood (1 Pet. 3:19–21; commentary on Gen. 6:5–7), but only after his prophetic warnings and pleas for repentance had been rejected.

6:1– 4 sons of God . . . daughters of men

Different ways of life differentiate "sons and daughters of God" from "sons and daughters of men" (TG, "Sons and Daughters of God"). Mixed marriages between "godly" and "earthly" partners, such as those between the daughters of the righteous and the sons of the wicked (Moses 8:14–15), contributed to the constant increase of rebels against righteousness.

As hinted in Genesis 6:3 and made clear in the restored records (Moses 8:17–20), the Lord granted humankind one hundred twenty years to repent in response to Noah's prophetic warnings rather than perish in the cleansing flood.

Rather than indicating that they were mythical giants and demigods, as some readers have imagined, the Hebrew name of these vaunted children of the mixed marriages, when they became "mighty men," merely supplied a rationale for unrighteous boasting by their parents and for rejecting Noah's warnings (Gen. 6:4; Moses 8:21). Their Hebrew name, *Nephilim*, is apparently derived from the verb *naphal*, "fall"; they are therefore thought by rabbinical commentators to have been "fallen ones" (rather than persons of gigantic stature; the Greek Septuagint rendered the Hebrew word as *gigantes*, for reasons unknown). *Nephilim* is one of four different Hebrew words translated "giants" in the King James Version of the Old Testament (Gen. 6:4*a*; BD, "Giants").

6:5– 8 God saw that the wickedness of man was great. . . . And it repented the Lord

The Hebrew word *JHVH (Jehovah)* is rendered as GOD in Genesis 6:5 and as LORD in Genesis 6:6, for reasons unknown.

Because children born on earth had little chance to learn to choose good from evil when "every man was lifted up in the imagination of the thoughts of his heart, being only evil continually" (Moses 8:22), most people growing up in those circumstances would become corrupted rather than gain exaltation. God in his justice and mercy could not continue to send his children to such an earth (Gen. 6:5, 13; cf. Moses 8:22).

According to Genesis, the Lord was "sorry" and "moved to pity" and to "have compassion" (Gen. 6:6*a*) on those who suffered in that evil society; but the inspired restoration of this passage indicates that it was Noah whom "it repented" (caused sorrow and regret to) and whose "heart was pained" because God's good earth and humankind had come to such despicable conditions (Moses 8:25).

The cataclysm involving all animate life on land is reported in many places in the scriptures (Gen. 6:13, 17; TG, "Earth, Cleansing of"; "Flood, Noah's"; BD, "Noah"). Its causes and effects help us understand the work of God with humankind in the past and prepare us for the future, for Jesus prophesied similar conditions to come near the end of the wicked world (Matt. 24:37–39; JS–M 1:41–43). The implication is that conditions can again get so bad in this world that continuation of its practices will be intolerable (TG, "Earth, Cleansing of").

6:8–10 Noah was . . . perfect in his generations, and Noah walked with God

The Hebrew word here translated *perfect* means "complete, whole, or having integrity" (Gen. 6:9*c*). Noah and his family were people of such quality (Moses 8:13, 27).

The first use of *generations* in verse 9 is to translate the

Hebrew *toledoth*, which means "genealogical lines," but the second use of *generations* here is to translate the Hebrew *doroth*, meaning "cycles" or years of time.

"Walked with God" is a metaphor used to describe a righteous way of life (Gen. 6:9*d*).

6:11–13 all flesh had corrupted his way upon the earth

In contrast to the integrity of the family of Noah, "all flesh" were "corrupt," that is, debased and degraded. The "work and glory" of God is "to bring to pass the immortality and eternal life of man" (Moses 1:39), but his children too often respond to things sensual and devilish instead. Thereby some descend to subbestial immorality rather than ascend to a godly immortality.

6:14–15 an ark of gopher wood. . . . The length of the ark shall be three hundred cubits . . .

Gopher is transliterated from a Hebrew word used only once in the Old Testament; it may designate a resinous wood, being related to *kopher* ("pitch"), a word that appears twice in this same verse; if so, it would be a water-resistant wood.

The dimensions of the ark indicate a very large vessel, approximately four hundred fifty by seventy-five by forty-five feet. Its construction was certainly a miraculous feat of engineering, possible only with divine help.

6:16 A window . . . door . . . ; with lower, second, and third stories shalt thou make it

Scant information prevents precise visualization of the openings in the ark. Levels of openings may be indicated, but no word for "stories" (printed in italics in the KJV) is given in the Hebrew description. The Hebrew word rendered *window* is a word for something shining or bright (Gen. 6:16*a*). Light and ventilation would of course be requisite in a vessel "tight like unto a dish, . . . tight like unto the ark of Noah," as the Book of Mormon describes both the ark and the Jaredite vessels. Those vessels were lighted by miraculously luminous stones (Ether 2:22–25; 3:1–6; 6:7).

6:17 all flesh, wherein is the breath of life

Man and beast, fowls and creeping things were mentioned (Gen. 6:7); "all flesh had corrupted his way upon the earth" (Gen. 6:12); a summary tells what died (Gen. 7:21–22). Mankind had become self-destructive through sin, but how other living things had become incompatible with proper earth life is not revealed. Certainly, though, a cataclysmic change on earth had become necessary.

6:18 with thee will I establish my covenant

Latter-day revelation tells that the covenant involves all future nations of earth (Gen. 6:18a). The eight souls "saved by water" (1 Pet. 3:20) to begin repeopling the world were the four couples mentioned here.

6:19–22 two of every sort . . . to keep them alive

At least one pair of *every* creature to be saved was to be taken aboard; more than one pair of some species was specified later (Gen. 7:2–3). Food to be stored for all these creatures and for the people would certainly have required another miracle; but Noah was directed by the Lord in all that he did, and only by His help was such a project possible at all.

7:1 Come thou and all thy house

Peter later understood that the few righteous souls of Noah's house were "saved by water" *from* the wicked world *by* the Flood. This was a "like figure" to baptism, to cleanse the earth (1 Pet. 3:20–21).

Peter also recorded the revelation that our merciful Redeemer went in the spirit, while his body was in the tomb, and preached to such spirits "in prison" as those "which sometime were disobedient, when once the longsuffering of God waited in the days of Noah" (1 Pet. 3:19–20). Thus they could learn the gospel, "live according to God in the spirit," and be justly "judged according to men in the flesh" (1 Pet. 4:6). Other scriptures tell how the Lord organized that great mission of mercy so that all who will listen may hear the gospel (D&C 1:11; 138:6–37; Isa. 24:22; John 5:25–29).

7:1–9; 6:3, 5, 6, 8, 11, 13, 22 Lord . . . God . . . God

Either *Lord* or *God*, given in capital letters, stands for Jehovah, whereas *God* can refer to either the Father or the Son. Various hypotheses have been contrived to explain such interchanges of the divine names, but lack of unanimity and consistency in their rationales leaves them unconvincing (see commentary on Gen. 2:4).

7:2–3 clean beast . . . by sevens, the male and his female

"Clean" describes the animals suitable for food or for sacrifice (BD, "Clean and Unclean"). For the year and more they would be aboard the ark (see commentary on Gen. 7:4–12), there could have been a need for more than one pair of each of the "clean" beasts (see Gen. 8:20).

7:4–12, 19–20 the rain was upon the earth forty days and forty nights

Rain, supplemented by "fountains of the great deep" (Gen. 7:11*b*), raised the water level to some twenty-two feet (fifteen cubits) above the mountains (Gen. 7:19–20; 8:5).

7:11 six hundredth year . . . second month

Note the date of the beginning of the deluge, and later the date of the end (Gen. 8:13–14), to avoid the common mistake of thinking the total duration of the Flood was only forty days. It actually lasted a year and ten days.

7:13–18 In the selfsame day entered Noah, and . . . the sons of Noah, and Noah's wife, and the three wives of his sons . . . into the ark; they and every beast. . . . And they went in unto Noah

Noah did not drive the animals into the ark, for after he and his family entered the ark, the beasts, cattle, creeping things, fowls, and birds "went in unto" him; and "they went in, . . . as God had commanded" (Gen. 7:14–16).

7:21–24 Noah only . . . and they that were with him

The Genesis account of the Flood concerns a universal cataclysm, not a local one, as confirmed by many other scriptures
(Gen. 7:21–24 and fn.; TG, "Flood, Noah's"; "Earth, Cleansing of";
BD, "Noah"). Besides the record of the Judaeo-Christian scriptures,
legends of such a deluge and renewal have been preserved by
other peoples. The concept is general that a man, his wife, and
their married children were saved (see almost any multivolume
commentary on the Old Testament).

*7:24; 8:1–14 prevailed . . . an hundred and fifty days . . . asswaged
. . . returned . . . decreased . . . abated . . . dried*

The Hebrew says the waters were "mighty" upon the earth
one hundred fifty days before they began to recede. Then for another one hundred fifty days the waters receded (Gen. 8:3), until
in the tenth month, mountaintops reappeared (Gen. 8:5; 7:19–20).
Noah waited forty days more and then made weekly checks until
the waters had abated and the land masses had dried enough that
the people and animals could leave the ark (Gen. 8:6, 10, 12). The
great flood had lasted one year and ten days (Gen. 7:11; 8:13–14).

8:15–19 Go forth . . . be fruitful and multiply

The people, animals, fowls, and creeping things disembarked
and launched life in this great earth-laboratory once more.

8:20–22 Noah . . . offered burnt offerings

With gratitude and supplication, Noah offered sacrifices in
worshipping God. The restored account records that Noah then
prayed that no such curse as the Flood would come again (JST
Gen. 9:4–6, as cited for Gen. 8:20*a*), and the Lord responded
(Gen. 9:8–17).

9:1–4 into your hand are they delivered

As in the days of Adam, so again in the days of Noah, God
blessed his children and gave them dominion over other living
creatures, not to abuse them but to use some for work and some
for food. But blood was not to be consumed (Gen. 9:4*b–c*). As

noted here and elsewhere in the scriptures, blood symbolizes mortal life; shedding the blood of man and needlessly shedding the blood of animals is forbidden (Gen. 9:4*a*, 6*a*; BD, "Blood"; D&C 49:21).

There is fear and dread between humankind and many other creatures on the earth today; but in an ideal age to come, enmity and fear between animals and man will no longer prevail (Isa. 11:6–9 and fn.).

9:5–7 *Whoso sheddeth man's blood*

Sin, violence, and bloodshed had been rampant before the Flood; but in the newly reborn world, preventive laws and warnings were issued against such evils, and punishment by execution for murder was prescribed. The sanctity of the human body derives in part from its having been created in the image of God (Gen. 9:6). Later a law was given that even the body of a person executed was to be safeguarded from degradation (Deut. 21:22–23 and fn.).

9:8–17 *I will establish my covenant with you*

As noted in Genesis 8:20–22, the Lord and Noah made a covenant and the rainbow became a token of their covenant that floods would never again be the Lord's instrument of cleansing the earth (Gen. 9:13, 17). Perhaps the Lord gave that assurance lest humankind thereafter seek to avoid punishment rather than seek to uphold righteousness (commentary on Gen. 11:4). The covenant also included a promise of Zion (Gen. 9:9*a*, 11*c*, 16*a*; Moses 7:51–52). Nevertheless, when the world in the last days becomes as wicked as it was in the days of Noah, it will again be cleansed—but by a baptism of fire (Matt. 24:37–51; Mal. 3–4).

9:18–27 *Japheth . . . shall dwell in the tents of Shem; and Canaan shall be his servant*

The sons of Noah and his wife were listed in Genesis 5:32; they were to become forefathers of the peoples who would inhabit the earth (Gen. 9:19), details of which follow in Genesis 10. Restored sources (Moses 8:12) indicate that Japheth was forty-two years older than Shem, and Shem was eight years older than Ham; thus, Ham was the youngest son (cf. Gen. 9:24). Just what Ham did to limit his spiritual privileges and those of his son Canaan is not indicated in the scriptures; but nonbiblical legends tell of his stealing Noah's sacred garment so that he might claim the authority granted to its legitimate possessor and pass it on to his sons. Some of this information correlates slightly with scripture (Abr. 1:21–22, 27); but, according to revealed principles (Alma 3:19; 13:3–7; Deut. 24:16; A of F 2; D&C 130:20–21), punishments or blessings come by one's own obedience or disobedience and not that of someone else. A curse of a family, clan, or people endures only as long as the way of life that caused it is perpetuated (TG, "Accountability"; "Chastening"; "Correction"; "Curse"; "Blessings"; "God, Justice of"; "Good Works"; "Inheritance"; "Justice"; "Punishment"; "Retribution").

It is not evident in history that early Canaanites were servants for any substantial time to Semites, but they were conquered and suppressed by Semitic Israel over a long period, beginning at the time of Joshua. In one notable case a Japhetic, or Indo-European people, the Medo-Persians, dwelt near Semites, the Babylonians. Eventually the Medo-Persians conquered Babylon and fostered the return of other Semites, the Judeans, to Jerusalem (2 Chr. 36:20–23; Isa. 44:28–45:4).

9:28–29 all the days of Noah were nine hundred and fifty years

Noah was the last to have a life span of more than nine hundred years, although Shem's was only somewhat less, at some six hundred ten years. Noah thus lived for fifty-eight years after Abraham's birth, and Shem lived for thirty-four years after Abraham's death. The next few generations, however, lived about half as long as Noah did, and after the Tower of Babel episode, half of that. What caused such long life at first and then the phased reductions has not been revealed. Although some hypotheses have been raised, neither research nor revelation has yet sustained any of them (commentary on Gen. 5:1–32).

10:1–5 Japheth . . . Gentiles . . . nations

Genesis 10 is commonly called the Table of Nations because it identifies several nations as descendants of the families of Noah's three sons and their wives. (They are more expressly identified in Josephus, *Antiquities of the Jews* 1.6.) Peoples of the Greek islands and peninsula and broadly northward through the Caucasus are generally the "Gentiles," or Japhetic nations. *Gentiles* is the word used to translate the Hebrew *goyim* ("nations" or "peoples"), which is any or all nations outside Israel (BD, "Gentiles"). There are prophecies about some of these peoples being involved in earth's final battles (Gen. 10:2*a–b*).

The work of Paul, missionary to the Japhetic "Gentiles," from Galatia to Ephesus, to Macedonia, Greece, and Rome, is well known; his letters to them are basic documents of Christianity (Acts 13–28; Epistles of Paul).

10:6–20 the sons of Ham

Ham's four sons and the nations attributed to them are Cush (Ethiopia), Mizraim (Egypt), Phut (Libya), and Canaan (Canaan). A daughter, Egyptus (Abr. 1:25), born to Ham and his wife Egyptus (Abr. 1:23), is not mentioned in Genesis, nor is her son who was the first "pharaoh" (Abr. 1:25–27) of the people of Egypt. An ancient wall painting in the tomb of Seti I of the Nineteenth Dynasty shows representatives of the four Hamitic nations as four races: black (Cush), copper-red (Mizraim), pink-white (Phut), and olive-tan (Canaan). An excellent color reproduction of this painting is in *Views of the Biblical World* (Jerusalem: International Publishing Co., Ltd., 1959), pp. 38–39.

The Old Testament records in Genesis 10:9 that Nimrod, of the family of Cush, is "a mighty hunter before the Lord"; other sources portray him as being against the Lord as a leader of the Babel rebellion (Gen. 10:10*b*; 11:1–9; Josephus, *Antiquities of the Jews* 1.4.2–3). The New Testament records that an early convert of Philip was an Ethiopian ("Cush") who was an important official in the court of Candace, queen of Ethiopia (Acts 8:26–40).

Descendants of Mizraim (Egypt) are seen mostly in Exodus, of course; but other interactions with them are seen throughout the Old Testament and some in the New Testament. Indeed, the New Testament records that the Holy Family took refuge in Egypt during the early years of Jesus' life (Matt. 2:13–18). The New Testament also records that Simon of Cyrene, which is a town of northern Libya (thus possibly making him a descendant of Phut), bore the cross of our Savior on the last part of the journey to Golgotha (Matt. 27:32).

The descendants of Canaan are seen most frequently in the early books of the Old Testament in their interactions and conflicts with the Israelite descendants of Shem.

10:21–32 children of Shem

It is with the descendants of Shem that the Bible history is mostly concerned; indeed they were the writers of most of the Bible and the Book of Mormon. They are the "Shemites," or Semites; and best known of them are the progeny of Shem's great-grandson Eber, or Heber—the "Heberites," or Hebrews. Shem was a forefather rather than the immediate "father" of all the children of Eber (Gen. 10:21–24).

Other scriptures briefly allude to the dividing of the earth in the days of Peleg (Gen. 10:25*a*–*b*); and a latter-day prophecy anticipates future changes in land masses and water bodies, making the earth "like as it was in the days before it was divided" (D&C 133:24).

From Shem, Ham, and Japheth, peoples of the nations of the world descended.

11:1–9 confound the language . . . scatter them abroad

Genesis 11 continues the account of the genesis of nations and peoples. Josephus, in *Antiquities of the Jews* 1.4.2–3, declared that Nimrod, grandson of Ham, "gradually changed the government into tyranny, seeing no other way of turning men from the fear of God, but to bring them into a constant dependence on his power. He also said he would be revenged on God, if he should have a mind to drown the world again; for that he would build a tower too high for the waters to be able to reach!" Genesis 11:4

indicates that the builders intended the tower to reach heaven and "make us a name, lest we be scattered abroad upon the face of the whole earth." But the Lord confounded their language and did scatter them (Gen. 11:7–8; Ether 1:33–43).

The biblical writer saw the name *Babel* as derived from a root word like the Hebrew *balal*, which means "to suffuse, mix, or confound." Others have seen it as a boastful name, "Gate of God," from *bab* ("gate") and *el* ("God").

Information about the pure language of Adam, its preservation by Jared's colony, and its superiority as a language is found in the restored scriptures (Ether 1:33–37; 3:22–28; 12:24–25; Moses 6:4–6). One prophet of the Old Testament prophesied the eventual restoration of the "pure language" (Zeph. 3:9; commentary on Gen. 5:1–32).

11:10–26 These are the generations of Shem

The recapitulation of Shem's descendants here traces only a single patriarchal line, from Noah's son Shem for ten generations to Abram (later Abraham). Peleg, in whose days "was the earth divided" (Gen. l0:25; 11:16–19), was the fifth generation, midway between Noah and Abraham.

11:26– 32 Terah begat Abram

A major figure in the history and destiny of the world, Abram, who became Abraham, is introduced in Genesis 11. The eleven chapters of Genesis, to this point, are an introduction to all the scriptures that follow. They provide selected bits of information about the Creation and the purposes of the earth, survey a few epochal events from thousands of years of history, and briefly sketch ten generations of patriarchs from Adam to Noah and ten more from Noah's son Shem to Abram. The remaining thirty-nine chapters of Genesis cover only about three hundred years and provide far more detail about Abraham and three generations of his descendants than was provided about all twenty generations of his ancestors.

Abraham's seed became the writers and major characters of the rest of the Old Testament, the New Testament, the Book of

Mormon, the Doctrine and Covenants, and the Pearl of Great Price. All of these scriptures contain history, doctrine, and prophecy of the missions of Abraham and his seed. Included among them is the central figure of all time, Jesus of Nazareth, the Messiah, the Divine Redeemer.

Some details about Abraham's family history are recorded in the Pearl of Great Price (Abr. 1–3). It tells that in the ancestral home in Ur, Abram's father Terah was not faithful to God and even threatened the life of Abram; but he did repent for a time and migrated with Abram when he and his family left Ur because of religious persecution and a famine. One of Abram's brothers, Nahor, accompanied the migration to the valley of a tributary of the upper Euphrates; they named the place Haran, for another brother, who had died in the famine. Two of the daughters of Haran became wives to their uncles, Nahor and Abram (if the one named Iscah in Gen. 11:29 is the same as Sarai, as attested by both Ibn Ezra and Josephus as well as earlier editions of Abr. 2:2). Lot, son of Nahor, continued with Abram beyond Haran to the land of promise. Terah, however, returned to his idolatry and remained in Haran, where he died (Abr. 2:1–21; Gen. 11:27–32).

12:1– 3 I will bless thee . . . and thou shalt be a blessing . . . and in thee shall all families of the earth be blessed

Abram had sought peace, righteousness, knowledge, the blessings of the righteous fathers, and the right to administer them; and he had become a high priest (Abr. 1:1–2). He had been saved by the Lord from a sacrificial death in Ur (Abr. 1:12–19; Fac. 1) and had been promised a new homeland (Abr. 2:3; Gen. 12:1). He had been called to a priesthood mission (Abr. 1:18–19) and had migrated from Ur in Chaldea to Haran (Abr. 1:1, 30; 2:4; Gen. 11:31–32; Bible Map 2).

In Haran certain aspects of the commands and promises of the Lord were reiterated as Abram's mission was further specified: he and his seed would bring blessings to all families of all nations (Abr. 1:19; 2:6, 9–11). These are "the blessings of the Gospel, . . . the blessings of salvation, even of life eternal" (Abr. 2:11). Understanding the mission of Abraham and his seed can facilitate understanding all of God's ways and intentions in working through "chosen" people throughout history.

12:4–5 Abram took Sarai, . . . Lot, . . . and the souls that they had gotten in Haran

Abram's great mission began with those souls "gotten" (Heb., lit., "made"; Abr. 2:15, "won") in Haran. With them they moved southward at the Lord's command (Abr. 2:5–6). They may have taken the trade route by way of Damascus and "won" another soul there, "Eliezer of Damascus," whom Abram later called "the steward of my house" (Gen. 15:2). They went on southward by way of Jershon (Abr. 2:16–17; possibly known later as Jerash).

Lot, son of Haran, was treated like a son and sometimes was called "brother" by Abram (Gen. 13:8; 14:14, 16). Sarai was also called Abram's "sister" (Gen. 12:11–13).

12:6–10 Sichem . . . Moreh . . . an altar unto the Lord

Sichem (Heb., *shkhem*, "one's upper back, neck, and shoulders") is spelled *Shechem* in all other occurrences in the Old Testament. The city is in a narrow valley between Mount Gerizim and Mount Ebal, at about 1870 feet above sea level; those two mountains are among the highest ("shoulders") of the land. (*Shechem* was also the name of the son of a leader in this area at the time of Jacob; Gen. 34.) A number of important events took place here in biblical times.

The "plain" (Heb., *'elon* "terebinth" or "oak") of Moreh was likely the terebinth or oak near Shechem mentioned in Genesis 35:4 and Joshua 24:26. *Moreh* means "guide" or "teacher" and is a good name for this place, for Abram built another altar unto the Lord there, and He appeared to Abram to teach him. Later, on a mount of a similar name in Jerusalem, Moriah ("Jehovah is my guide"), Abraham was taught by the Lord the greatest lessons of life (Gen. 22:2–18; Gal. 3:8; Jacob 4:5).

The Lord appeared and confirmed the promise of a land (Gen. 12:7). Further revelations clarify the blessing of a promised land, which would be possessed by Abraham's seed only under the condition that "they hearken to my voice" (Abr. 2:6; Gen.

17:7–9: "thou shalt keep my covenant"). They were to inherit the land "from the river of Egypt unto . . . the river Euphrates" (Gen. 15:18); yet Abraham was warned that his seed would be strangers in lands not their own for centuries, until the "iniquity of the Amorite" peoples dwelling in Canaan was "full"; only then could they justly be dispossessed (Gen. 15:7, 13–16, 18). These vital principles are reiterated throughout the scriptures: the Lord does not arbitrarily cause some people to suffer and be destroyed while others are blessed to prosper.

Thus in events recounted in Genesis, Exodus, and beyond, the families of Abraham, Isaac, and Jacob were "strangers" (Heb., lit., "sojourners") in Canaan and Egypt; indeed, they sojourned in Egypt "four generations" until the time of Moses (Gen. 15:16; Ex. 6:16–27). Only in Joshua's time, after wandering in the wilderness, did the Israelites come to "inherit" the promised land (Josh. 1:1–4).

Abram regularly built altars as he moved along, and he called upon the name of the Lord (Heb., lit., "called in the name of Jehovah"). From him Abram received guidance; and frequently, it is recorded, "the Lord appeared unto him" (Gen. 12:7–8; 13:3–4; Abr. 2:17).

Abram's first sojourn in Canaan was short because of a famine; however, before he left, the Lord gave him some great revelations about the universe of His creations and His ultimate purposes. He said, "I show these things unto thee before ye go into Egypt, that ye may declare all these words" (Abr. 3:15). These revelations were given through an instrument called "Urim and Thummim" (Heb. plurals used as abstract nouns to denote "light and perfection"), which the Lord had given him already in Ur (Abr. 3:1). Some of those revelations have been restored (Abr. 3–5).

12:11–13 Say . . . thou art my sister: that it may be well with me for thy sake

Abram and Sarai told no untruth in Egypt in identifying Sarai by her blood relationship rather than her marital relationship with Abram. Because they were descended from a common ancestor,

Terah (Gen. 11:26–32; 20:12; Abr. 2:23–25), according to their custom she could be called Abram's sister, just as Lot could be called his brother (Gen. 13:8; 14:14, 16). No special terms were used for such relationships as niece, nephew, cousin, granddaughter, grandson. Ancestors could be called "father" or "mother," and descendants could be called "daughters" or "sons" (as in Luke 3:8; John 8:39).

Abram was guided by the Lord to use this strategy (Abr. 2:22–25); its other purpose may have been to create an opportunity for Abram to teach the Egyptian leaders (Abr. 3:15).

12:14–20 he entreated Abram well for her sake

Sarai was nevertheless taken to Pharaoh's house but not as another wife, and she was returned (Gen. 12:19). Abram was treated well and made rich in goods (Gen. 12:16; 13:1–2). A good relationship developed between host and guest (Abr., Fac. 3 and fn.), but that status was not perpetuated forever. Pharaoh and his household were plagued until he called Abram in, restored his wife, and then sent the whole Semitic clan away with all their possessions.

13:1– 4 Abram went up out of Egypt . . . into the south . . . And . . . from the south even to Bethel

The "south" is the desert area south of Canaan, the *Negev* (or *Negeb;* Heb., lit., "dry, parched"). Thus they traveled eastward from Egypt to get to the "south" of Canaan.

Because Pharaoh sent them away with all their possessions, they left Egypt "very rich in cattle, in silver, and in gold" (Gen. 13:2; 12:20). The company doubtless hastened through the arid Negev and proceeded northward back to Bethel, to the altar Abram had made at first, to call again on the name of the Lord, as was his consistent practice (Gen. 13:4a–b). That was part of his mission, for the Lord had said, "Through thy ministry my name shall be known in the earth forever" (Abr. 1:19).

13:5–13 Let there be no strife . . . for we be brethren

When conflict arose between the herders of the many flocks

of Abram and Lot, a division of grazing land became necessary. Facets of the character of both men are evident in their actions (their status as "brethren" is explained in the commentary on Gen. 12:11–13). Abram stated his principles and made his offer, but Lot chose somewhat selfishly and unwisely (Gen. 13:8–13). He took advantage of Abram's generous offer and claimed what looked like a choice district for his livestock. Evidently climate and soil then were very different from what they were after the cataclysm that destroyed Sodom and Gomorrah (Gen. 19) and different from conditions in that dry valley now.

13:14–18 all the land . . . to thee . . . and to thy seed for ever

The Lord confirmed the promise of the land (Gen. 12:7), all around about where Abram stood, to become the first base of operations for him and his descendants. Recall the conditions under which Abraham's seed might possess the promised land "for ever"; it was not an unconditional grant (Gen. 13:15a; Abr. 2:6).

Mamre became Abram's home for some time. As was his custom, he built there an altar for worship (Gen. 12:7–8; 13:18c). Even today, visitors are shown the "Oaks of Mamre" or the "Oaks of Abraham" about a mile and a quarter north of Hebron.

14:1–12 these made war . . . And they took Lot . . . and departed

Lot had made a self-serving choice in taking the green valley of the Jordan and an unwise choice in pitching his family's tents near Sodom. The first of two misfortunes befell him when four allied Mesopotamian kings raided the lower Jordan valley, taking people and goods from the five kings of the area. Lot and his family and all their possessions were taken. Had his uncle Abram not rescued him, Lot's progeny would probably not have been known thereafter in Genesis.

14:13 Abram the Hebrew

Genesis 14 is the first chapter in the Bible to use the patronymic identification of Abram as a descendant of Shem through Eber, or Abram the Hebrew (see commentary on Gen.

10:21–30). Eber, or Heber, was one of Abram's ancestors in the patriarchal line who was still alive at this time, although he was five generations older than Abram. Thus Abram could be called a "Heberite," or Hebrew, as one in the clan of Heber at the time.

14:13 these were confederate with Abram

The last phrase of Genesis 14:13 could be more literally rendered from the Hebrew as "These were possessors of a covenant of Abram"; it would be interesting to know what their covenant included. It is evident from the action of the men who accompanied Abram and his troop to rescue Lot that they felt some loyalty and commitment to him.

14:14–16 when Abram heard that his brother was taken captive

When Abram heard that his "brother" (that is, his nephew; Gen. 12:5) was in trouble, he did not hesitate to form a small attack force of his three hundred eighteen servants and his neighbors (Gen. 14:13, 24). They pursued the captors and captives nearly two hundred miles. Near Damascus, they divided their group, attacked at night, and recovered all the captive people and goods. It was a miraculous victory for Abram, and he gave God credit for it upon returning home (Gen. 14:20).

14:17–24 And the king of Sodom went out to meet him . . . And Melchizedek king of Salem . . . priest of the most high God

The kings of the cities involved went out to meet Abram on his return (Gen. 14:2). Among them was a most noteworthy king, Melchizedek, a high priest, king of Salem (later called Jerusalem), prince and king of peace, king of righteousness (Gen. 14:18*a–d*; Heb. 7; Alma 13:14–19; D&C 107:2–4; Ps. 110:4). Melchizedek had ordained Abram to the high priesthood (D&C 84:14–17), and to him Abram paid a tithe of the goods God had blessed him to regain (Gen. 14:20).

The bread and wine (Gen. 14:18) were a ceremonial meal, elements of which were later used in the Passover and transmuted later still by Jesus into symbols of the salvation with which he has blessed all mankind.

The place of meeting, "the king's dale," may have been in either the Kidron or the Hinnom valleys, near the city of Salem. Salem, or Jerusalem, was called *Uru-salim* in the Tel-el-Amarna tablets, and the name can be translated "City of Peace." This meaning harmonizes with a Book of Mormon statement that "Melchizedek did establish peace in the land in his days; therefore he was called the prince of peace, for he was the king of Salem" (Alma 13:18; BD, "Melchizedek"; "Melchizedek Priesthood").

In contrast to that great priest-king, the earthly king of Sodom also went out to meet Abram. He must have been among those who had not fallen into the bitumen pits but rather had fled to the mountains (Gen. 14:10). He met Abram on his return (Gen. 14:17), and, with gratitude for the rescue of his people, offered him all the goods retrieved. But Abram had vowed to the Lord that the campaign was not for self-aggrandizement; therefore, he accepted compensation only for the supplies they had eaten and the service given by his three confederates from Hebron (Gen. 14:13, 24). The account of this historic event displays well the character of Abram.

15:1– 6 what wilt thou give me, seeing I go childless

Though the Lord had indeed been Abram's "shield" in the rescue of Lot and others and now reminded him of an "exceeding great reward" for his obedience (Gen. 15:1; Abr. 2:6), Abram was growing old and understandably felt that no other reward would be of lasting significance unless he received fulfillment of the promise of seed (Gen. 12:2; 13:16; Abr. 2:9–11). That seed would become the "great nation" and bless all families of the whole earth.

According to a custom described in the Nuzi tablets from eastern Mesopotamia, one born in a man's house could become his heir. Was Abram's heir to be one born to his steward, Eliezer of Damascus (Gen. 15:3)? Eliezer may have been one of the worthy converts "won" during their migrations (Abr. 2:15; Gen. 12:5).

It was an honest question, and the Lord gave Abram a clear

response, with details later: Abram would yet beget a son of his wife (Gen. 15:4–6; 17:15–17), and the promised multitude of seed would indeed be given. Despite their age (Abr. 2:14; Gen. 12:4; 16:3, 16; 17:1), Abram and Sarai had faith enough to believe the promise, and their faith itself became exemplary (Heb. 11:8–11). Further, according to an inspired restoration of this passage (Gen. 15:6a), when Abram learned that the Son of Man, the Messiah, would come, he believed that too, and he rejoiced (as Jesus later attested in John 8:56–58).

15:7–21 to give thee this land . . . in the fourth generation

In answer to Abram's desire for confirmation of the promise of the land, the Lord instructed him to sacrifice three animals, each of them three years old (two females and one male), and also a turtledove and a pigeon. The reasons for this selection and the unusual manner of sacrificing them are not revealed to us; but the number three can signify completeness or perfection.

In any case, when night came and a deep sleep fell upon Abram, he received a revelation that his seed would be sojourners ("strangers," or temporary inhabitants) in lands not theirs for four hundred years, and only in the "fourth generation" (Gen. 15:16a) would they return to inherit the land of promise. The explanation that "the iniquity of the Amorites is not yet full" (Gen. 15:16) indicates that people are not removed from the land of their natural inheritance until or unless they have become unworthy of being preserved in it. It is also true that people inherit a land by the hand of the Lord only when they are worthy of it. Those principles are stated in many scriptures (Abr. 2:6; Lev. 18:28; Deut. 4:25–31; 6:18; 1 Ne. 17:33–35; Ether 2:7–10).

For the origins of the Amorites (Gen. 15:16), see the descendants of Canaan, son of Ham, in the Table of Nations (Gen. 10:15–20).

That night, Abram saw a smoking incense burner and a flaming torch pass between the divided halves of the sacrificed animals, and a covenant was established between the Lord and Abram specifying the extent of the land of promise and the peoples who were being dispossessed. Sad to say, Israel, of

Abram's seed, were similarly dispossessed centuries later when they became unworthy.

16:1–3 Sarai . . . took Hagar . . . gave her to . . . Abram

"God commanded Abraham, and Sarah gave Hagar to Abraham to wife. And why did she do it? Because this was the law; and from Hagar sprang many people. This, therefore, was fulfilling, among other things, the promises" (D&C 132:34). Note that Hagar became another *wife* to Abram (Gen. 16:3). Later (Gen. 25:1–6), yet another family, children of yet another wife, became part of Abraham's seed. Abraham's mission call pertained to all the faithful among Abraham's seed, for the words of the calling were "I will make of thee a great nation, . . . and thou shalt be a blessing unto thy seed after thee, that *in their hands they shall bear this ministry and Priesthood unto all nations*" (Abr. 2:9, emphasis added; also vv. 10–11; emphasis added).

16:4–15 when she saw that she had conceived, her mistress was despised in her eyes

Conflict and near tragedy arose from the new union. Hagar had made the common assumption of the culture that pregnancy was a blessing and barrenness a curse, and so she looked down upon her mistress. Such attitudes may be seen in other instances (e.g., Gen. 30:1; 1 Sam. 1:1–20).

It is understandable that Sarai would find her low status, which seemingly had resulted from her generosity and obedience, to be intolerable. Abram gave her leave to do whatever "was good in her eyes" (Gen. 16:6*a*), and she punished Hagar. But human actions taken to satisfy some human sense of justice are not always just, and the Lord may intervene. When Hagar fled, she was told by an angel messenger to return and was reassured that she would bear a son, to be named Ishmael (meaning, "God will hear"). History records that from him came a nation. The prophecy about Ishmael may seem derogatory but does not malign his people (Gen. 16:12*a*).

Hagar humbly asked herself whether she had been properly attentive to the Lord who was so attentive to her welfare (Gen.

16:13) and commemorated the event and lesson by naming the place Beer-lahai-roi (Gen. 16:14*b*). Arabs claiming descent from Ishmael held annual festivities for centuries by the well so identified.

Hagar returned and bore Abram's first son, Ishmael, when Abram was eighty-six years old. Ishmael was not the son originally promised to Abram and Sarai, however, and was not designated as the one bearing birthright responsibility (Gen. 21–22).

16:16 Abram was fourscore and six years old

Note Abram's age at this event, and recall it later, when the narrative recounts Isaac's birth (Gen. 21:5).

17:1–9 walk before me, and be thou perfect . . . thy name shall be Abraham

It was a high point in Abram's life when the Lord next appeared; for he gave him a great preparatory challenge, a new name, and additional covenants. Identifying himself as *El Shaddai* (which may imply "the God whose bosom sufficeth" but is usually translated "God Almighty"), the Lord challenged Abram to walk before him in perfection. Some patriarchs before him had "walked with God," and two had been described as "perfect" (TG, "Walking with God"; "Perfection"). *Perfect* is used to translate the Hebrew *tammim*, which connotes wholeness, completeness, and integrity. Jesus later challenged his disciples, "Be ye therefore perfect, even as your Father which is in heaven is perfect" (Matt. 5:48; 3 Ne. 12:48).

On the occasion of this personal visitation to Abram, "God talked with him," renewed and expanded his covenant and gave him the new name *Abraham*, "Father of a Multitude" (Gen. 17:1, 3–5). The Lord promised him that he and his seed would be fruitful and multiply and become many nations and kings. Through them the everlasting covenant would be established. The promise of the land wherein they sojourned was again confirmed (Gen. 17:6–8). But to gain the blessings, Abraham and his seed after him had to keep the covenant (Gen. 17:9), perpetuating it by living according to its principles.

The restored version of Genesis explains that the old covenant of baptism made known in Adam's time (Gen. 17:3*a;* Moses 6:52–66; 7:11) had been corrupted, along with other ordinances, both in doctrine and practice. But now Abraham and his seed were commanded by the Lord, "Keep all my covenants wherein I covenanted with thy fathers," as well as those newly given them (JST Gen. 17:12; Gen. 17:7*a*); then circumcision was instituted as a sign of the covenant.

17:10–14 he that is eight days old shall be circumcised

As a sign of the covenant, circumcision would remind all fathers and mothers to teach children the laws and ways of the Lord, and it would remind all boys and men to perpetuate their covenants in purity. Circumcision continued as a sign of the covenant until the mission was extended to all nations in New Testament times (Acts 15:1–29; Gal. 5:6; 6:15; Col. 2:6–15).

According to the inspired restoration of these scriptures (Gen. 17:7*a;* JST Gen. 17:12), circumcision at the age of eight days would also remind parents that children become "accountable," when they are eight years of age, to keep the commandments in covenants made with the fathers. One might suppose those covenants would include the proper baptism of Adam's time (Moses 6:64–68) rather than the corrupted "baptism" that had evolved (JST Gen. 17:5–6), but that is not made explicit.

17:15–22 Sarah shall her name be. . . . I will bless her, and she shall be a mother of nations; kings . . . shall be of her

Sarai's new name foretold a change from her way of struggle and persistence to prevail. *Sarai* is derived from the Hebrew root *srh* ("prevail"), the same root from which the Hebrew *yisrael,* or *Israel,* was later derived. *Sarah,* "Princess," is the feminine form of the word meaning "chieftain," "chief," "ruler," "official," "captain," or "prince." Thus the promise "kings of people shall be of her" (Gen. 17:16) was a play on the meaning of her new name.

Abraham laughed (or rejoiced; Gen. 17:17*a*) upon receiving the promise of a son in his old age by his aged wife. He immediately expressed the hope that his son Ishmael would remain in

God's favor. The Lord gave a great promise regarding Ishmael and his descendants (Gen. 17:18, 20), and he also reassured Sarah and Abraham that they would indeed have a son to perpetuate the covenant and bear the birthright responsibility (Gen. 17:19, 21). His name would be *Yitzkhaq* ("he shall rejoice/laugh"; in English, *Isaac*, transliterated from the Greek, *Isaak*, which was pronounced EE-saak).

Note again the very personal nature of divine visitations to Abraham: "And he left off talking with him, and God went up from Abraham" (Gen. 17:22).

17:23–27 circumcised . . . the selfsame day as God had said

With the beginning of circumcision as the token of God's covenant with Abraham, both old and young men were circumcised on the same day, but the age thereafter for boys was eight days (Gen. 17:12). Ishmael's age of thirteen (Gen. 17:25) became the age for that initiation among his descendants and is still perpetuated in Islam (TG and BD, "Circumcision").

18:1–8 the Lord appeared, . . . and, lo, three men stood by him

In a quite extraordinary visitation, three men and the Lord next communicated with Abraham. The "three men" (Gen. 18:2) were addressed as "brethren," according to the inspired revision of the account (Gen. 18:3*a*). It was those three whom Abraham courteously addressed and for whom he and his wife prepared food, which they ate (Gen. 18:8, 22*a*; Joseph Fielding Smith, *Doctrines of Salvation* [Salt Lake City: Bookcraft, 1954], 1:16–17). Only after Abraham and Sarah took care of the duties of hospitality was the purpose of the visit made known, which was to reassure them concerning the promise of a son (Gen. 17:17).

18:9–15 Sarah thy wife shall have a son

Sarah's laughter in response to the surprising promise that a child would be born to her in her old age corresponds to that of Abraham earlier (Gen. 17:17–19); hence the child's name means either "he laughs" or "he rejoices" (Gen. 21:6*a*). The Lord's response to Sarah's laughter was a mild rebuke, and a truth was taught by a question, "Is any thing too hard for the Lord?" (Gen. 18:14).

18:16–33 Shall I hide from Abraham that thing which I do

The statement of the Lord indicating why he could trust Abraham and why he desired to let him know about the catastrophe coming to Sodom and Gomorrah is an impressive indication of God's esteem for that good man (Gen. 18:16–19).

In the inspired version of the account, the Lord sent the three "angels which were holy men" to Sodom to see that the iniquities of the people of that place were duly punished. They went to do so while Abraham conversed with the Lord (Gen. 18:22a; JST Gen. 18:19–23).

Consider why the Lord let Abraham go through the long process of pleading on behalf of those wicked places, knowing (as Gen. 19:29 implies) that it was Lot's family Abraham wished to save when he asked that the places be spared even if only as many as ten righteous could be found in them (Gen. 18:23–32). Evidently the Lord lets us exercise our intelligence and agency in order to develop, for if all things were done by the Divine initiative alone, there would be no challenges to help us grow in faith, hope, charity, intelligence, and judgment.

19:1–29 the Lord being merciful . . . brought him forth

When the three messengers arrived in Sodom (Gen. 19:1a–b; JST Gen. 18:19–23), they found evils there were indeed rampant—and were soon directed even against them (Gen. 19:5). A shocking problem is evident in the text that reports the conversation about the virgin daughters of Lot (Gen. 19:7–9); important corrections of that text are given in the inspired revision of it (Gen. 19:8a).

The crass condition of the men of Sodom and the spiritual lassitude of some members of Lot's family make it evident why mercy must not overrule justice and permit the wicked to escape the fruits of evildoing. The hesitant family of Lot could not justly be saved without some test of their faith and worthiness. Some did not accept the warning, and even Lot's wife looked back in spite of being led out by the hand and being duly warned (Gen. 19:14, 16–17, 26). She perished in the holocaust with the others who refused to heed. Jesus used this lesson in his prophecy about the end of our wicked world (Gen. 19:26; Luke 17:31–32); it concludes: "Remember Lot's wife."

19:30– 38 there is not a man in the earth to come in unto us

Lot's daughters' rationalizing their incest makes it appear that they too may have been imbued with the ways of Sodom. Their purpose could not justify such a means, for it was not a righteous way nor was it likely the only way.

Some commentators have supposed this account of illicit acts was contrived to impugn the Moabites and Ammonites; but that is a poor argument, for equally scandalous stories are preserved later concerning even the royal line of Judah. Doubtless such accounts were kept to provide vicarious experiences that should help others avoid such rationalization. There is, of course, no implication that because prominent people of the Bible did such things their actions were approved.

20:1–18 indeed she is my sister; . . . the daughter of my father, but not . . . of my mother

The incident involving Abraham and Abimelech parallels in several particulars a similar incident involving Pharaoh. Sarah was Abraham's "sister" in being of the same paternal line from Terah; but her maternal line was that of Haran's wife (commentary on Gen. 12:4–5, 11–13).

Why Abimelech took Sarah is not clear, but since he felt he had acted in integrity of heart and innocence of hands, the Lord intervened to save Sarah and spare Abimelech from sinning in ignorance, giving him correct information so that he could right the wrong (Gen. 20:3–7). Abimelech, like Pharaoh before him, learned through experience to respect the God of Abraham and not to obstruct his will. He showed generosity in seeking to compensate Abraham's group and in inviting them to stay wherever they pleased. Also, the affliction of his people was healed.

21:1– 8 Sarah conceived, and bare Abraham a son in his old age. . . . And Abraham circumcised his son

The Lord caused the miracle to happen: the promised son was born to Abraham and Sarah in their old age. They circumcised him at eight days of age as a sign of the covenant, as they had been commanded (Gen. 17:7–12, fn. 7a; JST Gen. 17:11–12).

Regarding his name, *Isaac,* see the commentary on Genesis 17:15–22; 18:9–15.

21:9–21 Sarah saw the son of Hagar . . . mocking. Wherefore she said . . . the son of this bondwoman shall not be heir with my son

After Isaac was born, named, circumcised, and weaned, and Ishmael had reached age fifteen or sixteen, trouble again arose between Sarah and Hagar, as it well might even though it should not. Sarah may appear to have been supersensitive about the status of her son and quite callous about the welfare of the second wife and first son of Abraham, but it is unwise to judge those matters from the limited information we have.

Abraham was naturally grieved by Sarah's demand that Hagar and her son be sent away, and only after receiving a revelation concerning Ishmael's destiny and Isaac's calling and responsibility did he let her be sent away. Apparently, however, the provisions he gave Hagar and Ishmael were inadequate, and it was by the Lord's intervention that tragedy was averted (Gen. 21:11–19).

God's concern and compassion for the individual are shown again in this episode. He "heard the voice of the lad" (v. 17), and the same "Living One Who Seeth" who had given guidance to Hagar in her need once before (Gen. 16:13–14) on this occasion provided life-giving water for her and her son. He also gave her assurance that Ishmael had an important destiny, which must have helped her in rearing him and securing a wife for him (Gen. 21:17–21).

21:22– 34 he called that place Beer-sheba; because . . . they made a covenant

Abraham's Philistine neighbors, acknowledging to Abraham

that "God is with thee in all thou doest" (Gen. 21:22), proposed that a covenant of peace be made between them. People could see in Abraham's way of life and in his prudence evidences of the power of the living God in his life. So they made the covenant and named the well—which Abraham had dug and which Abimelech's servants had taken over but then restored—*Beer-sheva* (anglicized, *Beer-sheba*), "Well of the Covenant." Abraham gave Abimelech seven lambs in token of that agreement. The Hebrew root *sheva* bears the meaning of "seven" and also of "swearing" an oath in making a covenant.

22:1–19 My son, God will provide himself a lamb

The vital episode in which the Lord "preached before the gospel unto Abraham" (Gal. 3:8, 24) let Abraham experience a terrible "similitude of God and his Only Begotten Son" (Jacob 4:5). Often this incident is seen only as a "test" of Abraham; certainly it did try him and prove him (Gen. 22:1*a*), and the "angel of the Lord" himself commended Abraham (Gen. 22:11–12, 15–18), confirming what he had declared earlier (Gen. 18:18–19). Because Abraham had already proved himself worthy in many ways and had been blessed by God for that, the main purpose of this episode may have been to let Abraham appreciate the mission of the Savior, "and he saw it, and was glad" (John 8:56). That is the point Jacob emphasized in the Book of Mormon (Jacob 4:5).

The mission of Abraham and his seed was and is to bear the priesthood and knowledge of the true and living God "in the earth forever" (Abr. 1:18–19). Thereby "shall all the families of the earth be blessed, *even with the blessings of the Gospel, which are the blessings of salvation, even of life eternal*" (Abr. 2:11, emphasis added; Gen. 12:3; 22:18). Abraham could know and teach the good news of salvation because the Lord had taught him. He would certainly have been in a perfect frame of mind to receive it after he said with prophetic faith, "My son, God will provide himself a lamb" (Gen. 22:8).

This epochal event occurred in "the land of Moriah . . . upon one of the mountains," the place that later became the Temple Mount (Gen. 22:2*a–d;* commentary on Gen. 12:6–10). A map of

Jerusalem (Bible Map 17) reveals that the Garden Tomb and the Hill of Golgotha are on a higher part of the same mount or ridge northwest of the temple site; thus it may be that the Savior, the divine Seed of Abraham, was offered nearly two thousand years later on a higher eminence of the same mount where the birthright son of Abraham was a "type" of Him.

22:20–24 Milcah . . . Nahor . . . Bethuel . . . Rebekah

Information reached Abraham about the family of his brother Nahor, who had stayed in Haran when Abraham migrated to Canaan. One of Nahor's granddaughters, Rebekah, later became the wife of Abraham's son Isaac (Gen. 22:23a–c).

23:1–20 after this, Abraham buried Sarah

Many years after the sacrifice, when Isaac had reached the age of thirty-seven years (calculated from information in Gen. 17:17; 21:5; 23:1; 25:20) and his mother was one hundred twenty-seven, Sarah died. The account of Abraham's purchase of a cave for her tomb in Machpelah gives additional insight into the character and reputation of Abraham. He was honest, considerate, persistent, and straightforward. The process of bargaining to make a purchase, or a contract, is still common in the Middle East, but usually the seller overstates the price rather than understates it. In this case the seller was trying to show favor and respect for the buyer; but the buyer, Abraham, was firm in doing what he considered to be right and just.

A shrine exists to this day at Machpelah, in Hebron, with cenotaphs for three patriarchs and their wives.

24:1–9 thou shalt go unto my country, and to my kindred, and take a wife unto my son Isaac

A proper wife for Abraham's birthright son was one who would believe in the true God and be able to bring up children in the faith to carry on the mission (Gen. 24:3c). The help of the Lord and the will of the young woman were both vital to the satisfactory completion of this mission of Abraham's servant (Gen. 24:3, 5, 7–8).

24:10–28 O Lord God of my master Abraham, I pray thee, send me good speed this day, and shew kindness unto my master Abraham

The servant took ten camels laden with gifts for the family and bride-to-be (BD, "Marriage," for the little that is known about wedding customs). He humbly supplicated the Lord for blessings for himself and his master, needing assurance of a safe journey and of guidance in selecting the bride, and then he set off.

The help he desired was given. A practical and significant sign from the Lord identified Rebekah as the right wife for his master Abraham's son, and the servant was duly grateful. Her gracious willingness to serve him must have been impressive. The writer of the account mentions that she was fair to look upon and adds the more important fact that she was a virgin (Gen. 24:16). The servant was assured that she would be an acceptable bride.

He gave Rebekah some impressive preliminary gifts and inquired about her identity; when he learned she was indeed of Abraham's brother's family, he thanked the Lord, and she went home to report (Gen. 24:22–28). More gifts were given later (Gen. 24:53).

24:29–50 Laban and Bethuel answered . . . The thing proceedeth from the Lord

Rebekah's brother Laban's mode of addressing Abraham's servant, and the response of both Laban and Bethuel, evidenced that they were still faithful worshippers of the true Lord (Gen. 24:31, 50–51). Abraham's servant had given a conscientious, faithful account of his mission, and they responded well.

24:51–60 And she said, I will go

Respect for the feelings and desires of the maiden involved was shown as Abraham had intended, for when she was asked directly, she affirmed that she would go to become the wife of Isaac (Gen. 24:5, 8, 57–58). The gifts of silver, gold, and raiment given the bride-to-be and the precious things given her mother and brother were doubtless part of the dowry, or *mohar* (Gen. 24:51–56; BD, "Marriage"). The bride was not "purchased" thereby; she was in no sense the chattel of the husband. Her demeanor in the home, her exercise of agency and will, her initiative and effectiveness, both as an individual and as a marriage partner, illustrate that she was truly a help meet for her husband.

As Rebekah, her nurse, and her maids departed, the parting wish and blessing of the family was perhaps more prophetic than they knew; for through her Abraham's seed was to become as numerous as the sands of the sea, so that they might eventually bless all families of the earth (Gen. 24:59–61; TG, "Seed of Abraham).

24:61–67 she became his wife; and he loved her

There is even a bit of romance in the account of the young couple's meeting and marriage. The details are quite nicely told, including the conclusion: "and he loved her."

Unfortunately, no details are given us about the marriage ceremony; but that may be understandable, for in our dispensation details of priesthood marriages (in the temple) are also not made public.

25:1–4 a wife . . . Keturah . . . bare . . . Midian

We could also wish for more details about Abraham's other family of six sons by Keturah, and especially about the possible ordination of Midian or someone in his line to the holy priesthood. The book of Exodus records that Moses married a daughter of Jethro, a priest of Midian; and latter-day revelation indicates that Jethro conferred the true priesthood upon Moses (Gen. 25:2b; D&C 84:6).

25:5–6 all . . . unto Isaac. . . . But unto the sons of the concubines, . . . Abraham gave gifts

Abraham gave the birthright leadership responsibility of his family to Isaac, but he may have given priesthood powers also to at least one of his other sons (see commentary on Gen. 25:1–4).

He gave gifts of material things to all of them and sent them to seek their fortune in the "east country."

Confirmation of Abraham's mission upon the head of Isaac by the Lord is seen later (Gen. 26:1–6), as is transmission of it by authority of the Lord from Isaac to Jacob (Gen. 28:10–22). It is significant that in the accounts of these ordinances, the hand of the Lord is emphasized more than the hand of man.

25:7–10 gave up the ghost . . . gathered to his people

A typical Old Testament description of the event and process of death, the passage recording Abraham's death illustrates a recognition that the spirit departed from the body and was reunited with family members whose spirits had gone before. Other examples of this concept can be found in other scriptures (TG, "Family, Eternal.") There are other interpretations of this description of death, but the credibility of this one merits its consideration.

Great honor has been attached to the name of Abraham in scriptures written hundreds and even thousands of years after his life was over. In Jesus' time some thought it sufficient for their salvation that they were descendants of Abraham. Jesus challenged that belief: "If ye were Abraham's children, ye would do the works of Abraham" (John 8:39). Paul assured his gentile converts in Galatia that by faith in Christ and baptism unto his righteous way, they became Abraham's children (Gal. 3:7–9, 26–29; Abr. 2:10). Abraham has indeed become the "father of the faithful" (D&C 138:41; 84:33–34; Gen. 17:5; Rom. 4:16; BD, "Abraham").

25:11 God blessed his son Isaac

The good relationship that Isaac maintained with the Lord is noted; details follow (Gen. 25:19ff). The well at Lahai-roi was an important place in the history of Abraham's family (Gen. 16:7–14).

25:12–18 these are the generations of Ishmael, Abraham's son

In the group record of Ishmael's descendants, twelve "princes"

(Heb., *nsi'im,* "ones elevated, chiefs") over his "nations" or clans are listed and their locations described.

The death of Ishmael is described in Genesis 25:17 in the same terms used to describe the death of Abraham in verse 8. That his death was recorded at the end of his family record does not necessarily mean that he died before the first events in the family record of Isaac, which follows.

25:19–26 these are the generations of Isaac, Abraham's son

This family group record continues the family history accounts that have been seen earlier in Genesis (cf. Gen. 5:1; 10:1) and may be seen later as well (1 Chr. 2–4). A variant account was used in Exodus (Ex. 6:14–30).

Like Abraham and Sarah, Isaac and Rebekah had to seek the Lord's blessing to start their family. When Rebekah did conceive and later felt conflict within, she asked the Lord the reason and meaning of it and received a revelation about the destiny of the twins she would bear. It appears later (Gen. 27) that she felt she had to help the younger child receive his destiny.

The first was named Esau (from a Heb. root meaning "hairy"), but his descendants were usually called *Edom* (Heb., "red"); both names recall his appearance as a newborn. The second twin was named *Jacob,* the meaning of which is "He shall follow at the heel," a Hebrew idiom meaning "he shall assail, overreach, or supplant"; his name was perhaps given by his mother Rebekah because of her revelation that he would acquire the birthright responsibility rather than the firstborn, Esau. The writer of the account saw significance in the fact that Jacob's infant hand took hold of his brother's heel, for the noun *'aqev,* "heel," is from the same Hebrew root as the name *Ya'aqov,* "Jacob."

25:27–28 Esau was a . . . hunter, a man of the field; and Jacob was a plain man, dwelling in tents.

Jacob's and Esau's were the contrasting ways of hunter and husbandman. *Plain* (Gen. 25:27*b*) is used here to translate the same Hebrew word that is often translated *perfect* (Gen. 6:9; 17:1), *perfect* meaning, ideally, a "man of integrity." This word was used to describe Noah and to inspire Abraham. Remember also Jesus' challenge to his followers to become "perfect" (Matt. 5:48). Jacob, like most of us, started out far from possessing that quality but achieved a degree of it later.

A quite superficial reason is recorded for Isaac's favoring Esau; Rebekah's favor of Jacob, on the other hand, may have been because of her revelation about his destiny. Their favoritism nonetheless held potential for tragedy—as it can in any family.

25:29– 34 I am at the point to die; and what profit shall this birthright do to me?

Surely Esau must have exaggerated somewhat, coming home from the hunt and saying he was hungry to the point of death and thus saw no "profit" in the birthright (Gen. 25:32). The writer of the account concluded that Esau "despised" it (Gen. 25:34). Jacob's asking his starving, dying brother to "sell" the birthright before giving him food is also surely exaggerated; but certainly Jacob did take advantage of the opportunity to offer food in return for the birthright.

26:1– 5 Sojourn in this land, and I will be with thee, and will bless thee; . . . and I will perform the oath which I sware unto Abraham thy father; . . . and in thy seed shall all the nations of the earth be blessed

Isaac was assured that he could remain during the cyclical drought in the Philistine-held coastal plains near Gerar. The Lord would bless him there and confirm upon him the blessings of Abraham. The revelation declared that Abraham qualified to retain his blessings by obeying the Lord—keeping his charge, his commandments, his statutes and laws (Gen. 26:5).

26:6–11 he said, She is my sister: for he feared

Recall the nearly parallel cases of Abraham and Sarah in Egypt (Gen. 12:13–20) and later in Philistine lands (Gen. 20:1–18). Isaac and Rebekah were double first cousins once removed, for they had a common ancestor and several closely related forebears; thus Rebekah could be called Isaac's "sister" in their manner of speaking, just as Sarah could be called Abraham's "sister."

This Philistine king was also named Abimelech; it means "father of a king" or "my father is king" and could be the title of a dynastic family. Isaac's experience with a king named Abimelech in Gerar was some sixty to eighty years after Abraham's.

26:12–33 We saw certainly that the Lord was with thee

Isaac's blessings helped him prosper in Philistia, and that prosperity aroused jealousy, fear, and acts of vandalism despite King Abimelech's proclamation. Nevertheless, Isaac lived the law of patience and forbearance that the Lord had given to the ancient patriarchs (D&C 98:23–32); and when the Philistines saw that the Lord continued to prosper him, they offered to make peace with him (Gen. 26:28–29). After patiently moving from well to well, Isaac finally went to the old well, Beer-sheba, where his father had made a covenant with the Philistines (Gen. 21:22–34). The Lord appeared at night and assured Isaac that he would continue to be blessed; so Isaac, like Abraham, built an altar and worshipped the Lord there. Another covenant was made with the Philistines; the name of the well was renewed, Beer-sheba, "Well of the Covenant"; and all parted in peace (TG, "Peacemakers"). This is an example of the way Isaac carried out the Abrahamic mission, making known by his way of life the name, ways, and powers of the Lord (Abr. 1:18–19; 2:6–11; commentary on Gen. 26:1–5).

26:34–35 Esau . . . took to wife . . . daughter[s] of . . . the Hittite: Which were a grief of mind unto Isaac and to Rebekah

Esau showed further disregard for the birthright (commentary on Gen. 25:34) by marrying Hittite women, who were unlikely to bring up his family with faith in the Lord (BD, "Heth"; "Hittites"). Esau's marriages were "a grief of mind" to his parents. Recall how their own marriage had been carefully and prayerfully planned and carried out (Gen. 24).

27:1–29 I shall bring a curse upon me, and not a blessing

Why Rebekah was so strongly motivated that she risked a curse upon her son or herself (Gen. 27:6–13) is difficult to know. Her revelation about his destiny (Gen. 25:21–23) may have been a factor, but deceit does not get blessings (D&C 82:10*a*; 130:20–21; TG, "Blessings"). It is not known whether she had ever shared her revelation with Isaac. Inasmuch as he was directed by the Spirit of the Lord, Isaac could not have given a patriarchal blessing to the wrong son. He did speak words conveying the birthright blessing while his hands were on the head of Jacob disguised as Esau; but that was by the will of the Lord. If the words spoken were to be confirmed and fulfilled, the Lord through Isaac would confirm them and Jacob would have to live worthy of fulfillment. Isaac did later confirm the promised blessing (Gen. 27:33; 28:1–5). Jacob's improved deportment and the Lord's confirmation of the blessing are shown later (Gen. 29–32).

27:30–33 yea, and he shall be blessed

When Isaac realized it was Jacob to whom he had given the blessing, he could have rescinded it and replaced it with a curse if he had been inspired to know Jacob was the wrong candidate (Gen. 27:12; D&C 56:4; 58:32; all fn.); yet he said, "Yea, and he shall be blessed" (Gen. 27:32). It is as if he realized at that moment, if not before, that Jacob had the potential to bear the birthright responsibility despite his existing faults. Patriarchal blessings may be given us today before we are fully worthy, but we also must live worthily before we can realize their fulfillment.

27:34–40 the fatness of the earth, and of the dew of heaven

Without mentioning that he had "despised his birthright" and traded it for food (Gen. 25:34), Esau bitterly denounced Jacob for being a "supplanter" who "took away" the birthright and then the blessing (Gen. 27:36*a*). He asked whether some blessing were not still available to him and received a promise of the bounties of the earth; moreover, his people were promised that they could sometimes free themselves from domination by Israel and have dominion themselves (Gen. 27:34–40). The vicissitudes of the strife between Edom and Israel are told from the book of Numbers on through the books of Kings—and that strife still goes on today.

27:41– 45 then will I slay my brother Jacob

Esau valued more highly what he had lost after it was gone, as many people do, and vowed violent revenge after the death of father Isaac. But the alert and resourceful Rebekah averted the double tragedy of loss of one son by murder and the other by the execution in accord with the law (Gen. 9:6); she proposed to Isaac that Jacob be sent away to find a proper wife in her ancestral homeland. Thus she would get Jacob away for "a few days" until Esau's anger cooled. He actually would be away for twenty years.

27:46 if Jacob take a wife of the daughters of Heth, . . . what good shall my life do me?

Knowing that their responsibility for perpetuating the Abrahamic mission would be frustrated if Jacob married as Esau had (Gen. 26:34–35), Isaac responded favorably to his wife's proposal.

28:1–5 Isaac called Jacob, and blessed him, and charged him

Isaac confirmed the future blessing upon the head of the son whom the Lord had allowed him to bless before he was fully worthy of it. The "blessing of Abraham" was explicitly transmitted this time. Isaac then gave strict instructions to Jacob on selecting a proper wife. They were much like those Abraham had given his steward for choosing a wife for Isaac (Gen. 24:1–9).

28:6– 9 Esau . . . took . . . the daughter of Ishmael . . . to be his wife

The reasons for Esau's taking a wife of Abrahamic descent in addition to his Hittite wives (Gen. 26:34–35) are clearly stated.

Note some confusion of the names of his wives in Genesis 36:2–3.

28:10–15 in thee and in thy seed shall all the families of the earth be blessed. I am with thee . . . and will bring thee again into this land

After walking more than sixty miles, Jacob slept on hard rocks; there he received a marvelous dream-vision from the Lord God of Abraham, divinely confirming the birthright promise and assuring him of a safe return to the land promised to Abraham's seed, where he could raise a family to fulfill their mission.

28:16–22 this is . . . the house of God . . . the gate of heaven

Awakening in this awesome ("dreadful") place of the Lord's presence, Jacob named it "House of God" (Heb., *Beth-el;* Gen. 28:19*a–b*). He resolved to pay a tithe of all his gains to God thereafter, out of gratitude for His blessings and promises (Gen. 28:22). Some commentators have failed to note that first the Lord offered the blessings (Gen. 28:13–15) and then Jacob responded to the offer, saying, "If God will be with me, . . . then shall the Lord be my God. . . . I will surely give a tenth unto thee" (Gen. 28:20–22). This is the second time tithing is mentioned in Genesis; the first is of Abraham's tithes given in gratitude for the blessings he had received in rescuing Lot and the other captives (Gen. 14:14–20).

29:1–12 Rachel came with her father's sheep

Upon Jacob's arrival among "the people of the east" (that is, Haran, in upper Mesopotamia), he providentially met Rachel, daughter of his uncle Laban, at the community well. Recall the similar circumstances under which Abraham's steward met for the first time Rebekah, who became the wife of Isaac and Jacob's own mother (Gen. 24:1–27).

The source of water was protected by a huge stone that could be rolled away only by several shepherds; but with strength born of eagerness to be of service (and perhaps to make a good impression), Jacob himself rolled it away and watered Rachel's sheep. He was a bit bold in that first meeting: he gave her an introductory kiss. He was following his father's instructions, however, in seeking out his mother's family to choose his wife.

29:13–20 I will serve thee seven years for Rachel

Jacob had taken into his own hands the means of gaining the birthright, and now he had nothing but his own hands to produce the needed *mohar,* or dowry, to gain a bride. There was no camel train laden with gifts as there had been when Abraham's steward negotiated for a bride for Isaac. Jacob's first seven-year contract with Laban seems to have worked out rather well. It is surprising to read that the seven years "seemed unto him but a few days" because of his love (Gen. 29:20); for a modern suitor, a few days would seem rather like seven years.

29:21–30 he took Leah his daughter, and brought her to him

Although it had been agreed that Jacob was working to marry Laban's younger daughter, Rachel, Laban contrived to have him marry the older daughter, Leah, who was described as "tender eyed." The contrast between her and Rachel, who is described as "beautiful and well favored" (Gen. 29:17), is less striking in Hebrew, in which Leah's eyes are described as "soft."

Perhaps Jacob's resentment was mitigated by a concession allowing him to marry Rachel after Leah's week of wedding festivities. But he also was "permitted" to work an additional seven years.

29:31–35 Rachel was barren. . . . And Leah conceived

A sort of "baby contest" began between the two wives (told in Genesis 30); in the course of it, Jacob gained two more wives, twelve sons, and at least one daughter. More than half of the children were mothered by the faithful but unfavored Leah. Note the significance in the name of each child, explained in a footnote to each, in Genesis 29 and 30.

30:1–24 God hearkened to her. . . . And she . . . bare a son

Again, as in two previous generations, the birthright son was born only after some delay, soul-searching, and sincere prayers to God. Rachel had turned first to her husband to demand children and had been called to repentance; she then turned to her sister

Leah to negotiate for some herbal remedies, only to find that Leah was blessed to bear another son (Gen. 29:31; BD, "Mandrakes"). Finally Rachel turned to God, and he responded to her supplications. When at last a son was born to Rachel, she named him Joseph (Heb., lit., "He shall add"), hoping for yet more; but the name was more prophetic still, for it may be derived from a verb meaning "He shall gather." That concept seems implied in statements in later scriptures (e.g., Deut. 33:17; D&C 58:45).

30:25– 43 when shall I provide for mine own house also?

Although Jacob's birthright at home should have included the right to a double portion of the parental property, he apparently did not wish to wait for the inheritance to make him economically self-sustaining. He showed admirable initiative in assuring his father-in-law that Laban need not *give* him anything but that the off-color animals among Laban's livestock should be his wages (Gen. 30:28, 32). He had already served fourteen years for his wives. Because his father-in-law wanted him to continue, Jacob proposed developing his own flocks and herds while continuing to work as before. Laban agreed, saying, "I have learned by experience that the Lord hath blessed me for thy sake" (Gen. 30:27). Just as Abimelech had learned from observing Isaac (Gen. 26:12–16, 23–26), so Laban had learned from watching Jacob the effects of the blessings of the Lord in a person's life. Jacob also was aware of those blessings.

Jacob's animal husbandry (Gen. 30:36–43) included the use of striped and spotted willows to engender conception of off-color animals, according to a superstition of the time. We know today that they could not have had any such effect, but similar superstitious beliefs and practices still persist in some places today. Jacob simply gave credit to the Lord for his increases in livestock (Gen. 31:6–10).

31:1–16 the Lord said unto Jacob, Return unto the land of thy fathers, and to thy kindred; and I will be with thee

Several factors let Jacob know he should leave at the end of his last six years of managing his father-in-law's flocks: Laban's sons manifested jealousy; the countenance of Laban was changed toward Jacob; Laban's daughters, Jacob's wives, were disaffected toward their father, feeling disinherited; and the Lord himself revealed that it was time for Jacob to return home.

Nothing is recorded here commending Jacob's twenty years of work for Laban, but it was noted later (Gen. 31:38–42).

31:17–55 Jacob stole away unawares. . . . Then Laban overtook Jacob

Though Laban learned of Jacob's departure three days afterward, he overtook him in seven days, at Gilead, on the way to Canaan. Laban complained of Jacob's departure without farewell amenities and accused someone of stealing his "gods" (Gen. 31:30). Rachel had indeed stolen her father's "images" (Gen. 31:19; Heb. *teraphim*; BD, "Teraphim"); they may have been deemed protectors of property ownership. Laban was restrained from punishing Jacob by a dream-revelation from God (Gen. 31:24); but he showed his resentment by identifying Deity to Jacob only as "the God of your father" (Gen. 31:29).

When Rachel's deed was neither confessed nor discovered, the two men made a peace agreement (Gen. 31:50–53), setting up boundary markers and invoking God's surveillance of their future acts toward one another. The matter was amicably concluded with a sacrifice by Jacob, a meal together, and even some good-bye kisses by Laban on the following morning before separating.

32:1–2 the angels of God met him

Another divine manifestation was granted Jacob, perhaps to prepare him for meeting and reconciling with his brother, Esau, after twenty years' separation. Jacob called the angels "God's host" and the place "Mahanaim" (Gen. 32:2a–b).

32:3–23 And Jacob sent messengers before him to Esau

To do what he could to assure peace between him and his brother, Jacob sent a message to Esau about his prosperous state—perhaps to suggest that he was not coming to claim any material inheritance. Distressed when he learned of Esau's approach with a company of four hundred, Jacob divided his company into two bands (Gen. 32:7, 2a–b; Heb., lit., "camps"). He hoped that at least one group might survive an attack, and he humbly and urgently prayed for God's protection (Gen. 32:9–12). Then he added works to his faith by sending generous gifts to Esau, to be delivered one group at a time with conciliatory messages, in the hope that strife might be averted (Gen. 32:13–23).

32:24–32 there wrestled a man with him

Jacob did not sleep that night after sending his families and attendants over the brook Jabbok. The brook's name means "the Wrestler," doubtless in commemoration of Jacob's experience that night, for while he tarried alone "there wrestled a man with him" who had divine power to bless him (Gen. 32:24a; compare the spiritual wrestling of Enos and Alma). Jacob would not let him go until he gave the blessing, even suffering physical injury while tenaciously holding on.

The "man" also had authority to change his name from *Jacob* (meaning "he shall supplant") to *Israel* (meaning "let God prevail"; Gen. 32:28a–d). The new name seems to symbolize the end of his past ways and contrast them with the way he could succeed as a true patriarch, by letting God prevail in guiding his emerging mission. Note also that during the night's experiences Jacob had "seen God face to face" and had been "preserved," not destroyed (Gen. 32:30). To commemorate that vision, Jacob named a place by the brook of his wrestling *Peniel*, "face of God." The "man" who wrestled with Jacob, and blessed him, and bestowed upon him a new name, was a man with authority from God; Jacob's seeing "God face to face" that night was an additional special experience.

33:1–16 Take, I pray thee, my blessing . . . because God hath dealt graciously with me, . . . and he took it

There were no traces of ill will between Jacob and Esau when they met twenty years after their conflict about birthrights; indeed, both the acts and words of each helped to create good will. If

Esau had come out with his four hundred men intending something else, Jacob's advance gifts helped him "find grace in the sight of" Esau, and the prayers of Jacob were answered (Gen. 32:8–12).

33:17–20 And Jacob came to Shalem, a city of Shechem

The little green valley of the Jabbok and the broader green valley of the Jordan must have looked good to Jacob's company, and they camped a while where the Jabbok enters the Jordan, at a place named *Succoth* ("booths"). There they built *succoth* (sheds made of posts supporting pole beams and joists and covered with willow branches), and they even built Jacob a house (Gen. 33:17).

When the group moved again it could have been up a western tributary to the Jordan, the Wadi Fari'a (or "Farah"; Bible Map 1) toward Shechem. Passing Tirzah, they could have turned south and in half a day reached *Shalem* ("fulfillment") near Shechem.

Jacob bought land there, the first that he owned in the whole land of promise. There he "spread his tent" and erected an altar to God, naming it "El is the God of Israel" (Gen. 33:20*a*). Jacob and his family doubtless hoped to enjoy some peace and fulfillment.

The New Testament (John 4:3–15) indicates that Jacob also dug a well there; at that well, Jesus taught first a woman of Samaria and then many people of that city. Modern tourists and others who come to worship there are still able to drink at "Jacob's well" in Nablus.

34:1–31 Shechem . . . defiled her. . . . Dinah's brethren . . . slew all the males. . . . Jacob said . . . Ye . . . make me to stink

Israel's peace in Shalem was short-lived. An act of risk followed by an act of lust, an attempt at recompense, an agreement made in duplicity, and a violent assault by sons of Israel—all caused Israel "to stink among the inhabitants of the land," so Israel had to move on. Jacob's remonstrance with his guilty sons (who had reasoned they were justified in using violence to revenge the honor of their sister) may seem mild, but there were deep and lasting effects (Gen. 49:5–7).

35:1–15 God appeared unto Jacob again . . . and blessed him

At God's command, Jacob was to take his family next to the hills of Bethel. Before departing he prepared them to receive covenant blessings by a spiritual and physical cleansing—burying any idolatrous things under an oak near Shechem. With gratitude for God's help, Israel went to Bethel and built an altar to worship the Lord, naming and anointing it *El-beth-el,* "God of the house of God." It was, for the time being, his temple. Blessings were renewed that had been given at the place of his wrestling, where he had received his new name (Gen. 35:9–10; 32:24–30). Abraham's blessings, previously conferred at that place, were confirmed upon Israel (Gen. 35:11–15; 28:10–15).

35:8 Rebekah's nurse died, and she was buried beneath Bethel under an oak

It seems that Jacob's mother's nurse, of a generation before (Gen. 24:59), had died and was buried near Bethel under an oak; hence, that place was called *Allon-bachuth,* "oak of weeping." It hardly seems possible that she could have lived long enough to come out to meet Jacob's company, dying at the time of the events recorded here.

35:16–21 Rachel travailed, and she had hard labour. . . . And Rachel died, and was buried in the way to . . . Bethlehem

A sad death followed a providential birth near Ephrath (Bethlehem), as the company moved southward; Rachel had trusted that the Lord would give her another son (Gen. 30:24), which He did, but she died in giving birth. The place is marked with a little shrine and a cenotaph in the outskirts of present-day Bethlehem.

Rachel named this son of her suffering *Benoni,* "son of my affliction"; but Israel renamed him Benjamin, "son of the right hand" (Gen. 35:18b–c), a hopeful and forward-looking name.

35:22 Reuben went and lay with Bilhah

Sadder still is the account of Reuben's instability of character, for by his breach of a basic moral law he lost his birthright (Gen. 49:3–4; 1 Chr. 5:1).

35:22–26 sons of Leah . . . Rachel . . . Bilhah . . . Zilpah

The twelve potential patriarchs, sons of Israel by four mothers, are listed in family groups; their births and the meaning of their names are recorded in Genesis 29:31 through 30:24.

35:27–29 Jacob came unto Isaac his father

Father Isaac, who had felt old twenty years before (Gen. 27:1–2) and had given the final birthright blessings at that time, did not die until he was one hundred eighty years old, many years after Jacob's return. Jacob's home in the land was Mamre, near Arbah, or Hebron, home of Abraham and Isaac (BD, "Hebron"; "Isaac"). Esau and Jacob, still at peace with each other, joined in performing the burial rites for their father Isaac.

36:1– 43 Now these are the generations of Esau, who is Edom

The names of descendants of Jacob's brother, Esau (also called Edom) and of Seir the Horite, a leader of the earlier inhabitants of the Arabah, have been preserved here. These are the neighbors with whom the Israelites interacted during most of the history recorded in the Old Testament. The "dukes" and "kings" of those peoples who lived long before the Israelites had kings are listed. The people of "Seir the Horite," who intermarried with the Edomites, may have been the first dwellers in the rock-hewn caves of the *sikh* that later became the cliff-carved city called *Sela* (Gr., *Petra*, "rock"). Visitors to that remote *sikh* ("wash," a gulch or canyon) today may see in the sandstone cliffs some of the sculpted temples, treasuries, and dwellings left there by the Byzantines, the Romans before them, the Nabataeans before them, and others of the Edomites and the Horites back to the beginning. The *Khorim,* or Horites, may indeed have been cave-dwellers, as *Khor* is a word used to mean "cave" (e.g., 1 Sam. 14:11; Job 30:6).

It would have been a blessing if the spirit of the meeting of Esau and Israel at Peniel (Gen. 33) and at the burial of Isaac (Gen. 35:29) could have prevailed, but most accounts of interaction between Israel and Edom from this time on report strife and contention. For that reason, some of the prophets have used the name *Edom* or its Latin form *Idumea* as a symbol and synonym for "the wicked world" (e.g., Isa. 34:5–6; Ezek. 35:15; 36:5; D&C 1:36).

37:1–11 Now Israel loved Joseph more

The explanation of Israel's favoring Joseph "because he was the son of his old age" may suggest Jacob was much older when Joseph was born than is accounted for in the records of his twenty-year sojourn in Haran.

In any case, favor with his father put Joseph into disfavor with his brothers. His telling the prophetic dreams to his brothers, certainly the action of an immature seventeen-year-old, only increased the disfavor, for the meaning of the dreams was plain enough. Note that whereas his brothers "envied" Joseph, his father "observed" (Heb., lit., "watched, guarded") the concepts in the dreams (Gen. 37:11).

37:12–36 they conspired . . . to slay him. Reuben . . . said, Let us not kill him. . . . Judah said . . . let us sell him

An evil inspiration surely motivated Joseph's brothers to seek to use violence to eliminate the source of their irritation. Years later, however, Joseph gave the Lord credit for taking him into Egypt and giving him high status there. It is evident that the Lord helped to bring good out of an otherwise evil situation. Even though the brothers' callousness about their younger brother and their aged father was not caused by the Lord, He could have influenced them through Reuben not to kill Joseph and caused Judah to think of selling him rather than abandoning him in the pit. The traders unknowingly took him to trials and opportunities in Egypt.

Two peoples related to Jacob's family, the Ishmaelites and the Midianites, were involved in the trade and transfer. The nature of their negotiations is not entirely understandable from the information we have been given (Gen. 37:28, 36).

38:1–30 Judah . . . said . . . She hath been more righteous than I

The sordid account of Judah and Tamar contains some genealogical facts pertinent to an important family line, that of King David (Ruth 4:18–22; Luke 3:33). Perhaps it can assure readers that they can excel in spite of problems in their ancestry; Jesus of Nazareth was born of that genealogical line.

There is also some satisfaction to one's sense of justice in that a self-righteous man, who was willing to have his daughter-in-law punished for adultery, had to face up to his own sins.

39:1–6 his master saw that the Lord was with him, and . . . made all that he did to prosper

Though sold to Potiphar to serve, Joseph did not become a common slave. With the Lord's gracious help, he was soon overseer of Potiphar's house and then of all he possessed.

Potiphar was captain of Pharaoh's guard. This Pharaoh may have been one of the foreign line of Semitic rulers, called *Hyksos,* who formed the Fifteenth through the Seventeenth dynasties of Pharaohs of lower Egypt. They ruled between 1720 B.C. and 1550 B.C., the period during which, it is almost certain, Joseph lived in Egypt (BD, "Pharaoh"). This possibility is important later in the history of Joseph's family (Gen. 41:45).

39:7–20 thou art his wife: how then can I do this great wickedness, and sin against God?

Potiphar's wife's lack of connubial loyalty and moral and personal character contrasts strikingly with Joseph's concern for God's law, decency, fairness, and right. But though he was fortified against her wiles "day by day," a time came when the temptress had an opportunity to make him yield or suffer the consequences of her easily contrived accusations. Her assertion in Genesis 39:17 that he came to "mock" her is more pointed in the original Hebrew, which could imply that he came to "play," or "toy," with her.

There may be a clue to Potiphar's evaluation of the situation in his putting Joseph in prison rather than summarily executing him. The Lord helped Joseph in that incident also.

39:21–23; 40:1–23 the Lord was with Joseph . . . and that which he did, the Lord made it to prosper

Certainly Joseph was rewarded by the Lord for doing right; he soon was made a leader in the prison. There again he performed exemplary acts such as giving aid, advice, and comfort; and he brought blessings from the God whom he served. One blessing from God enabled him to interpret the revelatory dreams of two fellow prisoners—and eventually helped get him out of prison.

41:1– 38 It is not in me: God shall give Pharaoh an answer

Patient service for two more years in prison was yet required of Joseph, however, until the butler whom he had helped finally mentioned him to Pharaoh (Gen. 40:14). Pharaoh's own troublesome dreams provided the opportunity.

Joseph shaved and groomed himself before appearing before Pharaoh. He immediately corrected Pharaoh's impression that Joseph of himself could "understand a dream to interpret it." Fulfilling a part of the responsibility of Abraham's seed, Joseph bore testimony of the Lord's name "in a strange land" (Abr. 2:6). He said that it was not he but God who could give an interpretation of the dreams. After giving the interpretation, Joseph explained that God had indeed shown what *He* was about to *do* in Egypt. Thus Pharaoh should understand that the idols of Egypt were bringing neither the plenty nor the dearth.

In recommending that Pharaoh select and appoint "a man discreet and wise" (Gen. 41:33) to collect one-fifth of the crops in the seven plenteous years to store up food against the famine years, Joseph did not suggest that he wanted the job for himself; it was Pharaoh who was impressed that they could not find another "such a one as this is, a man in whom the Spirit of God is" (Gen. 41:38).

41:39– 45 Thou shalt be over my house, . . . only in the throne will I be greater than thou

Pharaoh believed that the Spirit of the God Joseph served had shown Joseph truths that made him more "discreet and wise" than anyone else; therefore Joseph was made chief minister, appropriately attired, decorated, acclaimed, and given a new name, *Zaphnath-paaneah*—usually interpreted to mean "he who reveals that which is hidden" (BD, "Zaphnath-paaneah").

In view of the emphasis placed on proper marriage in previous generations of the seed of Abraham, it is likely that Joseph's wife also was chosen for him through the Lord's influence. It may be assumed that the priests were of the same lineage as the kings of the dynasty; thus, Asenath, daughter of the priest of On, who was given to Joseph as a wife, could have been Semitic (see commentary on Gen. 39:1–6; cf. Gen. 24:1–5; 28:1–5; D&C 86:8). Joseph and Asenath became the parents of Manasseh and Ephraim (commentary on Gen. 41:50–52).

41:46– 49 And he gathered up all the food of the seven years, . . . in the land of Egypt, and laid up the food in the cities

Joseph's wise implementation of his prophetic advice caused food to be stored throughout the land of Egypt during the seven good harvest years. The food was stored in cities in the farming areas (Gen. 41:48) and not all in one great central storage area for the whole country, as has sometimes been assumed.

"Corn" (Gen. 41:49) in King James English means "grain," not the American "maize" (BD, "Corn").

41:50–52 the firstborn Manasseh; . . . second . . . Ephraim

Joseph's work, his position of trust with Pharaoh, his marriage, and his children must have been a comfort, a joy, and a blessing to Joseph after all his years of lacking family love and appreciation. The name of his first child, *Manasseh,* may mean "causing to forget," as Joseph's comment suggests. *Ephraim* is from the Hebrew word for "fruit," with a dual suffix, suggesting double fruitfulness.

41:53–57 the seven years of dearth began . . . And Joseph opened all the storehouses . . . And all countries came

Note that Joseph retained control of distribution. Although at first glance his selling the grain rather than giving it away might seem unjust, anyone experienced in distributing aid knows of the problems and dangers inherent in a dole.

42:1–38 Joseph's brethren came, and bowed down themselves before him

Like many other foreigners who needed grain (Gen. 41:57), Joseph's brothers went to Egypt, where they bowed themselves before him, unknowingly fulfilling the old prophetic dream (Gen. 42:6*b*). Recognizing them and understanding their language, Joseph apparently seized the opportunity to test their integrity before divulging his identity. He challenged their claim that they were not spies but ten of one man's twelve sons—one of whom was at home "and one is not" (Gen. 42:13). Three days in jail with the prospect that only one would be allowed to return home must have terrified them. Then Joseph's release of all but one must have amazed them, as also his explanation that he did so because he had reverence for God. In addition, they had a new challenge: to return with their youngest brother to prove their veracity.

Note how guilty they felt regarding the lost brother, how Reuben chastised them, and how Joseph reacted—obviously not enjoying their suffering. Joseph may have held Simeon rather than Reuben, the firstborn son and natural leader, because he appreciated Reuben's attitude and remembered Reuben's effort to frustrate his brothers' violent intent and lack of compassion when they sold him (Gen. 42:21–24; 37:22, 29–30).

The return of Israel's money by Joseph was generous, but even that was looked upon suspiciously by the brothers as a plot whereby God might yet punish them.

Back home again, Reuben offered a sure pledge in order to persuade their aged father to entrust him and his brothers with

Benjamin on their return trip to get more food and redeem Simeon, but Jacob was afraid.

43:1–10 Judah said unto Israel . . . Send the lad with me, . . . I will be surety for him

The brothers did not go back to Egypt to obtain Simeon's release until their acute need of food persuaded their father to let them go in spite of his fear of losing Benjamin in addition to Simeon and Joseph. So Judah also volunteered to be surety for Benjamin. Recall that it had been Judah's suggestion years before that Joseph be sold so that his blood would not be shed (Gen. 37:26–27).

43:11–14 fruits . . . balm, . . . honey, spices, and myrrh, nuts, and almonds

How in a famine could any food or spices be available in Canaan for Israel's sons to take to Egypt? Cyclical droughts that may cause crops of grain and other annuals to fail do not ordinarily kill the trees that produce figs, dates, olives, nuts, and balm; shrubs and vines ordinarily survive and bloom, so some honey also is produced. Spices such as sage, oregano, or rosemary are produced by shrubs that survive most droughts.

43:15–34 Bring these men home, and slay, and make ready; for these men shall dine with me at noon

When the ten brothers, including Benjamin, returned to Egypt, they must have been amazed at being treated as honored guests, even having their feet washed before a noon meal and being seated according to rank in age. The money they brought back was not accepted by the steward: he said he had received it (he had indeed received it but had not kept it). Then what must they have thought of Benjamin's receiving a portion at dinner five times that of anyone else! If the brothers noticed that Joseph hurriedly left the room for a time, they could not likely have guessed he went out to weep—a second such occurrence (Gen. 43:30;

42:24). But he had one more test to perform before confessing his identity and reassuring them.

44:1–34 therefore . . . let thy servant abide instead of the lad

In the final test, Joseph contrived to cause Benjamin to be detained in Egypt. Judah proved true to his pledge—and more compassionate than he had been years before: he volunteered to take Benjamin's place rather than risk bringing down the gray head of their father in sorrow to the grave.

45:1–15 Then Joseph could not refrain himself

Joseph was so gratified that he wept again (Gen. 45:1–2; 43:30). Assured that they would not abandon their youngest brother and that they apparently were better men than they had been some twenty-five years before, Joseph divulged his identity. He hastened to reassure them that God had thus brought good out of that otherwise evil situation. Through Joseph, God had provided for the whole clan of Israel in the last five years of the famine. Father Jacob was to be brought, and all of his extended family could dwell in the good pasture lands of Goshen. Tender was their reunion.

45:16–24 the fame thereof was heard in Pharaoh's house, saying, Joseph's brethren are come; and it pleased Pharaoh

Pharaoh and his people were gracious to Joseph's family, but they had ample reason to be grateful: Joseph had not only saved the nation from the famine but had unified the whole land under a strong monarch (an achievement like that of the New Kingdom, in the Eighteenth Dynasty; but Joseph's time was much earlier than that).

Generously, Pharaoh urged Joseph to send for his father and all of his family and to have no concern about their goods in Canaan, "for the good of all the land of Egypt is yours" (Gen. 45:20). His generosity was shown in the goods and wagons he sent to help them move to Egypt. Pharaoh was solicitous, saying, "See that ye fall not out by the way" (Gen. 45:24).

45:25–28 Joseph is yet alive, and he is governor

It was understandably overwhelming to Jacob to learn that Joseph was not only alive but "governor over all the land of Egypt." Only when he heard what Joseph had said to his brothers and saw the Egyptian wagons could the aged father believe it.

46:1–4 I am God, the God of thy father: fear not to go down

At the southern outpost of their homeland, Beer-sheba, former home of Abraham and Isaac, God gave Jacob reassurance "in the visions of the night," tacitly sealing their covenant. He promised to go with Israel into Egypt, make them "a great nation," and bring them out again. In symbolic terms, God also promised Jacob that Joseph would attend him at his death (Gen. 45:4; 50:1–13).

46:5–27 besides Jacob's sons' wives . . . threescore and six

The fathers of the future twelve tribes of Israel were named along with their sons in a symbolic count of seventy; but their wives and their sons' wives, plus all the grandchildren, would have made a much larger total. Seventy is a tenfold multiple of seven, and seven symbolizes completeness. Note that Benjamin had the largest family—ten.

46:28–30 Now let me die, since I have seen thy face

Anyone who has a family can empathize with the emotions of gratitude, joy, and satisfaction in this family reunion. Jacob doubtless only intended to characterize his life as full and his wishes fulfilled when he cried, "Now let me die." He lived some seventeen more years (Gen. 46:30; 47:28).

46:31–34 when Pharaoh shall . . . say, What is your occupation? . . . say, Thy servants' trade hath been about cattle from our youth

So that this Semitic clan with their flocks and herds might have good grazing lands, and be as unobtrusive as possible among the Egyptians, Joseph advised his brothers to tell Pharaoh frankly that they were herdsmen. Evidently rough and rugged nomads were repulsive to the fastidious court class ("an abomination unto the Egyptians"), so Israel could be assured of being granted the grasslands in Goshen, as Joseph had hoped (Gen. 46:34; 45:10). Goshen lay in the eastern part of the Nile delta, allowing also a natural separation of the herdsmen from Egyptian tillers of the soil elsewhere up the river. Joseph's headquarters, if they were at the Hyksos capital Avaris, would have been nearby.

"Cattle" in King James English, as in the Hebrew word it translates, means the domesticated animals we call cattle, sheep, and goats.

47:1–6 in . . . Goshen let them dwell; and . . . make them rulers over my cattle

The delegation of Israelite brothers went to Pharaoh and did as Joseph had directed, and they were granted land as he had hoped. Appropriately, they were also given the job of caring for Pharaoh's livestock, whose flocks and herds were being much augmented by people trading for grain as the famine went on (Gen. 46:16–17).

47:7–12 Jacob blessed Pharaoh

When the old patriarch and shepherd was brought in for an audience with Pharaoh, Pharaoh was given a blessing by the patriarch. It was an unusual interaction between a leader with earthly power and a man with divine power.

Note how humbly Jacob responded to Pharaoh's inquiry about his age; perhaps he counted his one hundred thirty years as "few" because his father Isaac had lived to one hundred eighty and Abraham to one hundred seventy-five. Doubtless he counted his years as "evil" (Gen. 47:9b, "unpleasant") because of the loss of Rachel to early death, the disappearance of Joseph, and the trials incident to the famine.

The land of Goshen of Joseph's time was called "land of Rameses" by Moses (Gen. 47:11).

47:13–26 so the land became Pharaoh's

All Egypt was consolidated under Pharaoh as Joseph accumulated the people's money, livestock, and lands, and the people pledged their fealty (see commentary on Gen. 45:16–24). Seed was provided them for planting when conditions permitted; and four-fifths of the crop would be theirs thereafter, with one-fifth going to the government. Priestly possessions remained in the hands of the priests, however. Little is known from ancient Egyptian sources about the Hyksos period, and hence there is no confirmation of this biblical account of economic and political consolidation under Joseph's Pharaoh.

47:27–31 the time drew nigh that Israel must die . . . ; bury me not, I pray thee, in Egypt

For the remaining five years of the famine (Gen. 45:6, 11) and for twelve more years (seventeen in all; Gen. 47:28), Jacob lived with his extended family in Egypt. Then he called for Joseph, who of course managed everything, and arranged for burial in the family tombs in the cave Machpelah at Hebron in southern Canaan (Gen. 23:9, 19; 25:9; 49:30).

48:1–22 And now thy two sons, Ephraim and Manasseh, . . . are mine; as Reuben and Simeon, they shall be mine

Joseph took his sons to Jacob for patriarchal blessings. The patriarch reviewed for them the promises made by the Lord concerning Canaan and the return of Israel's people to it after he had made them "a multitude of people" (Gen. 48:4). He established the status of Joseph's two sons to be like that of his own first two sons, Reuben and Simeon, and declared that Joseph's issue thereafter would be called by the names of Ephraim and Manasseh, thus giving Joseph a double inheritance (Gen. 48:5*a*; 1 Chr. 5:1–2).

Although Joseph brought his firstborn conveniently to Jacob's right and the secondborn to his left, it was once again not priority of birth that determined the appointment to birthright leadership, for Ephraim was chosen. Note, however, that both would develop into great peoples, although Ephraim's descendants would be more numerous and found in "a multitude of nations" (Gen. 48:19). In poetic phrases, the grandfather-patriarch expressed his gratitude for the divine providence he had enjoyed and invoked it upon the boys. Dividing Joseph's heritage into two would give Joseph two "portions" in the future land of Israel.

49:1–2 Gather yourselves together, that I may tell you that which shall befall you in the last days

Jacob, who was Israel, next summoned all his sons that he might prophetically tell them their destiny in time to come. In the blessing of some was an indication of future tribal location and work. The heritage of some would be very good; some, not so good. Some blessings pertained to the individual being blessed; some, only to their progeny.

49:3– 4 Reuben . . . Unstable as water, thou shalt not excel

Reuben, the firstborn, received a sad evaluation and prognosis. Recall the deed recounted in Genesis 35:22, which characterized him as "unstable," but remember also his good qualities, shown in his attitudes and actions toward Joseph. Watch in the scriptures hereafter for information about his tribe, and note that his descendants will be among the one hundred forty-four thousand high priests of all the tribes of Israel sealed in preparation for the launching of the millennial kingdom of the Lord (Rev. 7:5; D&C 77:11).

49:5– 7 Simeon and Levi are brethren; . . . I will divide them in Jacob, and scatter them in Israel

Ominous words also were spoken to Simeon and Levi, whose depredations at Shechem were recalled (Gen. 49:6c, 7b); and they individually would not be distinguished, for Jacob indicted them as impulsive and violent. Yet it is again noteworthy that one's descendants are not impaired by ancestors' misdeeds. Simeon's descendants would continue among Israel, later largely "scattered" within Judah (Josh. 19:1, 9; Judg. 1:3). Levi's descendants later were appointed to the priesthood and rendered service among all of the tribes of Israel (Num. 3; Deut. 33:8–11; Josh. 21).

49:8–12 The sceptre shall not depart from Judah, nor a lawgiver from between his feet, until Shiloh come

The first of two detailed blessings is Judah's. Unlike the preceding three sons, he heard nothing about his own sins, qualifications, or individual destiny. He was told about the status of leadership his descendants would attain among the tribes, in the later nation of Israel, and in the messianic kingdom.

The lion is a symbol of rulership, and allusions to the "sceptre" and "lawgiver" envisioned the future Messiah. The royal power, beginning with David, would remain with his descendants until a divine lawgiver, "Shiloh" (Gen. 49:10c), would be born (indicated by the idiom "from between the feet"). The royal colt upon which he would ride and the "blood of grapes" which would stain his clothing identify the same figure spoken of in Isaiah 63:2 and Doctrine and Covenants 133:48—the Redeemer of Israel, the Savior. The last clauses of the blessing can be translated "His eyes shall be darker than wine and his teeth whiter than milk"; they imply his regal, distinctive countenance.

49:13–15 Zebulun . . . shall be for an haven of ships. . . . Issachar . . . the land . . . pleasant

The parts of the land of Canaan to be occupied by the tribes of Zebulun and Issachar are clearly indicated. The natural harbor north of Carmel, the good lands of the valley of Jezreel, and the plains of Megiddo were places of productivity but also of international conflict. Their inhabitants therefore suffered invasions and repressions. The area is mentioned in Isaiah's prophecy of the ministry of the Messiah (Isa. 9:1–4).

49:16–18 Dan . . . shall be . . . an adder in the path

Dan's name means "judged." His people's role as the first line of defense against invaders from the north may have been hinted at in this short blessing, but any such security would be temporal and temporary. It is better to await the salvation of the Lord.

49:19–21 a troop . . . royal dainties . . . goodly words

The military strife suffered by Gad and the prosperity of Asher's heritage can only be found later in the areas they inherited. Naphtali's inheritance was Galilee, the area of the later "goodly words" of Jesus, and the same envisioned by Isaiah, where "the people that walked in darkness have seen a great light" (Isa. 9:2). Perhaps the patriarch alluded to those events.

49:22–26 Joseph is a fruitful bough . . . whose branches run over the wall

As indicated already in the blessings upon the two branches of Joseph's family (see commentary on Gen. 48), they would be numerous and prosperous; here it is shown that their inheritance of land would be beyond the vineyards of Israel. Though adversaries harass them severely, they ultimately prevail, for their help comes from the God of Jacob. From Jacob, the Savior, the "Stone of Israel," the Good Shepherd, would come (D&C 50:44; commentary on Gen. 49:8–12). Jacob's blessings above and beyond those of his forefathers were invoked upon his birthright son (Gen. 49:26 and fn.; 1 Chr. 5:1–2; Deut. 33:13–18; D&C 133:30–32; 1 Ne. 3:4–22).

49:27 Benjamin . . . shall devour the prey, . . . divide the spoil

Benjamin's blessing may predict his descendants' prevailing, physically or spiritually, but it is difficult to know whether such descendants as King Saul or the apostle Paul could be meant. Applications of the blessing to the tribe of Benjamin are vague.

49:28–33 Jacob . . . yielded up the ghost, and was gathered unto his people

Jacob repeated his request for burial in Canaan and repeated his charge (Gen. 47:29–31). Then his spirit ("ghost") departed, to be "gathered unto his people" (Gen. 49:33a–b).

50:1–14 And Joseph went up to bury his father

With an extensive entourage and ceremony, the mourning for Jacob and his burial at Machpelah were accomplished. Forty days of embalming and seventy days of mourning in Egypt were followed by the long journey to Hebron in Canaan, seven days of mourning at the border beyond Jordan, and finally the burial in the cave at Machpelah.

50:15–21 ye thought evil against me; but God meant it unto good

Joseph responded with magnanimity to his brothers' entreaty for forgiveness and provided well for the whole extended family after the death of the old patriarch. The brothers had feared that only their father's presence had restrained Joseph from taking vengeance.

50:22–26 And Joseph saw Ephraim's children of the third generation; the children also of Machir the son of Manasseh were brought up upon Joseph's knees

Joseph's last fifty-five years and his grandfatherly roles are summed up in a sentence or two. Before his death, he reminded his people of the prophetic promises that one day they would return to the land of their inheritance. His last request was merely that his remains be taken with them and buried there in due time (Gen. 50:25b).

The inspired revision of the Genesis account includes some important prophecies by Joseph himself (Gen. 50:24a; JST Gen. 50:22–26). The Book of Mormon records prophecies that Lehi quoted from those made by Joseph (2 Ne. 3).

So ends the book of beginnings—Genesis.

EXODUS

Exodus tells how the Lord saved the Israelites from death in Egypt to prepare them for their life and mission in the promised land. Since through the seed of Abraham all nations are to be blessed (TG, "Israel, Mission of"), Israel needed rescue from spiritual and physical destruction in Egypt. The Lord's purpose was made evident when he said to Pharaoh through Moses: "Israel is my son, even my firstborn: . . . Let my son go, that he may serve me" (Ex. 4:22–23). The nature of Israel's relationship with the Lord was also clarified: "If ye will obey my voice indeed, and keep my covenant, then ye shall be a peculiar treasure unto me above all people; for all the earth is mine; And ye shall be unto me a kingdom of priests, and an holy nation" (Ex. 19:5–6). The Israelite people did not attain to consecration or broad priestly service, but a start was made. The rest of the Old Testament recounts Israel's efforts, successes, and failures. It also shows how the prophets tried to correct the people's faults and engender growth and goodness.

Various other scriptures allude to Exodus. Psalms 105 and 106 poetically overview the highlights; Nephi tells why the chosen people had not inherited the land generations earlier but were permitted to enter after the Exodus (1 Ne. 17:33–35; Gen. 15:13–16). Other scriptures reiterate and elucidate the eternal principles and doctrines recorded in revelations to Moses (TG, "Israel, Mission of"; "Law of Moses").

COMMENTARY

1:1–5 the children of Israel, which came into Egypt

The names of the twelve sons of Jacob who brought their families into Egypt are listed; "besides Jacob's sons' wives," seventy members of the extended family of Israel who entered Egypt were named previously in Genesis 46:3–27. Considering all the wives of all the sons and the husbands of all the daughters, as well as their children and grandchildren and spouses, the total of Israel's clan could have been hundreds (cf. 1 Chr. 4–8). Thus, in the fourth generation from Jacob (Gen. 15:16; Ex. 6:16–26), the Israelites could have been numerous enough to be called "a great nation" of those times (Gen. 46:3; Ex. 1:7).

Regarding the time that the children of Israel spent in Egypt, the apostle Paul evidently understood that there were four hundred thirty years from the time of Abraham's receiving the promise until the giving of the Mosaic law; this would make the "sojourn" in Egypt about two hundred fifteen years (Gen. 15:13; Gal. 3:16–17; Ex. 12:40–41 in the Greek Old Testament; confirmed by Josephus, *Antiquities of the Jews* 2:15:2; BD, "Chronological Tables"). Because Israel lived there in peace for seventy-one years of Joseph's life, one hundred forty-four years would have remained, some of them under Pharaohs of the favorable dynasty before the dynasty arose "which knew not Joseph" (Ex. 1:8; BD, "Egypt"; "Exodus"; "Pharaoh").

1:6–14 Israel . . . waxed exceeding mighty. . . . Therefore they did set over them taskmasters to afflict them

Several reasons are given for Israel's bondage: they became numerous, grew mighty, and became a potential military danger to Egypt; and a new king arose with no memory of Joseph and no reason to favor his people any longer (possibly the dynasty that replaced the Hyksos, about 1540 B.C.).

The name of one of the "treasure cities" of the time was Raamses (Ex. 1:11); this name has been cited as evidence that the

Pharaoh of the bondage of Israel was Rameses II (commentary on Gen. 47:11; BD, "Rameses").

1:12 the more they afflicted them, the more they multiplied and grew

It is plausible that the Israelites could suffer under bondage and oppression for a long time and yet grow ever stronger, in view of what has happened to modern Israelites, the Jews, during centuries of persecution and oppression. Until the Holocaust of the 1940s, they had become numerous in many lands.

1:15–22 midwives feared God, . . . saved the . . . children

Israelites who had knowledge of God and regard for the right are exemplified by the two courageous midwives who did not kill the male babies as they had been ordered, because they revered the heavenly King more than they feared the earthly one (Ex. 1:17, 21). The frustrated Pharaoh ordered "all his people" to kill the Hebrew babies; but God "dealt well with the midwives." "He made them houses" is a biblical phrase that can mean He blessed them with families; a similar expression is used later in a promise to David (Ex. 1:20–22 and fn.).

1:19 the Hebrew women are not as the Egyptian women . . . and are delivered ere the midwives come

The testimony of the midwives is quite credible about the contrast between some of the hardy Hebrew working women and some delicate Egyptian court women. Such a contrast is evident in pictures from ancient Egyptian tombs.

2:1–10 she had compassion on him, and said, This is one of the Hebrews' children

Moses was born under Pharaoh's decree of death for male Hebrew babies (Ex. 1:16, 22); but with courage and ingenuity, his parents kept him safe for a time and then put him in a reed basket on the river where his sister could watch until he was found by Pharaoh's own daughter. Compassionately she saved him, though she knew he was a Hebrew baby. It is likely that the Spirit of the Lord moved her to do so and also to accept "a nurse of the Hebrew women," although she must have known the "nurse" was the baby's mother. The name she gave him had appropriate meaning in both languages (Ex. 2:10*a–b*).

Some of Moses' education was doubtless given by his mother-nurse; for he later knew he was a Hebrew and he was concerned about his people. He was also "learned in all the wisdom of the Egyptians" (Ex. 2:11*a;* Acts 7:22; Josephus, *Antiquities of the Jews* 2:9:7).

2:11–15 when Moses was grown, . . . he went out unto his brethren

Moses was very distressed when he saw a fellow Hebrew being smitten by an Egyptian, and his hour of decision came. As he looked upon their suffering and perceived the crisis, he rose up and "slew" the Egyptian who was "smiting" the Hebrew. The same Hebrew verb translated *smiting* in verse 11 is translated *slew* in verse 12; it is a verb used to describe what soldiers do in battle. Thus Moses did to the Egyptian what he was doing to the Hebrew. His action destroyed a life but was in defense of a life. He "looked this way and that" (Ex. 2:12) before doing so; for he knew his action would not be condoned by any Egyptian.

Next day, however, when he tried to settle a conflict between two Hebrews, he was rebuffed with words that let him know his previous act was known, and he had to flee. In the New Testament, Stephen had information that caused him to say of Moses, "he supposed his brethren would have understood how that God by his hand would deliver them: but they understood not" (Acts 7:25).

Soon, Pharaoh "sought to slay Moses," and he fled to "the land of Midian" (Ex. 2:15), in the Sinai peninsula. This, too, proved to be a providential move.

2:16–22 Now the priest of Midian had seven daughters

In Midian Moses was blessed to find refuge with a true high priest of God, Reuel, or Jethro (Ex. 2:18; 3:1; 4:18; BD, "Jethro"). Through him Moses received the Melchizedek Priesthood, which had been transmitted through several generations from the time of Abraham (D&C 84:6–16). Recall that Abraham and Keturah had a son named Midian (Gen. 25:1–4).

Moses received Zipporah, a daughter of Jethro, as his wife, and she bore him children, the first of whom was named Gershom (Ex. 2:22*b*). There is no record of children by an earlier wife, an Ethiopian princess he is said to have married—a deed for which his brother and sister later found fault with him (Num. 12:1; Josephus, *Antiquities of the Jews* 2:10:2).

2:23–25 God remembered his covenant with Abraham

The time had arrived for Israel's redemption from bondage. The Pharaoh of Egypt who inaugurated Israel's enslavement had died, but the Israelites still suffered and cried unto God for relief. God chose this time to implement the next phase of his covenant with the seed of Abraham, so that they might implement their mission (Ex. 2:24*b*, 25*a*).

3:1– 6 the angel of the Lord appeared unto him in a flame of fire out of the midst of a bush

In the course of history, the presence of God has been shown by several phenomena: a mighty wind, a still small voice, a great thundering, a bright light, a flame of fire (see TG, "God, Privilege of Seeing"). A "flame of fire" in a bush manifested to Moses the presence of the Lord. After Moses' attention was thus focused, the Lord spoke and Moses heard the words from the flaming bush (Ex. 3:2*a–c*). Removing his shoes at that holy place was a way of showing reverence; it is still practiced in some holy places.

3:7–12 I will send thee unto Pharaoh, that thou mayest bring forth my people the children of Israel out of Egypt

The Lord is aware of the suffering and the prayers of people and He brings the relief that circumstances warrant. At the time Israel was in urgent need of a homeland, the occupants of Canaan were ripe in iniquity, and so the land could be made available to the Israelites if they could make themselves worthy of God's help (Gen. 15:16; Lev. 18:24–29; 1 Ne. 17:32–35).

The Lord's call required Moses to undertake a mission for which he humbly felt unqualified, but the Lord reassured him, saying, "Because I shall be with thee, this shall be a sign to thee that I have sent thee" (Ex. 3:12, translation mine).

The place where Moses was with his flocks, at "the backside of the desert" near "the mountain of God, . . . Horeb" (Ex. 3:1), was appointed by the Lord as the place to assemble the people, saying, "Ye shall serve God upon this mountain" (Ex. 3:12).

3:13–15 say unto the children of Israel, I AM hath sent me unto you. . . . The Lord God of your fathers . . . sent me

No doubt concerned about his rejection by the Israelites, who had asked him, "Who made thee a prince and a judge over us?" (Ex. 2:14), Moses asked the Lord how he should answer if they should ask for the name of Him who sent him. The Lord then revealed the sacred name *I AM* and *JHVH,* now traditionally pronounced "Jehovah" but shown in English Bibles by the substitute word LORD. Such pronunciations as "Ya-hoveh," "Yaweh," or "Yaveh" have been suggested. The name can mean "He who Is" and "He who causes to be." To Moses he identified himself in first person as "I AM THAT I AM" and bade Moses tell Israel, "I AM hath sent me unto you."

This revelation actually restored and explicated the divine name, for *JHVH* is found in Hebrew from the beginning of Genesis. In the days of Seth and Enos, the people began to "call upon the name of the Lord"; and the forefathers Abraham, Isaac, and Jacob all used that divine name (Gen. 4:26; Abr. 1:16; Gen. 22:14; 27:7; 28:13; commentary on Gen. 2:4).

3:16–22 I have surely . . . seen that which is done to you in Egypt; And . . . I will bring you up out of . . . affliction

The Lord knew, of course, about Israel's suffering, their need of leaders, the nature of the Pharaoh, the way to persuade him to let Israel go, and how Israel could be partly compensated for her years of servitude (Ex. 3:22a–b).

The "elders of Israel" (Ex. 3:16) were the patriarchal heads of the extended families, or clans, and were the natural leaders through whom Moses and the Lord could work. Though the Lord knew Pharaoh would not let Israel go into the wilderness to offer sacrifice, He allowed Pharaoh his agency to respond to Moses' request.

4:1–9 if they will not believe thee, neither . . . the first sign, . . . they will believe . . . the latter sign

Signs are used at times to teach and give proof, but miracles more often occur in compassionate service (BD, "Miracles"; TG, "Miracle"; "God, Manifestations of"; "Sign"; "Sign Seekers"). For the faithful, miracles are usually a reward of faith, to fulfill some urgent need (Mosiah 8:18; D&C 63:9–10).

4:10–17 I am not eloquent, . . . but I am slow of speech

The Lord, who "made man's mouth" was able to teach Moses what he should say (Ex. 4:11–12). He was not pleased with Moses' excuses and reluctance, but He still authorized Aaron to become Moses' spokesman. A spokesman for God is a prophet of God, and Aaron would be a prophet for Moses, who would "be to him instead of God" in conveying messages (Ex. 4:16*a–c*). This was the beginning of the "call of Aaron," and more about his call, ordination, and mode of service follows (Ex. 7:1–2; Lev. 8; Num. 3; Heb. 5:4).

4:18–20 Jethro said to Moses, Go in peace. And the Lord said, . . . Go, return into Egypt: for all the men are dead which sought thy life

Moses asked leave of Jethro, his employer and father-in-law, and he departed with Jethro's blessing, going under the Lord's direction.

A change of rulers had occurred in Egypt sometime during Moses' forty years with Jethro (BD, "Pharaoh").

The second of Moses' three periods of life, each forty years in length, was now finished (Ex. 7:7; Deut. 31:2; 34:7; Acts 7:23, 30).

4:21 but I will harden his heart, that he will not let the people go

This enigmatic statement is only "the word of God as far as it is translated correctly" (A of F 8; see the correction cited in Ex. 4:21*c*).

Harden is an English word used in the account of Moses' missions to translate three different Hebrew verbs. It is used as if the translators understood that God had planned and staged a dramatic sequence to demonstrate his powers, but that idea is not likely. One of those verbs is *khazaq,* in a form meaning "to make strong" or "to show to be strong" (Ex. 4:21; 8:15; 9:12; 9:35; 10:20). Another verb used is *kabad,* in forms meaning "to make heavy, weighty, important" (Ex. 8:32; 9:34; 10:1). The third is *qashah,* "to make harsh or hard" (Ex. 7:3). The translations are corrected in the Joseph Smith Translation (see fn. to the various passages cited above).

Incidentally, though there are many instances of the "hardening" of hearts recorded in the Book of Mormon, it is never said there that the Lord hardened anyone's heart. People made their own hearts hard, or Satan hardened them, but God did not do it.

4:22–23 Israel is my son, even my firstborn: . . . Let my son go, that he may serve me

This statement of the Lord shows his prime intent in saving Israel. "Firstborn" is here used figuratively; the firstborn in any family was customarily the one who bore the responsibilities of conserving the family's inheritance and perpetuating its way of life. The way of life to be perpetuated and the mission inheritance to be conserved by Israel, as Abraham's seed, has been frequently cited in the commentary above (TG, "Abrahamic Covenant"; "Israel, Mission of"; BD, "Abraham, Covenant of ").

4:20, 24–26 the Lord met him, and sought to kill him. . . . Surely a bloody husband art thou to me

As Moses and his family journeyed toward Egypt, something went wrong, but the words used here do not tell what it was. Surely if the Lord "sought to kill" a man He would not fail to do so. The inspired revision provides a better understanding of the matter. The phrase "bloody husband" is used later to translate a similar idiom that designated a recipient of the covenant of circumcision. Doubtless Moses, as a previous recipient, should have performed the rite on his son; Joseph Smith's inspired translation indicates that Moses was ashamed that he had not done so (Ex. 4:24a–c, 25b). After the operation, Zipporah returned with the children to the home of her father, Jethro, until Moses' rescue mission was over and the Israelites were encamped at Sinai (Ex. 18:1–6).

4:27–28 the Lord said to Aaron . . . , Go . . . to meet Moses

Aaron was personally "called of God" to begin his mission (Ex. 4:14–16, 27; Heb. 5:4). He accordingly went to the "mount of God" (Sinai) to meet Moses and be instructed.

4:29– 31 gathered together all the elders . . . And . . . spake all the words which the Lord had spoken unto Moses

Moses and Aaron instructed the Israelite elders and performed the miracles as they had been authorized (see commentary on Ex. 3:16). The grateful people believed, "bowed their heads and worshipped" (Ex. 4:31). As mentioned before, there are legitimate reasons for miracles, even though there are dangers in a doubter's "seeking for a sign" (BD, "Miracles"; TG, "Sign Seekers").

5:1– 9 Pharaoh said, Who is the Lord, that I should obey his voice to let Israel go? I know not the Lord, neither will I let Israel go

Pharaoh responded as anticipated (Ex. 3:19; 4:21–23). He asked a question, the answer to which he and many others have had to learn by hard experience. Many, like Pharaoh, who do not know the Lord, seem unwilling to learn about Him. Pharaoh even became vindictive, increasing the burdens, the beatings, and the demands made of his Israelite slaves.

5:10–23 neither hast thou delivered thy people at all

Disappointed and embittered because their suffering had

increased instead of being ended, the Israelites complained to Moses, who complained to the Lord.

6:1–8 but by my name JEHOVAH was I not known to them[?]

If a question mark were added (as bracketed above), the Lord's words would affirm what was noted before (3:13–15 above); for, ever since man's beginnings, His sacred name has been known. It was used throughout the epochs told of in Genesis. The Joseph Smith Translation confirms that fact (Ex. 6:3c).

In patience and mercy the Lord responded to Moses' urgent query and complaint: He had heard the "groaning" of Israel; he was remembering his covenant and would redeem them "with a stretched out arm" (meaning a manifestation of his identity and power). He would respond "with great judgments," implying there would be justifiable punishments for the oppressors.

6:9–13, 28–30 I am of uncircumcised lips, and how shall Pharaoh hearken unto me?

Moses dutifully repeated the divine promises to the suffering people, but they did not respond as he had hoped, and he was disappointed. He felt even more doubtful that the Egyptian leaders would listen, and lacked confidence in his ability as a communicator (Ex. 6:12a, 30a). But the Lord would yet turn Moses' humility and weakness into strength, and he would become a man "mighty in words and in deeds" (Acts 7:22; Ether 12:27).

6:14–27 These be the heads of their fathers' houses

The family history recorded here might well have been given in Exodus 1, but apparently it was placed here to further identify "Aaron and Moses, to whom the Lord said, Bring out the children of Israel" (Ex. 6:26). This history tells of four generations in Egypt as had been promised to Abraham: "in the fourth generation they shall come hither again" (Gen. 15:16).

7:1– 6 I have made thee a god to Pharaoh

"See, I have set thee in God's stead to Pharaoh" (Jewish Publication Society translation) is more correct and, incidentally, more in harmony with the Joseph Smith Translation (Ex. 7:1*b–c;* 7:2; cf. 4:15–16): a prophet is basically a spokesman.

7:7 Moses was fourscore years old, and Aaron fourscore and three years old

The comment on their ages seems to be a supplement to the family history inserted earlier (Ex. 6:14–27). Compare their ages to those of several Latter-day Saint General Authorities.

7:8–13 Shew a miracle for you

An alternate statement (Ex. 7:9*a*) clarifies the intent of Exodus 7:8–13. Pharaoh launched a contest between his miracle workers and Moses, and when his magicians won the first round, he "hardened his heart." Ungodly powers make possible such wonders as the magicians produced (Ex. 7:11–12; Matt. 7:22–23; 2 Cor. 11:13–14; D&C 50:1–3). It was thus necessary, over a period of time, to show Pharaoh many facets of God's omnipotence before he would finally recognize the unseen God, Jehovah (Ex. 9:13–17; 10:3).

7:14–25 the waters . . . in the river . . . shall be turned to blood

The first plague was announced, its purpose made clear, and it was performed; but Pharaoh was still impressed with the power of his own magicians and obdurate against the Lord's repeated commands.

Observe, as the account proceeds, that nine of the plagues occurred in three cycles of three, after which there was one final plague. The first in each cycle was announced to Pharaoh at the river in the morning, and when he did not yield, the plague came. The second plague in each cycle was announced with a warning, and when it came, Pharaoh supplicated for relief; but when respite was granted, he hardened his heart once again. The third plague in each cycle was inflicted without warning and Pharaoh's response was only a hardened heart.

8:1–15 Let my people go, that they may serve me. And if thou refuse . . . I will smite all thy borders with frogs

The second plague of the first cycle was announced and Pharaoh was warned; when he did not respond, the plague came. Although Pharaoh's magicians imitated it, he asked for relief and made his first promise to let Israel go. Yet, though Moses repeated the purpose of the plague and removed it, Pharaoh refused to keep his promise.

8:16–19 smite the dust . . . that it may become lice

The third plague then was sent without warning. The Egyptian magicians could not duplicate it nor counteract it, and they identified it as a manifestation of "the finger of God" (Ex. 8:19*a*); but Pharaoh remained obdurate.

8:20– 32 if thou wilt not . . . I will send swarms of flies

The fourth plague began the second cycle: Moses met Pharaoh at the waters in the morning and announced the next plague, which would afflict the Egyptians but not the Israelites. Then the plague came. The suffering prompted Pharaoh to seek relief and concede that Israel could perform a sacrifice "in the land." Moses explained that a sacrifice in that place would be an "abomination" to Egyptians (probably because it would involve cattle, which were sacred in Egypt). So Pharaoh further conceded that Israel could go out but "not go very far away," and humbly asked, "Intreat for me." Moses warned against duplicity again and removed the plague, but again Pharaoh recanted.

9:1– 7 if thou refuse . . . and wilt hold them still . . . there shall be a very grievous murrain

The fifth plague, second in the second cycle, came after an announcement and a warning. Pharaoh saw that only the cattle of the Egyptians were afflicted, whereas those of the Israelites were not; but he made no concession.

9:8–12 a boil breaking forth with blains upon man, and upon beast, throughout all the land of Egypt

The sixth plague came as had the third, without warning. Even the magicians suffered, but Pharaoh was stubborn and made no concession (Ex. 9:12*a*).

9:13–35 I will cause it to rain a very grievous hail. . . . Send therefore now and gather thy cattle

The seventh plague was announced at the river in the morning, as the first and the fourth had been. Pharaoh was specifically warned about exalting himself still (Ex. 9:17), and a general warning was given to the Egyptians. It saved those "that feared the word of the Lord among the servants of Pharaoh" (Ex. 9:20–21). Goshen, the land where the Israelites lived, was spared again. Pharaoh confessed his sin and asked again for intercession with the Lord, but his pride soon overcame his humility, for he "sinned yet more, and hardened his heart" (Ex. 9:34).

To understand Exodus 9:16 better, note that the words *cause* and *in* are in italics, meaning that they are added in the English translation and their equivalent is not in the Hebrew original. Leaving out those italicized words makes the meaning more like it was in Hebrew (Ex. 9:16 and fn.).

10:1–20 How long wilt thou refuse to humble thyself before me? let my people go, that they may serve me. Else, if thou refuse . . . , to morrow will I bring the locusts

The eighth plague, second in the third cycle, was preceded as usual by a warning, and the purpose of the plague was made clear. Once again Pharaoh responded inadequately, and the plague came. Pharaoh's heart was hardened again but not by the Lord (Ex. 10:1*a*).

The Lord intended that such accounts as this be kept in the scriptures to teach generations of his children about the evils of bondage and tyrants and the value of the divine gift of freedom (Ex. 10:2).

Even though the king's servants pleaded with him not to defy the God of Israel further, he could not humble himself to do so. For the second time, when the suffering became too great, he confessed sinning, asked forgiveness, and got relief, only to resume his hard-heartedness afterward.

10:21–29 darkness over the land of Egypt, even darkness which may be felt

The ninth plague, ending the third cycle, came in the usual pattern without warning. Compare the darkness described here to that in the Book of Mormon at the time of the Crucifixion (Ex. 10:21–23; 3 Ne. 8:20–23). Pharaoh proposed to let the Israelites go, but without their livestock; when that offer was rejected, he resumed his hard, resentful stance. Banned from seeing Pharaoh again, Moses gave a foreboding response: "Thou hast spoken well, I will see thy face again no more" (Ex. 10:29).

11:1–10 Yet will I bring one plague more . . . afterwards he will let you go

Moses received a revelation about a final plague and delivered the message while still in Pharaoh's presence.

Israel's asking for valuable things from the Egyptians could have been a means of some compensation for years of service in slavery (commentary on Ex. 3:16–22). When Pharaoh did not respond to the warning about the imminent death of Egypt's firstborn, Moses "went out from Pharaoh in a great anger" (Ex. 11:8).

A brief summary reviews the whole campaign for freedom and Pharaoh's responses (Ex. 11:1 and fn.).

12:1–14 Your lamb shall be without blemish . . . ; eat the flesh in that night . . . , and unleavened bread; and with bitter herbs

The Passover month became the "head," or chief, month of the year; but it is not the annual new year's day of the Jewish calendar, for the Jewish new year begins with the new moon nearest the autumnal equinox, whereas Passover is two weeks after the new moon following the spring equinox.

A yearling male lamb without blemish was to be chosen by each extended family; its blood on each doorpost and over the doorway would symbolize faith in the Lord's promise of liberation. Its flesh was to be roasted, not boiled, and eaten; none was to be wasted. All of this symbolized not only God's gift of earthly freedom but also his ultimate gift of eternal freedom from bondage, sin, and death (Ex. 12:14 and fn.; Isa. 53:4–7; 1 Pet. 1:18–21; TG, "Jesus Christ, Lamb of God"). Jesus turned the broken bread and wine of the Passover into symbols of his atoning sacrifice (Matt. 26:18, 26–29; Mark 14:12, 22–25; Luke 22:15, 19–20), thus perpetuating the significance of these emblems forever.

The day following the evening feast of Passover became a special Sabbath called "an high day" (John 19:31). That special Sabbath was one of the three days when Jesus' body lay in the tomb, while in the spirit world he "preached also to them that are dead" about redemption from sin and death (1 Pet. 3:18–20; 4:6; D&C 138:18–37). Through Him came an eternal Passover, the passing of sin and death.

12:15–20 Seven days shall ye eat unleavened bread

Unleavened bread was to be eaten each day, starting with the night of the slaughter of the lamb on the fourteenth day of the month of Aviv and continuing until the twenty-first. Both of those days became special Sabbaths every year. In later times, when Jews have lived in lands using other calendars (such as the Roman calendar we use), those Sabbaths are celebrated on whatever day of the week they occur, in addition to the regular Sabbath on Saturday (BD, "Feasts," for more about the Passover).

12:21–28 when your children shall say . . . , What mean ye by this service? . . . say, It is the sacrifice of the Lord's passover

The Israelites sacrificed the lamb as Moses instructed them and marked their doorposts with its blood. Though generally this practice has ceased, many Jewish families still observe some of the annual Passover rites, and they teach their children as they have been commanded to do, that they may know the meaning of liberty and value the freedom God has given. Christians too should value these gifts, as Paul suggested (1 Cor. 10:1–6; Gal. 5:1; 2 Ne. 2:26–27).

12:29–36 Rise up, and get you forth . . . ye and the children of Israel; and go, serve the Lord. . . . Also take your flocks and your herds, as ye have said, and be gone; and bless me also

Finally, after the last terrible plague had struck the Egyptian people, Pharaoh gave up his former posture of "I know not the Lord, neither will I let Israel go" (Ex. 5:2; 12:31–32).

The Israelites asked for valuables, and the Egyptians let them have such things as they required. A considerable amount was involved, for the word *spoiled* is used to translate the Hebrew *natzal,* meaning "stripped." Note later the consecration of some of the precious things for use in adorning the tabernacle (Ex. 25).

12:37–51 Israel journeyed from Rameses to Succoth, about six hundred thousand on foot that were men. . . . And a mixed multitude went up also with them; and flocks, and herds

It was a great host of people and animals that set out on the long, long journey toward the promised land. For four hundred thirty years, Abraham's descendants had been strangers or temporary sojourners in Canaan and Egypt (Ex. 12:40; commentary on Ex. 1:1–5).

By undergoing the initiatory ordinance of circumcision, those of the mixed multitude, including servants (Ex. 12:43–49), could convert and properly participate in the Passover, with "one law" for both "homeborn" and sojourner.

13:1–16 Sanctify unto me all the firstborn

A review of the purposes of the Passover and a command to perpetuate its lessons was given along with a command to sanctify all the firstborn of animals and people to the Lord. Three purposes of this dedication of the firstborn were to memorialize the deliverance from Egypt, to remember the ransom suffered by the firstborn of Egypt, and to provide personnel for divine service. The nature of that service and the redeeming of the firstborn by substituting the tribe of Levi for them is described later (Num. 3).

13:17–22 God led the people . . . through the . . . wilderness of the Red sea. . . . And the Lord went before them by day in a pillar of a cloud . . . and by night in a pillar of fire, to give them light

To travel "through the way . . . of the land of the Philistines," the coastal route, would have been short, but that was not the way God chose to lead Israel (Ex. 13:17*a*, 18*c*).

Note that Joseph's last request was fulfilled.

14:1–9 the Egyptians pursued after . . . and overtook them

Possible locations of some places on the route of the Exodus are known, but many can only be guessed at (Bible Map 3). No one now knows the exact place of Israel's crossing the Red Sea (Heb., lit., "Sea of Reeds"; the Greek Septuagint Bible, like earlier Greek geographers, called it the "Red Sea"). The crossing could have been through any of the lakes and swamps of Suez or through the northern tip of the Gulf of Suez itself. It would have been miraculous for such a multitude of people and livestock to get through anywhere.

Tragically, Pharaoh hardened his heart yet again (Ex. 14:4*a–d;* 8*a–b*). Doubtless the economic problems in Egypt caused by the loss of their slave labor were part of the concern (Ex. 14:5). A formidable army with chariots therefore pursued and overtook the terrified Israelites to return them to bondage.

14:10–18 Fear ye not, stand still, and see the salvation of the Lord

Pressed between the Egyptian army and the sea, the Israelites quite naturally grew frightened and then vituperative and sarcastic, but Moses stood firm in faith to strengthen them. Sometimes, when people can of themselves do nothing more, they must learn to "stand still, and see the salvation of the Lord."

14:19–31 the Lord caused the sea to go back by a strong east wind all that night, and made the sea dry land and the waters were divided

Both natural and supernatural forces responded to the Lord's commands as he led the former Israelite slaves out of reach of Pharaoh's army. The pillar of cloud caused darkness for the Egyptians but light for Israel (Ex. 14:20). The Egyptian armies perished as the waters returned.

Nephi wrote a helpful summary of the Lord's motives and methods, both miraculous and natural, in freeing Israel and guiding them through the wilderness and into the promised land (1 Ne. 17:23–35; Ps. 106:7–11).

15:1–21 The Lord is my strength and song, and he is become my salvation

A poetic song of praise and thanksgiving commemorated their triumphant exodus with the help of the Lord, who provided freedom and salvation. Typically, throughout the Old Testament, intense emotions were expressed in poetry: urgent supplications, blessings, praises, prophecy, or thanksgiving, and even (as in many of the Psalms) in outcries for vengeance. Thus the thoughts expressed may be noble and beautiful or strident and exultant, as seen in this song. One common feature of Hebrew poetry is parallelism, consisting typically of two complementary statements. Such parallel clauses may be similar in meaning, opposite to each other, progressive in building a concept, or bear some other matched relationship. Poetic diction, alliteration, and a rhythm pattern in words or syllables are also common, but these are not usually preserved by a translator. Other examples of poetry appear before this song of Moses in the biblical record (Gen. 4:23; 9:12–16; 27:27–29; 48:15–16; 49:1–27). Poetry is frequently used in prophecy in the Old Testament and predominates in Job, Psalms, Proverbs, Ecclesiastes, and the Song of Solomon.

The elderly Miriam, sister of Moses and his guardian when he was a baby on the river (Ex. 2:4–8), led out in the festive song and dance (Ex. 15:20–21).

15:22–27 And the people murmured against Moses, saying, What shall we drink?

After the singing and dancing were ended, the people's normal human needs became urgent, and their voices turned soon to murmuring. It would have been more reasonable to have lifted up their voices in supplication, with faith that they would receive God's help again, but the Lord heard them patiently and sweetened the bitter water of Marah; then he guided the hosts of Israel to the lovely oasis at Elim, with its dozen wells and scores of trees.

16:1– 8 Would to God we had died by the hand of the Lord in the land of Egypt, when we sat by the flesh pots, and when we did eat bread to the full; for ye have brought us forth into this wilderness, to kill this whole assembly with hunger

All that God has done does not teach people readily to trust in him for that which needs doing! The Israelites' pessimism, which returned soon after they left Elim, led them to prefer certainty of sustenance with slavery over freedom with responsibility. They had been six weeks in the desert, and their supplies had run out.

Moses tried to teach the people that both blessings and suffering can come from the Lord, and murmuring was not wise.

16:9– 36 Manna . . . was like coriander seed, white; and the taste of it was like wafers made with honey

The Lord provided food miraculously, for in the desert there could not have been sufficient natural food for such a multitude. It is useless to guess what the "manna" was; even the name they called it means "what is it?" (Ex. 16:15*a*). The quails seem not to have been provided constantly, but were provided again at a later crisis (Ex. 16:13*a*).

The instructions for keeping the Sabbath are the first recorded in the Old Testament since the beginning (Ex. 16:22–31; Gen. 2:1–3). Some did not follow the instructions and had to learn obedience by experience.

17:1–7 Israel journeyed from the wilderness of Sin . . . pitched in Rephidim: and there was no water for the people to drink

Sin here is a Hebrew word, not English, and is related to the name *Sinai;* the word probably refers to the series of valleys between the mountains southeastward from the coastal oasis Elim and inland to Rephidim and Sinai (Bible Map 3). In need of water, the people chided Moses again, and again they put the Lord to the test (Ex. 17:2*a–b*). They were not yet confident that their migration was directed by the Lord and that he would stay with them.

In the mountains of "Horeb" the Lord stood before Moses on a rock, which he struck "in the sight of the elders" and provided water miraculously. Moses named the place to commemorate their chiding, testing, and complaining (Ex. 17:7*a–c*).

17:8–13 Then came Amalek, and fought with Israel in Rephidim. . . . And Joshua discomfited Amalek

In their first war the Israelite warriors lacked confidence that the Lord would help them. Only when they could see Moses on the hilltop with the "rod of God" uplifted did they fight with courage and prevail. Aaron and Hur had to hold up Moses' hands. The young leader Joshua eventually became Moses' successor.

17:14–18 the Lord said unto Moses, Write this . . . in a book

Here is another statement that Moses wrote down an account of events and revelations in his time (Ex. 17:14*a*). And he erected a memorial altar (v. 15*a*).

18:1–12 Jethro rejoiced for all the goodness which the Lord had done to Israel

Moses was reunited with his wife and family after their long separation (Ex. 18:2–3; 4:20, 24–26) and with his wife's father, the high priest Jethro. Jethro offered a sacrifice to give thanks for the Lord's deliverance of Israel and ate a ceremonial meal with Moses and Aaron and with Israel's elders.

Note the names of the children of Moses and Zipporah; they

commemorate something of their status and the hopes their parents had for them. Very little is written about them and their descendants, except for their names in family history lists (Ex. 18:3–4 and fn.).

18:13–27 Moses sat to judge the people . . . from the morning unto the evening. . . . And Moses' father in law said, . . . Thou wilt surely wear away, both thou, and this people

Jethro suggested some valuable organizational changes and wisely recommended that Moses implement them if "God command thee so" (Ex. 18:19–23). Moses showed commendable humility and wisdom in accepting advice. The organization of people into groups with chief leaders and subordinate leaders was efficient; it has been used also in later times (Ex. 18:21 and fn.).

19:1– 6 ye shall be a peculiar treasure unto me . . . : a kingdom of priests, and an holy nation

Arriving at Sinai "in the third month" after being freed from Egypt, Israel was called anew to the mission of Abraham's seed (Ex. 19:5 and fn.). Moses was to prepare his followers to be a "peculiar treasure" (Heb., *segullah,* the personal treasury whereby a king operates, defends, and extends his kingdom). As a "kingdom of priests," the Israelites would be servants of the Lord with divine authority, "an holy nation" dedicated and committed to teach and serve. More instructions on the way of life they should live were given them from time to time.

19:7–13 Lo, I come unto thee in a thick cloud, that the people may hear when I speak with thee, and believe thee for ever. . . . the Lord will come down in the sight of all the people

If the people of Israel could have qualified for all the privileges offered them, they could have received the greatest of all revelations at Mount Sinai (Ex. 19:9*b*, 11*a*). Their preparation included cleanliness, commitment, and spiritual dedication.

19:14–25 Go down, charge the people, lest they break through unto the Lord to gaze, and many of them perish

Despite their attempts to prepare, the people trembled in anticipation and awe when a trumpet sounded "exceeding long." They apparently were not fully ready for the Lord to "come down in the sight of all the people," for he sent Moses to warn them (Ex. 19:11–12, 21). Some of their failings are given later (Ex. 20:18–19, 22; D&C 84:21–25; Deut. 4:10, 12, 33, 36; 5:22–26).

Even though they could not enter the Lord's presence, they did hear him speaking the Ten Commandments. It is well known, of course, that the Ten Commandments were later given to Moses on tablets of stone.

20:1– 6 And God spake all these words, saying, I am the Lord thy God. . . . Thou shalt have no other gods before me. Thou shalt not make unto thee any graven image

The first two commandments are essentially one. The Lord declared his identity as the One who freed them and forbade worship or acknowledgment of any other force, entity, or idea as a "god." The phrase "before me" is used here to translate the Hebrew *al-panai* ("against my face"); it permits no other deity whatsoever—neither in addition to, subordinate to, nor in contrast to the only true and living God. Anything else that people "worship" is forbidden in our time as urgently as it was in theirs (TG, "Idolatry, Idol").

Contrary to some interpretations, however, the law against making idols did not forbid the making of figures, statues, or motifs as decorations not for worship; it forbade making a *pesel,* which means specifically an idol. Thus, instructions were later given for making artistic and symbolic items for the ark of the covenant, for the tabernacle, and for the priestly garments (Ex. 25–26; 28). Later, adornments for the temple of Solomon were also made (1 Kgs. 5–6).

The word *jealous* now carries connotations not implied in the original word (Ex. 20:5*b*).

The Lord does not punish children for the sins of their

parents, but parental wrongs may affect their children's inheritance—socially, physically, materially, intellectually, spiritually, or otherwise—under his system of freedom, agency, and responsibility. Moreover, if children follow in the footsteps of parents in sinfulness or in hate and opposition to the Lord's way, the results are "visited" upon them. Nevertheless, when any sinner—or descendant of sinners—repents and keeps His commandments, God will show mercy and give help.

We believe we will be punished at the Judgment Day for our sins of which we have not repented and not for those of anyone else (Ex. 20:5*f*; Deut. 24:16; Ezek. 18; D&C 124:50; A of F 2).

20:7 *Thou shalt not take the name of the Lord thy God in vain*

The third commandment forbids swearing, profaning, or invoking the names of God for any false or vain purpose. It may also be understood to forbid using a name of the true God as a name for anything else.

Profanity is a common violation of this commandment. The prophets and Jesus admonished against it or any other inappropriate use of the divine names (Ex. 20:7*a–d*; Hosea 4:2; Matt. 5:33–37; D&C 63:61–64; 112:26; TG, "Profanity").

Furthermore, to make a covenant or promise in the name of the Lord and then break it is a way of taking his name in vain by our acts (TG, "Hypocrisy, Hypocrite").

20:8–11 *Remember the sabbath day, to keep it holy*

The fourth commandment admonishes God's children to rest on one day in seven and sanctify the day, commemorative of what he did after six periods of creation. The way to sanctify a day is to let the day sanctify us, and *sanctify* means "to dedicate to good and divine purposes," as the Lord did when he dedicated our world to good and divine ends (TG, "Earth, Purpose of"; "Man, Potential to Become like Heavenly Father").

This commandment we ought to obey gladly, with gratitude to God that he made a Sabbath for us to lay aside mundane things and learn to enjoy eternal things unencumbered by worldly concerns (TG, "Sabbath").

The principles underlying all of the first four commandments are embraced in one "first and great commandment" quoted by Jesus (Matt. 22:36–38; Deut. 6:5).

20:12 Honour thy father and thy mother: that thy days may be long upon the land which the Lord thy God giveth thee

The fifth commandment affirms that the home is the place where the good life is taught and learned. If parents teach children by precept and example, and if proper relationships are maintained between parents and children (TG, "Family, Children, Duties of"; "Family, Children, Responsibilities toward"), then every succeeding generation will honor their parents by living honorable lives, preserving and passing on the best of their heritage. In this way all may be preserved in the land and in eternity. When a rising generation rebels against the ways of God taught by good parents and chooses evil ways, then the character of the people and their culture deteriorate.

The commandment to honor one's parents is transitional between the commandments that govern human relationships with God (Ex. 20:2–11) and those that govern relationships with other human beings (Ex. 10:13–17).

20:13 Thou shalt not kill

The principles behind the last five commandments underlie the "second" great commandment quoted by Jesus (Matt. 22:39–40; Lev. 19:17, 33–34); no one who really loves a neighbor would do an act forbidden by these five commandments.

The fifth commandment forbids murder specifically (Ex. 20:13*a*). The evils of murder had been known since the beginning, when Cain slew Abel (Gen. 4:8–15). The sanctity of life was taught in the dispensation of Noah, and capital punishment for murder was prescribed (Gen. 9:5–6). Israel's sons knew that it was wrong to put Joseph to death (Gen. 37:17–22; 42:21–23). The revelation to Moses on Mount Sinai reiterated a known law.

Jesus reiterated it also and warned against either being angry or inciting anger, for anger might lead to violence and murder.

Modern revelation reiterates the law and the punishment (D&C 42:18–19; TG, "Murder").

Shedding innocent blood by anyone who has received the new and everlasting covenant is an unpardonable sin (D&C 132:27).

Participation in warfare is not murder in defensive circumstances (Ex. 17:8–16; Alma 43:47; D&C 98:33–37).

Unnecessary slaughter of animals is a related matter but is not murder (D&C 49:21*a;* JST Gen. 9:11).

20:14 Thou shalt not commit adultery

The seventh commandment prohibits abuse of God's system for procreation of human bodies for his children's earth life, even as the sixth commandment prohibits usurpation of God's prerogative for terminating life. It is the privilege and responsibility of a properly married man and woman to participate in procreative processes. If the organs and processes of procreation are misused or prostituted, it is, as Joseph said, a "great wickedness, and sin against God" (Gen. 39:7–9). We must avoid this sin and "anything like unto it" (D&C 59:6; Ex. 20:14*a*). It is punishable on earth and in heaven, but complete repentance can bring forgiveness (D&C 42:24–26).

20:15 Thou shalt not steal

The eighth commandment forbids taking the property of someone else without permission. Stealing includes robbery, burglary, shoplifting, plagiarism, embezzlement, cheating, or any other form of self-aggrandizement at the expense of others. This law is essential for a secure and peaceful society; the punishment for those who steal and do not repent may occur both in this life and in life after death (TG, "Fraud"; "Rob"; "Stealing, Stolen"; "Thief").

20:16 Thou shalt not bear false witness against thy neighbour

The ninth commandment specifically forbids false testimony,

but it is expanded in other scriptures to include all forms of lying, misrepresentation, or falsehood (TG, "Lying, Liar, Lie").

For liars who do not repent, the prognosis at the judgment bar of God is bad, for they are listed with the "abominable, and murderers, and whoremongers, and sorcerers, and idolaters," who "shall have their part in the lake which burneth with fire and brimstone" (Rev. 21:8; 22:15).

20:17 Thou shalt not covet

The tenth commandment forbids taking illicit delight in, or feeling an improper desire for, another's wife, property, status, or position. This commandment warns against desiring that which cannot be legally and morally acquired, and is thus a safeguard against committing other sins, such as adultery, lying, or stealing (Ex. 20:17*a–b*).

20:18–23 they removed, and stood afar off. And they said unto Moses . . . let not God speak with us, lest we die. . . . And the Lord said . . . Ye have seen that I have talked with you

The people were already awestruck by spiritual experiences at the beginning of the great revelation at Mount Sinai (commentary on Ex. 19:14–25), and at the end they moved "afar off," overwhelmed by the voice of the Lord as he spoke the commandments (Ex. 20:22; Deut. 4:33–36; 5:2–5, 22–30). It was an unusual revelation for a great assembly of people, and Moses comforted them. He explained that God's purpose was to "prove" them and to increase their reverence and their defense against sin (Ex. 20:20 and fn.). He again warned them against making any images of Him (Ex. 20:23*a;* Deut. 4:15–16).

20:24–26 An altar of earth thou shalt make unto me, and shalt sacrifice thereon

The Israelites were to honor the Lord in their way of life and offer their sacrifices only in the places where his name should be uttered—that is, places where the tabernacle would be set up as a portable temple with its holy place (Ex. 25–27).

Improper exposure of priests ascending steps to the great altar was to be avoided by the use of a ramp (Ex. 20:26*a*–*b*).

21:1–11 If thou buy an Hebrew servant

A poor person might contract to serve another person as a way to earn the necessities of life or to get out of debt. The regulations of such an agreement concern Hebrew servants—men, their wives, and families. They include provisions for protection of young women, for termination of service, and for liberation under certain circumstances, such as the sabbatical year.

21:12–27 He that smiteth a man, so that he die, shall be surely put to death. . . . Eye for eye, tooth for tooth, hand for hand, foot for foot

Equal retributive justice, with proper punishment for a number of types of abuses, was specified to prevent excessive punishment. Punishment for causing death and for abusing or cursing parents was very severe; however, people were also taught to do good to offenders and not merely to exact retribution (Ex. 23:4–5).

The retributive law most commonly cited in our time, supposedly to characterize the Mosaic law, is "an eye for an eye and a tooth for a tooth." But retributive law should have prevented undue punishments; it would be unfair to say it exemplifies the whole "law of Moses."

21:28–36 If an ox gore a man or a woman

Some instructions were given regarding responsibility for hazards connected with one's property, animals, or premises; they include principles good for any society.

22:1–15 If a man shall steal an ox, or a sheep

Several examples of restoration of stolen property clarify responsibilities in borrowing and lending.

22:16–20 And if a man . . .

A number of moral and religious laws are given here, each

related to one or more of the Ten Commandments. One involves a woman's rights if she is seduced. Another concerns a "witch," which was anyone who practiced sorcery or communion with evil spirits, but a Joseph Smith Translation emendation (Ex. 22:18*a*) makes it pertain to murder. The sexual offense of bestiality was not tolerated. Sacrificing to another god would, of course, break the first commandment.

22:21–31 Thou shalt neither vex a stranger, nor oppress him: for ye were strangers in the land of Egypt

The rule for treating strangers in the way Israelites would like to have been treated, as with other Mosaic laws, commended qualities of tolerance, kindness, consideration, honesty, mercy, gratitude, respect, and dedication.

23:1–9 If thou see the ass of him that hateth thee lying under his burden, and wouldest forbear to help him, thou shalt surely help with him

Here are more of the principles and practices taught in Moses' revelations to prevent cheating, getting involved in rash mob activity, or abetting evil causes (Ex. 23:1–3 and fn.).

To do good to an enemy ("him that hateth thee") is what Jesus taught (Matt. 5:43–48; Ex. 23:4–5); it was naturally part of our Lord's teachings for Moses' dispensation also. See again the essence of the Golden Rule (Ex. 23:9; 22:21).

23:10–13 six years thou shalt sow thy land . . . but the seventh year thou shalt let it rest and lie still

Sabbatical years of "rest" for the land allowed it to lie fallow to renew itself even as it provided food for the poor, who could harvest volunteer crops that grew.

Sabbath days should indeed "refresh" all working people and their animals. On the Sabbath, as at all times, only the true Giver of all things good should be credited with them.

23:14–19 Three times thou shalt keep a feast unto me in the year

These were three feasts of thanksgiving: the Feast of Passover commemorating liberation; the Feast of Harvest of the Firstfruits (*Shevuot,* "Feast of Weeks"), showing gratitude for the grains and other crops harvested early; the Feast of Ingathering, or late harvest (*Sukkoth,* "booths" or "tabernacles"), a week of thanksgiving for all crops and blessings.

The rule forbidding the cooking of a young goat in its mother's milk was intended to prevent a fertility cult practice (Ex. 23:19*b*). This rule, with many extensions, became a basic tenet in the *kashrut,* or "proper" (kosher), dietary practices of Judaism. To this day Jews who observe this rule keep dairy foods and meat foods strictly separated, neither preparing both in the same utensils nor serving them both at the same meal.

Practical reasons and spiritual purposes behind the strict statutes, ordinances, and performances are given in the Book of Mormon (Mosiah 13:28–32).

23:20– 33 I send an Angel before thee, to keep thee in the way, and to bring thee into the place which I have prepared

The promise of a guiding and guardian angel is quite analogous to the New Testament gift of the Holy Ghost—to guide, prompt, and comfort the faithful (TG, "Holy Ghost").

The divine help given the people of Israel in their preparation and return to the promised land was in accordance with the Lord's principle of blessing the worthy and letting the wicked suffer the fruits of their evil ways (1 Ne. 17:25–43).

Reasons were given for the Israelites' avoiding integration with the Canaanite peoples, their ways, and their worship (Ex. 23:32, 33*a*; Lev. 18).

24:1– 8 he took the book of the covenant, and read in the audience of the people: and they said, All that the Lord hath said will we do, and be obedient

Moses prepared the people so that he might be absent from them to commune with the Lord for forty days. He taught them the words of the Lord and also wrote them down. He built an altar and offered sacrifices, read all the words of the covenant to the people, and heard their promise to be obedient. He sprinkled the blood of the sacrifices upon the people to commit them to keeping the covenant (Ex. 24:1–8 and fn.). Nevertheless, they still were not strong enough to behave according to their promises, as will be seen (Ex. 32).

24:9–11 And they saw the God of Israel: . . . they saw God, and did eat and drink

The privilege of seeing God was granted to Moses, the Aaronic priesthood leaders, and seventy of the patriarchal elders of Israel. It was a personal experience during which they "did eat and drink" together in a covenant-making ceremony (TG, "God, Privilege of Seeing"). This is certainly one of the impressive Old Testament testimonies about the reality of God.

24:12–18 Come up to me into the mount, and be there: and I will give thee tables of stone, and a law, and commandments which I have written; that thou mayest teach them

Leaving the group of special witnesses with Aaron and Hur appointed to deal with matters that might arise, Moses and Joshua, "his minister" (that is, servant or assistant), ascended the mount. Joshua remained somewhere nearby (Ex. 32:15–18; 24:13), while Moses communed with God for a long period—"forty days and forty nights."

The fiery manifestation of the glory of the Lord on top of the mountain must have been an awesome sight for the people (Ex. 24:15–18); it should have kept them from the apostate revelry in which they soon involved themselves (Ex. 32).

25:1–9 Speak unto the children of Israel, that they bring me an offering: of every man that giveth it willingly . . . gold, and silver, and brass, And blue, and purple . . . and fine linen

The first thing revealed on the mount concerned a sanctuary for worship and divine communication. The people would be given the opportunity to contribute precious things they had brought from Egypt (Ex. 25:3–7; 11:1–2; 12:35–36) to adorn the sanctuary. The pattern of the structure was soon to be revealed (Ex. 25:9).

25:10–22 make an ark of shittim wood . . . and thou shalt put into the ark the testimony which I shall give thee

Specifications were given Moses for making a sacred box, using a desert acacia wood called *shittim,* overlaying it with gold, and placing on its golden cover two guardian cherubim whose wings would touch over the center (BD, "Cherubim"). Thus adorned, the top would be called "the mercy seat," and from it the Lord's communications to Moses would come. In the sacred box, or ark, the revealed laws, instructions, and other "testimonies" of the Lord would be kept (BD, "Ark of the Covenant").

25:23– 30 Thou shalt also make a table. . . . And thou shalt set upon the table shewbread before me alway

An acacia wood table overlaid with gold and equipped with rings and staves for carrying would provide a place for sacred shewbread (Heb., lit., "bread of presence"; Ex. 25:30*a;* BD, "Shewbread"). The religious significance and use of this bread is recorded later (Lev. 24:5–9).

25:31– 40 thou shalt make a candlestick of pure gold. . . . And six branches shall come out of the sides of it

The article described in this passage is the seven-branched menorah, or lamp fixture. It was not a candlestick as we understand that term; it had seven cups for oil with wicks for burning (BD, "Candlestick"). Many varieties of the menorah have been crafted from ancient times to the present, and it is one of the best known symbols in Judaism. An ancient carved image of it, as it was taken from Jerusalem by the Romans, may still be seen on the arch of Titus in Rome.

Note the emphasis that things be made according to the revealed "pattern, which was shewed thee in the mount" (Ex. 25:40).

26:1–30 Moreover thou shalt make the tabernacle

Specifications for making the tabernacle (Heb., *mishkan,* "dwelling") were then given to Moses. It would function as a portable temple. From the measurements for all of the curtains, boards, and so on, it can be calculated that the courtyard would be about seventy-five feet wide and one hundred fifty feet long; the tabernacle, fifteen by fifteen by forty-five feet, with the innermost, holiest place being a fifteen-foot cube. For a visual representation of all the posts, pillars, boards, curtains, and adornment, see any illustrated biblical encyclopedia.

26:31–37 the vail shall divide unto you between the holy place and the most holy

The first room was a holy place, but the innermost room was most holy (Heb., lit., "holy of holies"), and a beautifully colored "vail" divided them. The place of the sacred box, or "ark of the testimony," was in the inner room; other items were specified for the next room and for the outer court.

27:1–8 And thou shalt make an altar of shittim wood

These are the specifications for making a portable wooden altar, overlaid with brass and provided with brass grates, pans, and other accessories. The altar was to be seven and one-half feet square and four and one-half feet high with rings and poles for carrying it. The "horns" were symbolic extrusions of the four corners. Its use for burnt offerings is described later.

27:9–19 And thou shalt make the court of the tabernacle

The courtyard surrounding the tabernacle was to be enclosed by a fence with sockets holding upright pillars to support panels of fabric. The court was accessible to all worthy members of the congregation of Israel (BD, "Tabernacle").

27:20–21 command the children of Israel, that they bring thee pure oil olive beaten for the light, to cause the lamp to burn always

The Aaronic priests were to keep the menorah (seven-branched lamp) burning perpetually and keep everything in order in the tabernacle, or "tent of meeting" (Ex. 27:21*a*).

28:1 1 and they shall make holy garments for Aaron . . . and his sons, that he may minister unto me in the priest's office

Aaron and his sons were to wear special clothing, holy garments "for glory and for beauty." Aaron's special garments included a breastplate, apron (Heb., *ephod*), inner garment and outer robe, a bound cap, and a sash. Those who were to make the sacred clothing would be specially endowed with a "spirit of wisdom"; some spiritual gifts in Moses' time are comparable to those of New Testament times (Ex. 28:3; 1 Cor. 12:7–11).

28:5–29 And they shall take gold, and blue, and purple, and scarlet, and fine linen

Specifications were given concerning materials and modes of making all the items of clothing, including the beautifully adorned breastplate, which was to have two precious stones engraven with the names of the tribes of Israel (Ex. 28:9–12). A pocket in the breastplate over Aaron's heart was for the Urim and Thummim. This breastplate had some similarities to the Nephite breastplate but was of cloth rather than rigid materials (Ex. 28:15–30; JS–H 1:35, 59; D&C 17:1; BD, "Breastplate").

28:30 And thou shalt put in the breastplate . . . the Urim and the Thummim; and they shall be upon Aaron's heart

The Urim and Thummim (Heb., lit., "light and perfection") enlightened the mind of the prophet and gave him assurance of fulfillment (perfection) of covenant promises, according to some rabbinic commentaries. It was to help Aaron wisely judge the conflicts of the people and aid him in many other ways (TG and BD, "Breastplate"; "Urim and Thummim").

Abraham received revelations concerning the universe through such an instrument; also, an instrument called "interpreters" in the Book of Mormon and "Urim and Thummim" by Joseph Smith, assisted in translating unknown languages and in receiving other revelations. Their exact appearance and the nature of their operation is not known by anyone except the seers who are divinely appointed to use them.

28:31–35 thou shalt make the robe of the ephod all of blue

The sleeveless "robe of the ephod" slipped over the head and reached to the floor; the ephod, or apron, covered it in front, the ribbon of which was tied in the back, around the robe at the waist, according to rabbinic commentaries. Golden bells attached to the hem of the robe, interspersed with decorative pomegranates, would be heard by the worshippers as the priest performed his sacred services in the holy places.

28:36–43 Holiness to the Lord

The words on Aaron's cap would remind both the priest and the people that they were consecrated to the Lord by ordinances of the temple; the Hebrew word meaning "holiness" is *qodesh,* a noun formed from a root word meaning "dedicated," "sacred." Indeed, all the priestly garments "for glory and for beauty" should have helped people be reverent and dedicated in their temple worship.

29:1–9 And this . . . thou shalt do unto them to hallow them, to minister unto me in the priest's office

The ordinances prescribed for the priests who would officiate at the tabernacle (a temporary temple) included sacrificial offerings; washing and anointing; and clothing with the tunic, robe, ephod (apron), girdle (sash), and bonnet (cap). Thus Aaron and his sons were to be equipped (Heb., *milleh yad,* "fill the hand of"), or endowed, with the priesthood authority necessary to perform their sacred services.

29:10–46 Aaron and his sons shall put their hands upon the head of the bullock. And thou shalt kill the bullock

Procedures were given for certain meat offerings, portions of which were to be eaten by the priests and other portions dedicated as burnt offerings. The laying of the priests' hands upon the head of the sacrificial animal symbolically conveyed to it the sins of the worshippers, anticipating that a divine Redeemer would eventually take upon himself the sins of his followers (Moses 5:5–9). Part of the blood of the animals offered was also used symbolically, some of it being sprinkled on the worshippers to impute to them the benefits of the vicarious sacrifice offered on their behalf. A bit of the blood was put upon the ear, thumb, and toe of the high priest (Ex. 29:20). Perhaps it was to remind him to teach the people to listen to the Lord's commandments, to do them, and to walk in all his ways.

Daily offerings of one lamb in the morning and one in the evening would provide daily communication and renewal.

If the priests, properly ordained and consecrated, would do their work faithfully and all Israel would respond faithfully and keep the commandments of the Lord, then he would "dwell among the children of Israel, and . . . be their God" (Ex. 29:44–45). That promise also applies in this latter-day dispensation.

30:1–10 And thou shalt make an altar to burn incense upon

The altar of incense was to stand in front of the veil that separated the holy place from the holy of holies, where the sweet odor could symbolize pleasing communications from man to God (Ex. 30:7–9 and fn.; Rev. 5:8; 8:3–4).

30:11–16 then shall they give every man a ransom for his soul unto the Lord

A half-shekel "atonement" offering was required of everyone (Ex. 30:15–16). Remember that all these performances were only types and symbols of the divine redemption to come and did not of themselves bring salvation; they served to teach the people principles of repentance and redemption, commit them to faithful living, and strengthen their bonds with God. Sacrifice is an exercise in giving up something of worldly value in order to gain in heavenly values; it anticipates and embraces the blessings of the Atonement (Alma 25:15–16).

30:17–21 Thou shalt also make a laver of brass. . . . Aaron and his sons shall wash their hands and their feet thereat

The laver, or wash basin, was to be in the courtyard between the altar of burnt offering and the entrance to the holy place, so that the priests could cleanse themselves ceremonially before entering the tabernacle to minister in the other ordinances.

30:22–38 Take thou . . . principal spices . . . and of olive oil

Aromatic oil for anointing the tabernacle, its furniture, and the priests was to be prepared, as well as spice to be set before the ark of the covenant (Ex. 30:34–37). Things of pleasing sight and smell symbolized things of spiritual goodness, for they were "holy for the Lord" (Ex. 30:37).

31:1–11 I have filled him with the spirit of God, in wisdom, and in understanding, and in knowledge, and . . . workmanship

The gifts of the Spirit described here are like some in other dispensations (Ex. 31:3a–c). With them, Bezaleel would become chief artisan; he and his assistant would supervise all the "wise hearted" who would make all that had been commanded.

31:12–17 my sabbaths ye shall keep: for it is a sign between me and you . . . that I am the Lord that doth sanctify you

Sabbath observance is not only for rest, worship, renewing covenants, and remembering blessings; it is also a demonstration that there is a sanctifying covenant between God and man. It is a symbol to identify a worshipper of the true God.

31:18 And he gave unto Moses . . . two tables of testimony, tables of stone, written with the finger of God

Delivery of the stone tablets, with all the covenants divinely inscribed on them, came at the climax of forty days of divine instruction for Moses on the mount (Ex. 31:18a).

*32:1– 6 when the people saw that Moses delayed to come down . . . ,
the people gathered themselves together unto Aaron and said . . .
Up, make us gods*

Growing impatient and hopeless concerning Moses' return,
the Israelites desired divine images to "go before" them (Ex. 32:1).
The idea of a calf may have arisen from their memory of some
gods in Egypt, such as the Hathor cow and the Apis bull.
Ironically, after Aaron had fashioned the "molten calf" (Ex.
32:3–4), he sought to preserve the idea that it was a "feast to the
Lord" (Ex. 32:5) that they would celebrate by their offerings, their
eating and drinking, and their "play" before the calf.

32:7– 9 the Lord said . . . thy people . . . have corrupted themselves

They corrupted (Heb., lit., "debased") themselves through
idolatrous worship, whereas worship of the true God would exalt
them. Similar effects come still from certain worldly acts, in contrast to the value from true heavenly ordinances.

The Israelites did not make the golden calf in ignorance but
in "mischief" (Ex. 32:22), for they had been taught the Ten
Commandments and had promised to do "all the words which the
Lord hath said" (Ex. 20; 24:3–4).

*32:10–14 that I may consume them: and I will make of thee a
great nation*

Moses declined the Lord's offer to substitute him and his seed
for the apostate Israelites. If this offer was a test, Moses passed it
humbly, pleading with God for mercy for his erring people. As for
the Lord wanting to "consume" them and then "repenting," the
Joseph Smith Translation clarifies what He really said (Ex.
32:14a–b).

*32:15–18 the two tables of the testimony were in his hand: . . .
written on both their sides . . . And the tables were the work of God,
and the writing was the writing of God*

These divinely created tables bore the testimony and witness
of God to Israel that by living his laws they could fulfill a glorious

mission and attain glorious rewards, but such high and holy covenants were too much for them at that time.

32:19–20 Moses' anger waxed hot, and he cast the tables out of his hands, and brake them beneath the mount

In spite of Moses' plea for the Israelites (Ex. 32:11–13), he perceived by their actions that they were not worthy of God's holy covenants. He demonstrated his disappointment and their great loss by breaking the divinely engraven tablets. Then he destroyed their idol and obliged the people to drink the ashes of it, strewn on water, demonstrating the idol's lack of any power.

32:21–24 Moses said unto Aaron, What did this people unto thee, that thou hast brought so great a sin upon them?

Aaron had failed his duty by acceding to the people's rash demands. He excused his action as arising from "mischief" of the people and told the story as if it were a miracle, asserting, "there came out this calf" (Ex. 32:22, 24).

32:25 Moses saw that the people were naked

Naked may mean either "bare, uncovered," and exposed in their guilt before God; or "riotous, let loose" (Ex. 32:25a–b). The Israelites were evidently guilty of both. They had expressly committed themselves to keeping the Lord's covenants and commandments (Ex. 24:3–7) but had broken them anyway.

32:26–29 Then Moses . . . said, Who is on the Lord's side? . . . And all the sons of Levi gathered . . . unto him

Moses let any who were faithful to God identify themselves by coming unto him, and he charged them to execute the unfaithful. Their idolatrous apostasy was dangerous enough to Israel to warrant capital punishment (Deut. 13:6–9; Matt. 10:28).

32:30– 35 Ye have sinned a great sin: and now I will go up unto the Lord; peradventure I shall make an atonement for your sin

Even though they had sinned so grievously, Moses again

pleaded for forgiveness for the people, humbly taking responsibility for their failings. The Lord's reply was based on the principle that a person shall be punished only for his own sins (Ex. 32:33a–c). Moses was innocent of the Israelites' sin, because he had instructed them and committed them to obedience before leaving them (Ex. 24:3–4) and had left a leader over them. Atonement was available through the Lord's mercy, however, and He promised that His angel would again guide them. Nevertheless, the unrepentant guilty were plagued, because indeed "they made the calf, which Aaron made" (Ex. 32:35).

33:1– 6 Depart, and go up hence, . . . I will send an angel before thee; . . . for I will not go up in the midst of thee

The children of Israel were still called to their mission in the land of promise and would still be blessed with divine guidance. Nevertheless, many people had demonstrated by their actions at the time the commandments were spoken on Sinai and at the time of their presentation on tablets of stone that they did not have the capacity to "endure his presence" and to keep his commandments (Ex. 20:18–21; 32; D&C 84:22–26). They had forfeited the privilege of having the Lord "in the midst" of them (Ex. 33:5b).

33:7–10 And Moses took the tabernacle, and pitched it without the camp, afar off from the camp

Moses accordingly moved the tent of meeting, or "tabernacle of the congregation" (not yet the special tabernacle of testimony prescribed in Ex. 25–27 and built later, as recorded in Ex. 35–40), some distance outside the camp. The people watched in awe as the cloudy pillars descended, and Moses communed with the Lord.

33:11–23 the Lord spake unto Moses face to face, . . . And he said, I beseech thee, shew me thy glory

Moses asked that the Lord would still be with Israel and would show him the way to go. That request was granted (Ex. 33:14, 17), but his request to see the Lord in His glory was not.

There is a difference between seeing God face to face with one's spiritual eyes under the protective Spirit of God and having the power to behold all His glory. Thus it is not inconsistent that Moses talked with the Lord "as a man speaketh unto his friend" in previous revelations but yet was denied the request "Shew me thy glory." Note the privilege he did have, however (Ex. 33:11, 18–23 and fn.; Moses 1:2, 5, 9–11, 13–15; Ether 3:6–13).

34:1–9 the Lord said unto Moses, Hew thee two tables of stone like unto the first: and I will write upon these

Moses prepared the new stone tables as instructed and re-turned to the mount for a restoration of part of what had previously been given. Some privileges and powers of the higher priesthood and ordinances were not restored (Ex. 34:1*a–e;* D&C 84:19–27).

The Lord's name and something of his nature and ways of working with humankind were stated again. Important words are missing at the end of verse 7, and the word *generation* has been supplied in italics by the translators to replace the missing material (Ex. 34:7; Ex. 20:4–6, fn. and commentary). Moses accepted the revised covenant humbly and reverently.

34:10–17 Behold, I make a covenant: before all thy people I will do marvels, such as have not been done

Moses had pleaded that the Lord would remain with Israel on the journey and consider them still his special people (as stated in Ex. 19:5–6), forgiving their obstinacy, iniquity, and sinfulness. In response, the Lord promised to help Israel take an inheritance from the idolatrous people in Canaan (Gen. 15:13–16; 17:7–9; 1 Ne. 17:23–35); however, they had to keep their covenants and take to heart the "terrible" (awesome) things he would do with them. They were neither to marry nor worship with the idolaters, lest they be corrupted (Ex. 34:13–16 and fn.).

34:18–26 The feast of unleavened bread shalt thou keep

Instructions on some festivals and Sabbath observances are

reiterated (Ex. 34:18–26 and fn.). The special dietary law about meat and milk was also reiterated (commentary on Ex. 23:19).

34:27–28 the Lord said unto Moses, Write thou these words

Moses wrote the items reviewed (such as Ex. 34:10–26), but the Lord must have written upon the new stone tables the new covenant as promised (Ex. 34:1); thus "he" in the last sentence of 34:28 must refer to the Lord, not to Moses.

34:29– 35 when Moses came down from mount Sinai with the two tables of testimony . . . Moses wist not that the skin of his face shone

Moses' prolonged fast and his experience in the Lord's presence was unique in many respects, but radiation has been seen in other cases (Ex. 34:29*d;* Acts 2:1–3).

The word *shone* is used to translate the Hebrew verb *qaran,* which is from a noun meaning "horn." It here depicts radial beams of light, like the "horns" of morning—the rays seen over the horizon before sunrise. (A mistranslation in the Latin Bible of Michelangelo's time caused him to put horns on the head of his heroic statue of Moses!)

35:1– 3 And Moses . . . said unto them, These are the words which the Lord hath commanded, that ye should do them

Moses gathered the congregation and further delineated the Sabbath commandments. Orthodox Jewish worshippers still observe the restriction on lighting fires and related acts.

35:4– 9 whosoever is of a willing heart, let him bring it

All were invited to make voluntary contributions of valuable materials and precious stones for construction and embellishment of the tabernacle. The importance of exercising one's agency in making offerings is noted from time to time (Ex. 35:5*a;* Lev. 1:3). The contributions would have been from the jewels and precious things received by the Israelites before they left Egypt (Ex. 11:2–3; 12:35–36).

35:10–29 And every wise hearted among you shall come, and make all that the Lord hath commanded

Success in the sacred work depended on the willing hearted and wise hearted coming forth to perform it. Spiritual influences make people willing and wise (Ex. 35:21; 36:1–2). The people responded generously, both men and women, giving freely of their talents and material goods. This is a bright spot in Israel's history.

35:30– 35 See, the Lord hath called by name Bezaleel

People who were called by the Lord and filled with the Spirit, as were Bezaleel and Aholiab, not only developed their own skills in fine arts and crafts but taught others.

36:1– 7 all the wise men, that wrought all the work . . . spake . . . saying, The people bring much more than enough

In this great project the people did more than was required, for a change, and more than enough was contributed.

36:8– 38 And every wise hearted man . . . wrought the work of the tabernacle

The tabernacle and its furnishings were made in accordance with the instructions received (Ex. 26–31).

37:1– 38:20 And Bezaleel made the ark . . . the mercy seat . . . the table . . . the candlestick . . . the incense altar . . . the holy anointing oil, . . . the altar of burnt offering . . . the laver of brass, . . . and he made the court

All particulars of the project were completed. (Ex. 37:1–38:20 and fn.).

38:21– 31 This is the sum of the tabernacle, even of the tabernacle of testimony

A sum was made by Ithamar of all the gold, silver, and brass used in this great project directed by Bezaleel and Aholiab.

39:1–31 And of the blue, and purple, and scarlet, they made cloths of service . . . , and made the holy garments

Beautiful gems and colors in fabrics were used to make the garments and the breastplate, as specified.

All that good work, consecrated to the Lord (Ex. 39:30*a*), must have helped many to become a holy ("dedicated") people.

39:32–43 And they brought the tabernacle unto Moses

The beautiful new portable temple, with all its accoutrements, was reviewed and approved by Moses himself, and he blessed the workers.

40:1–16 And the Lord spake unto Moses, saying, On the first day of the first month shalt thou set up the tabernacle

Instructions were revealed for setting up, equipping, and dedicating the tabernacle for worship services and for washing, anointing, and clothing priests (BD, "Priests") so that they could properly officiate in the ordinances to be performed in the tabernacle.

40:17–33 And it came to pass in the first month in the second year, on the first day of the month, that the tabernacle was reared up

Moses caused everything to be erected and prepared as had been specified. The testimony was placed in the ark, and it was put in its holy place. The altars, lavers, and all implements were put in their places, ready for the dedicatory services.

40:34–38 Then a cloud covered the tent of the congregation, and the glory of the Lord filled the tabernacle

The Lord manifested his acceptance of the tabernacle as his "dwelling" on earth and as a place of worship and communication. When the glorious cloud filled the tabernacle, even Moses could not enter. Compare the spiritual phenomena similarly manifested when the first temple of the latter days was dedicated (Joseph Smith, *History of The Church of Jesus Christ of Latter-day Saints,* 7 vols., 2d ed. rev., edited by B. H. Roberts [Salt Lake City:

The Church of Jesus Christ of Latter-day Saints, 1932–51], 2:410). Thereafter, when the cloud moved from the tabernacle, the children of Israel moved; and when it stopped, they stopped and made camp. They should have felt very secure under such a divine favor (Ex. 40:36–38; but see Num. 10–11).

Thus ends Exodus, the record of the exit of Israel from Egypt. With many impressive, spiritual blessings and instructions the Lord prepared the children of Israel for their mission and life in the promised land. Just so will he prepare any who will accept him for service, life, and joy in his kingdom.

LEVITICUS

Leviticus was the priesthood handbook of the Levites and the Aaronic priests. It contains laws concerning offerings of animals, incense, and foods—laws given to the Israelites "to keep them in remembrance of God and their duty towards him" (Mosiah 13:30). These laws and offerings were as a "schoolmaster" to bring people by hope and faith unto the coming Redeemer and to salvation through him (Gal. 3:23–25).

Offerings of the flesh and blood of animals (called "carnal" offerings in Heb. 9:10) began in Adam's dispensation in "similitude of the sacrifice of the Only Begotten of the Father" (Moses 5:7). They continued until they were fulfilled by the Savior in Gethsemane and on the cross. Abraham, Moses, and the other prophets of the Bible and the Book of Mormon understood these concepts, but many of the people probably did not. Several passages of scripture, such as 2 Nephi 11:4–6; Jacob 4:4–6; Mosiah 13:27–35; Helaman 8:13–20; and Galatians 3, may help us appreciate the relationship of the offerings of flesh and blood to the Atonement (TG and BD, "Symbolism").

The moral and ethical laws in Leviticus commend respect, consideration, orderliness, and peace—principles promulgated also by the gospel in later dispensations. Some practical prescriptions for cleanliness and control of some diseases were also given to the Israelites.

Naturally, the people of Israel did not always obey the laws, but knowing them and the results of obedience or disobedience has helped many people, past and present, to live better lives. Knowing the law and its past effectiveness can help reduce the personal costs of learning by future experience.

Understanding Leviticus helps us rejoice in the sacrifice and atonement of our Savior, who fulfilled the Mosaic laws of sacrifice (Matt. 5:17).

COMMENTARY

1:1–9 let him offer a male without blemish . . . of his own voluntary will

Certain qualities of the sacrificial animals were symbolic, and proper attitudes of the worshippers were important. Laying hands upon the head of the animal before it was slain exemplified the transfer of suffering for sin, later done for us by the Savior. The ascending smoke and vapors from the burnt offering, as "a sweet savour unto the Lord" (Lev. 1:9), represented a communication of gratitude and supplication from earth to heaven. Other aspects of sacrificial worship are given later.

An overview of the three basic sacrifices—the sin offerings, burnt offerings, and peace offerings—is given in the Bible Dictionary (BD, "Sacrifices").

1:10–17 And if his offering be of the flocks, namely, of the sheep, or of the goats . . . And if . . . of fowls

The alternate burnt offerings were similar in purpose to those involving the large animals. The willingness to give up things of material value to gain things of spiritual worth was implicit in all sacrifices.

2:1–11 a meat offering unto the Lord . . . shall be of fine flour; and he shall pour oil upon it, and put frankincense thereon

The "meat offering" of fine flour could be called a "meal offering" because of the flour; *meat* in King James English means food in general, not flesh only; but the Hebrew word may be more simply translated as *tribute*. This offering could be either flour or unleavened cakes with oil. Only a portion was burnt, or made to "smoke upon the altar" (Lev. 2:2 in Hebrew). The remainder was to be used as food by the priests (Lev. 2:3, 10).

2:12–16 the oblation of the firstfruits

The "oblation of the firstfruits" was an offering of some heads of the first ripening grains (called "ears of corn" in Lev. 2:14, but it was not maize, or what Americans call "corn"). Heads of the nearly ripened grain were dried or parched by the fire, and the kernels were then threshed, or beaten free from the heads, to be offered by burning, along with oil and frankincense. Salt was essential, but the reason for it is not given (cf. Num. 18:19).

3:1–17 And if his oblation be a sacrifice of peace offering

Either male or female animals of the flock or herd could be used for the peace offering. The name of this offering in Hebrew is *shelamim,* which is related to the noun *shalom* ("peace") and the verb *shalam* ("to be entire, sound, safe, at peace"). As indicated later (Lev. 7:11–21), the peace offering could be used for giving thanks, making or concluding a vow, or for making other supplications. Only the fat was burned; part of the rest was used by the priests for food and part by the worshipper in a ceremonial meal.

4:1–35 If a soul shall sin through ignorance

Remedies were given for sins committed in ignorance of the law, whether by a priest (Lev. 4:3), a whole congregation (Lev. 4:13), a ruler (Lev. 4:22), or one of the people (Lev. 4:27). The offering was to be made whenever the sin became known. In any such case the priest was to offer the sacrifice on behalf of the guilty party to provide atonement and forgiveness. Ignorance of the law was no excuse, but penalties for breaking the law unwittingly were not as great as those for willful sinning.

5:1–19 if a soul sin, . . . and if it be hidden

Penalties were also prescribed for those who had heard a

sworn promise but would not attest to it, had touched something unclean without knowing it, or had uttered a rash oath without realizing it. According to his ability, a violator was to offer an animal, or two fowls, or some flour, and the priest would "make an atonement for him" so that the sin could be forgiven. Even if a serious trespass were committed "through ignorance" (Lev. 5:15–19), repentance and sacrifice could bring forgiveness.

6:1–7 If a soul . . . lie unto his neighbour

Lying about something found, wrongly held, or deceitfully acquired was sinful; such a sin required repentance, restoration of one-fifth more than its value, and also a trespass offering.

6:8–30 Command Aaron and his sons, . . . This is the . . . offering

Procedures were specified for the Aaronic priests' burnt offerings (Lev. 6:9–13), "meat" offerings (Lev. 6:14–18), initiation ceremonies (Lev. 6:19–23), and sin offerings (Lev. 6:24–30).

7:1–38 Likewise this is the law of . . . offering[s]

More specifications were given regarding trespass offerings, peace offerings, portions to be eaten and not to be eaten, types of flesh never to be eaten, portions to be given to the priest, and pertinent regulations (BD, "Sacrifices").

8:1–36 Take Aaron and his sons with him, and the garments, and the anointing oil. . . . And gather thou all the congregation

The public consecration of the Aaronic priests involved washing, anointing, and clothing them in priestly garments; afterward, sacrifices and a ceremonial meal were conducted. Note the use of the Urim and Thummim (Lev. 8:8 and fn.). The participants stayed at the tabernacle for a week (Lev. 8:33–35).

9:1–24 on the eighth day . . . Moses called Aaron and his sons, and the elders of Israel; And he said . . . to day the Lord will appear unto you

After the priests were consecrated (Lev. 8), certain offerings were made for the people. Then in accord with his promise to them (Lev. 9:4), the glory of the Lord was manifested at the tabernacle as "there came a fire out from before the Lord, and consumed . . . the burnt offering" (Lev. 9:24). The people shouted (Lev. 9:24; Heb., *ranan*, a "ringing cry of joy") and prostrated themselves in reverence.

10:1–7 Nadab and Abihu, the sons of Aaron . . . offered strange fire before the Lord, which he commanded them not . . . and they died before the Lord

The violation committed by two sons of Aaron and its tragic consequences are best understood in light of other scriptures regarding the perpetual fire to be kept for ritual purposes (Ex. 27:20–21; Lev. 24:1–4) and the incense to be burned every morning (Ex. 30:7–9). As to just what the sons of Aaron did wrong and why they were so summarily smitten, nothing is known beyond what is stated in the scriptures (consider Lev. 10:8–11).

10:8–11 And the Lord spake unto Aaron, saying, Do not drink wine nor strong drink, thou, nor thy sons with thee, when ye go into the tabernacle of the congregation, lest ye die

That this rule follows immediately after the record of the incident involving Aaron's sons may imply that intoxication caused them to fail in discerning "between holy and unholy, and between unclean and clean" (Lev. 10:10) in their sacred service.

In any case, this passage is a "word of wisdom" restricting use of intoxicants by the priests, for alcohol can distort one's discernment and discretion. It would surely impair one's ability to teach and one's spiritual dignity as a teacher (Lev. 10:11).

10:12–20 And Moses spake unto Aaron, and unto Eleazar and unto Ithamar, his sons that were left

Moses instructed the priestly leaders to finish the day's sacrifices and partake of the portions of the flesh offerings in the proper way. They did so, but Aaron felt he needed to be excused from partaking of the sin offering in his bereavement, and Moses agreed, perhaps out of compassion (Lev. 10:17–20).

11:1– 47 These are the beasts which ye shall eat among all the beasts that are on the earth

Doubtless sanitary and nutritional factors were among the criteria for designating clean and unclean flesh, but all the reasons are not known. Almost all the "unclean" beasts and fowl were carnivores. Some flesh can cause diseases unless it is thoroughly cooked, and that may have been a factor.

Servants of the Lord should not defile themselves in any way but be committed and clean. As the Lord declared, "Ye shall therefore be holy; for I am holy" (Lev. 11:45; 19:2).

12:1– 8 If a woman have . . . a man child . . . [or] a maid child

The "purification" rituals after childbirth would at least give a new mother time to recuperate. The forty-day purification following the birth of a boy was doubled for a girl, possibly to symbolize sanctification of both mother and daughter. Sanctification was completed by sacrifices, a burnt offering, and a sin offering; but the sin offering is no implication that conceiving or bearing children is sinful. Being thus sanctified through the sin offering could imply dedicating oneself to righteous parenthood (TG, "Marriage, Fatherhood"; "Marriage, Motherhood").

13:1– 46 When the plague of leprosy is in a man

The word leprosy was used in King James English as a generic term for various skin blemishes and diseases; the leprosy we know as Hansen's disease was certainly one of them. When approved by the priest, the sufferer of some skin conditions could be "cleansed" and freed from isolation (TG and BD, "Leper"; "Leprosy"). Leviticus 13 covers diagnosis and isolation; Leviticus 14 deals with remedies.

13:47–59 The garment also that the plague of leprosy is in

The word leprosy was used also for such conditions as mildew and mold in fabric, and specifications were given for getting such things clean and approved.

14:1– 32 the law of the leper in the day of his cleansing

Instructions were given for cleansing blemishes and getting the afflicted person declared clean. The isolation procedures (Lev. 13) and additional measures here prescribed could have prevented the spread of some infections; and the hope of forgiveness and atonement would have greatly relieved the afflicted (Lev. 14:31).

14:33–57 the plague of leprosy in a house

Scaling or crumbling mortar (such as might be caused by too much alkali) was also called "leprosy," and fungus-infested or rotting wooden parts of a house could be similarly identified. Some practical remedies were provided. (See fn. to Lev. 14:33–57 for alternate translations.)

15:1– 32 When any man hath a running issue out of his flesh

The cleansing of normal and abnormal discharges of the body was described. Not only was ritual cleansing symbolically meaningful but it was practical, basic hygiene.

16:1– 4 Thus shall Aaron come into the holy place

Aaron and his successors had to be properly prepared and clothed in the garments of the priesthood before entering the holy place beyond the veil of the tabernacle on the "day of atonement," the most holy day of the year (Lev. 16:2–34). The special clothing included linen underclothing ("breeches"), a robe ("coat"), sash ("girdle"), and cap ("mitre"); the priest was washed before being clothed in those garments of the priesthood.

16:5– 34 in the seventh month, on the tenth day of the month . . . shall the priest make an atonement for you

The tenth day of the seventh month was a special day each year: *Yom Kippur,* the Day of Atonement. Two goats were chosen and brought to the tabernacle, where one was selected by lot as a sacrifice and the other as a "scapegoat." The symbolism is clear: Aaron laid both his hands upon the head of one goat and confessed over him "all the iniquities of the children of Israel, . . . putting them upon the head of the goat," and sending the goat away into the wilderness. Symbolically, the goat carried away the iniquities of the people (Lev. 16:29–34; 23:26–32).

The English word *scapegoat* is not a translation but a substitute for the Hebrew word *azazel,* which may mean "entire removal," though it is variously interpreted.

17:1–9 What man soever . . . that killeth . . . And bringeth it not unto the door of the tabernacle

Sacrifices were not to be offered in the open field and never to "devils" (Heb., *se'irim,* "hairy ones," meaning either male goats or the legendary "satyrs"). Only proper sacrifices offered in the proper place were acceptable to the Lord.

17:10–16 whatsoever man . . . eateth any manner of blood

Blood, "the life of the flesh" (Lev. 17:11, 14), symbolized life itself, and consuming it was strictly forbidden. In sacrifices, it was "the blood that maketh an atonement for the soul." Fulfillment of the symbolism came when Jesus said, "This cup *is* the new testament in my blood, which is shed for you" (Luke 22:20; Lev. 17:11 and fn. *a–d*).

Spurious "mystery religions" have prescribed drinking the blood of sacrificial victims to ingest some life essence and extend the life of the participant. Such a concept may be a corruption of the revelation to Adam that the blood of a sacrificial animal was in similitude of the Savior's blood and by his blood mankind could gain eternal life (Moses 5:7–9).

18:1–5 After the doings of the land of Egypt . . . and after the doings of the land of Canaan . . . shall ye not do: neither shall ye walk in their ordinances

The Lord's people should live purely according to the laws and ordinances of the Lord to be saved in both time and eternity.

18:6– 30 None of you shall approach to any that is near of kin to him, to uncover their nakedness

Neither sexual relations, implied by the idiom "uncover their nakedness," between near relatives nor marriage between them was to be tolerated (Lev. 18:6–17).

Sexual activity with fertility idols such as Molech was forbidden, as were homosexuality and bestiality (Lev. 18:21–23).

Such practices had defiled the nations that were cast out of the land of promise, and such practices by the Israelites would cause them to be cast out also (Lev. 18:27–28; 1 Ne. 17:33–35).

19:1–2 Ye shall be holy: for I the Lord your God am holy

Translated here as *holy,* the Hebrew *qadosh* connotes being "set apart, consecrated, dedicated, sacred, sanctified"; hence the alternate translation, "ye shall be saints" (Lev. 19:2*a*). This chapter is a collection of concise reminders of the ways a dedicated, saintly people should live (Lev. 19:1–2 and fn.).

19:3 Ye shall fear every man his mother and his father

Fear is only one of the meanings of the Hebrew word *yareh;* it also means "stand in awe, honor, revere." This short verse ties together principles from the fourth and fifth commandments and emphasizes their origins with God.

19:4 Turn ye not unto idols, . . . I am the Lord your God

The first two of the Ten Commandments were concisely reiterated and divine authorship was again affirmed.

19:5– 8 And if ye offer a sacrifice of peace offerings unto the Lord, ye shall offer it at your own will

Individuals were to exercise agency in making peace offerings and promptly conduct the feast that followed them.

19:9–10 neither shalt thou gather the gleanings . . . thou shalt leave them for the poor and stranger

The right to glean the harvested fields was part of the Israelite welfare program (Lev. 23:22; Deut. 24:19–22; Ruth 2:2–22).

19:11–14 Ye shall not steal, neither deal falsely

Honesty and consideration in dealing with others and having reverence for God were required.

19:15–16 Ye shall do no unrighteousness in judgment

Justice was to be impartial, and gossip and false witnessing were not to be tolerated (Lev. 19:15–16 and fn.).

19:17–18 Thou shalt not hate thy brother in thine heart

No hatred was to be harbored against a neighbor, though rebuking him might be justified on occasion; the overruling passion should be love. When Jesus was asked, "Master, which is the great commandment in the law," he cited the one commending love of God (Deut. 6:5) and volunteered this commandment as "the second . . . like unto it" (Matt. 22:36–39; cf. D&C 121:41–45).

19:19 not gender with a diverse kind . . . not . . . mingled seed . . . neither . . . a garment mingled

The principle of keeping everything pure, unmixed, and undefiled was exemplified in laws about animals, plants, and fabrics.

19:20–22 whosoever lieth carnally with a woman that is a bondmaid

A particular violation of the seventh commandment was forbidden and procedures given for dealing with such a violation (Lev. 19:20b).

19:23–25 And when ye shall . . . have planted . . . trees

Israel was taught by revelation how to regulate development and harvest of fruit from new orchards.

19:26–28 blood . . . enchantment . . . heads . . . beards . . . cuttings

Aberrations in diet, ceremonies, grooming, and grieving were to be avoided.

19:29 Do not prostitute thy daughter

A particularly atrocious violation of the seventh commandment was condemned.

19:30–32 sabbaths . . . sanctuary . . . familiar spirits . . . the old

Religious and social rules were briefly summarized.

19:33–34 And if a stranger sojourn with thee . . . love him as thyself

As Jesus later taught, a stranger may be a neighbor and should be treated as one would like to be treated (Luke 10:25–37).

19:35–37 unrighteousness in judgment . . . weight . . . measure

Justice, fairness, and honesty in all dealings were emphasized. The final "I am the Lord" reasserts that such laws are not merely a product of people's experience, for God cares about how people treat each other.

20:1–5 Whosoever . . . giveth any of his seed unto Molech

Molech was a particularly abominable idol whose cult practiced human sacrifice; some later Israelite kings did participate in such abominations (Lev. 20:1–5 and fn.; BD, "Molech").

20:6–8 the soul that turneth after . . . familiar spirits . . . wizards

Israelites were urged to turn only to the Lord for guidance and to sanctify themselves and be saints; fortune-tellers can confuse and corrupt minds committed to the Lord (Lev. 20:6*a*).

20:9 every one that curseth his father or his mother

Recall the reasons for the fifth commandment (Ex. 20:12). *Curseth* is used here to translate a Hebrew word meaning "to make contemptible"; such an attitude and act would frustrate perpetuation of the way of life the Lord was trying to establish.

20:10–21 And the man that committeth adultery . . . shall surely be put to death

Punishments were prescribed for all the varieties of immorality prohibited by the laws (Lev. 18).

137

20:22–26 Ye shall therefore keep all my statutes . . . that the land, whither I bring you . . . spue you not out

Again the Israelites were warned that they who receive a chosen land from the Lord can keep it only by being true to his ways: "And ye shall be holy unto me, for I the Lord am holy." Chosen people must qualify by their righteousness to retain that status, and failing to do so can bring rejection. Blessings are earned by obedience to the laws upon which they are predicated (D&C 130:20–21; TG, "Accountability"; "Israel, Blessings of"; "Israel, Mission of").

20:27 A man also or woman that hath a familiar spirit, or that is a wizard, shall surely be put to death

"Wizards" (Heb., *yidd'onim,* "knowing ones") and others who claim to have ungodly supernatural sources of information can destroy souls; hence, the severe punishment (Lev. 20:27*a;* cf. Matt. 10:28).

21:1–9 Speak unto the priests . . . , There shall none be defiled for the dead . . . But for his kin, that is near

A priest should not perform the washing, dressing, and preparation of the dead for burial, except for his father, mother, son, daughter, brother, unmarried sister, and his wife (Lev. 21:2–3; inclusion of his wife was understood, according to rabbinic commentaries).

Neither should a priest show mourning by cutting part of his hair or beard, or slashing his flesh as some cults do. He is consecrated to God and should not profane himself, neither should he profane himself by marrying a prostitute or profane woman (Lev. 21:7). If a daughter of a priest became immoral, that would profane both her and her father (Lev. 21:9).

21:10–12 the high priest . . . , Neither shall he go in to any dead body

The anointed high priest was not to take care of the body even of his mother or father; neither was he to show mourning by uncovering his head or tearing his sacred garments. He was not to leave the sanctuary or profane it in any way when in mourning.

21:13–15 And he shall take a wife in her virginity

The high priest was to be an example of proper marriage.

21:16–24 No man that hath a blemish of the seed of Aaron . . . shall . . . offer the offerings of the Lord

Just as the offering was to be without blemish, in the similitude of the Only Begotten Son of the Father, so also was the priest who offered the sacrifice to be without blemish, in similitude of the Father who offered his Son. (This parallelism is not explicit here but may be deduced from such scriptures as John 3:16 and Jacob 4:5.) Nothing in modern revelation, however, bars one who is physically impaired from holding any priesthood office or functioning in any priesthood ordinance, in or out of the temple.

22:1–16 Whosoever he be of all your seed . . . that goeth unto the holy things . . . having his uncleanness upon him, that soul shall be cut off from my presence

Any priest who was "unclean" by reason of diseases or touching unclean things was not to handle the sacred things; neither was any unqualified person to partake of holy things.

22:17–25 Ye shall offer at your own will a male without blemish

Proper attitudes of the worshippers and proper qualities of offerings were again specified. As mentioned before, worshippers must perform sacrifices of their own free will (Lev. 1:3).

The offerings were to symbolize the ultimate, perfect Redeemer who was to come. Perhaps all worshippers did not understand this symbolism, and it was essential that they all be given the chance to do so (cf. Mosiah 13:30–32).

22:26–31 whether it be cow or ewe, ye shall not kill it and her young both in one day

Some compassionate considerations for perpetuation of life

were to be observed in offering the young firstborn of the herd or flock. And again, no one was to be forced to make offerings.

22:32– 33 Neither shall ye profane my holy name; but I will be hallowed . . . : I am the Lord which hallow you

Whatever is done to revere the Lord and respect sacred things will help to sanctify the doer (Lev. 22:32*a–b*).

23:1– 44 These are the feasts of the Lord, even holy convocations

The Jewish year has twelve months (moons), alternating thirty and twenty-nine days in length (to total 354 days). About nine times every twenty-five years an extra month is added to keep that lunar year in phase with the solar year. For this reason the holidays of the Jewish year do not occur on fixed dates on our modern calendar.

Leviticus 23 outlines the sabbaths, feasts, fasts, and other holy days of the Jewish year. Most of the holy days were special sabbaths and could occur on any of the days of the week: Passover and Unleavened Bread (Lev. 23:5–8); Firstfruits (Lev. 23:9–14); Feast of Weeks, or Shevuot (Lev. 23:15–21); Blowing of Trumpets, New Year, or Rosh Hashanah (Lev. 23:23–25); Atonement, or Yom Kippur (Lev. 23:26–32); Ingathering, Tabernacles, Booths, or Sukkoth (Lev. 23:33–44); the eighth day of Sukkoth was a special sabbath, later called Rejoicing in the Law, or Simchas Torah (Lev. 23:39). Some of these holy days had been introduced earlier (Ex. 12:1–27, 23:14–19; Lev. 6:5–34). Celebrations such as Hanukkah, Purim, and Tishah-b'Ab came later (BD, "Calendar"; "Fasts"; "Feasts").

24:1– 4 bring unto thee pure oil olive beaten for the light

Special oil was to be prepared for perpetual burning in the menorah, the seven-branched lamp of the Tabernacle.

24:5– 9 thou shalt take fine flour, and bake twelve cakes

More direction was given on preparing and displaying the

shewbread, or "bread of the presence" (cf. Ex. 25:30; 35:13; 39:36).

24:10–16, 23 And the Israelitish woman's son blasphemed

In an incident of blasphemy, Israelites sought that "the mind of the Lord might be shewed them" regarding punishment; otherwise the summary punishment of the son of an Egyptian man and an Israelite woman might have been presumptuous (Lev. 24:12, 23).

24:17–22 And he that killeth

Punishments for murder and for killing animals were again declared, as was the law of equal retribution, "tooth for tooth" (cf. Ex. 20:13; 21:24; 22:10–13; and commentary; TG, "Capital Punishment"; BD, "Blasphemy").

25:1–7 in the seventh year shall be a sabbath of rest unto the land, a sabbath for the Lord

In the sabbatical year the Israelites were neither to sow, to prune, nor to harvest—except to gather enough volunteer produce to supply the needs of the family, servants, and "strangers" (nonresidents who might need food); they should show gratitude for their land and their freedom (Deut. 5:6, 12–15; BD, "Sabbatical Year").

25:8–24 ye shall hallow the fiftieth year, and proclaim liberty throughout all the land . . . : it shall be a jubile unto you

Jubile, or jubilee, from the Hebrew yovel ("the trill of the ram's horn"; Lev. 25:9a), has come to mean "rejoicing". It was a signal to proclaim liberty for servants in bondage, and the return of a heritage to its rightful heirs. Thus land was conveyed only for the number of years remaining in each half-century after the jubilee, and no one was to take advantage of either buyer or seller in calculating those years (Lev. 25:10, 14–17).

Note the words that were later inscribed on the bell that became the Liberty Bell of the United States of America (Lev. 25:10):

"Proclaim liberty throughout all the land unto all the inhabitants thereof."

25:25– 34 If thy brother be waxen poor, and hath sold away some of his possession, and if any of his kin come to redeem it

Redemption of land by a kinsman (Heb., *go'el,* "redeemer") was an alternative to waiting for the jubilee to get former possessions back. This concept is well illustrated in the book of Ruth (TG, "Redeem, Redeemed.")

A house in a walled city could be sold and become the permanent property of the buyer if it was not redeemed within a year, but there were exceptions in villages and Levite cities (Lev. 25:29–33).

25:35–55 if thy brother be waxen poor, . . . then thou shalt relieve him; yea, though he be a stranger, or a sojourner

Principles were prescribed to protect the poor from slavery among Israelites and provide for redemption of any in bondage to others.

26:1–26 If ye walk in my statutes, and keep my commandments, and do them; Then I will give you rain . . . , and the land shall yield her increase

In the land of promise, Israelites would enjoy prosperity and security only if they obeyed the laws that justified the blessings. The principle of agency lets people choose their goal or their way, but ways lead to certain ends whereas goals require certain ways. There are consequences to all laws, physical and spiritual.

26:27– 46 if ye will not for all this hearken unto me, but walk contrary unto me; . . . I will scatter you among the heathen

Reiterated here was the prophetic warning that Israel must qualify for the blessings of living in a promised land or be driven out as were others before them (recall Lev. 18:24–28). But they or their descendants could be gathered again upon remembering and fulfilling God's covenants, for he will certainly remember and perform his part (Lev. 26:40–46).

27:1– 34 When a man shall make a singular vow, the persons shall be for the Lord by thy estimation

Rules were given about people and things dedicated unto the Lord. Valuation in shekels was required to redeem and to show gratitude to the Lord for granting some request. Amounts were established for persons of various age groups, for animals, houses, and fields. Firstlings of beasts, already designated as an offering to the Lord, would be redeemed at an increased value. Likewise, the tenth part of the increase of crops, flocks, and herds was already the Lord's tithe; to redeem grains or fruits would cost extra, and animals that were the designated tithe were not redeemable.

Leviticus shows us the laws governing Saints in former days. Many of them embrace principles that still apply to us, and many describe practices that anticipated the plan of redemption that we are blessed to know.

NUMBERS

The book of Numbers is an account of the census and organization of the migrating tribes of Israel and an overview of some of the tribulations suffered by them as they traveled in the wilderness toward the land of promise. They were to endeavor by obedience to the law to become "a peculiar treasure" unto the Lord, "a kingdom of priests, and an holy nation" (Ex. 19:5–6). They suffered because they repeatedly lapsed into doubt, insecurity, and complaints about their condition rather than trusting constantly in the Lord and humbly supplicating him for the satisfaction of their needs. They knew that God lives and had helped them many times but fell to doubting and wondering whether he would help again. Thus even today we may learn applicable lessons from Numbers.

The history of most of Israel's forty-year sojourn in the wilderness is covered in the book of Numbers. Exodus ended at the dedication of the tabernacle at Sinai during the first month of the second year, and Numbers begins with events on the first day of the second month (Ex. 40:17; Num. 1:1). Numbers ends, and Deuteronomy begins, during the fortieth year after Israel left Egypt (Num. 33:38–49; Deut. 1:1–5).

Many later scriptures allude to events recorded in the books of Moses. Psalm 105 reviews events from Genesis and Exodus; Psalm 106, from Exodus and Numbers. Psalm 107 generalizes about people's struggles and hopes as they sought the land of promise; it tells of their blessings when they turned to repentance and faith in the Lord. In the New Testament, Hebrews 3:7–19 reviews history and lessons from the book of Numbers. Indeed, some one hundred twenty items quoted in the New Testament are from the books of Moses (BD, "Quotations").

COMMENTARY

1:1–16 Take ye the sum of all the congregation . . . after their families . . . every male . . . From twenty years old

The census council included a leader from each tribe who was appointed to count all males of age to go to war. Members of the council were identified by divine revelation.

1:17–46 and they declared their pedigrees after their families, by the house of their fathers

After all the generations spent in Egypt, it is noteworthy that the Israelites' identification as extended families was still possible. The tribal totals ranged from Benjamin's 35,400 to Judah's 74,600; Joseph's total, combining Manasseh and Ephraim, was 72,700. The grand total was 603,550 men twenty years old and over, excluding the Levites. Levites were not subject to military duties, so their census is separate (Num. 3). By estimating the number of women and children, one could arrive at a total near three million. Such a multitude is thought to be possible in view of the numbers given and implied at the time of Israel's entering Egypt (commentary on Gen. 46:5–27). Divine help would indeed have been required to get such a host across the sea, provide them with food, and manage them in their many crises.

1:47–54 thou shalt not number the tribe of Levi . . . But thou shalt appoint the Levites over the tabernacle

The Levites were numbered later (Num. 3) and appointed to assemble the tabernacle at all the long-term camping places, conduct services, and disassemble and carry the parts of the tabernacle and its furnishings. (Their duties in the land of Israel are shown quite well in the books of Chronicles.)

2:1–31 Every man . . . shall pitch by his own standard, with the ensign of their father's house: far off about the tabernacle

Those chosen to encamp on the east side of the tabernacle and to be first in the line of march were the tribes of Judah, Issachar, and Zebulon. (Recall from Gen. 29:35 and 30:17–20 that these were three of Jacob's sons born to Leah.)

On the south side, and next in line when traveling, were the tribes of Reuben, Simeon, and Gad. The first two were of Leah, and Gad was from Zilpah, Leah's maid, who also was a wife of Jacob (Num. 2:10–16; Gen. 29:31–33; 30:9–11).

In the center of the camp, and of the march, were the Levites, including the Aaronic priests and the bearers of the tabernacle (Num. 2:17).

On the west side of the tabernacle in camp and following it on the march, were the descendants of Ephraim, Manasseh, and Benjamin. Rachel was the grandmother of Ephraim and Manasseh and the mother of Benjamin (Gen. 30:22–24; 35:16–20; 41:50–52).

On the north side and bringing up the rear in the march were the descendants of Dan and Naphtali, sons of Bilhah, Rachel's maid and wife to Jacob (Gen. 30:5–8) and Asher, another son of Leah's maid Zilpah (Gen. 30:12–13). They were numbered in tribes according to the names of the ancestral fathers but arranged in groups identified with the ancestral mothers.

2:32–34 These are those which were numbered of the children of Israel by the house of their fathers

A summary of the census and the organization of the camp and the march concludes Numbers 2.

3:1–4 These also are the generations of Aaron and Moses

The four sons of Aaron, consecrated to serve in the priests' office, are listed, and the tragic death of two of them is reiterated (Num. 3:4 and fn.).

3:5–13 Bring the tribe of Levi near, . . . before Aaron the priest, that they may minister unto him

Aaron and his sons were appointed to serve in the priests' office and the rest of the Levites were to assist them, doing the service that the firstborn sons of all Israel had previously been appointed to do (Ex. 13:2; Num. 3:10, 12, 23–39; 8:16–19).

In earlier times, the patriarchs, such as Abraham, Isaac, and Jacob, had the authority to perform the ordinances of sacrifice without the aid of other priests. Even after the priesthood organizational change noted here, the patriarchs of each family continued in their functions in governing their families and tribes as seen in all the ancient scriptures.

3:14–39 Number the children of Levi after the house of their fathers, by their families: every male from a month old and upward

The three sons of Levi were Gershon, Kohath, and Merari (Num. 3:17a). The total of the numbers in the three Levite families was 22,300, rounded off to 22,000 (Num. 3:39).

The duties of each of the three Levite family groups, their places of encampment, and their positions in the line of march, were described in connection with the enumerations of each of them.

Eleazar, son of Aaron, was made "chief over the chief" (Heb., lit., "prince of the princes") of the Levites to oversee all their work (Num. 3:32).

Encamped in front, east of the tabernacle, were Moses, Aaron, and his sons, "keeping the charge of the sanctuary" (Num. 3:38).

3:40–51 Number all the firstborn of the males of the children of Israel . . . and . . . take the Levites for me . . . instead of all the firstborn

The total number of Levites thus taken into religious service (22,000) closely approximated the number of firstborn (22,273). The extra 273 of the firstborn not redeemed by a Levite replacement were redeemed by a tribute of five shekels each, which was given to the priesthood leaders (Num. 3:46–51).

4:1– 45 Take. . . from among the sons of Levi . . . From thirty years old and upward even until fifty years old

The Levites of specified ages were appointed to perform sacred service during twenty years of their life. More details are given concerning the work of each of the three family groups in dismantling, transporting, and reassembling the sacred tabernacle.

4:46– 49 All those that were numbered of the Levites, . . . From thirty years old and upward even unto fifty years old, . . . were eight thousand and five hundred and fourscore

The total, at the time of the census, of all Levites of the specified age to serve, was 8,580.

5:1– 4 put out of the camp every leper, and every one that hath an issue, and whosoever is defiled by the dead

Exclusion from the regular camp was required of all with diseases or "uncleanness." Steps had earlier been specified for restoring those who could be cleansed (Lev. 12–15).

5:5–10 When a man or woman shall commit any sin . . . to do a trespass against the Lord

Regulations are repeated concerning recompense of things taken unlawfully; repentance and forgiveness procedures are clarified.

Trespass is often used in the King James Version Old Testament to translate Hebrew words denoting guilt, unfaithful behavior, and treachery, whereas *sin* is usually used to translate Hebrew roots meaning to err, miss the mark, miss the way, or otherwise break the divine commandments. The words may be used either synonymously or to supplement each other (BD, "Sacrifices," paragraphs on trespass or guilt offerings, and sin offering).

5:11– 31 If any man's wife go aside, and commit a trespass against him, And a man lie with her carnally, and it be hid from the eyes of her husband, . . . and she be defiled, and there be no witness against her

Trial by ordeal seems strange; perhaps it was not as traumatic as ordeals involving torture. Suffering would of course ensue; it is to be hoped that an innocent wife would not have been entrapped by the procedure. Whether this passage truly preserves a revealed process is difficult to know now. Better procedures are certainly recommended in our dispensation for all leaders and members, male and female.

6:1–21 When either man or woman shall separate themselves to vow a vow of a Nazarite, to separate themselves unto the Lord

In the Hebrew, both the noun *Nazarite* and the verb *to separate,* here and in subsequent verses, are from the same root; thus he or she is separated, or set apart, from an ordinary life's work and instead is consecrated to the service of the Lord. What manner of service was given is not here specified, but some historical examples include Samson (who was not an exemplary Nazarite), Samuel, John the Baptist, and Paul. (Note Paul's way of concluding his Nazarite vow; Acts 18:18; 21:23–24; cf. Num. 6:13–21; BD, "Nazarite.")

In the latter-day Church the name *Nazarite* is not used, but a host of people are "set apart" from part of their daily work to give a variety of types of service; and missionaries consecrate full time to the Lord for a period of life, somewhat in the Nazarite tradition. Do not confuse *Nazarite* with *Nazarene;* the latter is an inhabitant of Nazareth. The two words are from two different Hebrew roots, *Nazareth* being derived from a word meaning "branch."

6:22–27 Speak unto Aaron and unto his sons, saying, On this wise ye shall bless the children of Israel

Here is recorded a lovely priesthood blessing for use in Israel. It is still used by ministers of various faiths in our time. In the Hebrew, the supplication for peace asks not for mere quiescence but for a condition of satisfaction and fulfillment.

7:1–89 it came to pass on the day that Moses had fully set up the tabernacle, and had anointed it, and sanctified it . . .; That the princes of Israel . . . brought their offering

The inventory of offerings from each of the twelve princes, or leaders, of the twelve tribes of Israel is impressive in the variety, quantity, and value represented.

The descendants of Joseph were divided into two tribes and named after his two sons; hence there were twelve tribes besides the Levites.

The order of the presentation was again according to the tribes' ancestral mothers (commentary on Num. 2).

8:1–4 the seven lamps shall give light over against the candlestick

The awkward phrase "over against" can better be translated "in front of"; the lamp atop each of the seven branches of the menorah was to be set up with the wick forward, to "give light in front of the menorah." It is so rendered in some translations other than the King James Version.

8:5–26 Take the Levites . . . and cleanse them. . . . and the children of Israel shall put their hands upon the Levites

The Levites, who had been taken by the Lord to serve in place of the firstborn of all the tribes (Num. 3:40–51), were to be given certain initiatory ordinances, including a ceremonial sprinkling with "water of purifying" (cf. Num. 19), shaving, and washing their clothes. Then, by the laying on of hands, a sin offering, and a burnt offering, the Levites were consecrated for their service in the tabernacle. Each was set apart for a period from age twenty-five. There was evidently a five-year preparatory period before working *in* the tabernacle (Num. 8:24–25; cf. 4:3).

9:1–14 keep the passover at his appointed season

In the first month of the second year of liberty, Israel celebrated the Passover. Some individuals, defiled by caring for a dead body, asked how they could participate. Moses asked the Lord and received direction. Those who rightly desired to keep the

Passover and were thus hindered could keep it one month later, in the second month (Num. 9:6–12).

9:15 23 So it was alway: the cloud covered it by day, and the appearance of fire by night. And when the cloud was taken up . . . the children of Israel journeyed

A manifestation by day and night showed the presence of the Lord in the camp and indicated the direction they should travel.

10:1–10 Make thee two trumpets of silver . . . for the calling of the assembly, and for the journeying

Trumpets were made of hammered silver, doubtless from the precious metals brought out from Egypt (Ex. 12:35–36). The ram's-horn trumpet, or *shophar,* became common later (Josh. 6). Some signals assembled the people; others, the princes only. There were signals for resuming the journey, gathering for defense, and assembling for rejoicing or for solemn worship services.

10:11–28 on the twentieth day of the second month, in the second year . . . the cloud was taken up . . . And the children of Israel took their journeys out of the wilderness of Sinai

The journey toward the promised land resumed one year, one month, and twenty days after the Israelites were freed from bondage in Egypt. They moved in the order they had been instructed to follow (cf. Num. 2).

10:29– 32 And Moses said unto Hobab . . . come thou with us . . . forasmuch as thou knowest how we are to encamp in the wilderness, and thou mayest be to us instead of eyes

Hobab, brother-in-law of Moses, was persuaded (though at first he declined) to accompany Israel as a guide to choose routes and campsites (Num. 10:29*a;* 10:31*a*). Later he and his family became heirs to land in Israel (Judg. 1:16; 4:11; 1 Sam. 15:6; 2 Kgs. 10:15; 1 Chr. 2:55; BD, "Kenites"). Jeremiah cited them as exemplary for integrity (Jer. 35). The present-day Druze tribes in Lebanon, Syria, and Israel claim to be descendants of them.

10:33–36 the ark of the covenant of the Lord went before them in the three days' journey, to search out a resting place

The Israelites were divinely guided on their first march with the pillar of cloud over them and the ark before them, although the tabernacle and its sacred implements were normally to be in the middle of the host in traveling and in camping (Num. 2:17). Their camps are listed in Numbers 33.

11:1–15 when the people complained, it displeased the Lord . . . Moses also was displeased

The people's complaints were sometimes burdensome, especially when they showed ingratitude (Num. 11:1, 10).

When they complained about manna and wished for the succulent and flavorful foods of Egypt (Num. 11:4–5), both Moses and the Lord were exasperated, and Moses cried out for help to bear his leadership burdens (Num. 11:14–15).

11:16–29 the Lord said unto Moses, Gather unto me seventy men of the elders of Israel . . . : and I will take of the spirit which is upon thee, and will put it upon them

Recall the previous seventy who were privileged to go up the mount and become divine witnesses, seeing the Lord, eating and drinking together there (Ex. 24:1–11). When this new group of seventy elders met at the tabernacle by appointment and the Lord endowed them with the Spirit Moses possessed, they were blessed with the gift of prophecy. It came even upon two of them who did not meet at the appointed time and place. Some, including Joshua, objected when those two also were endowed with the Spirit; but Moses accepted them, wishing indeed "that all the Lord's people were prophets, and that the Lord would put his spirit upon them" (Num. 11:29; TG, "Holy Ghost, Gifts of").

11:30–35 there went forth a wind from the Lord, and brought quails from the sea . . . two cubits high

The Lord miraculously provided quail for the flesh the people craved and let their gluttony cause their own punishment. They gathered all they desired and more than they needed; so many died of overindulgence that their burial place was commemorated as "the graves of lust" (Num. 11:32, 34*a;* on "homers," BD, "Weights and Measures").

12:1–16 Miriam and Aaron spake against Moses because of the Ethiopian woman whom he had married

Aaron and Miriam in their declining years seem to have objected to the idea that Moses was the sole spokesman for the Lord, and they justified their fault-finding by berating him for his marriage in Egypt to an Ethiopian. Josephus (*Antiquities of the Jews* 2:10:2) indeed recorded an account of such a marriage, proposed by the princess and the king of Ethiopia for military and political reasons, but the Bible mentions it nowhere else. That marriage is not to be confused with his marriage in Midian to Zipporah, daughter of the high priest Jethro (Ex. 2:15–22).

Note Moses' humility under criticism (Num. 12:3; cf. Matt. 11:29). The fault-finding by Miriam and Aaron against the Lord's anointed was wrong, and He chastised them. Moses pleaded that Miriam be healed, and she was.

The Lord's evaluation of Moses is noteworthy (Num. 12:6–8).

13:1–25 Send thou men, that they may search the land of Canaan

Advance scouts were chosen, representing each of the twelve tribes, and they were sent from the wilderness of Paran through the Negev (Num. 13:3; Bible Map 3; Num. 13:17, 22*a*). Searching the land from the wilderness of Zin in the south to Rehob on the way to Hamath in the north of the land of Canaan, they sought to determine the strength of defenses, productivity of the land, and the quality of its produce (Num. 13:18–20). Of the twelve scouts, most is recorded about Joshua of Ephraim and Caleb of Judah (Num. 13:6, 8; Joshua is here called Oshea, which in Hebrew is *Hoshea'*, meaning "Save!"; whereas he is usually called Joshua, in Hebrew, *Jehoshua'*, meaning "Jehovah is Salvation").

Returning by way of Hebron and the brook or valley of *Eshcol* (Heb., lit., "a cluster of grapes"), they brought a good report of the productive land and a large cluster of grapes, carried on a staff between two men, to prove it (Num. 13:23).

13:26–33 surely it floweth with milk and honey; . . . Nevertheless the people be strong . . . , and the cities are walled, and very great

The scouts returned to Israel in the desert area of Paran, at a place later called Kadesh-barnea (Num. 32:8), and brought good news and bad. When the people recoiled at the descriptions of mighty peoples and cities to be overcome, only Caleb of Judah and Joshua of Ephraim sought to persuade them positively and strengthen their faith (Num. 13:30; 14:6–10). Others of the scouts used exaggeration to discourage the children of Israel from entering the promised land (Num. 12:31–33).

14:1–10 wherefore hath the Lord brought us unto this land, to fall by the sword? . . . Let us make a captain, and let us return into Egypt

Most of the people responded with bitter sarcasm, rebellion, and rejection of the Lord's leadership; like many people before and since, they preferred slavery with security to freedom with challenges and responsibilities.

Moses and Aaron were overwhelmed at the people's preference to die or return to Egypt. Joshua and Caleb tore their clothing in a sign of deep sorrow and tried to induce more faith and courage; but the people were in a mood to stone them.

14:11–12 And the Lord said. . . , How long will this people provoke me? and how long . . . ere they believe me . . . ? I will smite them . . . and will make of thee a greater nation

The matter became a new test of Moses' character, faith, humility, and power as the appointed leader of Israel. He passed it, as he did the earlier incident of the golden calf (Ex. 32:10–12).

14:13–19 Pardon, I beseech thee, the iniquity of this people

Reasoning as he had with the incident of the golden calf, Moses sought forgiveness for the people so that the Lord might become better known to them for His patience and mercy and not be discredited for lacking capacity to bring up His people.

14:20– 39 I have pardoned according to thy word. But . . . Surely they shall not see the land which I sware unto their fathers

Some clemency was granted, but the rebellious ten scouts responsible for the "evil report" and the people's consequent rebellion died by a plague (Num. 14:36–37). The faithless older people were all sentenced to live out their years in the unrelenting wilderness, with only the hope that their children and grandchildren would inherit the land of promise.

14:40– 45 Go not up, for the Lord is not among you

Some repented of their rebellion the next morning and went to Moses, confessing they had sinned and claiming to be ready to go to the promised land. But it was too late to repent; and when some also defied the warning not to go without the Lord, they fell prey to the Amalekites and the Canaanites.

15:1– 31 When ye be come into the land of your habitations, which I give unto you, And will make an offering

More instructions were given about offerings and covenants, with provisions for redemption if errors were committed in ignorance by Israelites or by strangers. "But the soul that doeth ought presumptuously," whether he were Israelite or convert, was to be excommunicated because such had "despised the word of the Lord" (Num. 15:30–31).

15:32– 36 they found a man that gathered sticks upon the sabbath

This case in point shows the severe punishment of one who presumptuously broke the Sabbath.

15:37– 41 make them fringes in the borders of their garments . . . that ye may look upon it, and remember all the commandments of the Lord

The Israelites made garments with fringes to remind them to remain "holy": sanctified unto the Lord.

16:1–50 Korah . . ., and Dathan and Abiram . . . took men: . . . two hundred and fifty princes . . . men of renown: And they gathered themselves together against Moses and against Aaron

Quite amazing is the account of a willful mutiny and bid for power by the Levite leader Korah, his two associates from the tribe of Reuben, and "two hundred and fifty princes" of Israel.

Korah was a member of the Kohathite family of Levites, who were bearers of the sacred ark and other sacred implements (Num. 16:1, 9; 4:18–20, 34–37; 7:9); but he sought the *high* priesthood also (Num. 16:10*a*) and accused Moses and Aaron of arrogating power to themselves (Num. 16:3, 13). Moses disavowed any usurpation of power or any intent to assume prerogatives through his priesthood and challenged the rebels to come out to the tabernacle, where the Lord could indicate who his chosen were. The mutineers gathered, with all the congregation they could influence, to stand against Moses and Aaron (Num. 16:19). When punishment for all seemed imminent, those with Moses pleaded that only those actively challenging him be punished, and the Lord advised all to depart from the rebel leaders before the punishment from God fell upon them. A "new thing" happened, so that all survivors might know it was not any coincidence that they who stood with Korah, Dathan, and Abiram perished (Num. 16:29*a*). When some of those who were spared complained about the fate of those who were punished, they also suffered a plague—which was stayed only when Moses and Aaron interceded (Num. 16:47–48).

17:1–13 take of every one . . . a rod according to the house of their fathers . . . twelve rods: write thou every man's name upon his rod. And . . . write Aaron's name upon the rod of Levi

Rods representing the tribes were placed in the tabernacle overnight, so that the Lord could indicate his chosen priesthood leader and "take away their murmurings" from those who followed the rebels (Num. 17:5, 10). The people were impressed but seem to have overreacted with fear (Num. 17:12, 13*c*).

18:1–7 And the Lord said unto Aaron, Thou and thy sons and thy father's house . . . shall bear the iniquity of the sanctuary: and . . . of your priesthood

It appears that the Lord's making the Aaronic leaders responsible to keep unauthorized persons and activities away from the sanctuary (Num. 18:1*a*) was a consequence of the rebellion (Num. 17).

18:8–19 This shall be thine of the most holy things, reserved from the fire

Portions of certain offerings were reserved for the priests and members of their households to eat. Perhaps that is why salt was part of certain offerings, serving to symbolize preservation of wholesomeness as it preserved food and enhanced its flavor (Num. 18:19; Lev. 2:13).

18:20–32 Thou shalt have no inheritance in their land, . . . I am thy part and thine inheritance. . . . But the tithes of the children of Israel . . . I have given to the Levites to inherit

In addition to using some parts of certain sacrifices for food, the Levites (including Aaron's progeny) could use the tithe offerings for support. These were "heave offerings," symbolizing things "lifted up" unto the Lord and returned by him to the priests for their use. The heave offerings were part of their inheritance, so they were to offer up a tithe from it. Thus were they compensated for their service (Num. 18:26–31).

19:1–22 it shall be kept . . . for a water of separation: it is a purification for sin

Ashes of a certain sacrificed animal were to be put into a vessel with water as "water of separation" to be used in "purification for sin" by Israelites who necessarily or inadvertently handled the body of a dead person (Num. 19:9, 17).

That the specified animal was a heifer (a young cow, a potential giver of life) and red (the color of blood) may have made her ashes a symbolic counteragent for contact with death.

20:1 the people abode in Kadesh; and Miriam died there

Miriam was older than Moses, for she was his guardian when he was left as a baby in an ark for Pharaoh's daughter to find (Ex. 2:1–9). Recall also that as "the prophetess" (Ex. 15:20–21) she led the women of Israel in celebration and praise of the Lord after the miracle at the Red Sea had freed them from Egyptian bondage. Recall also that Moses had pleaded for mercy toward Miriam and besought her healing from punishment when, in her old age, she questioned his leadership at Hazeroth (Num. 12:1–16).

20:2–13 Take the rod, and gather thou the assembly together, . . . and speak ye unto the rock before their eyes; and it shall give forth his water

Lack of water caused the people once again to accuse Moses and the Lord of leading them into the desert to perish.

Anyone who has visited the dry Negev and Arabah valley, in the vicinity of the so-called "spring of Moses," can appreciate how desperate people would feel without water in such an area.

To meet the need, Moses was commanded to *speak* to a rock. He disobeyed, apparently not believing sufficiently (Num. 20:8–12, 24), and struck the rock with his symbol of power, the rod, as he had done once before—when he had been told he should do so (Ex. 17:6–7). He also took honor to himself, saying, "Must we fetch you water out of this rock?" (Num. 20:10; 27:14; Deut. 32:51). Moses' punishment teaches us that great leaders must especially be exemplary in every way (Deut. 3:23–27; 4:21–23; 34:10).

20:14–21 Let us pass . . . through . . . by the king's highway

Moses appealed to Edom, descendants of Esau, for peaceful passage through the land, promising not to damage fields, vineyards, or water sources; Edom refused, threatening Israel and accepting no promises (Num. 20:18–21). So Israel turned south instead of east, passing again through part of the dry deserts.

20:22–29 the Lord spake unto Moses and Aaron in mount Hor, . . . saying, Aaron shall be gathered unto his people: . . . strip Aaron of his garments, and put them upon Eleazar his son

When the children of Israel arrived at Mount Hor, the time came for Aaron to die, but his priesthood garments and office were first transferred to his son Eleazar.

Aaron and Moses were reminded of their failure to show faith, obedience, and recognition of the Lord's blessing at Meribah (Num. 20:10, 24).

Israel halted their march for a month at Mount Hor to mourn the death of Aaron; this would show honor to him.

21:1–3 king Arad the Canaanite . . . fought against Israel, and took some of them prisoners

The Israelites' early encounter with a Canaanite clan proved symbolic and prophetic of what would happen to Israel in Canaan later.

21:4–9 And they journeyed . . . by way of the Red sea . . . and the soul of the people was much discouraged because of the way. And the people spake against God, and against Moses

The long journey, the prospect of death in the wilderness, the frequent lack of water, and even the diet of manna became causes of rebellion. When venomous serpents were added, however, the people repented of their rebellion, and the Lord provided escape from death through a test of faith and obedience: A symbolic bronze serpent was raised on a pole and all who would look up could be saved. A Book of Mormon writer pointed out that "because of the simpleness of the way, or the easiness of it, there were many who perished" (1 Ne. 17:41). Jesus made of this incident a symbol both of his crucifixion and of the truth that all who will look up to him in faith and obedience may have everlasting life (John 3:14–15).

21:10–35 And the children of Israel set forward

Toils and travels, conflicts and conquests, continued along the

Israelites' journey past Edom, around Moab, and through some other kingdoms east of the Dead Sea. Accounts of these events were once written in "the book of the wars of the Lord" and rehearsed in proverbs of the people (Num. 21:14–15; 27–30). Kings who refused to allow peaceful passage through their lands were vanquished and their cities possessed for a time; however, the Lord deemed the Moabites and Ammonites, descendants of Lot, still the rightful possessors of their lands, and though Israel had strife with them in passing, their lands were not taken from them (Deut. 2:9, 19).

22; 23; 24 Balak . . . king of the Moabites . . . sent messengers therefore unto Balaam . . . to Pethor . . . saying . . . Come now therefore, . . . curse me this people; for they are too mighty for me

The words from Numbers 22:1–6 indicate that Israel's advance toward Moab frightened King Balak. Knowing somehow that in Pethor was a people who believed in the same God as the Israelites, he assumed that with the "rewards of divination" and sacrifice he could persuade their God to curse Israel and thus remove their threat. It was a vain idea.

Pethor is thought to have been near Haran; descendants of Abraham's brother, Nahor, and his son Laban, lived there in the time of Abraham, Isaac, and Jacob; remnants of their culture may have remained (Abr. 2:1–6; Gen. 11:31–32; 22:20–24; 24; 28–31). In any case, the prophet Balaam was found, and he sought instructions from the Lord. Naturally, the instructions were that Israel was not to be cursed (Num. 22:12); however, the "rewards of divination" (Num. 22:7) must have motivated Balaam to importune until he was permitted to go. He ignored even a unique warning given through the animal he rode (Num. 22:20–35). When he arrived, he tried three times through ever more opulent sacrifices to change the Lord's mind; when he blessed Israel three times instead, Balak was exasperated, and they parted (Num. 22:36–24:14). Yet though he had blessed the Israelites, Balaam did give Balak some insidious counsel on overcoming them (Num. 24:14–25; 31:16). His advice worked to a degree, as is shown in

Numbers 25. The evil counsel of Balaam was cited centuries thereafter (2 Pet. 2:15; Rev. 2:14).

25:1–18 the people began to commit whoredom with the daughters of Moab. . . . And Israel joined himself unto Baal-peor

The "daughters of Moab" must have been the women who "caused the children of Israel, through the counsel of Balaam, to commit trespass against the Lord in the matter of Peor" (Num. 31:16).

The twin sins of idolatry and adultery were later causes of Israel's apostasy, overthrow, and exile. The seemingly extreme countermeasures undertaken by Aaron's grandson Phinehas did engender some repentance in Israel.

26:1–65 Take the sum of all the congregation of . . . Israel, from twenty years old and upward, . . . able to go to war

Another military census was taken before the conquest of Canaan. Note that the men of military age were again numbered according to tribal membership, and the Levites were still exempt.

After nearly forty years of travel, suffering, and death in the wilderness of all the people who had been twenty years of age or more when the Israelites left Egypt, the people numbered 601,730, compared to the former 603,550; the death rate had exceeded the birth rate by 1,820. This census also served in apportioning inheritances for the twelve tribes (Num. 26:51–56).

The Levites had increased from 22,000 to 23,000 (Num. 3:39; 26:62).

27:1–11 If a man die, and have no son, then ye shall cause his inheritance to pass unto his daughter

Again a problem was solved through revelation. Land inheritances usually passed to sons because daughters would go away to live with their husbands; but in this case, a father without male heirs had died and his daughters brought the question of inheritance to Moses, Eleazar, and the princes of Israel. Moses "brought their cause before the Lord," and a law was established to give women rights of inheritance. Israel was very early among the nations of the world in establishing such rights.

27:12–14 Get thee up into this mount Abarim, and see the land

The time was coming for Moses to see the land of promise before being released from his life's mission—after being reminded that he had once failed to do as he had been directed (Num. 27: 14c).

"This mount Abarim" can be translated "this mountain of the fords"; it is the mountain range east of the Dead Sea, which runs north to a point overlooking the fords of the River Jordan that lead into Canaan. The particular mountain peak to which Moses went for the view was named Nebo (Num. 33:47; Deut. 32:49).

27:15–23 And Moses spake . . . , Let the Lord, the God of the spirits of all flesh, set a man over the congregation

Before going up to the mount, Moses prayed for a successor to be appointed so the people would not be "as sheep which have no shepherd" (Num. 27:17) after his departure. Joshua's appointment was exemplary; note the process of selecting, instructing, presenting, and ordaining him (vv. 18–23 and fn.).

28:1–31 My offering, and my bread for my sacrifices made by fire, . . . shall ye observe to offer unto me in their due season

A few more points of procedure in daily, weekly, monthly, and yearly offerings were revealed to Moses for Israel to observe in the land of promise.

One was a "drink offering" of wine, to be "poured unto the Lord" to accompany the several offerings, including the Passover lamb (Num. 28:7, 10, 14, 15, 24, 31). Later, Jesus' followers were instructed to eat the broken bread and drink the Passover wine in order to always remember him and his blood that was poured out to seal the ultimate atoning covenant (Luke 22:17–20).

29:1–40 And in the seventh month . . . an holy convocation

Held on the first day of the seventh month of the Israelite

calendar, the holy convocation signaled by "blowing the trumpets" later became known as the "head of the year"—Rosh Hashanah (Num. 29:1–6). On the tenth day of the same month, "ye shall afflict your souls" (with fasting) and "not do any work therein." This holy day became the most solemn of the annual high holy days; it was known as Yom Kippur, the "Day of Atonement" (Num. 29:7–11). From the fifteenth day on, for eight days total, extensive sacrifices and feasting were celebrated in the wilderness; later this period became the happy celebration of Sukkoth, "Booths," or the Feast of Tabernacles, ending on the eighth day with Simchas Torah, "rejoicing in the Torah" (Num. 29:12–40; BD, "Feasts"). No sacrifices have been offered since the destruction of the temple at Jerusalem by the Romans.

On the intent of many offerings and laws in the Mosaic dispensation, see the summary in the Book of Mormon (Mosiah 13:27–35).

30:1–16 These are the statutes, which the Lord commanded Moses, between a man and his wife, between the father and his daughter, being yet in her youth

A series of revelations about the binding and releasing of vows was summarized (Num. 30:16).

Vows should be kept faithfully by all, but under certain circumstances a woman or a girl might be released from a vow she had made.

31:1–54 Avenge the children of Israel of the Midianites

There had been a grisly destruction of the kings, all the men, some of the women, and all the male children in five tribes of Midianites who had been involved in the corruption of Israel on the occasion of the Balak and Balaam incident. Balaam himself was killed in open warfare against the people of Israel, whom he had once unwillingly blessed (Num. 22–24; 31:8, 16).

The killing of women and children along with the men and the keeping of certain virgin girls along with some booty does not seem just nor in keeping with a law later clearly pronounced (Deut. 24:16).

Certain valuables were offered as "an oblation for the Lord," which should have prevented private looting and provided for adorning the tabernacle (Num. 31:50–54 and fn.).

32:1– 42 The children of Gad and the children of Reuben came and spake . . . saying, . . . let this land be given unto thy servants for a possession

When the tribes of Gad and Reuben, who were herdsmen and shepherds, requested their inheritance in the lands already conquered east of the Jordan, Moses warned them against the attitude of their fathers forty years before, who had feared to invade the promised land (Num. 32:6–15; 14:1–10). The applicants for the concession disavowed any intention of leaving the body of Israel. They promised to establish their families in the lands they requested and then provide soldiers to help conquer the rest of the land. Moses approved that agreement and also assigned half the tribe of Manasseh to that area (Num. 32:33).

33:1– 49 These are the journeys of the children of Israel

Moses wrote a review of the journeys of the Israelites "by the commandment of the Lord" (Num. 33:2). It mentions the Lord's judgment upon the Egyptians and their gods, the Exodus, and Israel's many moves and camps. Most of them are not reported in Exodus or Numbers. Unfortunately, the locations of most of the sites mentioned are not now known, but the very list vividly illustrates their toils and travels.

33:50–56 drive out all the inhabitants . . . , and destroy all their pictures, . . . molten images, and . . . their high places

There was to be an orderly division of the land, and the Israelites were warned about the dangers of leaving Canaanites there. For information concerning justifications for driving out the inhabitants and for destroying some things, see footnotes (e.g., Num. 33:52*a–c*).

34:1– 15 this is the land that shall fall unto you for an inheritance, even the land of Canaan with the coasts thereof

Moses received information on the ideal boundaries of the

lands west of Jordan to be inherited by the remaining nine and one-half tribes. The allocations to Gad, Reuben, and half of Manasseh on the east bank are also mentioned (Num. 34:13–15; Bible Map 5, with tribal names in red). Some of the eastern areas were not held long, and some areas were not actually conquered until King David's time.

34:16–29 These are the names of the men which shall divide the land unto you

Eleazar, at the head of the priesthood, and Joshua, at the head of military and related operations, were to chose ten tribal leaders to divide the land for the nine and one-half tribes. A comparison of the names of this group with the names of previous representatives of the twelve tribes, such as those who offered tribal offerings (Num. 7), or those chosen to explore the land (Num. 13), reveals that all the names in this group are new except Caleb. Others of the older generation had all perished during the years of wandering.

35:1–5 Command the children of Israel, that they give unto the Levites . . . cities to dwell in

Forty-eight cities were allocated to the Levites throughout all twelve tribal areas, four cities in each, so that priesthood services would be available throughout all of Israel (Num. 35:1–5 and fn.; Josh. 21).

35:6–15 among the cities which ye shall give unto the Levites there shall be six cities for refuge

The remarkable provision of a sanctuary for anyone accused of killing, in order that they might be fairly tried and either punished or freed, was a significant safeguard of human rights at such an early time. The uses and locations of the sanctuaries, three west and three east of the Jordan River, are later specified (Josh. 20).

35:16–34 he is a murderer: the murderer shall surely be put to death

Guidance was given for determining whether a homicide was

murder or not, and the executioner was specified (TG and BD, "Murder"; "Capital Punishment"; "Guilt").

The law requiring more than one witness was another safeguard of justice. A safeguard against random violence and vengeance was also given (Num. 35:30, 33–34).

36:1–12 only to the family of the tribe of their father shall they marry. So shall not the inheritance of the children of Israel remove from tribe to tribe

Even though daughters could inherit property (Num. 27:1–11), complications might arise if the daughters married outside their ancestral tribe and their property became the heritage of their children; hence this advice that, though daughters were free to "marry to whom they think best," it would be preferable for them to marry within their own tribe (Num. 36:6).

36:13 These are the commandments and the judgments . . . in the plains of Moab by Jordan near Jericho

The final verse of the book of Numbers is its concise summary and conclusion.

Thus Israel was numbered, tried, and prepared to enter the land promised long before to be given to Abraham's seed when the iniquity of the old inhabitants was full—but on the condition that his seed remain worthy (Gen. 15:7, 13–18; Lev. 18:1–5, 24–30; Abr. 2:6; 1 Ne. 17:23–35).

Moses was with the people in their last camp before he ascended Mount Nebo and departed (Deut. 34). Then the Israelites, under Joshua, crossed the Jordan River into the promised land (Josh. 1–4).

DEUTERONOMY

The opening declaration of the book of Deuteronomy and some statements within it identify it as Moses' farewell, which he delivered beyond Jordan before he ascended Mount Nebo and departed from Israel and from the earth. It is also a review of some teachings he had given to the people at several places in the wilderness from the time they were near the Red Sea until they camped in Moab (Deut. 1:1–5).

Deuteronomy is an English word derived from a Greek word meaning "second law."

Along with detailed reviews of revelations recorded in the earlier books of Moses, Deuteronomy provides some new revelations appropriate to Moses' time but still valuable to us in the latter days. Indeed, it is marvelous how useful this book is now, more than three millennia later, for doctrine, reproof, correction, and instruction in righteousness, as Paul in his time said of scripture (2 Tim. 3:16).

There is a later reference to "the book of the law in the house of the Lord" (2 Kgs. 22:8), which helped engender a religious reform by young King Josiah, who lived about 621 B.C. Some scholars think Deuteronomy may have been that book.

Numerous statements are found within Deuteronomy itself concerning the writing and preservation of its contents and the reading of parts of it to the people in Moses' time; watch for them in the text and in the commentary.

In Deuteronomy, the cross-references given in the footnotes are particularly useful in locating previous accounts of events and teachings. They are also helpful in calling attention to reiteration of doctrines, admonitions, or organizational structures. It is helpful to read both the account in Deuteronomy and the earlier one, as they may supplement each other; often they differ in emphasis (e.g., Deut. 1:23a).

COMMENTARY

1:1–5 These be the words which Moses spake unto all Israel

A general introduction to the book of Deuteronomy, the first five verses may have been supplied by an editor after Moses' time, but the verses confirm that the book contains Moses' words in Moab and at various times and places from the Red Sea to the Jordan.

1:6– 8 The Lord our God spake unto us in Horeb, saying

Speaking to Israel, Moses recalled the Lord's command of forty years before that had directed them to start their great trek from Horeb, or Sinai, toward the promised land (Deut. 1:5–8 and fn.).

1:9–18 I spake unto you at that time, saying, I am not able to bear you myself alone. . . . So I took the chief of your tribes, wise men, and known, and made them heads over you

Moses reminded the children of Israel of the organizational structure he had introduced to govern them in the wilderness.

1:19– 46 our brethren have discouraged our heart, saying, The people is greater and taller than we; the cities are great

In reviewing Israel's first approach to the promised land, the mission of the spies, and the people's response to their report, Moses emphasized the responsibility of the generation he was addressing, for some of them had been young at the time of the events he reviewed. In his farewell, Moses' purpose was evidently to emphasize the people's responsibility in much that had happened and would happen (e.g., Deut. 1:26–46).

2:1– 3:11 the space in which we came from Kadesh-barnea, until we were come over the brook Zered, was thirty and eight years

Moses reviewed their long trek, the goodness of the Lord to them, the directions and the restrictions He had given them, the adversaries they had encountered, and the aid they had received. He reminded them of the reasons for the death of all the older generation during their time in the wilderness.

The Joseph Smith Translation is helpful in an additional verse: "But Sihon king of Heshbon would not let us pass by him; for he hardened his spirit, and made his heart obstinate, that the Lord thy God might deliver him unto thy hand, as he hath done this day" (JST Deut. 2:30).

Some ancient cultures were named who had lived earlier in parts of the land of promise. Their lands had been inherited by the people of Esau (Edom), Moab, and Ammon; and it was emphasized that these peoples, who were related to Israel, were not to be deprived of their lands, except in cases where they refused to let Israel pass through on the way to their own inheritances (Deut. 2:1–3:11 and fn.).

The "giants" could have been the large peoples who frightened the earlier Israelite scouts (Deut. 2:11; 3:11).

3:12–22 this land, which we possessed at that time, gave I unto the Reubenites . . . Gadites . . . and . . . Manasseh

The boundaries were delineated on the east of Jordan in Moses' time for the inheritances of the tribes of Reuben, Gad, and Manasseh (Num. 32 and fn.; Bible Map 5).

What the Lord had helped Israel to do should have given them hope of help in the future (Deut. 3:21–22).

3:23–29 I besought the Lord at that time, saying, . . . I pray thee, let me go over, and see the good land that is beyond Jordan

Moses regretted his loss of the privilege of entering the

promised land and pointed out again that the people bore part of the blame (Deut. 3:26; 1:37; Num. 20:12; 27:12–14). And then he reviewed for them the appointment, ordination, and charge of Joshua to lead them into the promised land (Deut. 3:28; Num. 27:15–23).

4:1– 4 Now therefore hearken, O Israel, unto the statutes and unto the judgments, . . . for to do them, that ye may live

Israel could possess the promised land and be preserved therein only through hearkening to the Lord's commandments, with no additions or deletions—an admonition relevant also to later dispensations (Deut. 4:2a).

The Israelites were warned against such moral and religious infidelity as that at Baal-peor (Deut. 4:3a–b).

4:5– 8 Keep therefore and do them; for this is your wisdom and your understanding in the sight of the nations

Here is an excellent statement of the mission of Israel and of every true believer in the Lord and his gospel. It is related to Jesus' basic charge to believers: "Let your light so shine before men, that they may see your good works, and glorify your Father which is in heaven" (Matt. 5:16; Deut. 4:5–6).

4:9–24 Only take heed to thyself, . . . lest thou forget the things which thine eyes have seen, and lest they depart from thy heart . . . : but teach them thy sons, and thy sons' sons

Further admonitions included a reminder of their great and unique privilege of hearing "the voice of the words" of the Lord when he first gave the covenants and commandments on Mount Sinai, before "he wrote them upon two tables of stone" (Deut. 4:12; 4:13e; 4:10a).

The Israelites had been granted the privilege of *hearing* the Lord so that they could know for themselves, bear record of him, live his laws, and teach others; those who did so would be blessed and preserved. They had not been granted the privilege of *seeing* him lest they corrupt themselves and make a graven image to represent him (Deut. 4:15–16; Ex. 20:23). The Israelites and their seed should remain "unto him a people of inheritance" (Deut. 4:20). To reemphasize the seriousness of that responsibility, Moses recalled again the consequences of their infidelity, for which they and he had suffered (Deut. 4:20–24).

4:25– 40 Did ever people hear the voice of God speaking out of the midst of the fire, as thou hast heard, and live?

After such great blessings, if the Israelites of that time or any time should forget God and turn from him, they would be scattered (Deut. 4:27–28); yet in later times if any would seek the Lord, turn to him, and be obedient to his laws, the covenant would be renewed (Deut. 4:29–31). Israel then and now should know that the Lord let his voice be heard and his miraculous help be seen so that his people might "keep therefore his statutes, and his commandments" that all may "go well" with them; then their days would be prolonged in his service (Deut. 4:33–40).

4:41– 43 Then Moses severed three cities on this side of Jordan . . . That the slayer might flee thither

The three cities of refuge for the tribes east of the Jordan were appointed as promised (Num. 35:9–34).

4:44– 49 These are the testimonies, and the statutes, and the judgments, which Moses spake unto the children of Israel after they came out of Egypt, On this side Jordan

This summary of the place and content of Moses' farewell review is thought by some to be the end of his first speech to Israel on the occasion. More reviews follow.

5:1–5 And Moses called all Israel, and said unto them, Hear, O Israel . . . The Lord our God made a covenant with us in Horeb . . . not . . . with our fathers, but with us, even us, who are all of us here alive this day

Beginning the second part of his review, Moses summoned Israel and reminded the rising generation to whom he spoke of a truth that is as valid today as it was then: the covenant made on Sinai is valid for "us, even us, who are all of us here alive this day" (Deut. 5:3). The covenant was delivered to all Israel as a personal revelation (Deut. 5:4).

5:6–21 I am the Lord thy God . . . Thou shalt have none other gods before me

Moses included in his review of revelations the Ten Commandments received on Sinai. There are some differences from their form in Exodus 20; for example, in keeping the Sabbath day, we should remember times of servitude and be grateful for liberty (Deut. 5:15). Also, Deuteronomy urges us to "Honour thy father and thy mother . . . that it may go well with thee" (v. 16). In Hebrew "Thou shalt not covet" not only forbids one to "take pleasure in" the wife of one's neighbor but also admonishes (with a different Hebrew verb) not to desire his properties (Deut. 5:21*b*; Ex. 20:17*a*).

5:22–27 we have seen this day that God doth talk with man, and he liveth

It had been a special privilege for the multitude to hear all that great revelation, spoken to them by the voice of God, and delivered later through Moses on tables of stone. See their testimony of it and of their appreciation for the privilege (Deut. 5:24, 26). It was indeed so awe-inspiring that they had humbly asked to receive any further word from God through the prophet (Ex. 20:18–19; Deut. 5:27).

5:27–33 speak thou unto us all that the Lord our God shall speak unto thee; and we will hear it, and do it

Moses reminded all who were old enough to remember, and all who had been born or reared since that time, that they had promised to be obedient and keep the commandments (Deut. 5:27; Ex. 24:7). The Lord had heard their promise and expressed his wish that "there were such an heart in them, that they would" do so for their own good (Deut. 5:28–29; D&C 20:18–20). The

Lord had then sent the people to their tents while he taught Moses all the "commandments, and the statutes, and the judgments" to be passed on to the people, promising that if they would hearken and "walk in all the ways which the Lord your God hath commanded," they would live long, and all would be well with them (Deut. 5:30–33).

6:1– 4 Now these are the commandments, the statutes, and the judgments, which the Lord your God commanded to teach you . . . Hear, O Israel: The Lord our God is one Lord

Moses opened his overview of divine laws with a proclamation: "Hear, O Israel: JEHOVAH is our God; JEHOVAH is one" (Deut. 6:4, translation mine). The first word, *hear*, is *shema* in Hebrew, so the whole verse is called the Shema by Jews; they recite it on special occasions, and the deeply religious desire to repeat the verse at the moment of death. They do not, of course, pronounce the name *Jehovah* but use a substitute, *Adonai,* which means "my Lord."

The law of God is for man's good: "Observe to do it; that it may be well with thee" (Deut. 6:3).

6:5 thou shalt love the Lord thy God with all thine heart, and with all thy soul, and with all thy might

This primary law, if obeyed completely along with another "like unto it," would engender living in harmony with all the laws of God and teachings of his prophets, as Jesus said (Matt. 22:34–40; Lev. 19:18, 34). Loving God with heart, soul, and might would motivate us to behave in total harmony with him—mentally, spiritually, and physically.

6:6–25 these words . . . shall be in thine heart: And thou shalt teach them diligently unto thy children

Several admonitions in Deuteronomy 6:6–25 help promulgate the divine laws the Israelites received. Some symbolic reminders derived from them have been developed in Judaism and used in worship and teaching for many centuries; dialogues from the last of them are repeated during the Passover Seder (Deut. 6:8–9, 20–26). Jesus quoted an admonition from Deuteronomy during the trials and tests administered by Satan (Deut. 6:16; Luke 4:12).

7:1–5 Neither shalt thou make marriages with them . . . For they will turn away thy son from following me, that they may serve other gods

The most fundamental reason for Israelites not to marry out of the faith was so they would not adulterate their spiritual heritage and fail in their mission. The warnings against idolatrous practices still apply today to our trends in materialism and hero-worship. Marriage in the faith to raise up faithful children is still vital (Deut. 7:3*a;* TG, "Idolatry").

7:6–16 For thou art an holy people unto the Lord thy God

Holy people are those consecrated to the Lord's service to carry out the Abrahamic mission (Deut. 7:6*a–d*). Great are the blessings of the Lord to all who live his law and serve him.

7:17–26 If thou shalt say in thine heart, These nations are more than I; . . . Thou shalt not be afraid of them

The Lord's promise of help in overcoming worldly opposition has relevance for the Lord's people in latter days also, if they seek to overcome evils and replace them with righteous ways of life (Deut. 7:17–26 and fn.).

8:1–20 remember all the way which the Lord thy God led thee these forty years in the wilderness, to humble thee, and to prove thee

Moses reviewed for Israel the purposes of the tests in the wilderness and reminded the people again of the gracious gifts of the Lord. He described the beautiful and provident land they could expect if they would live worthily, and he gave them dire warnings lest they forget God's providence and boast, "My power and the might of mine hand hath gotten me this wealth" (Deut. 8:17). Israel would be no more blessed and preserved in the land than were the nations who went before if they behaved as those nations (Deut. 8:20; Lev. 18:24–30).

9:1– 6 but for the wickedness of these nations the Lord doth drive them out from before thee

Moses and the Lord wanted Israel to know that it is not because of favoritism that one nation is displaced by another by the hand of the Lord. It was earlier revealed to Abraham that his seed could not inherit the land promised as long as "the iniquity of the Amorites is not yet full" (Gen. 15:16; 1 Ne. 17:33–35). Even in Moses' time, Israelites were only relatively righteous compared to Canaanites; thus, they were warned not to pride themselves on their own supposed worthiness (Deut. 9:4–5).

9:7–29 Remember, and forget not, how thou provokedst the Lord thy God to wrath in the wilderness: from the day that thou didst depart out of the land of Egypt, until ye came unto this place

Lest they become proud, Moses reminded the Israelites of their apostasy at Sinai while he was on the mount for forty days and of their later complaints about lack of water, meat, and trouble-free entry into the promised land. Yet, he also reminded them, they were the Lord's people and greatly favored.

10:1–5 At that time the Lord said unto me, Hew thee two tables of stone like unto the first, and come up unto me, and make thee an ark of wood

Moses reviewed for them how and why a second set of tables of divine law was given: "save the words of the everlasting covenant of the holy priesthood" (Deut. 10:2b; D&C 84:17–26). Note that the tablets were kept in the ark Moses had made.

10:6–11 At that time the Lord separated the tribe of Levi

Although he had resumed the review of their journeys and the death of Aaron, Moses returned to an event that had occurred before the journey from Sinai began, when the Levitical priesthood was installed and the Aaronic priests began their ministry (Deut.

10:6, *8a–b*). He told Israel how he had pleaded for them on the mount the second time that they might not be destroyed because of their perfidy.

10:12–22 And now, Israel, what doth the Lord thy God require of thee, but to fear the Lord thy God, to walk in all his ways, and to love him, and to serve the Lord thy God with all thy heart and with all thy soul

With a marvelous summary of the way that worshippers of the Lord should live, Moses began to review the principles that matter most in relationships with God and with each other.

11:1–9 Therefore thou shalt love the Lord thy God, and keep his charge, and his statutes, and his judgments, and his commandments, alway

Again Moses challenged the Israelites whose eyes had seen all the marvelous things the Lord had done, trying to motivate them to live according to the commandments reviewed for them that day so that they could be blessed.

11:10–17 For the land, whither thou goest in to possess it, is not as the land of Egypt, from whence ye came out

Crops in Egypt had been irrigated in various ways from the Nile river—in some cases by an apparatus operated by the feet—but the new land of Israel would be "a land of hills and valleys, and drinketh water of the rain of heaven." Anyone who has lived in the near-desert conditions of Israel (and of Utah) knows that it is a blessing when there is adequate rain and snow in their seasons; without them, people cannot live there (BD, "Rain").

11:18–21 Therefore shall ye lay up these my words in your heart and in your soul

Again they were asked to remember and apply the laws, symbolically binding them on the hand, keeping them as "frontlets" between the eyes. Those phrases mean they were to abide by the words of the Lord in their thoughts, desires, and actions. They were to think of them going out and coming in, and teach them to each rising generation (cf. Deut. 6:4–12).

11:22–25 There shall no man be able to stand before you

Keeping God's commandments would also assure Israelites of possession of the land and the capacity to replace those "greater nations and mightier" (Deut. 11:23) who "had rejected every word of God, and . . . were ripe in iniquity" (1 Ne. 17:32–35).

11:26– 32 Behold, I set before you this day a blessing and a curse; . . . the blessing upon mount Gerizim, and the curse upon mount Ebal

Moses set out the parameters of free agency: to reach good ends, there are required actions; ignoring the requirements, or indulging in other actions through other motivations, may bring bad ends. Agency never was the right to do whatever one wishes and get whatever one wants.

The children of Israel were to gather in the center of the land of promise, in a valley at Shechem between Mount Ebal on the north and Mount Gerizim on the south; half were to be on the slope of each mountain to hear from Ebal lists of evils that would lead to curses and from Gerizim lists of good deeds that would bring blessings. This place for launching the commonwealth of Israel was also the place of Abraham's first altar in the land of promise, and it was the place of Jacob's first camp upon arriving back from Haran, where he also built an altar (Deut. 11:29*a–b;* Gen. 12:6–7; 33:18–20). An area there was called the "plains of Moreh" (or oaks of Moreh), and *moreh* means "director, teacher," just as *torah* means "direction, or doctrine." Both are from *yareh,* "to point out, give guidance." It was thus a place where the Lord gave guidance and direction to Abraham, Jacob, and their descendants (Gen. 12:6; Deut. 11:30).

12:1– 32 These are the statutes and judgments, which ye shall observe to do in the land, which the Lord . . . giveth thee

Idol worship was to be destroyed and true worship would

finally be established in a "place which the Lord your God shall choose"; that place would be Jerusalem, a fact not revealed at this time but later (Deut. 12:5*a–b*).

Better discipline in diet, behavior, and worship was anticipated, with people living the laws of God and not each doing whatever is "right in his own eyes." Most certainly they must avoid the abominations of the Canaanites—but they did not always avoid them (Deut. 12:8, 31*a–c*).

13:1–18 If there arise among you a prophet, a dreamer of dreams, . . . saying, Let us go after other gods, . . . Thou shalt not hearken unto the words of that prophet, or that dreamer

The people of Israel were given a warning (not unlike another given thousands of years later in the latter days) to safeguard them against prophets inspired by the wrong spirits. Such were condemned to death, even if they were family members. It was the same warning in different terms that Jesus later gave his followers that a false teacher is more to be feared than a murderer. Infidelity to God is degenerative because it engenders infidelity to all his principles, laws, and doctrines (cf. D&C 50:1–8; Matt. 10:28).

14:1–21 the Lord hath chosen thee to be a peculiar people unto himself. . . . Thou shalt not eat any abominable thing

In this review of clean and unclean meats, remember that it is ceremonial and symbolic "uncleanness" that is considered. Non-Israelites were not bound by these specifications; therefore, to give to the alien or stranger an animal not slaughtered in the *kosher* manner, or one that had been killed accidentally, could be helpful in some circumstances. If done carelessly or for profit, however, it would be unjustifiable, and the Joseph Smith Translation indicates it was forbidden (Deut. 14:21*a–b*; Lev. 11; BD, "Clean and Unclean"; on meat with milk, Deut. 14:21*c*).

14:22–29 Thou shalt truly tithe all the increase

The tithe, or tenth, of all increase, was ordinarily contributed "in kind"; but if the contributor lived too far from the place specified to take it, he could instead sell the tithing goods, carry the proceeds to the place of worship, and there purchase "whatsoever thy soul lusteth after" (in the KJV, the phrase "lusteth after" is used to translate a word meaning simply "desires" or "yearns for"). Therewith he could make his contributions and prepare the thank-feast associated with tithe-paying. Some of the food items contributed were to be used by the priests and Levites, and some were given to the poor (BD, "Levites," "Tithe"; TG, "Tithing").

The use of wine and other fermented fluids called "strong drink" may surprise latter-day worshippers who are not to use them, but they were permitted in ceremonial exercises in ancient Israel; only excessive or improper use was forbidden (TG, "Drunkenness"; "Temperance"; "Word of Wisdom"). Fermented drinks were not to be used by the priests in service and not by Nazarites at all (Deut. 14:26; Lev. 10:9–11; Num. 6:2–4).

15:1–6 At the end of every seven years thou shalt make a release

Israelites were not to exact repayment of loans from fellow Israelites beyond any sabbatical year; however, they were not expected to release strangers from their responsibility to repay. If Israelites would obey God's commandments, they would be blessed with prosperity and be able to lend to others and have no need of borrowing from them (Deut. 15:1a–b; 15:4a; Ex. 21:1–6; TG, "Sabbatical Year").

15:7–11 thou shalt not harden thine heart, nor shut thine hand from thy poor brother

Israelites were to be charitable always and were not to slacken when the sabbatical year was nigh because they feared loss of repayment. As Jesus later said, the poor will always be with us (Matt. 26:11; Deut. 15:11).

15:12–18 in the seventh year thou shalt let him go free

Recall the detailed regulations of the release of Hebrew servants (Lev. 25:35–55).

15:19–23 All the firstling males . . . thou shalt sanctify unto the Lord

The sanctification and sacrifice of a portion of each firstborn male among the clean animals was followed by a ceremonial meal in which the remaining flesh was roasted and eaten (Deut. 15:19–23, fn., and commentary). The injunction regarding blood was reiterated (Deut. 15:23; Gen. 9:4; Lev. 3:17; and commentary).

16:1–17 Three times in a year shall all thy males appear before the Lord thy God in the place which he shall choose

The three major annual feasts were reviewed (Ex. 23:14–17; Lev. 23; and commentary; BD, "Feasts").

Although only males (Deut. 16:16) were ordered to worship at the central place—which was Jerusalem for much of the biblical period after Solomon—all the holy days have become family affairs and are kept by men, women, and children in home and synagogue.

16:18–20 Judges and officers shalt thou make . . . Thou shalt not wrest judgment

Here is another reminder of the system of judges, introduced and amplified earlier; there is much in scripture about righteous judges and judgment (Ex. 18:13–26; Deut. 1:9–18; TG, "Judge"; "Judgment"; "Justice").

16:21–22 Thou shalt not plant thee a grove of any trees near unto the altar of the Lord thy God

The prohibition against planting groves near their places of worship was to prevent them from becoming shrines of fertility cults. Apostasy and adopting Canaanite religious practices was a constant problem for Israelites in the land of Canaan and became a major cause of Israel's decline and destruction centuries later (Deut. 16:21–22 and fn.).

17:1 not sacrifice . . . any bullock, or sheep, wherein is blemish

It is not known how well Israelites understood that sacrificial animals had to be perfect to be in similitude of the divine Redeemer to come, but it is a good point for us to appreciate (Lev. 1:10; Mosiah 13:31–32).

17:2–7 If there be found among you . . . man or woman, that hath. . . . gone and served other gods, and worshipped them

The strict laws and severe punishments pertaining to idolatry were particularly important while the worship of the Lord was being established (Deut. 13:1–18 and commentary).

17:8–13 If there arise a matter too hard for thee in judgment. . . . being matters of controversy within thy gates

Matters of judgment were part of the responsibility of the priests and Levites, along with teaching and officiating at the altars of the Lord. Theirs was a vital part of the Israelite government (Deut. 16:18–20 and commentary).

17:14–20 When thou art come unto the land . . . and shalt say, I will set a king over me

A prophetic anticipation of kings in Israel restricted and instructed those future rulers. They were to educate themselves to remain humble and obedient by reading every day in their own copy of the laws of God. The principles apply to kings, and to all of us, but it is evident later that neither Saul, David, nor Solomon lived out their lives in accord with them; and only a very few kings after them did so.

18:1–8 The priests the Levites, and all the tribe of Levi . . . shall eat the offerings of the Lord

The provisions for the Levites' sustenance were summarized (Deut. 18:1–8 and fn.).

18:9–14 When thou art come into the land . . . thou shalt not learn to do after the abominations of those nations

Moses again condemned the spiritualistic divination by the

peoples of the land Israel was about to take over (Deut 18:9–14 and fn.).

18:15–22 The Lord thy God will raise up unto thee a Prophet . . . like unto me; unto him ye shall hearken

The special spokesman for God thus anticipated was to be Jesus himself. In the last days others would also have *some* leadership responsibilities like those of Moses (Deut. 18:15*b;* D&C 103:16; 107:91).

19:1–10 Thou shalt separate three cities . . . that every slayer may flee thither

A review was given of the procedure for guaranteeing the right of a just trial to one who may have caused another's death (Num. 35:9–34; Deut. 4:41–43; Josh. 20).

19:11–21 at the mouth of two witnesses, or . . . three witnesses, shall the matter be established

Israel was reminded of some important procedures for judging those charged with murder or other evils.

20:1– 4 When thou goest out to battle against thine enemies . . . be not afraid of them: for the Lord thy God is with thee

Faith in God could give Israel assurance in their struggles and confidence in their destiny. Some dramatic fulfillments of these promises are recorded later.

20:5– 9 let him go and return unto his house, lest he die

Generous exemption from military service was granted anyone newly establishing a home, and even one faint at heart could be excused from battle!

20:10–18 When thou comest nigh unto a city to fight against it, then proclaim peace unto it

Cities outside Canaan, if they negotiated peacefully, could become tributaries to Israel and be left intact. Canaanite cities were to be destroyed because of the likelihood of corrupt peoples corrupting Israel (Deut. 20:15–18).

20:19–20 thou shalt not destroy the trees

During times of siege and conquest, trees that produced food were not to be cut down, but other trees might be cut down to make siege implements.

21:1–9 If one be found slain in the land . . . , lying in the field, and it be not known who hath slain him

People in a city near a field where a homicide victim was found were to make a special sacrifice and let all citizens declare whether they were innocent of the homicide; and if all so declared, the Lord was supplicated not to hold the city guilty.

21:10–14 among the captives a beautiful woman, . . . that thou wouldst have her to thy wife

Permission was given to marry certain captives, but because that would be an exception to the law forbidding marriage with peoples of the land, it has been supposed to pertain to peoples other than the Canaanites, although no reason for it was declared (Deut. 7:3–4).

21:15–17 If a man have two wives, one beloved, and another hated, . . . he may not make the son of the beloved firstborn before the son of the hated, which is indeed the firstborn

Favoritism was not to be shown the child of a favorite wife in the matter of inheritances; thus justice would not be denied.

21:18–21 If a man have a stubborn and rebellious son . . . a glutton and a drunkard . . . all the men of his city shall stone him with stones, that he die; so shalt thou put evil away from among you

Discipline and punishment could be severe within a family. It is to be hoped this kind of execution was seldom used.

21:22–23 if a man have committed a sin worthy of death . . . and thou hang him upon a tree: His body shall not remain all night upon the tree

"According to Rabbinical commentaries, to leave a body hanging was a degradation of the human body and therefore an affront to God, in whose image man's body was made" (Deut. 21:23*a*). An alternate translation of "he . . . is accursed of God" is "it is an affront to God." Note the urgent observance of that law at the time of Jesus' crucifixion (Deut. 21:23*a–c*).

22:1–12 Thou shalt not

Moses reiterated a series of rules against keeping lost animals, passing by a brother who needs help, transvestite deceit, robbing a nest and killing its occupant, failing to protect against hazards at home, sowing mixed seeds, plowing with a mixed team of animals, and mixing fabrics in a garment. Some of these were for obvious practical purposes; some perhaps reminded Israel of the urgent principle of purity.

The "fringes" on garments were reminders of covenants (Deut. 22:12*a*).

22:13–30 If any man take a wife, and go in unto her, and hate her, And give occasions of speech against her, and bring up an evil name upon her

A man must not impute unchastity to his wife or commit adultery with another's wife or with a virgin. If rape was committed in a field, out of the city, so that a damsel's outcry would not be heard, he who does it is to be considered guilty, but she is free. If a man was intimate with a virgin not betrothed, he must pay a heavy fine, marry her, and never "put her away." Finally, the prohibition against incest was reiterated (Deut. 22:13–30 and fn.).

23:1–8 shall not enter into the congregation of the Lord

In the Church in the latter days there are no restrictions against converting and baptizing any worthy person, so proscriptions set out here are not in force. Indeed, even in Old Testament times, Ruth, a Moabitess, accepted the God of Israel, married in Israel, and became an ancestress in a most important line (Ruth 1:4, 16; 4:9–13, 18–22; Matt. 1:1–17).

It is not clear why the Moabites and Ammonites were not to "enter into the congregation of the Lord" whereas Edomites and Egyptians were acceptable (Deut. 23:7–8). Physical impairments, lineage, or faults of one's parents would not keep anyone from baptism, priesthood, or temple covenants today.

23:9–14 any man, that is not clean by reason of uncleanness

The regulations here pertained not only to ritual uncleanness but also to practical matters of keeping the body and clothing clean of excretions. Even a way to dispose of body wastes was described. Such procedures could be helpful still in many undeveloped countries.

23:15–25 Thou shalt not

Another list of rules provided sanctuary for refugees as well as forbade prostitution, usury, failure to pay vows, and illicit harvesting.

24:1–25 When a man hath

Reviewed were rules for annulment, military exemption, pledges, stealing, quarantine, oppressing servants, individual responsibility, fairness, and gleaning.

It was decreed once again that individuals shall be punished only for their own sins (Deut. 24:16; Ezek. 18; A of F 2; Ex. 20:5–6 and commentary).

25:1–18 If there be

Moses reviewed punishments for crimes, moderation of punishments, provisions for widows, and rules on fairness, violence, honesty, and vengeance. In the book of Ruth is an example of levirate marriage in accord with this law and also an example of the prescribed procedure for those unwilling to accept that responsibility (Deut. 25:5–10; 25:9a).

26:1–15 take of the first of all the fruit

When offering the firstfruits of the land in their first harvest, the Israelites were to recall the history of their many blessings from the Lord and pay their tithes. Worthy individuals could well preface their supplications for blessings with a declaration of innocence and righteousness.

26:16–19 Thou hast avouched the Lord this day to be thy God . . . And the Lord hath avouched thee . . . to be his peculiar people

Moses ended the review with a reiteration of the covenant. The purpose of divine law is to help covenant people improve in their lives and mission and help others become servants of the Lord (Deut. 26:18*a;* D&C 100:15–17).

27:1– 3 when ye shall pass over Jordan . . . set thee up great stones, and plaister them with plaister: And thou shalt write upon them all the words of this law

A monument to be built where the Israelites crossed over Jordan would remind succeeding generations about the blessings of the Lord in leading them into the promised land (Josh. 4; 8:30–36).

27:4–26 And there shalt thou build an altar unto the Lord

The altar and the monument were two separate structures, not just one. When Israel arrived in the promised land, a general conference was to be held between two mountains, Gerizim and Ebal; this is a review of the revelation about that conference, with more details on the curses that would result from evil-doing (Deut. 27:11–26; cf. 11:26–32; Josh. 8:30–35).

28:1– 68 if thou shalt hearken diligently . . . all these blessings shall come on thee, . . . if thou wilt not hearken . . . all these curses shall come upon thee, and overtake thee

One-fifth of this chapter is a more complete catalog of the material, physical, and spiritual blessings to be earned by living according to the law; the remaining four-fifths of the chapter detail the curses that come from ungodly behavior, including a return to bondage.

These alternative blessings and curses characterize what some call "the deuteronomic idea," but they are common in all the scriptures and are in force in the latter days (Deut. 28:15–68; D&C 41:1; 59; 130:20–21; TG, "Blessings"; "Obedience"; "Punishment"; "Disobedience").

29:1–28 These are the words of the covenant, which the Lord commanded Moses to make with the children of Israel in the land of Moab, beside the covenant which he made with them in Horeb

If the covenant of Horeb was mainly a covenant of sacrifice to God, then this was mainly a covenant of obedience to God. Obedience would help people prosper, and disobedience would put people into bondage like that of Egypt, even a scattering abroad. All nations would know that the Israelites had forsaken the covenant of the Lord God of their fathers if they were exiled.

29:29 The secret things belong unto the Lord . . . but those things which are revealed belong unto us

Moses urged all of Israel to learn and then to act in accord with all that God has revealed and be ready for more revelation.

Many mysteries "belong unto the Lord," for humankind does not yet know or understand everything; but those things that have been revealed should be learned and heeded, for our benefit. In later dispensations it has been promised that as more light is needed, it will be given (D&C 121:26–31).

30:1–20 when all these things are come upon thee, . . . And [thou] shalt return unto the Lord thy God, and shalt obey his voice . . . then the Lord thy God will turn thy captivity

Moses prophesied the scattering and the gathering of Israel; and for every person then or now the principle is clear: "See, I have set before thee this day life and good, and death and evil" (Deut. 30:15). It is the eternal principle of agency: Choose what you will, and do what you must to get it; or do what you will, and content yourself with what you must get. The Lord plainly set before Israel the alternatives, and he pleaded with the people to love him enough to obey his voice; for only thereby would any people be free from captivity.

31:1–8 the Lord hath said unto me, Thou shalt not go over this Jordan . . . The Lord thy God, he will go over before thee

Nearing the end of his farewell address, the great leader Moses, then one hundred twenty years old, encouraged the Israelites to be strong and faithful so the Lord could lead them into the promised land. Moses knew well enough the reasons that he himself could not enter with them, but he was not negative; he encouraged the people and Joshua, the new leader, to be strong and trust in the Lord, who would go with them and not fail them.

31:9–13 Moses wrote this law, and delivered it unto the priests the sons of Levi, which bare the ark of the covenant

Internal evidence indicates that Moses wrote these scriptures during his life, provided for their preservation, and ordered their public review every seven years.

31:14–23 Behold, thy days approach that thou must die

As preparations for Moses' farewell were made, Joshua was summoned with him to the tabernacle to receive his calling and charge. Note that Moses was told he would die and sleep with his fathers (Deut. 31:14, 16; but see Deut. 34:5–6 and commentary).

Moses was then instructed by the Lord to write certain memorable things into a song and teach it to the people. It would help them remember vital facts (Deut. 31:19, 21; 32).

31:24–30 Take this book of the law, and put it in the side of the ark of the covenant . . . that it may be there for a witness

Moses finished writing the laws of the Lord in a book and preserved it in the sacred ark, which was in the tabernacle and the temple for centuries as a witness to right and wrong for all.

32:1– 47 And Moses came and spake all the words of this song in the ears of the people

In typical parallel lines of Hebrew poetry the song began:

Give ear, O ye heavens, and I will speak;
and hear, O earth, the words of my mouth.

Then, with many such paired phrases, Moses reminded the people of the divine origins of true doctrine, the sure dependability of the Lord's justice, his compassion in having "bought" them and brought them as a father from bondage, their favored status and responsibility, the divine help given them in the wilderness despite their rebelliousness, warnings that God is "jealous" of his chosen servants (vitally concerned with their welfare), the traumas of his punishment if people are negligent in behavior, the inferiority of other religions, and the Israelites' lamentable state if they forsake the true God and he forsake them. Moses spoke these things to the people and to Hoshea (Joshua), admonishing them to set their hearts upon all that he had testified and teach their children accordingly. It would not be a vain thing for them; it would be their way to life.

32:48–52 Get thee up into this mountain . . . and behold the land of Canaan

Moses was directed to a mountain overlooking the Jordan crossing (Heb., *avarim;* English, *abarim;* Deut. 32:49; Num. 27:12–13 and commentary); a high point was Mount Nebo, from which he could view the land of promise. Then he would depart from this world (Deut. 34:5–6). Moses had trespassed against the Lord, failing to sanctify Him when bringing forth water from the rock, but even in death he would leave a lesson for the benefit of others' lives (Deut. 32:51a–b, 52).

33:1–25 And this is the blessing, wherewith Moses the man of God blessed the children of Israel before his death

Using again the types and parallels of Hebrew poetry, Moses left a blessing for the twelve tribes of Israel, as Jacob had done before his death (Deut. 33:1c). He began by reviewing briefly the Lord's help given from Sinai to Seir, and in Paran in between, to his "saints," those sanctified by commitment to their covenants with him. When Moses delivered the law to them, "he was king in Jeshurun" (Deut. 33:5; Heb., lit., "uprightness").

The sequence of the tribes in the blessing follows generally a geographical sweep, proceeding with tribes to be located in the south, center, and north parts of the land. Many of the blessings mention natural resources or other geographical features of the areas.

Reuben was blessed only that his tribe would not dwindle in number; this was a nominal blessing for the son who could have been the birthright bearer (Gen. 49:3–4; 1 Chr. 5:1).

Simeon was not mentioned here but was later, in the distribution of the land adjoining Judah (Josh. 19:1, 8–9; Judg. 1:3, 17).

Judah was blessed to be heard of the Lord, to be self-reliant, and to be helped against adversaries. His blessing by Jacob anticipated the line of kings and the Messiah as his descendants (Gen. 49:8–12).

Levi had been made the priesthood-bearing tribe, and the breastplate bearing the divine Urim and Thummim was to be kept and used by the chief priest. Though one great Levite, Moses, had "proved" (tried) the Lord at Massah and Meribah (striking the stone for water), and though the Levites would not be a familial unit like the others because they were scattered among all the other tribes, they would be preserved to teach all Israel, administer justice, and officiate at altars in offering sacrifices.

Benjamin would be near the future holy dwelling of the "beloved of the Lord." That, of course, would be at Jerusalem, whose temple site would lie along Benjamin's east border.

Joseph was given a multifaceted blessing; it alluded to lands and precious things "of the ancient mountains" and the "lasting hills." It included promises of leadership, glory, and the power ("horns") to gather the other tribes at last from all ends of the earth (Deut. 33:13–17 and fn.). It is apparent that the mission of

Joseph's seed through Manasseh and Ephraim was to be far-reaching in time and in eternity.

Zebulun and *Issachar* were foreseen enjoying their homes and surroundings, and with good reason: their settlement would be in the choice valley of Jezreel, with good water from surrounding mountains, good soil, and a river that emptied into Israel's only natural harbor.

Gad would inherit the land already allotted them east of Jordan by Moses. Their territory was extensive, including the border lands of Israel, which was to be guarded as a lioness guards her terrain.

Dan was also blessed as to territory, something of a "leap" northeastward from Bashan on a common route of travel and invasion. Moses made no mention of Dan's original allocation on the Mediterranean coast, near Philistine country (Josh. 19:40–48; Judg. 18).

Naphtali was to inherit the sea (Deut. 33:23*b*) and its surrounding district in Galilee, a rich area agriculturally.

Asher, in the northern highlands, would be rich in olive oil production; the bars, or defense (Deut. 33:25*a*), of this northern boundary tribe of Israel would be strong.

33:26–29 There is none like unto the God of Jeshurun

Jeshurun ("the upright") was an idealistic title for Israel in this benediction in praise of the God of righteousness. The last half-dozen poetic strophes combine Moses' praise of God with felicitation of Israel.

34:1–4 And Moses went up . . . unto the mountain of Nebo . . . And the Lord shewed him all the land

Moses did at last see the promised land, which can be seen from the peak called Nebo on the mountain "divide" (Heb., *Pisgah*) east of the north end of the Dead Sea. Tribal territories named in Deuteronomy 34 include some of those given earlier in the tribal blessings. It has been supposed that Joshua was the author of this last chapter of Deuteronomy.

34:5–8 So Moses the servant of the Lord died there in the land of Moab

The writer of these verses understood that Moses "died" and that the Lord buried him; but he simply may not have known how Moses departed from this earth, just as the Nephites did not know of Alma's death and burial: they understood that Alma, like Moses, had been "buried by the hand of the Lord"; but they also had scriptures which said "the Lord took Moses unto himself" and supposed that "he has also received Alma in the spirit, unto himself" (Alma 45:18–19). What is meant in Jude 1:9 regarding Satan and Michael disputing over the "body" of Moses is not now evident.

Moses and Elijah appeared to Jesus and three apostles on the Mount of Transfiguration; Elijah is known to have been taken from earth without the ordinary process called death; thus it may be that both Elijah and Moses were "transfigured" and had not "died" in the ordinary sense (2 Kgs. 2:11; Matt. 17:3).

34:7–8 Moses was an hundred and twenty years old when he died; his eye was not dim, nor his natural force abated

No commentary is needed on that remarkable statement.

There was probably much more than mere ceremonial weeping and mourning for Moses during those thirty days. The people must have been sad indeed as they watched their great leader depart for the last time from camp and ascend the gray-white hills east of the Dead Sea to the heights of Nebo, never to return to them.

34:9 Joshua . . . was full of the spirit of wisdom; for Moses had laid his hands upon him: and the children of Israel hearkened unto him, and did as the Lord commanded Moses

It is gratifying to read this report; would that such a report could still have been made many years later in Israel.

34:10–12 And there arose not a prophet since in Israel like unto Moses, whom the Lord knew face to face

Recall the earlier prophecy regarding the Messiah as a prophet like unto Moses (Deut. 18:15, 18). There were other prophets like Moses in some ways, but no one altogether like unto him.

Joshua was well able by nature, endowment, and divine appointment to take over as leader of the Israelites, even though he was not the equal of Moses in intimacy with the Lord. Each leader appointed by the Lord has an endowment to perform his own mission, if he will faithfully try.

The book of Deuteronomy fittingly concludes the Torah, the teachings, guidance, and testimony of Moses, prophet of the Lord.

JOSHUA

The book of Joshua recounts Israel's preparations to enter the promised land (Josh. 1–4). It covers the conquest as it proceeded westward, southward, and northward, and then the conquest was consolidated (Josh. 5–12). It describes the allocation of areas to each tribe and the responsibilities each tribe bore (Josh. 13–22). It reports Joshua's farewell and his charge to Israel to be true to God in keeping all their covenants with Him (Josh. 23–24).

The book also portrays the effects a people's needs and challenges have upon their courage and faith. It shows the value of having a strong, inspired, faithful leader over a nation.

To understand why Israel conquered and settled Canaan, we must know the nature and purposes of the covenant promises to Abraham and his seed (BD, "Abraham"; "Abrahamic Covenant"). The promise of a land was not fulfilled in patriarchal times because the resident peoples were still worthy to keep their homeland. Only when Canaanite evils became rampant were the heirs of Abraham—the Israelites—led in (Gen. 15:13–16; 1 Ne. 17:23–35; Lev. 18). Even then, many Israelites were not as righteous as they needed to be to fulfill their Abrahamic mission (Deut. 9:4–6; Lev. 18:24–28).

COMMENTARY

1:1–9 Now after the death of Moses . . . the Lord spake unto Joshua the son of Nun, Moses' minister

In the first recorded revelation to Joshua as Israel's leader, the Lord gave him his life's mission: to lead Israel into the land of their inheritance. The Lord promised help and encouraged him.

The boundaries of the promised land were reviewed (Josh. 1:1–9 and fn.). Israelite control did not reach all those boundaries until the time of David and Solomon.

The Lord's encouragement of Joshua and his admonitions about daily scripture study are applicable still.

1:10–18 Prepare you victuals; for within three days ye shall pass over this Jordan, to go in to possess the land

At last Israel was to make immediate preparations for the long-awaited event. The tribes of Reuben and Gad and half of the tribe of Manasseh were committed to helping the other tribes in the conquest before settling down east of the River Jordan, and they responded favorably to Joshua's leadership, even repeating the Lord's own encouraging words, "be strong and of a good courage" (Josh. 1:18).

2:1–24 Joshua . . . sent out . . . two men to spy secretly, saying, Go view the land, even Jericho. And they went, and came into an harlot's house, named Rahab, and lodged there

Though the spies lodged in a public house where strangers commonly came and went, they were detected. The innkeeper, because of her convictions, proposed that she would help save them and they would in turn help save her and her family. She felt assurance that the Lord God of Israel is the only and universal God. Her faith and works on their behalf were remembered in Israel on into New Testament times (Josh. 2:1*a;* 2:9–11). She remained with Israel and may have been the Rahab who was the mother of Boaz, who married Ruth, as recorded in the genealogy of Jesus (Josh. 6:25; Matt. 1:5*a*).

The spies returned confidently to Joshua and assured him, "The Lord hath delivered into our hands all the land" (Josh. 2:24).

3:1–17 as . . . the feet of the priests that bare the ark were dipped in the brim of the water, . . . the waters which came down from above stood and rose up upon an heap

The time for crossing the River Jordan was set in advance; and the significance of the Lord's stopping the water for Israel was pointed out (Josh. 3:5, 10–17). Simply translated, the account is clear: "the waters flowing down from above stopped; they rose up as a heap very far away at Adam, the city that is beside Zarethan, and those [waters] that went down toward the sea of Arabah, the Salt Sea, were completely cut off, and the people passed over, opposite Jericho" (Josh. 3:16; translation mine). The city called Adam, now Tel ed-Damieh, is near a narrow channel with high clay banks that dam up the water when they collapse. It was a miracle that the waters were cut off as promised (Josh. 3:11–16; 4:21–24).

4:1–13 Take you hence out of the midst of Jordan . . . twelve stones

A monument was to be built of twelve stones taken from the riverbed where the priests bearing the ark had stood. In fact, a marker was built in the middle of the river where the priests had stood, but a monument was built at their night lodging place so that future generations might be taught trust in the Lord (Josh. 4:3, 6–9, 19–24).

The contingent from Reuben, Gad, and half of Manasseh preceded the rest of Israel, demonstrating that they were keeping their promise to Moses. Their forty thousand troops were only part of those numbered earlier (Num. 26:7, 18, 34). Perhaps some were left to guard the cities and camps occupied by the families of the two and one-half tribes that settled east of the Jordan.

4:14–24 On that day the Lord magnified Joshua in the sight of all Israel

The events of that day must have assured Israel that the Lord was with the leader he had provided them.

The first encampment in the land of promise was established on the day of preparation for the Passover, the "tenth day of the first month" (Josh. 4:19; 5:10–11; TG, "Passover"). The camp formed a great circle *(Gilgal)* around the ark of the covenant on the approach to Jericho. There the monument of twelve stones was erected and the purpose of it reiterated.

5:1 when all the kings of the Amorites . . . and all the kings of the Canaanites . . . heard that the Lord had dried up the waters of Jordan from before the children of Israel . . . their heart melted

The anticipated effects began to be realized (Josh. 4:24).

5:2–9 circumcise again the children of Israel

The generation born in the wilderness had not been circumcised; performing that ordinance renewed Israel's commitment and consecration.

5:10–15 the children of Israel encamped in Gilgal, and kept the passover . . . in the plains of Jericho

The first Passover kept by the Israelites in Canaan took place forty years after the Passover was inaugurated in Egypt on the eve of Israel's march to freedom (Josh. 5:10a; Ex. 12:11; Num. 28:16; 32:13; Deut. 29:5). The children of Israel crossed the Jordan "on the tenth day of the first month, and encamped in Gilgal" on the day each family was to select a lamb in preparation for the Passover (Josh. 4:19; 5:10; TG and BD, "Passover"). On the next day, after the Passover, they ate unleavened cakes made with grain from the previous year's harvest in Canaan, and the manna ceased to fall.

A heavenly messenger came "as captain of the host of the Lord" to reassure Joshua and Israel. The divinity of the messenger is indicated by his instructions to Joshua, which, like those that Moses had been given at the burning bush, were to show reverence because the place had become holy (Josh. 5:13–15a–b). His message was encouraging, and Joshua was reverent and grateful.

6:1–19 the Lord said unto Joshua, See, I have given into thine hand Jericho . . . And ye shall compass the city

So it was ordered, and so it was done. Joshua commanded the priests to carry the sacred ark of the covenant with the people in daily marches around the city. The blowing of the trumpets was the only sound heard during the march each day; only on the completion of the seven rounds on the seventh day did the people shout (Josh. 6:10, 16).

One important instruction given before the attack required that all of the city be devoted (Heb., *cherem*) either to destruction or to holy purposes (Josh. 6:18*a*). That would prevent individual Israelites from becoming selfish looters and yet preserve some things of value for the benefit of all the congregation, under the control of the priesthood.

6:20–27 So the people shouted when the priests blew with the trumpets: and . . . the wall fell down flat

As visitors may see today, Jericho was a tiny walled city with a circumference of less than a mile. The Israelite army could probably have walked seven times around Jericho in half a day on the seventh day of the siege. When the city was opened up and the army stormed over the fallen walls, the Israelites kept their promise to Rahab: she and her family were spared, and they dwelt in Israel (Josh. 6:25).

Joshua's curse of the site was prophetic of later events there (Josh. 6:26*a–b*).

7:1–5 Achan . . . took of the accursed thing

Trouble arose when one man disobeyed orders and kept some valuable contraband. As a lesson, divine help was withdrawn, and Israel suffered a defeat in the next siege, at Ai. Achan's individual punishment came later (Josh. 7:19–26).

7:6–15 Get thee up; wherefore liest thou thus upon thy face?

Joshua tore his clothes, fell to the earth before the ark, and asked why this failure had occurred after all the promises. The answer was a sharp reprimand for Joshua's implication that the Lord had failed Israel. Then he gave Joshua instructions for identifying the tribe and family of the individual responsible.

7:16–26 Achan, the son of Carmi, the son of Zabdi, the son of Zerah, of the tribe of Judah was taken

The dramatic procedure must have caused everybody to suffer in apprehension of possible guilt, and they would have learned thereby.

There is some ambiguity in the account of the punishment that followed; the alternation of the pronouns *him* and *them* make it difficult to tell whether or not the whole family suffered as accomplices in the sin of Achan. Most likely the Israelites stoned him only and burned the contraband things. Unless the whole family had been accomplices, it would have been a breach of the principle of justice to stone all of them for his sin (Deut. 24:16).

Note the word-play on the Hebrew names *Achan* and *Achor,* which mean "trouble." Achor was thereafter remembered as the place where he who had caused Israel trouble was himself caused to suffer (Josh. 7:25, 26*a*).

8:1–29 Fear not, neither be thou dismayed—I have given into thy hand the king of Ai, and his people, and his city

The Lord's earlier encouragement was reiterated, so Joshua proceeded with the conquest of Canaan. He used the stratagem of ambush and decoy to draw the people out of Ai and nearby Bethel to conquer them. A hilltop ruin near modern Beitin (Bethel) is called *Et Tell,* "the ruin-heap."

8:30–35 half of them over against mount Gerizim, and half of them over against mount Ebal

On Mount Ebal Joshua built an altar of whole stones and wrote upon it a copy of the law of Moses as the Lord had previously commanded (Josh. 8:32; Deut. 27:2–8). Consider the importance of literacy in Israel in the promulgation of the laws of God.

Also in accord with the instructions Moses had given, in that valley between the mountains Gerizim and Ebal, with half the people on each side and the ark in the middle, the children of Israel "read all the words of the law, the blessings and cursings" (Josh. 8:34). The blessings for keeping the law were read from Mount Gerizim, and the cursings for breaking the law were read from Mount Ebal, as the Lord had commanded Moses (Deut. 27:12–13).

9:1–27 the Hittite, and the Amorite, the Canaanite, the Perizzite, the Hivite, and the Jebusite . . . gathered themselves together, to fight with Joshua and with Israel . . . the inhabitants of Gibeon . . . did work wilily

As the fame of the God of Israel and Joshua's armies spread, some peoples united to fight, but others contrived to save themselves. The Hivites of Gibeon, the next probable target of Israel after Ai and Bethel, came out dressed as peoples from far away and proposed a treaty; Joshua accepted it and made peace. Such subterfuge was not necessary; Gibeon could simply have accepted an overture of peace from Israel and become a "tributary" to Israel, a status similar to what they negotiated (Deut. 20:10–12).

10:1–14 when Adoni-zedek . . . heard how Joshua had taken Ai, and had utterly destroyed it; as he had done to Jericho . . . and how . . . Gibeon had made peace with Israel . . . they feared

Adonizedek, Jebusite king of Jerusalem (BD, "Jebus"), sent word to four other kings of city-states that all should punish Gibeon for its capitulation and all should oppose Israel. His plan was to no avail (Gen. 15:16; Ex. 23:28–33; Josh. 2:24; 10:14; 1 Ne. 17:33–35; Bible Map 4).

The miracle of the extension of light may have been performed so the combined Amorite resistance could be broken in a single siege to leave no time for armies to regroup and prolong the carnage (Josh. 10:12*a*; Hel. 12:15).

10:15–43 But these five kings fled, and hid themselves in a cave at Makkedah

After defeating the coalition of southern kings, Joshua quickly followed through by capturing the kings and reducing all their defenses. "And all these kings and their land did Joshua take at one time, because the Lord God of Israel fought for Israel"; it would not have been possible without divine help (Josh. 10:42).

11:1–15 when Jabin king of Hazor had heard those things . . . he sent to Jobab king of Madon, and to the king of Shimron, and to the king of Achshaph, And to the kings that were on the north of the mountains, and of the plains

The peoples of the north mobilized against Israel as those of the south had done, and they met a similar fate. Even the stronghold of Hazor fell, which "beforetime was the head of all those kingdoms" (Josh. 11:10). Hazor today is a ruin that may be seen by visitors.

These violent activities, aided and abetted by the Lord, may be understood only in context of the conditions and the situation as explained in the scriptures (e.g., 1 Ne. 17:33–35).

11:16–23 So Joshua took all that land . . . Joshua made war a long time with all those kings

The major cities fell quickly, but many Canaanite villages and country inhabitants kept Joshua busy for years, and the tribes moving into their areas later had to continue the struggle. The gigantic Anakim, who had frightened Joshua's fellow spies more than forty years before, were vanquished, except for those in the Philistine cities of Gaza, Gath, and Ashdod on the southern coastal plain. One giant, Goliath, was prominent later, in David's time (Josh. 11:22; Num. 13:21–33; Deut. 2:10–12; 1 Sam. 17).

Mention of the "mountains of Judah" and the "mountains of Israel" shows a division of northern Israel from Judah in the south, perhaps foreshadowing the geopolitical division that developed centuries later, after Solomon's reign (Josh. 11:21; 1 Kgs. 12).

12:1– 6 these are the kings of the land, which the children of Israel smote . . . on the other side Jordan . . . Them did Moses the servant of the Lord and the children of Israel smite

Joshua reviewed those defeated under Moses, including the

giant Og, king of Bashan; the defeats provided lands for peoples of Reuben, Gad, and half of Manasseh (Num. 21:21–30).

12:7–24 And these are the kings of the country which Joshua and the children of Israel smote on this side Jordan on the west

The existence of some thirty-one kings in such a small land as Canaan emphasizes that each governed only a small fortified city-state. Some of them can be located on a map (Bible Map 5).

13:1–33 there remaineth yet very much land to be possessed

All the cities that had been brought under Israelite control were listed, and then the areas not possessed through Joshua's campaigns were enumerated. Among them were the Philistine cities of the coastal plain, the Shephelah, and strongholds on the Carmel ridge; some northern coastal and inland cities; and some of the Phoenician area farther north. A vital gateway city, Beth-shan, in the Jordan valley leading toward the Jezreel valley, and other cities also remained unconquered (Josh. 17:16; Judg. 1:19, 21, 27–35). All those cities were promised to Israel, but the distribution of inheritances to nine and one-half tribes west of the Jordan was to proceed immediately, and the previous distribution of land to two and one-half tribes who were east of the Jordan was confirmed.

Although no single area was given for Levi, Levitical cities in the areas of all the other tribes were later specified in keeping with Moses' instructions. Priesthood services in teaching, judging, and officiating in the worship practices were provided for all the other tribes by the priests and other Levites; they needed to be available throughout all Israel (Josh. 13:33; 21; Num. 35).

Among the slain was Balaam, the Aramean prophet who went against the will of the Lord and in the end openly fought against Israel. His infidelity and betrayal were cited in the scriptures centuries later (Josh. 13:22; Num. 31; 2 Pet. 2:15; Jude 1:11; Rev. 2:14).

14:1–5 By lot was their inheritance, as the Lord commanded

Joshua 14 begins to describe the allocation of inheritances, called "countries" in verse 1, for all twelve tribes in the lands of Canaan. There were twelve inheritances, even though the Levites were to live among all the tribes, for Joseph's descendants became two tribes, Ephraim and Manasseh (Gen. 48:5, 19–20).

14:6–15 Then the children of Judah came unto Joshua in Gilgal: and Caleb . . . said unto him

Caleb was Judah's spokesman and a survivor of the older generation (Num. 34:18–19); recall that he and Joshua were the only faithful scouts forty-five years before. In Caleb's old age, his faith was still unwavering and his courage undaunted; he asked for the very location that had frightened his fellow spies—the city of Hebron and its environs (Num. 13:22–33; 14:24).

15:1– 63 This then was the lot of the tribe of . . . Judah

The inheritance drawn by lot for the large tribe of Judah was in the south and included the territory Caleb had asked for. The area allotted to Judah was large enough that part of it was shared with Simeon (Josh. 19:1–9; Gen. 49:5–7).

Note that the Jebusites of Jerusalem could not be driven out even though their king had been killed. Jerusalem's subjection to Israel came much later, in the days of young King David (Josh. 10:23–26; 15:63; 2 Sam. 5:1–10; 1 Chr. 11:4–8).

16:1– 4 And the lot of the children of Joseph

The inheritances for Joseph's descendants were first generalized and then specified, one each for Ephraim and Manasseh.

16:5–10 And the border of the children of Ephraim

Ephraim was assigned the center of the land, but failed to heed Moses' commandment from the Lord and settled among the Canaanite peoples. This practice became common with each tribe and brought disastrous repercussions as the peoples intermarried and some Israelites turned from the Lord (Josh. 16:10; Lev. 18:1–5, 24–28; Deut. 7:1–5; Judg. 2).

17:1–18 There was also a lot for the tribe of Manasseh

Joseph's descendants through his two sons were more numerous than Judah's (85,200 to 76,500, according to Num. 26:22, 34, 37); so their land east and west of the Jordan, including the highland wooded areas Joshua invited them to take over, was greater in area than Judah's. In fact, the combined inheritances of Ephraim and Judah were over one-half of the whole land.

Manasseh also failed to remove all Canaanites from the land.

18:1–10 And there remained . . . seven tribes, which had not yet received their inheritance

After the large tribes had taken lands, the remaining seven were apparently reluctant to venture out and occupy theirs. In a grand gathering at Shiloh, where Israel had set up the old tabernacle in a permanent place, Joshua ordered representatives to explore the remaining areas and report. Then he divided among them the cities, villages, and geographical features listed. Recall that both Jacob and Moses, in blessing the twelve tribes, had anticipated some of these tribal locations, their resources, and ways of life (Gen. 49; Deut. 33).

18:11–28 And the lot of the tribe . . . of Benjamin came up

The Benjamites' territory fell between that of Judah and Ephraim. The word *coast* also means "border" (Josh. 18:28.)

19:1–9 And the second lot came forth to Simeon

Simeon's allotment was in the southern part of Judah's territory (Josh. 15 and commentary)

19:10–16 the third lot came up for the children of Zebulun

Zebulun's inheritance was in the hilly central region of western Galilee, north of the Jezreel valley.

19:17–23 the fourth lot came out to Issachar

Issachar's inheritance was next to, and southeast of, Zebulun; Moses had blessed both of those tribes in one statement (Deut. 33:18–19).

19:24– 31 the fifth lot . . . the tribe of . . . Asher

Surprisingly little was said of the resources or advantages of Asher's seacoast and harbor location; both Moses and Jacob had given hints of them (Gen. 49:20; Deut. 33:24–25).

19:32– 39 The sixth lot came out to the children of Naphtali

Naphtali occupied much of the Galilee area. Moses spoke of the area as "full with the blessing of the Lord" (Deut. 33:23); Isaiah foresaw that people who "walked in darkness" in areas of Zebulun and Naphtali should see "a great light," anticipating the Savior's mission there (Isa. 9:1–2; Matt. 2:23; 4:13–16).

19:40– 48 the seventh lot came out for the tribe of . . . Dan

The original allocation for Dan was in largely unconquered Philistine territory between Judah and Ephraim. Later scriptures suggest that it was never really possessed by Dan and tell more about the Danites' conquering cities in northern Canaan (Josh. 19:47; Judg. 18:1, 27–29).

19:49–50 children of Israel gave an inheritance to Joshua

The Israelites, guided by inspiration, showed Joshua honor and gratitude by giving him a city in his tribal area of Ephraim. He was eventually buried there (Josh. 19:50*a*).

19:51 These are the inheritances which Eleazar the priest, and Joshua the son of Nun, and the heads of the fathers of the tribes of the children of Israel, divided for an inheritance by lot in Shiloh before the Lord, at the door of the tabernacle

This summary tells concisely what was done, by whom, where, and under whose authority.

20:1–9 Appoint . . . cities of refuge, whereof I spake unto you by the hand of Moses

Review Moses' revelations on this important provision for safeguarding justice (Num. 35:6–15; Deut. 4:41–43). It would provide a haven for any innocent person unjustly charged and establish a system for examining charges and determining guilt.

21:1– 42 Then came . . . the Levites . . . saying, The Lord commanded by the hand of Moses to give us cities to dwell in, with the suburbs thereof for our cattle

A survey of the tribal locations of the forty-eight Levitical cities shows one combined tribal area with thirteen such cities, one with ten, another with thirteen, and one with twelve. Cities for the descendants of Aaron were also named, one of which was made a city of refuge. The rest of the Levitical cities for the descendants of Kohath were named, also including a city of refuge. The Levitical cities for the descendants of Gershon were next, including three cities of refuge. Finally the Levitical cities for the descendants of Merari were named, including a city of refuge. The total, forty-eight, included all six of the cities of refuge—three of which were east of the Jordan River and three west (BD, "Cities of Refuge").

21:43– 45 the Lord gave unto Israel all the land which he sware to give unto their fathers . . . And the Lord gave them rest round about, according to all that he sware unto their fathers

Everyone at this point was at peace, but the mopping-up operations did not thereafter go as intended, and the Lord could not justly fulfill his part of the covenant if the people did not continue to do their duty; therefore, a different assessment of the state of things was given later (Josh. 23:13).

22:1– 34 Then Joshua called the Reubenites, and the Gadites, and the half tribe of Manasseh

Joshua summoned representatives of the tribes who were to live east of the Jordan in order to bless them and charge them to be faithful to the Lord; then he sent them to their inheritances across the river. There they built a great altar, not for sacrifice, but as a monument, a symbolic witness so that future generations could be taught about their relationship with the Lord and their oneness with the Israelites west of Jordan. It was to remind them of the altar of sacrifice at the tabernacle in Shiloh.

Ironically, the western tribes, seeing it from afar, thought it was an altar erected to an idol, and they worried that the Lord might punish not only the offenders but all of Israel, as at Achor (Josh. 22:20*a*). They mustered troops, but fortunately the princes and priesthood leaders determined the true purpose of the stone altar-like monument, and war was averted.

23:1–16 And it came to pass a long time after . . ., that Joshua waxed old . . . And Joshua called for all Israel

In his old age (he died at age one hundred ten; Josh. 24:29), Joshua called the first of two assemblies to give his farewell instructions and a charge. He repeated the promises and urged Israel not to backslide and affiliate with Canaanite remnants, lest they suffer as they had been warned (Josh. 23:12–13 and fn.; Lev. 18:24–30).

Joshua spoke poetically of his approaching death (Josh. 23:14*a;* cf. Job 10:21; 16:22) and added one more warning.

24:1–28 Joshua gathered all the tribes of Israel to Shechem

Joshua's valedictory address was at Shechem, in the center of Israel's new land, a few miles north of Shiloh. As Moses had done, Joshua reviewed the reasons why the people should remain faithful and grateful to God for his blessings. He spoke of the Lord's help given in Egypt, at the Red Sea, in the wilderness, in the struggles against such opponents as King Balak and the false prophet Balaam, and in the conquest of the land. A high point in his speech, and a great gem in the Bible, is his final testimony and resolution (Josh. 24:14–15).

The people covenanted to be faithful, and Joshua wrote a record of it in a "book of the law of God." He set up another stone memorial to bear witness of the covenant, and the Israelites did keep it for a time, until that generation passed away (Josh. 24: 26–28, 31; Judg. 2:7–11). Sadly, the same cannot be said of many of their descendants, as they are portrayed in the books of Judges, Samuel, and Kings.

24:29–31 after these things, . . . Joshua . . . the servant of the Lord, died, being an hundred and ten years old

Joshua's death could have been about twenty-five years after he led the invasion of Canaan, assuming he was the age of his friend Caleb (Josh. 14:7–10). Their example and influence were one cause of the fidelity of that generation.

24:32 And the bones of Joseph, which the children of Israel brought up out of Egypt, buried they in Shechem

Joseph's request that his body be buried in the promised land was at last fulfilled: his body was buried in the first parcel of land owned by Jacob in the land of promise, purchased from the people of Shechem (Josh. 24:32a; Gen. 33:18–19).

Jacob's well was known in New Testament times in that vicinity (John 4:5); and it, as well as a cenotaph for Joseph nearby, can still be visited in Shechem.

24:33 And Eleazar the son of Aaron died; and they buried him

It was truly the end of an epoch in Israel when Joshua, the successor to Moses, and Eleazar, son of Aaron, were both gone.

Joshua was a man of vision, courage, wisdom, fairness, spiritual power, and energy. Inspiring words from his book have been cited by preachers and teachers throughout the ages (e.g., Josh. 1:6–9; 24:15). His name, appropriately, means "Jehovah is Savior."

JUDGES

The book of Judges covers the first centuries of Israel's cycles of success and failure in the newly occupied land of Israel, where they should have become "a peculiar treasure . . . a kingdom of priests, and an holy nation" (Ex. 19:5–6); by the end of the book, the Israelites' failure to fulfill the mission of Abraham to bring blessings to "all the families of the earth" is manifestly evident (TG, "Israel, Mission of," "Abrahamic Covenant"; BD, "Abraham, Covenant of").

The first two chapters in the book of Judges review the situation at the close of Joshua's era and preview the coming cycles of success and failure in Israel's efforts to be God's exemplary nation. Details follow about several of the judges (Heb., *shophetim,* "leaders, defenders, judges"). Most of them were raised up by the Lord to supplement the priestly leaders in governing Israel, but some who were not raised up by the Lord are also covered. One of them was Jephthah, a somewhat tragic man whom the people themselves summoned to lead them. A different tragic case is Samson, who was called of God even before his birth but seems to have failed his divine calling. The book concludes with a few examples of the extremes of evil that developed during periods of Israel's deep apostasy when "every man did that which was right in his own eyes" (Judg. 17:6; 21:25).

COMMENTARY

1:1–15 Now after the death of Joshua . . . Israel asked the Lord, saying, Who shall go up for us against the Canaanites first

Although the narrative of the book of Judges begins "after the death of Joshua," some events prior to his death are reviewed.

When Israel asked who should begin to occupy their lands, the Lord responded that Judah should go. The men of Judah invited men of Simeon to accompany them, and they attacked Bezek, Jerusalem, Hebron, and Debir. The mutilation of Adoni-bezeq was a common enough practice, but it hardly seems justifiable by Israel. It is surprising that Adoni-bezek could moralize about it and count it as just (Judg. 1:7).

Though Jerusalem was breached and burned, it was still held by Jebusites until King David's time (Judg. 1:8, 21; Josh. 15:63; 2 Sam. 5:4–9; 1 Chr. 11:4–9).

Debir, or Kirjath-sepher, near Hebron, was within the inheritance of Caleb of Judah; part of this account was told before (Josh. 15:13–19).

1:16 And the children of the Kenite, Moses' father in law, went up . . . with the children of Judah . . . and dwelt among the people

A promise by Moses was fulfilled when the Kenites, a special Abrahamic clan, went into Judah (Judg. 1:16; Num. 10:29–32; BD, "Kenites").

1:17–20 And Judah went with Simeon his brother, and they slew the Canaanites

Further clearing of Canaanite territory by the armies of Judah and Simeon are here recounted. But Gaza, Askelon, and Ekron were Philistine cities whose "valley" (coastal plain) could not be overcome because of their iron-bound chariots; indeed, the Philistines remained dominant there sporadically in the reigns of David and Solomon.

1:21 And the children of Benjamin did not drive out the Jebusites that inhabited Jerusalem

Jerusalem, or some part of it, was conquered by Judah, but it appears that not all of the city was purged of Jebusites. Part of the city lay within Judah's inheritance and part within Benjamin's, so some reports may pertain only to one part.

1:22–29 And the house of Joseph . . . went up against Bethel

Some of the territories of Ephraim and Manasseh had been previously occupied but not divested of Canaanites. Additional efforts to remove them are recounted, but those efforts were never entirely successful (Judg. 1:27–29; Josh. 16; 17).

1:30– 36 Zebulun . . . Asher . . . Naphtali . . . Dan

The tribes of Zebulun, Asher, Naphtali, and Dan also failed to drive out all former inhabitants but instead dwelt among them; and the ways of those inhabitants became temptations and "thorns" in their sides as Moses had warned, Joshua had reiterated, and an angel later reinforced (Num. 33:55; Josh. 23:13; Judg. 2:1–3). The Israelites' adoption of Canaanite morals and religious practices became one of the causes of Israel's eventual overthrow (TG, "Apostasy of Israel").

The neighboring Ephraimites ("the house of Joseph") subjected some of the Amorites, but the Danites had difficulty with their inheritance south of Ephraim and later moved to a northern outpost (Josh. 19:40–48; Judg. 1:34–36; 18).

2:1– 6 And an angel of the Lord came up from Gilgal to Bochim

The first part of Judges 2 also recounts some events that occurred before Joshua's death; it is possible that this is the message from the earlier angelic visit. Note that it was given in the first person as a message from the Lord himself, warning against adopting Canaanite ways (Josh. 5:13–15).

2:7–9 And the people served the Lord all the days of Joshua, and all the days of the elders that outlived Joshua, who had seen all the great works of the Lord, that he did for Israel

This summary repeats a previous one. The people of that generation served the Lord, but transmission of faith and responsibility to the next generation did not succeed well (Josh. 24:31; Judg. 2:7, 10–13).

2:10–23 and there arose another generation after them, which knew not the Lord, nor yet the works which he had done

Here is the regrettable report of apostasy and its results, though the Lord raised up leaders to combat it. A preview tells of the cycles of repentance, prosperity, apostasy, suffering, and repentance again, which continue throughout the book of Judges. Because the Israelites did not long remain righteous after any of the judges the Lord raised up, he could not cause them to prosper.

3:1–7 these are the nations which the Lord left, to prove Israel

The angel had warned that because the Israelites had not driven out the Canaanites and Amorites but had made treaties with them and had not destroyed their places of worship, the Lord would not do it for them (Judg. 2:1–6). Thus those peoples and their ways were the tests "to prove Israel." Israel tended to fail the tests.

3:8–11 Therefore the anger of the Lord was hot against Israel, and he sold them into the hand of Chushan-rishathaim

For eight years, the Israelites suffered and repented; then they were given a "deliverer" (Heb., *moshia'*, "a rescuer, or savior") who led them in a war to free them from their oppressor. This first "judge" was Othniel, nephew of Caleb (Judg. 1:13). Note that it was the Spirit of the Lord that gave him power to lead Israel.

The oppressor is not well identified, for he is called by a derogatory name in Hebrew, meaning "Cushite of the double wickedness." He was king of a place called, in Hebrew, "Aram of the double rivers," here rendered in English as *Mesopotamia*. It may have been in Aramea, near two tributaries of the Euphrates.

After that war, Israel had rest for forty years, a number which often represents a lifetime or career of one individual.

3:12–30 the children of Israel did evil again . . . and the Lord strengthened Eglon the king of Moab against Israel

Eglon (Heb., lit., "round one"), an obese king of Moab, was the next oppressor of a part of Israel, occupying an area near Jericho, or "the city of palm trees." He was opposed by an Israelite "deliverer" named Ehud, a Benjamite. The bold personal attack of Ehud upon Eglon is told in gory detail. Eighty years of rest followed.

3:31 after him was Shamgar the son of Anath

No details are known about Shamgar, the next deliverer of Israel. He had a Hittite or Philistine name and was the son of Anath, whose name is that of a Canaanite goddess. Perhaps he was a Philistine rebel. His weapon, an "ox goad," would have been effective as a short stabbing spear, having a staff six to ten feet long and a point of metal or stone. His name appears again in a poetic review of conditions before Deborah's term as a judge (Judg. 5:6).

4:1–9 Israel again did evil . . . when Ehud was dead. And the Lord sold them into the hand of Jabin king of Canaan . . . And Deborah, a prophetess . . . judged Israel at that time

The account of Deborah's time as a judge ties back to Ehud's time, ignoring Shamgar.

Rather than a few verses, as with some of the judges, two chapters were written about Deborah, the only female judge of Israel and a prophetess (TG, "Prophetess"; "Holy Ghost, Gifts of"). She was a wife and mother (Judg. 4:4; 5:7) who provided advice and judgment for people who came to her home between Ramah and Bethel in Ephraim. She called Barak, a man of Naphtali, for

213

the campaign against Sisera, captain of King Jabin's Canaanite hosts from the area of Hazor. Barak was reluctant to serve unless the prophetess herself went to battle with him. She consented but prophesied that the honors of the campaign would go to a woman (not referring to herself; Judg. 4:17–21).

4:10–24 Barak called Zebulun and Naphtali . . . and Deborah went up with him

It seems that only the oppressed tribes were involved in the respective campaigns recounted in the book of Judges; there is seldom any indication that all of Israel acted together. Ephraim, Naphtali, and Zebulun (Judg. 4), together with Benjamin and Issachar (Judg. 5), are listed as participants in the campaign under Deborah and Barak; the participation of Reuben, Dan, and Asher was doubtful.

With Deborah giving the commands and Barak leading the armies, battle was joined and victory was won. But the final coup was administered by Jael, wife of Heber, a Kenite; wielding a hammer and a tent peg, she ended the life of the Canaanite captain, Sisera. (Driving tent pins and pitching tents were part of a woman's work among the nomads.) A graphic account of her deed, in dramatic poetry, follows in the next chapter.

5:1–31 Then sang Deborah and Barak . . . on that day, saying

The victory poem of Deborah and Barak, aside from dramatic details about the death of the enemy, is chiefly a song of thanks and praise to the Lord. Some stanzas also extol valor in the armies and the preeminence of Deborah (Judg. 5:7, 12, 15). The bold courage of the Kenite woman, Jael, is praised, in contrast to the poignant bereavement of the mother of Sisera (Judg. 5:24–30).

Literarily, Judges 5 is highly reputed as poetry. Paired reiterations tell the death of Sisera (Judg. 5:27).

Remembering what the function of the priesthood should have been (Num. 27:21), we conclude that the priests were either failing or ignored as spiritual advisers; a good woman, Deborah, became the messenger of the Lord to Israel.

The name *Deborah* (meaning "bee") and its diminutive forms (e.g., Debbie) have been popular in many cultures since her time.

6:1–10 And the children of Israel did evil in the sight of the Lord: and the Lord delivered them into the hand of Midian

Again, instead of a single verse or only a few to characterize the career of a judge, three chapters deal with one great leader, Gideon—and one with his terrible successor, his son Abimelech.

The era began with seasonal raids on crops and herds by peoples of the east and south, including Midianites and Amalekites. Before calling Gideon as a judge to lead Israel when they cried out, the Lord raised up a prophet to declare to them that their failure to keep their covenants was the cause of their lack of divine protection (Judg. 6:7–10).

6:11–24 Gideon threshed wheat by the winepress, to hide it from the Midianites. And the angel of the Lord appeared unto him

When Gideon was called, he was first greeted by an angel with complimentary words. Gideon responded with irony: "If the Lord be with us, why then is all this befallen us? and where be all his miracles which our fathers told us of?" (Judg. 6:13). But the Lord's message from the angel was still positive: if Gideon would serve God with his might, God would be with him and help him do what he was called to do (Judg. 6:16). Gideon was too overwhelmed and humble to accept immediately; he asked for a sign that the message really was from the Lord. There is a difference between asking for signs out of an urge to be gratified and asking because of the desire to discern; so, as a sign, the Lord let the angel turn a meal provided by Gideon into a miraculous burned offering. (On the problem of discerning whether a messenger is from the Lord or not, see 2 Cor. 11:13–15; 1 Jn. 4:1–2; D&C 129.) Then Gideon was more overwhelmed with awe, gratitude, and fear, but the Lord graciously comforted him and gave him peace; wherefore, Gideon built a memorial altar and named it *Jehovah-shalom,* meaning, "Jehovah is peace."

6:25– 32 throw down the altar of Baal that thy father hath, and cut down the grove that is by it: And build an altar unto the Lord thy God upon the top of this rock

Gideon was to start the reform by destroying idolatry at home and restoring there the worship of the true God. He did so, and after his father's timely repentance, they demonstrated the impotence of idols. Later, the power of the true God was demonstrated (Judg. 7:1–23). His new name was a challenge to Baal (Judg. 6:32).

6:33– 40 Then all the Midianites and the Amalekites and the children of the east were gathered together, . . . But the Spirit of the Lord came upon Gideon, and he blew a trumpet . . . And he sent messengers throughout all Manasseh . . . Asher . . . Zebulun . . . and unto Naphtali

The reformation and restoration were launched immediately. The people of his community gathered to Gideon, and then those of his own large tribe and of the neighboring tribes to the north, for the enemy was gathered in the important north-central valley of Jezreel.

Additional signs were granted Gideon to indicate the time for action and to give assurance that the Lord would save Israel (BD, "Miracles").

7:1–25 Then Jerubbaal, who is Gideon, and all the people that were with him, rose up

The enemy was numerous and their camels without number, but the sizable Israelite army of 32,000 assembled from the four tribes was reduced by command of the Lord to a mere 300—so that the help of the Lord might be very apparent. Then, against the formidable camel-mounted marauders, with whom hand-to-hand combat could have been disastrous, the Lord gave Israel miraculous success. When the rout began, Gideon summoned Ephraimite warriors and sent them to cut off the enemy retreat across the Jordan at Beth-bara, which they did.

8:1–21 men of Ephraim said unto him, Why hast thou served us thus, that thou calledst us not, when thou wentest to fight

Despite the miraculous defeat of the main army, Gideon had needed cooperation to stop some of the retreating forces at the Jordan and to overtake the leaders responsible for the years of plundering. The Ephraimites had helped, but they were insulted that they had not been called earlier to participate. Gideon wisely complimented them sincerely on their vital contribution, and they were satisfied.

Inhabitants of Succoth, beyond the river, refused to provide food for the soldiers with Gideon; they were warned and later punished; so also were the people of Penuel, some seven miles farther on. Finally, the fleeing Midianites were caught beyond Jogbehah, at least fifty miles from the crossing of the river. Those who feared to help Gideon lest the Midianites return were punished (Judg. 8:7, 16), and the Midianite leaders were eliminated.

8:22–28 I will not rule over you, neither shall my son rule over you: the Lord shall rule over you

Gideon clearly understood his role in the Lord's government, and refused personal aggrandizement. He honored the Lord with a new ephod (part of the garment of the chief priest in Israel) made of precious things gathered from the smitten soldiers of the enemy; unfortunately, it later became a "snare" because people idolized it (Judg. 8:27).

8:28–35 and the country was in quietness forty years in the days of Gideon

Gideon's life was exemplary and his contributions noteworthy, but after his death the people returned to idolatry, apparently having forgotten the help of the Lord through Gideon.

9:1–57 And all the men of Shechem . . . made Abimelech king

Ignoring or forgetting the teachings of the Lord and Gideon, some people still wanted a king. Abimelech, one of seventy or more sons of Gideon, was not like his father; he wanted to be king, and he murdered his brothers and others to achieve that end. He hired followers with silver from an idol's shrine, and an evil spirit attended his reign. He is not usually counted as one of the judges in Israel and certainly was not raised up by the Lord. His reign, his end, and the response of God to his evils need no explication.

10:1–5 And after Abimelech there arose—

Brief records were preserved of two more judges and defenders of Israel: Tola, of Issachar, and Jair, a Gileadite, probably of Manasseh in Gilead. Those two judges may have ruled in peace, for no details are given.

10:6–18 And the children of Israel did evil again . . . and served Baalim, and Ashtaroth, and the gods

Peace and prosperity usually allowed indulgences and aberrations to develop—not an uncommon phenomenon. The results were usually the same: loss of worthiness and morale, and then loss of liberty. In this case the Philistines from the west and the Ammonites from the east invaded. When the Israelites repented and cried to the Lord for relief, he let them learn a lesson from life—advising them to cry to the gods they had chosen to serve. When they further repented, the Lord was grieved for their misery, but this time he only prepared them to fight for their own deliverance.

11:1–40 Jephthah the Gileadite was a mighty man of valour . . . And they said unto Jephthah, Come, and be our captain

So the people themselves chose a leader, an outcast, a son of a harlot but yet a "mighty man of valour." He accepted the appointment as leader only after the people assured him he could remain as such after the crisis was removed. He knew the history of Israel's invasion of Moabite and Ammonite lands under Moses after their kings had refused his request for peaceful passage (Judg. 11:13–25 and fn.). Naturally the Ammonite king rejected Jephthah's overtures and prepared for war.

Jephthah was acquainted with the Lord's powers and had faith in his help, but he mistakenly believed he could secure that help by promising to offer as a burnt sacrifice whatever might come out from the doors of his house to meet him.

He did indeed succeed in the campaign, and when his beloved daughter came to meet him, he tragically felt he must fulfill his vow. Because the Lord does not require human sacrifice, it may only be hoped that she was dedicated to the service of the Lord rather than sacrificed as a burnt offering (Judg. 11:34–37; Jer. 32:35).

12:1–7 the men of Ephraim gathered . . . and said unto Jephthah, Wherefore . . . didst [thou] not call us to go with thee?

When the Ephraimites complained because Jephthah had not let them join in his campaign against Ammon, he countered that they had been invited but had sent no help. There was a brief period of strife as he chastised them for their presumption and petulance. Some of them tried to escape back to their lands west of the Jordan, but Jephthah's forces identified them by their dialect: they pronounced *shibboleth* as *sibboleth*. Because they had crossed over Jordan to fight against Jephthah, they were put to death.

A brief note recorded Jephthah's death after six years of rule. He was cited, however, even into New Testament times, as one of the historic exemplars of great faith (Heb. 11:32–34).

12:8–15 and after him—

Jephthah was followed by three judges who are briefly mentioned and who judged Israel seven, ten, and eight years, respectively. The number of sons and daughters and the number of animals seem to be facts relevant to status.

13:1–25 And the children of Israel did evil again in the sight of the Lord; and the Lord delivered them into the hand of the Philistines forty years

Thus begins a four-chapter account of forty years of Philistine oppression and the miraculous rise of a leader who became a folk hero but not a valiant leader. He was Samson, who was blessed with power whereby he could have delivered Israel. An angel promised a son to a Danite woman, and she was instructed to prepare for him before birth and dedicate him to serve the Lord as a Nazarite. He should have become one of Israel's greatest judges, but he did not.

The gracious second visit of the herald to confirm the promise to the woman's husband and the divine acceptance of their offering left them awestruck. His promised birth, his blessings as he grew, and his early actions in Philistine country as moved upon by the Spirit of the Lord looked auspicious. He was named Samson (Heb., *Shimshon,* perhaps from *shemesh,* "sun").

14:1–20 Samson went down to Timnath, and saw a woman . . . of the daughters of the Philistines

Samson seems to have behaved whimsically. His parents must have been distressed when their foreordained Nazarite son desired to marry someone not of Israel, disregarding the laws of Moses. They may be forgiven for failing to understand it as a motivation "of the Lord" that Samson "sought an occasion against the Philistines" (Judg. 14:4); for the Lord hardly needs to set up an occasion to take action against oppression.

In violating Nazarite standards in his proposed marriage and his behavior otherwise (Num. 6), he must have been moved by some spirit he assumed to be the Spirit of the Lord. His proposed marriage, the impossible riddle and betrayal, and the slaughter of thirty men to pay off a silly vow seem unlikely ways to free Israel or bring blessings from God.

15:1–20 Samson visited his wife . . . And her father said, . . . I gave her to thy companion

Samson's incendiary raid out of the frustration of his wish to return to his riddle-ruined marriage and his subsequent slaughter of "a thousand men" with the jawbone of an ass also seem inappropriate actions for a Nazarite. Samson's story appears to be that of a popular hero from the apostate days of the rule of the judges.

His prayer for water was one of two prayers mentioned in the story of his life.

Lehi is the English rendering of the Hebrew *lechi,* meaning "cheek," "jaw," or "jawbone," and is so used in this chapter.

16:1–3 Then went Samson to Gaza, and saw there an harlot, and went in unto her

Samson's next act, after spending half a night with a harlot in the Philistine city of Gaza, was to slip out and pull up the city gates, gateposts and all, and carry them about forty miles into Judah, to a hill near Hebron—no service to God or fellowman.

16:4–31 afterward . . . he loved a woman in the valley of Sorek, whose name was Delilah

Samson developed a passion for another Philistine woman, Delilah, who enticed him and he teased her, until at last he disclosed the secret of his strength and she betrayed him. The Philistines then bound, tortured, and taunted him until he prayed one more prayer; his last "service" was to slay more in his death than he had slain in his life. He is said to have judged Israel twenty years, but no record of that service is given. He was a man foreordained, but not disciplined, to do good (Judg. 16:31; D&C 3:4).

17:1–13 his mother took two hundred shekels of silver, and gave them to the founder, who made thereof a graven image and a molten image

Here is another account from apostate times in Israel: "In those days there was no king in Israel, but every man did that which was right in his own eyes" (Judg. 17:6 and fn. *a–c*). It was no doubt the lack of informed and conscientious priesthood leaders rather than lack of a king that caused Israel to flounder.

A young Levite from Bethlehem of Judah went to Ephraim, where he was employed by Micah as his private priest, in his house of gods, to officiate at his idolatrous altars in the name of the Lord. The characters of this story seem to have sinned more in ignorance than by intent; for there would be no point in knowingly dedicating so much silver to molten and graven images as an insult to God and then hoping for his blessing (Judg. 17:4–5, 13).

18:1–31 In those days there was no king in Israel: and . . . the tribe of the Danites sought them an inheritance to dwell in

Again the lack of a "king in Israel" was given as a kind of apology for bad behavior. Such tribal pillage as the Danites' taking an Ephraimite's idols and priest and then raiding a town of peaceful Sidonians is especially disconcerting when committed by a people whom God had called to become "a kingdom of priests, and an holy nation" (Ex. 19:6).

The Danite move north (Josh. 19:47–48; Judg. 18:7, 27–28) established Israel's northern outpost, and the extremes of a stretch of territory were thereafter described as "from Dan even to Beersheba" (Judg. 20:1; 1 Sam. 3:20; 2 Sam. 3:10; 17:11). Many conquests have occurred at Dan, as shown by a *tell* (a mound of the ruins of a succession of cities, destroyed and built atop one another) called "Dan" in northern Israel, in a beautiful little river valley. It is a pleasant park, reminding one today of the peaceful place that attracted the Danite band three thousand years ago.

A final irony is recorded: Micah's idolatrous priest was probably a descendant of Moses (Judg. 18:30*a*).

19:1–30 in those days, when there was no king in Israel, . . . a certain Levite . . . took to him a concubine

The synopsis at the head of the chapter covers briefly this account of some evil people (except for one charitable old man). "Certain sons of Belial" sought to violate and kill a migrant Levite but accepted instead his concubine, whom they raped and abused until she could hardly return to the house where they lodged. There she died; that she was dead before the Levite cut her to pieces is only to be hoped (Judg. 19:28; 20:5–6).

Nothing excuses the lack of morals, decency, faith, courage, or compassion shown by the host and guest, who offered a daughter and a concubine to the violent men at their door to save themselves; it bespeaks the terrible apostasy of the time. All involved were "sons of Belial" (BD, "Belial")!

20:1– 48 Then all the children of Israel went out, and the congregation was gathered together as one man . . . Then said the children of Israel, Tell us, how was this wickedness?

There was general revulsion and outrage against the Benjamites who committed the sin and crime described above; but as often occurs in popular uprisings, the punishment went to extremes, and tens of thousands on both sides were slain. In the end, most of the Benjamites were wiped out.

One can only wonder what mode of inquiry was used in asking the Lord's advice and consent for these actions; whatever it was, the leaders felt they were justified for the time being (Judg. 20:18, 26–28, 35).

21:1–25 And the people came to the house of God . . . And said, O Lord God of Israel, why is this come to pass in Israel, that there should be to day one tribe lacking in Israel?

Repenting of their rash punishment of one sin, they prayed, sacrificed, and then took extreme vengeance on another segment of Israel (some from Jabesh-gilead who had not joined in the former action), killing everyone except four hundred virgins to provide wives for the remaining Benjamite men. More amazing still, it is recorded that they repented that the Lord had caused one tribe to be destroyed (Judg. 21:3, 15). Could they really have blamed the Lord for it all and made amends by inviting the remaining men of Benjamin to wait in hiding for the annual dances in the vineyards near Shiloh, so that they could catch wives to replace their wives and children slain in the first *putsch?*

The book ends with a repetition of the apology "in those days there was no king in Israel: every man did that which was right in his own eyes" (Judg. 21:25). Although it is repeated only in the last few chapters of the book of Judges, that statement characterizes many of the cycles of apostasy during the centuries from Joshua until Samuel—a period about as long as the time from the Pilgrims in America to the present day.

RUTH

The book of Ruth serves as an appendix to the book of Judges. It tells of some nobler events that "came to pass in the days when the judges ruled" (Ruth 1:1). It is reassuring to read about Israelites of that time who were good, even exemplary—showing faith, love, loyalty, generosity, and devotion to duty. Perhaps they represent many other Israelites of the time whose family history we do not have.

The first two chapters introduce a family, their situation, characters, problems, and options for solutions. Bereavement, followed by some good decisions and admirable actions, moves the story to a climax. The third chapter shows how Israel's welfare laws facilitated the exercise of goodwill, agency, and enterprise to accomplish good ends. The final chapter records the results, the immediate benefits, and the historic developments.

COMMENTARY

1:1–2 there was a famine in the land. And a certain man of Beth-lehem-judah went to sojourn in the country of Moab, he, and his wife, and his two sons

All of the names in these introductory verses are significant: *Beth-lehem-judah* names a community in the usually pleasant, productive hills and dales south of Jerusalem; *Beth-lehem-judah* means "house of bread" or "place of food" in Judah. The other name for the area, *Ephratah* (Ruth 4:11), connotes "fruitfulness."

Nevertheless, an intense cyclical drought and famine caused a family of Ephrathites to leave the area and seek sustenance in Moab.

The name *Elimelech* means "my God is king" and characterizes the religious loyalty of the man and his family.

Naomi means "pleasantness, sweetness," and though this good woman later became so depressed that she thought *Mara* ("bitter sorrow") would be a more appropriate name, she recovered her pleasantness and showed wisdom and faith as well.

Mahlon is possibly derived from *mahlah,* implying "illness," and seems to have anticipated his short life.

Chilion is possibly derived from *kalah,* which has one root meaning "to be ended, spent, consumed," also anticipating a short life and early death.

1:3 And Elimelech Naomi's husband died; and she was left

Tersely the account of Naomi's triple bereavement begins.

1:4–5 they took them wives . . . and they dwelled there about ten years. And Mahlon and Chilion died also

And tersely the account continues. Marriage of the sons to Moabite women was not forbidden because Moabites were an Abrahamic people (BD, "Moab"), but a return to the true faith was essential.

1:6–13 Then she arose with her daughters in law, that she might return from the country of Moab

Options for the three widows' survival were limited. For Orpah and Ruth, there was the possibility of another marriage; for Naomi there could be security and redemption under the marriage laws of Israel (Gen. 38:8; Lev. 25:23–28, 35; Deut. 25:5–6), but Naomi was not very optimistic. She felt that the hand of the Lord was against her and recommended that her daughters-in-law return to their families (Ruth 1:11–13, 20–21).

1:14–18 And they lifted up their voice, and wept again: and Orpah kissed her mother in law; but Ruth clave unto her

The tension between love and loyalty on the one hand and

an uncertain future on the other led Orpah to choose to return to her parents' home and hope for another marriage.

Ruth chose differently. Her testimony shows that her loyalty and love for Naomi and Naomi's God were real; her declaration thereof is radiant (Ruth 1:16-17). Interestingly, *Ruth* means "companion."

1:19–22 when they were come to Beth-lehem . . . all the city was moved about them, and they said, Is this Naomi?

Naomi's rather gloomy return and pitiful prospect made her feel more like *Mara* (Ruth 1:20*a-b*).

Their arrival "in the beginning of barley harvest" (probably late April) was propitious, however, and prospects soon improved.

2:1–16 Naomi had a kinsman of her husband's, a mighty man of wealth . . . and his name was Boaz

The name *Boaz* means "in him is strength, swiftness, quickness" (Ruth 2:1*a*).

The younger widow, Ruth, volunteered to go out as a gleaner to secure food for both herself and her mother-in-law (Ruth 2:2*a*), and it was indeed a blessing that she was guided to the field of Boaz, a "kinsman." The good qualities of Boaz may be seen in the way he greeted the workmen, in his inquiry about the foreign gleaner, and in his generous treatment of Ruth after learning she was the Moabite daughter-in-law to Naomi. Ruth's humility and appreciation are also noteworthy. It is evident here, as it was earlier, that she had become a converted follower of the true God (Ruth 1:16; 2:12).

2:17–23 So she gleaned in the field until even, and beat out that she had gleaned: and it was about an ephah of barley

Naomi was impressed with the amount of grain Ruth had gleaned and threshed (nearly two-thirds of a bushel) and the leftover parched grain from Ruth's lunch. She was yet more pleased to learn whose field Ruth had gleaned and recognized the blessings of the Lord in all that had happened.

A kinsman had the right to purchase (redeem) the land of a deceased relative, marry his widow, and produce offspring—the first of whom would be the heir of the man who had died. Thus a "redeemer" could restore to a widow a degree of security and status she could not of herself attain and even provide for continuation of the seed. Understanding this meaning deepens our appreciation for the prophets' use of the word *redeemer* (Heb., *go'el*) to characterize our Savior (TG, "Jesus Christ, Redeemer").

Naomi recognized all the potential and guided the follow-up action throughout the harvests.

3:1–5 Then Naomi her mother in law said . . . My daughter, shall I not seek rest for thee, that it may be well with thee?

Naomi suggested that Ruth consider a levirate marriage (Ruth 3:1*a*). It was proper for Naomi to propose this option because she was the responsible parent. She knew the threshing would be done during the time of evening breezes. For Ruth to return thereafter and lie at his feet as a humble servant would bring her status to Boaz's attention, and Naomi was confident that he would tell Ruth what to do. There would have been moral danger in such proceedings except for the known character of Ruth and Boaz—in which Naomi implicitly trusted.

3:6–9 And he said, Who art thou? And she answered, I am Ruth thine handmaid: spread therefore thy skirt over thine handmaid; for thou art a near kinsman

When Boaz awoke from his sleep by the pile of grain (which he and the others were guarding, as was customary at harvest time), he was startled by Ruth's presence. She was direct in her response, for the Hebrew word meaning "skirt" is also the word meaning "wing." Her request therefore was not unlike our idiom, "take me under your wing": it was a proposal of marriage.

*3:10–18 And he said, Blessed be thou of the Lord, my daughter:
. . . fear not; I will do to thee all that thou requirest: for all . . . doth
know that thou art a virtuous woman*

Boaz responded graciously, generously, and properly, appreciating her honest choice in seeking security for herself and her mother-in-law. But there was another *go'el* with a precedent claim that he would respect, so he promised sincerely to do the redeemer's duty by this virtuous woman if the other man refused.

He sent with her a quantity of grain as a token to her mother-in-law near morning, while it was yet too dark for anyone to recognize her, thus safeguarding her reputation. Naomi comprehended fully, confident the matter would be concluded that very day.

*4:1–10 Then went Boaz up to the gate, and . . . the kinsman . . .
came by . . . And he turned aside, and sat down*

The proceedings were duly accomplished according to the law. The writer has not even preserved the name of that kinsman who was willing to redeem the property but not to marry the widow and raise up a son to the name of the dead. The heir of the dead man would get the redeemed property, and thus it would not increase the redeemer's estate; hence he said selfishly, "I cannot redeem it for myself, lest I mar mine own inheritance" (Ruth 4:6).

*4:11–12 And all the people . . . said . . . The Lord make the woman
that is come into thine house like Rachel and like Leah*

The wish of the witnesses at the gate for the bride-to-be proved to be prophetic: the marriage would indeed be as fruitful as that of their ancestral grandmothers and that of the young widow Tamar, who bore an ancestor of Boaz (Ruth 4:18a).

*4:13–17 So Boaz took Ruth, and she was his wife: and . . . the Lord
gave her conception*

The wishes of the witnesses were complemented by the blessings of the women upon Naomi and Ruth in celebrating the birth of the baby. The Moabitess Ruth, who did indeed come into the congregation of the Lord (despite Deut. 23:3), became part of the royal line of Judah; numbered among her descendants would be kings of Israel and Judah and our Redeemer, King of the world.

4:18–22 Now these are the generations of Pharez

A writer after the birth of David may have added this genealogical list to clarify all the connections from Pharez through Boaz to David. (David's history begins in 1 Sam. 16.)

Thanks to the Lord may appropriately be offered for inspiring the writing and preservation of the book of Ruth; it provides more inspiration than does most of the book of Judges.

FIRST SAMUEL

The first book of Samuel contains a historic announcement: "all Israel from Dan even to Beer-sheba knew that Samuel was established to be a prophet of the Lord" (1 Sam. 3:20). For the first time since the days of Moses and Joshua, the tribes became somewhat united, first under the prophet Samuel and then under the first two kings, Saul and David. Samuel was an inspired judge and a prophet, able to motivate the people to defense or to repentance. He influenced Israel to begin again to become the holy people they were called to be (Ex. 19:5–6).

When the people first requested a king (1 Sam. 8), Samuel reasoned with them, comparing civil government to the government of the Lord and warning them against it; but they persisted, and the Lord granted their wish. Samuel was inspired to choose Saul, of whom he said, "See ye him whom the Lord hath chosen, that there is none like him among all the people?" (1 Sam. 10:24).

But Samuel and Saul were not able to convert Israel to be the "peculiar treasure" and "holy nation" intended (BD, "Abraham, Covenant of"; "Peculiar"). Samuel's own sons diminished his potential effectiveness, and Saul deteriorated from a man of faith and humble confidence to one imbued with vain jealousy, violence, and spiritual degeneration to the tragedy of his suicide.

As Saul's behavior worsened, the Lord, through Samuel, chose and prepared David to become king (1 Sam. 16). Saul jealously tried to assassinate David, and finally, without divine guidance or hope, Saul went into his last battle against the Philistines and died by his own sword.

Some facets of this part of Israel's history are exemplary, but many are not.

COMMENTARY

1:1–2 Now there was a certain man . . . and his name was Elkanah . . . And he had two wives; the name of one was Hannah

Elkanah and Hannah were the parents-to-be of Samuel. According to later genealogical lists, Samuel's father was of the tribe of Levi living in Ephraim. Samuel did function as a priest as well as a prophet (1 Chr. 6:16–28).

1:3–18 And this man went up . . . yearly to worship and to sacrifice unto the Lord of hosts in Shiloh

The first book of Samuel opens with the situation that led to his birth as a child of promise. As with Sarah, Rebekah, Rachel, and others, Hannah was not blessed with children at first, despite her prayers and sacrifices. She and her husband took the matter to the Lord when they went to worship at Shiloh, the site of the old tabernacle of the congregation (Josh. 18:1; BD, "Tabernacle"). Childlessness was considered a curse and motherhood a blessing, so Hannah prayed in deep sorrow, promising that if she had a son he would be given as a Nazarite to the Lord. The old priest, Eli, mistook her profound emotion for drunkenness (1 Sam. 1:11*d;* BD, "Nazarite"). She protested that she was not such a "daughter of Belial" (BD, "Belial"), and Eli relented and promised she would be blessed.

1:19–28 Elkanah knew Hannah his wife; and the Lord remembered her. Wherefore . . . she bare a son, and called his name Samuel, saying, Because I have asked him of the Lord

The name *Samuel* (Heb., *Shmu'el)* could be a contraction of "heard of God" or even "requested from God." True to her promise, and with gratitude, Hannah gave Samuel into the care of the priestly family at Shiloh after he was weaned.

2:1–10 And Hannah prayed, and said, My heart rejoiceth in the Lord, mine horn is exalted in the Lord

Hannah's poetic song of thanksgiving, with its prophetic insight and appreciation, is in some ways like Mary's (Luke 1:46–55). In poetic parallels and figurative phrases she praises God, his powers, and goodness. Her language is sometimes terse but always clear; for instance, she knows that birth, life, death, and resurrection are all prerogatives of the Lord (1 Sam. 2:5–6). She prophesies of the ultimate kingdom, when the Lord will be acclaimed as ruler, judge, and kingmaker. The "horn" symbolizes the power of the "anointed" one. Hannah was a prophetess.

2:11 And the child did minister unto the Lord before Eli

Simply translated, the Hebrew says, "And the lad was serving the Lord within the presence of Eli the priest."

2:12–17 Now the sons of Eli were sons of Belial; they knew not the Lord

Belial was an epithet meaning "worthlessness, evil"; the English translators capitalized it as if it were a cognomen for Satan, and, indeed, in New Testament times, Paul apparently so used it (2 Cor. 6:15; BD, "Belial"). The immoral and blasphemous acts of the sons of Eli justified the label.

2:18–21 But Samuel ministered before the Lord . . . girded with a linen ephod

In contrast to Eli's own sons, the child Samuel was dutiful in his training and service. He wore the new robe his mother made for him each year and the apronlike ephod (BD, "Ephod"). Eli blessed Samuel's happy parents to have more children, and Samuel grew "with the Lord" (1 Sam. 2:21, translation mine).

2:22–25 Now Eli was very old, and heard all that his sons did unto all Israel

Eli knew of his sons' grave violations not only of their priestly privileges (they had the right to certain portions of flesh and other food items offered in sacrifice, but they took more than allowed and demanded choice parts) but also of the commandments (their abuse of women worshippers emulated the behavior of the priests of fertility cults in Canaan). The priest reproved his sons, but he did not effectively restrain them. The tragic results of his failings and their faults became evident later (1 Sam. 2:27–36; 3:11–14; 4:12–22).

2:26 And the child Samuel grew on, and was in favour both with the Lord, and also with men

Again Samuel's good development was contrasted to that of Eli's sons. Compare the brief description of Jesus' growing up (Luke 2:52).

2:27–36 And there came a man of God unto Eli, and said

The Lord knows what people are wont to do, and he communicates warnings through his spokesmen. The "man of God" who warned Eli is typical of many such prophets throughout the Old Testament; their names are sometimes given, but often they are not. His message was plain and must have been devastating to hear.

The promised "faithful priest" was Samuel, but thereafter another priestly line was to be established (1 Sam. 2:27–36 and fn.; BD, "Eli"; "Zadok").

3:1–15 And the child Samuel ministered unto the Lord before Eli. And the word of the Lord was precious in those days; there was no open vision

Samuel's ministry as a prophet, priest, and judge was needed in those apostate times. The downward spiral of apostasy in the days of the judges left the "word of the Lord" and "open vision" "precious"—both rare and valuable.

Young Samuel was sleeping near the doors he was to open each morning at the tabernacle—where the ark of God was— when a new dispensation dawned. He heard his name called, and after two calls and some confusion he learned from Eli that it could be a call from the Lord. He received first the bad tidings for Eli.

3:16–18 Then Eli called Samuel, and said, . . . What is the thing that the Lord hath said unto thee?

Samuel feared to report until Eli adjured him to hide nothing of the Lord's message. When Eli did receive the dread warning, he humbly accepted it, saying, "He is Jehovah; what is good in his eyes let him do!" (1 Sam. 3:18, translation mine). Eli was a well-meaning man who had not been firm enough with his sons and in humility felt his punishment was just.

3:19–21 And Samuel grew, and the Lord was with him, and did let none of his words fall to the ground. And all Israel from Dan even to Beer-sheba knew that Samuel was established to be a prophet of the Lord.

Thus began a new dispensation. The Lord continued to reveal his word to Samuel at Shilo and to fulfill it. "Let none of his words fall to the ground" means the Lord let none of his words fail. News of the new prophet in Israel soon spread.

4:1–11 And the word of Samuel came to all Israel

But before Samuel could teach the Israelites to repent and thus qualify for divine assistance, they tried to enlist the Lord's help by taking the ark out to battle. Instead, the armies of the Israelites were decimated, and the Philistines, stimulated by fear, captured the ark. Truly, the ark had no place in battle. Its proper use was in its holy place in worship and communication with the Lord (BD, "Ark of the Covenant"; "Mercy Seat"). Later, Samuel was able to teach Israel how to get the help of the Lord to "deliver [them] out of the hand of the Philistines" (1 Sam. 7:3).

4:12–18 And when Eli heard the noise of the crying, he said, What meaneth the noise of this tumult? And the man came in hastily, and told Eli

A messenger from the war gave a threefold tragic report: Israel had fled before the Philistines because of a great slaughter, Eli's two wicked sons were dead, and—the ultimate shock to him—the ark had been taken. Eli collapsed, fell backward from his seat by the gate at Shilo, and died.

The old tabernacle at Shilo ceased to be a sanctuary at that time. In King Saul's time, there was something of a shrine at Nob, some twenty-five miles southward. Destruction of the tabernacle thereafter, though not recorded here, was still being told centuries later (Jer. 7:12; 26:6).

4:19–22 His [Eli's] daughter in law, Phinehas' wife, was with child, near to be delivered: and when she heard the tidings . . . bowed herself and travailed; . . . And she named the child I-chabod, saying, The glory is departed from Israel

There is pathos in the account of the birth and naming of Ichabod, grandson of Eli. The wife of the infamous Phinehas appears to have been a righteous woman. She knew that her husband and father-in-law were both dead, but she lamented especially that "the glory is departed from Israel: because the ark of God was taken." With her last breath she named her baby *Ichabod,* meaning "Where is the glory?" (1 Sam. 4:21*a*).

5:1–12 And the Philistines took the ark of God, and brought it from Eben-ezer unto Ashdod . . . [and] to Ekron

The victorious Philistines with some awe placed the ark of the Lord as a trophy in the temple of Dagon at Ashdod; but when they and their idol suffered as a result, they passed it on to the Philistines at Gath and then to Ekron. When the people in those cities were smitten, they proposed to send the ark "again to his own place" (1 Sam. 5:11, 6*a*).

6:1–21 And the ark of the Lord was in the country of the Philistines seven months

The Philistine priests and diviners recommended that the ark be sent back to Israel with an offering of golden images of the tumors they had suffered and of the "mice that mar the land"

(1 Sam. 6:5); but they also suggested the things be sent in a way to test whether there was really supernatural power associated with it. If cows not trained to work were yoked to the cart to carry the ark while their calves were confined at home and if the cows then pulled the cart up the road to Israel, the Philistines would know that a supernatural power was involved. The cows went indeed, bearing the trespass offering on behalf of all five Philistine city-states (1 Sam. 6:17).

Of the men of Beth-shemesh who were smitten for the sacrilege of looking into the ark, the Hebrew account states: "And he smote among the people seventy men, fifty thousand men" (1 Sam. 6:19; literal translation mine). That is not a proper Hebrew expression of the number 50,070, and Josephus (*Antiquities of the Jews* 6:1:4), as well as some Hebrew manuscripts, reads simply, "seventy men." Some translate the Hebrew as "seventy men, fifty chiefs"; but though the words for "thousand" and "chief" are of the same root, they are not the same form. The village of Beth-shemesh could hardly have had 50,070 inhabitants; so the problem remains, and we can believe the account "as far as it is translated correctly" (A of F 8).

7:1–2 And the men of Kirjath-jearim came, and fetched up the ark of the Lord, and brought it into the house of Abinadab . . . and sanctified Eleazar his son to keep the ark of the Lord

Nothing is given at this point about the identity of the man in whose house the ark was kept for twenty years; however, Josephus asserts he was a Levite by birth. Oddly enough, Beth-shemesh was a Levitical city, but Kirjath-jearim was not.

Note that Israel felt the loss of the Spirit (1 Sam. 7:2).

7:3–14 And Samuel spake unto all the house of Israel, saying, If ye do return unto the Lord with all your hearts, then put away the strange gods and Ashtaroth from among you, and prepare your hearts unto the Lord, and serve him only: and he will deliver you out of the hand of the Philistines

Samuel sought to renew the covenant, gathering all of Israel for a great conference at Mizpeh, in fasting and prayer. For a time the Israelites did put away the Baalim and Ashtaroth (male and female idols) to serve the Lord only. They experienced the promised blessing when the Philistines attacked again, for Samuel told them to pray while he offered a sacrifice of supplication. The Lord "thundered with a great thunder . . . upon the Philistines, and discomfited them" (1 Sam. 7:10). The Philistines were driven out and did not attack again during Samuel's administration. After Samuel was replaced by a king, however, the Philistine depredations resumed.

7:15–17 And Samuel judged Israel all the days of his life.

Samuel served Israel by traveling from city to city, including his home city of Ramah, where he also built an altar for worship.

8:1–5 when Samuel was old . . . he made his sons judges

Unfortunately, Samuel's sons were not of his character, and they perverted judgment for bribes. That was one factor that led the people to ask for a king; but they also wanted a king to lead them like the kings who led the other nations.

8:6–22 they have not rejected thee, but they have rejected me, that I should not reign over them

Perhaps partly because the Israelites had suffered attacks by neighboring kings for generations, they felt a need for a king to judge them and lead them in battle; but it was tragic that they thereby rejected direct leadership by the Lord. Nevertheless, the Lord instructed Samuel to grant their request, respecting their agency even though it would not be best for them (D&C 88:65). If their priests had been faithful, the people responsible, and the judges fair, the Israelite government after Moses and Joshua could have been a peaceful theocracy. Samuel's warning speech about the dangers of monarchy was inspired. His warnings pertain not only to kings but also to autocrats or dictators. Yet the people insisted; so, under the Lord's command and guidance, Samuel selected a king.

Centuries later, when Israel had indeed become like other

nations spiritually as well as politically, they were conquered and exiled.

9:1–27 there was a man of Benjamin, whose name was Kish, . . . And he had a son, whose name was Saul, a choice young man

Even though the people had made a bad choice in rejecting the Lord that he "should not reign over them" (1 Sam. 8:7), and though the Lord had directed Samuel to "protest solemnly unto them" (1 Sam. 8:9) and they refused to hearken, yet in wisdom and grace the Lord appointed a choice candidate for king in Israel (1 Sam. 9:2). The narrative is clear about the meeting of Samuel and Saul and the preparation of Saul for his awesome responsibility.

In addition to the historical shift in the terms *prophet* and *seer,* here mentioned, there are some specific differences in the meaning of the two titles (1 Sam. 9:9; BD, "Prophet"; "Seer").

10:1–16 Then Samuel took a vial of oil, and poured it upon his head, and kissed him, and said, Is it not because the Lord hath anointed thee to be captain over his inheritance?

Saul of Benjamin was called by prophecy and anointed by the prophet of the Lord to become king in Israel. It was done in secret first so that the choice of the Lord could be properly disclosed in public later (1 Sam. 9:25–27; 10:1, 17–27).

The term *captain* is used to translate the Hebrew word *nagid,* meaning "leader" or "prince."

The Israelites are called the Lord's "inheritance" in a metaphor implying that they should be his servants from generation to generation (1 Sam. 10:1; Deut. 32:9: 1 Kgs. 8:51–53).

Kings properly chosen to rule in Israel were anointed with oil to become king, and in that sense they were the anointed of the Lord (Heb., *meshiach,* "messiah"); but only the divine Messiah will be the ultimate King.

God gave Saul "another heart" when "the Spirit of God came upon him" (1 Sam. 10:9a; 10:10); contrast his behavior under the aegis of that Spirit with his behavior after the Spirit departed and another spirit "not of the Lord" came upon him (1 Sam. 16:14–16 and fn.).

The "prophesying" by a company of prophets who met Saul was the chanting of poems or songs as psalms of praise with accompaniment by musical instruments. Prophets may preach, teach, admonish, praise, predict, or warn—as inspired by the Lord. Saul was inspired to join the company of prophets temporarily.

10:17–27 Samuel called the people together unto the Lord to Mizpeh

Samuel gathered Israel to Mizpeh again for a historic event (recall 1 Sam. 7:5–12). He reminded them that they had in one sense rejected their God, who had so often saved them, by insisting on an earthly king; but he then demonstrated the Lord's choice of a king for them, indicating the tribe, family, and person. Saul was finally found hiding among the baggage of the people. He was an impressive choice, standing head and shoulders above other men.

Samuel not only announced the Lord's choice of king but also made the occasion a kind of constitutional convention, for he "told the people the manner of the kingdom, and wrote it in a book, and laid it up before the Lord" (1 Sam. 10:25). Recall the prophetic instructions for Israelite kings given by Moses (Deut. 17:14–20). The consenting, sustaining voice of the people was also a factor, as seen in the installation of kings Saul, David, Solomon, and Rehoboam (1 Sam. 10:24).

Samuel then sent the people home, and Saul went home also, but "there went with him a band of men, whose hearts God had touched" (1 Sam. 10:26).

Another evidence of Saul's humble character was shown when "he held his peace," even when certain unbelievers ("children of Belial") despised him and gave him no presents. Later in life, it will be seen, he lost that admirable humility.

11:1–13 Then Nahash the Ammonite came up, and encamped against Jabesh-gilead

An Ammonite who threatened the Israelites east of the Jordan and proposed to blind their right eyes and enslave them, as a stigma upon Israel, was the first to challenge King Saul. The Spirit of God came upon Saul when he heard the threat, and he met the challenge with decisiveness and dispatch. The prophet Samuel was still associated with him in leadership (1 Sam. 11:7).

When King Saul had vanquished the foe, some enthusiastic supporters wanted to punish those who had rejected him; but Saul showed magnanimity towards his people and humble recognition of the help of God, saying, "There shall not a man be put to death this day: for to day the Lord hath wrought salvation in Israel" (1 Sam. 11:12–13; 10:27).

11:14–15 Then said Samuel to the people, Come, and let us go to Gilgal, and renew the kingdom there

This time "all the people" sustained and confirmed Saul as king. They made this new start at Gilgal, where Israel had first entered the promised land, and a monument to the Lord's help was raised (Josh. 4:19–24).

12:1–25 And Samuel said unto all Israel

Samuel clarified his role and status with the people, challenging them to indict him if he had treated anyone unrighteously. He reminded them that the Lord had delivered them from bondage, and he recalled some of the leaders the Lord had provided, reassuring them that though they had turned from the Lord as their only King, he would not reject them if they were obedient to his laws and revelations (1 Sam.12:1–15). Samuel gave them a miraculous demonstration of the Lord's ratification of his words, and then, while they remained in their humbled state, he assured them that he would continue to teach them the Lord's "good and the right way" (1 Sam. 12:16–23). He ended with a warning and a challenge to the new kingdom of Israel.

13:1 Saul reigned one year; and when he had reigned two years over Israel

Problems of chronology arise here. How much time passed from Saul's anointing as a young man, who was out seeking his father's lost asses (1 Sam. 9:15–10:10), until the time of the public announcement at Mizpeh? (1 Sam. 10:17–26.) Also, how much time elapsed from that announcement until the Ammonite war and the public sustaining of King Saul at Gilgal? (1 Sam. 11:14–15). The problems arise because the translation of 1 Samuel 13:1 states "Saul reigned one year; and when he had reigned two years," the events related in chapter 13 occurred; but Saul was by then a mature man with a mature son, Jonathan, in the army with him (1 Sam. 13:3, 16). Perhaps these events happened two years after the confirmation of Saul's kingship at Gilgal.

13:2–22 And Jonathan smote the garrison of the Philistines that was in Geba

Much time must have passed since the Lord "discomfited" the Philistines at the launching of Samuel's ministry at Mizpeh, after which they "came no more into the coast of Israel . . . all the days of Samuel" (while he was sole leader; 1 Sam. 7:10–13). Jonathan seized the initiative and smote the garrison, but when Israel prepared to follow up, the Philistines mustered such a formidable force that the Israelites melted away. Saul needed Samuel and the Lord, and when the prophet did not appear at the appointed time, the king offered an offering without priesthood authority. When Samuel did arrive, he saw the king's assumption of priestly prerogatives as a very serious innovation and warned Saul that he and his family would not continue as rulers in Israel; indeed, the Lord had already chosen another.

Thus it was that a disheartened, poorly equipped king and a mere six hundred soldiers faced the Philistine invader. Lack of metal armaments in Israel were part of the problem, for the Philistines kept a monopoly in iron work. Only Saul and Jonathan had swords; the weapons of the others would have been of wood and stone (1 Sam. 13:19–23).

14:1–23 And Jonathan said to the young man that bare his armour, Come, and let us go over unto the garrison of these uncircumcised: it may be that the Lord will work for us: for there is no restraint to the Lord to save by many or by few

In spite of all, the courageous and faithful Jonathan launched a private raid that routed the Philistines. The Lord did save by only a few. Meanwhile, Saul wondered about the noise among the enemy, found out about Jonathan's absence, and joined the pursuit. Israelites rallied who had hidden or deserted (1 Sam. 14:21*a;* 14:22*a*).

14:24–52 the men of Israel were distressed that day: for Saul had adjured the people, saying, Cursed be the man that eateth any food until evening, that I may be avenged on mine enemies. So none of the people tasted any food

Conscience-stricken, King Saul had tried to get the Lord's help in battle by proclaiming a fast, but obviously the time for preparation was past and the time for action was at hand—as evidenced by Jonathan. Yet after Jonathan's raid and the resultant rout, Saul asked the Lord whether he should follow up and break the Philistine power. He received no answer and assumed the Lord was angry with Israel. Learning that Jonathan had eaten some food, Saul reasoned that the Lord was angry with Jonathan and he must be punished, even though he had not known of the fast and the Lord had helped him rout the Philistines. Saul had deteriorated in spirit since the time when he had refused to punish even the offenders who had opposed him (1 Sam. 11:1–15). Fortunately, the will of the people could still prevail over the will of the king, and Jonathan was saved.

A summary of Saul's former achievements, his family, and his connections concludes the chapter.

15:1–35 I remember that which Amalek did to Israel . . . Now go and smite Amalek, and utterly destroy all that they have

The episode with Amalek was one more challenge for King Saul. The account of it has some problems, however. Although it is true that the Amalekites in the days of Moses were the first to attack Israel in the wilderness, punishment of their descendants several centuries later was not according to God's law (Deut. 24:16).

It is not clear that Saul's saving some animals for sacrifice was a capital sin, although the lesson taught is valid: "to obey is better than sacrifice, and to hearken than the fat of rams" (1 Sam. 15:22). Saul's confession, "I have sinned . . . because I feared the people, and obeyed their voice," does indicate an uncharacteristic weakness in leadership. But the dread message to Saul was final: "the Lord hath rent the kingdom of Israel from thee this day, and hath given it to a neighbor of thine." That decree stood even though Saul humbly sought forgiveness and though Samuel himself mourned for him (1 Sam. 15:28–31, 35).

The old prophet Samuel then resolutely took a sword and "hewed Agag in pieces before the Lord." The verb translated by the phrase "hewed in pieces" occurs only in this place in the Bible, and its meaning is not certain. "Before the Lord" may mean he did it by the altar.

The last problem passage states that "the Lord repented that he had made Saul king" (1 Sam 15:35). It is well known that the Lord "will not lie nor repent"; that truth is stated only six verses earlier (1 Sam. 15:29). The Joseph Smith Translation renders verse 35 as "the Lord rent the kingdom from Saul whom he had made king over Israel" (JST 1 Sam. 15:35).

16:1–16 the Lord said unto Samuel, How long wilt thou mourn for Saul . . . ? fill thine horn with oil, and go . . . to Jesse the Bethlehemite: for I have provided me a king among his sons

Samuel mourned Saul's deterioration and rejection, but he accepted it and obeyed the Lord's errand to go anoint a future king. Samuel knew that Saul would be jealous of his successor's royal status and likely violent because of his rejection and replacement by someone better (1 Sam. 13:13–14; 15:28); therefore only his sacrificial duty was announced. It is curious that the elders of Bethlehem were fearful of the prophet's errand and inquired if it were peaceable (1 Sam. 16:4–5).

Even in a prophet's evaluations, we can note the difference between man's power to discern and God's power to know (1 Sam. 16:7).

After David was anointed, "the Spirit of the Lord came upon David from that day forward"; but for other reasons, "the Spirit of the Lord departed from Saul" (1 Sam. 16:13–14). The incongruity of an "evil spirit from the Lord" is removed in the Joseph Smith Translation text (1 Sam. 16:14–16*a*).

16:14–23 command thy servants . . . to seek out a man, who is a cunning player on an harp; . . . when the evil spirit . . . is upon thee . . . he shall play . . . and thou shalt be well

It is a classic irony that David, the one chosen to replace Saul, was also the one chosen to heal his spiritual affliction.

Unfortunately, David's status as a loved and trusted comforter and armor-bearer to the king soon changed—and tragically.

17:1–54 Now the Philistines gathered together their armies to battle . . . And there went out a champion out of the camp of the Philistines, named Goliath

The story of David and Goliath is one of the best known stories in the Bible, so probably little comment on it is warranted. Note the circumstances that took David's brothers into the army and David back to his shepherd's work for a time but then brought him into the crucial contest of champions (1 Sam. 17:12–37).

David's faith and his experiences in guarding his flocks left him surprised at the Israelites' fear of the blasphemous challenger, Goliath—and perfectly confident that he could meet such a challenge. It is of course not surprising that some, especially his brothers, scoffed; indeed, it is somewhat surprising that Saul believed in David. Saul had been a very religious man, however, and there were still times when the evil spirit did not dominate him.

Naturally Saul thought it well to arm David as well as possible, and David put the armor on. It is not surprising that when he "assayed [tried] to go" in it, he could not. He could not trust it either, for he had not "proved" it; so he trusted what he had proved: his sling and stones and his faith in the Lord (1 Sam. 17:37, 45).

The covenant relationship of Israel and the Lord was evidently known to David; he believed that if the Israelites did what was required, God would do his part to save them, for his own sake as well as for theirs (1 Sam. 17:45–47). The outcome is well known.

17:55–58 And when Saul saw David go forth against the Philistine, he said unto Abner, . . . whose son is this youth?

It appears that Saul had forgotten whose son David was (1 Sam. 16:18–21), perhaps because of his spiritual and mental illness; or it may have been that Saul was so impressed with David that he wished to learn more about his background. (One hypothesis holds that this inconsistency remains from two unco-ordinated traditions—if that is of any value.)

18:1– 4 the soul of Jonathan was knit with the soul of David

One admirable development in the story of Saul and David was the covenant of love and cooperation between Jonathan and David, who ordinarily should have been rivals. The knowledge of David's appointment to become king created no jealousy in Jonathan. Indeed, the transfer of his robe, garments, girdle, sword, and bow to David seems to symbolize Jonathan's willing yielding of his natural claim to the throne, which he made explicit later (1 Sam. 23:17).

18:5–16 And Saul eyed David from that day and forward

Although Saul at first trusted David and sent him on important military missions, David's conscientiousness and success soon aroused Saul's jealousy. It is pathetic to see the character of the formerly strong, noble, and yet humble Saul degenerate into one of fear, insecurity, envy, jealousy, and anger.

18:17–30 her will I give to thee to wife

Saul attempted to contrive David's death at the hands of the enemy while he was securing tokens of success in combat with a hundred or more of them. David, unsuspecting, went out to battle with the Philistines and returned with twice the number required. As a reward, Saul gave his daughter Michal to David as a wife.

Several times it is mentioned that "David behaved himself wisely"; doubtless his faith, the Spirit of the Lord, and his intelligence made his wise and confident actions possible. But David's good qualities only disturbed Saul more and more.

19:1–24 And Saul spake to Jonathan his son, and to all his servants, that they should kill David

The noble Jonathan, loyal both to his father and to David, dissuaded Saul from shedding innocent blood (1 Sam. 19:5–6), and for a time David and Saul were together "as in times past." But David's success in another war revived Saul's jealous and evil spirit. Forsaking all reason, promises, and responsibilities, he tried to kill David with a javelin while David played music to soothe him. The Joseph Smith Translation emends that report: "And the evil spirit which was not of the Lord was upon Saul" (JST 1 Sam. 19:9). Michal, the daughter by whom Saul had hoped to entrap David, was a true wife to David and sent him away at her own peril. Saul accepted her reasons for a time but later took vengeance.

Saul next attempted to seize David at Samuel's dwelling place at Naioth, in Ramah, where David had taken refuge. A spiritual phenomenon saved him from the emissaries and even from Saul himself. A religious exercise of singing or chanting praises to God was again called "prophesying" (1 Sam. 19:20–24; commentary on 1 Sam. 10:1–16). Saul joined in but was soon apparently overcome by the evil spirit, which caused him to strip and lie inert.

20:1– 42 And David fled from Naioth in Ramah, and came and said before Jonathan, What have I done? what is mine iniquity? . . . So Jonathan made a covenant with the house of David

Jonathan offered to do anything David required, so they planned signals to indicate danger for David. Thus Jonathan made a covenant of friendship "with the house of David" in full faith that David would show kindness to the house of Jonathan forever; and both promises were kept (1 Sam. 20:14–17, 42; 2 Sam. 9; 21:7). The covenant was made in full knowledge that David was the heir-apparent to the kingship, which Jonathan approved in spite of his father's outrage (1 Sam. 20:30–34; 23:17). Mutual trust and personal regard, not sentiment or politics, were at the foundation of their covenant.

21:1–9 Then came David to Nob to Ahimelech the priest

The shrine at Nob, where a number of men of the priestly clan of Eli remained, seems to have substituted for the tabernacle at Shiloh, which ceased to function after the ark of the covenant was taken away (1 Sam. 5). At Nob, the priests had the hallowed bread, or shewbread (BD, "Shewbread"), an ephod (part of the high priest's garments), and Goliath's sword, which was apparently preserved there as a memento of David's earlier triumph in the name of the Lord. When David persuaded the priest to let him and his men have some of the sacred bread and take the sword, the priest was blameless, for he had no reason to know David was fleeing from the king. (Recall Jesus' use of this event in justifying to the Pharisees his disciples' picking and eating grain on the Sabbath; Matt. 12:1–4). Saul's Edomite herdsman who observed the favors done for David contributed to a tragedy later by testifying, for his own reasons, against the priest (1 Sam. 21:7; 22:9–19).

21:10–15 And David arose, and fled that day for fear of Saul, and went to Achish the king of Gath

It may seem strange that David would take refuge with the Philistines, but because Saul was the enemy of both Achish and David, David may have hoped Achish would treat him as an ally. When he heard the servants of Achish declaring his former exploits and his heirship to the throne, David contrived a way to appear to be harmless so that he could flee.

22:1–2 David . . . escaped to the cave Adullam: . . . And every one that was in distress . . . in debt, and . . . discontented, gathered themselves unto him

Fellow refugees and malcontents who joined him at Adullam in the valley of Elah became a nucleus of supporters that increased steadily (1 Sam. 23:13).

22:3–5 And David went thence to Mizpeh of Moab

David sought sanctuary for his parents in Moab, which the

king of Moab granted. Whether David's great-grandmother Ruth's having been a Moabitess had any bearing on this choice of refuge is not known. Possibly the Moabite king was willing to befriend David because of his prowess and his being Israel's future king. David also had the help of a prophet named Gad to advise him.

22:6–23 Saul said unto his servants . . . will the son of Jesse give every one of you fields and vineyards, and make you all captains

Saul bitterly resented that many of his people, and even his own son, appeared to be more loyal to David than to him. But his challenging questions gave an opportunity to Doeg, his Edomite servant, to ingratiate himself with Saul by telling of the help David had received from the priest at Nob (1 Sam. 21:7; Ps. 52). Enraged, Saul caused the whole priestly clan there to be slain by the same Edomite when the Israelite soldiers would not lift their swords against priests. Eighty-five priests, the whole city of Nob, and all their animals were slain. Only the priest Abiathar escaped, and he joined David. David regretted the tragedy and retained Abiathar as his priest for most of the rest of his career (1 Sam. 22:20*a*).

23:1–15 Then they told David . . . the Philistines fight against Keilah . . . Therefore David inquired of the Lord, saying, Shall I go and smite these Philistines? And the Lord said, . . . Go

Guidance from the Lord was important to David. A warning later helped him escape from Keilah, when citizens who were more loyal to Saul than to David would have betrayed him there.

23:16–18 and thou shalt be king over Israel, and I shall be next unto thee; and that also Saul my father knoweth

How and when Saul and Jonathan learned that David would be king is not recorded, but they knew before this time (1 Sam. 23:17*a*). The commitment of Jonathan is again evident.

23:19–29 Then came up the Ziphites to Saul to Gibeah, saying, Doth not David hide himself with us

The people of Ziph, a town of Judah south of Hebron, would

have betrayed David to Saul, but someone told David, and he fled a few miles farther south to the desert of Maon to escape. While another Philistine raid diverted Saul, David's little band retreated eastward, down the wadis toward the Dead Sea, and encamped at a rare freshwater spring, En-gedi.

24:1–22 David [was] in the wilderness of En-gedi. Then Saul took three thousand chosen men . . . and went to seek David

The wilderness of En-gedi was one of two places where David refused to lift up his hand to remove "the anointed of the Lord" (1 Sam. 24:6; 26:10–12). Saul's repentance upon hearing David's message and seeing the evidence that David could have killed him was probably sincere, but it did not last. Saul did confirm, however, that he knew David would be the next king; and he obtained David's oath and promise not to destroy Saul's name and seed (1 Sam. 24:20–22; 23:16–18).

David and his men took the precaution to remain at En-Gedi.

25:1 And Samuel died; and all the Israelites were gathered together, and lamented him

Only this simple statement tells the end of the life and work of the great prophet Samuel. Possibly David went to Ramah for the burial of his friend and patron, but he then took refuge farther south in the Negev, in the deserts of Paran.

25:2–44 there was a man in Maon . . . and the man was very great . . . the name of the man was Nabal; and . . . his wife Abigail

Hearing that a wealthy herdsman of Maon was shearing near Carmel (about a mile northward), David and his men went to him for supplies. Shearing time, like harvest, was a time for generosity, and David hoped for favors because his band had really done the shepherds no harm and had given them protection (1 Sam. 25:7, 15–16, 21). But the man was "churlish" (Heb., lit., "hard, rough"); his name was *Nabal* (Heb., lit., "foolish"), and foolish he was. Except for the wisdom and insight of Abigail, David's band would surely have punished Nabal (1 Sam. 25:3, 18, 23–35). As it was, his rage appears to have caused a stroke, and he died ten days later (1 Sam. 25:36–38).

David was grateful to the Lord and impressed with Abigail. He sought her hand in marriage, and she hastened to accept (1 Sam. 25:39–42). Another wife of David, Ahinoam, is mentioned, as well as Michal, who was taken from him by Saul.

26:1–25 And the Ziphites came unto Saul . . . saying, Doth not David hide himself in the hill of Hachilah

The Ziphites, who lived four miles north of Carmel, tried again to betray David to Saul (recall 1 Sam. 23:19–29); but again David escaped and could have slain Saul but for his principles. Note his conviction that only the Lord should remove the Lord's anointed (1 Sam. 26:8–11, 23). Once again Saul confessed his faults and this time acknowledged the great things done by David.

27:1–12 And David said in his heart, I shall now perish one day by the hand of Saul: there is nothing better for me than that I should speedily escape into the land of the Philistines; and Saul shall despair of me

The Bible does not tell only of the exemplary activities of the heroes but tells frankly about their faults as well. Surprisingly, David appears not to have asked counsel of the Lord, either directly or through a priest or prophet, whether he could trust Saul's promise (1 Sam. 26:21). He sought refuge with Achish of Gath on his own. For a year and four months, he and his band of six hundred lived in Philistine lands, deceiving their host by raiding non-Israelite peoples while appearing to Achish to be raiding cities of Judah. The ruse worked, and Achish trusted David to be his ally and Israel's enemy forever (1 Sam. 27:12).

28:1–2 And Achish said unto David, Know thou assuredly that thou shalt go out with me to battle

Because Achish trusted David, he was willing to set him in battle against the Israelites and make him his personal bodyguard

(1 Sam. 28:2*a*). The account of Achish and David is interrupted here but is resumed later (1 Sam. 29).

28:3 Now Samuel was dead . . . And Saul had put away those that had familiar spirits

The short reprise of Samuel's death and of Saul's elimination of others supposed to know about the future sets the stage for Saul's last tragic episode.

28:4–25 And the Philistines gathered themselves together, . . . and Saul gathered all Israel together

The doleful account of the end of King Saul recounts his futile last battle. He could not get divine guidance through legitimate avenues, so he turned to the spurious diviners he had banished in his better days (1 Sam. 28:3, 7 and fn.). There is no reason to suppose that the Lord, who had refused to respond to Saul through legitimate avenues, would then send him a bona fide revelation through the diviner at En-dor. Her vision of "gods ascending out of the earth" may well have been an apparition of the forces of evil that wished to bring about a formerly good man's destruction. Note that Saul himself did not see the "Samuel" described by the medium; he assumed it to be the former prophet (1 Sam. 28:13–14). The message, ostensibly from Samuel, overwhelmed Saul, for it was a combination of truths he could not deny with predictions he could not dismiss. Ironically the compassion of the diviner-woman then persuaded the fear-racked and emaciated Saul to take nourishment and rest to prepare for his dreadful and fateful day.

29:1–11 Now the Philistines gathered together all their armies to Aphek: and the Israelites pitched . . . in Jezreel

More than forty miles separated the Philistines gathering on the coastal plain from the Israelites in the rich north central valleys of Jezreel. Though David had won the confidence of Achish, the other princes of the Philistine confederacy were skeptical of his loyalty to their cause, so David was not allowed to go into battle against Saul and Israel.

30:1–31 when David and his men were come to Ziklag . . . the Amalekites had . . . smitten Ziklag, and burned it

David's city of refuge was raided by the ever-threatening Amalekites while he was away. He sought divine guidance through the priest Abiathar, with the ephod, and was assured that he should go to the rescue of his people (1 Sam. 30:8).

David's men found abandoned a sick Egyptian servant of the Amalekites, revived him with food and drink, and with his help found the raiders; they recovered all the captives and goods.

Some of David's men, exhausted by the eighty-mile trek from Aphek to Ziklag and on to Besor (1 Sam. 29:1–3, 11; 30:1, 10), could not continue. Therefore David established the generous principle that they also serve who watch the camp and goods while others fight (1 Sam. 30:22–25).

From Amalekite spoil, taken in addition to their own goods, David and his men sent favors to friendly elders in cities of Judah, doubtless for political reasons (1 Sam. 30:26–31).

31:1–13 Now the Philistines fought against Israel: and the men of Israel fled . . . and fell down slain in mount Gilboa

Saul was wounded, his sons were dead, and when he was unable to persuade his armorbearer to kill him, he became one of the few suicides reported in scripture; his loyal armorbearer followed him in death (1 Sam. 30:1–6; see a different account in 2 Sam. 1:1–10, given by an Amalekite who hoped for favors from David). The Philistines made their deepest inroads into Israel at that time, taking many cities. When they found the bodies of Saul and his sons, they sent his head and armor as trophies to Philistine temples and cities and fastened the bodies to the wall at Beth-shan. The inhabitants of Jabesh-gilead, to honor the great Saul they had known in former times (1 Sam. 11), retrieved the bodies, burned them, and buried the remains under a tree in their city. David's eulogy and lament for Saul and Jonathan follow in 2 Samuel 1:17–27.

So ends the first book of Samuel. Obviously it was not all written by Samuel, for his death was recounted before the end of the first book and the second book of Samuel follows. Perhaps the books covering an era influenced by him were given his name, much as the plates of Nephi continued to be written long after Nephi's death (Book of Mormon Index, "Plates of Nephi, Large").

SECOND SAMUEL

The second book of Samuel continues the narrative of the first book of Samuel, which ended with the death of Saul and the succession of David. Like that of Saul, the history of David is heroic but ultimately tragic, though in ways and for reasons that are quite different. The prophet Samuel's announcement of David's call was "the Lord hath sought him a man after his own heart" (1 Sam. 13:14). And yet, after his moral and spiritual downfall, David had to be admonished and reproached by the prophet Nathan: "Wherefore hast thou despised the commandment of the Lord, to do evil in his sight? . . . by this deed thou hast given great occasion to the enemies of the Lord to blaspheme" (2 Sam. 12:9, 14).

The second book of Samuel opens with an account of Saul's death that is different from the one recorded in 1 Samuel 31:1–6. The second account was reported by an Amalekite, whose motives and whose role in Israel's ranks can only be guessed. Second Samuel continues with David's installation as king over Judah first and then over all Israel. It relates his zealous actions in restoring the ark to a central place in the kingdom and in Israel's religious life. It tells of his extension of the kingdom to the promised boundaries; but it also recounts the indulgences and sins that led to his fall from honor and grace.

Many of the psalms of the Old Testament are identified with David and allude to situations in his life reported in the books of Samuel. Some historical information, supplementary to these accounts, is found in the first book of the Chronicles; such information is cross-referenced in the footnotes to 2 Samuel.

The powers of good, which help one to be good, and the powers of evil, which persuade one to be evil, are both well illustrated in the narratives about David in all his roles—shepherd boy, minstrel, armor bearer, hero, captain, fugitive, king, mighty warrior, sinner, penitent, and poet (BD, "David").

COMMENTARY

1:1–16 on the third day . . . a man came out of the camp of Saul with his clothes rent, and earth upon his head

A lone Amalekite went to David in Ziklag to report the death of Saul and his sons and the defeat of Israel's armies. He claimed credit for aiding Saul in his suicide and brought a royal crown and bracelet to verify his claim, perhaps hoping for favors from David (2 Sam. 4:10). But he did not know David's beliefs about the Lord's anointed, and he suffered for his presumption.

David and his men mourned for Saul, for Jonathan, for the people of the Lord, and for the house of Israel (2 Sam. 1:12).

1:17–27 David lamented with this lamentation over Saul and over Jonathan his son

Verse 18 (set in parentheses) is difficult to understand, though easy to translate: "And he said to teach the sons of Judah [the] bow; behold it is written in the book of the upright" (translation mine). It seems to be a kind of superscription, like those introducing some of the psalms, but it is difficult to relate it to what follows—a lament over Saul and Jonathan—although a bow of Jonathan is mentioned. Perhaps it was kept as a psalm of lament in the book of Jasher.

David honored Saul for his good characteristics and omitted mention of his faults. He probably did not have to invent compliments, however, for it is quite possible that in the early years of Saul's reign (only hints of which were given in 1 Sam. 13:1), his administration fostered peace and prosperity. Jonathan's loyalty to his father, as well as his fidelity to David, are reflected in David's lament. The tragedy of Jonathan, slain in his prime, his earthly potential cut short, is poignantly portrayed. The concluding verse powerfully declares the futility of war.

2:1–4 David enquired of the Lord, saying, Shall I go up into any of the cities of Judah?

David asked divine guidance when accession to his great responsibility was imminent. Apparently he desired to know where first to proclaim his kingship and was told to go to Hebron. It was sacred as the home of father Abraham and was central to the territory of Judah. When the ten northern tribes were won over, a more central capital was chosen.

No information is recorded about how the people of Judah were assembled or how the anointing was administered. Only a single verse tells of the inauguration, and it also tells of David's learning that Gileadites from Jabesh-gilead had buried the bodies of Saul and his sons (2 Sam. 2:4a-c).

2:5–7 David sent messengers unto . . . Jabesh-gilead, and said . . . Blessed be ye of the Lord

Contrast David's attitude and acts toward the Gileadites, who had treated Saul's body with respect, with what he said and did to the Amalekite who claimed to have expedited Saul's death (2 Sam. 1:14–16).

2:8–11 Ish-bosheth Saul's son was forty years old when he began to reign over Israel . . . But . . . Judah followed David

Abner, the head of Saul's armies, championed Saul's surviving son as king over Israel, temporarily separating nearly ten northern tribes from Judah, until David won them over, seven years later (2 Sam. 5:1–5). Permanent division came eighty years later, at the end of Solomon's reign (1 Kgs. 12).

2:12–32; 3:1 Abner . . . and the servants of Ish-bosheth . . . went . . . to Gibeon. And Joab . . . and the servants of David . . . met together by the pool of Gibeon

The two military leaders representing the forces of Saul and

David, respectively, took some initiative to determine which king should reign over all Israel. The grim "play" to determine dominance was futile: twelve young soldiers from each side engaged in a duel with short swords, each holding his opponent by the hair with one hand and wielding the sword with the other. Naturally, all the soldiers were killed. (Such a strange encounter has been confirmed by a sculptured stone bas-relief found in Gozan.)

Saul's forces were beaten in the ensuing general battle. A tragic encounter between the old soldier Abner, leader of the northern army, and the young Judahite Asahel, brother of Joab, the captain of David's army, resulted in the young man's death. Joab later sought vengeance and nearly frustrated David's negotiations for the reunion of all Israel (2 Sam. 3:12–39).

In the ensuing long war, David's side became the stronger.

3:2–5 And unto David were sons born in Hebron

Two wives went with David to Hebron (2 Sam. 2:2), and four others are accounted for here. One son born to each of the six wives is named.

3:6–21 Ish-bosheth said to Abner, Wherefore hast thou gone in unto my father's concubine? Then was Abner very wroth

A break between Abner and Saul's son Ish-bosheth offered David an unexpected opportunity to unite all the tribes of Israel. Ish-bosheth's accusation of Abner, his friend and military champion, was tantamount to accusing him of seeking to be Saul's heir. So incensed was Abner that he committed himself to making David king over all Israel (2 Sam. 3:8–10). Abner's power and influence in Israel could have made the transition easy from Saul's rule to David's.

Saul's earlier separation of Michal from David had been unjust, but a reunion by duress, under the conditions here noted, could only bring added sorrows (2 Sam. 6; 21).

3:22–35 when Joab was come out from David, he sent messengers after Abner . . . and smote him

Joab's vengeance upon Abner engendered neither justice nor peace; indeed, it would have thrown the two Israelite factions into open warfare had David not been able to convince the northern Israelites that he had not instigated Abner's assassination.

The first line of David's poetic lament for Abner could mean "has a just man thus been deceived and put to death?" (2 Sam. 3:33). His lament, followed by a brief fast and mourning, impressed the people of northern Israel.

3:36–39 And all the people took notice of it, and it pleased them: as whatsoever the king did pleased all the people

Ironically, David's political fortunes were enhanced, not impaired, by Joab's rash interference, even though he took no action against Joab and Abishai. Something about David "pleased all the people."

4:1–12 Rechab and Baanah, went . . . to the house of Ish-bosheth

The power behind King Ish-bosheth, son of Saul, was Abner; so with Abner gone, nothing held that kingdom together. It is not surprising that opportunistic assassins tried to gain favor with David by destroying Ish-bosheth, but they did not know David's principles. They were punished as had been the Amalekite who claimed to have killed Saul (2 Sam. 1:1–16).

Mephibosheth is here introduced—a little lame prince, son of David's staunch friend Jonathan. David later became his guardian (2 Sam. 4:4a).

5:1–5 Then came all the tribes of Israel to David unto Hebron, . . . and they anointed David king over Israel

There were many factors—divine, military, and personal—in David's success as king and he remained popular throughout his reign. Note that he became king through a covenant ("league") made with the elders of Israel, and he was anointed; thus, Israel continued for a time as a divinely guided constitutional monarchy (1 Sam. 10:25).

5:6–10 And the king and his men went to Jerusalem unto the Jebusites

David wisely chose Jerusalem for his capital; it was on the

border between northern Israel and Judah and was still held by Canaanite Jebusites (2 Sam. 5:6*a*).

The Hebrew word rendered *gutter* may mean "a tunnel or shaft." A shaft relevant to this scriptural account was in fact discovered by Sir Charles Warren in 1867. It ascends from a channel fed by the spring Gihon to carry water inside the walls of the ancient fortress of Jerusalem, which was located on a little ridge known as Ophel, southeast of the present Old City of Jerusalem. Joab may have gone into the spring, through a lateral channel, and up the shaft into the city to open the gates to his men. The Jebusites had been so confident of their hilltop fortress that they had boasted even the "lame and the blind" could withstand invaders. David berated the defenders, calling them all "the lame and the blind" (2 Sam. 5:8).

Here is the first mention of *Zion* in the Old Testament. It was once found in Genesis (the JST version of which is Moses 7:18–69). Zion may have been the place of "the pure in heart" in Melchizedek's time (JST Gen. 9:21–25; 14:25–40; Alma 13:17–19; TG and BD, "Zion").

5:11–12 Hiram king of Tyre sent messengers to David, and cedar trees, and carpenters, and masons: and they built David an house

This era in Israel's history was the beginning of a long and mutually beneficial relationship between Israel and the Phoenician cities of Tyre and Sidon. In the reigns of David and Solomon, Israel received much excellent cedar wood and many skillful Phoenician craftsmen; Israel sent agricultural produce to them. In modern times, until 1982, a mutually advantageous trade relationship again existed between modern Lebanon and Israel.

5:13–16 David took him more concubines and wives out of Jerusalem, after he was come from Hebron, and there were yet sons and daughters born to David

The polygamy of patriarchal times was still practiced, especially by rulers, and David exercised that prerogative (a comment on which is made in modern scripture, D&C 132:38–39). Note among his children the names Nathan and Solomon. Luke traced a genealogy for Joseph, husband of Mary, through this Nathan

(Luke 3:23–38); he should not be confused with the prophet Nathan of David's time. Matthew gave the royal line as descending through Solomon to Joseph (Matt. 1:1–16; TG, "Jesus Christ, Davidic Descent of"; BD, "Genealogy"; "Joseph"). Joseph is said to have been a cousin to Mary, so his lineage would also have been hers, and hence, of Jesus.

5:17–25 But when the Philistines heard that they had anointed David king . . . all the Philistines came up to seek David

When all the Philistines realized what some rulers of their city-states had anticipated (1 Sam. 29:4–9), they attacked Israel through the valley of Rephaim, which runs eastward toward Jerusalem. With the guidance of the Lord, David drove them back, first by a frontal assault and then by a surprise attack from the rear. He eventually controlled the Philistines even more completely than had Saul, and he restrained them as in the early part of Samuel's administration.

6:1–11 And David . . . went . . . to bring up . . . the ark of God

Saul had once asked for the ark to be brought (1 Sam. 14:18) but must not have secured it, for it remained in the house of Abinadab, who had dedicated his son Eleazar to care for it after it was returned from the Philistine cities (1 Sam. 6:21; 7:1–2). Perhaps Abinadab's house in Gibeah was still in the Philistines' sphere of influence until David vanquished them (2 Sam. 5:17–25), and he felt free at last to take the ark to Jerusalem, his new capital in Israel.

David assembled a great congregation from all Israel for the festive entourage, which he and other musicians led. But when Uzzah, who drove the oxcart that carried the ark, put forth his hand to steady it, he was smitten and died. David was so frightened that he left the ark at the home of the Levite family of Obed-Edom for three months until it was evident that blessings of the Lord, not curses, attended it (2 Sam. 6:11–12). A metaphor has arisen out of that incident: one who seeks without proper authority to correct the Church or its leaders is said to be trying to "steady the ark" (D&C 85:8).

6:12–19 And it was told king David, saying, The Lord hath blessed the house of Obed-Edom. . . . So David went and brought up the ark of God . . . into the city of David with gladness

David gathered his courage and arranged for Aaronic priests and other Levites to take the ark into Jerusalem, the new "city of David" (1 Chr. 15:2ff.; 16:4ff.). They placed it in a "tabernacle" (Heb., *tent*) specially pitched for it and offered unto the Lord burnt offerings and peace offerings. Food was given to all the multitude (2 Sam. 6:19*a*).

6:20–23 Then David returned to bless his household. And Michal the daughter of Saul came out to meet David

David, clad in a linen ephod, danced as the procession moved along; his action seemed improper to Michal, his restored wife, and their relationship further deteriorated (2 Sam. 6:14, 20*b–c;* BD, "Ephod").

7:1–29 the king said unto Nathan the prophet, . . . I dwell in an house of cedar, but the ark of God dwelleth within curtains

When David's conscience stirred him to build a house for the ark, Nathan immediately gave his personal approval, but a revelation from the Lord sent him back to David with different orders. David was occupied with warfare and bloodshed (1 Chr. 22:8; 28:2–3; 1 Kgs. 5:3), but he was promised perpetuation of his "house" (his progeny) and assured that his son would build a proper temple. The blessing on the Davidic throne and kingdom "forever" anticipated the Messiah (2 Sam. 7:13).

David humbly submitted to the Lord's will and gratefully went into the tent of the ark, where he "sat before the Lord" and uttered a psalm of gratitude, praise, and supplication (2 Sam. 7:18–29).

8:1–14 Of Syria, and of Moab, and of . . . Ammon, and of the Philistines, and of Amalek, and of . . . [the] king of Zobah

David extended his control of nations around Israel to the bounds described by Moses and promised to Abraham (Gen. 15:18; Num. 34; Deut. 1:7). He received "gifts" (tribute) from those nations and put "garrisons" or occupying forces in the dominant nations to the north and south—Syria and Edom. It may be assumed that his conquests completed the action begun by Moses and Joshua because "the Lord preserved David whithersoever he went" (2 Sam. 8:6). But the Lord is not arbitrary or capricious in preserving some people and destroying others (Gen. 15:5–8, 16–21; Ex. 23:28–32; Deut. 7:9–10; Josh. 2:24; 2 Ne. 17:33–37; Abr. 2:6).

8:15–18 And David reigned over all Israel; and David executed judgment and justice unto all his people

David's quality of rulership in his early years is impressive. Imagine what could have been accomplished had he continued so until the end of his life.

A recorder (Heb., *mazkir,* "remembrancer," probably the secretary who prepared documents or communications) and a scribe (Heb., *sopher;* cf. *sepher,* "book"; probably the historian or archivist) were among the first government officials named. The duty of record keeping had from the beginning been established among the "people of the Book" (Moses 6:5; Abr. 1:31; Ex. 24:4; Deut. 31:9; TG, "Scriptures, Writing of").

Descendants of some of David's religious leaders served from this period on (BD, "Abiathar"; "High Priest"; "Zadok").

9:1–13 And David said, Is there yet any that is left of the house of Saul, that I may shew him kindness for Jonathan's sake?

This is the story anticipated earlier about David's befriending the handicapped son of his friend Jonathan. That son, Mephibosheth, was five years old at Saul's death but at this point he was mature and had a son of his own, named Micha (2 Sam. 9:6a, 12). Ziba also appears later (2 Sam. 9:2a).

10:1–19 And David's servants came into the land of the children of Ammon

A gesture of kindness by David was misinterpreted in Ammon, and his messengers were grossly insulted. War was the result. The details in this chapter are probably of the wars summarized earlier, involving Ammon, Syria, and others mentioned in both accounts (2 Sam. 8:1–12). This chapter introduces a tragic development in David's personal life.

11:1–27 David sent Joab, and his servants with him, and all Israel; and they destroyed the children of Ammon. . . . But David tarried still at Jerusalem

The "time when kings go forth to battle" in the Near East was in late spring, after the rains ceased (2 Sam. 11:1). This chapter gives further information on the wars, their inception, and the events that occurred in Jerusalem at the time of Joab's campaign beyond Jordan.

It was unusual for the king to remain at leisure at home while his men were in the field; and it was bitterly ironic that he would take advantage of the beautiful wife of his neighbor, one of his thirty-seven "mighty men" (2 Sam. 23:8, 39). Uriah was a Hittite, evidently a believer, whose name means "Jehovah is my light." He was a man of such integrity that his very dependability was used to bring about his death.

It is shocking that leisure and lust led David to adultery and contrived murder. It is shocking that a man may be ever so good, great, and eminent and yet indulge inclinations that subvert and defeat his better nature and impair his eternal potential. Even though it is disturbing, it benefits us that the Bible tells frankly the good and the bad about both heroes and villains.

12:1–14 thou hast . . . taken his wife to be thy wife, and hast slain him with the sword of the children of Ammon

The Lord sent Nathan to David, and the prophet told David a parable about a sin similar to but less serious than David's. When David condemned it, Nathan turned that condemnation upon him: *Attah ha ish*—"Thou art the man" (2 Sam. 12:7). The words must have crashed in upon David's conscience with withering weight.

No doubt his repentance was sincere, as many of his psalms attest, but who can repent enough to restore a life and restore a woman's virtue? The consequences were immutable (2 Sam. 12:10–12, 13a-b).

David prayed that his soul would not be left forever in "hell" (Ps. 16:10; Heb., *sheol,* "the spirit world"; in this case, the spirit prison). That hope is provided by our divine Redeemer, who raises every soul from the disembodied state by resurrection. But the eternal state of resurrected souls differs according to worthiness, and the eternal destiny of unrepentant doers of such sins as adultery and murder is not good (Ps. 16; 51; Heb. 6:4–6; Rev. 22:14–15; D&C 132:39).

Another evil arises when cynics look at the sins of reputedly religious people; they may rashly generalize that all such are hypocrites (2 Sam. 12:14).

12:15–25 And the Lord struck the child that Uriah's wife bare unto David, and it was very sick

The child of the illicit union did not live long, and the parents suffered, but there is no reason to suppose the child was punished for the sin of the parents. Death must come at one time or another, and it can be a blessing to an individual at whatever time the Lord appoints. The parents did suffer remorse and bereavement. David's hopeful fasting, mourning, and praying before the baby's death, but not after, is understandable, although such behavior was not customary.

David's hope to "go to him" in death was not realistic (2 Sam. 12:23). He could not hope to go to the kingdom of glory to which innocent children are heirs (TG, "Salvation of Little Children").

David apparently promised Bathsheba that her next son would be heir to the throne (1 Kgs. 1:17; 1 Chr. 22:9).

12:26–31 And Joab fought against Rabbah of the children of Ammon, and took the royal city

Joab completed the conquest of Ammon and sent for David to lead the forces into the capital city, lest Joab himself be acclaimed as ruler. Regardless of his other faults, Joab was always loyal to his king, and the king rewarded him. Punishment for Joab's sins came later (1 Kgs. 2:5–6, 28–34).

13:1–19 Absalom the son of David had a fair sister, . . . and Amnon the son of David loved her

As Nathan had foretold, evils soon arose in David's family. The first was Amnon's illicit lust and incest, abetted by a "subtil" friend's suggestions. But lust turns quickly to hate; only true love endures, and it was not love that Amnon felt.

Note the admirable compassion, wisdom, patience, and persuasiveness of Tamar, caught unwittingly in Amnon's trap. She pointed out rationally why, for his sake and for hers, he should not do such an immoral deed. But he forced her; she could then only rend the garments of her virginity and mourn, with the hope that someone would help her.

13:20–39 And Absalom her brother said unto her, Hath Amnon thy brother been with thee?

Absalom and Tamar were the children of David's wife Maacah; Amnon was the child of David and Ahinoam (2 Sam. 13:4; 3:2–3). It seems from his question that Absalom must have known something of Amnon's infatuation. But he did not seek justice through the procedures of the Mosaic law (Lev. 20:10–17). He undertook a private vendetta, after which he took refuge at his grandfather's house for three years. David sorrowed both for the dead son and the fugitive; and yet more tragedies developed.

14:1–20 Now Joab . . . perceived that the king's heart was toward Absalom. And Joab sent to Tekoah, and fetched thence a wise woman

The loyal but usually unscrupulous Joab sought to play a pacifying role, attempting to reconcile David and Absalom. It seems he was honestly trying to bring back some happiness to the king, who, after three years, was still yearning for Absalom.

The "wise woman" ingeniously persuaded the king to end the banishment of the son whom he loved but who had taken the law into his own hands. The woman showed knowledge of the concept of divine atonement, declaring that God doth "devise means, that his banished be not expelled from him" (2 Sam. 14:14).

14:21–33 the king said unto Joab, . . . go therefore, bring the young man Absalom again

Joab's persuasion got Absalom back from his foreign refuge, but David refused to reconcile with him, and Absalom remained ostracized for two more crucial years. The bitterness engendered in Absalom during that time spawned ideas of revolt by the handsome and popular prince (2 Sam. 14:25; 15:1–12). Only by violent means and harsh words did he finally get audience with his father the king; but it was too late, and ultimate tragedy was inevitable.

15:1–37 Absalom prepared him chariots and horses, and fifty men to run before him. And Absalom rose up early, and stood beside the way of the gate: . . . when any man . . . came to the king for judgment, then Absalom called unto him

So began a process by which "Absalom stole the hearts of the men of Israel" (2 Sam. 15:6). It was easy demagoguery for Absalom to tell every person who had a controversy that if he were in power, he would provide justice. With feigned piety and shameless deceit, Absalom set the stage for his own coronation in Hebron, his birthplace and the base of David's long-standing power.

But the strategy didn't succeed: David still had some powerful and loyal friends, including the priests Zadok and Abiathar; a faithful foreigner, Ittai the Gittite; the wise counselor Hushai; and, of course, the old soldier Joab. All these took crucial roles in a war resisting Absalom's coup.

No clear reason is given for David's abandoning his strong citadel at Jerusalem in the face of attack. His concern later for his son Absalom leaves the impression that he was probably reluctant to confront him in open battle. He tried by subterfuge to delay Absalom's campaign, sending Hushai to counter the advice of his former counselor Ahithophel, who stayed with Absalom.

16:1–4 And when David was a little past the top of the hill, behold, Ziba the servant of Mephibosheth met him

Apparently Ziba wanted to ingratiate himself with David to

gain back the lands and possessions of his former master, Saul. Ziba administered them on behalf of the lame prince, Mephibosheth, son of Jonathan (2 Sam. 9). Ziba's ruse was that Mephibosheth was trying to become king. The sequel to his connivance is given later (2 Sam. 19:24–30). Ziba arrived with pack animals and provisions at a time when they were needed, and David rewarded him later for that.

16:5–14 when king David came to Bahurim, behold, thence came out a man of the family of . . . Saul, whose name was Shimei, . . . he came forth, and cursed still as he came

When a ruler falls, there are generally adversaries who then feel free to express their grievances. David chose to endure Shimei's curses (2 Sam. 16:10–12). Joab and Abishai were often intemperate men, and David countered with more moderate action; however, we learn later that David smarted under Shimei's curses and tempered mercy with what he felt to be justice (1 Kgs. 2:8–9).

16:15–23; 17:1–24 when Hushai . . . David's friend, was come unto Absalom, . . . Absalom said to Hushai . . . why wentest thou not with thy friend?

David had sent Hushai to counter the counsel of Hushai's former peer, Ahithophel, who was with Absalom (2 Sam. 15:31–37). Ahithophel did not make as favorable an impression on Absalom's men as did Hushai, who was secretly trying to gain time for David's forces to assemble and organize. Had Ahithophel's advice been followed, David could well have been killed in battle.

Hushai's emissaries, who were given information by priests loyal to David, barely escaped detection (2 Sam. 17:15–22) but carried Hushai's advice to David, and he escaped across the Jordan River to consolidate his forces.

Ahithophel, whose advice to Absalom would have been advantageous had it been followed, felt so dishonored that he committed suicide—one of the few recorded in the Old Testament (1 Sam. 31:4).

17:24–29 Then David came to Mahanaim. And Absalom passed over Jordan, he and all the men of Israel with him

Some time had passed, apparently, for both forces were organized for battle. Absalom chose Amasa, a relative of Joab, as captain of his host. David was strengthened by friends, both Israelite and non-Israelite. Barzillai brought vital equipment and supplies, and for his help was later rewarded. He proved to be a generous man not seeking rewards (2 Sam. 17:27*b*).

18:1–33 And the king commanded Joab and Abishai and Ittai, saying, Deal gently for my sake with . . . Absalom. And all the people heard when the king gave all the captains charge concerning Absalom

David was persuaded not to go into battle because he would be the prime target of the rebels, but he was anxious that his rebellious son be spared. It is hardly surprising that Joab again took matters into his own hands and put Absalom to death, presuming to protect the king's interests even if he had to disobey his commands. This deed was more rationally motivated than some of his previous acts had been; but administering justice by executing Absalom was not his prerogative, nor was it lawful.

Note the mention of Absalom's pillar in verse 18; a structure by that name still stands in the Kidron valley of Jerusalem, but it is a structure of less ancient origin.

Ahimaaz, son of Zadok the priest, attempted to cushion the blow in telling the king his son Absalom was dead, but to no avail; the messenger sent by Joab arrived first and gave the sad news. Tragedy had been in the making for a long time in the lives of David and Absalom, and now it had come. In his poetic lament, David wished in vain that he had died in place of his son.

19:1–8 this day I perceive, that if Absalom had lived, and all we had died this day, then it had pleased thee well

Joab saw that David would be utterly forsaken if he did not change his demeanor. He used harsh sarcasm to bring David back to reality. So David arose, sat at the gate, and thanked his people.

19:9–15 why speak ye not a word of bringing the king back?

In the general confusion of the rebellion, involving people who had supported Absalom and those who either had remained loyal to David or were returning to him, David sent the priests Zadok and Abiathar to the elders of Judah to ask why they were slow to invite him to come back. Then David appointed Absalom's former military chief to be captain of his host, perhaps in hope of reconciling the factions. In any case, he won over the men of Judah, and they invited him and all his servants to return.

19:16–23 And Shimei . . . hasted and came down with the men of Judah to meet king David

Shimei, who had cursed David when he left Jerusalem, probably typifies those who needed to make reconciliation with David; he confessed he had sinned and wanted to be the first of all the "house of Joseph" to make amends (2 Sam. 19:20; 16:5). Abishai recommended execution, but David pardoned Shimei for the time being (but see 1 Kgs. 2:8–9).

19:24–30 Mephibosheth the son of Saul came down to meet the king

Protesting that Ziba had deceived and slandered him, Mephibosheth pleaded for reconciliation (2 Sam. 19:24–30 and fn.). Whether he or Ziba was most blameworthy was not evident, and David simply restored both to their former status. Mephibosheth generously offered to let Ziba take all the property; perhaps he assumed he could return to the status he had formerly enjoyed in the house of the king (2 Sam. 9:10).

19:31–40 Now Barzillai was a very aged man, even fourscore years old

Old, affluent, and gracious Barzillai was duly thanked for his support but did not accept the king's offer of perpetual sustenance in Jerusalem. Arrangements were made to reward his family later, and after the accession of Solomon, those plans were implemented (2 Sam. 19:38; 1 Kgs. 2:7).

19:41– 43; 20:1–2 And, behold, all the men of Israel came to the king, and said . . . , Why have our brethren the men of Judah stolen thee away

After Judah consented to accept King David once again, Judahite leaders went out to him without notifying the northern Israelites (19:8–15, 41). So, when David returned to his capital, their mutual jealousies erupted in political strife. One Benjamite summoned the northern Israelites in a movement for secession; it was a temporary breach but a harbinger of things to come (1 Kgs. 12).

20:3 his concubines, whom he had left to keep the house

According to the law, a father's wife or concubine should not be taken by a son (Deut. 22:30; 2 Sam. 15:16; 16:20–22); hence, the women whom Absalom had taken lived "in widowhood" thereafter.

20:4–13 Then said the king to Amasa, Assemble me the men of Judah within three days . . . So Amasa went to assemble the men of Judah; but he tarried longer than the set time

Amasa was appointed as promised but he was too slow, and Joab's brother Abishai was dispatched to deal with Sheba and the rebels. Joab voluntarily appeared with foreign mercenaries of the royal guard, who were loyal to him notwithstanding his replacement. When Amasa at last came on the scene, Joab summarily assassinated him, just as might have been anticipated. The soldiers, momentarily stunned, soon followed Joab again.

20:14–22 And he went through all the tribes of Israel . . . to Beth-maachah

After a long march northward through all the Israelite territories to a city near Dan where Sheba had taken refuge, Joab began a siege. Again a "wise woman" played a saving role. By her intercession, the men of the city delivered Sheba's head to Joab. The rebellion was over, and Joab returned to Jerusalem—and to the king.

20:23–26 Now Joab was over all the host of Israel

So Joab was again chief of David's officers and men. The list is about the same as before except that a man was placed over the tribute, the conscripted laborers, an innovation of David's reign, and a man was appointed in place of David's sons as "chief ruler" (2 Sam. 8:18).

21:1–14 there was a famine . . . It is for Saul . . . because he slew the Gibeonites

This terrible story can be true only so far as it is translated correctly. It is the first of several apparently appended accounts that are not necessarily in historical sequence (2 Sam. 21–24). If this account is accurate, it must have occurred in a time of David's spiritual deterioration. The law does not sanction putting sons or grandsons to death for the sins of a father (Deut. 24:16; Num. 35:33). Thus it could not have been a revelation from the Lord to David that all Israel was then suffering a famine because Saul had slain some Gibeonites, thereby breaking Joshua's promise that they might live in Israel. Neither the laws of cause and effect nor the principles of divine justice are evident in this story.

It is traumatic to read of the innocent mother, thereafter guarding the bodies and bones of innocent sons from scavenger birds and beasts. It is also repulsive to read that after all these merciless acts were committed, "God was entreated for the land," implying that the famine ceased because of those acts (2 Sam. 21:14). This is apostate theology, akin to that of a Canaanite Baal.

The name *Michal* must be a mistake for *Merab,* for she was the daughter of Saul who had been given to Adriel (2 Sam. 21:8; 1 Sam. 18:19). If they were indeed sons of Michal, or even if they were sons of Merab whom Michal had "brought up" for Adriel, that was one more sad episode in the relationship of David and Michal.

21:15–22 Moreover the Philistines had yet war again with Israel

The triumphs over four giant sons of "the giant in Gath" may have been in a war already noted (2 Sam. 21:22; 8:1). They appear to be hero-stories appended here.

22:1–51 David spake unto the Lord the words of this song in the day that the Lord had delivered him out of the hand of all his enemies, and out of the hand of Saul

This psalm from an earlier period of David's life is found also in the book of Psalms (Ps. 18) but with some differences in wording. It beautifully gives thanks and praises the might of the Lord for His control of all things in the earth and sky, the seas and winds.

Note mention of "a bow of steel" some four hundred years before the bow of steel of Nephi (2 Sam. 22:35*b*).

23:1–7 Now these be the last words of David

This excellent psalm is presented as "the last words of David" (but see 1 Kgs. 2:1–10).

David's claim that "the Spirit of the Lord spake by me, and his word was in my tongue" is creditable for his younger days when he was a man after the Lord's own heart (1 Sam. 13:14). It was the Spirit of the Lord, or Holy Ghost, that moved the prophets of old to speak the words of God (2 Pet. 1:21). Many of the psalms are prophetic and were cited or alluded to by Jesus himself (BD, "Quotations from the Old Testament found in the New Testament").

23:8–39 These be the names of the mighty men whom David had

Here are more appended anecdotes; they tell the deeds of David's "mighty men" (Heb., *gibborim,* "great ones, heroes"). The best known story tells of three friends who fulfilled the king's nostalgic wish for a drink of water from the well at the gate of his old home in Bethlehem. They risked their lives going through enemy lines to get it; but it then seemed to David too precious to drink, and he offered it to the Lord as a libation poured out upon the ground (2 Sam. 23:13–17).

24:1–25 again the anger of the Lord was kindled against Israel, and he moved David against them to say, Go, number Israel and Judah

This chapter presents some mistaken concepts of the Lord's

272

ways, perhaps arising in the time when David was struggling for the Spirit of the Lord (Ps. 51, esp. v. 11). An inconsistency is seen in the Lord's already being angry at Israel but causing David to do something He disapproved of so that He would have an excuse to punish Israel. The other account of this episode, in 1 Chronicles 21, records that it was Satan who moved David to take the offensive census. There is no explanation why a census was offensive, unless it signified putting trust in the arm of flesh instead of trusting in the Lord.

The Lord is said to have offered a choice of three punishments: seven months of famine, three months as a fugitive for David, or three days' pestilence for everybody. The pestilence was chosen, but then the Lord "repented him of the evil" and David showed Him the injustice of punishing the innocent (2 Sam. 24:16–17). Finally, even though the Lord had "repented" and told the destroying angel it was enough, the prophet Gad advised David to buy a threshing floor from Araunah the Jebusite (in Jerusalem), build an altar there, and offer offerings. David did so, and "the Lord was intreated for the land, and the plague was stayed from Israel" (2 Sam. 24:21–25). The site of this offering became the place upon which Solomon later built the temple (2 Sam. 24:18; 2 Chr. 3:1). This account is dubious but not because of the translation; all its problems are present also in the Hebrew account, but it is strange doctrine.

So end the books of Samuel. As we have noted, they were written in part by others and named for Samuel, the great prophet of that era, whose death was recorded before the end of the first book (1 Sam. 25:1; BD, "Samuel"; "Samuel, Books of"). They are vital sources for the history of the consolidation of Israel and the rise of the monarchy; they show the character of some great leaders and prophets; and they portray the situations out of which many of the great psalms of Israel were written. And certainly some of the best known of all Bible narratives are in the books of Samuel.

FIRST KINGS

The first book of the Kings continues the narratives of the second book of Samuel. In fact, in their subtitles the books of Samuel are "otherwise called" the first and second books of the kings; thus the subtitle of this book is "Commonly Called the Third Book of the Kings," and the four books are presented as a continuum.

The first half of the first book of the Kings (1 Kgs. 1–11) relates the transmission of the kingdom from David to his son Solomon. It recounts Solomon's consolidation and further expansion of the kingdom and the establishment of Jerusalem as the religious capital with a glorious new temple. It accounts for Solomon's acquisition of wealth and fame. But then Solomon declined and fell, as did the previous two kings.

The second half (1 Kgs. 12–22) illustrates what Jesus once said: "Every kingdom divided against itself is brought to desolation; and every city or house divided against itself shall not stand" (Matt. 12:25). Ancient Israel deteriorated, lost the concept of the divine Abrahamic mission of Israel, and lost the blessings promised those who faithfully perform it.

Parallel accounts are found in 2 Chronicles 1–20 but with more details about Judah than about northern Israel.

It is said that Solomon "spake three thousand proverbs; and his songs were a thousand and five" (1 Kgs. 4:32). Most of the book of Proverbs is indeed attributed to Solomon.

COMMENTARY

1:1– 4 Now king David was old and stricken in years

David had indeed grown old. His beautiful young wife Abishag was later innocently involved in a political action by a brother of Solomon (1 Kgs. 2:13–34).

1:5–10 Then Adonijah the son of Haggith exalted himself

Adonijah might logically have assumed that he should succeed his father, David. He was David's fourth son (2 Sam. 3:2–5); two elder brothers, Amnon and Absalom, were already dead; a third, called Daniel or Chileab (1 Chr. 3:1; 2 Sam. 3:3), is not spoken of in the record after the sons of David are listed; and Solomon was younger than Adonijah.

But no one could properly make himself king in Israel. One was to be called prophetically and anointed, as were Saul and David. Surprisingly, Adonijah had the support of the priest Abiathar, King David's long-time friend, and he also had the support of the redoubtable Joab, David's staunch defender. But he did not have the support of Zadok, the chief priest, nor was he called to the kingship through Nathan the prophet. Neither did he have the support of Benaiah, one of the three mightiest of David's thirty mighty men and Joab's chief rival (2 Sam. 23:20–22). But Adonijah did not invite his brother Solomon to his coronation (1 Kgs. 1:19, 26).

1:11–53 Didst not thou, my lord, O king, swear unto thine hand-maid, saying, Assuredly Solomon thy son shall reign after me

Bath-sheba and the prophet Nathan knew that David had told Solomon the Lord had promised his birth, his peaceful reign, and his building of the temple (1 Kgs. 1:13*a*). They also knew it was urgent that David should be told of Adonijah's usurpation. Bath-sheba therefore reminded him, and Nathan confirmed what she said, giving more facts about Adonijah's intentions. All of this, with the gentle sarcasm in Nathan's last question, brought a re-sponse (1 Kgs. 1:27).

Adonijah's coronation feast at the spring En Rogel, about half a mile down the Kidron valley from the spring Gihon, was interrupted, as were his royal hopes. The priest Abiathar, last of the line of Eli, was cut off from his priesthood position.

The prophet Nathan, with the chief priest Zadok and the military leader Benaiah, who was to replace Joab, summoned the royal bodyguard and the people to follow Solomon as he rode the king's mule down to the spring Gihon, water-source for Jerusalem, where Solomon was anointed and proclaimed king.

Adonijah and his followers saw that their cause was lost and their lives in danger, so the pretender fled for sanctuary to the ark, where he clung to the horns of the altar for safety until he was assured that if he would prove worthy, he might be saved. Solomon was judicious and tolerant, and for a time there was peace.

2:1–11 Now the days of David drew nigh that he should die

David gave Solomon his farewell charge; a poetic version reports more detailed blessings, transcending Solomon's reign and anticipating the Messiah (Ps. 72). Hearkening to the charge could indeed have made Solomon an outstanding king under the covenant promise of the Lord to David and his descendants (1 Kgs. 2:4). Less saintly were David's dying requests for Solomon to punish Joab and Shimei for past deeds, but he did remember to reward Barzillai's family.

The king's death is recorded simply and his reign briefly reviewed. His burial "in the city of David" (1 Kgs. 2:10) was unusual; burials were typically outside Israelite cities. The traditional site of his burial is venerated to this day on "Mount Zion" southwest of the Old City of Jerusalem, where many people visit David's cenotaph every day.

2:12–46 Then sat Solomon upon the throne of David

Solomon immediately executed the punishments requested by his father. He also soon found grounds to put to death Adonijah, the erstwhile usurper of the throne, for Adonijah provided a reason himself. He should have known that anyone who acquired a wife of a former king would appear to be the royal heir. Why the mother of Solomon presented Adonijah's request to her son is not recorded; perhaps she acted simply out of kindness. But Solomon was suspicious of Adonijah and with autocratic dispatch decreed his death.

Abiathar is a tragic figure (1 Kgs. 2:26–27 and fn.). The sole survivor of Saul's purge of Eli's priestly family, he was embraced sympathetically at first and served David well, but he chose unwisely to support Adonijah and was terminated from his priestly service by Solomon. How the king got authority over the priesthood is not recorded.

Joab's championing of Adonijah had left him vulnerable to Solomon, and he sought sanctuary at the tent set up by David to house the ark, clinging to the horns of the altar and rashly saying, "Nay, but I will die here" (1 Kgs. 2:30). So there he was executed at Solomon's command by the new military leader, Benaiah (1 Kgs. 2:28–35).

Shimei, who had cursed David but had been given a reprieve, was restricted to the city of Jerusalem. Almost inevitably an occasion arose for which he could also be put to death.

3:1–2 building his own house, and the house of the Lord, and the wall of Jerusalem

The king's need for royal housing and the people's need for a temple because they were still sacrificing on mountain tops provided reasons enough for Solomon's major building projects (2 Kgs. 5–7). Marriage of an Egyptian princess to an outsider was a rare concession from Egypt, and Solomon gave his Egyptian wife special treatment (2 Kgs. 3:1).

3:3–4 And Solomon loved the Lord . . . a thousand burnt offerings did Solomon offer upon that altar

Solomon himself had made abundant offerings to the Lord on one of the "high places," but a proper place of worship chosen by the Lord had been anticipated since Moses (Deut. 12:1–6). That was reason to build the temple, even though worship on hilltops, common in all of Canaan, had been acceptable to the Lord in patriarchal times.

3:5–15 In Gibeon the Lord appeared to Solomon in a dream . . . and God said, Ask what I shall give thee

King Solomon may be seen at his best in this event. When given the opportunity in a dream to ask the Lord for whatever he desired, he asked only for ability to understand and judge fairly. Because of his choice, he was promised other blessings. The recorded commendation of David is a problem in view of his moral deterioration, but the emphasis is upon his loyalty to the Lord in never turning to other gods. Some later references specify that his heart was right in the eyes of the Lord *except* in his sins against Uriah and Bath-sheba. Such references commend his behavior in his better days rather than approving his whole life.

3:16–28 Then came there two women, that were harlots, unto the king, and stood before him

In this famous illustration of Solomon's wisdom, it is surprising that his solution to the question worked out at all. Normally two women who both desired the same baby would *both* have objected to the crude suggestion that it be cut in two. His wisdom must have been in his insight to see that one would be brazen enough to consent. Naturally the true mother gave in rather than consent to the death of the child.

4:1–28 So king Solomon was king over all Israel

A huge government bureaucracy began to develop in Solomon's reign; the first officers are listed here. Evidence of the size of it is shown in the quantity of provisions for each day and in the numbers of horses and horsemen (1 Kgs. 4:22–28). It is surprising that Abiathar is listed as a priest (1 Kgs. 4:4; 2:27). Possibly the Nathan whose sons are named was the prophet who aided in Solomon's coronation; such appointments for his sons would have shown gratitude to him (1 Kgs. 4:5).

Solomon reorganized his nation into twelve administrative districts, preserving some of the old tribal units but altering others. Two of his twelve procurement officers were sons-in-law (1 Kgs. 4:11, 15). These officers were to collect the people's contributions of food for the royal household.

The boundaries of the promised land, anticipated in the covenant with Abraham, were reached (1 Kgs. 4:21*b*).

4:29–34 And God gave Solomon wisdom and understanding exceeding much, and largeness of heart

The Hebrew phrase "largeness of heart" denotes power and breadth of understanding. Evidence for some of the king's talents is shown by the number of his proverbs and songs. Obviously our book of Proverbs does not contain all the compositions attributed to Solomon.

5:1–18 And Hiram king of Tyre sent his servants unto Solomon

The favorable trade relationship, which began between King David and King Hiram, became advantageous to both nations in Solomon's time (2 Sam. 5:11–12). The Israelites had never developed cutting and carving skills in wood and stone anciently, possibly because of an overgeneralized interpretation of the laws against making graven images. Agricultural products, such as grain and oil, were among the Israelite goods that were traded to the Sidonians for their excellent cedar and for the labors of their skilled workmen.

Most of the common laborers would have been state slaves from other lands. The Israelite workers, sent to the places in which the trees and stones were cut, "ruled over the people that wrought in the work" (1 Kgs. 5:13–17; 9:20–23; 2 Chr. 2:17–18; 8:7–9).

6:1–10 in the four hundred and eightieth year after the children of Israel were come out of . . . Egypt, in the fourth year of Solomon's reign . . . he began to build the house of the Lord

This date is important in calculating much biblical chronology. The wilderness wandering was forty years long, and the reigns of Saul and David were each forty years. That would leave only three hundred sixty years for all the events recorded in the books of Joshua, Judges, Ruth, and Samuel. The terms of the judges cannot be added end to end, as that would total more than three hundred sixty years, so it is apparent that some of the judges were contemporaries serving in different parts of the land during terms that overlapped.

Details about the size and features of the temple show that it was not a large edifice, but its architecture and adornment must have been beautiful. The floor plan was that of the tabernacle of the congregation but with all its dimensions doubled (BD, "Temple of Solomon"; "Tabernacle").

The building materials were cut and shaped before being brought to the site, so that the work might go on with reverent quietness there.

6:11–13 And the word of the Lord came to Solomon

Another revelation came to Solomon, emphasizing that blessings would come to him and the people for keeping the covenants and obeying the laws, ordinances, and statutes.

6:14–38 So Solomon built the house, and finished it

The central holy places were most ornate, with such features as the large cherubim, which were fifteen feet in height and width and made of olive wood overlaid with gold. They were placed with their wings over the gold-covered ark and its smaller cherubim.

None of the carved and engraved objects violated the first two of the Ten Commandments, which forbade the making and worshiping of carved or cast *idols* (Ex. 20:4 and commentary).

Building the temple took seven years.

7:1–12 But Solomon was building his own house thirteen years, and he finished all his house

Nearly twice as much time was required to build Solomon's residence, which included housing for government officials and for Solomon's wives.

7:13–51 Solomon sent and fetched Hiram out of Tyre. He was a widow's son of the tribe of Naphtali, and his father was a man of Tyre, a worker in brass

This Hiram, of course, was not the king Hiram of Tyre (5:1–12) but a craftsman "filled with wisdom, and understanding, and cunning to work all works in brass" (1 Kgs. 7:14; 2 Chr. 2:14). His creations in cast metal included two colossal bronze pillars to stand in front of the temple proper. Whether these were reminiscent of the pillars erected from time to time by the patriarchs in remembrance of special blessings is not known (1 Kgs. 7:15–21; Gen. 28:18–22; 31:13, 51–52).

A font of bronze was set on the backs of twelve bronze oxen. It was used for the ceremonial "washing of priests" (2 Chr. 4:2–6; BD, "Temple of Solomon"; "Baptism"). Temples built in antiquity by various peoples had basins for water to be used in ceremonial ablutions, if not baptism. Recall that true baptism had ceased by Abraham's time and had been replaced with apostate practices (Gen. 17:7a; JST Gen. 17:3–7). Whether baptism was restored and practiced in Solomon's temple has yet to be revealed, but outward washings symbolic of inner cleansing were common (TG, "Wash, Washing"; BD, "Temple of Solomon").

Ore for the extensive bronze work may have been found in what has come to be called King Solomon's mines near Eilat (the site of which is known). Much material for building the temple had been gathered and dedicated by King David (1 Kgs. 7:51b).

8:1–11 Then Solomon assembled the elders of Israel, . . . that they might bring up the ark of the covenant of the Lord out of the city of David, which is Zion

Attended by priests, elders, and tribal leaders, the ark of the covenant, the tabernacle, and the holy vessels of the tabernacle were brought up from the little citadel of David, then called Zion, to the new temple. It was higher on the ridge north of the old citadel, and it also came to be called Zion. The old portable tabernacle of the wilderness, last used at Shiloh and retained for a time at Gibeon, was brought with all its vessels to the temple compound. (What ultimately became of it is not recorded.) A tent had been pitched by David to shelter the ark and other sacred things in his city (2 Sam. 6:17; 2 Chr. 1:4–5).

The two tables of stone remained in the ark; it would be interesting to know where the other sacred objects and writings were (1 Kgs. 8:9; BD, "Ark of the Covenant").

After the ark was in place, a glorious cloud indicated the presence of the Lord and his acceptance of the temple.

8:12–21 Then spake Solomon, . . . I have surely built thee an house to dwell in

Solomon began the services by blessing the congregation and thanking the Lord for the many blessings that had made it possible for him to build the temple. It had been eagerly anticipated by his father David and others since Moses received revelations about it (2 Sam. 7:1–13; Deut. 12:5–7; BD, "Temple of Solomon").

8:22–53 And Solomon stood before the altar of the Lord in the presence of all the congregation of Israel, and spread forth his hands toward heaven: And he said, Lord God of Israel

The dedicatory prayer by King Solomon is the best indication of the breadth and depth of his faith, his philosophy of life, and his regard for eternal values. He recognized that the great God could not be confined to his little temple, but it would be a place where the king, priests, and people could come before Him. It was a place where people could make covenants and receive promises. Solomon knew they would be blessed if they kept their covenants and punished if they broke them. He outlined several situations of need in which the people might come and supplicate the Lord; or, if compelled to be away, they might look toward the temple and be heard and blessed, being forgiven as necessary. Strangers might pray toward this house and be blessed. Solomon arose after his prayer before the altar; he had been kneeling on his knees—a mode of prayer we still use.

8:54– 61 when Solomon had made an end of praying . . . he stood, and blessed all the congregation of Israel

As Solomon blessed the congregation, he reminded them of good things the Lord had done for them and their ancestors and prayed that all might live accordingly, keeping their hearts perfect with the Lord by keeping his statutes and commandments. He prayed for all people of the earth to know that the Lord is the only true God, thus showing that he knew of the mission of Abraham and Israel (TG, "Israel, Mission of").

8:62–66 And the king, and all Israel with him, offered sacrifice before the Lord

This account means not that the king and people officiated at the altars but that they provided the sacrifices and participated in the worship services. Recall that King Saul officiated in offering a sacrifice and was condemned for arrogating unto himself the authority to do so (1 Sam. 13:9–14).

It appears that this offering was a festival "peace offering" in which some of the fat was burned upon the altar, the priests received a portion for food, and the remainder of the animal was eaten by the families on whose behalf it was sacrificed (Lev. 3; 7:11–21). It does not appear that the "continual burnt offering" was involved in this celebration (Ex. 29:38–42; Lev. 6:8–13; 8:18–21; Num. 28:3–8).

The festival for the first seven days of the seventh month would have included the solemn Day of Atonement. The second seven days would have been the joyful Feast of Tabernacles, or Sukkoth, ending on the eighth day with Simchas Torah, "Joy in the Torah" (BD, "Fasts"; "Feasts").

9:1–9 And it came to pass, when Solomon had finished the building of the house of the Lord . . . That the Lord appeared to Solomon the second time

The effects of keeping or breaking one's covenants were reiterated in a revelation confirming the covenant promises made at the temple dedication. David was again cited as an exemplar of integrity of faith in the Lord, having never turned to other gods (recall, however, that by his sins he fell from his exaltation; D&C 132:39; BD, "David").

9:10–14 at the end of twenty years . . . king Solomon gave Hiram twenty cities in the land of Galilee

It appears that Solomon was unable to pay all his construction costs and was obliged to give King Hiram of Tyre twenty cities, mostly along the coastland of western Galilee from the place of the present Arab village of Kabul northward and adjoining Phoenician lands below Tyre. The cities did not please Hiram, and he called them *Cabul* (1 Kgs. 9:13*a*). Nevertheless, they seem to have more than paid the debt, for Hiram sent Solomon six score talents of gold—a very large amount. It is possible, however, that this was the gold used in adorning the temple.

9:15–25 And this is the reason of the levy which king Solomon raised; for to build the house of the Lord, and his own house, and Millo, and the wall of Jerusalem, and Hazor, and Megiddo, and Gezer

Solomon's levy that enabled him to build so extensively was heavy for the people to bear. The word in Hebrew that is translated here as *levy* means "conscripted labor," the chief sources of which were the non-Israelites left in the land, for Solomon did not require the children of Israel to be "bondmen."

When all the work was finished, Solomon's wife who was Pharaoh's daughter moved up to her new house (1 Kgs. 9:24; 3:1).

At last the people of Israel might fulfill their hopes and the Lord's commandments that they should gather at appointed seasons each year to worship and to sacrifice in the place which He had chosen (1 Kgs. 9:25; Deut. 16:16).

9:26–28 And king Solomon made a navy of ships in Ezion-geber, which is beside Eloth, on the shore of the Red sea. . . . And they came to Ophir

Little is known about the place called Ophir or its gold or even whether it was the source of gold for the temple. One may wonder at the resources Solomon used in building and in foreign exchange, but they were burdensome and oppressive to the people (1 Kgs. 12:4).

10:1–13 And when the queen of Sheba heard of the fame of Solomon concerning the name of the Lord, she came to prove him with hard questions

The call of Abraham was that through the ministry of him and his seed, the name of the Lord should be "known in the earth forever" (Abr. 1:19). Just how Solomon gained fame in relation to the name of the Lord is not stated, but it must have something to do with the temple he built and with his reputed wisdom.

Because both "Sheba" and "Ophir" were named in connection with the descendants of Shem through Joktan, brother of Peleg, both being sons of Eber, father of the Hebrews, it is plausible that their descendants still dwelt in the Arabian peninsula and that this queen of Sheba came from there (Gen. 10:21, 25–30).

A long dynasty of kings of Ethiopia, which ended with Haile Selassie (1891–1975), claimed descent from the queen of Sheba and Solomon, but no evidence for that claim is given in this biblical account.

The "hard questions" (Heb., lit., "riddles") presumably were to prove Solomon's intellect, knowledge, and wisdom. The queen was impressed and gave him lavish gifts. He responded by giving her "all her desire, whatsoever she asked," and she returned home (1 Kgs. 10:13).

10:14–29 Now the weight of gold that came to Solomon in one year was six hundred threescore and six talents of gold

The weight of six hundred sixty-six talents would be very great (BD, "Weights and Measures"). One can only marvel at the opulence implied by that amount of gold.

Sources of many chariots, horses, and wealth are given. (A place-name is mistranslated "linen yarn"; 1 Kgs. 10:28*a*.)

With all his wealth, military power, and renowned wisdom, Solomon had an unequaled opportunity to make known the name of the true God, for "all the earth sought to Solomon, to hear his wisdom, which God had put in his heart." But only in the story of the queen of Sheba is evidence given that he followed through (1 Kgs. 10:24; 1–13).

11:1–8 King Solomon loved many strange women, together with the daughter of Pharaoh, women of the Moabites, Ammonites, Edomites, Zidonians, and Hittites

This passage declares Solomon's violation of a basic law.

Every Israelite was warned that a foreign wife might turn away his heart and that of their children after other gods, and Solomon's many wives and concubines did turn away his heart so that it was no longer perfect with the Lord (1 Kgs. 11:2–3; Deut. 7:3–4).

Again the heart of David was commended for being perfect with the Lord, his God, but only his fidelity in worship was so commended. Solomon's violation of the marriage laws led to his breaking the first and second of the Ten Commandments; David's breach of the tenth led to his breaking the sixth and seventh. Grievous results followed in both cases.

11:9–13 And the Lord was angry with Solomon, because his heart was turned from the Lord God of Israel

Solomon's faults and the response of the Lord to them makes it difficult to believe that he was permitted to continue enjoying his kingdom because of the merits of his father David, whereas his son Rehoboam would suffer the division of his kingdom because of the violations of his father. Such is stated here as a revelation, but it is possible that the information has not been transmitted accurately through the centuries. The principle of individual responsibility is that everyone is to be punished for his own sins (Deut. 24:16; Ezek. 18:20; A of F 2).

11:14– 40 the Lord stirred up an adversary unto Solomon

It is not surprising that some peoples who had been conquered by David and compelled to pay tribute to Solomon rebelled as soon as they saw an opportunity to do so. Such were Hadad of Edom and Rezon of Damascus, Syria (1 Kgs. 11:14–25). One rebel who became a major force in the future of the kingdom of Israel was Jeroboam, an Ephrathite, or Ephraimite, of Zereda in the hill country of Ephraim. Jeroboam's leadership abilities and ambition were factors, but the prediction of Ahijah the prophet that he would become king over ten of the tribes set him on his path. Though he had been a trusted foreman over the laborers of the tribes of Joseph during Solomon's building projects, Solomon sought to kill him when his future status was made known. It was not unusual that a refugee such as Jeroboam would be harbored for a time in another land (1 Kgs. 11:26–40).

11:41– 43 And Solomon slept with his fathers

A rather terse note, without any eulogy, tells of Solomon's death. Although he reigned forty years, few details are told of his reign after his building was completed. Neither has he been cited as a hero or exemplar in later scripture. The "book of the acts of Solomon" is not available to give other facts about him (1 Kgs. 11:41).

12:1–15 And Rehoboam went to Shechem: for all Israel were come to Shechem to make him king

The people gathered for the coronation at Shechem, a central city in northern Israel, rather than the capital at Jerusalem, and asked for relief. Their proposal was simple: if the new king would reduce the taxes and quotas of labor conscription, they would accept him and serve him. Ironically, this son of Solomon refused an offer that the father of Solomon would have felt fortunate to receive. It took David seven years to win the northern tribes and unite all Israel (2 Sam. 2:4; 3:1; 5:1–5).

So Rehoboam rejected the wise but conservative counsel of the elders and acted on the despotic suggestions of his peers. That action marked the beginning of the end of the united nation of Israel, as it became a house divided against itself.

12:16–20 So when all Israel saw that the king hearkened not unto them, the people answered the king, saying, What portion have we in David?

With a short rallying song, the people departed to their own tents. Rehoboam failed to take the rupture seriously and sent his supervisor of the labor draft into the camps of Israel; but when the officer was stoned to death, Rehoboam fled to Jerusalem. Only the tribe of Judah and some of Benjamin accepted his leadership. The northern ten tribes of Israel made Jeroboam king, as had been prophesied (1 Kgs. 11:29–31; 12:20).

12:21–24 when Rehoboam was come to Jerusalem, he assembled all the house of Judah, with the tribe of Benjamin

Only Judahites had shown loyalty to Rehoboam at the assembly in Shechem, but some Benjamites joined them, perhaps because Jerusalem was virtually on the border between the tribes of Judah and Benjamin.

Thanks to the inspired advice of a "man of God," a prophet, who warned Rehoboam against making war on the northern tribes to force them back under his subjection, Rehoboam's military forces turned back. His action is surprising—and commendable—but it also confirmed the divided state of Israel.

The southern Israelite nation of Judah thereafter included the tribes of Judah and Simeon, some of the tribe of Benjamin, and all the faithful of the tribe of Levi (Josh. 19:1, 9; Judg. 1:3, 17; 1 Kgs. 12:21; 2 Chr. 11:1, 5–14).

12:25–33 Then Jeroboam built Shechem in mount Ephraim, and dwelt therein

Northern Israel was led into idolatry by King Jeroboam, and was provided with an apostate, non-Levite priesthood. Jeroboam did not simply *lose* his faith in Jehovah (1 Kgs. 14:1–20) but willfully created golden-calf idols and false priests to compete with the true religion and temple at Jerusalem for his own political purposes (1 Kgs. 12:27–33). He even made priests for "devils," causing the true priests in all the tribes of Israel to flee to Jerusalem (2 Chr. 11:13–15*b*, 16–17; Lev. 17:7).

The "ten tribes" to the north were really nine and a fraction, for there were thirteen, total, counting the Levites and reckoning Joseph as two: Ephraim and Manasseh.

13:1–34 And, behold, there came a man of God out of Judah by the word of the Lord unto Bethel: and Jeroboam stood by the altar to burn incense. And he cried against the altar in the word of the Lord

Note the prophecy about Jeroboam's idolatrous altar and watch for its fulfillment (1 Kgs. 13:2*a*). And observe that the miraculous punishment of King Jeroboam, followed by the miraculous healing of his afflicted hand, did not cause him to turn from his wicked ways (1 Kgs. 13:4–10, 33).

There are problems in the account of an "old prophet" trying the integrity of the man of God from Judah, and the results seem unfair; but there is a general lesson: if one knows by revelation what he should do, he must not let anything dissuade him. There is precious little comfort in the honor the old prophet bestowed upon the dead corpse of the man of God from Judah (1 Kgs. 13:18b, 21–32).

So, despite a prophetic warning that cost a righteous man's life, neither the king nor the people repented, and others followed in the sins of Jeroboam, going from bad to worse until they were destroyed.

14:1–20 Abijah the son of Jeroboam fell sick. And Jeroboam said to his wife . . . disguise thyself . . . and get thee to Shiloh: behold, there is Ahijah the prophet, which told me that I should be king

Here may be evidence that Jeroboam still had faith in the prophet who had appointed him, and in the Lord—not in his own idols. A poignant, dramatic, and tragic narrative, it foreshadows the course of northern Israel during the ensuing two hundred years. Jeroboam continued his idolatry, despite the prophet's warning. Likewise, king after king of Israel perpetuated the sins of Jeroboam, despite continuing prophetic warnings, until their related evils, from within and without, destroyed them (1 Kgs. 16:31; 2 Kgs. 3:3; 10:29; 13:6, 11; 14:24; 15:9, 18, 24, 28; 17:22).

14:21–24 Rehoboam was forty and one years old when he began to reign, and he reigned seventeen years in Jerusalem

All was not well in Judah's religious life either, even though Rehoboam had repented and obeyed a prophet at the beginning of his reign (1 Kgs. 12:21–24). His mother was an Ammonitess whom King Solomon had married, so Rehoboam's religious upbringing may not have been ideal. His violations of God's laws included worship of images in the old high places and groves (Heb., *asheroth,* "female fertility images") on the hills and under the green trees; there were also sodomites and cultic prostitutes. These evils always signified apostasy in Israel.

14:25–31 Shishak king of Egypt came up against Jerusalem: And he took away the treasures of the house of the Lord, and the treasures of the king's house

Shishak had been Jeroboam's friend, so perhaps Rehoboam's treasures and the costly things of the temple from Solomon's time seemed fair game to him (1 Kgs. 14:25*a*).

The second book of Chronicles provides more history about the kings of Judah, and a number of Rehoboam's additional accomplishments are recounted there (2 Chr. 11–12).

15:1– 8 Now in the eighteenth year of king Jeroboam . . . reigned Abijam over Judah

The chronology of the kings of each of the two Israelite nations is correlated in the record of the royal succession of the other.

The second king of Judah after the division of the kingdom perpetuated the sins of his father, Rehoboam (but see 2 Chr. 13). Abijam's very name honors *Yam,* the Canaanite god of the sea; it means "Yam is my father"—certainly an apostate name for David's great-grandson. Abijam was compared, as are many of the later kings of Judah, with David, who was commended for his worship of the true God and for general goodness except for his sins against Uriah the Hittite (1 Kgs. 15:5*c*).

15:9–24 And in the twentieth year of Jeroboam king of Israel reigned Asa over Judah . . . . And Asa did that which was right in the eyes of the Lord |

At last Judah had a righteous king and was blessed during his long reign (the account in Chronicles adds some important details; 2 Chr. 14–16). Asa even "removed" his idolatrous mother Maachah "from being queen" (1 Kgs. 15:13). Such good kings as Asa made the difference between the unstable conditions in Israel and the relatively more stable conditions in Judah during much of the ensuing three centuries.

15:25–34 And Nadab the son of Jeroboam began to reign over Israel . . . and Baasha smote him . . . and reigned in his stead

The house of Jeroboam ended, as had been prophesied (1 Kgs. 14:7–14). Nadab was replaced by a usurper, Baasha, the first of many usurpers in northern Israel. Although he fulfilled the prophecy against Jeroboam, Baasha himself perpetuated the same idolatrous ways.

16:1–7 the word of the Lord came to Jehu . . . against Baasha

The Lord continued to send prophets to warn Israel's kings, but they continued to be idolatrous, as had Jeroboam; also, a wicked man who slays a wicked man is not justified thereby.

16:8–14 In the twenty and sixth year of Asa king of Judah began Elah the son of Baasha to reign over Israel . . . two years

Only two years passed until another assassin killed the son of the first assassin-king, wiped out his family, and reigned. As Jesus later said, "all they that take the sword shall perish with the sword" (Matt. 26:52).

16:15–20 In the twenty and seventh year of Asa king of Judah did Zimri reign seven days

An army captain, Zimri, who slew his drunken king, was soon opposed by another captain, Omri. The desperate Zimri burned the royal residence and perished in it.

16:21–28 Then were the people of Israel divided into two parts; half . . . followed Tibni . . . and half followed Omri

Omri's faction prevailed, and he reigned twelve years—six in Tirzah and six more in a new capital, Samaria, which remained the capital of northern Israel until the Assyrians conquered Israel in 722 B.C. Other sources, such as inscriptions of Mesha, king of Moab, and the annals of Shalmaneser III, held Omri in some regard for his military prowess; but the Bible reports that he did more evil than all that were before him.

16:29–34 In the thirty and eighth year of Asa king of Judah began Ahab the son of Omri to reign over Israel . . . twenty and two years. And Ahab . . . did evil . . . above all that were before him

Ahab, who outdid his father's records for evil, is also better known than his father, Omri. Six chapters tell of his evils despite warnings by the great prophet Elijah. That prophet's mission continued throughout Ahab's life and after his death (1 Kgs. 17–22; 2 Kgs. 1–2).

One fateful move by King Ahab was to marry Jezebel, daughter of a king of Zidon (1 Kgs. 16:31). She was an avid worshipper of Baal and powerfully influenced Ahab. Their marriage, their descendants, and the way of life they engendered had evil effects upon both Israel and Judah for the next fifty years.

Recall the prophecy of Joshua about the man who would rebuild Jericho (1 Kgs. 16:34*a*).

17:1–7 And Elijah the Tishbite, who was of the inhabitants of Gilead, said unto Ahab

Here is a brief introduction to Elijah, a great prophet for his time and for the future. His name means "My God is Jehovah," appropriate to his mission to bring Israel back to God. He was first called by the Lord to warn King Ahab and Israel. He was a rugged and dramatic prophet from Gilead, from the city of Tishbe, the exact location of which is not known. His first attempt to awaken people to their need for the Lord and to teach them their duty to Him came during a drought and famine, which lasted nearly three years (1 Kgs. 17:1; 18:1). Elijah was provided with food miraculously during the drought, until the brook near where he lived dried up and he was told to move.

17:8–24 Arise, get thee to Zarephath, which belongeth to Zidon: . . . I have commanded a widow woman there to sustain thee

Jesus later observed, "Many widows were in Israel in the days of Elias. . . . But unto none of them was Elias sent" (Luke 4:25–26); he was making the point that no prophet is accepted in his own country. This widow in a neighboring land believed in the Lord and in Elijah, his prophet; she gave him food as he requested and was rewarded.

During the three years of drought, Elijah performed a miracle that is rare in the Old Testament: restoring life.

18:1–18 the word of the Lord came to Elijah in the third year, saying, Go, shew thyself unto Ahab

At length there was a crucial confrontation between Ahab and Elijah—and Israel and the Lord. Apparently almost all the Israelites had departed from the Lord, and Jezebel had had slain all the prophets of the Lord whom she could find. It is ironic that Ahab's own chief steward, Obadiah, hid and saved a hundred of them. Only after being persuaded that the Lord and Elijah would confront Ahab was Obadiah willing to take him before the prophet (1 Kgs. 18:15). Sarcastically Ahab asked if Elijah was the one who had troubled Israel; Elijah responded that the king and his family had troubled Israel by following Baal for evil.

18:19– 40 Now therefore send, and gather to me all Israel unto mount Carmel, and the prophets of Baal . . . and the prophets of the groves

Hundreds of prophets of Baal and the fertility goddess Asherah (wrongly translated as "the groves") were called to this confrontation. The question for Israelites was "How long halt ye between two opinions?" which implied a dangerous double-mindedness (1 Kgs. 18:21*a*). It was Elijah's dramatic way of trying to turn the hearts of the children of Israel back to the covenants of the Lord with their forefathers. (Elijah's latter-day mission is similar; JS-H 1:39; BD, "Elijah".)

The drama became intense as the prophets of Baal called on their idol all morning, jumped on the altar, and slashed themselves until their blood gushed out—but all to no avail. Elijah taunted them that their god must be talking, busy, on a journey, or sleeping, because he did not respond. Then Elijah soaked the altar with water and prayed simply that it be made known that the God in Israel lived and had supreme power. His hope was that people might realize the Lord is God and turn from idolatry. When supernatural fire consumed the offering, rocks, dust, and water, the people fell prostrate and confessed that the Lord is God. With public opinion temporarily on his side, Elijah had the idolatrous prophets executed (1 Kgs. 18:40; Deut. 13:1–11; 17:1–7).

18:41– 46 And Elijah said unto Ahab, Get thee up, eat and drink; for there is a sound of abundance of rain

In a further dramatic demonstration of the Lord's power and benevolence, Elijah had his servant watch while clouds rose and came inland from the sea, promising rain. Elijah ran before the chariot of the king, as if to show that Elijah and the Lord were at last guiding Ahab. The drought was broken, as rain indeed came.

19:1–18 Ahab told Jezebel all that Elijah had done . . . Then Jezebel sent a messenger unto Elijah, saying, So let the gods do to me, and more also, if I make not thy life as the life of one of them

Elijah was disappointed that Jezebel's power over the king and people was unbroken. He felt he had failed and was discouraged to the point of giving up his life because the people had gained no real conviction by the miraculous demonstration. Apparently he wanted to return to the place where the dispensation of Moses had begun. He walked a hundred miles from Jezreel to Beersheba and then on into the desert southward.

The Lord interceded and twice sent an angel to urge Elijah to arise, eat, and drink. Thus strengthened, he went two hundred miles farther, to Horeb, or Sinai, where the divine law had been given to Moses six centuries before.

The dramatic forces of nature did not get through to him—neither strong wind, earthquake, nor fire. Only the "still small voice" caused him to hearken and respond. He repeated his lament, but he respected the Lord's continuing confidence in him and accepted His call to return to his mission. A new king was named for Syria, Jehu was to be anointed as king for Israel, and

Elisha was to become a prophet with him as a companion for the remainder of his mission and then his replacement.

As for Elijah's fear that he was the only believer left in Israel, the Lord assured him that there were still thousands who had not bowed in faith or affection for Baal.

The trek from Horeb to Damascus would have been well over five hundred miles, and Elijah didn't undertake it immediately; Elisha anointed the kings later (2 Kgs. 8:7–15; 9:1–13.)

19:19–21 So he . . . found Elisha . . . and cast his mantle upon him

The temporary passing of Elijah's mantle to Elisha symbolized his calling; later it was permanently bestowed (2 Kgs. 2:8, 13–14). Note that Elisha was required to leave all that he had to perform his new calling (cf. Matt. 4:18–22).

20:1– 43 Ben-hadad the king of Syria gathered all his host together: and there were thirty and two kings with him . . . and besieged Samaria, and warred against it

This chapter tells of two encounters between Israel against Syria and a coalition of others while Ben-hadad was still king in Damascus. Because of their unconscionable aggression and blatant confidence against the God of Israel, the coalition forces were repulsed, once by an Israelite army with a group of young princes at the head, and again a year later, even though Israel's armies were like "two little flocks of kids" compared to the enemy hosts. A prophet advised King Ahab of Israel on the first strategy, and "a man of God" reassured him it was the Lord's power being challenged in the second (1 Kgs. 20:28, 13, 22); therefore, victory came in both. But when Ahab chose to accept Ben-hadad's concessions, one of the "sons of the prophets" symbolically warned him he had done wrong in releasing an important prisoner of war and would suffer at his hand (1 Kgs. 20:35–43 and fn.).

21:1–29 Naboth . . . had a vineyard . . . hard by the palace of Ahab king of Samaria

Little comment is needed on this account of a covetous and

petulant king, his aggressive and unscrupulous wife, and their confrontation with Elijah, the prophet of God.

Ahab is shown behaving like a spoiled child, frustrated by Naboth's insistence on his rights.

Jezebel was bold, sarcastic, and boastful in her action. Her plan to proclaim a fast and charge Naboth with blasphemy was cynical and diabolical, for by it she could get his land all in the name of piety. Naboth's vineyard would escheat to the king for lack of a living legal heir (1 Kgs. 21:15–16; but see 2 Kgs. 9:26). In her opinion, who could object?

Objection did come, however, by the word of the Lord through Elijah the prophet, for Jezebel's criminal acts were divinely known. In the confrontation, the king's exclamation and the prophet's response were in character for each. As the dynasty of the first despot of Israel, Jeroboam, had been eradicated, so too would be the dynasty of Jezebel and Ahab (1 Kgs. 21:17–24 and fn.).

The concluding statement is problematical, because Ahab, Jezebel, and their family did suffer as Elijah had predicted (1 Kgs. 21:25–29; 22; 2 Kgs. 9–10).

22:1– 40 Jehoshaphat the king of Judah came down to the king of Israel

In Ahab's ambitious campaign to retake the city of Ramoth-gilead, beyond the Jordan River, it is surprising that he was joined by the pious king of Judah, Jehoshaphat. The reason for such an alliance is not evident, but it is noted later that Jehoshaphat's son married a daughter of Ahab and Jezebel. Perhaps Judah hoped to get northern Israel back into the old union; and perhaps Ahab hoped to subjugate Judah.

The difference between the ostentatious religion of Ahab and the humbler faith of Jehoshaphat was shown in the latter's seeking guidance from prophets. The true prophet Micaiah offered first only a sarcastic repetition of the false prophets' assurance to Ahab, but when pressed by Ahab for the truth, he did give him the Lord's message of doom. Micaiah used a metaphor portraying the Lord asking who would persuade Ahab to undertake this campaign and fall therein, explaining that a "lying spirit" was allowed in the minds of all Ahab's false prophets that they might do so (1 Kgs. 22:19–23). Ahab refused to believe Micaiah's prophecy and his explanation of the false prophets' message, and he sent Micaiah to prison until his return. Undaunted, Micaiah declared, "If thou return at all in peace, the Lord hath not spoken by me. . . . Hearken, O people, every one of you" (1 Kgs. 22:28). Despite problems in the account as transmitted, it is a valuable demonstration of the working of false and true prophecy.

Jehoshaphat's personal humility and faith must have qualified him for protection; else the Syrian captains dispatched to kill the king of Israel would not have bypassed anyone dressed in royal robes, whoever he was. Divine power also seems evident in their unknowingly striking Ahab with an arrow (1 Kgs. 22:32–36). Thus Israel's worst king died and "the dogs licked up his blood" as predicted (1 Kgs. 22:37–40; 16:30).

22:41–50 Jehoshaphat the son of Asa . . . reigned twenty and five years in Jerusalem. . . . And he walked in all the ways of Asa his father . . . doing that which was right in the eyes of the Lord

Only Jehoshaphat's failure to destroy the old "high places" of idolatrous worship was recorded against the good record of this king of Judah. A few more of Jehoshaphat's deeds are told, including his wise refusal to collaborate with King Ahaziah, son of Ahab, in a gold-seeking venture. Note how many relatively good kings ruled in Judah in contrast to Israel.

Jehoshaphat's death and the rise of Jehoram, his son and successor, are briefly noted here, but crucial events are recorded later from the few years Jehoram lived and reigned (2 Kgs. 8:16–24).

22:51–53 Ahaziah the son of Ahab . . . reigned two years over Israel

Three verses preview the short reign of Ahaziah in the ways of his father and mother and of the former king Jeroboam. More details are recorded in 2 Kings.

Events recorded in the first book of the Kings began with the prosperous times of Solomon, in which Israel had unlimited opportunities to carry out their divine mission, but neither king nor people performed well, and the kings of northern Israel abandoned all such holy responsibilities after the division of the kingdom. The book ends with tales of terrible decadence in northern Israel, which occasioned the rise of two of the Bible's great prophets to counter the decay. Both of those prophets, Elijah and Elisha, continued into the first years reported in the second book of Kings. That book also reports further problems in both Judah and Israel, which caused the Lord to send Isaiah, Jeremiah, Hosea, and the other "writing prophets" of the Old Testament. Thus there is much to be learned from the books of the Kings as a warning both to worshippers and to adversaries of the true God in earth's latter days.

SECOND KINGS

The second book of the Kings continues from the first book the account of the Lord's efforts through his prophets to turn the hearts of Israel back to a righteous way of life and their Abrahamic mission. The first thirteen chapters continue the accounts of the efforts of Elijah and Elisha, but the people failed to repent, except for brief periods, and in time Elijah and then Elisha passed on. The next four chapters tell of the degeneration, fall, and dispersion of the northern ten tribes of Israel, despite the early "writing prophets" Isaiah, Hosea, Amos, and Micah. Those four chapters, plus three more, record the reigns of several kings of Judah, a few of whom were relatively good and to some degree heeded such prophets as Isaiah and Micah (BD, "Chronology"). The remaining chapters tell of the degeneration, fall, and exile of Judah to Babylon, despite all the writing prophets, including Isaiah, Micah, Jeremiah, and Ezekiel.

COMMENTARY

1:1 Then Moab rebelled against Israel after the death of Ahab

An ancient inscription confirms that Ahab's father, Omri, did conquer Moab and exact tribute from that nation all his days (BD, "Mesha"; "Moabite Stone"). Ahab maintained that dominion, but at his death the Moabites sought freedom. The inscription makes it appear that Moab vanquished and practically destroyed Israel—

an exaggerated claim compared to the biblical account of those events (2 Kgs. 3:4–27).

1:2–18 Ahaziah fell down through a lattice . . . and was sick: and he sent messengers, and said . . . Go, enquire of Baal-zebub the god of Ekron whether I shall recover

This dramatic episode shows how deeply apostate this Israelite king had become and how vigorously the Lord, through his prophet Elijah, tried to correct the presumption of such a king, even though it involved removing some servants of the king from this life. (Such action is not always warranted; recall Jesus' response to James's and John's request to employ it in his behalf; Luke 9:51–56.)

Because of his attitudes and actions, Ahaziah died after only two years of rule, as the true prophet had predicted. He was replaced by his brother Jehoram, since he had no son (2 Kgs. 1:17; BD, "Jehoram or Joram"; both Israel and Judah had kings with the same name during part of the same period).

The name of the idol god Baal-zebub appears as "Beelzebub" in the New Testament (Matt. 12:24), where he is referred to as "the prince of the devils." The name means "Lord of flies," and he was the Philistine god of both disease and healing.

2:1–18 And it came to pass, when the Lord would take up Elijah into heaven by a whirlwind, that Elijah went with Elisha from Gilgal

Before Elijah departed, his loyal young companion and heir, Elisha, requested a double portion of Elijah's spiritual gifts, a request that may be understood in light of the law of inheritances (BD, "Inheritance"). The birthright son inherited a double portion of property as well as more responsibility than other sons; thus Elisha asked, in effect, to be made Elijah's spiritual heir. The "mantle" of Elijah, which had earlier been placed symbolically on Elisha, was now given to him (1 Kgs. 19:19; 2 Kgs. 2:13).

Little is known of Elijah's passage "by a whirlwind into heaven"; but he retained the calling and power to fulfill some exceptional missions back on earth (2 Kgs. 2:10–11; Mal. 4:5–6; Matt. 17:3, 11; John 1:21; JS–H 1:38–39; D&C 110:13–16).

Elijah is transliterated in the New Testament as *Elias,* from its Greek spelling. The name *Elias* is also used as a title for other servants (BD, "Elias"; "Elijah").

The "sons of the prophets" seem to have been subordinate to Elijah and Elisha (BD, "Schools of the Prophets").

2:19–22 the men of the city [of Jericho] said unto Elisha . . . this city is pleasant . . . but the water is naught, and the ground barren

In the first of many "good turn" miracles, Elisha "healed these waters" so that the city spring would be useful to the people and the land. Tourists still visit "Elisha's Spring" next to the ancient mound, or "tell," of Jericho.

Elisha worked much as Jesus later worked—with compassion to help people in need.

2:23–25 he went up from thence unto Bethel: and . . . little children . . . mocked him

Youths, rather than little children, disrespectfully challenged Elisha to ascend ("go up"), as they perhaps had heard that Elijah had ascended (2 Kgs. 2:23a). When he "cursed them in the name of the Lord" (2 Kgs. 2:24), he called upon the Lord to punish them (compare the imprecation in Jude 1:9); it is the opposite of blessing someone in the name of the Lord. The bears did not kill the offenders, as some commentaries assume, but "tare," or lacerated, them.

3:1–27 Jehoram the son of Ahab began to reign over Israel in Samaria the eighteenth year of Jehoshaphat king of Judah

When Jehoram, a son of Ahab, followed his brother Ahaziah as king, he did away with Ahab's Baal and in other ways did somewhat better than his parents had. His cleaving to the sins of Jeroboam means that he failed to eliminate the idolatrous shrines at Bethel and Dan, erected a century earlier by King Jeroboam.

In view of the heavy tribute that Israel required from Moab, it is not surprising that Moab sought to free itself at this moment of apparent weakness in Israel. Jehoram sought the aid of Jehoshaphat of Judah in the resulting conflict. It was for the righteous Jehoshaphat's sake that Elisha felt he could ask the Lord for a miracle when water was needed by the armies of Israel and Judah and their allies from Edom (2 Kgs. 3:13–14). Presumably the minstrel who played for them set a worshipful atmosphere for Elisha's supplication. Elisha hoped the people who benefited from the miracle would gain faith that if they qualified, the Lord could easily deliver the Israelite armies (2 Kgs. 3:15–18).

The miraculous supply of water appeared to the Moabites to be blood when they saw it from far away, and they thought their enemies had slain each other. The Moabites, hoping for plunder, attacked. Then Israel "rose up," decimated the Moabite army and laid waste their cities, farms, and wells. The sacrifice by the king of Moab of his son and heir upon the wall of a Moabite city made it unnecessary for Israel to continue the siege. They and their allies ceased further action and went home; however, the lifting of the siege may have been the "victory" of which King Mesha boasted in the inscription on the Moabite Stone (commentary on 2 Kgs. 1:1).

4:1–7 Now there cried a certain woman of the wives of the sons of the prophets unto Elisha

This compassionate miracle enabled a righteous widow to pay her debts and save her sons from slavery. In its creative nature and compassionate purpose, it also resembles some of Jesus' deeds.

4:8–37 it fell on a day, that Elisha passed to Shunem, where was a great woman

This is the second case of the rare miracle of the raising of the dead (recall 1 Kgs. 17:17–24). Charity, goodwill, and compassion characterize the prophet Elisha's response both to the good woman's generosity and to her sore vexation.

Elisha's mode of resuscitating the child is interesting, but the fact that he prayed first is vital (2 Kgs. 4:33–37).

4:38– 41 Elisha came again to Gilgal: and there was a dearth

When Elisha stopped to visit a group of sons of the prophets in a time of dearth and they tried to prepare food, they unknowingly put a noxious gourd into their stew. Such a gourd, still known in the Jordan valley, can be used in small amounts as a laxative, but in large quantity it can cause death. Elisha knew how to remedy its effects.

4:42– 44 there came a man . . . and brought the man of God bread of the firstfruits

Elisha was inspired to share the offering of twenty loaves with a hundred people and miraculously multiplied the bread to do so—as Jesus later did (2 Kgs. 4:42–44 and fn.).

5:1–27 Now Naaman, captain of the host of the king of Syria, was a great man . . . and honourable, because by him the Lord had given deliverance unto Syria . . . but he was a leper

This is the account of a captive Israelite maid whose compassion and faith instigated an international incident and an act of God in the healing of a Syrian captain. Note his qualities and her compassion and faith. But when Naaman went to Jehoram of Israel, Ahab's son, who had no faith in the Lord's power to heal, Jehoram "rent his clothes" in fear. Somehow apprised of King Jehoram's consternation and Naaman's need, Elisha intervened. Then when Naaman refused to bathe in the Jordan, his servants saw the wisdom of humbly obeying the prophet's command and persuaded the captain to yield. Of course the captain's gratitude knew no bounds when his flesh became as clean as a little child's. He even pleaded to be permitted to worship the Lord in Syria and to be forgiven when required to accompany his king to the Syrian house of worship of another god.

Tragedy developed in the matter, however, when the prophet's servant, Gehazi, could not resist an opportunity to enrich himself a little bit. Secretly and by deceit he did so; but he was exposed and punished by the prophet and the Lord. Gehazi would likely have lost his position with the prophet as a result;

his appearance in a later account (2 Kgs. 8:4) may mean that the events are not compiled in chronological order. Of course, it could be that he repented and was forgiven and cleansed.

6:1–7 But as one was felling a beam, the axe head fell into the water. . . . And the man of God said, Where fell it?

In another helpful miracle, Elisha relieved the distress of one who lost the iron head of a borrowed axe in the water. Miraculously, the iron axe head floated and was retrieved.

6:8–23 Then the king of Syria warred against Israel, . . . And the man of God sent unto the king of Israel, saying, Beware

Presumably this event was in the days of a Syrian king other than the one of the previous chapter (2 Kgs. 5). Here the prophet Elisha functioned as a spy, able to inform the king of Israel of the movements of the enemy. He was also able to avoid capture by the Syrian invaders (cf. Alma 16:5–6; 43:23–24). Indeed, he was able to reassure his fearful servant by asking the Lord to let the servant see (spiritually) the superior defenses of the Lord. Then he led the enemy blindly right into the middle of Israelite head-quarters in Samaria! And as if that were not enough, he recommended to the Israelite king that he feed the enemy and release them, overwhelming them with such kindness that these bands of Syria did not again go up against Israel. Attacks came from others, however (2 Kgs. 6:24).

6:24–7:20 after this . . . Ben-hadad king of Syria . . . went up, and besieged Samaria. And there was a great famine in Samaria

Ben-hadad's siege of Samaria was probably in a later time, as mentioned above.

The intense suffering of the people in the Israelite capital city of Samaria led to cannibalism (2 Kgs. 6:28–30; cf. Lev. 26:29). The king was horrified but blamed the prophet Elisha and the Lord. He angrily asked why he should wait for the Lord any longer and vengefully planned to punish the prophet (2 Kgs. 6:31, 33).

Despite the king's false assumptions and accusations, the Lord showed mercy upon the suffering people, announced the end of the siege through the prophet Elisha, and caused the Syrian attackers to flee. A miracle made them think that the Hittites from the north and the Egyptians from the south had been "hired" to attack them, and they fled (2 Kgs. 7:6–7).

Though the four lepers who found the abandoned supplies thought at first only of their own needs, conscience motivated them to share the goods, lest they suffer for their selfishness.

The king's messenger who doubted Elisha perished as Elisha had predicted (2 Kgs. 7:2, 17–20).

8:1– 6 Then spake Elisha unto the woman, whose son he had restored to life, saying, Arise, and go . . . wheresoever thou canst sojourn: for the Lord hath called for a famine . . . seven years

The righteous woman of the earlier encounter was warned to go where food could be found during the famine (2 Kgs. 8:1*a*).

It is amazing that a king would be interested in Elisha's good deeds and that Elisha's former servant Gehazi would be interviewed about them. But it was obviously all brought about by the hand of the Lord, for out of these events the righteous woman was restored to her home and land.

8:7–15 And Elisha came to Damascus; and Ben-hadad the king of Syria was sick

Just why the accession of Hazael was prophesied by Israelite prophets under the direction of the Lord is not clear. Recall that Elijah was earlier called to go and "anoint Hazael to be king over Syria" (1 Kgs. 19:15). Whether he did so himself or passed that assignment to his successor Elisha is not recorded.

In any case, Elisha's message was ominous: the king could certainly recover but would surely die, and Hazael would be king. Hazael took part of the message to his master, Ben-hadad, and then committed murder to fulfill the rest of it. Elisha's further message that Hazael would one day oppress Israel was denied by Hazael, but it was nevertheless fulfilled by him later (2 Kgs. 8:12*a*) in a divine punishment of Israel's unrighteousness.

8:16–24 in the fifth year of Joram the son of Ahab king of Israel . . . Jehoram the son of Jehoshaphat king of Judah began to reign

This brief review of the reign of Jehoram, son of Jehoshaphat, picks up his story from the point at which it was first raised (1 Kgs. 22:50). The earlier incident from Jehoshaphat's time (2 Kgs. 3:4–27) was recorded out of chronological order.

The names *Joram* and *Jehoram* are interchangeable. For a time Israel and Judah had kings of the same name. Joram of Judah was a brother-in-law to Joram of Israel, having married Athaliah, daughter of Ahab and Jezebel. Through that marriage the worship of Baal from Ahab's and Jezebel's family was introduced into the royal house of Judah.

8:25–29 In the twelfth year of Joram . . . king of Israel did Ahaziah the son of Jehoram king of Judah begin to reign

Ahaziah, when he became king of Judah, followed the ways of his mother, a daughter of Ahab and Jezebel. Athaliah is once called the "daughter of Omri," but Omri was her grandfather. That a Jehoram/Joram was succeeded by an Ahaziah in Judah at about the same time an Ahaziah was succeeded by a Jehoram/Joram in Israel adds to the confusion (BD, "Chronology," pp. 637–38).

Ahaziah of Judah went with Joram of Israel to war against Syria and then visited him in Jezreel while he recovered from a wound. There both of these descendants of Ahab were assassinated by Jehu (2 Kgs. 9:14–29).

9:1–37 Elisha the prophet called one of the children of the prophets, and said unto him . . . look out there Jehu . . . Then take the box of oil, and pour it on his head, and say, Thus saith the Lord, I have anointed thee king over Israel. Then open the door, and flee, and tarry not

Elisha gave careful instructions for the installation of a new king of Israel to replace the apostate dynasty of Ahab. But the young messenger did not follow instructions: after anointing the Israelite army captain Jehu, he charged him to "smite the house of Ahab" and repeated Elijah's former prophecy that "the dogs shall eat Jezebel" (2 Kgs. 9:5–10; 1 Kgs. 21:23). Jehu undertook that charge with vigor, conspiring against Joram of Israel and slaying him in the very field that Ahab and Jezebel had taken from Naboth (2 Kgs. 9:21; 1 Kgs. 21:1–24). Next, he overtook and slew the fleeing Ahaziah of Judah and went on to Jezreel to confront Jezebel. Knowing of previous assassinations of royalty by an army leader, Jezebel adorned herself as queen and warned him of the fate of Zimri, one of those army usurpers. Undaunted, Jehu called for allies in the royal house to cast Jezebel down, and he left her body to be consumed as had been prophesied, relenting only later to send someone to bury any remains.

10:1–11 And Ahab had seventy sons in Samaria. . . . Then he wrote a letter . . . saying . . . take ye the heads of the men your master's sons, and come to me to Jezreel

After writing one letter challenging those loyal to the house of Ahab to appoint another king of that house, Jehu wrote another letter telling them to behead all of Ahab's lineage and take the evidence to Jezreel. He used the heads as evidence that others were with him against Ahab's family.

Jehu's bloody purge was not by Elisha's command, although it did somewhat follow the charge disobediently added by the prophet's young messenger (2 Kgs. 9:1–3, 6–10). The prophet Hosea later prophesied vengeance upon Jehu's house for violent excesses (Hosea 1:4).

10:12–14 Jehu met with the brethren of Ahaziah king of Judah . . . And they took them alive, and slew them

Forty-two of the seed of Ahab through Athaliah, mother of King Ahaziah of Judah, were next in Jehu's purge.

10:15–28 call unto me all the prophets of Baal, all his servants, and all his priests

Taking Jehonadab, son of Rechab, as a witness, Jehu called together the prophets and priests of Baal for a great sacrifice and then made them the sacrificial victims. Thus Jehu sought to destroy Baal in Israel.

10:29–31, 34–36 Howbeit . . . Jehu departed not from after them, to wit, the golden calves that were in Bethel, and that were in Dan

It seems incongruous that this reformer, appointed by a prophet and proud of his zeal for the Lord, would fail to clear out the idolatry introduced in Israel a hundred years earlier by the first king of northern Israel. He purged the seed of Ahab, but how well did he serve the Lord? We do not have the book that chronicles his further acts and might. He reigned twenty-eight years and began another short dynasty in Israel.

10:32–33 In those days the Lord began to cut Israel short: and Hazael smote them

Hazael of Syria began his wars against Israel as prophesied by Elisha, who had anointed him (2 Kgs. 8:7–15).

11:1–3 when Athaliah the mother of Ahaziah saw that her son was dead, she arose and destroyed all the seed royal

There was yet more bloodshed in Judah because of the house of Ahab. His daughter Athaliah, widow of King Joram of Judah and mother of King Ahaziah, seized the opportunity afforded by Jehu's having killed her sons. She killed all remaining heirs so that she might rule alone; only one little grandson, Joash, son of the dead King Ahaziah, was saved with his nurse by his aunt Jehosheba/Jehoshabeath, sister of King Ahaziah and wife of the high priest Jehoiada (2 Chr. 22:11). The terrible grandmother, Athaliah, reigned in Judah for six years, instituting some of the Baalism of her mother, Jezebel, and it was never completely destroyed thereafter.

11:4–21 And the seventh year Jehoiada sent and fetched the rulers . . . and shewed them the king's son

When Joash (also called Jehoash) was seven years old, the high priest Jehoiada aligned the military leaders for a coup, killed

Athaliah and destroyed her ways (for a time), and restored the Davidic monarchy. It was a blessing for Judah that there were still enough faithful people to rally to the high priest for this reform.

12:1–21 In the seventh year of Jehu Jehoash began to reign; and forty years reigned he in Jerusalem

All the days of the good priest Jehoiada, the young king reigned in righteousness except for his failure to remove the old sacrificial altars on the common "high places." There people continued to burn incense and offer offerings—sometimes to the Lord but too often to idols.

King Jehoash/Joash, with the help of Jehoiada, also revised the system for channeling money-offerings at the temple into their proper use, for it was evident that the priests had not maintained the temple as they should have done (2 Kgs. 12:4–16; 2 Chr. 24:4–14).

Judah felt the rampaging power of Hazael of Syria when apostasy followed the death of the good priest Jehoiada. Despite his early righteous deeds, King Jehoash/Joash was eventually assassinated because of his unrighteous deeds. Nevertheless, his son was made king. More details are given in the books of Chronicles (see esp. 2 Chr. 24).

13:1–9 In the three and twentieth year of Joash . . . of Judah . . . Jehoahaz the son of Jehu began to reign over Israel

Although he was described as being like most of the kings of northern Israel, Jehoahaz did turn to the Lord under the oppression of Syria, and in His mercy the Lord gave Israel a "saviour," or deliverer. The king was spared, with a few horsemen, chariots, and a small army of foot soldiers; when he died, his son Joash/Jehoash succeeded him. (Note again that kings in Judah and Israel have similar names; BD, "Chronology.")

13:10–13 In the thirty and seventh year of Joash king of Judah began Jehoash the son of Jehoahaz to reign over Israel

Joash/Jehoash of Israel fought with Amaziah of Judah and did evil as usual. Yet he did recover some cities from Syria (2 Kgs. 13:12, 15; 2 Chr. 25:17–24).

13:14–21 Now Elisha was fallen sick of his sickness whereof he died. And Joash the king of Israel came down unto him, and wept

One wonders whether Elisha was the "saviour" sent in response to Joash/Jehoash's earlier prayer (2 Kgs. 13:5). The king did seem to feel respect for the old prophet and grief at his death.

Symbolic acts done by the king with arrows were interpreted by the prophet as harbingers of temporary triumphs over Syria but not of lasting peace. The great power given by the Lord to Elisha was exemplified a year after his death, when a man hastily buried in his tomb was revived again (2 Kgs. 13:21).

13:22–25 But Hazael king of Syria oppressed Israel all the days of Jehoahaz

This addendum to the first half of the chapter clarifies the Lord's reasons for helping Israel at that time and tells the fulfillment of Elisha's last prophecy (2 Kgs. 13:18–19).

14:1– 6 In the second year of Joash son of Jehoahaz king of Israel reigned Amaziah the son of Joash king of Judah

Amaziah was another of Judah's kings who reigned righteously except for failing to take away the altars on the high places. He followed the principles of justice in dealing with those who assassinated his father (2 Kgs. 14:5–6; Deut. 24:16).

14:7 He slew of Edom in the valley of salt ten thousand, and took Selah by war

Judah vanquished Edom in the Arabah ("valley of salt") and recovered the rock-hewn city of Selah (Petra). There is much additional information in the parallel account in Chronicles (2 Chr. 25:5–13).

14:8–16 Then Amaziah sent messengers to Jehoash . . . king of Israel, saying, Come, let us look one another in the face

Judah's strange invitation to northern Israel to do battle was ill-advised and resulted in disaster for Judah's army; part of the city wall of Jerusalem and the temple were damaged. This was the only time Israelites plundered the temple of the Lord.

The death of Joash/Jehoash of Israel is again reported here (2 Kgs. 13:13; 14:15–16).

14:17–22 Now they made a conspiracy against him in Jerusalem

Assassination of a king in Judah did not result in a change of dynasty, though it usually did in northern Israel. It seems that in Judah there were always people who felt the Davidic dynasty should be preserved.

Here only the beginning of the reign of Azariah is told, including his recovery and rebuilding of the port of Elath; more is given later (2 Kgs. 15:1–7; 2 Chr. 26). Also called "Uzziah" (2 Chr. 26:1*a*), he reigned righteously for a number of years; but he usurped priestly authority, was smitten with leprosy, and was restricted to a separate house (2 Chr. 26:16–21). His son Jotham was "over the king's house, judging the people of the land" until Azariah/Uzziah's death, according to 2 Chronicles 26:21. That source also indicates that Isaiah may have been the recorder of some of this information (2 Chr. 26:22).

14:23–29 In the fifteenth year of Amaziah the son of Joash king of Judah Jeroboam the son of Joash king of Israel began to reign in Samaria

Although reproached with the usual charge of idolatry, this new Jeroboam, of a different family from the first, must have been fairly capable. He reigned longer than most of Israel's kings, and in his administration he restored parts of the borders of Israel with guidance from the prophet Jonah (2 Kgs. 14:25*a*). The book of Jonah does not report his service at home; it pertains only to his foreign mission to Nineveh.

The prophet Amos also did his work in the days of these kings, Amaziah/Uzziah of Judah and Jeroboam of Israel (Amos 1:1; 7:10–13).

15:1–7 In the twenty and seventh year of Jeroboam king of Israel began Azariah son of Amaziah king of Judah to reign

A few more details about the last years and the disease of Azariah are given here, but much more is recorded in Chronicles (2 Chr. 26).

The name *Azariah* means "Jehovah is my helper"; his other name, *Uzziah,* means "Jehovah is my strength."

15:8–12 In the thirty and eighth year of Azariah king of Judah did Zachariah the son of Jeroboam reign over Israel in Samaria six months

Zachariah, the fourth king of the house of Jehu, was assassinated rather soon, and thus the promise of the Lord was fulfilled (2 Kgs. 10:30; 15:12). None of the four kings was credited with righteousness or noteworthy contributions. We do not have the "book of the chronicles of the kings of Israel" (2 Kgs. 15:11, 15). Our books of Chronicles seem rather to be chronicles of the kings of Judah.

15:13–16 Shallum . . . began to reign in the nine and thirtieth year of Uzziah king of Judah; and he reigned a full month in Samaria

Again one who took the throne by the sword lost it by the sword. After one month, the assassin Shallum was himself assassinated, and Menahem reigned in his stead. The prophet Hosea said of these times: "By swearing, and lying, and killing, and stealing, and committing adultery, they break out, and blood toucheth blood" (Hosea 4:2). The last phrase in Hebrew implies "violence upon violence." Consider areas in the world in the last days that could be similarly described.

15:16–22 In the nine and thirtieth year of Azariah king of Judah began Menahem . . . to reign over Israel, . . . ten years

King Menahem also committed "evil in the sight of the Lord," such as his mutilation of pregnant women in Tirzah. But he held the throne for ten years by exacting money from wealthy Israelite men and paying huge tribute to Pul (Tiglath-pileser), king of

Assyria. Within fifty years the next king of Assyria would conquer northern Israel's ten tribes and carry them away captive when they failed to pay tribute.

15:23–26 In the fiftieth year of Azariah king of Judah Pekahiah the son of Menahem began to reign over Israel . . . two years

Menahem's "dynasty" was also shortened by assassination. Pekah, one of the king's captains, killed Menahem's son King Pekahiah and replaced him.

15:27–31 In the two and fiftieth year of Azariah king of Judah Pekah . . . began to reign over Israel . . . twenty years

Note how much longer the kings of Judah lasted, as a rule, than the northern Israelite kings. The Davidic monarchy was often more righteous and the government more stable.

The threat of Assyria grew ever more intense. The old enemies, Israel and Syria, were both threatened—and became allies. Israelites of the tribes in Gilead and Galilee were taken into captivity by Assyria some twenty years before the rest were taken.

The book of Isaiah reports that Pekah of Israel combined with Rezin of Syria to resist Assyria. They tried to persuade Judah to join the coalition and failed; and in the time of Ahaz, king of Judah, they threatened to overthrow him and put a king on the throne who would cooperate with them. Through Isaiah, the Lord assured Ahaz that the plot would fail, and the two threatening kings, whom he characterized as "tails of these smoking firebrands" would soon be taken away (Isa. 7:1–16).

During these times of political disruption, religious degeneration, and moral corruption, the great "writing prophets" of the Old Testament preached repentance and wrote their books. Some of them came before the fall of Israel, and some a hundred and thirty years later, before the fall of Judah. Their warnings and pleas for the people to repent, along with their assurance of the future fulfillment of God's purposes, have come down to us because of their special relevance for the last dispensation.

Among the earlier group were Hosea, Amos, Micah, and

Isaiah. Hosea pleaded with the northern ten tribes to return to Jehovah and emphasized His loving concern for them. Amos, a shepherd from Judah, preached in Israel in the very court of the second King Jeroboam, condemning injustices done to the poor by powerful religious and political leaders. The eloquent Micah gave warnings for his times, as well as recording his visions of the birth of the Messiah and of the last days of the earth. But the dean of all the early writing prophets was Isaiah, who prophesied at Jerusalem, advising kings and commoners and addressing messages to both Judah and Israel. These prophets and their messages are discussed in commentaries on their respective books.

15:32–38 In the second year of Pekah . . . king of Israel began Jotham the son of Uzziah king of Judah to reign

This was the beginning of Jotham's reign proper, after his taking over during the last years of his incapacitated father, Uzziah (2 Kgs. 15:1–7). The pressure on Judah by Syria and Ephraim (northern Israel), mentioned above, is reported here (2 Kgs. 15:37). More of the works of Jotham in building defenses and in warfare are recorded in Chronicles (2 Chr. 27).

16:1–20 In the seventeenth year of Pekah . . . Ahaz the son of Jotham king of Judah began to reign

Ahaz was the worst of the Davidic kings. He had the great prophet Isaiah to advise him and would have done better by accepting his advice.

The phrase "made his son pass through fire, according to the abominations of the heathen" (2 Kgs. 16:3) does actually mean that he offered a son to a fire-belching idol. He also performed other idolatrous practices.

Ignoring both Isaiah's assurance about an attack by Syria and Israel and his warning about the growing dangers from Assyria (Isa. 7), Ahaz tried a pressure-play against the Syrians and northern Israelites by giving tribute to Assyria's king, even adopting his religion, to curry favor with him. This Ahaz, a descendant of David and Solomon, even removed the lavers from their bases and the "sea" (font) from the brazen oxen of the temple to satisfy the king of Assyria.

The Chronicles account expands the brief note about Ahaz's death to explain that he was buried in Jerusalem but not in the sepulchres with the other kings (2 Kgs. 16:20; 2 Chr. 28:27).

17:1– 6 In the ninth year of Hoshea the king of Assyria took Samaria, and carried Israel away into Assyria

Hoshea, the last king of the northern ten tribes of Israel, conspired against King Pekah and slew him in the twentieth year of King Jotham of Judah; but Hoshea began reigning years later, in the twelfth year of the reign of Jotham's son Ahaz (2 Kgs. 15:30; 17:1). The account concedes that the evil he did was not as bad as the evil done by the kings before him. He paid Assyria tribute as three kings before him had done, but like Pekah before him, he could not keep Assyria appeased. When he tried to get Egypt's help against Assyria, Shalmaneser of Assyria imprisoned him and besieged the capital city, Samaria, for three years. Finally Shalmaneser took the city and sent thousands of Israelites into slavery in the areas listed. Thus they became "the lost ten tribes of Israel" (2 Kgs. 17:6b–c).

17:7–23 For so it was, that the children of Israel had sinned against the Lord their God . . . Yet the Lord testified against Israel, and against Judah, by all the prophets . . . saying, Turn ye from your evil ways, and keep my commandments

This summary of the reasons for the downfall of Israel shows clearly that the chosen people had failed to do what they had been chosen to do (TG, "Israel, Mission of"). Also summarized are the mission of the prophets, the reasons their mission did not succeed in saving Israel, and the reasons the Lord allowed the ten tribes to be taken into exile (cf. 2 Kgs. 15:27–31).

17:24– 41 And the king of Assyria brought men from Babylon, and from Cuthah, and from Ava, and from Hamath, and from Sepharvaim, and placed them in the cities of Samaria instead of the children of Israel

A mixture of peoples became the "Samaritans"; doubtless

some Israelites were also among them. The Israelite religion was nominally retained because when predatory beasts began to flourish after the human population was reduced, a mixed religion evolved: some inhabitants sacrificed to the Lord to protect them from predators but still served their own gods.

18:1–8 in the third year of Hoshea . . . Hezekiah the son of Ahaz king of Judah began to reign. . . . And he did that which was right in the sight of the Lord

The contrast of Hezekiah of Judah with Hoshea of Israel is striking. They differed in their efforts to defend their countries, their religious attitudes, their response to the prophets, and in their fates, for Hezekiah was righteous.

18:9–12 in the fourth year of king Hezekiah, which was the seventh year of Hoshea . . . Shalmaneser king of Assyria came up against Samaria . . . And at the end of three years they took it

The writer of this passage reviewed the fall of Israel (2 Kgs. 17:7–23) and reiterated the reason for the fall: "Because they obeyed not the voice of the Lord their God, but transgressed his covenant" (2 Kgs. 18:12). The nations and cities named are those to which the Israelites were at first scattered.

18:13–37 Now in the fourteenth year of king Hezekiah did Sennacherib king of Assyria come up against all the fenced cities of Judah, and took them

Ten years later Judah was tested again by Assyria, under a new king. For a time Hezekiah had to pay an enormous tribute out of the palace and temple treasures. Sennacherib's records on a stone cylinder found by archaeologists confirm the amount of gold as thirty talents but claim eight hundred talents of silver rather than the three hundred reported in the Bible (cf. BD, "Sennacherib").

During those years of crisis, Isaiah the prophet warned Judah against depending on the armed might of Egypt, recommending trust in the Lord instead (Isa. 30–31). When Sennacherib sent three of his leaders from besieging the fortress city of Lachish to persuade the people of Jerusalem to capitulate, Isaiah advised Hezekiah to resist and rely on the Lord (2 Kgs. 19; Isa. 36–37).

The Assyrian Rabshakeh's propaganda was diabolical. He taunted the people of Judah with offers of horses if they could find riders for them. He used vulgarity to frighten them with the horrors of famine. He promised to take them to a land better and more productive. He asserted that the Lord would not help them because Hezekiah had ordered altars on the high places destroyed—wrongly assuming that those altars were for worship of the Lord. He claimed that the Lord had sent Sennacherib to destroy Judah—in a twist on the warning of Israel's prophets that if the people did not repent they would be captured. He boasted that the Lord could not defend Jerusalem against Assyria even if he wanted to do so, citing the failure of gods of other lands to defend them. Obedient to the king, the people held their peace. Hezekiah's steward Eliakim, the scribe Shebna, and the recorder Asaph reported the pleas and threats to King Hezekiah, who turned to the prophet and the Lord and indeed received help (2 Kgs. 18:37; 19; Isa. 37).

19:1–7 when king Hezekiah heard it . . . he . . . went into the house of the Lord . . . And he sent . . . to Isaiah the prophet

In Jerusalem, the beleaguered king requested that the prophet ask the Lord to punish the blasphemy uttered by the Assyrian spokesman Rabshakeh. The reply of the Lord, through the prophet, was concise, precise, and reassuring: the attacker would suffer a "blast" from the Lord, hear a "rumor," return home, and fall by the sword there.

19:8–13 So Rab-shakeh returned, and found the king of Assyria warring against Libnah

Sennacherib had trouble, too. Rabshakeh found that the Assyrian army had left Lachish and was battering away at Libnah. (Both were important hilltop fortress cities about twenty-five miles west-southwest of Jerusalem.) News had arrived that the king of Ethiopia was coming to resist Assyria's empire-building war. So

Rabshakeh was sent back to Jerusalem to try again to impress upon Judah that no gods had stood successfully against Sennacherib, this time delivering the message by letter to King Hezekiah.

19:14–19 And Hezekiah received the letter . . . and read it: and . . . went up into the house of the Lord, and spread it before the Lord

Faithful Hezekiah literally opened the letter to the Lord and humbly told him of Sennacherib's reproach and boasting. Hezekiah knew the Assyrian gods "were no gods," whereas the Lord alone is God; he therefore sought salvation from him.

19:20–34 Then Isaiah . . . sent to Hezekiah, saying, Thus saith the Lord . . . That which thou hast prayed to me against Sennacherib king of Assyria I have heard. This is the word that the Lord hath spoken concerning him

The Lord's answer through Isaiah the prophet was that He had indeed permitted the Assyrians to destroy some peoples (2 Kgs. 19:25–26; Isa. 10:5–19); but because of Sennacherib's reproach, he must be hooked, bridled, and taken away (2 Kgs. 19:28). The people of Judah were then to return to their lands, eat the volunteer crops for a year, and resume sowing and reaping; the people could again "take root downward, and bear fruit upward" (2 Kgs. 19:29–30). The boastful king of Assyria would neither shoot an arrow into Jerusalem nor build siege banks against the walls. His fate had already been pronounced by Isaiah (2 Kgs. 19:7).

19:35–37 And it came to pass that night that the angel of the Lord went out, and smote in the camp of the Assyrians an hundred fourscore and five thousand

The deliverance came as promised; a plague decimated the Assyrian forces and the remnant fled. The annals of Sennacherib, recorded on stone, confirm his departure from Judah without capturing Jerusalem; and though the Assyrian account boasts of the booty he took out, it does also confirm that after returning to

Nineveh, Sennacherib was assassinated by two of his sons and replaced by a third.

*20:1–11 In those days was Hezekiah sick unto death. And the
prophet Isaiah . . . came to him*

King Hezekiah had an abscess and illness which, if allowed to
run its course, would have caused his death; but just as any of us
might do, the king prayed humbly and sincerely to be healed. He
was found worthy to be healed, and the prophet Isaiah was directed to tell him so. The account here reports the king's asking
what sign would assure him that the Lord would heal him and
that he could go to the temple in three days; Isaiah's account reports that the king asked only what sign would show that he
would indeed yet go up to the temple. Why he asked for a sign
and did receive it is not indicated (2 Kgs. 20:8–11; Isa. 38:22).

*20:12–19 At that time Berodach-baladan . . . king of Babylon, sent
letters and a present unto Hezekiah: for he had heard that
Hezekiah had been sick*

The seemingly compassionate mission of messengers from
Babylon may have had some strategic purpose. Babylon had been
under Assyrian oppression, having been subdued by Sennacherib
earlier, ca. 740 B.C.; so Judah's cooperation with Babylon in a rebellion against Assyria could help them both. In any case, Hezekiah
unwisely showed the Babylonians his treasures and powers; when
Isaiah heard of it, he prophesied that Babylonians would one day
carry them away captive to Babylon. "Sons" in the Bible does not
always mean immediate progeny (2 Kgs. 20:18); a century later,
some third- and fourth-generation descendants of King Hezekiah
would be captured and exiled or killed (2 Kgs. 24–25).

King Hezekiah was submissive and grateful that peace and
truth would prevail in his days.

*20:20–21 And the rest of the acts of Hezekiah, and all his might,
and how he made a pool, and a conduit*

In the brief summation of Hezekiah's other accomplishments

is mentioned an engineering feat now called Hezekiah's tunnel (2 Kgs. 20:20; 2 Chr. 32:1–4, 30). That tunnel has been rediscovered and can be traversed by anyone who wishes to wade through its six hundred yards of cool waters, some places calf-deep and other places hip-deep. The "Siloam inscription"—named for the pool into which the water-course empties—engraved in the stone wall of the tunnel is an important and fascinating ancient Hebrew document. It describes how the workers started at each end of the proposed tunnel and worked until they met, deep under the old lower city of Jerusalem (BD, "Hezekiah"; "Hezekiah's Tunnel").

An earlier water course and pool in the time of Hezekiah's father Ahaz was a surface water system, remnants of which have also been found (Isa. 7:3; 22:11).

21:1–9 Manasseh was twelve years old when he began to reign, and reigned fifty and five years . . . And he did that which was evil in the sight of the Lord

Despite the virtues of Hezekiah and his religious reforms (told in more detail in 2 Chr. 29–32), Judah reverted to idolatry when he was dead. Hezekiah's son Manasseh, being so young when his father died, may have been influenced by factions who had smarted under the righteous regime of his father; perhaps they yearned for relaxed moral ways and the carnal fertility rites of the Baal cults. These had always attracted the less dedicated of the Lord's people, in spite of warnings by the prophets. *Asherah,* often translated as "grove," was not a grove of trees but a fertility goddess thought to dwell in, or be represented by, a tree. She was sometimes a female consort of Baal. Altars for the "host of heaven" were for constellation-based worship. The terrible worship of Moloch, which also was resumed, required infants to be cast into a fire-belching idol. Note also the people's superstitions.

Thus under Manasseh the people of Judah did more evil than the nations that the Lord had destroyed in the land, notwithstanding prophetic warnings about such behavior (Lev. 18:26–28). During the years from Manasseh to his great-grandson Zedekiah, those prophecies were all fulfilled (2 Kgs. 24–25).

21:10–15 And the Lord spake by his servants the prophets, saying, Because Manasseh king of Judah hath done these abominations . . . I am bringing such evil upon Jerusalem and Judah

The prophets of these times included Zephaniah, Habakkuk, Jeremiah, Ezekiel, and others not named in the Bible, including Lehi of the Book of Mormon.

The metaphors about a line, a plummet, and a dish are easily understandable—they involve straightness, uprightness, and cleansing—and the forecasts of the results of iniquity are plain. The summation that generations of Israelites since Moses had done so much evil is sobering and ominous to contemplate.

21:16–18 Moreover Manasseh shed innocent blood very much

Since the shedding of innocent blood was in addition to the other sins Manasseh engendered in Judah, the phrase may well refer to blood purges of hosts of those who opposed young Manasseh. Very little about his life and deeds for the fifty-five years of his reign is recorded. His death and burial in his garden, not in the tombs of the previous kings, is simply told.

In the Chronicles, an account not corroborated either here or in the prophetic books tells of Manasseh's being taken captive by captains of the army of the king of Assyria to Babylon, where he suffered and repented and then was returned to finish out a much more righteous reign in Jerusalem. That account raises some historical problems (see 2 Chr. 33:11–18).

21:19–26 Amon was twenty and two years old when he began to reign, and he reigned two years . . . And he did that which was evil in the sight of the Lord, as his father Manasseh did

Amon was as bad as or even worse than his father, and his servants conspired against him and slew him (cf. 2 Chr. 33:21–24). Yet loyalty to the royal house of David was still strong, so people slew the conspirators and put Amon's young son Josiah on the throne.

22:1–20 Josiah was eight years old when he began to reign, and he reigned thirty and one years . . . And he did that which was right in the sight of the Lord

The young son and grandson of wicked kings, Josiah was religious and righteous and became a great reformer in Judah. Early in his reign he arranged that the money collected at the door of the temple be used for its intended purpose to repair and maintain the temple.

Josiah's reforms increased after a scribe found the book of the law in the temple. When the king heard words from the book, telling what people should do and what would befall them if they did evil instead, he rent his clothes in repentance and asked his scribes and Hilkiah the priest to inquire of the Lord whether His wrath would fall upon all for their many violations. They may have read warnings in the books of Moses (Lev. 18:26–28; 26:21–46; Deut. 4:23–30; 28:58–68) and feared they were applicable to Israel in their time. Rather than making a direct inquiry by prayer or going to the holy place in the temple, the priest and scribes went to "Huldah the prophetess" for her interpretation. She confirmed that the wrath of God would surely fall if the people of Judah continued their wickedness; but because the young king was a true reformer, it would not happen in his reign. Huldah was a "wise woman" like those of earlier accounts (2 Kgs. 22:18–20; Judg. 4:4–5; 2 Sam. 14:2; TG, "Prophetess").

The prophet Jeremiah began his ministry in the thirteenth year of King Josiah, but no contact between them is mentioned in his early days (Jer. 1:2). The prophet Zephaniah also lived in that period (Zeph. 1:1).

23:1–30 And the king went up into the house of the Lord, and all the men of Judah and all the inhabitants of Jerusalem with him, and the priests, and the prophets, and all the people, both small and great: and he read in their ears all the words of the book of the covenant

With administrative skill, King Josiah launched a great reform involving all the people and the leaders. He led out by teaching them about their covenants with God and renewing them. He caused all the idolatrous facilities to be destroyed, including the infamous altar at Beth-el set up by the first king of northern Israel—thus fulfilling a prophecy about it (2 Kgs. 23:15; 1 Kgs. 12:25–29; 13:1–2). Yet in burning the bones of former idolatrous priests of the place, he identified and honored the bones of a man of God (1 Kgs. 13:23–32). In that same eventful year the Passover was celebrated as it had not been celebrated for centuries (2 Kgs. 23:22–23). Finally, the spiritualists and their abominations were put away, and the land was cleansed for the first time in centuries. But the pendulum swinging from evil kings to good kings had not stopped. The Lord knew that Judah would revert to evil after Josiah's death and be destroyed because of it (2 Kgs. 23:26–27).

It is tragic that the zealous Josiah lost his life in a vain attempt at intervention in international affairs. Perhaps he feared the rise of Egypt more than he feared the decadent Assyria against whom the king of Egypt was going to fight. As it turned out, Assyria was overthrown and Nineveh conquered by Babylon three years after Josiah's death (BD, "Chronology," p. 639.)

The death of young Josiah after thirty-one years of remarkable action must have been a bitter disappointment for the righteous people in Judah. It may well have hastened the resurgence of un-righteous forces that dominated the last two decades of that nation. Quite understandably, the prophet Jeremiah lamented the death of the righteous King Josiah (2 Kgs. 23:29–30; 2 Chr. 35:24–25).

23:31–34 Jehoahaz was twenty and three years old when he began to reign; and he reigned three months in Jerusalem . . . And he did that which was evil in the sight of the Lord

Josiah's first son and his immediate successor, Jehoahaz, was unacceptable to King Necho of Egypt, who dominated Judah after killing Josiah. He demanded tribute and took King Jehoahaz to Egypt, where he died.

Jeremiah of Libnah, identified as the father of Jehoahaz's mother, is not Jeremiah of Anathoth, the prophet (2 Kgs. 23:31; Jer. 1:1).

23:34–37; 24:1–7 And Pharaoh-nechoh made Eliakim the son of Josiah king in the room of Josiah his father, and turned his name to Jehoiakim . . . Jehoiakim was twenty and five years old when he began to reign; and he reigned eleven years in Jerusalem

The new puppet-king's first name, *Eliakim,* means "El [God] shall establish," and his new name, *Jehoiakim,* means "Jehovah shall establish," but he was untrue to both names and sinned as had his forefathers (2 Kgs. 24:1–5; Jer. 36).

The Pharaohs' giving a new name to subjected people is not unusual, but it is noteworthy that they acclaimed the Lord (Jehovah) in this case. In some cases when the followers of a "powerful" god were conquered, the conquerors sought to appease that god by sacrifices or honors, lest he avenge himself. That may have been the reason for honoring Jehovah specifically rather than God generally by this change of name.

During the last three years of his stormy reign, Jehoiakim became a vassal of Babylon instead of Egypt, for Babylon expanded its domain throughout all the Fertile Crescent. Jehoiakim undoubtedly would have been purged by Babylon, but he died at an early age and was replaced by his son, Jehoiachin, who reigned for a few months.

24:8–16 Jehoiachin was eighteen years old when he began to reign, and he reigned in Jerusalem three months

The young King Jehoiachin was besieged almost immediately and was taken away—along with his mother, the servants, the princes, the craftsmen, and the treasures from the temple and palace—in the eighth year of Nebuchadnezzar's reign, about 597 B.C. (More is told about Jehoiachin and the treasures in Ezra 1:7–11.) This group of ten thousand exiles may have included young Ezekiel, who became a prophet in exile (Ezek. 1:1–2). Daniel had likely been taken earlier (ca. 605 B.C.; Dan. 1:1–2).

It is evident that the Babylonian policy of control was to carry away all the leading citizens and leave the common people to produce agricultural goods for tribute.

24:17–20 And the king of Babylon made Mattaniah his father's brother king in his stead, and changed his name to Zedekiah

The king's new name retained the name of the Lord, for *Mattaniah* means "gift of Jehovah" and *Zedekiah* means "righteous is Jehovah." It may be that declaring Jehovah just or righteous was also intended to honor him, as in the Egyptians' changing the name of their Judahite puppet-king from *Eliakim* to *Jehoiakim*.

Zedekiah's grandfather, Jeremiah of Libnah, was not Jeremiah of Anathoth, the prophet (2 Kgs. 24:18; 23:31).

Zedekiah was the last king of the Davidic line before the Messiah, who came six hundred years later (the Book of Mormon gives the date of his appointment as 600 B.C.; 2 Kgs. 24:18*a*). And yet, despite everything, Zedekiah also did evil in the sight of the Lord. Ignoring the advice of the prophet Jeremiah, he rebelled against Nebuchadnezzar and suffered for doing so (2 Kgs. 24:19*a;* 24:20*a-b;* 25:1–21).

As indicated in the books of Jeremiah and his contemporaries, the Lord sent prophets to warn the kings of Judah to repent and seek his help rather than try to free themselves. Ironically, when Babylonian oppression did become worse, the king and the people blamed, maligned, and punished the prophets of God (Jer. 1:18–19; 32; 38).

25:1–7 in the ninth year of his reign . . . Nebuchadnezzar king of Babylon came . . . And the city was besieged unto the eleventh year of king Zedekiah . . . And the city was broken up

So, as the prophets had warned, Judah was conquered after a two-year siege of Jerusalem, and its leaders, warriors, and people were killed or captured. Zedekiah was triply tortured as his sons were killed in his sight, his eyes were put out, and he was taken in chains to Babylon. Other sources record that his daughters were not carried off by the Babylonian conquerors but were taken to Egypt by a group of Jewish refugees, as was Jeremiah the prophet (Jer. 43:5–7). The Book of Mormon indicates that a son of Zedekiah named Mulek escaped by sea with a group that ended up in the western hemisphere (Omni 1:14–19).

*25:8–21 And in the fifth month, on the seventh day of the month
. . . he burnt the house of the Lord, and the king's house, and all
the houses of Jerusalem*

Just a month after the invaders broke in, the temple was destroyed. It had stood since King Solomon's time, nearly four hundred years before. It was the end of an epoch for Jerusalem. Only the poor of the land were left to produce crops.

Valuable brass and bronze works of the temple compound were broken up and taken to Babylon. Many fine vessels were taken intact, however, and eventually were returned to the second temple, which was built in Jerusalem some seventy years later (2 Kgs. 25:13–17; Ezra 1:7–11; 7:19; 8:24–36).

Certain religious leaders and others who had somehow been missed earlier were also taken and slain, but Jeremiah the prophet was sought out by Nebuchadnezzar's leaders of the siege and was permitted to do whatever he chose—perhaps because he had advised the kings not to fight against Babylon to save themselves (2 Kgs. 25:18–21; Jer. 39:11–14).

*25:22–26 for the people that remained in the land of Judah, . . .
Nebuchadnezzar . . . made Gedaliah . . . ruler*

Gedaliah seems to have been a good man, but one Ishmael "of the seed royal" conspired against him; to the regret of most of the remnant of Judah left in the land, Ishmael slew him and many others. Much more detail was given by Jeremiah concerning that remnant, their fate as refugees in Egypt, and the future also of Egypt (2 Kgs. 25:26; Jer. 40–44).

*25:27–30 in the seven and thirtieth year of the captivity of
Jehoiachin king of Judah, . . . Evil-merodach king of Babylon . . .
did lift up the head of Jehoiachin king of Judah out of prison*

The favor granted to the former king of Judah is unexplained, unless the new Babylonian king found it politic to make with him a sort of government-in-exile to help control the Jews in Babylon. A grandson of Jehoiachin named Zerubbabel (1 Chr. 3:17–19; Ezra 2:1–2; BD, "Zerubbabel") was later made governor of the Jews who were permitted by the Persians to return to Judah; and his lineage continued on down to Joseph and Mary (his name is spelled *Zorobabel* in Matt. 1:12). According to Chronicles, Jehoiachin was eight years old rather than eighteen, as recorded in Kings, when he was taken to Babylon (2 Chr. 36:9; 2 Kgs. 24:8). He would therefore have been either forty-five or fifty-five years old when he was freed from prison. He may have been divinely preserved to perpetuate the Davidic line into which the Messiah would be born.

It is evident from the book of the prophet Ezekiel and the book of Ezra that the Jews in Babylon were kept together, not scattered as had been the ten tribes of Israel taken captive by the Assyrians a century earlier.

Jeremiah had prophesied that the Babylonian captivity would last seventy years (Jer. 25:8–11; Dan. 9:2). Seventy years passed from the time the first captives were taken until the first company returned. Also, it was seventy years from the date of the destruction of the first temple in Jerusalem to the date of the dedication of the second.

There is much sobering historical information in the books of the Kings. Knowing the events traced therein can make more understandable the books of the prophets of Israel, provide background for the remaining historical books of the Old Testament, and enhance our appreciation of the New Testament, the Book of Mormon, and the latter-day scriptures.

FIRST CHRONICLES

The books of the Chronicles repeat some of the information in the books of Samuel and Kings but add details having particular religious significance. The chronicler emphasized the Davidic kingdom, so after the division of the kingdom, Chronicles deals predominantly with the nation of Judah (BD, "Chronicles").

The first nine chapters of 1 Chronicles review the genealogy from Adam to David and to Saul and also some details of such related lines as those of Levi, particularly of Aaron. The remaining nineteen chapters give historical information about King Saul's last battle, death, and burial and continue with the reign of David, often emphasizing items of spiritual or religious significance somewhat more than do the books of Samuel and Kings.

Sources of information are cited fairly frequently, showing that the Israelites were always "people of the book," who regularly kept records from which the chronicler drew or to which he referred from time to time.

COMMENTARY

1:1– 4 Adam . . . Noah

The ten patriarchs from Adam to Noah have the same Hebrew names as in Genesis, but in the English translation the spelling of some is slightly different. Only the genealogical lines leading to

Abraham and Israel are given; hence, the descendants of Cain are not listed.

1:5–16 Japheth . . . [and] . . . Ham

The patriarchs of the Japhetic and Hamitic lines, and the nations that originated from them, are named.

1:17–54 the sons of Shem

The overview of some Shemite (Semitic) peoples includes the descendants of Abraham through Ishmael, the descendants of Abraham's sons by Keturah, and the descendants of Isaac's son Esau, including the Edomite kings.

2:1–2 These are the sons of Israel

The twelve sons of Israel (Jacob) are all listed, but the remainder of this chapter and the next deal only with the descendants of Judah.

2:3–55 The sons of Judah

Among the descendants of Judah, the most attention is given to the ancestry of David and Caleb, with some collateral lines.

The Kenites were descendants of Moses' brother-in-law. The word *scribes* is used to translate *Sopherim,* which should not be translated here; the Sopherim in this case were the three clans of Kenites who lived at Jabez. They were all of the house of Rechab, which was important in Israel in actions later on (1 Chr. 2:55*b–c*).

3:1–24 Now these were the sons of David

The ancestors of Jesse through David (1 Chr. 2:3–17) and on to David's descendants of the royal line are named, down to the last king to reign. The Davidic line continues through Jeconiah (or Jehoiachin) to Zerubbabel, who was made "governor" of the Jews that returned from Babylon (Ezra 2:2; 3:2, 8; 5:2). Several generations of Zerubbabel's descendants are then given. (Regarding his lineage down to Joseph and Mary, see 1 Chr. 3:19*a*.)

4:1–23 The sons of Judah; Pharez

Sons is usually used to translate the Hebrew word meaning "descendants"; thus, Pharez himself was a son and the rest were other descendants. In some cases the "father" of people who were the settlers of a place is given, such as "the father of Bethlehem" (1 Chr. 4:4; cf. 2:50–54).

4:24– 43 The sons of Simeon

The Simeonites, who shared territory with Judah (Josh. 19:1, 9; Judg. 1:3, 19), are genealogically and geographically identified.

5:1–26 Now the sons of Reuben the firstborn of Israel

A parenthetical explanation before the list of Reuben's descendants explains his loss of the birthright to the "sons of Joseph"; therefore, though his is the lineage of "the firstborn of Israel," it is not the birthright lineage (1 Chr. 5:1*a–d*). It is clarified that Judah's is the royal line, and Joseph's is the birthright line.

Descendants of Reuben, Gad, and half the tribe of Manasseh who lived east of the Jordan River went to war against the "Hagrites," descendants of Hagar and Abraham through their son Ishmael. The Israelites were helped by the Lord because they put their trust in him (1 Chr. 5:20). The chronicler drew a lesson from their later history, however, to explain that the Lord permitted the king of Assyria to exile them because they transgressed against Him.

6:1– 81 The sons of Levi; Gershon, Kohath, and Merari

Though Kohath was not first in order of birth, he was probably first in importance to the chronicler because he was the forefather of Moses, Aaron, and Miriam; his descendants through the priestly line of Aaron are given (1 Chr. 6:2–15).

All of Levi's sons are listed again and some of the descendants through the firstborn, Gershom, along with the sons of the lastborn, Merari. Before detailing any of those, however, the chronicler outlined the Kohathite descent of Samuel the prophet, certifying his priestly lineage (1 Chr. 6:22–28 and fn.). Descendants of

Merari who provided music and other services in the tabernacle are named (1 Chr. 6:29–48).

Again the writer returned to the line of Aaron and his descendants as far as Zadok, who officiated at the altars of sacrifice after the time of David (1 Chr. 6:49–53). Finally, a review is given of the Levitical cities where the priests and other Levites lived among all the tribes of Israel (1 Chr. 6:54–81 and fn.).

7:1– 40 the sons of

In no particular order genealogically or geographically, information about six of the tribes of Israel is given, beginning with some families of Issachar and their "soldiers for war." Similar information is given about some families of Benjamin (1 Chr. 7:1–12). But only the immediate sons of Naphtali are listed, and some wives and families of the sons of Manasseh. Several of Ephraim's descendants, deeds, and dwelling places are named. Finally, Asher's sons, their descendants, and the number of men of war are given, as with the tribes of Issachar and Benjamin.

8:1– 40 Now Benjamin begat . . .

The names of Benjamin's descendants and the movements and locations of some of their clans provide the lineage of Kish and the family of Saul, Israel's first king (1 Chr. 8:33–40).

9:1 So all Israel were reckoned by genealogies; and, behold, they were written in the book of the kings of Israel and Judah

The "book of the kings of Israel and Judah" evidently are not the present books of 1 and 2 Kings, for they do not contain all the genealogies. Neither do the preceding chapters of 1 Chronicles, for Zebulun and Naphtali were omitted and others only briefly mentioned.

9:2– 44 And in Jerusalem dwelt of the children of Judah, and of the children of Benjamin, . . . Ephraim, and Manasseh . . . , and of the priests

A few leaders from four tribes who were living for a time in

Jerusalem are listed; then many priestly and Levite groups are named and their ecclesiastical work is identified. The remaining verses repeat information given before (1 Chr. 9:35–44; cf. 8:29–38); perhaps they were intended as an introduction to the chapter about the end of Saul's family.

10:1–14 Now the Philistines fought against Israel; and the men of Israel fled from before the Philistines

The account of Saul's final battle against the Philistines parallels the one in Samuel, except where that account is more detailed (cf. 1 Sam. 31:7, 10). At the close of the chapter, Chronicles gives as the reason for Saul's rejection and death his having asked counsel of one who had a familiar spirit. No mention is made of his having transgressed in offering an offering, decreeing the death of Jonathan, disobeying commandments regarding the Amalekites, seeking to kill David, and slaying all the priests at Nob because one of them had helped David. All those deeds are condemned to some degree in the books of Samuel (1 Sam. 13:12–14; 14:43–45; 15:9–24; 19–26).

11:1–9 Then all Israel gathered themselves to David unto Hebron . . . and David made a covenant with them in Hebron before the Lord; and they anointed David king over Israel

Chronicles here passes over the first seven years of David's reign, in which only Judah and part of Benjamin accepted him as king (2 Sam. 2–4), and goes directly to his making the covenant to become the anointed king over all Israel (but see 1 Chr. 13:23–40).

In this account of how David's forces penetrated and conquered Jerusalem, Joab "went first up, and was chief," which was not told before; other items in the account in Samuel were omitted here by the chronicler (1 Chr. 11:6–7; cf. 2 Sam. 5:7–9).

11:10– 47 These also are the chief of the mighty men whom David had, who strengthened themselves with him in his kingdom, and with all Israel, to make him king

This passage may be a summary of the efforts of David's

"mighty men," who helped him to become king of all Israel during the "seven years and six months" he reigned in Judah only (2 Sam. 5:5; 23:8). The rest of the account of David's mighty men parallels the previous accounts (1 Chr. 11:15–20; cf. 2 Sam. 23:8–39 and commentary).

12:1–22 Now these are they that came to David to Ziklag, while he yet kept himself close because of Saul

Most of this information was not given before (cf. 2 Sam. 27). It may account in part for Saul's military weakness during the times he pursued David. Some men of Benjamin, Saul's own tribe, are the first listed; then follow some of Gad, more from Judah and Benjamin, and some from Manasseh. Note the poetic statement of commitment (1 Chr. 12:18).

12:23– 40 And these are the numbers of the bands that were ready armed . . . and came to David to Hebron, to turn the kingdom of Saul to him

The earlier account generalizes that "all the elders of Israel came to the king to Hebron; and king David made a league with them in Hebron" (2 Sam. 5:3; cf. 1 Chr. 11:1–9). The chronicler gave here more details about the number of armed men from all the tribes, including both halves of Manasseh and the priests and Levites. They all went to David, from both near and far, carrying supplies on their beasts of burden, "to turn the kingdom of Saul to him" (1 Chr. 12:23).

13:1–14 And let us bring again the ark of our God to us

This chapter resumes the history of David's reign, after the interruption listing his mighty men and the numbers of armed men from all the tribes (1 Chr. 11:10–12:40). David was concerned that taking the ark to Jerusalem "be of the Lord our God" and that all of Israel approve; specific mention that "the priests and Levites" should all be gathered has also been added (2 Sam. 6:1–2; cf. 1 Chr. 13:2–3).

14:1–17 Now Hiram king of Tyre sent messengers to David, and timber of cedars, with masons and carpenters, to build him an house

Information given here about trade with Tyre and the wives of David is also given in the account in Samuel (2 Sam. 5:11–25; cf. 1 Chr. 14). One chapter in Samuel records the two phases of moving the ark; two chapters record it here (2 Sam. 6; cf. 1 Chr. 13; 15).

15:1–29 And David made him houses in the city of David, and prepared a place for the ark of God, and pitched for it a tent

Concluding what was begun in 1 Chronicles 14:1 about David's buildings in Jerusalem, the first verse of chapter 15 resumes the account of moving the ark to Jerusalem to the tent prepared for it.

Material here adds to what was given in the account in Samuel (2 Sam. 6:11–12; cf. 1 Chr. 15:2–24) and explains that David arranged for "the children of Aaron, and the Levites" to carry the ark properly during the last part of the journey so that he would avoid such an offense as occurred while it was being transported on the cart (1 Chr. 13:9–14). On the other hand, less is said here about the friction between David and Michal (2 Sam. 6:20–23; cf. 1 Chr. 15:29). In Chronicles there is more of the commendable and less of the deplorable about David.

16:1–43 So they brought the ark of God, and set it in the midst of the tent that David had pitched for it: and they offered burnt sacrifices and peace offerings before God

The account in Samuel speaks only of David's making offerings to the Lord; according to the chronicler, all apparently participated (1 Chr. 16:1; cf. 2 Sam. 6:1–18). Nor does the account in Samuel mention the Levites appointed to minister before the ark of the Lord, to record events, and to thank and praise the Lord. A psalm written by David for the occasion is given here but is not in Samuel (1 Chr. 16:7–36; cf. 2 Sam. 6; but see Ps. 105:1–15).

Additional information here tells of the priests and Levites appointed to officiate before the ark of the covenant.

17:1–27 David said to Nathan the prophet, Lo, I dwell in an house of cedars, but the ark . . . remaineth under curtains

This chapter is very similar to 2 Samuel 7. The differences are sometimes merely rhetorical; for example, a command here was a question there (1 Chr. 17:4; cf. 2 Sam. 7:5). But a related verse in a later chapter gives a reason *why* David should not build the temple: he had been a man of war and bloodshed; his son, a man of peace, would build it (1 Chr. 22:8–9).

18:1–17 Now after this it came to pass that David smote

First Chronicles 18 parallels 2 Samuel 8 but omits an enigmatic detail (v. 2 in both accounts) about certain Moabites' being put to death. That the brass booty David took was used by Solomon to make the "brasen sea" of the temple is told only here (v. 8 in both accounts). There are a few other differences in wording.

19:1–19 David sent messengers . . . So the servants of David came unto the land of . . . Ammon to Hanun, to comfort him

The accounts here of compassion, misapprehension, insult, and revenge are essentially the same as in Samuel, except for the record of mercenaries hired by the Ammonites when attack by Israel was imminent (2 Sam. 10:6; cf. 1 Chr. 19:6–7).

20:1–8 at the time that kings go out to battle, Joab led . . . the army, and wasted the country of the children of Ammon

This brief chapter corresponds to 2 Samuel 11 for part of the first verse, then omits the story of David and Bathsheba, and resumes the same wording thereafter (2 Sam. 11; 12:1–26, 30–31; cf. 1 Chr. 20:1–3). Chronicles omits all mention of the tragedy of Amnon, Tamar, and Absalom; Absalom's attempted usurpation and his death; and the aftermath of the tragedy of Amasa and Joab in the Sheba rebellion. The account of the famine and the resultant execution of four of Saul's descendants is omitted here; so is the pathetic story of Rizpah. After mention of a Philistine giant before whom David "waxed faint," the parallels resume (2 Sam. 13:1–21:17; then 21:18–22; cf. 1 Chr. 20:4–8). It is obvious that the chronicler had no desire to record incidents bearing on David's sins, failings, and weaknesses.

21:1–30 And Satan stood up against Israel, and provoked David to number Israel

Nonetheless, this chapter does speak of one of David's "sins"—the census he ordered to determine his military strength—but the first verse essentially blames the sin upon Satan (cf. 2 Sam. 24:1). The account in Samuel says that because the Lord was angry at Israel he "moved David against them to say, Go, number Israel and Judah"; both accounts record David's repentant spirit (2 Sam. 24:1, 10; 1 Chr. 21:8, 17). The chronicler made both David and the Lord look better by selecting what to emphasize. But the lesson taught by both accounts is clear: governments that calculate their military might for vain purposes do indeed bring much suffering upon their people.

22:1–19 Then David said, This is the house of the Lord God, and this is the altar of the burnt offering for Israel

The acquisition of a site on a hill above the old city of David and the building of an altar there are attested in both accounts (2 Sam. 24:18–25; 1 Chr. 21:24–26). This chapter adds details about the preparation of materials and the briefing of David's son Solomon for his work on the temple.

Although no complete parallels to this chapter are found in the books of Samuel and Kings, some points there are elucidated here; see footnoted references to them (1 Chr. 22:16, 2*a*, 4*a*, 5*a*, 7*a*, 9*a*–*b*, 10*a*).

A poetic passage records a blessing of the Lord upon David's promised son Solomon; it has a nice play on the related Hebrew words translated as *Solomon, peace,* and *quietness—Shlomo, shalom,* and *sheqet* (1 Chr. 22:9–13).

23:1 So when David was old and full of days, he made Solomon his son king over Israel

This single verse sums up an event detailed in 1 Kings 1 and 2. The spiritual confirmation of the appointment of Solomon is told in much detail in 1 Chronicles 29, but Adonijah's attempted coup was not recorded by the chronicler.

23:2–32 And he gathered together all the princes of Israel, with the priests and Levites

The remainder of this chapter sets forth the divisions of priests and other Levites as they were organized to work in the temple, somewhat as they had served in the old tabernacle of the congregation. It overviews the work of the descendants of Levi's sons Gershon, Kohath—including a rare mention of descendants of Moses (1 Chr. 23:12–20)—and Merari. Finally, some assignments made "by the last words of David" (1 Chr. 23:24–32) are noted.

24:1–19 Now these are the divisions of the sons of Aaron

Two sons of Aaron died without children, so the descendants of the two remaining sons, Eleazar and Ithamar, represented respectively by Zadok and Ahimelech, are here recounted. Their twenty-four periods of service were determined by lot—sixteen periods being covered by descendants of Zadok and eight by those of Ahimelech.

24:20–31 And the rest of the sons of Levi were these

Other descendants of Kohath, the forefather of Moses and Aaron, are listed, starting with the descendants of Kohath's son Amram (1 Chr. 24:20; cf. 23:12) and continuing with other sons of Kohath's brother Merari (1 Chr. 24:26–30; cf. 23:21). These Levites also cast lots for the order of their service.

25:1–31 Moreover David and the captains of the host separated to the service of the sons of Asaph, and of Heman, and of Jeduthun, who should prophesy with harps, with psalteries, and with cymbals

Prophesy is used here in its ancient sense of inspired utterance in song or otherwise of praises, admonitions, chastisements, or, occasionally, predictions. Only in modern English does *prophesy* mean only "to predict."

The inspired musicians for temple service were identified by name and then allocated by lot to the periods of service in twenty-four courses, as were the priests.

26:1–32 Concerning the divisions of the porters: . . . treasures, . . . outward business

"Porters" were keepers of the "ports," or gates and doors, of the temple compound. They too were Levites, and their assigned places were also determined by casting lots.

Also accounted for are those chosen as officers over the temple treasuries and those over "the outward business," which is understood to have been procurement of materials. Some were assigned to tribes west of Jordan; others, to the two and one-half tribes east of Jordan.

27:1–34 the chief fathers and captains of thousands and hundreds, and their officers that served the king

The military defense services were organized into twelve "courses," so each group of twenty-four thousand served for one month of the year.

Why the "ruler" of Gad and Asher is omitted from the list of the tribal rulers is not known. But the reason David's census did not count those under twenty years of age is recorded (1 Chr. 27:23–24).

Various other officers are named, such as those over the king's treasures, the cultivated fields, vineyards, olive trees, herds (cattle), camels, and flocks (sheep and goats).

David's counselors or advisers, including those with responsibility over his children, were named. Finally, Joab was named as general of the king's army (1 Chr. 27:32–34).

28:1–8 And David assembled all the princes . . . and the captains . . . and the stewards . . . with the officers, and with the mighty men, and with all the valiant men, unto Jerusalem

The king explained to all the leaders how he, whom the Lord

had chosen out of the chosen tribe of Judah to be king, had wanted to build a temple and was forbidden to do so but was promised a son who would reign and would build it. That king and his people would prosper and be preserved if they were obedient to the Lord.

28:9–21 And thou, Solomon my son, know thou the God of thy father, and serve him with a perfect heart and with a willing mind

The old king charged his son with the work of the kingdom and instructed him on "the pattern of all that he had by the spirit, of the courts of the house of the Lord, and of all the chambers round about" (1 Chr. 28:12). David claimed divine revelation as the source for the instructions—"all in writing by the hand of the Lord upon me, causing me to be wise in understanding all his task" (1 Chr. 28:19, translation mine).

David charged Solomon in the words the Lord had spoken to Joshua: "Be strong and of good courage" (1 Chr. 28:20; Josh. 1:6, 9) and challenged him to work with every willing and skillful man.

29:1–9 for the palace is not for man, but for the Lord God

The "palace" is the temple to be built under Solomon's leadership; *palace* is used here to translate a Persian word meaning "great house."

David continued to describe precious things he had gathered in preparation for building the temple. He challenged tribal leaders and other people to contribute; they responded with good hearts and offered willingly to the Lord—for which the king rejoiced.

29:10–19 Wherefore David blessed the Lord before all the congregation

This little psalm makes a significant theological statement: it speaks of the Lord God as "father, for ever and ever," great in power, glory, and majesty, head of the kingdom, exalted above all, the source of all riches, honor, and strength. It asserts that humility is becoming to mortals, for they are "strangers"—that is, temporary sojourners—on the Lord's earth.

David humbly offered with an upright heart all that he and the people were giving to the Lord and supplicated him to keep uprightness "for ever in the imagination of the thoughts of the heart of thy people, and prepare their heart unto thee." He then asked that the Lord give Solomon "a perfect heart" to keep the commandments and do all things well, including the building of the temple (1 Chr. 29:17–19).

29:20–25 And all the congregation blessed the Lord God of their fathers, and bowed down their heads, and worshipped the Lord, and the king.

This was surely the highest point of righteous resolve ever reached by Israel. Solomon's reign should have been a golden age in implementing the mission of Israel, for many peoples of the world would know of King Solomon of Israel and could have seen what living a pure religion led by the true and living God could do for people. But little of Israel's mission is seen in the record of Solomon's reign.

Worshipped translates a Hebrew word that means the people "prostrated themselves before" the Lord and his newly appointed king (1 Chr. 29:20).

Because Solomon had been proclaimed and accepted as king previously, he was here confirmed "the second time," and "anointed . . . unto the Lord" as Israel's earthly leader; Zadok, the chief priest, was Israel's spiritual leader. The record concludes with a brief statement of the golden age that followed—for a time (1 Chr. 29:22–25; 23:1; 1 Kgs. 1:33–39).

29:26–30 Thus David the son of Jesse reigned over all Israel. And . . . he reigned over Israel . . . seven years in Hebron, and thirty and three years . . . in Jerusalem

David's good qualities—and none of his sins—are eulogized, in keeping with the tone of the rest of the Chronicles accounts. It would be interesting to have the source-books named, in addition to the book of Samuel, for further details.

A certain air of peace and assurance comes through in the books of Chronicles because of their emphasis on the goodness of the Lord and the good characteristics of his servants. It is worthwhile for such historical accounts as the books of Judges, Samuel, and Kings to tell all facets of the people's attitudes and activities, but it is also worthwhile to have some records that select their best aspects.

SECOND CHRONICLES

The second book of the Chronicles, like the first book, is concerned with events of religious and ecclesiastical significance. Indeed, "the two Books of Chronicles are counted as one in the Hebrew canon" (BD, "Chronicles"). Historical interest centers on the Davidic dynasty, so the record here deals mostly with the kingdom of Judah after the division of the kingdom; the northern kingdom of approximately ten tribes of Israel is mentioned only in reports of interaction with Judah.

Source books used by the writer of Chronicles continue to be cited, but of them only the books of Kings are now known. Even though Chronicles is historical information chosen for discernible purposes and the source books cannot be examined, it is also a valuable religious and historical resource that complements the books of Kings and provides background on the times and people of the Book of Mormon prophet Lehi.

The first nine chapters of 2 Chronicles deal with achievements of Solomon in his reign over the united kingdom of Israel, with emphasis on the building of the temple, the work of the priests and Levites, and the reinstating of the Mosaic sacrifices and rituals. The remaining chapters cover the reigns of Solomon's descendants from Rehoboam to Zedekiah, ending with the commencement of the Babylonian captivity. The closing verses anticipate the return of many Judahites to their homeland from Babylon by the grace of God through the sympathy of King Cyrus of Persia. Thus the book anticipates its sequels, the books of Ezra, Nehemiah, and Esther.

COMMENTARY

1:1– 6 Solomon the son of David was strengthened in his kingdom, and the Lord his God was with him, and magnified him

After notifying all of Israel, the new king and all the congregation went about six miles northwestward from Jerusalem to Gibeon, to the centuries-old tabernacle of the congregation, which had been "made in the wilderness" and used in Moses' time. It had been erected first at Shilo and used there throughout the time of the judges (Josh. 18:1). Later, according to this Chronicles account only, it was established at Gibeon (2 Chr. 1:3). The ark of the covenant, however, had been taken to Jerusalem by David and placed in a tent he prepared for it (2 Sam. 6:17; 1 Chr. 15:1). Solomon and his people offered "a thousand burnt offerings" on the brasen altar of the ancient tabernacle, being still at the "great high place" at Gibeon (2 Chr. 1:6; 1 Kgs. 3:4).

1:7–12 In that night did God appear unto Solomon, and said unto him, Ask what I shall give thee

These verses relate Solomon's vision and his humble request for wisdom, knowledge, and judgment, and the resultant blessing slightly more concisely than the account in 1 Kings 3:6–13.

1:13 Then Solomon came from his journey to the high place that was at Gibeon to Jerusalem

The words *from his journey* have been added in the English translation; they do not translate anything in the Hebrew text, but there are problems in the narrative if the Hebrew is translated literally, and the addition harmonizes this account with that in Kings (1 Kgs. 3:15).

1:14–17 And Solomon gathered chariots and horsemen: and he had a thousand and four hundred chariots, and twelve thousand horsemen. . . . And Solomon had horses brought out of Egypt, and linen yarn

Chronicles again gives more information than does Kings

about the prowess of the new king and the great numbers of horses and chariots, even though such were forbidden by the law of Moses (Deut. 17:14–17; 1 Kgs. 4:26).

The Hebrew does not mention linen yarn, but says, literally, "And he brought out the horses which were for Solomon from Egypt and from Kue [Cilicia]; the purchases of the king from Kue he received at a price." (2 Chr. 1:16–17; 1 Kgs. 10:28*a*).

2:1–18 Solomon determined to build an house for the name of the Lord, and an house for his kingdom

The chronicler omitted the account of Solomon's decision concerning two mothers' dispute over a baby (1 Kgs. 3–4). He also omitted accounts of the king's reorganizing his country into twelve districts, the tallies of supplies required for the royal officials, and the statements about the king's worldly wisdom and went immediately to the account of the building of the temple. On this subject, however, Chronicles gives more information than does the account in Kings, especially concerning negotiations with the king of Tyre (cf. 1 Kgs. 5).

3:1–17 Then Solomon began to build the house of the Lord at Jerusalem in mount Moriah, where the Lord appeared unto David

The chronicler did not tell how many years had passed since the Exodus, as did the author of Kings, but told more about the place in which the temple was built on Mount Moriah (2 Chr. 3:1*a-d*). In general this account is briefer (cf. 1 Kgs. 5–6).

4:1–22 he made an altar of brass . . . Also . . . a molten sea . . . for the priests to wash in

This chapter contains important information about the "sea," or font (2 Chr. 4:6; cf. 2 Kgs. 7:23–25). Its purpose is simply stated in Hebrew: "and the sea [was] for washing, for the priests, in it." Commentary from the ancient rabbis indicates that it was indeed used for immersions, such as the Torah prescribes for purification. Washing facilities were also needed for the cleansing of various illnesses. The font may have been used in ordinances such as those on the Day of Atonement (Lev. 15; 16:23–24; BD, "Fasts," paragraphs about the Day of Atonement; "Purification").

See the commentary on 1 Kings 7:13–51 regarding baptism.

5:1–14 Then Solomon assembled the elders of Israel, and all the heads of the tribes . . . unto Jerusalem, to bring up the ark of the covenant of the Lord out of the city of David, which is Zion

The report is virtually the same here and in Kings regarding the moving of the ark and its precious contents to its new shrine in the temple of Solomon. Descriptions of performances by singers and other musicians are not found in Kings, however. The sign of the presence of "the glory of the Lord" manifested in the cloud is recorded in both (cf. 1 Kgs. 7:51; 8:1–11).

As observed before, the name *Zion* was eventually applied to all Jerusalem and was so used by the prophets. Only in more recent times has it been used specifically for a place outside the southwest corner of the "old city" of Jerusalem.

6:1– 42 Then said Solomon . . . I have built an house of habitation for thee, . . . And the king . . . blessed the whole congregation

This account adds one item about the Lord's having chosen Jerusalem and one about Solomon's "brasen scaffold" upon which he knelt down upon his knees in prayer. This, with its parallel (2 Chr. 6:13; cf. 1 Kgs. 8:54), is the first time kneeling in prayer has been mentioned. His supplications in the closing verses are added, but some important words of the dedicatory prayer are not found in Chronicles (cf. 1 Kgs. 8; and commentary).

7:1–3 Now when Solomon had made an end of praying, the fire came down from heaven, and consumed the burnt offering

This miraculous manifestation is not recorded in Kings. Recall the similar manifestation when the temple site was first secured by David (1 Chr. 21:26). Manifestations of the glory of the Lord are known also in the latter days (cf. D&C 109:12, 37).

7:4–11 Then the king and all the people offered sacrifices before the Lord

These spiritually awesome and festive events took place in the seventh month (2 Chr. 5:3; 7:10). The first twenty-three days of the month are "high holy days" in Judaism (Num. 29).

Much of this information is found also in Kings (1 Kgs. 8:62–66; 9:1; and commentary).

7:12–22 And the Lord appeared to Solomon by night, and said unto him, I have heard thy prayer, and have chosen this place . . . for an house of sacrifice

In this second night-vision granted to Solomon by the Lord (recall 2 Chr. 1:7), he was assured that his supplications had been accepted and the blessings he had sought would be given according to Israel's needs and worthiness (compare promises with requests; 2 Chr. 7:13–15; 6:26–31). The rest of the assurances and warnings are like those in Kings (cf. 1 Kgs. 9:3–9).

8:1–18 And it came to pass at the end of twenty years, wherein Solomon had built the house of the Lord, and his own house, That the cities which Huram had restored

This overview has fewer details about the mundane and more about the religious. An interesting difference may be seen in the mention of the special house built for Solomon's wife from Egypt. The Chronicles account declares it was built because "the places are holy, whereunto the ark of the Lord hath come," perhaps implying that she who had worshipped the deities of Egypt ought not dwell in holy places near the temple (2 Chr. 8:11; 1 Kgs. 9:24).

The items that pertain to worship practices and priesthood services have no counterpart in Kings. For other items of significance, see the commentary on 1 Kings 8–9.

9:1–12 And when the queen of Sheba heard of the fame of Solomon, she came

This incident is also reported in Kings, but it is somewhat

different there. The account in Kings indicates that "when the queen of Sheba heard of the fame of Solomon concerning the name of the Lord, she came to prove him with hard questions." Chronicles does not mention her interest in "the name of the Lord" but is explicit that she indeed praised the God "which delighted in thee to set thee on his throne, to be king for the Lord thy God" (1 Kgs. 10:1; cf. 2 Chr. 9:8).

9:13–28 And king Solomon passed all the kings of the earth in riches and wisdom

The parallels with Kings continue, with reiteration of the opulence and power of King Solomon and a reflection of Solomon's fulfillment of the Lord's promise to Abraham about the land to be occupied (2 Chr. 9:26; 1 Kgs. 4:21; Gen. 15:18).

9:29–31 Now the rest of the acts of Solomon, first and last, are they not written in the book

Citing three books in which the rest of Solomon's deeds were recorded and going directly from the summation of his greatness to the brief account of his death, the chronicler did not include any of some forty verses of 1 Kings 11 about the king's seven hundred wives and three hundred concubines or the shrines made for their gods and goddesses and the worship of them. Neither did he tell of the Lord's castigation of Solomon and the resultant troubles as enemies rose up against him, nor of the rise of Jeroboam, nor of the division of the kingdom prophesied by Ahijah the Shilonite, nor of Solomon's heir Rehoboam losing the kingship of ten of the tribes of Israel to Jeroboam (cf. 1 Kgs. 11:28–31). And, unfortunately, the three other books that are cited about the deeds of Solomon are not now known.

10:1–19 And Rehoboam went to Shechem: for to Shechem were all Israel come to make him king

All the events of this chapter are recorded in Kings (1 Kgs. 12:1–19), though not verbatim. It appears that the chronicler did not protect Rehoboam's image as he usually did Solomon's.

347

11:1– 4 he gathered . . . fourscore thousand chosen men . . . that he might bring the kingdom again to Rehoboam. But the word of the Lord came to Shemaiah the man of God

Beyond these four verses, the corresponding chapters in Kings and Chronicles have little in common (1 Kgs. 12:21–24; and commentary).

11:5–17 And Rehoboam dwelt in Jerusalem, and built cities for defence in Judah

The chronicler concentrated on Rehoboam's administration and his building of defenses and on the virtues of the work of the true priests, many of whom left the northern kingdom and went to Judah, rejecting the ways of Jeroboam, who had set up apostate shrines and a false priesthood mentioned here but detailed in Kings. The migration of "the priests and Levites that were in all Israel" to the southern kingdom augmented that kingdom to include all of Judah and Levi, most of Simeon, and part of Benjamin (2 Chr. 11:13–14; cf. 1 Kgs. 12:25–33; and commentary).

11:18–23 And Rehoboam took him Mahalath . . . to wife, and Abihail . . . And after her he took Maachah the daughter of Absalom; . . . he took eighteen wives, and threescore concubines. . . . And Rehoboam made Abijah the son of Maachah the chief, to be ruler among his brethren

This account would have genealogical importance if it was certain that Maachah, the mother of Abijah, was indeed the daughter or granddaughter of Rehoboam's uncle Absalom, but the name of Abijah's mother and the name of her father are given later as "Michaiah the daughter of Uriel of Gibeah" (2 Chr. 13:2). About the many wives of Rehoboam, see 2 Chronicles 11:23*b*.

12:1–16 when Rehoboam . . . had strengthened himself, he forsook the law of the Lord, and all Israel with him

Religious instability developed in both the king and the people. The account of this apostasy in Judah, the warnings of Shemaiah the prophet, the attack by Shishak of Egypt, and the resultant loss of treasures of the king's house and the temple are told in more detail here (cf. 1 Kgs. 12:21–31).

The death notices identify Rehoboam's son and heir as *Abijah* here but as *Abijam* in Kings. It is more than a slight spelling variant: *Abijah* means "my father is *Yah*" (a short form of Yahweh, or Jehovah); but *Abijam* means "my father is *Yam*" (a Canaanite god of the sea). It is not surprising that the chronicler used the faithful name rather than the idolatrous one. The evaluation of Rehoboam does contain both positive and negative elements, however.

13:1–22 Now in the eighteenth year of king Jeroboam began Abijah to reign over Judah

This picture of King Abijah is very different from the one in Kings (cf. 1 Kgs. 15:1–8), in which he was shown to be sinful like his father and engaged in war all his years as king. Here he is depicted as a valiant champion of the Lord, calling on Jeroboam and northern Israel to repent and return to the true priesthood and worship of the living God. Then when Jeroboam would have overwhelmed him by a stratagem and by superior numbers, the priests sounded the trumpets and the men of Judah shouted a battle cry (the same Hebrew word used in Josh. 6:16), attacked the enemy before and behind, and won a victory with the Lord's help (2 Chr. 13:13–18). Thus the chronicler left a lesson from the life of true *Abi-jah,* not false *Abi-jam.*

The conclusion also claims Abijah recovered some northern Israelite areas unto Bethel and its environs in his short and war-filled reign of two or three years.

14:1–15 So Abijah slept with his fathers . . . and Asa his son reigned in his stead. And Asa did that which was good and right

Three whole chapters here give far more credit to Asa and his worthy actions than the mere sixteen verses in Kings, which tell only briefly of his religious reforms and deal mostly with his war with northern Israel's king Baasha (1 Kgs. 15:9–24).

Chronicles reports Asa's removing idolatrous facilities and practices, strengthening Judah's northern borders, and fighting a defensive war against "Zera the Ethiopian" (Heb., *Cushi;*

probably an Arabian tribe rather than the distant Ethiopians of the Nile), which he won after a humble prayer. The tally of troops involved is told in huge round numbers. A question may arise concerning the troops of Judah smiting cities and taking spoil; it may be that only cities occupied by Zera's forces or by other invaders were thus taken.

15:1–19 And the spirit of God came upon Azariah . . . And he went out to meet Asa, and said unto him . . . the Lord is with you, while ye be with him . . . but if ye forsake him, he will forsake you

This prophetic call renewed the spirit of reform in Judah and Benjamin, reminding the people that the parts of Israel that had forsaken the true God were without true priests and without law.

King Asa's religious reforms resulted in an important historical development: not only people of Judah and Benjamin but also people of Ephraim, Manasseh, and Simeon came out of Israel in great numbers when they saw that the Lord was with good King Asa. Simeon already shared an inheritance with Judah (Josh. 19:9; Judg. 1:3); but Ephraim and Manasseh were Judah's neighbors to the north. These migrations in the late 900s B.C. could account for the presence in Jerusalem in the late 600s of such descendants of Joseph as Lehi, Laban, and Ishmael (1 Ne. 5:14–16; 6:2; 2 Ne. 3:4; Alma 10:3). This migration is historically significant, for the tribes of Ephraim and Manasseh were among the northern Israelites conquered, exiled, and "lost" by Assyria more than a century before Lehi's time (TG, "Israel, Joseph, People of"; BD, "Joseph").

A summary of the religious conversions in Judah tells of the people's renewal of the covenant with the God of their fathers and the good results of it; however, some became extremists and put to death any who would not join.

16:1–16 In the six and thirtieth year of the reign of Asa Baasha king of Israel came up against Judah, and built Ramah

This event is related also in Kings (1 Kgs. 15:16–24), but Chronicles adds that Hanani, a seer, chastised King Asa for employing Syrians to fight for him rather than trusting in God as he had in previous wars. It is sad to see that in his old age Asa resented prophetic advice, became angry, imprisoned the seer, and oppressed his people. Three years after the war began, Asa contracted a disease and, failing again to return to his former faith in the Lord, he perished. His vanity may be seen in his being buried in a sepulchre that he had had made for himself.

17:1–6 And Jehoshaphat his son reigned in his stead . . . And the Lord was with Jehoshaphat

Jehoshaphat was another king of Judah more honored in Chronicles than in Kings. Besides the usual phrases describing good behavior, it is said that "his heart was lifted up in the ways of the Lord"—a good description of the inner exaltation a righteous person may feel.

17:7–11 Also in the third year of his reign he sent . . . Levites . . . and with them Elishama and Jehoram, priests

This mission to all the cities of Judah by nine Levites and two priests, who had the book of the law of the Lord with them, resembles missions undertaken from time to time among peoples of the Book of Mormon (cf. Alma 21:16ff.; 37:8–10; Hel. 15:4–10). The results for Judah's internal and external peace and security were phenomenal.

18:1–34 Now Jehoshaphat had riches and honor in abundance, and joined affinity with Ahab

The accession of Jehoshaphat is barely mentioned in Kings (1 Kgs. 15:24; 2 Kgs. 3:7, 12). While King Jehoshaphat was ruling righteously and productively in Judah, as recorded only in Chronicles, Elijah was ministering in northern Israel, as recorded only in Kings (1 Kgs. 17–22). Perhaps Elijah's mission is not reported in Chronicles because he was sent to the northern tribes under King Ahab to call them to repentance.

In any case, with slight differences in the introduction, the account of the war with Syria is similar in both books (cf. 1 Kgs. 22).

There are helpful changes here concerning the problem of the Lord sending a "lying spirit" (2 Chr. 18:21–22 and fn.).

Neither here nor in Kings was the righteous prophet Micaiah further identified nor his fate revealed.

The death and burial of Ahab and the succession to his throne are told in more detail in Kings; see the commentary on 1 Kings 22:34–40.

19:1–11 And Jehoshaphat the king of Judah returned to his house in peace to Jerusalem

Jehoshaphat returned "in peace," but he was reproved for helping the unrighteous Ahab by "Jehu the son of Hanani the seer," who served as a prophet in both Israel and Judah (1 Kgs. 16:1–4; 2 Chr. 16:7–10). Nevertheless, he did commend the king's righteous deeds, which included a great mission tour from south to north (Beer-sheba to Ephraim), in which he regulated the functions of judges, Levites, and priests according to the law and the principles of justice, reverence of the Lord, and courage. These accounts resemble some in the Book of Mormon, such as those concerning King Mosiah and Alma.

20:1–30 It came to pass after this also, that the children of Moab, . . . Ammon, and with them other beside the Ammonites came against Jehoshaphat to battle

This account also is like accounts in the Book of Mormon, in the writings of Nephi, Mosiah, Alma, or Helaman. There is no equivalent in Kings.

Note the faith of the king and the people and the prayer of the king. He recalled God's promises from the time of the patriarchs until Solomon and the mercy shown Moab and Edom in the time of the migration of Israel under Moses and then supplicated the Lord's help. The spirit of prophecy enabled a certain Levite to deliver the Lord's reply, and for it the king and the people gave thanks and praise to the Lord. King Jehoshaphat's faithful admonition the next day and his appointment of singers to lead the people in worship were appropriate responses.

Apparently residents of the area under attack came out of ambush and confused the enemy so that various peoples among the invaders fell upon each other as in Gideon's day (2 Chr. 20:22–23 and fn.). Thus King Jehoshaphat and his people were saved; and with the goods they took from the enemy dead, they returned to Jerusalem, thanking the Lord.

20:31–37 And Jehoshaphat reigned over Judah . . . twenty and five years . . . And he walked in the way of Asa his father

This summary notes that like Asa, Jehoshaphat did mostly commendable deeds; but one aberration is recorded. As with his help for Ahab, so here his collaboration with Ahab's successor Ahaziah was recompensed with a loss (2 Chr. 20:36–37; but see 1 Kgs. 22:48–49).

21:1–20 Now Jehoshaphat slept with his fathers . . . And Jehoram his son reigned in his stead

The death of Jehoshaphat and his replacement by Jehoram are mentioned. Among the accounts of the deeds of Elisha is the account of Jehoshaphat's collaboration with Israel's King Jehoram (1 Kgs. 22:50; 2 Kgs. 3; 8:16–25).

Jehoshaphat was liberal in giving wealth to his sons, and he was too liberal in another sense when he secured a daughter of Ahab and Jezebel as a wife for his heir. Jehoram murdered his brothers and fostered idolatry. A miraculous but fateful warning in writing came "to him from Elijah the prophet," who had been translated before this time (2 Chr. 21:12–15; 2 Kgs. 2–3).

There were attacks and plundering by Arabians and remnants of the Philistines, and finally, as predicted, death came by a degenerative disease. His eight-year reign brought suffering to Judah; and his wife, a true daughter of Jezebel and Ahab, brought even more death and suffering (2 Chr. 22:10–12; 23).

22:1–9 And the inhabitants of Jerusalem made Ahaziah his youngest son king in his stead

Ahaziah (also called Jehoahaz, which has the same meaning;

2 Chr. 21:17*a*) was made king by the people. He was the son of the wicked King Jehoram and a part-Canaanite woman, Athaliah, and grandson of the terrible Ahab and Jezebel (2 Chr. 22:2 and fn.). But he didn't last long as king; his affinity for the ways of the house of Ahab and for his cousin Jehoram/Joram of Israel brought about his death within a year. This account in Chronicles of his life and death differs from the longer account in Kings, but both show how the house of Ahab was eliminated by the hand of Jehu (2 Chr. 22:5–9; 2 Kgs. 8:25–29; 9:27–29; 10:12–14).

22:10–12 But when Athaliah the mother of Ahaziah saw that her son was dead, she arose and destroyed the seed royal of the house of Judah

This terrible grandmother killed her grandchildren and others to eliminate all the Davidic heirs and reign by herself for about six years; however, one baby boy, Joash, was saved by his aunt Jehoshabeath, wife of Jehoiada the priest (2 Chr. 22:11–12). According to 2 Kings 11:1–3, she was a daughter of King Joram of Judah and hence "the sister of Ahaziah."

23:1–15 in the seventh year Jehoiada strengthened himself . . . and gathered the Levites . . . to Jerusalem. . . . And all the congregation made a covenant with the king in the house of God

The chief of the priests and the Levites carefully made plans, removed Athaliah, and crowned a descendant of David to assume the throne of Judah. Note the proper anointing, the crowning, and the charge (2 Chr. 23:11*a*).

Athaliah had seized the throne by treason and violence, but at her removal she cried treason. Her terrible acts had been unjust; her removal was just, though violent.

The accounts here and in Kings differ in some details but complement each other. The main difference is that in Kings Jehoiada is reported as working through military leaders; in Chronicles they appear to be armed Levites, who could act within the restricted temple areas (2 Chr. 23:6–7; 2 Kgs. 11:4).

23:16–21 And Jehoiada made a covenant between him, and between all the people, and between the king, that they should be the Lord's people

This account details the removal of idolatrous shrines and functionaries and the reinstatement of proper religious and civil leaders. Since "all the people rejoiced," there must have been virtually no supporters of the rule of Athaliah, the only non-Davidic ruler in the history of Judah (cf. 2 Kgs. 11:17–20).

24:1–27 Joash was seven years old when he began to reign, and he reigned forty years . . . And Joash did that which was right in the sight of the Lord all the days of Jehoiada the priest

The account in Kings is more explicit that the young king did that which was right "all his days wherein Jehoiada the priest instructed him" (2 Kgs. 12:2). But after all the work of organizing the people, collecting the proper contributions, and refurbishing the temple was finished, and years had passed, Chronicles records that Jehoiada died, the evils returned, and Jehoiada's son Zechariah was killed "in the court of the house of the Lord" by command of the king (2 Chr. 24:15–22; 2 Kgs. 12:19–20). A similar crime involving a similar name is referred to in Matthew 23:35 and Luke 11:51; but they are not the same (*Teachings of the Prophet Joseph Smith,* sel. Joseph Fielding Smith [Salt Lake City: Deseret Book Co., 1938], p. 261).

Chronicles explains more fully than Kings that the servants of King Joash slew him after his apostasy and his treachery to Zechariah, son of his mentor and champion Jehoiada (2 Kgs. 12:19–20).

25:1–28 Amaziah was twenty and five years old when he began to reign, and he reigned twenty and nine years in Jerusalem

This account corresponds with that in Kings about Amaziah beginning his reign commendably by observing the law in punishing the guilty but sparing their innocent family members (2 Chr. 25:1–4; 2 Kgs. 14:1–6; Deut. 24:16).

Chronicles then records an event that is not given in Kings, showing how Amaziah's military might was built from Judah, Benjamin, and a hired army from Ephraim against the advice of a "man of God." When, at last, he heeded that prophet's warning and sent the Ephraimite army back, they became angry and raided some cities of Judah on the way home.

Another report not in Kings tells of an apostate innovation by King Amaziah in honoring the gods of Edom, perhaps to appease them because he had conquered Edom (2 Chr. 25:14–15). He then disregarded a prophet's warning, which accounts in part for his vain challenge and disastrous war against northern Israel (2 Chr. 25:14–24; 2 Kgs. 14:8–14). Israelites even plundered the temple in that war.

The remainder of Amaziah's life, in which he was unfaithful to the ways of the Lord and was slain through a conspiracy, are related both here and in Kings.

26:1–23 Then all the people of Judah took Uzziah, who was sixteen years old, and made him king in the room of his father

Again the people of Judah maintained some stability by keeping the Davidic dynasty when they overthrew a bad king. Young King Uzziah did mostly that which was right, while a prophet was able to influence him (2 Chr. 26:4–5). His name means "the Lord is my strength"; he was also called Azariah, meaning "the Lord is my helper"; so his names were appropriate to the good aspects of his life (2 Kgs. 14:21–22; 15:1–7). Supplementing the brief account in the book of Kings, Chronicles tells of his successes against old enemies, his building projects, his promotion of agriculture, and his development of defenses "invented by cunning men" (2 Chr. 26:15).

But then came the old scenario so common here and in the Book of Mormon: "when he was strong, his heart was lifted up to his destruction: for he transgressed against the Lord his God" (2 Chr. 26:16). His transgression was like that of King Saul; he assumed priestly prerogatives and burned incense upon the altar. When he was corrected, he flew into a rage and was punished with leprosy. For the rest of his life the government was in the hands of his son Jotham, who later succeeded him as king (2 Chr. 26:15–23).

The note about Isaiah the prophet having written an account of the rest of the acts of Uzziah is important information about another service of one of the great writing prophets (2 Chr. 26:22; Isa. 1:1; 6:1).

27:1–9 Jotham was twenty and five years old when he began to reign, and he reigned sixteen years in Jerusalem

The sixteen years of Jotham's rule included his time as regent during his father's years of banishment because of leprosy. Chronicles mentions Jotham's building projects in the hills and forests of Judah; the books of Kings and the book of Isaiah describe the beginning of attacks on Judah by northern Israel and Syria, who later tried to force Judah into their coalition against the great threat of Assyria (2 Kgs. 15:37; Isa. 7:1–9).

Prophecies in these times were written in the books of Hosea, Amos, Micah, and Isaiah. Jonah had been sent by the Lord on a mission to Assyria before the others began their work at home (2 Kgs. 14:25). Usually, each prophetic book gives the names of the kings in whose times the prophet served.

28:1–15 Ahaz was twenty years old when he began to reign, and he reigned sixteen years in Jerusalem

These years were crucial for Judah. The chronicler stated that Ahaz "did not that which was right"; indeed, had he reigned any longer than sixteen years, Judah may well have been conquered by Assyria when northern Israel was. Both Kings and Chronicles attest that he even sacrificed children to his idols (2 Chr. 28:3; 2 Kgs. 16:3).

In due time the Lord allowed Syria and Israel to attack Ahaz (2 Chr. 28:5–8; 2 Kgs. 16:1–9), but their stated intent was to force Ahaz into their alliance against Assyria.

The remarkable episode of women and children being taken captive by Israel after an attack and then returned because of the admonitions of the prophet Oded was not reported by the other books. It is typical that Chronicles bears testimony of the effects of prophetic admonitions in Israel (2 Chr. 28:8–15).

The accounts here are brief but show how desperately Ahaz tried to save his kingdom from the relatively minor threat of Syria and Ephraim (a name sometimes used for all of northern Israel); but in doing so he subjugated his kingdom to Assyria, a much greater danger. He made bad choices politically, morally, and religiously; the prophet Isaiah tried to dissuade him from that course, but to no avail (Isa. 7:1–9).

It was providential for Judah that King Ahaz died and was replaced by his son Hezekiah, who responded to Isaiah's prophetic guidance; thereby, Judah was saved from captivity by Assyria (2 Chr. 29–32; 2 Kgs. 18–20; Isa. 36–39).

29:1–36 Hezekiah . . . in the first year of his reign . . . opened the doors of the house of the Lord, and repaired them

Some details about the temple and worship not recorded in Kings are preserved here (cf. 2 Kgs. 18). Hezekiah corrected evils and innovations of his father, King Ahaz. He caused the doors of the temple to be opened again and repaired, the priests and Levites to be gathered and sanctified, the temple compound to be cleansed of "filthiness," and the people to be prepared to renew their covenants with God (2 Chr. 29:3–11). When that was all done, the rulers, priests, and people came to the temple with their offerings and musical instruments. Festive worship services and sacrifices were conducted. When all was set in order, the king rejoiced with all the people.

30:1–27 And Hezekiah sent to all Israel and Judah . . . that they should come to the house of the Lord at Jerusalem, to keep the passover unto the Lord God of Israel

This chapter records events comparable to those in the lives of Mosiah and Alma in the Book of Mormon. It has no parallel in Kings. This Passover must have been kept before Israel was conquered by Assyria, during the time that Hoshea ruled Israel and Hezekiah ruled Judah (1 Kgs. 18:1; 17:6).

Some two hundred fifty years had passed since the division of the northern Israelite tribes from the tribes of Judah and others in the south when King Hezekiah and the true priesthood leaders courageously attempted to reconcile all of Israel with the Lord.

It is a delight to read about the counsels of the king, princes, priests, and people and the letters of invitation sent out by proclamation to all Israel from Dan to Beer-sheba. There were appeals and admonitions for a righteous return to the Lord. Chronicles realistically reports the responses, unfavorable in some areas but favorable in Asher, Zebulun, and Manasseh as well as Judah. Priesthood service was extended to the multitude from Ephraim, Manasseh, Issachar, and Zebulun, so that all might be properly cleansed and participate in the Passover, the Feast of Unleavened Bread, and the prayers of supplication to the Lord. The Lord graciously healed the people, and the king commended the Levites who had "taught the good knowledge of the Lord" (2 Chr. 30:22).

The rejoicing, peace offerings, and confessions continued another seven days beyond the normal Passover time. Joy and blessings prevailed such as had not been seen since Solomon's time.

31:1–21 Now when all this was finished, all Israel that were present went out to the cities of Judah, and brake the images in pieces, and cut down the groves, and threw down the high places and the altars out of all Judah and Benjamin, in Ephraim also and Manasseh, until they had utterly destroyed them

Having thus destroyed Baalism and other idolatry for a time, Judah and some repentant neighbors among the tribes to the north were organized by the king for proper worship. Chronicles details Hezekiah's reformation, whereas Kings provides only generalizations (2 Chr. 31:20–21; cf. 2 Kgs. 18:4–7).

32:1–8 when Hezekiah saw that Sennacherib was come, . . . He took counsel with his princes and his mighty men

Preliminary to this threat, as the book of Kings relates, Hezekiah had rebelled against paying the tribute to Assyria that had been begun by Ahaz before him (2 Kgs. 16:5–10; 18:7, 13–14). The Assyrian King Sennacherib came to subject Judah as Tiglath-pileser and Shalmaneser had subjected the nations to the north and east (BD, "Chronology," p. 638, displays the century of Assyrian threats and conquests of their neighbors, including Syria and Israel).

Hezekiah's work in preparing his people, both spiritually and temporally, against Assyria is quite impressive. Disparagement of trusting in "the arm of flesh" rather than trusting in the power of God is found also in the book of Jeremiah and in the Book of Mormon, whose writers came out of Jerusalem a little over a century after Hezekiah's time and in the time of Jeremiah (2 Chr. 32:8; Jer. 17:5; 2 Ne. 4:34; 28:31).

32:9–23 After this did Sennacherib . . . send his servants to Jerusalem . . . saying . . . Whereon do ye trust . . . ?

Sennacherib's propaganda attack on the people of Judah in their own language is told more vividly, with all the indelicate details, in other biblical records (2 Kgs. 18:17–36; Isa. 36; and commentary). There was a second propaganda attack; Isaiah's two responses and the blasphemy against the Lord are noteworthy, and it is surprising that Chronicles gives only a hint of the prophet's involvement (2 Chr. 32:20–21; cf. 2 Kgs. 19; Isa. 37). It does summarize how the Lord helped in the days of Hezekiah and how the people showed their gratitude.

32:24–26 In those days Hezekiah was sick to the death, and prayed unto the Lord

The king's illness, his prayer, the answer by the prophet, the "sign" given him, and his recovery are more detailed in the other accounts (Isa. 38; 2 Kgs. 20:1–19; and commentary).

32:27–30 This same Hezekiah also stopped the upper watercourse of Gihon, and brought it straight down to the west side of the city of David

While applauding Hezekiah's honors and riches, these verses also give credit for a remarkable engineering feat—a tunnel that may still be seen and traversed (commentary on 2 Kgs. 20:20).

32:31–33 Howbeit in the business of the ambassadors of the princes of Babylon

On the king's unwise indulgence of visitors, Chronicles says little compared to Isaiah 39 and 2 Kings 20:12–20. The incident was evaluated by the chronicler as a test, "to try him."

The note about the king's death is about the same in Kings; it is not mentioned in the book of Isaiah.

33:1–10 Manasseh was twelve years old when he began to reign, and he reigned fifty and five years . . . But did . . . evil in the sight of the Lord, like unto the abominations of the heathen

This evil king of the line of David could not be overlooked, but the chronicler left only a brief record (cf. 2 Kgs. 21:1–16 and commentary) that includes nothing of the dire warnings given by the prophets.

33:11–20 Wherefore the Lord brought . . . the captains of the host of the king of Assyria, which took Manasseh

This surprising account is only in Chronicles; it tells of a king of "Assyria" going to Judah, taking Manasseh captive to "Babylon," and after a period of suffering and repentance, letting him return to Jerusalem. Who it could have been and what made such a circumstance possible are unknown. The account was attested in a "book of the kings of Israel" (2 Chr. 33:18), but it is not our present book of Kings. The Apocrypha of the Old Testament contains a beautiful prayer of repentance and supplication called the Prayer of Manasseh. Its origins are also not known.

In any case, the evil done by Manasseh began an evil way of life in Judah that never abated, though one good king tried to overcome it. The decadence thus begun resulted in the captivity and exile of Judah.

33:21–25 Amon was two and twenty years old when he began to reign, and reigned two years in Jerusalem

This wicked king emulated none of the late reforms accredited to his father but followed all his predecessor's evil ways instead (2 Chr. 33:2–10, 22–23). It is surprising that his father's reign lasted fifty-two years but no surprise that Amon's lasted only two.

After the pendulum had swung from relatively good kings to the bad king Ahaz, to the good king Hezekiah, to the bad kings Manasseh and Amon, it came back to one last good one—Amon's young son Josiah.

34:1–32 Josiah was eight years old when he began to reign, and he reigned in Jerusalem one and thirty years. And he did that which was right in the sight of the Lord

Since it was "the people of the land" who made Josiah king at age eight (2 Chr. 33:25), perhaps they also provided him advisers and motivation for good. In the eighth year of his reign, he began to seek the Lord. Thus, at age sixteen he was getting a religious base, and by age twenty he began to "purge Judah," including Jerusalem and cities round about, in Simeon, and even northward into former territories of Ephraim, Manasseh, and Naphtali, and "throughout all the land of Israel" (2 Chr. 34:3–7). Because Assyria had taken the ten tribes of northern Israel into captivity some eighty years earlier (BD, "Chronology," p. 638), Josiah's cleansing in the north must have been undertaken among whatever Israelites there were among the other peoples Assyria had sent in (2 Kgs. 17:22–24).

After this detailed introduction to the life and work of young King Josiah, Chronicles essentially parallels the other account (2 Kgs. 22–23 and commentary); there are some differences in order and in emphasis, however. The emphasis in Chronicles is on the king's part in getting the people to renew their "covenant of God," turn from all abominations, and serve him (2 Chr. 34:31–33; cf. 2 Kgs. 23:3).

35:1–19 Moreover Josiah kept a passover unto the Lord in Jerusalem

This Passover is summarized in three verses in the account in Kings (2 Kgs. 23:21–23). The Chronicles account characteristically gives more details, including the names and functions of many of the priests and Levites who conducted the revival of this important high holy day. It is evident from this account that the Levites still performed their teaching functions and other duties in the worship services.

35:20–27 After all this . . . Necho king of Egypt came up to fight against Carchemish by Euphrates: and Josiah went out against him

Some thirteen years later the good King Josiah met his doom at the hands of the forces of Pharaoh Necho of Egypt, for he held the great Passover in the eighteenth year of his reign and reigned thirty-one years in all (2 Chr. 35:19; 34:1). Before reporting Josiah's death, the book of Kings summarizes his contributions (2 Kgs. 23:24–25). Chronicles adds the significant observation that Jeremiah the prophet "lamented for Josiah" (2 Chr. 35:25); well might he do so, for during the twelve years of the subsequent reigns of two of Josiah's sons, a grandson, and another son, Jeremiah and other prophets received little response. These were the times of the prophet Lehi (1 Ne. 1).

36:1– 4 Then the people of the land took Jehoahaz the son of Josiah, and made him king

This son of Josiah reigned only three months before Necho deposed him and took him in "bands" to Egypt, where he died (2 Kgs. 23:31–34).

36:5– 8 Jehoiakim was twenty and five years old when he began to reign, and he reigned eleven years . . . and he did . . . evil

Appointed by Egypt, King Jehoiakim, another son of Josiah, was deposed by Babylon after three years and taken away to Babylon. There is no mention of this exile in Kings, and neither account tells of his burial; but Jeremiah condemned him and prophesied for him an ignominious death and burial (Jer. 22:18–19). He was succeeded by his young son, Jehoiachin.

36:9–10 Jehoiachin was eight years old when he began to reign, and he reigned three months and ten days

Even the short reign of this one grandson of good King Josiah was "evil in the sight of the Lord." Perhaps he merely assumed the throne, for Nebuchadnezzar took him and other prominent people, along with some precious materials, to Babylon. There he was later raised up as a sort of king in exile (2 Kgs. 25:27–30).

36:11–21 Zedekiah was one and twenty years old when he began to reign, and reigned eleven years . . . And he did that which was evil . . . and humbled not himself before Jeremiah the prophet speaking from the mouth of the Lord

Zedekiah was not the brother (2 Chr. 36:10) of Jehoiachin but his uncle (2 Kgs. 24:17–18). The account in Kings records that his name was changed from Mattaniah to Zedekiah. Like most of his predecessors, he resisted the warnings and advice of the prophets, such as Jeremiah (2 Chr. 36:12, 14–16; cf. Jer. 21; 37:1–10; 38).

Jeremiah prophesied that the Babylonian exile of Judah would last seventy years (2 Chr. 36:21*b*).

36:22–23 Now in the first year of Cyrus king of Persia, that the word of the Lord spoken by the mouth of Jeremiah might be accomplished, the Lord stirred up the spirit of Cyrus

The writer of Chronicles anticipated the decree by Cyrus of Persia at the end of the ensuing seventy years and after Babylon's overthrow. Details of that decree are told in the books of Ezra and Nehemiah. The seventy years of captivity may be calculated either from the time the first group of exiles left Judah until the first group returned or from the time of the destruction of the temple until it was rededicated after being rebuilt.

The books of Chronicles have much value and relevance to our own latter day, for they contain examples of the blessings that follow obedience to the Lord as well as vivid warnings against disobedience to him in their record of the kings of Israel and Judah.

EZRA

The book of Isaiah the prophet, who lived more than two hundred years before Ezra, records a remarkable prophecy about the return of the Jews from what had been Babylon by permission of Cyrus, the conqueror of Babylon: "Thus saith the Lord . . . of Cyrus, He is my shepherd, and shall perform all my pleasure: even saying to Jerusalem, Thou shalt be built; and to the temple, Thy foundation shall be laid" (Isa. 44:24, 28). That prophecy, and another one recorded by Jeremiah some seventy years before the return, began to be fulfilled in the early days of Ezra by edict of Cyrus (Jer. 25:12; 2 Chr. 36:22–23; Ezra 1:1–2).

Persian treatment of conquered peoples was the opposite of the Babylonian method of exiling captive peoples. Under the inspired and much more humane system of the Persians, captive peoples were permitted to return to their homelands, and the redemption of Judah and Jerusalem was made possible. Nevertheless, the return of hundreds of people was not without vicissitudes, internal and external; and in the accounts of their exodus and migration, different qualities of character in people—statesmen, laymen, priests, and prophets—may be seen.

The first two chapters of the book of Ezra report an edict permitting Judah's return, the response of some who chose to do so, and the willingness of others to help them return. The next two chapters tell how the former exiles began rebuilding their desolated homeland. There the Samaritans, residents of Judah who were of mixed descent, proposed to help rebuild the temple; but upon being rebuffed by the Jews, they began to impair the work. Chapters 5 and 6 tell of the prophets Haggai and Zechariah encouraging the people to rebuild the temple. Continual opposition by the Samaritans led to a search of the royal Persian records for the Jews' authority to build the temple and the city; Cyrus's enabling edict was confirmed, work was resumed, and the temple was completed on the third day of Adar, 516 B.C., which was indeed seventy years after Babylon destroyed the great temple of Solomon. The last four chapters record that some years later, about 458 B.C., Ezra himself was commissioned to go to Jerusalem, where he carried out great reforms (BD, "Chronology," p. 640).

COMMENTARY

1:1– 4 Now in the first year of Cyrus king of Persia, that the word of the Lord by the mouth of Jeremiah might be fulfilled, the Lord stirred up the spirit of Cyrus . . . that he made a proclamation throughout all his kingdom

At the end of 2 Chronicles a historic proclamation by Cyrus was announced; it is here repeated and elucidated (2 Chr. 36:22–23; Ezra 1:1–4). The edict launched the fulfillment of prophecies of two great prophets of earlier times regarding Babylon's demise and the return of the Jews (Jer. 25:11–12; 29:10; Isa. 44:28; 45:1–4; 13–14; 47).

The "first year of Cyrus" refers to his first year of ruling over the area that had been Babylon, about 537 B.C.; he had begun to reign in his native Elam twenty years before. His responsiveness to "the Lord God of heaven" who is "the Lord God of Israel" and his assertion that "he is the God" could have been consistent with a Zoroastrian-like belief that all gods are one, though known by different names among various peoples; but it likely arose out of pure inspiration. Josephus states that when Cyrus read Isaiah's prophecies "and admired the divine power, an earnest desire and ambition seized upon him to fulfil what was so written" (*Antiquities of the Jews* 11:1:1–2).

It was anticipated that though some Jews would desire to return to Judah, some would choose to remain in Babylon, now ruled by Persia. The Jews who remained were admonished in the edict of Cyrus to help those who returned and to contribute toward rebuilding the house of God. A sizable Jewish community did remain in Mesopotamia, and there have been some Jews in that region on through time to the present.

1:5–11 Then rose up the chief of the fathers of Judah and Benjamin, and the priests, and the Levites, with all them whose spirit God had raised, to go up to build the house of the Lord which is in Jerusalem

Only the general tribal identity of the people in the first group of returning exiles is given. Among them, priests and Levites would fill particularly important roles in building and operating the second temple.

Those who assisted the returning Jews ranged from the common people to King Cyrus himself. He sent vessels that had been taken from Solomon's temple by Nebuchadnezzar. Note the astonishing number of them.

"Sheshbazzar, the prince of Judah" is generally considered to be the same person as "Zerubbabel," although the two names are from different linguistic roots and have different meanings (Ezra 1:8, 11; 5:14, 16; 2:2*b*. For Zerubbabel's genealogy, see 1 Chr. 3:16–19; BD, "Zerubbabel").

2:1–70 Now these are the children of the province that went up out of the captivity . . . and came again unto Jerusalem and Judah, every one unto his city

These were the first company of exiles who returned under Zerubbabel and ten other leaders. Zerubbabel was of the royal lineage, a grandson of Jehoiachin. Jeshua may be the same man identified by Haggai the prophet as Joshua, a leading priest (Hag. 1:1; 2:2, 4). The Nehemiah listed here is likely not the one appointed to be governor nearly ninety years later and introduced in the book of Nehemiah (see BD, "Chronology," p. 640). The exiles were identified, some by the names of families or clans (Ezra

2:3–19), others by cities or areas of origin (Ezra 2:20–35), others by their priestly families (Ezra 2:36–39), and others by their Levite families (Ezra 2:40–42). The Nethinim were possibly descendants of the Gibeonites who became servants of Israel, some having been Solomon's servants (Ezra 2:43–58; Josh. 9:3, 22–23; 8:20). Some did not know their genealogy or even whether they were of Israel; and several priests with doubtful genealogy had to wait for a high priest possessing the Urim and Thummim to certify their right to the priesthood (Ezra 2:59–63). The outcome is not recorded.

The total number of exiles in this group (42,360) is not the same as the sum of the numbers in each subgroup (29,818), nor the same as that given later (Neh. 7:66). Various reconciliations have been proposed, but the matter has not been resolved conclusively.

Apparently these exiles returned to the localities where they or their parents or grandparents had lived and resumed the work of producing food and providing shelter and later helping to rebuild Jerusalem. More is told in the next chapter about assemblies for worship there (Ezra 3:1–7) and also about the appointment of priests, Levites, and others to live and work in Jerusalem (Ezra 3:8–13; Neh. 11:1–2).

3:1–7 And when the seventh month was come . . . the people gathered themselves together as one man to Jerusalem

The high holy days—Rosh Hashanah, Yom Kippur, Sukkoth, and Simchas Torah—were evidently celebrated in the first twenty-three days of the seventh month, although not all of the high holy days are mentioned in these verses (Ezra 3:1–7 and fn.; Num. 29).

The general leader, Zerubbabel, and the priestly leader, Jeshua, constructed an altar at the temple site so that burnt offerings and other sacrifices could be made. The worshippers were motivated partly by fear of the peoples round about and turned to the Lord with sacrifices and supplications for security. Regular daily and monthly worship services were resumed after the Feast of Tabernacles (Sukkoth), which ends the high holy days.

Although the altar was now reconstructed and in use, reconstruction of the temple came later. Money was given to builders and agricultural exports were sent to providers of materials in Lebanon in preparation for construction work on the house of God to begin.

3:8–13 Now in the second year . . . in the second month, began Zerubbabel . . . and Jeshua . . . and . . . the priests and the Levites . . . to set forward the work of the house of the Lord

When the foundations of the temple were laid, people rejoiced, praised the Lord, and sang—but some wept. Doubtless some wept for joy; but some wept because the new structure was "as nothing" compared to the glorious first temple (Hag. 2:3; Ezra 3:12*a–b*).

4:1– 6 the adversaries of Judah . . . said unto them, Let us build with you . . . Then the people of the land weakened the hands of the people of Judah, and troubled them

It is difficult to know whether the "people of the land" really wanted to seek the Lord or were "adversaries of Judah" from the beginning and had selfish motives. They were descendants of people who lived there when the ten tribes were taken away by Assyria and replaced by other peoples brought in from many nations, who intermixed both blood and faith with the remnant Israelites (2 Kgs. 17). They were active adversaries during the reigns of Cyrus, Ahasuerus, Artaxerxes, and Darius I (BD, "Chronology," p. 640). The first interruption of the work on the temple lasted about fifteen years (ca. 536–521 B.C.).

4:7–24 And in the days of Artaxerxes [they] wrote Bishlam, Mithredath, Tabeel, and . . . their companions, unto Artaxerxes king of Persia

Several of the Samaritan leaders wrote to the Persian King Artaxerxes about "damage" to his dominion that might result from reconstruction of the "rebellious city" of Jerusalem. When the history of that city was researched, the warnings appeared to be well founded, so Artaxerxes issued an edict that the Jewish reconstruction at Jerusalem must cease. And the work on rebuilding the city of Jerusalem did cease until the reign of Darius (Ezra 4:5, 24; 5–6). Ahasuerus, or Xerxes, reigned from about 486 through 465 B.C., and Artaxerxes, 465 through 423 B.C.

The language shifts from Hebrew to Aramaic (Ezra 4:8–6:18) in reporting these letters and their results; Hebrew is then resumed for the rest of the book of Ezra except for one other Aramaic passage (Ezra 7:12–26; BD, "Aram, Aramaeans"; "Aramaic"). Aramaic, the official language of the Persian empire, was the language of international communication and trade for centuries. Later the scriptures were orally translated and explained to the people in that language (Neh. 8).

5:1–17 Then the prophets, Haggai . . . and Zechariah . . . prophesied unto the Jews . . . in Judah and Jerusalem . . . Then rose up Zerubbabel . . . and Jeshua . . . and began to build the house of God which is at Jerusalem

In 520 B.C. the people of Judah, encouraged by the prophets Haggai and Zechariah, resumed work on rebuilding the temple. Tatnai, the local governor under Persia, challenged the builders on account of Artaxerxes' edict (Ezra 4:21–23) and demanded the names of the leaders who were directing the building (in Ezra 5:4, *we* should be *he,* according to the Septuagint, which makes better sense). When the governor's complaint went to Darius, however, it also contained the Jews' assertion that Cyrus had earlier authorized the work and aided them in building the house of God in Jerusalem, and they requested that a search be made for Cyrus' decree (Ezra 5:6–17).

6:1–18 Then Darius the king made a decree

Indeed, King Darius made two decrees: that the decree of Cyrus be sought, and when found, that it be vigorously implemented. Tatnai, the governor "beyond the river," may well have regretted having ever brought up the matter, for he was commanded to cease his obstruction and even contribute to the building project.

The Persian King Darius seems, like Cyrus, to have felt some motivation to please "the God of heaven" and "the God that hath caused his name to dwell there" in Jerusalem. With the king's political and economic help and with the spiritual guidance of the prophets Haggai and Zechariah complementing the work of the priests and Levites, the work prospered and was finished within six years, about 516 B.C. (Ezra 4:24; 6:6–15; BD, "Darius"). The dedicatory services were not as grand as those for Solomon's temple (1 Kgs. 8), but they were joyous, and the sacrifices were resumed. The festivities were held in the month of Adar, an early spring month at the approach of the Passover season of renewal.

6:19–22 And the children of the captivity kept the passover upon the fourteenth day of the first month

Two weeks after the dedicatory services and throughout the third week of Nisan (also called "Aviv"), the Passover and the Feast of Unleavened Bread were observed with special rejoicing at Judah's delivery from bondage. Indeed, the Jews had reason to be grateful to the Lord for the actions of the Persian kings Cyrus, Darius, and others who reigned over what had been the oppressive empires of Assyria and Babylon. Ezra may imply that the oppressive governor Tatnai was, metaphorically, a "king of Assyria" (Ezra 6:22).

7:1–28 Now after these things, in the reign of Artaxerxes . . . Ezra went up from Babylon; and he was a ready scribe

This event came some sixty years after the temple dedication and the Passover discussed above, for it was "in the seventh year of Artaxerxes the king," the second king of that name in Persia, according to the biblical record (Ezra 7:7; ca. 458 B.C.; BD, "Chronology," p. 640). Ezra undertook the fifteen-hundred-mile, four-month-long journey from Persia to Jerusalem that same year. He was a "ready scribe" (BD, "Scribe"). *Ready* is used to translate a Hebrew word meaning "fast," implying that he was efficient at copying and expounding the scriptures. He was a "son" (descendant) of Seraiah, who died at the capture of Jerusalem nearly one hundred years before (2 Kgs. 25:18–21), and thus of the lineage of

Aaron through Eleazar. He was well qualified by birth and preparation "to seek the law of the Lord, and to do it, and to teach in Israel statutes and judgments" (Ezra 7:10).

Ezra's remarkably generous commission was from King Artaxerxes (Longimanus, 465–421 B.C.; not the Artaxerxes of Ezra 4:7, who is designated as Pseudo-Smerdis in secular histories; BD, "Chronology," p. 640). His commission is another Aramaic portion of this book (Ezra 7:12–26). It granted him all his requests and gave him official sanction to take other priests, Levites, and people with him and to carry the precious things that "the king and his counsellors" sent "unto the God of Israel, whose habitation is in Jerusalem" (Ezra 7:15). He was also to take materials for offerings by the people and priests.

The king's motivation is quoted frankly: "For why should there be wrath against the realm of the king and his sons?" Accordingly, whatever else was needed was made available "out of the king's treasure house" and from "all the treasurers which are beyond the river," and no one was to tax the priestly leaders and servants. Because ecclesiastical and secular government were all one, Ezra was also to set up magistrates and judges, teach them the laws of God, and punish anyone disobedient to the laws of God and the king (Ezra 7:20–26).

No wonder this ready scribe and priest, who had prepared his heart for his mission, ended this part of his account with thanks to God, who had "put such a thing as this in the king's heart." He bore this testimony: "I was strengthened as the hand of the Lord my God was upon me, and I gathered together out of Israel chief men to go up with me" (Ezra 7:27–28).

8:1–36 These are now the chief of their fathers, and this is the genealogy of them that went up with me from Babylon, in the reign of Artaxerxes the king

Ezra identified the families, or clans, who voluntarily came with him, gathered them together, and summoned leaders and Levites, who were men of understanding and ministers for the house of God. They felt blessed with success "by the good hand of our God" over them.

Before setting out, Ezra gathered his company and called for a fast that they might find the right way to go in safety, for he was reluctant to ask the king for a military escort in view of his testimony that the hand of God would be upon them for good. Ezra "separated," or set apart, responsible leaders to whom he weighed out precious things for which they would be responsible until they were delivered to the house of God. The company departed on the twelfth day of the first month and were delivered "from the hand of the enemy," arriving safely in Jerusalem (Ezra 8:21–32).

They rested (quite understandably) three days and then weighed in all the precious things they had weighed out, finding all in order. Ezra and his company next "delivered the king's commissions unto the king's lieutenants, and to the governors," who implemented them (Ezra 8:36*a*–*b*).

Ezra is seen as a very conscientious, orderly, and efficient leader in these accounts as well as the later accounts recorded in the book of Nehemiah.

9:1–15 Now when these things were done, the princes came to me, saying, The people of Israel, and the priests, and the Levites, have not separated themselves from the people of the lands, doing according to their abominations

When Ezra learned that the people and their priesthood leaders were again intermarrying with unbelieving people of the land, he felt both concern and shame. It worried him that the laws of Moses had so soon again been broken, for it indicated that the lessons of their history had not been learned. Intermarriage with other cultures had led to changes in their religion, neglect of the divine law, and apostasy. Israel must remain dedicated as the "holy seed" for the Lord's planting (Ezra 9:2; Ex. 19:6; Lev. 19:2; Deut. 7:6). The Lord's purpose in calling a consecrated, dedicated "seed" was, and is, to provide exemplars and messengers to all families of all nations, so that "all that will hear may hear" (D&C 1:11; Gen. 12:3; Abr. 2:9–11).

In his prayer, Ezra confessed his shame and concern for his people and recognized the grace and patience of God. He contrasted the Lord's grace with the infidelity, carelessness, and rebelliousness of Israel (Ezra 9:4–15; compare the prayer of Nephi, son of Helaman, in Hel. 7:6–29).

10:1– 44 Now when Ezra had prayed, and when he had confessed, weeping . . . the people wept very sore

The people were surprisingly responsive, and a spokesman for those who had transgressed the laws proposed that the people make a covenant to repent. Ezra charged them to "swear that they should do according to this word," and they did so. Accordingly, all the people were assembled, even though it was in the ninth month (November-December), the time of the heavy winter rains. When all agreed to take action, Ezra wisely observed that it was something they could not do then and there in the rain, but rulers could be appointed and violators identified. So in about four months the matter was done (the "first month" is Nisan, or Aviv, which falls in March-April). Records were made of the names of all involved.

Ezra was indeed a good leader; in nine months (recall Ezra 7:4), he had accomplished much reform, and more of his mission is yet to be told in the book of Nehemiah.

The book of Ezra, which begins with events in history some eighty years before the time of Ezra's appointment by Artaxerxes, covers an exciting and challenging period of Israel's long and tortuous history. The Israelites were weak, returning from a period of bondage without means of adequate security or support. Those who were seventy years old and older could barely have remembered being taken away to Babylon as little children, and the younger generations would only have known of their homeland from the stories of their parents and grandparents. They must be admired for their commitment and sacrifice, their trek of some fifteen hundred miles, and their toil to provide food and shelter again in the promised land. But it took Ezra, a strong, dedicated leader, to get them organized and functioning satisfactorily. Accounts of their continued rebuilding in Jerusalem and of their further reforms are told in the next book, named for the next great leader, Nehemiah.

NEHEMIAH

The book of Nehemiah is a colorful record that continues the account begun in the book of Ezra about the return of the Jews from Babylon. It begins much as a journal would: "The words of Nehemiah the son of Hachaliah" (Neh. 1:1). There are many good word-pictures of the personality and character of the man Nehemiah, who had been cupbearer to the king of Persia and was later governor of Judah. This loyal and altruistic man was able with faith, resourcefulness, capability, and persistence to take constructive action, counter opposition, and improve the condition of his people. One project, undertaken along with that "ready scribe" Ezra, was to collect and preserve scrolls that became the Holy Scriptures of Judaism—our Old Testament.

The first seven chapters of the book of Nehemiah tell how he, the Jewish cupbearer to the Persian King Artaxerxes, was commissioned to go to Jerusalem to rescue the city and province from resurgent deterioration. He organized the repairing of the walls and gates, which had again been broken down.

The next three chapters record a vital event—the gathering, reading, and explication of the books of the Law to the Jews of the return. That was part of the canonization of the Law, the Prophets, and the Writings. And it brought about the first oral translations of Hebrew scripture into another language; they were the first Aramaic Targums.

Chapter 11 and most of 12 (vv. 1–26) list the people who had returned to Judah from areas of Babylon after it became part of the Persian empire. The remainder of chapter 12 (vv. 27–47) tells of their completion of the wall around Jerusalem and of its dedication. Perpetual support for priesthood leaders was implemented according to the Law; but all the reforms were not continued. Chapter 13 records that after a time back in Persia, Nehemiah returned to Jerusalem to complete his life's mission of reform and stabilization.

The apocryphal book of 1 Esdras contains much of the information that is in the books of Ezra and Nehemiah but with a few differences in sequence and some additional material.

COMMENTARY

1:1–11 The words of Nehemiah . . . in the month Chisleu, in the twentieth year, as I was in Shushan the palace

The book begins with the memoirs of Nehemiah, a Jew in a favored and trusted position in the Persian palace as cupbearer, who was responsible to safeguard the king. The year was about 445 B.C., twenty years after the accession of Artaxerxes (Ezra 7:1; BD, "Chronology," p. 640).

The bad news Nehemiah had received from one of his "brethren" in Jerusalem may have been an account of the condition of the walls and gates that had still not been reconstructed since the return of some of the Jews ninety years before; but more likely the report reflected deterioration and destruction done after the rebuilding work had been partly accomplished.

Though he himself held a position of security and honor, Nehemiah empathized with his countrymen who lived in poor circumstances. He worried about their welfare and was in such distress the king perceived it. Knowing well the promises of the scriptures and the powers of God, Nehemiah fasted and prayed.

2:1–8 in the month Nisan, in the twentieth year of Artaxerxes . . . the king said unto me, Why is thy countenance sad . . . For what dost thou make request?

About four months later, in the springtime, his worry and the king's concern brought Nehemiah to his life's mission in Jerusalem. He had tried not to appear sad in the king's presence, but the king was perceptive and offered help.

Nehemiah's requests show that he was a practical man and a knowledgeable administrator. He prepared to go to Judah and Jerusalem, equipped politically and economically to accomplish all the reconstruction work needed.

2:9–20 Then I came to the governors . . . and gave them the king's letters. . . . And I went out by night . . . and viewed the walls of Jerusalem, which were broken down, and the gates

He proceeded very logically to assess what was needed, gain the people's cooperation, and neutralize the opposition whenever possible. Facing his adversaries with faith and courage, he sought to accomplish what the Lord had put into his heart to do (Neh. 2:12). More about the adversaries is told later (Neh. 4; 6).

3:1–32 Then Eliashib the high priest rose up with his brethren the priests, and they builded the sheep gate . . . And next unto him builded the men of Jericho. And next to them

The leaders and people responded positively to Nehemiah's testimony that the hand of God was good upon him (Neh. 2:18). Nehemiah's record concisely reports what each of the groups undertook and performed. Some were identified by their family, some by their city of origin, some by their Levite affiliation, and some by their crafts or professions.

The position of each segment of the wall and gates cannot now with certainty be located with respect to the present "Old City" of Jerusalem (Bible Map 17); but the first five verses may refer to the north wall and gates, the next seven to the west, the next two to the south, the next fourteen to the southeast, and the last five to the east. Acquaintance with the terrain and with features to which the gates give access makes those identifications plausible.

4:1–23 But . . . when Sanballat heard that we builded the wall, he was wroth, . . . and mocked the Jews

Sanballat was the Samaritan leader (BD, "Samaria"; "Samaritans";

"Sanballat"). He, with an "Ammonite," certain "Arabians," and others, opposed Nehemiah's work; they scoffed at it, belittled it, and later (Neh. 6) engaged in intrigue to stop it. Nehemiah took action to meet that opposition: he prayed, set out guards and defenders, kept the workmen armed and encouraged their faith, and kept a trumpeter at hand to summon help if needed. Thus with vigilance, day and night, he moved the work forward despite problems external or internal.

5:1–19 And there was a great cry of the people and of their wives against their brethren

The effectiveness of Nehemiah's leadership is seen again in his response to the complaints of the poor and of the recently returned exiles who were impoverished by drought, taxes, debts, and many other demands upon their means and labor to help build the wall. Evidently the Jews who had returned earlier had greater wealth, and the poorer ones had borrowed from them. Unable to repay, they had indentured sons and daughters into service or bondage. Nehemiah's anger, rebuke, persuasion, and good example brought about relief.

He was exemplary also in refusing to accept perquisites as governor, receiving only the necessary food and wine from the people to sustain his officers and servants.

Nehemiah's short prayers (Neh. 5:19; 6:9, 14, etc.) maintained his relationship with the Lord. They were practical and sought for things he could not achieve alone.

6:1–19 Sanballat and Geshem sent unto me, saying, Come, let us meet together

When the walls had all been repaired, the inveterate enemies made further attempts to destroy Nehemiah; but neither an assassination plot, false accusations of sedition, nor the treacherous suggestions of an inside "friend" moved him. Nor did the compromising suggestions of some false friends among the nobles of Judah succeed against this worldly-wise and spiritually alert leader.

It is amazing that the walls could have been repaired by the sixth month, Elul, after fifty-two working days (Neh. 6:15).

7:1– 4 when the wall was built, and I had set up the doors . . . I gave my brother Hanani, and Hananiah the ruler of the palace, charge over Jerusalem

Apparently to supplement the work of two other men (Neh. 3:9–12), each of whom ruled half the district of Jerusalem, Nehemiah appointed his brother and another God-fearing man to regulate the opening and closing of the gates and to organize "watches," or home-guards, throughout the city.

Many homes had yet to be rebuilt and occupied, a condition they remedied later (Neh. 11).

7:5–73 And my God put into mine heart to gather . . . nobles, . . . rulers, and the people, that they might be reckoned by genealogy. And I found a register of the genealogy of them which came up

From a record of those who had come back earlier, Nehemiah made up a list like that of Ezra, but with a few variations; he gave also a few more details in the closing verses about the offerings given by leaders, including "the Tirshatha"—the governor, Nehemiah himself (cf. Ezra 2:1–70).

Once again the Urim and Thummim was needed for revelation (Neh. 7:65; Ezra 2:63; BD and TG, "Urim and Thummim").

The "seventh month" after Nehemiah began his mission was the month of Tishri, the time for high holy days (Neh. 7:73; 8).

8:1–18 And Ezra the priest brought the law before the congregation . . . upon the first day of the seventh month

What Ezra had been doing since the days of his great reformation (Ezra 9–10) is not recorded, but at this point in the history of the return, he reappeared on what has become Rosh Hashanah, "Head of the Year." He was asked by the people to bring out the scroll of the law of Moses. With awe the people stood up when he opened the scroll, and when he finished the blessing before reading, they raised their hands and responded "Amen, Amen," bowed down to the ground, and worshipped the Lord.

As he read, those on the stand with him "caused the people to understand" (Neh. 8:7–8). It is possible that the explaining and paraphrasing was done in Aramaic, and thus the *Targums*, or translations in Aramaic, originated. That language, which is closely related to Hebrew, was learned by the Jews in exile in Babylon (BD, "Aramaic").

Ancient traditions attribute to Ezra the collection at this time of all the scrolls of the Law, the Prophets, and the Writings; the Talmud asserts that by inspiration he rewrote books which were missing. It is quite well established that this was a period of collection and primary canonization of the great Hebrew Scriptures of the Jews, our Old Testament (BD, "Canon"; "Ezra"; "Nehemiah"; "Synagogue, the Great"; "Talmud").

As the reading continued, the Jews learned again of the Feast of Sukkoth, "Booths," or "Tabernacles"; so they celebrated their own exodus and return from bondage while renewing the original commemoration of the exodus from Egypt. Though this feast had been observed in the first year of the return of Zerubbabel's group (Ezra 3:4–5), never since Joshua had it been so fully kept as it was on this occasion (Neh. 8:17*a–c;* BD, "Feasts," paragraph on the Feast of Tabernacles). During this special time, Ezra read to them from the scriptures daily.

9:1–38 Now in the twenty and fourth day of this month the children of Israel were assembled with fasting . . . And the seed of Israel separated themselves from all strangers, and stood and confessed their sins, and the iniquities of their fathers

Two days after the annual high holy days concluded, these grateful children of Israel held a day of fasting and commitment, sealing the covenants they had renewed. There was scripture reading for one-fourth of the day, with confessions and worship during another fourth. Then some of the Levites who had explained the previous reading, along with others, stood on the platform and prayed aloud on behalf of all (Neh. 8:7; 9:4–5). They praised the Lord and recalled his blessings to Abraham, including the promise of a land. They reviewed God's blessings given in the days of Moses despite Israel's many rebellions; and they reviewed blessings given in the land of promise, including the "saviours" in the days of the judges (Neh. 9:27*d*). They confessed that in the days of the kings many sins had been committed despite the admonitions of the prophets, and the exile had resulted. They confessed their faults and supplicated God's mercy, forgiveness, and renewal of the covenant, to which they wished to be sealed (Neh. 9:32–38; 10:1 ff.).

10:1–27 Now those that sealed were, Nehemiah, the Tirshatha, the son of Hachaliah, and Zidkijah

The leaders who thus renewed their covenants included Nehemiah, the governor, and certain priests and Levites who were listed by name. The "rest of the people" included priests, Levites, temple workers—"every one having knowledge, and having understanding" of the oath and covenants (Neh. 10:28, 29*a–e*).

The Mosaic covenant embraced many aspects of daily life and religious commitment (Neh. 10:29–39 and fn.).

11:1–36 the rulers of the people dwelt at Jerusalem: the rest of the people also cast lots, to bring one of ten to dwell in Jerusalem the holy city, and nine parts . . . in other cities

Because too few had returned to Jerusalem to rebuild homes (Neh. 7:4), people besides the civil and religious leaders were chosen by lot to help build and defend it. Those who had voluntarily come into the city to do so were esteemed by all.

Certain leaders from Judah and Benjamin are listed by name, as well as the temple maintenance workers and ordinance workers. Other temple workers, such as singers, servants, Levites, and their overseers, are also named.

Then "the residue of Israel" and the villages where they dwelt are outlined (Neh. 11:20–36).

The people also remembered with appreciation—and sought to implement—the Persian kings' edicts that the temple should be rebuilt, be adequately supplied, and function to the honor of the Lord God (Neh. 11:23–24; Ezra 6:8–12; 7:12–28).

12:1–26 Now these are the priests and the Levites that went up with Zerubbabel . . . and Jeshua

Some of the priests and Levites were previously listed (cf. Ezra 2:1–2; Neh. 10:3–9). The Jeremiah and the Ezra named in the first verse were not Jeremiah the prophet nor Ezra the scribe.

12:27– 47 at the dedication of the wall of Jerusalem

The wall was finished near the end of Elul (Neh. 6:15), which was just before the celebration of the high holy days in the first three weeks of Tishri—"the seventh month" (Neh. 8). The date of the festival to dedicate the wall is not recorded, but one tradition places it on the twenty-fifth day of Kislev, about two months after the celebration of Sukkoth, or Tabernacles; that would correspond with a date nearly three centuries later when the temple was rededicated in the time of the Maccabees, in 165 B.C. (BD, "Chronology," p. 642; "Maccabees"; "Temple of Zerubbabel"). If that dating is correct, it gives a double reason for the annual Jewish celebration of the Feast of Hanukkah, or Dedication, which continues to the present (BD, "Feasts," paragraph on the Feast of Dedication, p. 673).

One group, led by "Ezra the scribe" (Neh. 12:36), walked on the west wall southward, then eastward on the south wall, then northeastward and northward to the stairs leading up to the temple (Neh. 12:31–37). The other group went with Nehemiah (Neh. 12:38) northward along the west wall, then eastward along the north wall, and finally southward along the east wall until both groups met at the entry and "gave thanks in the house of God" (Neh. 12:38–40). There was such rejoicing they could be "heard even afar off" (Neh. 12:43).

Appointments were made for the chambers for the treasures, offerings, tithes, and so forth; and the singers were organized for service. Daily portions of supplies for them and for the priests and Levites were also appointed.

13:1–9 they read in the book of Moses . . . and therein was found written, that the Ammonite and the Moabite should not come into the congregation of God . . . But in all this time was not I at Jerusalem: . . . I came to Jerusalem, and understood of the evil

Although at the great conference of dedication, the faithful had read and committed themselves to all that they should and should not do, this chapter tells of evils that had crept in while Nehemiah was back at the court of Artaxerxes for twelve years (Neh. 13:6).

First was a situation in which Tobiah, the inveterate opponent of the Jews, had allied himself to Eliashib, the chief priest (Neh. 13:4, 28; cf. 2:10; 4:7; 6:1, 12–19). Through his scheme, Tobiah had been given living quarters in "a great chamber" of the temple compound (Neh. 13:5). When Nehemiah returned to Jerusalem and "understood the evil that Eliashib did for Tobiah," he cast him and his household goods out and had the chambers cleansed (Neh. 13:7–9, 28).

13:10–14 I perceived that the portions of the Levites had not been given them

Furthermore, the offerings for the Levites had become delinquent again, so the Levites had left the temple service to earn their living in the fields. Nehemiah immediately appointed "treasurers" to keep track of contributions, and the people resumed contributing their tithing.

13:15–22 In those days saw I in Judah some treading wine presses on the sabbath, and bringing in sheaves, and lading asses

Despite the covenant renewal a few years earlier (Neh. 10:29–31), the Sabbath was again being broken through labor and commerce. Nehemiah perceived that these evils were the fault of the leaders and reminded them that such behavior had brought the punishments of God upon their forefathers. He corrected them, set guards to close the gates on the Sabbath, and appointed Levites there to maintain them.

Note again Nehemiah's little prayers (Neh. 13:14, 22).

13:23–31 In those days also saw I Jews that had married wives of Ashdod, of Ammon, and of Moab: And their children spake half in the speech of Ashdod, and could not speak in the Jews' language

Although the people had resolved to "walk in God's law" and not intermarry with peoples outside the covenant (Neh. 10:29–30), the practice still prevailed. Nehemiah reminded the Jews that even the great King Solomon was caused to sin by his unbelieving wives, and he corrected the violators vigorously (Neh. 13:25–26 and fn.). Finally, Nehemiah prayed again for the Lord's confirmation of his work in constraining people to honor their priesthood and the covenant of the priesthood (Neh. 13:29*b*).

In the last of the little personal prayers, he hoped he would be remembered for the good he had tried to do (Neh. 13:31).

Just as some chapters of 2 Chronicles resemble Book of Mormon accounts of leaders undertaking great missions, so also in some ways does the book of Nehemiah. It may profitably be read for good teachings, interesting and important narratives, and basic doctrines.

ESTHER

Once it happened that the crafty was taken in his own trap, the falsely condemned were saved, and the worthy were rewarded. It is not always so. Perhaps this story has endured because it has given the comfort of hope to other oppressed people. Although God is not expressly mentioned in the book of Esther, there appears to be evidence in it of the God whom Job describes, who can "set up on high those that be low; that those which mourn may be exalted to safety. He disappointeth the devices of the crafty, so that their hands cannot perform their enterprise" (Job 5:11–12). There was, in a crisis, fasting, which can imply prayer. And divine foreordination may be implied by the challenging question: "Who knoweth whether thou art come to the kingdom for such a time as this?" (Esth. 4:14).

The first chapter of Esther sets the stage for Esther's dilemma. The second tells how she became a queen in Persia and how her cousin and guardian, Mordecai, attained honorable status. The adversary, Haman, is introduced in the third chapter, and the development moves quickly toward a crisis. The fourth chapter tells how Queen Esther was faced with a challenge and rose to meet it. The fifth and sixth chapters become tense as Esther's plan and Haman's plot progressed simultaneously and Esther barely managed to execute her plan in time to save her people from Haman's plot. The last chapters show how he who planned to destroy others was himself destroyed, and the Jews gained a victory over those who had sought to destroy them. The festival of Purim, still celebrated by Jews to this day, was thereby originated, according to this account.

Numerous commentaries are available on the book of Esther; it has been the subject of much criticism as well as much commendation. There are more differing versions of it, more Targums of it, and more Midrashes on it than on any other book in the Bible. Yet it is the only Old Testament book not found in the Dead Sea Scrolls.

COMMENTARY

1:1– 8 Now it came to pass in the days of Ahasuerus . . . In the third year of his reign

The name *Ahasuerus* is an English transliteration of the Hebrew spelling of the Persian king's name—*Khshayarsha;* the common Persian-to-Greek-to-English transliteration of it is *Xerxes* (BD, "Ahasuerus"; "Xerxes"; "Chronology," p. 640). He is thought to have reigned 486–465 B.C. If so, he lived earlier than the commission of Ezra (458 B.C.) and Nehemiah (444 B.C.).

He is introduced as a vain king, showing off "the riches of his glorious kingdom," at a royal feast for the realm's princes, nobles, and their servants in a celebration lasting one hundred eighty days! Added glamour and opulence were shown in a "feast unto all the people that were present in Shushan the palace, both unto great and small, seven days." Yet a quality of justice in the king was shown in that he compelled no one to imbibe.

1:9–22 But the queen Vashti refused to come at the king's commandment

Queen Vashti had her own standards and refused to be displayed before the reveling royal guests. The crisis that ensued is almost humorously related as it tells how the principals and counselors made urgent plans to avoid a wifely rebellion throughout the realms. Accordingly, the queen was banished, that she might "come no more before king Ahasuerus"; and her royal estate was given to someone "better than she."

2:1–20 Then said the king's servants . . . Let there be fair young virgins sought . . . And let the maiden which pleaseth the king be queen instead of Vashti

A queen-contest was held to seek Vashti's replacement. Young women were gathered from all realms by government officers. There is no indication that Esther's guardian, Mordecai, offered her, but she also was taken into the contest.

Mordecai was a great-grandson of Kish, a Benjamite "who had been carried away from Jerusalem with the captivity . . . with Jeconiah king of Judah," ca. 598 B.C., some one hundred twelve years before. He regarded his fair cousin as "his own daughter" (Esth. 2:5–7).

No reason is given for Mordecai's advice that she hide her Jewish identity, but disclosure of it at a crucial time in the events became vital. Mordecai's own Jewishness was known, however, and that became a critical factor.

The process of Esther's being chosen queen needs little analysis or explanation. Questions may arise about a good Jewish girl being taken in marriage by a gentile king, but it may have been because the Lord was preparing her opportunity to save her people.

Esther's name is interesting. Her Hebrew name was *Hadassah,* which is also the name of a hardy, perennial ground cover plant called myrtle. It bears five-petal flowers that are like little blue or white stars; *Esther* is an English rendition of a Persian word meaning "star." That name also appears sometimes as *Ishtar,* the name of the goddess-companion to *Marduk,* which name has the same root as *Mordecai.* Some symbolism therein may be significant.

An eminent Jewish women's organization for social and civic service is called by the name "Hadassah."

2:21–23 two of the king's chamberlains . . . sought to lay hand on the king . . . the thing was known to Mordecai, who told it unto Esther . . . and Esther certified the king thereof in Mordecai's name

This incident became a vital link in the later elevation of Mordecai as a hero and the degradation of Haman as a villain.

3:1–15 After these things did king Ahasuerus promote Haman . . . the Agagite. . . . And all the king's servants . . . bowed, and reverenced Haman. . . . But Mordecai bowed not, nor did him reverence

Potential for conflict is suggested in Haman's identity as an "Agagite" (recall 1 Sam. 15:9, 33) and Mordecai's descent from "Kish, a Benjamite" (recall 1 Sam. 9:1; 10:21); for Israel's first king, Saul, was a son of Kish, a Benjamite, and his downfall came after he spared Agag, a king of Israel's inveterate enemy the Amalekites. Whether the names are metaphors in the book of Esther, or indicate actual genealogical descent, the parallelism is symbolic.

Mordecai's refusal to bow and "reverence" Haman may not have been a gratuitous affront. It could have been Mordecai's obedience to the first of the Ten Commandments and the reason that he "had told them that he was a Jew" (Esth. 3:4).

Haman has become the prototype of many who have sought "to destroy all the Jews," both because his pride was damaged and because he hoped for material and political gain thereby. Evaluate both Haman's rationales in acquiring the king's consent and the king's unquestioning concession. Haman generalized reasons why a certain people should be destroyed but did not identify them. He promised great contributions to the king's treasuries without disclosing sources of the treasure, though it might have been assumed he planned to kill men, women, and children and "take the spoil of them for a prey." To determine an auspicious day for such a deed, a lot *(pur)* was cast. Annually, to the present day, Jews have commemorated Purim on the thirteenth and fourteenth day of the twelfth month, Adar (Esth. 3:7, 13; 9:26–32).

4:1–17 Mordecai rent his clothes . . . and cried with a loud and a bitter cry; . . . Then was the queen exceedingly grieved

At first Queen Esther was troubled only by Mordecai's deep mourning, for she did not know the cause, and she sent clothing so that he could go to her and explain. Then came the dread surprise and challenge. She had to appeal to the king for her people, facing whatever personal danger there was in approaching the throne without the king's invitation.

Religious faith and commitment in the characters of both Mordecai and Esther are implicit in his challenge to her and in her response (Esth. 4:13–17).

5:1–14 Now it came to pass on the third day, that Esther put on her royal apparel, and stood in the inner court of the king's house . . . when the king saw Esther . . . she obtained favour . . . and the king held out to Esther the golden sceptre that was in his hand

Note Esther's procedure of entering, approaching as properly as possible, extending a disarming invitation to *both* Haman and the king to a banquet, using her opportunity to ask a favor by asking only for another opportunity to please, and awaiting the strategic moment for her ultimate appeal.

Note also the continuing rise in Haman's anticipations and his wife's complicity with him for a time (but see Esth. 6:13). Anyone reading this narrative for the first time might well begin here to suspect that Haman's vainglorious enjoyment of his status, along with his anticipation of totally gratifying his ire and avarice, would one day be frustrated.

6:1–14 What shall be done unto the man whom the king delighteth to honour?

The next development was ironic, as the sleepless king happened to hear again of Mordecai's unrewarded service and Haman happened to be the one who was asked by the king what might be done for someone deserving honors. With overwhelming frustration Haman learned that it was not himself but his adversary who would be honored—and he, Haman, must conduct the ceremony on the very day he would have sought permission to hang Mordecai. With unexplained insight, Haman's wise men and his wife had foretold that "if Mordecai be of the seed of the Jews," Haman would indeed perish (Esth. 6:13).

To a literary analyst these ironic and fateful developments might seem only to be elements of good storytelling; but to a believer in God, they may appear as evidence of divine intervention, even though it is not declared explicitly in this book.

7:1–18 the king said again unto Esther on the second day . . . What is thy petition, queen Esther? . . . Then Esther the queen answered . . . let my life be given me at my petition, and my people at my request

The countermoving actions collided in a dramatic climax. The king could scarcely contain himself when he realized it was death for all his favorite wife's people that Haman had planned. Recall what had been asked and granted (Esth. 3:4–11). Haman added insult to injury, begging the queen's mercy by prostrating himself on her reclining couch; the already enraged king saw that as a desperate assault. When a chamberlain revealed that Haman had built gallows fifty cubits high for Mordecai, the sentence was instant: Haman must hang thereon.

8:1–17 And Esther spake yet again before the king, . . . to put away the mischief of Haman . . . and his device . . . against the Jews

Though Mordecai had been advanced to the post once held by Haman, it was Esther who again risked approaching the king to save her people; for any edict issued in the king's name could not be revoked and they had to devise a way to give the Jews authority to fight for their lives against those who might still try to implement the first edict on the thirteenth day of Adar. So a second edict was sent out to all. Note a superficial "conversion" effect, as "many of the people of the land became Jews; for the fear of the Jews fell upon them" (Esth. 8:17); however, the word translated with the phrase "became Jews" occurs here only, and since it is not the word usually used to describe religious conversion, it may simply mean that some "judaized" themselves by sympathetic actions.

9:1–19 the Jews had rule over them that hated them

Considerable carnage ensued as the Jews and the people who helped them stood against "the enemies of the Jews." Five hundred were slain in the palace compound, three hundred in the rest of Shushan, and seventy-five thousand throughout the other provinces. The sons of Haman were slain, perhaps to avert their later organizing for vengeance; but the hanging of their bodies the next day (Esth. 9:13) would not have been justified by the Law or the Prophets (Deut. 24:16; Ezek. 18:19–21).

In contrast to the intent of Haman to "take the spoil of them for a prey" (Esth. 3:13), no plunder was taken by the Jews who "stood for their lives" in Shushan and in the provinces (Esth. 9:15–16).

"Sending portions one to another" was, and remains, one of the customs of the Jews in the season of Purim.

9:20–32 And Mordecai wrote . . . that they should keep the fourteenth day of the month Adar, and the fifteenth day . . . , yearly . . . Wherefore they called these days Purim after the name of Pur

The festival of Purim commemorates the day that was appointed by lot *(pur)* for the destruction of Jews in Persia and was reversed to become a day of salvation and joy.

10:1–3 And all the acts of his power . . . and the declaration of the greatness of Mordecai . . . are . . . written in the book of the chronicles of the kings of Media and Persia

The book ends with a brief summary of the relationship of Mordecai to the king and the people, showing forth Mordecai's greatness and benevolence.

The book of Esther is a dramatic paradigm of commitment, courage, redemption, and the overthrow of evil.

JOB

The book of Job deals with the interrelationships of man with man and man with God in problems involving human suffering, human needs, and the Lord's concerns and powers. It demonstrates the inadequacy of the simple thesis that anyone who sins will suffer and anyone who suffers must have sinned.

A prose prologue occupies the two introductory chapters of this masterwork. It shows some prerogatives of God and some of the adversary, Satan, as they affect man. The testing and trying of the man Job reveal some essential facts about the nature and purposes of earth life.

A long poetic dialogue between Job and his friends occupies the main body of the work (Job 3–31). In Job's misery and dismay, and in his desperate search for the reasons for his suffering, he has become a type for mankind. By his integrity, endurance, and perseverance and by his ascendant hope through faith, though he didn't know of any cause or purpose in such suffering, he has become an exemplar for any of us who suffer.

Job's "friends" spoke many truths about the evils of sin, the foolishness of irreverence, and the wisdom of being moral and good; but their diagnoses of Job's predicament were simplistic and their prescriptions nonapplicable. Moreover, those friends failed to show compassion or give comfort; indeed, in their zeal to motivate Job to repent, they increased his suffering by heaping upon him many false charges of wickedness. In the course of three series of charges and replies, Job and his friends explored many facets of God's vast, varied, and intricate creations and learned of his powers, might, and justice.

A kind of addendum (Job 32–37) presents some analyses and prescriptions by Elihu. His evaluations portraying his insight into God's concern for man, and his assurance that a ransom would be provided, capture some truths about salvation, but he did not add much to the main body of the work.

The last four chapters of the book of Job report the Lord's responses to and remonstrance with Job, challenging him with many hard questions and showing him that He indeed cares and is in control but is not always rightly perceived. Job humbly submitted to God's primacy with frank acknowledgments. A prose epilogue represents Job's recompense in double restorations of what he had lost and gives promise of ultimate satisfaction of the demands of justice through God's might and mercy.

Other scriptures also deal with the problem of misery suffered by everyone, including the righteous people of earth, in contrast to the pleasures enjoyed by some of the wicked; some of them are Jeremiah 12; 20; 26; 32; Habakkuk 1; Malachi 3; and D&C 121; 122.

COMMENTARY

1:1–5 There was a man in the land of Uz, whose name was Job; and that man was perfect and upright, and one that feared God, and eschewed evil

The "land of Uz" could have been the home of some of the descendants of Shem (Gen. 10:22–23; 1 Chr. 1:17) as "men of the east" along borders of the eastern Arabian desert (Job 1:3, 13–19). Job's friends came to him from Teman, Shua, and Buz; and the names of such places or people are known (Job 2:11; Ezek. 25:13; Gen. 22:21; 25:2), but these only give superficial clues to the localities involved. The events appear to have been in patriarchal times, for Job offered sacrifices as a patriarchal leader without need for any priests.

The Hebrew word *tam,* rendered here as *perfect,* means "whole," "complete," "having integrity" (TG, "Perfection").

1:6–11 there was a day when the sons of God came . . . before the Lord, and Satan came also among them

The scriptures indeed tell of a time when all the children of God gathered in the Council in Heaven, and Lucifer was there until he became "Satan" (Heb., *ha-satan,* "the adversary"), opposed to God's plans (TG, "Council in Heaven"; BD, "Devil"; "War in Heaven"). Satan is shown here in his role of testing Job, as he may test every earthbound soul. Because the narrative of Job is a particular example of the general predicament of man, any of us may relate Job's experiences to the tests and trials we have in life.

1:12–22 the Lord said unto Satan, Behold, all that he hath is in thy power; only upon himself put not forth thine hand

In the first terrible "test," Job lost his possessions, servants, and children but still was able to accede humbly to God's prerogative to give him all he had and to take it all away.

2:1–10 Again there was a day when . . . Satan came also

We know of no second Council in Heaven, but it may be that the ongoing interaction between God, mankind, and the Devil is here particularized to Job's case, for it is true that any of God's children on earth are tested and tried again and again. Satan can challenge, use, and abuse the God-given agency of man to work for his own gain.

Job's second terrible test, after he had lost all his possessions and family, was loss of health and relationships, including his wife, who bitterly suggested he "curse God, and die" to get relief from his terrible ills. Job's response to his wife can be read as gentle remonstrance that it was not like her to propose something the uninformed or foolish would propose. Thus Satan's second supposition failed. He had assumed that under the value-for-value ("skin for skin") principle, Job would give up his integrity for relief, curse God, and die (Job 2:4–5).

394

2:11–13 Now when Job's three friends heard of all this evil . . . they came . . . to mourn with him and to comfort him

The friends had compassionate intent, but so terrible was Job's condition they could hardly recognize him and could only sit with him silently for a week, as if in mourning for the dead. That was probably the best service they did for him.

3:1–26 After this opened Job his mouth, and cursed his day

The poetic part of the narrative begins with the first outcry of complaint from Job. He still neither blamed nor questioned God but simply wished himself nonexistent—unborn, stillborn, or dead in infancy. Here is poignant poetry, expressing Job's questions and yearnings and ending in quiet lament.

As with any of us, ills came upon him, even though he had not been lax or careless (Job 3:25–26).

4:1–21 Then Eliphaz the Temanite answered and said . . . thou hast instructed many, and . . . strengthened the weak hands . . . and . . . the feeble knees. But now it is come upon thee, and thou faintest

In a somewhat compassionate remonstrance, the first friend tried to suggest that what Job had done for others he should be able to do for himself in his trials. Eliphaz may even have attempted reassurance in his assertion that the righteous are not cut off and that only those who "sow wickedness, reap the same" (Job 4:8).

Perhaps reacting to Job's complaint that there is no purpose in the life of one "whom God hath hedged in," Eliphaz claimed a mysterious revelation that had warned him about a man presuming to be "more just than God . . . more pure than his maker." Neither angels nor mortals could so qualify (Job 3:23; 4:12–21). But where was any evidence that Job was guilty of that presumption?

5:1–27 I have seen the foolish taking root

Eliphaz continued, warning Job in a third-person reference to "the foolish" who suffer losses to themselves and their families. Trouble, he asserted, is as natural to man as it is for sparks to fly upward. Then he made a first-person proposal: "I would seek unto God, and . . . commit my cause" (Job 5:8). Praising God's great powers, mercies, wisdom, and ability to save, correct, and make whole, Eliphaz ended his first attempt to help by assuring Job of what God would do. Note the proverbs in Job 5:17–18.

6:1–30 But Job answered and said, Oh that my grief were throughly weighed

In his first response, Job expressed only dismay at suffering "the arrows of the Almighty" and "the terrors of God." In a series of rhetorical questions, all of which would reasonably be answered no, he almost sarcastically implied that it was not reasonable that his request for a declaration of cause, or for a grant of relief, could continue to be met by divine silence. Even destruction or death seemed more acceptable (Job 6:1–13).

Then he turned his attention to friends and friendship and what they should provide for a suffering peer. His friends had been as "a brook" (Heb., *nachal*), a water course that flows only seasonally, and in summer, when they are most needed, the waters "pass away" (Job 6:15). He pleaded with the friends to deliver him, teach him, or utter "right words" to help him understand wherein he had erred—and not to reprove. He asked that they give him a reply without iniquity, for he felt there was no iniquity in his claims. He had not asked for any other gift, reward, delivery, or redemption (Job 6:19–30).

7:1–21 Is there not an appointed time to man upon earth? Are not his days also like the days of an hireling?

With no more words for his erstwhile friend, Job was again preoccupied with his seemingly endless misery, asking whether he could not hope, as a servant or indentured worker could hope, for an end to his term of debt and receive his release. His days and nights seemed endless in his suffering. It appeared that life had come to an impasse, and he must make his cause heard (Job 7:1–11).

He again addressed God with bitter questions and complaints, almost implying that God had unreasonably visited misery upon him every morning, trying him every moment.

It would be better to translate the Hebrew word rendered "I have sinned" as "*If* I have sinned" (Job 7:20). Job's desperate questions follow, as does his pitiable request for pardon of his unknown transgression before his death.

8:1–22 Then answered Bildad the Shuhite, and said, How long wilt thou speak these things?

Bildad's first attempt to help only increased Job's misery. Rhetorically asking if God be unjust, Bildad implied that Job's children were destroyed because they had sinned and assured him that if he were "pure and upright," he would be well. Bildad even intimated that by returning to uprightness, Job's "latter end" would make his former prosperity seem small (Job 8:1–7).

He recommended observing history and nature for evidence that things work by principles of cause and effect. His picture of the fate of those who forget God or who are hypocrites must have tortured Job, for it was the image of Job in his suffering. Ironically, Bildad's pious declaration that "God will not cast away a perfect man" reminds the reader that the Lord called Job "a perfect and an upright man" (Job 8:20; 1:8).

9:1–35 Then Job answered and said, I know it is so of a truth; but how should man be just with God?

In responding to the second friend, Job affirmed that he knew all the principles Bildad had pronounced and knew man was not comparable to God in justice or in creative powers. What he did not know was the way to get God's favorable response on his own behalf. As for the "perfect," Job concluded that God destroys both the perfect and the wicked. He even thought God would "laugh at the trial of the innocent." He had to assume "the earth is given into the hand of the wicked," and justice was nowhere to be seen. Then he boldly asked, "If not, where, and who is he [God]"? (Job 9:1–24).

By this time, Job's hope had faded until he felt nothing he could do would help. He despaired of trying to communicate directly and knew of no arbiter to help him. Pitifully he wished to be relieved and to speak without fear (Job 9:25–35).

10:1–22 My soul is weary of my life. . . . I will say unto God, Do not condemn me; shew me wherefore thou contendest with me

Job's soul-searching continued as he asked God in several ways why he would oppress a living being of his own creation, because He knows all already and has no need to test their quality (Job 10:3–13).

Job was "full of confusion" about whether he would be found wicked or righteous, wondering why he had been born and why he was still alive; he hoped only for a little respite before sinking permanently into "a land of darkness, . . . and of the shadow of death, without any order, and where the light is as darkness" (Job 10:14–22).

11:1–20 Then answered Zophar the Naamathite, and said, Should not the multitude of words be answered? and should a man full of talk be justified?

The third friend, Zophar, failed to consider Job's suffering or its cause but seized upon what Job was saying in his misery and made Job's very claim of innocence the evidence of his guilt. He charged that Job's soul-searching was vain, asking, "Canst thou by searching find out God?" He implied that since the extremes are "as high as heaven" and "deeper than hell," it is useless to ponder the nature of God at all (Job 11:1–12).

Zophar's prescription for relief was "prepare thine heart, and stretch out thine hands toward him"—a worthy admonition; but that was what Job had been doing. His friend's depiction of Job's possible blessed relief was also good, but his warning of what would befall Job if he remained wicked was merciless (Job 11:13–20).

12:1–25 And Job answered and said, No doubt but ye are the people, and wisdom shall die with you. But I have understanding as well as you; . . . yea who knoweth not such things as these?

Round one ends with Job's response to his third friend. Job could not resist sarcasm about their continuous platitudes and gratuitous charges. He felt he had as much understanding as they, but it availed nothing; he had been an upright man who called upon God and yet suffered misery and scorn. Contrariwise, robbers and "they that provoke God" seemed to be secure (Job 12:6).

Nonetheless, as to the greatness of God's work, the very beasts, fowls, and other creatures do declare it. The marvelous senses of man also show it (Job 12:7–12). God controls all, governs all, influences all, and is superior to all princes, judges, and mighty men. Without him, they wander and grope in the dark (Job 12:13–25).

13:1–28 Surely I would speak to the Almighty, and I desire to reason with God. But ye are forgers of lies, ye are all physicians of no value

Job resumed castigating his erstwhile friends, wishing they had enough wisdom to quit trying. Why should they presume to speak for God and speak falsely? Let him deal with his problem himself and take responsibility for his life.

This was the turning point in Job's test, and it eventuated in his supreme testimony (expressed six chapters later). Key to that process of recovery and reconciliation is his statement of trusting in God even though he suffer death at His hand, for God would also provide salvation. He would be no hypocrite but order his case, and God would justify him. He would not hold his tongue lest he perish.

Note Job's confidence in God and in himself. That kind of integrity and confidence is consistent with the kind of man he was before the test began. A hypocrite does not have that consistency. But Job was still hurting, and he needed two concessions lest he perish: let God ameliorate his sufferings and then disclose his iniquities or other causes of his trouble. He asked what value the alternative had (Job 13:20–28).

14:1–22 Man that is born of a woman is of few days, and full of trouble. . . . But man dieth, . . . and where is he? . . . If a man die, shall he live again?

By means of observations and questions (Job 14:1, 10, 14) Job meditated on life and its brevity, inadequacies, and frustrations. Again he asked for respite. He reasoned that even as a tree that is cut down will sprout again from the root, so there must be hope that death and the grave are not the end of man. That being true, he could hope for relief in death, after which he could rise and respond to God at His call at the appointed time (Job 14:1–15).

Job's testimony grew as he persisted in faith and thought, and therein he also was exemplary. But all of that notwithstanding, he was constrained by his predicament to lament his prevailing mortal condition, for the cause of it was still unknown to him (Job 14:16–22). Watch his progression (Job 16–17; 19; 23).

15:1–35 Then answered Eliphaz . . . Should a wise man utter vain knowledge, and fill his belly with the east wind?

Eliphaz's second speech was the beginning of the second round of dialogues. In contrast to Job's growing firmness, faith, and trust, this "friend" grew more truculent. He sarcastically charged Job with prating about his wisdom, and yet Eliphaz touted the wisdom he and the other friends and elders possessed. He repeated charges (Job 15:14–16; 4:17–19) and gave a litany of the woes of the wicked, implying that Job was of such a "congregation of hypocrites" (Job 15:17–35).

16:1–17:15 Then Job answered and said, I have heard many such things: miserable comforters are ye all

As inconsistent friends, they deserved the ironic epithet: "miserable comforters"! Job shamed them with brief summaries both of what they had done and of what they should have done instead of adding to his trouble.

Though he lapsed for a time into reviewing injustices he had suffered, yet again he forged a spiritual step forward, for when he felt near death and the grave, he was not willing to have earth cover him and his history. He was inspired to know he had a "witness" in heaven and a "record" on high and resolved again that regardless of what friends said, he would appeal to God. In that confidence he appealed to God to make a pledge of surety for future justice, for no others could assure him in their lack of understanding. Job must have felt some assurance from his growing testimony, for he expressed confidence that "upright men" would eventually be astonished at his experiences, and the truly "innocent" would eventually turn against hypocrisy. The righteous, with clean hands, "shall be stronger and stronger" (Job 17:5–9).

Job still had his afflictions and his accusers to endure and felt dismayed because of them, but it is evident in his next response that he did become stronger and stronger until he reached his supreme testimony (Job 19:23–27).

18:1–21 Then answered Bildad . . . and said, How long will it be ere ye make an end of words?

The second friend's second speech sarcastically implied that it was useless for friends to say anymore until Job stopped resisting them with angry words; but Bildad went on anyway, rehearsing again how the wicked must suffer and perish, their strength and confidence fail, and their posterity be cut off. All this he applied to Job as one of the wicked who do not know God. Ironically, Bildad did not know that Job was learning and speaking more truth about God than were Bildad and his friends.

19:1–29 Then Job answered and said, How long will ye vex my soul, and break me in pieces with words?

Bildad had complained about Job's repeated denials of his friends' words (Job 18:2–3), but Job pleaded for respite from their false accusations, which broke him "in pieces" again and again while his errors remained hidden even to himself.

He returned to reviewing his experience, how he had cried out but found no justice, how he had lost property, lost his friends and family, including his estranged wife, and suffered the taunts of children and others so that he could barely exist. He appealed to his friends for pity and respite from their exacerbation of what God had brought upon him.

Then came Job's triumph of faith, and as he felt it, he wished it could be recorded indelibly. He testified: "And I, I know my

Redeemer lives and afterward upon the dust shall He arise; then after even this my skin is destroyed, yet from my flesh shall I see God, whom I, even I, shall see for myself and mine eyes behold, and not another. My inmost feelings conclude it" (Job 19:25–27; translation mine).

The meaning is quite clear. Even though the Hebrew says not "in my flesh" but "from my flesh," it can mean "by means of my flesh." The Book of Mormon expresses the concept thus: "In our bodies we shall see God" (2 Ne. 9:4 and fn. *a–b*).

Job warned his friends to cease persecuting him and look within themselves for the root of the matter. He advised them to anticipate punishment, for "there is a judgment" coming (Job 19:29).

20:1–29 Then answered Zophar . . . , I have heard the check of my reproach, and the spirit of my understanding causeth me to answer

Zophar must have been thinking of what he would say in his second turn and failed either to hear or to understand Job's great testimony of the Redeemer. Perhaps he had heard only the appeal and the warnings spoken by Job (Job 19:2–3, 28–29); if he had heard the testimony, his evaluation of it as a "triumphing of the wicked" was pathetically insensitive. He went on with his litany of heartless words about the horrible end such a person would earn. Recall that the prologue testified of no such deeds by Job, so how did Zophar presume to speak for God in this indictment?

21:1–34 Job answered and said, Hear diligently my speech, . . . be astonished, and lay your hand upon your mouth

Job knew that his friends would not understand the evidence he was about to put before them, but at this point, beginning the third and last round of the dialogues, he was ready to declare the other half of the dilemma: "Wherefore do the wicked live, become old, yea, are mighty in power"? His observations are detailed and specific about the things wicked people enjoy despite their impudence toward God. Job didn't countenance their mode of operation, but he saw no evidence that they suffered for it. He listed a series of situations in which divine justice and punishment do not, in this world, fall upon the wicked; and he asserted there is neither justice nor comfort in the notion that punishment is laid up for their children. He asked whether anyone should presume to teach God knowledge—implying He surely knows all, even though His justice is not evident yet in this world.

He charged that his friends had not really observed life because they had not seen how the wicked have prospered without being condemned, chastised, or deprived of honorable burial and "sweet" rest in death. Thus, since the friends' answers to his problems were based on false premises, their "comfort" had been in vain.

22:1–30 Then Eliphaz . . . answered and said, . . . Is it any pleasure to the Almighty, that thou art righteous?

The translation of the Hebrew here is difficult, but Eliphaz seems to have used his third turn to imply that Job's self-proclaimed righteousness was not acceptable to God and asked sarcastically whether God would refrain from reproving him for fear of him or would negotiate with him on his judgment! Then he launched into another list of evil deeds he assumed Job had done to cause him to suffer "snares" and "darkness."

Eliphaz rightly asserted that God judges from the vantage point of the "height of heaven" and that "the old way which wicked men have trodden," claiming prosperity in spite of their defiance of God, is scorned by righteous men. But he once more appealed to Job to acquaint himself with God and be at peace: to receive God's law, "return to the Almighty," and be blessed.

23:1–17 Then Job answered and said, . . . Oh that I knew where I might find him! that I might come even to his seat!

Did Job find Eliphaz's last effort at comfort inane? He answered him not a word but instead pondered more deeply and with more confidence than before on his relationship with God. In his suffering he wished again that he knew where he might find God and how he might come before His judgment seat; but with confidence that he could present his cause to God and receive His answer, he did not fear that God would use His great power against him: "No; but he would put strength in me." Job would be able to present his case and be delivered. He felt confidence, even though he had gone forward and backward, right and left, and had not contacted God: "But he knoweth the way that I take: when he hath tried me, I shall come forth as gold." Job perceived then that he was undergoing a test.

Job knew in his integrity that he had lived in God's good ways, and though God would take His own time to perform whatever was "appointed" for him, leaving him troubled and afraid, yet his heart was being softened by the things he suffered in "darkness." By this testimony Job also made progress.

24:1–25 Why, seeing times are not hidden from the Almighty, do they that know him not see his days?

Job went on pondering the injustices of this world, wondering why "they that know him" go on in their unrighteous ways. He reviewed a whole catalog of unrighteous deeds commonly done again and again and observed that though the oppressed groan and cry out, God does not respond (Job 24:12*a*). Job's consternation rose as he reviewed more of earth's injustices and inconsistencies, asking at last that if his observations were not true, someone might arise and demonstrate the truth to be otherwise.

25:1– 6 Then answered Bildad . . . and said, . . . How then can man be justified with God?

The second speaker of the third round had no answers. Without understanding the miracle of redemption, he could not know how man can be justified with God. He terminated the dialogue with a brief reiteration of some imponderables about Deity.

Three men with three tries would have symbolized completeness; but the inconclusiveness of their arguments is typified by the early expiration of the series without a third speaker.

The total impossibility of man's ever achieving justification by himself (without a divine Redeemer) is, ironically, truly declared in Bildad's last assessment of man; in Hebrew his hyperbolic metaphor is in two different words, which may be translated *worm* and *maggot*.

26:1–14 But Job answered and said, How hast thou helped him that is without power? how savest thou the arm that hath no strength?

In contrast to the shortened arguments of the friends, Job continued, and in two-times-three added chapters he extolled the might of God, maintained his "integrity," marveled at the wonders of creation, recalled the goodness of life as it was when blessed by God, lamented his continuing condition, and offered admission of any guilt, beseeching God to identify the problem (Job 26–31).

Job began this last series of six dissertations with a practical evaluation of the negative contributions of the three human comforters. He did it tersely, ending with a frank question: How had they helped someone in need? Indeed, whose spirit had actuated them?

Then Job changed the subject, to consider God's marvelous management of other phenomena and functions in the universe. He maintains surveillance over everything—the nebulous (wrongly translated *dead* in Job 26:5), things deep in the seas, in the underworld (*sheol*, "hell," "the spirit world"), in the infinities of space, and on and on from the clouds and rain to the mystic powers of the great deep, symbolized by the forces of chaos (Heb., *rahab*, wrongly translated by the phrase "the proud" in Job 26:12; cf. Isa. 51:9). "The crooked serpent" may be a metaphor for the unorganized materials in primeval chaos out of which the Creators formed the earth and its environs (Job 26:13; Isa. 27:1; Abr. 3:24).

27:1–23 Moreover, Job continued his parable, and said

Parable (Heb., *mashal*) is used here in a sense different from the usual one, but its use is plausible, because one root of *mashal* has a basic meaning of "represent, be like"; thus biblical "proverbs" often contrast two similar yet opposite concepts.

Job continued expressing his concepts of God, declaring that though deprived of "judgment" (that is, justice) for a time by the Almighty who had "vexed" his soul, he had maintained his integrity. Job knew the wicked and the hypocrite could not hope for blessings. Indeed he questioned whether they would ever delight themselves in, or call upon, God. He promised to teach "by the hand of God" certain truths the friends should have observed. He decried all wickedness, deceit, and hypocrisy and described what will result from such evils. He truly expected for the wicked what his friends had falsely expected for him.

28:1–28 Surely there is a vein for the silver, and a place for gold where they fine it. . . . But where shall wisdom be found?

Seemingly in a little respite, Job meditated a while on the treasures of the Lord's creations. Among physical treasures, man can find ores in the earth and water, find crops for making bread, find stones and precious things by digging paths where no other creature has trod, make channels for rivers, and bind the floods; but where is wisdom found? Wisdom may also be found, and "the place of understanding," but not by man unaided; it may not be bought by gold or the other precious things, and its price is above that of rubies. "Whence then cometh wisdom?" "God understandeth the way thereof." After all His creative works, He says to man, "Behold, the fear of the Lord, that is wisdom; and to depart from evil is understanding" (Job 28:13–28).

"Fear of the Lord" is reverence for Him; access to reverence is through humility, work, study, and faith.

29:1–25 Oh that I were as in months past, as in the days when God preserved me; When his candle shined upon my head, and when by his light I walked through darkness

Job then returned to consider his predicament and his future for the final time (Job 29–31). He recalled his former state when the Almighty blessed him and he walked by God's light: with confidence, prosperity, friendship, and respect, he had been able to help the needy, judge wisely, guide the blind and lame, and be as a father and a counselor to all. All were once attentive to his words and grateful for his counsel and comfort.

30:1–31 But now they that are younger than I have me in derision

In contrast to his blessed state as a giver and a guide to the lowly, now the lowest and meanest made him their "song" and their "byword." Since God had apparently broken his ties with Job, the unworthy abandoned restraint in their relationships with him; even God had become "cruel" to him (Job 3:11, 20–21). Job used to weep for those in trouble; but in his own trouble, only evil came to him, and his cries were unanswered, as if they were the cries of wild creatures. The conclusion is a poetic description of his utter desolation.

31:1– 40 Let me be weighed in an even balance, that God may know mine integrity

This is the crux of the matter: God is the supreme judge of man, and man's supreme quality is integrity. Job had made a covenant and felt he had kept it (Job 31:1–6). He was ready to sum up his case, making a frank provisional confession of any evil committed unawares. The list tacitly embraces many biblical morals by proscribing seven typical sins of neglect as well as seven typical unrighteous ways of behaving, each preceded by "if" (Job 31:7–34).

Job had supplicated God's judgment and afterward yearned for His verdict. The Hebrew translated here by the phrase "and that mine adversary had written a book" would relate to the first part of the verse better if it were translated literally: "and a book were written by the man who accused me." Job wished to know not only the verdict but also the charges (Job 31:4–6, 35–37). With two more imprecations against himself "if" he had mistreated even his land or had not been grateful or considerate, he ceased to speak (Job 31:38–40).

32:1–22 Then was kindled the wrath of Elihu

Elihu is not introduced in the prologue nor during Job's inter- action with his three friends. Neither is he mentioned afterward, in the speeches of the Lord (Job 38–41), though the other three are (Job 38–41); nor is he in the epilogue (Job 42:7–17). His iden- tity as a "Buzite" suggests he was related to Job and to Abraham (Job 1:1 and commentary; Gen. 22:20–21). The name *Elihu* means "He is my God."

Many have thought him not properly a part of the original cast and narrative and that his speeches were added by some other author. It will be evident, however, that this section contributes important items doctrinally, as the author no doubt intended, noting some wrongs and deficiencies in the discourses of the others and anticipating some to come.

Despite his youth compared to the previous three friends of Job, Elihu ventured to speak, for his was an even more important source of wisdom, saying: "There is a spirit in man: and the inspiration of the Almighty giveth them understanding." With that qualification he begged their attention to his answers and his opinions; he was eager to speak and would try to do so fairly, without either flattery or respect of persons (Job 32:6–22).

33:1–33 Wherefore, Job, I pray thee, hear my speeches, and hearken to all my words. . . . I am according to thy wish in God's stead: I also am formed out of the clay

It is not presumptuous for a man, if he is properly authorized, to speak for God; and Elihu's authorization is indicated (Job 32:8; 36:1–2). He did confess he would give his own opinion also (Job 32:10, 17).

Elihu began by citing Job's former claim to be clean, innocent, and without transgression, and thus unjustly punished (Job 33:9–11; 10:7; 16:17; 23:10–12; 31). In this charge, Elihu overstated what Job claimed; indeed, it was the Lord who had described Job in such terms (Job 1:8). But Elihu claimed Job was not just in his presumption that he was punished but innocent. Though God had not responded, Elihu suggested that it is His prerogative to give answers and explanations when and how He may choose. Man may not at first perceive His responses, as they may be in a dream or by inspiration. Indeed, it is God who keeps man's soul from perishing even though He may let him suffer as Job had. He will be gracious and deliver him. Elihu gave intimations of divine ransom, restitution, and deliverance from "the pit." Compare Job's own testimony (Job 33:18–30; 19:25–27).

34:1–37 Furthermore Elihu answered and said, . . . Job hath said, I am righteous: and God hath taken away my judgment

It is evident in Elihu's continuing remonstrance that he was not inspired to know the special nature of Job's test at the hands of Satan. Yet he seems to have known that Job was being "tried" (Job 34:36)—perhaps as all mortals are tried. In any case he considered Job too hasty in deciding that God had taken away His justice; the same Hebrew word may mean both "judgment" and "justice."

In poetic words Elihu characterized God's powers, wisdom, and judgments; he felt it was wrong for Job to assume that there is not a reward for good work by a man who delights himself with God. He knew it is God's prerogative to take away the "spirit and . . . breath" of man when it is time for him to perish, for God knows what a man does and brings him to proper judgment.

Finally, Elihu commended Job for bearing chastisement though he felt he had not sinned and complimented him for being willing to be taught; but he warned that God's response might not be according to Job's own expectations (Job 34:31–33). Elihu said what the Lord later said, that "Job hath spoken without knowledge" and multiplied "words against God" (Job 34:35–37; 38:2; 40:2; 42:3).

35:1–16 Thinkest thou this to be right, that thou saidst, My righteousness is more than God's?

The translation of this key question is not certain, but this brief chapter continues to emphasize that Job had multiplied words without knowledge (Job 35:16; 34:35–37; references cited above). Some prophetic insight and advice reinforce what Job himself had resolved (Job 35:14; 13:15).

36:1–33 Elihu also proceeded, and said, Suffer me a little, and I will shew thee that I have yet to speak on God's behalf

A literal translation of the Hebrew is simpler: "I will show thee that there are yet words for God." Elihu promised to ascribe righteousness to God and teach nothing false, for the One perfect in knowledge (that is, God) was with them.

He then proceeded to teach some well-known truths: God is

powerful and wise and despises no one; he is just in discipline and rewards the obedient; Job could have had relief before had he not been so litigious; God teaches us, but we don't know all his powers yet.

37:1–24 At this also my heart trembleth. . . . Hear attentively the noise of his voice, and the sound that goeth out of his mouth

Elihu continued in awe of great manifestations of God in nature, when "God thundereth marvellously with his voice" and brings snow or rain. Indeed, the word rendered here as *noise* means more precisely "rumbling, turbulence." He observed that God certifies to man the power to appreciate the phenomena of nature, which God controls for his all-wise purposes.

Elihu again admonished Job to observe the equilibrium in all things ordered by God, the one "perfect in knowledge." Then he concluded, echoing some facts from nature of which the friends and Job had spoken and anticipating some that the Lord was about to speak in the ensuing chapters.

38:1– 41 Then the Lord answered Job out of the whirlwind

At last the Lord spoke to Job. He did not immediately give him comfort but led him through extensive reviews of what he could know of God that he might not again darken counsel "by words without knowledge" (Job 38:2; commentary on Job 34:35–37). These reviews and teachings conclude with comfort for Job, including confirmation of his correct deeds and words, correction of the "friends," and double restoration for his losses.

There was some reproach in the first words of the Lord, asking Job for unimaginable details about his whereabouts at the time of Creation and his knowledge and understanding of it, alluding even to the Council in Heaven, which no mortal remembers (Job 38:3–7, 7*b*).

The whole review is in superb Hebrew poetry. It refers to God's creation and management of the seas, clouds, light, and darkness; the "springs of the sea" and the "gates of death"; the sources of light and of snow and hail; the functions of light, wind, and weather; germination of seeds; cycles of freezing and thawing; the orders and places of the constellations; the "ordinances of heaven"; and the provisions for all the creatures of the earth (Job 38:8–41).

39:1–30 Knowest thou the time when the wild goats of the rock bring forth? or canst thou mark when the hinds do calve?

Searching questions for Job review the marvelous intricacies of the Lord's creations.

40:1–24 Shall he that contendeth with the Almighty instruct him? he that reproveth God, let him answer it

So at last came Job's long-sought opportunity for dialogue with God (cf. Job 23:3–6). He had known it would be no equal match, and, as he had anticipated, he was overwhelmed. Humbled, he confessed that he had spoken without sufficient knowledge or understanding. Though he had prated about demanding answers, he was not inclined to speak any further.

The Lord continued the lessons as He had begun them and asked Job another searching question: "Wilt thou also disannul my judgment? wilt thou condemn me, that thou mayest be righteous?" (Job 40:8). Such a challenge could have arisen out of Job's many statements about the lack of evidence of justice in the good and evil experienced by both the wicked and the righteous during earth life.

Then the Lord challenged Job to deck himself with majesty, forget his former anger, and deal out justice to "every one that is proud" and "abase him." If he could do it, the Lord would confess that Job could also save himself (Job 40:10–14).

The lessons continued with poetic descriptions of great beasts; *behemoth* means "beasts," but the hippopotamus may be the particular beast that is intended here. All these God had made, as well as man, but they move and function without man's intervention.

41:1–34 Canst thou draw out leviathan with an hook?

God continued to question Job, turning next to an unknown

monster "leviathan" (see Isa. 27:1 for a metaphorical use of this name; it may here refer to a crocodile). The questions reflect man's inability to communicate, negotiate, or play with such a beast. The questions point out man's incapacity to attack this creature or subdue it or even to stand at the sight of it, and part of the lesson is this: if man dare not stand before one of God's great creatures, who can stand before Him? (Job 41:1–10). The point is driven home with further details of all the marvelous body parts and capabilities of the beast.

42:1–17 Job answered the Lord . . . therefore have I uttered that I understood not; things too wonderful for me, which I knew not

Job knew indeed that the Lord could know and do everything. Remembering the Lord's challenge that he hear and answer, Job confessed having spoken of things he neither knew nor understood. He at last knew by his own experience the great difference between hearing *of* the Lord and *seeing* Him; and he repented of all his misapprehensions (Job 42:1–6).

Eliphaz and the other two friends then received a shocking message, whereas Job was commended: "Ye have not spoken of me the thing that is right, as my servant Job hath." Quite appropriately, the friends had to offer up burnt offerings and have Job pray for them. The Lord graciously accepted the repentance of all and released Job from the captivity of his afflictions when he had prayed for his friends—another exemplary lesson.

The book of Job provides what may be taken as an allegorical lesson of hope for all of us, in the afterlife: "the Lord gave Job twice as much as he had before"; family members were reunited, gifts were given, possessions were doubled, and Job's family was extended. The daughters' names are common nouns for three things of beauty—a bird, a plant, and an adornment.

Thus the account of Job and his friends ends with the characters of the drama at last in heavenly peace, though when the story began, some were in idyllic innocence but palpable ignorance. It dynamically characterizes the struggles of mortality as Job represents each mortal soul in this world.

PSALMS

The psalms of Israel were the worship songs of Israel. They were part of the temple worship services, chanted to the accompaniment of strings, pipes, or percussion, and they continue to be so used in synagogues and churches. They are songs of praise and thanks, lament and supplication, instruction and exhortation; and they express yearnings for the righteous rule of the Lord. They were structured for chanting—often in responsive form, with a line for the leader and a parallel line for the congregation. That structure may involve synonymous, antithetic, synthetic, and other forms of parallelism. Many of the psalms are prophetic, which is one reason some eighty-five quotations from thirty-four of them are quoted in the New Testament (BD, "Quotations").

The one hundred fifty psalms are divided into five sections, each of which ends with words of praise and thanksgiving to God. A superscription, at the head of many psalms, identifies their source or collection, their author, and often the accompaniment, such as "To the chief Musician [the collection], on Neginoth [the instrument], A Psalm of David [the author, or literary type]" (Ps. 4). Features of the book of Psalms are outlined in the LDS Bible (BD, "Psalms"), including descriptions of instruments that accompanied the singing of the psalms.

413

COMMENTARY

1:1–6 Blessed is the man that walketh not in the counsel of the ungodly

The book of Psalms starts out praising and commending life in harmony with the ways of the Lord. Indeed, the first line of this psalm is like a title or a thesis statement. Note the parallel progression in the sequence: neither walketh, standeth, nor sitteth with the ungodly, the sinners, or the scornful.

"Meditate day and night" poetically admonishes one to let every thought and act be tempered by principles of right from the law of the Lord (Ps. 1:2*b*). Note the contrast in the similes describing the godly person, compared to the ungodly (Ps. 1:3–6, and fn.).

2:1–12 The kings of the earth set themselves, and the rulers take counsel together, against the Lord, and against his anointed

The adversaries become angry, make plots, and imagine vain things against the Lord; but his word is a "rod," which shall teach some, persuade some, judge all, and condemn some. Those ultimately condemned will indeed be "broken" by his word (Ps. 2:9 and fn.).

The admonition "Kiss the Son" is an odd idiom that does not use customary terms; it can be translated "worship in purity," after which the last clause follows naturally: "Blessed are all they that put their trust in him" (Ps. 2:12).

3:1–8 A psalm of David, when he fled from Absalom his son

The superscription to this psalm in the English translation is the first verse in the Hebrew. The events are told in 2 Samuel 15–18.

The word *selah* is thought to be an instruction for the musicians accompanying the psalm. It occurs in some psalms but not in all. Often it occurs at a transition in the thought. In this psalm it comes after David's distress is told and then after the divine source of his relief is announced.

In two verses David tells of the comfort of God's care: namely, temporal salvation when enemies are smitten and eternal salvation as a blessing upon the Lord's people (Ps. 3:7–8).

4:1–8 Hear me when I call, O God of my righteousness

The superscription prescribes accompaniment upon *neginoth,* or stringed instruments.

David gives thanks for help received, wonders why many mortals go wrong, testifies that the Lord hears him, and admonishes the unbelievers who "love vanity, and seek after leasing." *Leasing* is an archaic English word meaning "to tell lies." They should worship the Lord and put trust in him, for he gives the light of his countenance to the righteous and gives joy, peaceful sleep, and safety.

5:1–12 Give ear to my words, O Lord, consider my meditation

The musical accompaniment is *nehiloth,* possibly a flute.

In this psalm of supplication, after the salutation, the worshipper expresses confidence in his contact with the Lord and summarizes truths about Him for the benefit of fellow worshippers. (On "leasing," Ps. 5:6, see commentary on Ps. 4:2.)

After a statement of confidence and reverence, there is supplication for divine guidance as a safeguard against faithless enemies and another expression of confidence that the Lord hears and gives protection.

6:1–10 O Lord, rebuke me not in thine anger . . . Have mercy upon me, . . . heal me

The musical accompaniment is *sheminith,* strings, or "eighth" string.

Though the nature of the writer's illness is unknown, anyone suffering from spiritual, mental, or physical ills may find this psalm of supplication comforting—especially when critics blame the sufferer for causing the problem and there is need for reconciliation, mercy, and healing.

7:1–17 save me from all them that persecute me

Shiggaion is not an instrument but a variety of poetry. "Cush the Benjamite" was perhaps a servant of Saul.

David's suffering as a refugee, after Saul became a jealous

adversary, could have been the cause of this outcry in prayer. It expresses urgency, trust in the Lord, submissiveness if guilty of offense, indignation against wicked persecutors, and confidence that divine justice will punish the wicked. Anyone who has suffered persecution may identify with the essence of this psalm (cf. D&C 121:1–6).

8:1–9 O Lord our Lord, how excellent is thy name in all the earth!

Gittith was perhaps an instrument or a tune of the grape harvest and winepress, which is the meaning of a similar word in Hebrew.

Messianic psalms usually anticipate the second coming of Jesus Christ on earth, but this one sings praise to the reigning Lord, who is Jehovah, Master and Creator of all.

The Hebrew name of the book of Psalms is *Sepher Tehillim,* "Book of Praises"; and Psalm 8 certainly is full of *tehillah,* "praise," for the Creator of the universe and what he does with "babes" and with mankind. A human, made in the image of God, is certainly "less than the gods" (Ps. 8:5*a*) but is given opportunity to earn "glory and honor."

"Dominion" over others of God's creatures gives God's children opportunities to learn the ways of godliness (Ps. 8:6–8). They violate their dominion if they exploit animals or resources selfishly.

9:1–20 I will praise thee, O Lord, with my whole heart; I will shew forth all thy marvellous works

Muth-labben may mean "death of the son," which perhaps describes a melody.

The first verse is a thesis statement in "synthetic parallelism," in which the second line reinforces and builds upon the first.

In addition to the themes announced in the chapter heading, this psalm of praise expresses gratitude for help against enemies, reassurance in times of trouble, gratitude for salvation, and confidence that the Lord shall prevail over wicked or unbelieving nations.

Higgaion may specify a pause; and *Selah,* a musical interlude (Ps. 9:16).

10:1–18 Why standest thou afar off, O Lord? why hidest thou thy-self in times of trouble?

The question asked by this psalm has been asked by poets, patriarchs, and prophets from Enoch and Job to Abraham, Samuel, Jeremiah, Habakkuk, and Joseph Smith. This world is a laboratory for the children of God to use their agency, learn by experience, develop the power to discern, and create good while combatting evil; but it may seem to some that time goes by without divine intervention. Eventually, the wicked, who think God will not notice their wickedness, will be abashed, but the humble must develop patience and confidence in God.

11:1–7 In the Lord put I my trust: how say ye to my soul, Flee as a bird to your mountain?

The righteous feel confident in taking a stand rather than in fleeing. Even though the moral foundations of society may decay, the Lord is still available "in his holy temple," and his "throne is in heaven." He sees the trials of the righteous and punishes the unjust violence of the wicked. Because he is righteous, he loves righteousness.

The Joseph Smith Translation applies this psalm to the ultimate situation of the wicked world just before the coming of the Lord, when the righteous will have to flee and take refuge until he destroys evil and establishes right (Ps. 11:1*a*).

12:1–8 Help, Lord; for the godly man ceaseth; for the faithful fail from among the children of men

On *sheminith,* see commentary on Psalm 6.

Continuing the theme of Psalm 11, this one portrays situations in which the moral foundations of society have failed, the vile are exalted, and the Lord is the only source of help. The Lord's ways will provide refuge against all evils, for his words are pure.

13:1–6 How long wilt thou forget me, O Lord? for ever?

As David did when Saul was pursuing him (1 Sam. 19–27), the righteous, when oppressed, may wonder how long the oppression will continue, but they will be restored to confidence in the Lord and be grateful to him.

14:1–7 The fool hath said in his heart, There is no God

An emended version of Psalm 14 is in the Joseph Smith Translation (Ps. 14:1*a*). A slightly different version is Psalm 53, in which Deity is called *God* (Heb., *Elohim*) rather than *Lord* (Heb., *Jehovah*) in verses 2, 4, and 6.

This psalm is an outcry about a time of widespread apostasy, when the righteous yearn for salvation and restoration. Joseph Smith's translation of the psalm makes it a time of yearning for the coming of the Lord to bring salvation, destroy wickedness, and reign in righteousness.

15:1–5 Lord, who shall abide in thy tabernacle? who shall dwell in thy holy hill?

This essential question and answer pertain to those who enjoy the Spirit of the Lord in this life and may dwell in his celestial kingdom in the life to come. It provides a short sampling of the qualifying godly virtues.

"He that sweareth to his own hurt, and changeth not," is one who makes covenant promises and keeps them, even if he suffers some costs or disadvantages thereby (Ps. 15:4).

16:1–11 Preserve me, O God: for in thee do I put my trust

Michtam identifies this psalm and also Psalms 56 through 60. They do not seem to have much in common, so it is not certain what the name implies, but the root of *Michtam* is a poetic word for "fine gold"; thus, these may be "golden psalms."

The concern in Psalm 16, as in Psalm 15, is for ultimate salvation and exaltation in the presence of the Lord. The psalmist humbly recognizes that his own goodness is not equal to that of the Lord but hopes it will be like that of the Saints in whom the Lord delights. Idolaters are at the other extreme.

The hope for salvation from the disembodied state parallels the hope expressed in the psalm of Nephi, with the prophecy of resurrection of the Holy One (Ps. 16:10*a, d*). Prophetically, David knew that spirits would not forever be left in *she'ol* ("hell," the world of the unembodied), because the Holy One would counteract "corruption" (disintegration) by resurrection and teach "the path of life" leading to "fulness of joy."

17:1–15 Hear the right, O Lord, attend unto my cry

One may pray with David in this psalm that the judgment of the Lord will find in him no transgression and that one's honest effort to do good will succeed with the help of the saving hand and the loving kindness of the Lord. Thereby one can aspire to protection from evildoers and their fate and hope to awaken from death in the likeness of the Lord.

The "apple of the eye" is the pupil, a most precious part; hence protecting it is a simile for taking great care (Ps. 17:8).

18:1–50 I will love thee, O Lord, my strength. The Lord is my rock, and my fortress, and my deliverer

The superscription tells the historic situation out of which this prayer of thanksgiving and praise arose (2 Sam. 22).

The poetic beauty of Psalm 18 is evident with a little help from the chapter heading and the footnotes; however, one problematic metaphor refers to the presence of the Lord coming like a thunderstorm, riding upon a cherub. The cherubim on the ark of the covenant in the tabernacle and the temple had wings, eyes, and legs meant to symbolize supreme, divine powers (BD, "Cherubim"; D&C 77:4). Thus, by his powers the Lord saves the believer. Many truths are beautifully spoken by David in Psalm 18 (see esp. vv. 24, 28, 30, 35, 46).

19:1–14 The heavens declare the glory of God; and the firmament sheweth his handywork

This poetic masterpiece combines appreciation for the testimony of the universe and its functioning with appreciation for the scriptures. The continuing evidences of the intelligent Creator seen in nature are symbolized, and the ennobling potentials of the laws and statutes of the Lord in the scriptures are summarized (Ps. 19:1–11). But in spite of such impressive testimonies, one may slip into insensitivity and sin; against that danger, David supplicated the Lord (Ps. 19:12–14).

One statement from this psalm is used in Handel's *Messiah* (chorus no. 39, G. Schirmer ed.), to characterize the ultimate spread of the gospel (Ps. 19:4, as quoted in Rom. 10:18).

20:1–9 The Lord hear thee in the day of trouble; the name of the God of Jacob defend thee

This blessing invokes the help of the heavenly King and thanks him for salvation for his people and anointed leaders in warfare, literal or figurative. The last verse is two poetic lines in Hebrew (translation mine):

> O Lord, bring salvation;
> O King, answer us when we call.

21:1–13 The king shall joy in thy strength, O Lord; and in thy salvation how greatly shall he rejoice

As a sequel to Psalm 20, this psalm gives thanks for the Lord's answer to the supplications offered in that one. Some verses relate to King David but some to the future Messiah. The last half appears to anticipate the cleansing of the earth in preparation for the messianic reign.

22:1–31 My God, my God, why hast thou forsaken me?

The *Aijeleth Shahar* of the superscription may have been a melody; it is not an instrument. It means "deer of dawn," or more properly, "doe of dawn," because the first word is feminine.

The opening words of Psalm 22 were quoted by Jesus on the cross, and other verses pertain to his suffering there (Ps. 22:7–8, 13–18). This psalm alludes to some things suffered by King David (Ps. 22:2–6, 19–25), but it is as if in his suffering he had a vision of the suffering of the "Son of David" who would come as the Savior; thus David spoke prophetically for him who would suffer all things. When Jesus quoted the first lines of this psalm, it was as if to announce that he was about to fulfill all of its prophecies (Ps. 22:1*a–c*, 7–8, 13–18). The psalm concludes with a prophecy of the millennial reign of the Lord on earth.

Handel's *Messiah* uses excerpts of Psalm 22 as a tenor recitative and a chorus (see chorus nos. 27 and 28; Ps. 22:7–8).

23:1– 6 The Lord is my shepherd; I shall not want

Psalm 23 is probably the best known of all the psalms, even among peoples beyond the Judaeo-Christian cultures.

The beauty and simplicity of the Hebrew is hard to translate into another language, but the rendition in the King James Version is a beautiful approximation. There are many layers of symbolism: thus, "thy rod and thy staff" is not just synonymous parallelism; the rod was a weapon, an aid in times of conflict; the staff, a walking stick useful in all times and ways of life.

In the last two verses, the poet saw himself as a guest of the divine Shepherd, which status he hoped to retain forever.

24:1–10 The earth is the Lord's, and the fulness thereof; the world, and they that dwell therein

Psalm 24 is another well-known psalm. Verses 1 through 4 are used in a modern musical setting entitled "The King of Glory," by J. A. Parks, and verses 7 through 10 are used in Handel's *Messiah* as the stirring herald chorus (no. 31).

Historically, this psalm is thought to commemorate the establishment of Jerusalem as the capital of Israel by King David after he had conquered the Jebusites (2 Sam. 5:6–10; 6; 1 Chr. 11:4–9; 15). He built there a place for the ark of the covenant before the temple of Solomon was built. The festive entry of the ark therefore represented the coming of the Lord as "the King of glory."

The psalm's prophetic value is better known as the herald of the coming of the Messiah to earth to rule as Lord of lords and King of kings. That is to happen in the rebuilt Jerusalem and in the New Jerusalem in the western hemisphere (Ezek. 40–48; Ether 13:5–6; TG, "Jerusalem, New"; "Zion"). Proper qualifications for the citizens of that kingdom are given (Ps. 24:3–6). Renewal of the old earth is implied and its creation is recalled (Ps. 24:1–2;

Gen. 1:2, 9). The "heads" of the gates will be high to admit the Messiah, the "King of glory," and the redeemed of Israel (Ps. 24:7–10, 7a; TG, "Jesus Christ, Second Coming").

Meanwhile, since the restoration of the gospel and the reorganization of the kingdom of the Lord on earth, all who desire to enter his kingdom may go up to a temple of God for worship and make covenants of eternity there, qualifying to do so by living in the way prescribed and by making the preparatory covenants.

25:1–22 Unto thee, O Lord, do I lift up my soul. O my God, I trust in thee

Psalm 25 is an acrostic: each verse begins with a word whose initial letter is in the Hebrew alphabetical order, which, unfortunately, is lost in translation. That pattern makes this psalm a song of praise and supplication, covering the qualities and blessings the worshipper desires, as it were, from *A* to *Z* (in Hebrew, from *aleph* to *tau*). Several psalms have this alphabetic pattern: 34, 37, 111, 112, 119, and 145.

The twenty-two verses list blessings and petitions any humble person would like. Many virtues lauded here are commended also in other scriptures (Ps. 25 and fn.).

26:1–12 Judge me, O Lord; for I have walked in mine integrity: I have trusted also in the Lord

Psalm 26 is a prayer suitable for any person of integrity who tries to keep the commandments, shuns evil, and loves to go to the house of the Lord with other good people.

27:1–14 The Lord is my light and my salvation; whom shall I fear?

Psalm 27 is reassuring to read, recite, or sing in any of the melodies to which it has been set. Anyone who loves the Lord has felt similar needs and rejoiced in blessings such as these. Light and salvation are the great gifts from the Savior.

28:1–9 Unto thee will I cry, O Lord my rock; be not silent

These are short prayers for help, thanks for help received, and appeals for the salvation of the Lord's people. The Lord is the only sure protection against "workers of iniquity, which speak peace to their neighbours, but mischief is in their hearts."

29:1–11 Give unto the Lord the glory due unto his name

Worship and praise are expressed in this work of art. The power of the Lord is seen in a thunderstorm sweeping in from the Mediterranean Sea, over the coastline and up the highlands of northern Israel and southern Lebanon, where the forests and their animals respond to the tempest of lightning, thunder, wind, and rain. It ends in peace afterward, on land, on sea, and in the people's hearts.

The symbolism is cast in chiastic poetry; compare the content of the first verses with the last, the second with the next to last, and so on to the middle; alone at the apex, the Creator's awesome power is symbolized in the flash of lightning.

30:1–12 I will extol thee, O Lord; for thou hast lifted me up, and hast not made my foes to rejoice over me

As a psalm of thanksgiving for deliverance, Psalm 30 recalls the many occasions in which the Lord had saved David, but its use as a "song at the dedication of the house of David" (superscription) is not corroborated in the books of Samuel or Chronicles.

Many can apply parts of this psalm to their own experience. All of it could be used at times to express relief and gratitude.

31:1–24 In thee, O Lord, do I put my trust; let me never be ashamed: deliver me in thy righteousness

His times of suffering, illness, and persecution seem to be reflected in David's supplication for relief and in his gratitude for the rewards of his trust in the Lord. Some of the situations he suffered and some of his expressions of grief and gratitude are like those of other scripture writers (Ps. 31 and fn.). The words "Into thine hand I commit my spirit" were spoken by the Lord at his death on the cross (Ps. 31:5a).

The closing admonitions and encouragement are of value for the Saints or any other reader.

32:1–11 Blessed is he whose transgression is forgiven, whose sin is covered

The word *Maschil* in the superscription may mean "making wise"; but the contents do not seem to be especially so directed, except that anyone who has repented and has been forgiven is wiser than he was. The Joseph Smith Translation (Ps. 32:1*a*) says "blessed are they whose transgressions are forgiven, and who have no sins to be covered," which may be taken as an exhortation to continual repentance, for who of us is without sin? This psalm is an excellent expression of gratitude for the redemption and atonement provided by our Savior.

David's gratitude for forgiveness of sins and transgressions confessed here cannot pertain to his sins against Bathsheba and Uriah, for they included murder, a sin not subject to forgiveness (1 Jn. 3:15; D&C 42:18; 132:39).

33:1–22 Rejoice in the Lord, O ye righteous

The theme of gratitude and praise to the Lord is resumed with enthusiastic admonishments to sing and play in praise of his name, his words, his righteousness and justice, his creative acts, and his counsel. He is praised as the God of all inhabitants of the earth: "Blessed is the nation whose God is the Lord."

No defense against any enemy is sure except the help of the Lord, and the prayer concludes by seeking that help.

34:1–22 I will bless the Lord at all times: his praise shall continually be in my mouth

Like Psalm 25, this is an alphabetic acrostic song, with twenty-two short sentences praising the Lord, giving thanks to him, and counseling to live his ways. Some verses have become proverbial (Ps. 34:13, 14, 19). Verse 20 was probably intended to complete the thought of verse 19; but by itself it is looked upon as prophetic (v. 20*a*).

35:1–28 Plead my cause, O Lord, with them that strive with me: fight against them that fight against me

Psalm 35 is another psalm of imprecation by David against his enemies, probably reflecting his years seeking refuge from King Saul. He sought the Lord's punishment for those who had laid snares for him (figuratively speaking), spoken as false witnesses against him, returned evil for good, or hypocritically mocked and hated him. Confident that the Lord perceives all injustices, David looked forward to His righteous judgment and justice.

36:1–12 The transgression of the wicked saith within my heart, that there is no fear of God before his eyes

The phrase "saith within my heart" is a Hebrew idiom meaning "it seems to me."

The first verse introduces this psalm. It continues with four verses about wickedness, which it contrasts with the reverence for God felt by the righteous in appreciation of his mercy, righteous judgment, loving kindness, and providence. It ends with a prayer against "workers of iniquity."

37:1– 40 Fret not thyself because of evildoers, neither be thou envious against the workers of iniquity. . . . Trust in the Lord, and do good; so shalt thou dwell in the land

Dealing somewhat with the problem Job dealt with, this psalm admonishes patience under the oppression of seeming injustice and recommends faithful trust combined with good deeds, assuring that justice will ultimately prevail. Compare it with Psalm 73.

Many verses of Psalm 37 are constructed as proverbs with two parallel parts using either synonymous or antithetical clauses. Among them are many gems, for example, verses 5, 7, 8, 10, 11, 39, and 40.

38:1–22 O Lord, rebuke me not in thy wrath: . . . For mine iniquities are gone over mine head: as an heavy burden they are too heavy for me

Anyone who has gone against some principle for a time and

then finally committed something quite unacceptable may find comfort in Psalm 38, which speaks of remorse, repentance, and hope for redemption; read especially verses 4, 5, 13, 17, 21, and 22.

39:1–13 I said, I will take heed to my ways, that I sin not with my tongue

Jeduthun, the "chief Musician," may have been an earlier musician, a father, and the leader of a group of singers in the time of David (Ps. 39, superscription; 1 Chr. 16:41–42; 25:3, 6; 2 Chr. 29:14).

A sequel to Psalm 38, this one repeats some items and adds expressions of regret for delayed confessions and corrections. Anyone who has sinned and repented can identify with the supplications. Phrases from the psalm are set in the soul-searching *German Requiem* op. 45 by Johannes Brahms (Ps. 39:4, 7).

40:1–17 I waited patiently for the Lord; and he inclined unto me. . . . He brought me up also out of an horrible pit

Whatever the personal experiences of David had been to elicit this psalm of thanksgiving for a past rescue from evil and a supplication for future redemption, it is a pattern for similar prayers for most of us. For the "wonderful works" the Lord has done for those who have made Him their trust and for saving errant ones from the "horrible pit," the psalmist is also thankful. We too may feel delight in doing the Lord's will, in testifying of him, and teaching his ways as missionaries. Many would join David in praying for the future and ultimate deliverance. Parts of this psalm, especially the beginning, have also been set to music and sung in modern times.

41:1–13 Blessed is he that considereth the poor: the Lord will deliver him in time of trouble

The opening words of Psalm 41 and some that follow appear to have been spoken by David in almost Job-like agony. Regardless of his confessions and repentance, he had been suffering still because of his sins. His enemies, and even his "own familiar friend" in whom he trusted, had "lifted up his heel" against him. That was prophetic of what the Lord suffered on earth (Ps. 41:9; John 13:18). David knew the Lord would uphold him in integrity, and he deeply desired eternal redemption.

This psalm ends what is considered to be the first division of the book of Psalms; each division ends with a similar expression of praise and solemn amens (Ps. 41:13; 72:19).

42:1–11 As the hart panteth after the water brooks, so panteth my soul after thee, O God

On *maschil,* see commentary on Psalm 32.

The striking simile with which Psalm 42 opens expresses the yearning of a soul to return to the temple and to the presence of God. It begins a collection of worship songs identified with "the sons of Korah." Korah, a Levite descended through Kohath, died in a cataclysm following a rebellion, but his children did not die (Num. 16; 26:11). Their descendants were singers in the temple (2 Chr. 20:19; BD, "Korah"). Ten psalms are similarly identified: 42, 44–49, 85, 87, 88.

The poignant yearning of the author is portrayed, comparing his disquiet and depression in estrangement from the presence of God to the primeval deep (*tehom;* Gen. 1:2); but he acknowledges that the Lord's loving kindness could alleviate his suffering (Ps. 42:5–11).

43:1–5 O send out thy light and thy truth: let them lead me; let them bring me unto thy holy hill, and to thy tabernacles

This little psalm, the only one in this section without any superscription, is considered a continuation of Psalm 42. Ultimate trust in God demonstrates qualities of character in this writer, like unto the qualities of Job.

44:1–26 our fathers have told us, what work thou didst in their days, in times of old. . . . But thou hast cast off, and put us to shame; and goest not forth with our armies

On *maschil,* see commentary on Psalm 32.

The theme statements from verses 1 and 9 of Psalm 44 lament that though the people of Israel knew of the power of God to do marvelous things for his people and they proclaimed him their king, he did not always respond to their needs and cries. So also in the present, people sometimes wonder why they have many afflictions, as in the history of the Latter-day Saints in Missouri and Illinois; but at the right time and in the right way, help is given according to God's wisdom.

45:1–17 I speak of the things . . . touching the king

More than a few questions have arisen regarding this "song of loves": why is it called a *Maschil* (wisdom psalm), what do *shoshannim* (lilies) have to do with its rendition, and why was it written by or for the sons of Korah? On Korah, see commentary on Psalm 42; on *maschil,* commentary on Psalm 32.

A Targum of Psalm 45 interpreted it as prophesying the King Messiah. Christians have followed that meaning, which is sustained by several expressions in verses 2, 6, and 17; problems for that interpretation arise, however, in verses 5, 8, 9, and 12. The "daughter" addressed could be the Lord's chosen people, and "daughter of Tyre" would represent other peoples giving homage (Ps. 45:10–15); but the origins and purposes of this psalm are not entirely clear.

46:1–11 God is our refuge and strength, a very present help in trouble

Alamoth, in the superscription, means literally "maidens," but it is thought also to have designated a high-pitched instrument.

Another of the Korahite songs, this is a well-known and much-loved psalm. It expresses faith in God in poetic and beautiful phrases frequently cited and quoted, especially verses 1, 4, 5, 9, and 10. Compare the river and the city of verse 4 with those of the celestialized Jerusalem (Ps. 56:4–5; Rev. 22:1–3).

47:1–9 shout unto God with the voice of triumph. For the Lord most high . . . is a great King over all the earth

This psalm not only characterizes the Lord's kingship over

creation in general but also prophetically anticipates his reign over the peaceful millennial world. If it seems ethnocentric (esp. Ps. 47:3–4), remember that the "people of the God of Abraham" include faithful converts from all nations—all families of the earth (Ps. 47:3–4, 9; Abr. 2:6–11). All peoples shall be under the government of the righteous, under the King Messiah.

Terrible means "causing awe" (Ps. 47:2).

48:1–14 Beautiful for situation, the joy of the whole earth, is mount Zion . . . the city of the great King

Continuing the messianic anticipations of the previous two Korahite psalms, this one sings of the glory of Zion, city of God's government over the future peaceful earth. The fear and retreat of unconverted peoples may reflect actions alluded to in latter-day prophecy also (Ps. 48:4–7; D&C 45:70).

49:1–20 They that trust in their wealth, . . . None of them can by any means redeem his brother, nor give to God a ransom

The themes expressed in verses 6 and 7 of Psalm 49 are developed by other declarations in the psalm, one of King David's expressions of his eternal hope for redemption from the grave through the power of God (cf. Ps. 16:10).

The contrapuntal theme is that wealth gives sufficient assurance in which to trust forever, for possessions in houses and lands would remain in the family forever (Ps. 49:6–11); but the nature of mortal life is transitory in contrast to the hope expressed by one who believes in the Redeemer (Ps. 49:15, 20).

50:1–23 Our God shall come, and shall not keep silence: . . . He shall call to the heavens from above, and to the earth, that he may judge his people

Psalm 50 is one of a dozen didactic (instructional) psalms attributed to or collected by Asaph and his descendants. Asaph was a Levite in the days of David and Solomon who was appointed to lead the musical parts of the worship services in the tabernacle and the temple; his descendants continued so to serve (BD, "Asaph"). The other songs of Asaph are Psalms 73 through 83.

In essence, Psalm 50 states that the righteous should not think they need do nothing more than offer their sacrifices, and the wicked who have covenanted falsely or given consent to immorality should not think God will overlook their evils. It is a sharp warning to any who tend to forget God but gives comforting promises to those whose worship and ways are right.

51:1–19 Have mercy upon me, O God, . . . blot out my transgressions. Wash me throughly from mine iniquity, and cleanse me from my sin

In this psalm David has asked for more than he could receive. For his adultery alone he could perhaps in time have made amends and received forgiveness, but murder—causing the death of his friend and neighbor Uriah, as related in 2 Samuel 11 and 12—is not forgivable (Ps. 51:14; D&C 42:18; 132:39; TG and BD, "Adultery"; "Murder"). His sins are somewhat overgeneralized and understated, for they were not only against God but also against Bathsheba and Uriah. Furthermore, by his deeds he gave "great occasion to the enemies of the Lord to blaspheme"; and his lament that he was conceived in sin cannot excuse his deeds (2 Sam. 12:14; Ps. 51: 4–5; Moses 6:55).

Nevertheless, all that he said about the mercy and grace of God, extended in forgiveness and redemption, is beautiful and true for any who have sinned, felt in the burning of conscience the urgent need to repent, and accepted cleansing through repentance and receiving forgiveness. Their effective sacrifices are "a broken spirit: a broken and a contrite heart," and the divine Redeemer relieves all except the unpardonable sin (Ps. 51:17*a–b*).

52:1–9 Why boastest thou thyself in mischief, O mighty man? . . . Thy tongue deviseth mischiefs; . . . Thou lovest evil more than good

On *maschil,* see commentary on Psalm 32.

The situation identified in the heading is history (1 Sam. 21–22), and the deeds of Doeg the Edomite were worse even than those reflected in this psalm. Nevertheless, this psalm could help evildoers learn more wisdom and help the innocent refrain from tasting evil.

53:1– 6 The fool hath said in his heart, There is no God

Mahalath, meaning "sickness," may identify a tune for this spiritual lament. On *maschil,* see commentary on Psalm 32.

The use of the name *God* (Heb., *Elohim*) instead of *Lord* (Heb., *JHVH*) may have made this psalm suitable for public worship outside the temple.

In Psalm 53, a situation different from that in its counterpart, Psalm 14, results from God's intervention (Ps. 53:5; cf. Ps. 14:5–6; JST Ps. 14).

54:1– 7 Hear my prayer, O God . . . For strangers are risen up against me

On *neginoth,* see commentary on Psalm 4; on *maschil,* commentary on Psalm 32.

The "strangers" who rose against David were the "Ziphims" of the superscription. They were inhabitants of "the wilderness of Ziph" who tried, for their own advantage, to betray David into the hands of Saul (1 Sam. 23:15, 19–29). An attack on Israel from another quarter diverted Saul from pursuing David in Ziph, and this psalm reflects David's relief.

Ziphim is the Hebrew plural; *Ziphites* would be the English plural.

55:1–23 For it was not an enemy that reproached me; . . . But . . . a man mine equal, my guide, and mine acquaintance

David's dismay at people who had been close to him turning against him foreshadows events of the later years of his reign (Ps. 55:12–14, 20–21; 2 Sam. 15–20). To David's credit, he was then more the poet than the soldier, and he mounted campaigns reluctantly against his son Absalom and against the rebel Sheba. Rather than turning vindictive, as Saul had done, David wrote psalms such as this one and through them and through prayer sought relief. With artful figures he expressed his yearning to get away from strife and insecurity.

Words of this psalm are combined with others (Ps. 55:22; 16:8; 108:4) in lyrics by Julius Schubring. Set to a beautiful melody by Felix Mendelssohn, the hymn is entitled "Cast Thy Burden upon the Lord" (*Hymns* [Salt Lake City: The Church of Jesus Christ of Latter-day Saints, 1985], no. 110).

56:1–13 Be merciful unto me, O God: . . . Mine enemies would daily swallow me up

The accompaniment for Psalm 56 is *Jonath-elem-rechokim,* an instrument or a tune called "Dove of silence of those far away." On *michtam,* see commentary on Psalm 16.

When David fled to Gath to escape Saul's pursuit, he found that his reputation from the days of Goliath made him suspect there (1 Sam. 21:10–15). It seemed that on every hand there was someone to swallow him up, and again he turned to God for salvation and security.

57:1–11 my soul trusteth in thee: yea, in the shadow of thy wings will I make my refuge

Al-taschith means "destroy not" and may identify the tune to accompany this psalm. On *michtam,* see commentary on Psalm 16.

David hid from Saul in a cave just after the incident cited above (Ps. 56; cf. 1 Sam. 21:10–15; 22:1–9). In calamitous circumstances, he turned instinctively to God as a young bird returns to the wings of its mother. David's heart was steadfast in confidence in God, and he praised him for his mercy and power.

58:1–11 Do ye indeed speak righteousness, O congregation? do ye judge uprightly, O ye sons of men?

On the superscription, see commentary on Psalms 16 and 57.

Out of no one situation but a series of injustices he was suffering, David questioned the judgment of congregations and of individuals. He recalled much inequity and used fierce metaphors to ask God to reduce his enemies' power to do him harm, to cause them to melt or creep away. In the Middle East, thorns are burned under cooking pots as fuel, so this metaphor suggests that unjust words and actions, which hurt like thorns, will be removed by the Lord as by a whirlwind before they burn and brew further harm. When God exerts righteous judgment and avenges the righteous, they shall rejoice.

59:1–17 Deliver me from mine enemies, O my God: defend me from them that rise up against me

On the superscription, see commentary on Psalms 16 and 57. For historic background, see 1 Samuel 19:11–18.

Psalm 59 is another outcry for deliverance from enemies, workers of iniquity, and violent men. David hoped that all who caused him suffering for reason other than his own sins would be punished. Their overthrow would be easy for the Lord, and David was sure that divine action would precede any he might take. He anticipated some would die and some would wander, frustrated in their enterprise of evil. In relief, David sang thanks and praise to God.

The poetry of Psalms is typically done with few words in Hebrew; hence these songs are often terse, concise, even cryptic.

60:1–12 O God, thou hast cast us off, thou hast scattered us, thou hast been displeased; O turn thyself to us again

On *michtam*, see commentary on Psalm 16.

The Hebrew *shushan* means "lily" and is used for any lily, including iris. The plural form of *shushan* is *shoshannim*. *Shushan-eduth* means "lily of testimony"; it seems to be intended to teach by a review of many occasions wherein the Lord had helped David. The situation described in the heading is one of conflict (cf. 2 Sam. 8:9–13). The point is plain: without the help of God, the people may be overcome. Times when help has been given are recalled, and prayers are raised for resumption of such help.

61:1–8 From the end of the earth will I cry unto thee, ...: lead me to the rock that is higher than I

On *neginah*, see its plural, *neginoth*, in commentary on Psalm 4.

Rather than a cry in distress, this psalm is a hopeful and worshipful prayer for salvation from a higher source, for a return to the presence of God, and for preservation of self and progeny through his mercy and truth. For these blessings, David would praise the Redeemer forever and keep His covenants.

62:1–12 Truly my soul waiteth upon God: from him cometh my salvation

On the "chief Musician," *Jeduthun,* see commentary on Psalm 39.

With supreme confidence in the salvation of God, David saw those who would diverge from it as "a bowing wall" or "a tottering fence" and as hypocrites. The "rock" is frequently a metaphor for Deity, connoting firmness, strength, immovability, and dependability (Ps. 61:2; 62:2, 6, 7; TG, "Jesus Christ, Rock"). In his Rock, David trusted for help and for salvation.

63:1–11 O God, thou art my God; early will I seek thee: my soul thirsteth for thee, my flesh longeth for thee in a dry and thirsty land, where no water is

David was in the wilderness of Judah, which is a dry and thirsty land, when he was fleeing from Absalom (2 Sam. 15:28–29); indeed he had dwelt in such an environment for many years previously. His desire for the spirit of God was like thirst, and he trusted in him for help and justice.

64:1–10 Hear my voice, O God, in my prayer: preserve my life from fear of the enemy

As David was asking for help, whether against earthly enemies or against spiritual adversaries, so may we also.

65:1–13 O thou that hearest prayer, unto thee shall all flesh come

Psalm 65 is a psalm and a lyrical song.

Zion ("Sion") is God's dwelling, and all who are ultimately redeemed to dwell there will sing his praises. All will come to the true God in prayer. All who come unto him, all whose iniquities have been purged away and who are therefore chosen by him, will dwell in his courts. By awesome ("terrible") things in righteousness, the God of our salvation will restore confidence. He who created all, controls all, and will make earth productive and life abundant for his people.

66:1–20 Come and see the works of God: he is terrible in his doing toward the children of men

Psalm 66 is a lyrical song.

The Hebrew word translated *joyful noise* means "an outcry in joy or need." In King James English, *terrible* was adequate to translate the Hebrew, but its connotations make it inaccurate in our day; *awe-inspiring* is more suitable now (Ps. 66:3, 5).

Because of all the awe-inspiring works of God, all shall worship him and sing to the honor of his name. God's miraculous saving of Israel at the Red Sea is hinted at, and his overruling power is proclaimed; therefore the people are invited to acknowledge him as the sustainer of life. All who have been tested, tried, and proved faithful will be saved. Then all may go to the house of worship and to the temple with their offerings and fulfill their vows.

Psalm 66 concludes with a testimony.

67:1–7 That thy way may be known upon earth, thy saving health among all nations

Psalm 67 is a lyrical song.

On *neginoth,* see commentary on Psalm 4.

The theme of this excellent psalm, stated in the second verse, is missionary work; it is the essence of the original call of Abraham. He and his seed are to minister unto all families of all nations; they are to bring knowledge of the name, blessings, and power of the only true and living God (TG, "Abrahamic Covenant"). Thereby all nations shall be blessed. This psalm is a prayer for God's blessing to help the faithful fulfill that mission. Then all nations may sing for joy, when God shall govern the nations and all shall worship him.

435

68:1–35 Let God arise, let his enemies be scattered: let them also that hate him flee before him. . . . But let the righteous be glad; let them rejoice before God

Psalm 68 is a lyrical song.

The conversion of all peoples is anticipated in this psalm as well (cf. Ps. 67); the enemy of righteousness shall melt away and the Lord shall reign over all (Ps. 68:4; Heb., *JAH,* short form of *Jehovah*). He will bring justice and salvation. Historical manifestations of his works are cited, and the great company of missionaries who publish his word in preparation for his coming are anticipated (Handel, *Messiah,* no. 37).

Metaphors express the prophecy of the Lord's subduing the earth by ascending "on high" via the cross and the Resurrection, whereby he "received gifts for men" in the Atonement so that all may come unto him (Handel, *Messiah,* no. 36). He is "the God of salvation," for unto him belong "the issues from death," meaning all who arise from death. He is the Savior, Eve's "Seed," who did "bruise" or "wound" the head of the adversary (Gen. 3:15; Ps. 68:19–20, 21*a*).

In less lovely terms are described the final wars in which right, personified as Israel, conquers all, and even such as Egypt and Ethiopia worship the Lord (Ps. 68:31*a*). All kingdoms of the earth shall sing praises unto the Lord when his people shall have fulfilled their mission to bring blessings to all peoples in all nations.

69:1–36 I sink in deep mire, where there is no standing: I am come into deep waters, where the floods overflow me

On *Shoshannim,* see commentary on Psalm 45.

David's cry for help continues, but then in his own trouble, he seems to have envisioned the Savior's rejection by his people, his cleansing the temple, and his sufferings through the Crucifixion (Ps. 69:7–21 and fn.). David called down justice upon his adversaries; a phrase he used was later applied to Judas Iscariot (Ps. 69:25 combined with Ps. 109:8 in Acts 1:20). David humbly prayed for salvation "on high" along with the humble and poor, and he looked to the time when Zion shall be redeemed and the cities of Judah be built, so that the seed of the Lord's servants may inherit it and "they that love his name shall dwell therein" (Ps. 69:29–36 and fn.).

70:1–5 Make haste, O God, to deliver me; . . . and let such as love thy salvation say continually, Let God be magnified

Continuing the supplications of Psalm 69, this psalm, whose purpose is "to bring to remembrance," also looks forward urgently to the Lord's salvation and deliverance.

71:1–24 In thee, O Lord, do I put my trust: let me never be put to confusion. . . . Cast me not off in the time of old age

Reminiscent of his prayers for forgiveness (Ps. 32; 51), this song from David's old age eloquently tells of his yearning to retain the comfort of the presence of the Lord and repeats his hope for redemption (Ps. 71:9, 18). Again, he may have hoped for more than he could be given, in view of what he had done to his friend Uriah and his wife Bathsheba (Ps. 71:21; 51:14; D&C 42:18; 132:39).

72:1–20 Give the king thy judgments, O God, and thy righteousness unto the king's son

The "king" and the "king's son" was Solomon, son of David, as the superscription says; but prophetic elements in this prayer apply really to the ultimate "Son of David," the Messiah. It is evident in retrospect that Solomon's reign did not achieve the ideal conditions and the glory described here (Ps. 72:4, 7–8, 12, 14). They will be achieved only by the divine Messiah.

Psalm 72 ends with a doxology typical of the ending of each of the five sections of the book of Psalms. An added verse announces the end of "the prayers of David," but that seems to pertain only to the prayers in this section, for another prayer is labeled with his name (Ps. 86) and several more are labeled "A psalm of David."

73:1–28 Truly God is good to Israel, even to such as are of a clean heart. But as for me, my feet were almost gone; my steps had well nigh slipped

On the superscription, see Psalm 50.

The theme of Psalm 73 is a familiar one in the book of Psalms and in the book of Job. More than half its verses describe common evidences that the wicked are not immediately punished by God for wickedness, and some do prosper in this world. Some even question whether God knows what is going on (Ps. 73:3–16). Only in the sanctuary (the temple) could the psalmist gain assurance about the end of the wicked and understand the final justice of God; then he felt humbled and ashamed of his premature judgment. As a result he expressed a strong resolution to trust in God, who like a father holds one by the hand, gives guidance and counsel, and afterward rewards one in glory. The psalm ends with a trusting and comfortable commitment to "the Lord God" (Heb., *Adonai JHVH*).

74:1–23 O God, why hast thou cast us off for ever? why doth thine anger smoke against the sheep of thy pasture?

On the superscription, see Psalm 50.

A national cataclysm, such as the overthrow and captivity of Judah by Babylon, is portrayed in this lament (Ps. 74:3–4, 6–8, 10). After the death of Jeremiah and Ezekiel, the people in captivity, as well as any left back home, were without a prophet (Ps. 74:9–11; cf. Lam. 2:3, 9), although Daniel was in the court of the kings of Babylon and Persia and did pray for the return of Judah when the time for it came (Jer. 25:12; Dan. 9:2). But despite impatience for relief, the author could still express great faith in God's powers, trusting that He cared for His people and their covenant mission; he knew God would not let them pray in vain nor let the enemy triumph.

75:1–10 Unto thee, O God, do we give thanks, . . . for that thy name is near thy wondrous works declare

Psalm 75 is a psalm and a lyrical song. On *Al-taschith,* see commentary on Psalm 57; on *Asaph,* commentary on Psalm 50.

After the opening declaration of thanks to God, the author quotes words of God regarding His coming judgment and His universal control. The psalm cites confidence in the power of God and contrasts it with the foolishness of the wicked, who lift up their "horn" (prate about their own power). The "cup" in the hand of God symbolizes His rewards and punishments. The psalm concludes with praise for the Lord and assurance that the wicked shall perish and the righteous win.

76:1–12 In Judah is God known: his name is great in Israel. In Salem also is his tabernacle, and his dwelling place in Zion

On *neginoth,* see commentary on Psalm 4; on *Asaph,* commentary on Psalm 50.

This psalm of praise and thanks alludes to times when the enemy was repulsed and the righteous saved. It speaks of the early Salem of Melchizedek and relates it to the ultimate Zion. When the Lord shall arise to save the meek of the earth at the end of times, the wrath of man shall turn to praise or be restrained. Then all will covenant with God and worship him whose power is awesome; he will vanquish princes and kings.

77:1–20 I cried unto God with my voice, . . . and he gave ear unto me. In the day of my trouble I sought the Lord

On *Jeduthun,* see commentary on Psalm 39; on *Asaph,* commentary on Psalm 50.

In the first half of Psalm 77, the psalmist expresses despair and dismay in a time of trouble, when help seems not to be coming, and then makes a humble confession of inner infirmity. In the second half, he speaks of the works of old, the wonders God has always done in bringing relief, and sings praises to Him.

78:1–72 Give ear, O my people, to my law . . . Which we have heard and known, and our fathers have told us

On *Maschil,* see commentary on Psalm 32; on *Asaph,* commentary on Psalm 50.

A review of Israel's history forms the body of this didactic psalm, touching vital events from the "testimony in Jacob" to the appointment of David, but most of the details pertain to the Lord's hand in events in Egypt and the wilderness. It condemns Israel's failure to appreciate his help and be loyal to him.

The Lord gave to his people his law (Heb., *Torah*, "guidance," "instruction") and certified it by his testimony (Heb., *'eduth*, "witness"). The law and the testimony were to be perpetuated from generation to generation so that Israel might excel over earlier, rebellious generations. Yet there was infidelity in "Ephraim," the birthright tribe, and among others who neither kept the covenant nor obeyed the law. Ungrateful for all the miracles of deliverance by the plagues in Egypt and the sustenance in the wilderness the Lord had provided, they were punished as in the years of wandering.

The Lord led them to the border of the "sanctuary," the promised land, and helped them enter the land by going up with them against the enemy; and they divided it for their inheritance. Yet they "tried" and provoked the Lord and kept not his law nor remembered his testimony; therefore, he forsook the sanctuary established at Shilo and abandoned the leadership of Ephraim there. Because of the apostasy and decay of the tribes of northern Israel, he let them be taken into captivity. He retained Judah, the house of David, and established headquarters in "mount Zion," where he maintained and prospered the people of Judah for a time.

The purpose of the psalm, at the time it was written, may have been to teach and warn the people of Judah in later years to be true to the covenant and the law, so that they might return from Babylon and be saved for their destiny.

79:1–13 O God, the heathen are come into thine inheritance; thy holy temple have they defiled; they have laid Jerusalem on heaps

On *Asaph,* see commentary on Psalm 50.

Psalm 79 does not continue the history of Judah from where Psalm 78 left off; but like Psalm 74, it laments the Babylonian invasion and the destruction of the country of Judah, the city of Jerusalem, and the temple. The people in their misery prayed for forgiveness and mercy and asked that the horrors of destruction, death, scorn, unburied bodies, and captivity imposed by "the heathen" be avenged.

80:1–19 O Shepherd of Israel, . . . Before Ephraim and Benjamin and Manasseh stir up thy strength, and come and save us

On *Shoshannim-Eduth,* see the commentary on Psalm 60; on *Asaph,* the commentary on Psalm 50.

Psalm 80 seems to have been a prayer in the temple at the ark of the covenant on behalf of some of the tribes of Israel when the Assyrian invasion was threatening in the decade before 721 B.C. Poetic references to God's transplanting Israel from Egypt and cultivating her in the promised land are followed by supplications of help for the people once chosen. The two images of God, as Shepherd of Israel and as keeper of the vineyard, characterize the intimate relationship of the people with God in better times in Israel.

81:1–16 Sing aloud unto God our strength: . . . Blow up the trumpet in the new moon, in the time appointed

On *Gittith,* see commentary on Psalm 8; on *Asaph,* commentary on Psalm 50.

Psalm 81 urges the people to resume proper worship, remembering the Israelites who went into Egypt in the time of Joseph and later came out by the hand of the Lord. The poet spoke for the Lord, reviewing his help in the Exodus, his law given them, their failure to respond, and his abandonment of them to wickedness and exile. The psalm ends with a review of what the Lord could have done with Israel, thus implying what he could do in their release from exile. Traditionally, this psalm has been used in celebration of the Feast of Tabernacles because of its references to the exile and the return, which that feast celebrates.

82:1–8 God standeth in the congregation of the mighty; . . . How long will ye judge unjustly, and accept the . . . wicked

On *Asaph,* see commentary on Psalm 50.

Essential theology is found in this little psalm. Its purpose is to show that God is the ideal judge and that human judges, because they are of divine parentage, should follow his example. If they do not, they perish as do earthly princes. The poet appealed to men to improve and appealed to God to execute justice and rule the nations.

Recall Jesus' use of Psalm 82:6 against his assailants who accused him of blasphemy in claiming to be the "Son of God" (John 10:32–37; cf. Gen. 1:26–27; Luke 3:38). His citation of the fatherhood of God and sonship of man as "written in your law" implies that all the inspired books are part of the *Torah.*

83:1–18 Keep not thou silence, O God: . . . For, lo, thine enemies make a tumult

Psalm 83 is a lyrical song. On *Asaph,* see Psalm 50.

This last of the psalms of Asaph is another cry for God to defend himself and his reputation by defending his people. All of the neighboring and related peoples are listed—descendants of Esau, Ishmael, Lot, Hagar, and others of the inveterate enemies of Israel. A review of previously vanquished enemies follows, with the fate they suffered because they sought to possess Israel, the "habitations of God" (Ps. 83:12; *houses* is a mistaken translation). Various catastrophes were invoked upon them.

The one positive result was that other peoples might seek the Lord and know that he whose name is Jehovah is over all the earth. This name is rarely transliterated in full, but it is done here to make the meaning precise. Usually the word *Lord* is substituted (commentary on Gen. 2:4).

84:1–12 How amiable are thy tabernacles, O Lord of hosts!

On *Gittith,* see commentary Psalm 8; on the sons of Korah, commentary on Psalm 42.

Rendered as "How lovely is thy dwelling place, O Lord of hosts," stanzas 1, 2, and 4 of this psalm are adapted to the beautiful *German Requiem* by Brahms (op. 45). This refreshing and inspiring Korahite psalm expresses the comfort of being spiritually in harmony with the Lord and physically in his temple. It is indeed better to be a doorkeeper in the house of God than to dwell in the homes of the wicked.

85:1–13 Lord, thou hast been favourable unto thy land: . . . Turn us, O God of our salvation

This psalm of the sons of Korah speaks of the early return of Judah from the Babylonian captivity, for which the people were grateful; but they needed God's further favor to strengthen them for the arduous tasks of reconstruction. It expresses confidence in God's favor and help and poetically describes the cooperation between earth and heaven.

In the latter-day restoration of the gospel, literal fulfillment of prophecy was seen in the retrieval of inspired scriptures from their vault in the earth and companion revelations being sent from heaven to establish God's kingdom on earth again (Ps. 85:11*a–b*).

86:1–17 Bow down thine ear, O Lord, hear me: for I am poor and needy

On this additional prayer of David, see commentary on Psalm 72.

Psalm 86 expresses dismay at sins within and enemies without. The word *holy* does not quite convey the concept of the Hebrew word *chasid,* which connotes "loving kindness." The whole psalm is an expression of deep love and comfort in the presence of God. The request to be taught right ways, with a resolution to walk therein, is exemplary; they need only to be followed by equivalent actions. But David still needed help against proud and violent enemies, from whom only God could save his soul.

87:1–7 The Lord loveth the gates of Zion. . . . Glorious things are spoken of thee, O city of God

Psalm 87 is a poetic prophecy of the messianic age, when the Lord shall reign in Zion, the city of God, over those born there and those who know him, though they were born in the lands of former enemies—Rahab (Egypt), Babylon, Philistia, Tyre, and Ethiopia.

88:1–18 O Lord God of my salvation, . . . Let my prayer come before thee

Psalm 88 is a lyrical song. On the sons of Korah, see commentary on Psalm 42; on *Mahalath Leannoth,* "sickness to oppress," commentary on Psalm 53; on *Maschil,* commentary on Psalm 32. Heman may be associated with Ethan the Ezrahite referred to in 1 Kings 4:31.

This psalm is more like the bitter laments of Job; even the suggested accompaniment was doleful. Part of the author's depression seems to have come from his feeling that the Lord brought him to his misery and that his prayers had not been answered; moreover, his friends, acquaintances, and loved ones had been put far from him. In spite of all, however, he did attribute "lovingkindness" and the power of salvation unto the Lord.

89:1–52 I will sing of the mercies of the Lord for ever: with my mouth will I make known thy faithfulness to all generations

Ethan the Ezrahite began at the opposite end of the spectrum of mood and spirit from Heman the Ezrahite of Psalm 88, but they each wrote a *Maschil,* a psalm to engender wisdom. After the opening verses of praise for the Lord's mercies (Heb., lit., "the loving kindness of Jehovah"), the author quoted promises made to David's seed to be established forever (Ps. 89:1–4*a*). Because the Messiah was to be of that lineage, the continuing words of praise are appropriate to his creative and controlling powers.

Ethan spoke of blessings to the people who shall hear the joyful sound heralding the Lord and walk in the light of His countenance. The psalmist recounted more of the promises made to David and his seed; and though it is evident that some were fulfilled by David and his people when they were worthy, the truly glorious promises remain to be fulfilled by the Messiah.

David himself sinned and so did his descendants; for their sins, all Judah and their king had been "cast off and abhorred" by the Babylonian conquest; land, people, and king had been covered with shame. Hence, the psalmist asked "How long, Lord? wilt thou hide thyself for ever?" He prayed urgently for the time to be short until there would be an outpouring of loving kindness and an end to the time of reproach.

The doxology and amen close both this psalm and the third part of the book of Psalms.

90:1–17 Lord, thou hast been our dwelling place in all generations. . . . from everlasting to everlasting, thou art God

The superscription attributes this psalm to Moses. Some of the concepts and phrasing are comparable to poetic chapters of Deuteronomy, such as the song of Moses and his final blessings (Deut. 32, 33). A hymn by Isaac Watts, "O God, Our Help in Ages Past" (*Hymns,* 1985, no. 31), was inspired by it.

Psalm 90 speaks of the Creation and of man's brief mortal life. Man's years are as a moment to God; his iniquities may cause his sudden removal by God's justice, or His anger. The psalm asks that humankind may seek for wisdom and that God may have mercy upon us to bring us to joy after affliction. It asks that we may come to know God's work and glory, that his beauty will be upon us, and that the work of our hands will be blessed (Ps. 90:12–17, 16*a*).

91:1–16 I will say of the Lord, He is my refuge and my fortress: my God; in him will I trust

This song of trust in the Lord is a sequel to Psalm 90. It begins with assurances to those who stay close to the Lord and resolve to trust in him for protection. Then the Lord's protection is exemplified in easily understood symbols and images. Satan used one of these promises of protection in tempting Jesus (Ps. 91:11–12; Luke 4:10).

The Savior's promises to all who set their love upon him include the blessings of deliverance and salvation (Ps. 91:14–16).

92:1–13 It is a good thing to give thanks unto the Lord, and to sing praises unto thy name, O most High

The first third of this Sabbath worship psalm and song expresses praise and appreciation for the help and good given by the Lord to the righteous. The second part contrasts with it the way the "brutish" and the wicked respond to the Lord and the way he affects their lives. The third segment tells of ways the Lord helps the righteous overcome their enemies and increases their power so that they may flourish and grow in the courts of the Lord and bear fruit even in old age—all of which demonstrate the firmness and uprightness of the Lord.

Figuratively, "horn" symbolizes power; righteous strength can be increased by commitment through an anointing, as implied in verse 10; this concept pertains to latter-day anointings also.

93:1–5 The Lord reigneth, he is clothed with majesty

Ascending parallelism is used to build to two climaxes: the first portrays the Lord's creative power and the second shows the Creator mightier than the mightiest things he created. The conclusion affirms that all witnesses to those truths are very sure and that holiness characterizes his "house."

94:1–23 Lift up thyself, thou judge of the earth: render a reward to the proud

Psalm 94 begins with the observation that until the Lord reigns everywhere, wickedness and injustice do at times triumph; this psalm is another cry for divine justice. Some think that the Lord does not see or heed; but the Creator who made eyes and ears knows, and his chastening and instruction in the law are therapeutic. The psalm concludes with gratitude and praise for divine help, mercy, inspiration, protection, and eventual elimination of evil.

95:1–11 O come, let us sing unto the Lord: let us make a joyful noise to the rock of our salvation

Here begins a series of six psalms with the same purpose as Psalm 93—to assemble worshippers and sing praises to the Lord.

"Let us make a joyful noise" means simply "shout joyously" to recognize the greatness of the true God and his power over everything. People ought not harden their hearts against his truths, nor seek to test or prove him as did the generation that provoked him and consequently had to wander forty years in the wilderness.

96:1–13 O sing unto the Lord a new song . . . all the earth

Only the Lord deserves praise; all the gods of other nations are only idols. Therefore all kindreds ought to worship the Lord "in the beauty of holiness"—a lovely phrase and concept. The time will come when the world shall know that the Lord reigns; then heaven and earth will rejoice—even the seas, the fields, and the woods. The Lord will come to judge with righteousness and truth.

97:1–12 The Lord reigneth; let the earth rejoice

All of the phenomena of nature proclaim the Lord's power and goodness; hence, they who worship idols must surely be confounded, and the idols be cast down before him. The earth is cleansed by fire before his coming. Worshippers of God can be glad, love him, hate evil, be enlightened and preserved, and give thanks.

98:1–9 O sing unto the Lord a new song; for he hath done marvellous things

Continuing the series begun with Psalm 95, which sings about the Creator and the Shepherd, this psalm sings of the Lord's victory in providing salvation "in the sight of the heathen"—salvation to be seen in "all the ends of the earth." All creation is invited to join in acclaim of his salvation and his righteous judgment.

99:1–9 The Lord reigneth; let the people tremble

In proclaiming the Lord's reign, Psalm 93 speaks of his majesty; Psalm 97 invites all earth to rejoice; and Psalm 99 invites reverence for his awe-inspiring ("terrible") name.

The judgment which the divine King loves establishes justice, equity, and righteousness.

Historic exemplars—Moses, Aaron, and Samuel—are mentioned among others with whom the Lord communicated and whom he blessed or punished as needed. Hence, all are admonished to worship him at his temple (Heb., lit., "his holy hill"), for he is "holy" (Heb., *qadash*, "set apart, consecrated").

100:1–5 Make a joyful noise unto the Lord all ye lands. Serve the Lord with gladness: come before his presence with singing

Psalm 100 is another "psalm of praise," with an invitation to all the earth to "shout unto the Lord," serve him happily, and worship him with exultant singing. The rest of this well-known psalm reminds all to be thankful that he made us and provides for us; he is merciful and good to us; and his truths are eternal.

101:1–8 I will sing of mercy and judgment: . . . I will behave myself wisely in a perfect way. O when wilt thou come unto me?

Psalm 101 is another "Psalm of David." Like so many other Davidic psalms, it contains a host of righteous resolutions by a ruler who hopes to be worthy of the Lord's help in ridding his house and the land of evil.

102:1–28 Hear my prayer, O Lord, . . . For my days are consumed like smoke

This psalm is a Job-like supplication in the first half, speaking not only of a time of personal suffering but also a time of national suffering in exile when Israel longed to return to Zion. It is a prayer that the people shall be gathered together and shall serve the Lord in his glory. Then the seed of the Lord's servants shall be established in his presence.

103:1–22 Bless the Lord, O my soul: and all that is within me, bless his holy name

Psalm 103 is yet another "Psalm of David."

Bless is used to translate the Hebrew *barak*, which means "to kneel" to extend adoration, good will, or benefits. Usually it is God who blesses mankind; but the concept that man can also bless God appears occasionally. This psalm and the next start with the same exhortation to adore and show appreciation to God.

Psalm 103 lists many aspects of the Lord's benevolence toward humanity, not only throughout the brief mortal life but throughout eternity. To those who "keep his covenant" and "remember his commandments to do them," mercy and righteous justice are extended forever. The psalm concludes with an exhortation to all the Lord's angels, all his hosts and ministers, and all his works in all parts of his dominion to "bless the Lord."

104: 1–35 Bless the Lord, O my soul. O Lord my God, thou art very great

For the meaning of the admonition to "bless" the Lord, see commentary on Psalm 103.

Psalm 104 expresses adoration of the Lord for beauty, goodness, and functional practicality shown in all nature. It is one of the best such expressions in all scripture. It would be good for reading in "the woods and forest glades," or "from lofty mountain grandeur," as the hymn "How Great Thou Art" asserts (*Hymns,* 1985, no. 86). This psalm speaks of God's functions in creation, providing water, causing food to grow, establishing the changing seasons, providing day and night; indeed, it acclaims his making and controlling all things of earth and sea. For all these, any singer of this psalm can praise the Lord, meditate in sweet thought, avoid sinfulness, bless the Lord, and thank him.

105: 1– 45 O give thanks unto the Lord; call upon his name: . . . sing psalms unto him: talk ye of all his wondrous works

Psalm 105 is the first of three longer psalms that review major incidents from the history of the seed of Abraham through Israel as reasons for giving thanks to the Lord. This one advocates not only giving thanks and praise to the Lord but also glorying in his holy name and seeking for his strength. And of course, recognition of the Lord's goodness redounds to one's own good.

The blessings are listed mainly in chronological order, with some variations, and are plain enough to be easily recognized, beginning with the covenant of the Lord with Abraham, Isaac, and Jacob.

Some historical transitions are abrupt as the mode and the

purposes of bringing Joseph into Egypt are reviewed. Israel's entry into Egypt and the developments there are briefly covered. Then the mission of Moses in the negotiations with Pharaoh, the plagues, the Exodus, and the beginnings of the wilderness wandering are presented. Note the emphasis on the benevolence of the Lord, with a little about the weaknesses of the people.

106:1– 48 Praise ye the Lord. O give thanks unto the Lord; for he is good: . . . Who can utter the mighty acts of the Lord?

Although this psalm continues from Psalm 105 with more history, the intent of Psalm 106 is to remind the Israelites of past sins they had committed despite the Lord's blessings and to urge them to repentance, good behavior, and fidelity, with assurances of the Lord's future help. Comments on divine help in Egypt to free the Israelites and help them cross the Red Sea are followed with reminders of their ungrateful rebellions and infidelity. Also, in moving to the promised land, the Israelites often failed to obey. The psalm reviews the many times they failed, suffered oppression, repented, and received deliverance. Finally, the end of the psalm asks for another deliverance from bondage "among the heathen." That is followed by a doxology that concludes this psalm and the fourth section of the book of Psalms.

107:1– 43 O give thanks unto the Lord, for he is good: for his mercy endureth for ever. Let the redeemed of the Lord say so

Whatever the basis was for dividing the book of Psalms into five sections, it was obviously not subject matter or type of literature; indeed, the division seems somewhat arbitrary, for this first psalm in the fifth section continues the review of Israelite history begun in Psalm 105. Psalm 107 covers the gathering of the Israelites in Egypt from all directions and details their wandering in the wilderness after their deliverance from Egypt.

From time to time the psalmist exclaimed, "Oh that men would praise the Lord for his goodness" (Ps. 107:8, 15, 21, 31). After each outcry, he presented another aspect of God's goodness and contrasted it with man's failure to show appreciation by behaving with consistent goodness. Typically, "fools" among mortals do badly and could do better. "They that go down to the sea in ships" feel awe and a need for the Lord; hence, they respond better to him. Another wish that humankind would praise the Lord and obey him is amplified by allusions to his helping Israel in the wilderness and establishing them in the promised land. A final generalization contrasts "princes" with "the poor."

108:1–13 O God, my heart is fixed; I will sing and give praise, even with my glory

This little song of praise and supplication repeats parts of previous psalms (Ps. 108:1*a*, 6*b*). No doubt it is attributed to David because the earlier psalms were. Its essence is that the worshipper's "heart is fixed" (steadfast) in its resolve to praise and thank God that His beloved people will receive help in trouble and finally "do valiantly."

109:1–31 Hold not thy peace, O God of my praise; For the mouth of the wicked and the mouth of the deceitful are opened against me: they have spoken against me with a lying tongue

Reminiscent also of previous psalms of David (Ps. 25; 69), Psalm 109 is a prayer for help against adversaries who are difficult to combat, especially those who repay "evil for good" (Ps. 109:3–4*a*). Verse 8 of this psalm is combined with verse 25 of Psalm 69 to describe in Acts 1:20 the punishment of Judas Iscariot. Requests for punishment may not seem to be suitable matters for ritual; vengeance is truly best left to the Lord. The admonition "Let them [the wicked] curse, but bless thou" sums up the message of this psalm.

110:1–7 The Lord said unto my Lord, Sit thou at my right hand, until I make thine enemies thy footstool

King David prophesied of the Messiah in this psalm, calling him a priest "after the order of Melchizedek" (Ps. 110:1*a–e*, 4*b–d*; Heb. 5:6; 7:17, 21). Because the Lord (Jehovah) spoke this promise to King David, He was obviously speaking of His own role on earth and His own ultimate victories over all enemies.

David understood that the priesthood of Melchizedek is different from that of Aaron; and we understand from modern revelation that the true name of the Melchizedek Priesthood is "the Holy Priesthood, after the Order of the Son of God" (D&C 107:1–4). *Melchizedek* means "King of Righteousness"; thus the name is doubly appropriate.

Psalm 110 is difficult to interpret because of the names and because of the description of future bloody victories in the destruction of kings, resulting in many "dead bodies," but the psalm may speak symbolically of the demise of the kingdoms of this world and the perishing of all the wicked.

111:1–10 Praise ye the Lord. . . . The works of the Lord are great

Psalm 111 is the first of the Hallelujah Psalms, which comprise Psalms 111 through 113 in one set and Psalms 146 through 150 in another. Each begins with the Hebrew word *hallelujah,* meaning "praise ye Jehovah."

Three varieties of the Lord's "works" described in Psalm 111 are more specific in Hebrew: his "deeds," his "work," and his "wonders," each of which is exemplified. The poet started each clause with a different letter of the Hebrew alphabet, and all twenty-two letters are used in the ten verses. This acrostic pattern suggests that the Lord's works in the world for the good of his people cover the whole spectrum from *aleph* to *tav* (from *A* to *Z*).

112:1–10 Praise ye the Lord. Blessed is the man that feareth the Lord, that delighteth greatly in his commandments

The second of this trio of Hallelujah Psalms praises the Lord for blessings to his "seed," people made righteous by his righteous ways. These also are arranged in an alphabetic, acrostic pattern. The scope of these psalms may be seen in the variety of topics footnoted.

113:1–9 Praise ye the Lord. Praise, O ye servants of the Lord, praise the name of the Lord

The third of this set of Hallelujah Psalms starts with a triple entreaty and ends with a hallelujah. The reasons for praising the Lord are briefly generalized and then particularized with examples.

114:1–8 When Israel went out of Egypt

Perhaps the most familiar subject of praise and cause for worship in Israel was the historic rescue from Egypt. Psalm 114 points to that event as the beginning of the nation of Israel—later two nations, Judah and Israel. It poetically portrays the drama of seas, mountains, and rocks responding to the controlling powers of God.

115:1–18 Not unto us, O Lord, not unto us, but unto thy name give glory, for thy mercy, and for thy truth's sake

The contrast of the living God to idols and idol worshippers to worshippers of the true God is artistically done, as is the summary of idols and their makers. That leads to a threefold exhortation to all Israel, to the priestly tribe of Aaron, and to all those who reverence the true God to trust in him. Reassurance through history and testimony is presented.

The closing verses urge people to worship the Lord now and not to put it off until their bodies are dead and in the grave, where they cannot speak. Latter-day revelation assures us, however, that "the dead" can praise him in the spirit world (Ps. 115:17*a;* D&C 138:14–19).

The psalm ends with a resolution to "bless the Lord from this time forth and for evermore." The last phrase is "Praise the Lord"—in Hebrew, *hallelujah.*

116:1–19 I love the Lord, because he hath heard my voice and my supplications. Because he hath inclined his ear unto me

Psalm 116 expresses gratitude for relief from some of the common problems of life—sorrow at death, pain of conscience, disillusionment. But because there is relief through communication with the Lord and through his merciful attention to "the simple," a profusion of sincere expressions of gratitude follows—which many readers can echo. Some verses would be appropriate meditations during sacrament services (Ps. 116:12–14). The psalm ends with *hallelujah*.

117 O praise the Lord, all ye nations

This briefest of the psalms anticipates fulfillment of the mission of Abraham's seed, when all peoples in all nations shall worship the Lord. All will at last appreciate God's merciful kindness and truth.

118:1–29 O give thanks unto the Lord; for he is good: because his mercy endureth for ever

Psalm 118 expresses gratitude to the Lord and confidence in him, as do many others; it may have been the psalm Jesus and the Twelve sang at the Last Supper (Matt. 26:30). Note how many verses apply to that situation.

Two other connections with New Testament events are also evident. One is the phrase "Save now" (Ps. 118:25), which translates a compound word in Hebrew, *hoshia' na*, meaning "O save us now"; it is anglicized to *Hosanna*. Recall the Hosanna Shout at the triumphal entry of Jesus into Jerusalem (Matt. 21:9; Mark 11:9–10; John 12:12–13). The second is the passage "the stone which the builders refused is become the head stone of the corner" (Ps. 118:22), which is quoted with reference to Jesus (Luke 20:17; Acts 4:11; 1 Pet. 2:6–7).

Psalm 118 may have been composed at the time the second temple was dedicated, at the time of Haggai and Zechariah, and could have been sung at the Feast of Dedication (*Hanukkah*) in the time of the Maccabees. It could well be sung in temple dedications in our day: "the Lord is my strength and song, and is become my salvation" (Ps. 118:14). This psalm begins and ends with one acclaim: "his mercy endureth for ever."

119:1–176 The twenty-two, eight-verse segments of this long psalm are addressed separately in this commentary

Only one psalm separates the shortest, Psalm 117, from the

longest, Psalm 119, which is an acrostic poem with eight verses for each of the twenty-two letters of the Hebrew alphabet. The theme of this long psalm is that blessings follow those who obey the law, the statutes, and the testimonies of the Lord and who live in reverence before him (cf. Ps. 19:8–10). One Hebrew letter and its name appears above each eight-verse segment.

119:1– 8 ALEPH [pronounced AL-eff]. . . Blessed are the undefiled in the way, who walk in the law of the Lord

The first two verses are parallel statements of the theme: "Blessed are they that keep his testimonies." The Hebrew word *ntzr*, here translated *keep*, means "to watch over, protect, preserve." Thus should one's own testimony, born of the witnesses of the Lord, be treasured and nourished while one walks in the way of the Lord.

119:9–16 BETH [pronounced baet] . . . Wherewithal shall a young man cleanse his way?

The answer to this universally useful question is simple, but its ramifications are profound: by watching and guarding himself, and by obeying the Lord's word from the scriptures and the prophets.

119:17–24 GIMEL [pronounced GIE-mel] . . . Deal bountifully with thy servant, that I may live, and keep thy word

The simple sweetness of the supplications that follow befit a person desiring to be righteous.

119:25–32 DALETH [pronounced DAH-let] . . . My soul cleaveth unto the dust: quicken thou me according to thy word

There is physical, moral, and spiritual symbolism in this statement of man's being *of* this earth-dust but yearning for heavenly sublimation (Ps. 119:25*b;* TG, "Man, Natural, Not Spiritually Reborn"; "Man, New, Spiritually Reborn"). The psalmist expressed his conversion to the Lord's ways in the remaining verses, using the same word (Heb., *davaq*) to declare that he had "*stuck* unto thy testimonies" as he had formerly *"cleav[ed]* to the dust," or world (Ps. 119:25, 31).

119:33– 40 HE [pronounced hey] . . . Teach me, O Lord, the way of thy statutes; and I shall keep it unto the end

The worshipper prays for understanding, guidance, protection, understanding—to keep true to the Lord's ways, for which he had longed and which he adopted.

119:41– 48 VAU [pronounced vav] . . . Let thy mercies come also unto me, O Lord, even thy salvation, according to thy word

It truly is by the Lord's grace we are saved (Ps. 119:41; cf. 2 Ne. 25:23); hence all we can do may well be done with gratitude, having been set "at liberty" (Ps. 119:45; John 8:32; Gal. 5:1). Then we will bear testimony of the blessing by word and deed, as promised in the concluding verses.

119:49–56 ZAIN [pronounced ZAH-yin] . . . Remember the word unto thy servant, upon which thou hast caused me to hope

Word is by extension *message* and in context here, *promise.* The remaining verses testify that the petitioner has remembered the Lord's good promise and has maintained hope through afflictions, derisions, and horrors in the course of his life's pilgrimage. Throughout all he was comforted, as the Lord promised.

119:57– 64 CHETH [pronounced khaet] . . . Thou art my portion, O Lord: . . . The earth . . . is full of thy mercy

In life's vicissitudes one may ask for the Lord's mercy when trying to repent; and any who have had that experience may well also have awakened "at midnight" and given thanks for his mercy in judgment. There is security in being a companion of others who "fear" (revere) the Lord.

119:65–72 TETH [pronounced taet] . . . Before I was afflicted I went astray: but now have I kept thy word

He who went astray is grateful for the affliction that helped him cease going astray and begin to learn the law. That theme is reiterated, describing how most mortals feel as they strive to become just and moral (Ps. 119:67, 71). The proud forge lies and have unreceptive hearts.

119:73–80 JOD [pronounced yud; *rhymes with* could] . . . *give me understanding, that I may learn thy commandments*

It is a process to learn the commandments and become "sound in [the] statutes"; hence, it is comforting to have company along the way. One achieving soundness need not be ashamed.

119:81–88 CAPH [pronounced caf] . . . *My soul fainteth for thy salvation: but I hope in thy word*

Unjust persecution of humble followers of the Lord by "proud" adversaries may make their souls almost faint; but hope for divine salvation quickens (makes alive again) their testimony through the grace of the Lord's loving kindness.

119:89–96 LAMED [pronounced LAH-med] . . . *Unless thy law had been my delights, I should then have perished in mine affliction*

The thesis of this segment appears in the middle of it. Through the Lord's word, faithfulness, and ordinances, the afflicted one learned the law and will never forget it. He now belongs to the Lord, who will save him. The wicked shall not destroy him now, for with the witnesses of the Lord, he has seen the goal of all perfection, and the Lord's commandment is broad enough to help him reach it.

119:97–104 MEM [pronounced maem] . . . *Thou through thy commandments hast made me wiser than mine enemies*

He loves the law of the Lord, for divine commandments have made him wiser than the enemy and more understanding than the teachers and the elders. Therefore he has resisted evil and been guided by the Lord's judgments. The Lord's words are sweet, and His precepts increase understanding.

119:105–12 NUN [pronounced noon] . . . Thy word is a lamp unto my feet, and a light unto my path

This pair of synonymous metaphors is often quoted; there are other memorable passages in this segment also. The writer, like many of us, relies on the Lord's guidance to help him through all afflictions. He offers his offerings and trusts he can keep the Lord's statutes even to the end.

119:113–20 SAMECH [pronounced SAH-mekh] . . . Uphold me according unto thy word, that I may live: and let me not be ashamed of my hope

The author loves the Lord's law and the security He provides against evildoers. He trusts he will be upheld in his hope, for the wicked are trodden down and are purged away. He is so inspired with awe that he trembles in humility before the Lord.

119:121–28 AIN [pronounced EYE-yin] . . . It is time for thee, Lord, to work: for they have made void thy law

Despite all the blessings and successes he has experienced in righteous living, the writer still finds it evident (as Job so often declared) that the wicked prosper and even triumph. So it is time for the Lord to take a hand and sustain the righteous; the writer has full confidence in His commandments and precepts.

119:129–36 PE [pronounced pay] . . . Thy testimonies are wonderful: therefore doth my soul keep them

In other words, "the witnesses [evidences] of thee are marvelous, therefore doth my soul retain them." The writer loves the Lord's words, commandments, mercy, guidance, and deliverance. He supplicates the Lord's favor and weeps when he goes astray.

119:137–44 TZADDI [pronounced TSAHD-dee] . . . Thy word is very pure: therefore thy servant loveth it

With great appreciation for the Lord's judgments, testimonies, and revealed word, the psalmist is overwhelmed that his enemies could have forgotten them. He feels humble but does not falter in trying to keep the precepts and the true law. Despite the trouble and anguish he has experienced, the Lord's commandments are his delight, and his righteous testimonies are eternal. Because the Lord gives him wisdom, he shall live.

119:145–52 KOPH [pronounced koef*] . . . I prevented the dawning of the morning, and cried: I hoped in thy word*

Prevent, from the Latin *prevenire,* "to come before," is used here in that original sense. With help from the footnotes, we can see the intended meaning: in morning and evening he turned *first* to his prayers to be true to the ways of the Lord and be protected from the evildoers. Though his enemies threaten mischief, he trusts forever in the Lord's testimonies.

119:153–60 RESH [pronounced raysh*] . . . Consider mine affliction, and deliver me: for I do not forget thy law*

This section of the psalm supplicates for deliverance, protection, and salvation from afflictions, persecutors, and transgressors. The psalmist never sought help as an entitlement but pleaded for it in hope of divine mercy, trusting in the Lord's judgments forever.

119:161–68 SCHIN [pronounced sheen*] . . . Princes have persecuted me without a cause: but my heart standeth in awe of thy word*

Troubles were created by civil governments anciently also. Those who lie (Ps. 119:163) can cause much persecution. Yet the word of the Lord and his law give peace through consistent prayer; the love of his precepts and testimonies brings about salvation.

119:169–76 TAU [pronounced tav*] . . . I have gone astray like a lost sheep; seek thy servant; for I do not forget thy commandments*

As a conclusion to the whole psalm, from *aleph* to *tau,* the author sums up the human predicament. He seeks true salvation through the mercy of the Lord by obedience to His commandments and through divine assistance obtained by prayer.

120:1–7 In my distress I cried unto the Lord, and he heard me

Psalm 120 begins a series of fifteen psalms, each of which is called, with some variations, "A Song of degrees." That is a plausible translation, but *ma'aloth* is from the root word *'alah,* meaning "to ascend," and it can also mean "steps." Perhaps these psalms were songs for going up the steps to the temple, or for pilgrims going up to Jerusalem, or for exiles going up to the promised land again.

Perhaps a clue to the purpose of the psalm is found in verse 5: the author (and hence any singer of the psalm) laments about sojourning in "Mesech" and "Kedar." Those were places associated with Japhetic and Ishmaelite peoples (Ps. 120:5*a–c*) and hence symbolized being in exile, or away from Zion; thus the song is a prayer for deliverance from evils of the outside world. It is a prayer to rise above all that—to be exalted—in the spirit, at least, out of the worldly presence of "him that hateth peace" (Ps. 120:6).

121:1–8 I will lift up mine eyes unto the hills, from whence cometh my help

This "song of ascent" is a prayer for exaltation above worldly dangers. The "hills, from whence cometh my help" are the mountains of the Lord's house; thus it is made clear that "my help cometh from the Lord" (Ps. 121:1–2). This psalm, which is almost as well known as Psalm 23, "The Lord is my shepherd," gives the same assurance of protection in the walks of life but in a different idiom. It is another beautiful song.

122:1–9 I was glad when they said unto me, Let us go into the house of the Lord

This is a "psalm of ascents" for obvious reasons—going up for temple worship. It is as applicable now as it was when it was written. The messianic New Jerusalem, or Zion, and the ultimate temple are clearly envisioned. Many workers in latter-day temples already feel like singing this song of exaltation.

123:1– 4 Unto thee lift I up mine eyes, O thou that dwellest in the heavens

Again a theme of "lifting up" predominates. Beautiful similes make real the relationship of a humble servant to the Lord our God and Master. And humble faith can lift up the oppressed from the contempt or scorn of the haughty "that are at ease."

124:1– 8 If it had not been the Lord who was on our side . . . Then they had swallowed us up quick

The poetry of Psalm 124 is characterized by a progressive, "stair step" parallelism that enhances symbols of divine help lifting souls up out of the waters of oppression, out of the stream of "proud waters," and out of the snare of the bird catchers. Much uplift can indeed come "in the name of the Lord."

125:1–5 They that trust in the Lord shall be as mount Zion, which cannot be removed, but abideth for ever

The "mount Zion, which . . . abideth for ever" is the celestial Zion; they that trust in the Lord shall thus be exalted. This is another song of ascent, a song of exaltation, a song of seeking a celestial home. The discerning judgment of the Lord upon the good and bad is clear.

126:1– 6 When the Lord turned again the captivity of Zion, we were like them that dream

The return of Judah from Babylon after it was conquered by Persia (ca. 538–537 B.C.) was like a dream come true; but though "the Lord [had] done great things" for them, there was yet "captivity" in mortality itself, from which they desired redemption. If they who sow in tears go forth in life to sow "precious seed," then the Lord will lift them up with joy as they come "bringing . . . sheaves" to the Judgment Day. Redemption from Babylon was like a dream; but redemption from the wicked world of "Babylon"

(D&C 1:16) will be a dream come true. Thus this psalm too sings of the ultimate elevation of man by the Lord.

127:1–5 Except the Lord build the house, they labour in vain that build it: except the Lord keep the city, the watchman waketh but in vain

A "house" may be either a domicile or an extended family; in either case, except it be done in the ways of the Lord and by His power and blessing, they indeed labor in vain that build. It was so of the great King Solomon, who builded great "houses" but did many things that were not of the Lord (D&C 132:38; Jacob 2:23–24) and were therefore in vain.

After making the point in general, the psalm makes it specific with regard to the family, for children "are an heritage of the Lord" and "the fruit of the womb is his reward" (Ps. 127:3). Those who know how "families can be forever" through celestial marriage recognize this as a psalm about exaltation.

128:1–6 Blessed is every one that feareth the Lord; that walketh in his ways

This psalm about a reverent, obedient husband and wife, their children, and their children's children—all of whom are promised that "the Lord shall bless thee out of Zion"—is more clearly about family exaltation. It is clearly a song of "ascent" or exaltation.

129:1–8 Many a time have they afflicted me from my youth, . . . yet they have not prevailed against me

A person who has suffered persecution, imprisonment, and torture by the lash or people with ethnic memories of suffering may well hope for "Zion," when the Lord will "cut asunder the cords of the wicked." But those who hate "Zion" shall perish. In this prophetic psalm the righteous rise above evil conditions; it is truly a "song of ascent."

130:1–8 Out of the depths have I cried unto thee, O Lord

This psalm is the cry of a sinner begging to be lifted out of depths where he can hardly feel hope, even in the Lord, because of his many iniquities. It is reminiscent of Jonah's testimony: "I cried by reason of mine affliction unto the Lord, and he heard me; out of the belly of hell cried I, and thou heardest my voice" (Jonah 2:2).

The Hebrew word translated *depths* in verse 1 of Psalm 130 is a word that implies deep water; but the author knows that the miracle of forgiveness is available and is reverent in that knowledge. A beautiful metaphor expresses Israel's hope for just such a miracle of redemption.

131:1–3 my heart is not haughty, nor mine eyes lofty

A brief disclaimer of pride is uttered in this song labeled "of David"; then that virtue of humility and its blessings are sought for Israel as a whole. As for being a "psalm of ascent," Jesus pronounced the same principle illustrated in this psalm: "whosoever shall exalt himself shall be abased; and he that shall humble himself shall be exalted" (Matt. 23:12).

132:1–18 Lord, remember David, and all his afflictions: How he sware unto the Lord . . . ; Surely I will not come into the tabernacle of my house . . . Until I find out a place for the Lord

With allusions to the commitment of David and the people of his time who secured a place for the temple and prepared to have it built so that they might "go into his tabernacles" to worship, this "song of degrees" supplicates the Lord to return to his place, possibly at the time of the return from Babylon, when the second temple had not yet been built. Reminders of the Lord's promises of a Davidic ruler then become prophetic anticipations of the Messiah (Ps. 132:11–18). Thus Psalm 132 returns to the topic of Psalm 122—the yearning to *go up* to Zion and to the temple, there again to be able to worship the Lord.

133:1–3 Behold, how good and how pleasant it is for brethren to dwell together in unity

Words of this psalm have become a popular folk chant in the modern nation of Israel. This short Davidic psalm of exaltation yearns for the ideal age of Zion to come, with the blessings of peace, love, and "life for evermore" in true exaltation.

134:1–3 Behold, bless ye the Lord, all ye servants of the Lord . . . Lift up your hands in the sanctuary, and bless the Lord

The last "song of going up" (or "song of degrees") is set in the temple, and the worshippers are invited to conclude the service by lifting their hands in the sanctuary to bless the Lord. The officiator then asks that the Lord bless them "out of Zion."

135:1–21 Praise ye the Lord

This psalm of praise begins almost like the "little" Hallelujah Psalm, Psalm 113; the Hallelujah Psalms are Psalms 111 through 113 and 146 through 150. The second admonishment, "Praise ye the name of the Lord," is not entirely synonymous with the first, for his very name, Jehovah, connotes creative power, and divine power is exerted by those (of the priesthood) holding the right to invoke it. The sacred name was never to be used "in vain" for unauthorized purposes or by unauthorized spokesmen (Ex. 20:7 and commentary).

The worshippers in the temple are urged to praise and thank the Lord for appointing Israel as his "peculiar treasure" (Ps. 135:4b–c; BD, "Peculiar"), for with that treasure he extends his kingdom, defends his kingdom, and operates his kingdom.

Historical evidence of some aspects of the Lord's greatness are cited. Then with a transition from what the Lord can and will do for his people, the praise continues in a comparison with, and ridicule of, dumb idols that have nonfunctioning limbs and organs. It is clever irony to say "they that make them are like unto them: so is every one that trusteth in them." Again, all worshippers are urged to bless the Lord. All should participate—the houses of Israel, Aaron, Levi, and all in Zion at Jerusalem. The psalm ends with one more *hallelujah,* "Praise ye the Lord."

136:1–26 O give thanks unto the Lord; for he is good: for his mercy endureth for ever

The opening words of Psalm 136 and succeeding verses have

been repeated in liturgical adulations by Jewish and Christian worshippers for ages. They are followed by a review of the Lord's might and works from the Creation through the Exodus, the establishment of Israel in the promised land, and some cases of redemption from enemies. They recognize the universal providence of God and give thanks to him as "the God of gods" and "the God of heaven." The refrain in every verse declares him worthy of praise because "his mercy endureth for ever" (the Hebrew is even more clear: "for to eternity [is] his lovingkindness").

137:1–9 By the rivers of Babylon, there we sat down, yea, we wept, when we remembered Zion

The Israelite singers hung their harps upon the willows in Babylon and could not sing a song of Zion as demanded by their captors; but the psalmist composed a lament about that event. Many have since set the lament to music and sung it (see, for example, *Hymns: The Church of Jesus Christ of Latter-day Saints* [Salt Lake City: Deseret Book Co., 1948], no. 55).

With bitterness the psalmist hoped for punishment for the Edomites, who applauded and encouraged the Babylonian conquerors of Judah (Ps. 137:7*a–b;* Obad. 1, on Edom's doom). Perhaps only people who have known or felt some of the effects of the twentieth-century holocausts wrought upon Jewish people and others understand the bitterness.

138:1– 8 I will praise thee with my whole heart: before the gods will I sing praise unto thee

Before is used here to translate the Hebrew *neged,* which means "face to face, confronting, opposite." The "gods" were the idols of Babylon; the psalmist in exile defied them by worshipping the living God not only in front of them but also toward God's holy temple. Worship toward the holy temple by Israelites in need, by the absent armies of Israel, by "strangers" in other lands, or by captive Israelites in exile was a mode of worship suggested by Solomon in his dedication of the temple (1 Kgs. 8:35–50). He prayed that the Lord would hear and bless them all. A confident testimony asserts that the Lord always does answer prayers and will be worshipped by other peoples, including their kings. "Though the Lord be high, yet hath he respect unto the lowly: but the proud he knoweth afar off."

Note the Joseph Smith Translation emendation of the final testimony and supplication (Ps. 138:7–8*a*).

139:1–24 O Lord, thou hast searched me, and known me. . . . If I ascend up into heaven, thou art there: if I make my bed in hell, behold, thou art there

The omniscience of the Lord is dramatically declared in this famous psalm, and the gratitude of those who are comfortable in the presence of the Lord is beautifully stated. It is marvelous and comforting that there is no hiding place God does not know. The psalmist expresses trust in God and desire for his help in the process of repentance.

There are many gems in this literary jewel, especially verses 2, 9, 10, 14, 17, and 18; every reader will find other favorites as well.

140:1–13 Deliver me, O Lord, from the evil man: preserve me from the violent man

Only a person who has suffered much from many enemies would compose so many prayers for protection against the ungodly and beseech the vengeance of God upon them. The psalmist cried out to the Lord in ardent supplications and ended with a confident testimony.

141:1–10 Lord, I cry unto thee: make haste unto me; give ear unto my voice, when I cry unto thee

This psalm is the second of this series of Davidic prayers for help. It asserts that reproof of a righteous person can be tolerated—indeed it is good for one—but asks for divine retribution for unjust judges and workers of iniquity, who have let the bones of the righteous be scattered even at the grave's mouth. The author hoped they might fall into their own gins (traps) and snares, while he enjoyed the Lord's protection.

142:1–7 I cried unto the Lord with my voice; . . . I poured out my complaint before him

On *Maschil,* see commentary on Psalm 32.

The third of this series of outcries describes the desperate straits David found himself in because of persecution; he had no source of help save the Lord (cf. 1 Sam. 22; 24). The prayer expresses the psalmist's confidence in salvation from the Lord.

143:1–12 Hear my prayer, O Lord, . . . in thy faithfulness answer me

The fourth Davidic psalm in this series urgently beseeches rescue from deep depression, but again it expresses complete confidence in the Lord, not only for rescue but for guidance, teachings, and revival. Hope persists because of the Lord's loving kindness and his mercy.

144:1–15 Blessed be the Lord my strength, . . . My goodness, and my fortress

This composite "psalm of David" has parts from many others (some of which are footnoted). Accordingly, it reiterates familiar themes, such as deliverance in battle, the weakness of a man without God, deliverance from enemies, praise to God for victory, supplications for help against alien influences, and prayers for prosperity.

145:1–21 I will extol thee, my God, O king; and I will bless thy name for ever and ever

The whole book of Psalms is called, in Hebrew, *Tehillim,* "Praises"; but only this one is called "David's Psalm of praise" in a superscription. The last of this series of eight psalms of David, Psalm 145 is also a prelude to the remaining group of Hallelujah Psalms, each of which begins with *hallelujah,* "praise ye Jehovah."

This psalm praises the Lord's name, greatness, mighty acts, awesome powers, great goodness, grace, compassion, patience, mercy, and righteousness—familiar themes throughout the book of Psalms. Like many others, it declares the dependability of his help, available to all who humbly and honestly seek it. The alphabetic acrostic pattern suggests the comprehensiveness of the Lord's power.

146:1–10 Praise ye the Lord. Praise the Lord, O my soul

Psalm 146 begins the final group of Hallelujah Psalms.

Trust in the Lord is contrasted against trust in any "princes" or other mortals. Then, as in many psalms, the virtues of the Lord are reviewed, and his reign in the eternal Zion is anticipated. *Hallelujah,* "praise ye the Lord," ends the psalm.

147:1–20 Praise ye the Lord: for it is good to sing praises unto our God; for it is pleasant; and praise is comely

The first statement of Psalm 147 is a refreshing assertion. Much of the rest of the psalm identifies facets of the Lord's goodness, power, and mercy. Pleasant word-pictures portray the cycles and functions of nature under the Lord's hand. Revelations to Israel, the scriptures, go forth to the world from the Lord through his chosen people (Ps. 147:19–20). The psalm ends with *hallelujah.*

148:1–14 Praise ye the Lord. Praise ye the Lord from the heavens: praise ye him in the heights

Starting with an exhortation that angels, the hosts of the heavens, and the orbs of the skies praise the Lord, the author admonishes all creations of earth and all leaders and peoples to do likewise, for the Lord's "glory is above the earth and heaven." The Lord exalts the powers ("horn") of his people and the qualities of his covenant ones ("saints") of Israel. The psalm ends as it began, with *hallelujah.*

149:1–9 Praise ye the Lord. Sing unto the Lord a new song, and his praise in the congregation of saints

The praise of the Lord and a new song shall be in the congregation of the virtuous, the "saints."

Psalm 149 is an avowal of the relationship between God and

his people. Israel will rejoice and praise the Lord, whereas he will "beautify the meek with salvation" (cf. "blessed are the meek" in Matt. 5:5; 3 Ne. 12:5). Then secure from present and ultimate dangers, the Saints will be joyful when awake, secure when asleep, and have power to resist and bind unbelievers and former oppressors. This psalm, too, ends as it began, with *hallelujah*.

150:1–6 Praise ye the Lord. Praise God in his sanctuary: praise him in the firmament of his power

This final, grand hallelujah psalm begins each clause with *hallelu,* "Praise ye." The place of "his sanctuary" is stated in a synonymous parallel as "the firmament of his power"—the heavens. Because of "his excellent greatness," all instruments of music and all living things are summoned to his praise. Then both the psalm and the book of Psalms end with one last hallelujah.

This is the book of Psalms, the book of praises, testimonies, supplications, outcries of despair, hope, confidence, and gratitude, and even more praises. They are voiced by ordinary people, priests, a king, other leaders, exiles. Their language is sometimes strange to us but often strangely familiar. Their times were different, long ago; but in the present many things are like their times. Thus the psalms are valuable for history, for heritage, and for worship.

PROVERBS

The book of Proverbs contains much that is attributed to King Solomon. It is a treasured collection of Hebrew wisdom literature derived mostly from the experiences of humankind and written by wise and faithful men and women to epitomize rules of good behavior and to commend their virtues. The book contains less material accredited as divine revelation and more attributed to human observation than do the books of the Prophets; but some inspired advice is included, and ways of thought, speech, and action pleasing to the Lord are commended. Much of it no doubt originated with men and women inspired by the Lord, and in that sense they were prophetic.

Solomon was credited with God-given wisdom and understanding exceeding that of "all the children of the east country, and all the wisdom of Egypt"; it is recorded that "he spake three thousand proverbs, and his songs were a thousand and five" about relationships between nature, man, and God (1 Kgs. 4:29–43).

Three sections of the book of Proverbs are labeled as the proverbs of Solomon. Whether these are all of his compositions, or whether all that are attributed to him are really his, are matters of some speculation, but no doubt much that is in this book was written by Solomon. Other authors are identified in the headings.

The book of the Proverbs is divided into five parts. The first part, Proverbs 1 through 9, is called "the Proverbs of Solomon"

(Prov. 1:1); it contains didactic poems longer than the two-line couplets that make up the body of Proverbs proper. The poems arc largely advice from father to son; they include some dissertations on wisdom.

The second section, Proverbs 10 through 24, is also—and perhaps more aptly—entitled "the Proverbs of Solomon" (Prov. 10:1); it contains formal, pithy, poetic couplets. There is no evident organization of most of the subjects of the verses and chapters of this section; but there is a collection of short aphorisms, one or more verses in length, that is introduced by an explanatory admonition and covers a variety of moral and social matters (Prov. 22:17–24:34).

The last three sections together are shorter than either of the first two. Proverbs 25 through 29, the third section, is introduced as "also proverbs of Solomon, which the men of Hezekiah king of Judah copied out" (Prov. 25:1); it contains proverbs, maxims, and other aphorisms. The fourth section, Proverbs 30, is called "the words of Agur the son of Jakeh, even the prophecy" (v. 1); it too contains a variety of moral and religious observations and admonitions. The fifth section, Proverbs 31, is called "the words of king Lemuel, the prophecy that his mother taught him" (Prov. 31:1); it is a renowned poetic summary of the virtues of a good woman and wife.

The Hebrew title of the whole book, *Mishlei,* is a plural form of *mashal,* whose root means "to represent, be like, be similar." Many proverbs do indeed treat similarities using parallel clauses with a synonymous, antithetic, or synthetic relationship.

COMMENTARY

1:1– 6 To know . . . To receive . . . To give . . . To understand

The title and purpose of the compilations are stated, together with some values for those who receive them.

1:7–9 The fear of the Lord is the beginning of knowledge

Fear in this context means "humility, reverence"; reverent humility is a state of mind in which a person can be taught, retain what is learned, and apply that learning in wise ways. Many useful rules are found in these verses.

1:10–19 My son, if sinners entice thee, consent thou not

The first of many admonitions to youth warns against joining gangs for bloodshed and pillage.

1:20–23 Wisdom crieth without; she uttereth her voice in the streets

The parent or teacher laments when the naive, the scorner, or the foolish reject wisdom, instruction, and reproof.

1:24–33 Because I have called, and ye . . . set at nought all my counsel, . . . I also will laugh at your calamity

This passage of Proverbs is one that contains the Lord's words. When and why he will not respond to prayers is made clear.

2:1–9 My son, if thou wilt receive my words, . . . and apply thine heart to understanding; . . . Then shalt thou understand the fear of the Lord, and find the knowledge of God

Father-to-son advice in these verses provides a preventive for loss of the Lord's help (cf. Prov. 1:24–33).

2:10–22 When wisdom entereth into thine heart, and knowledge is pleasant unto thy soul; Discretion shall preserve thee, understanding shall keep thee

True wisdom will safeguard one from "the way of the evil man" and the "strange" woman (Prov. 2:12, 16a); it will lead one in the way to good, whereas the wicked will suffer destruction.

3:1–12 My son, forget not my law; but let thine heart keep my commandments . . . So shalt thou find favour and good understanding in the sight of God and man

Fatherly advice in this case corresponds with divine instruction and commends a way of life that many humble people have applied with confidence and comfort (Prov. 3:5–6). When all does not go well, divine catharsis is available (Prov. 3:11–12).

3:13–26 Happy is the man that findeth wisdom, and the man that getteth understanding

Wisdom is personified in this segment of Proverbs 3; metaphors state some truths effectively and beautifully. The declaration about the Lord's own use of wisdom, understanding, and knowledge in creating and controlling earth and heaven is good theology (Prov. 3:19–20; cf. TG, "God, Intelligence of"; "God, Omniscience of"; "God, Wisdom of"). Wisdom also helps mankind to acquire the blessings of the Lord (Prov. 3:21–26).

3:27–35 Withhold not good from them to whom it is due

Miscellaneous maxims and admonitions against parsimony, mischief, belligerence, envy, perverseness, scornfulness, and other wicked ways finish this chapter. Several types of parallelism are skillfully used.

4:1–27 Hear, ye children, the instruction of a father. . . . Enter not into the path of the wicked, and go not in the way of evil men

A father teaches gems of wisdom about the family, getting wisdom and understanding, and retaining instruction. Positive recommendations make up the first half of this chapter; warnings against negative ways, the second half. Poetic metaphors and similes convey wise teachings (all fn.).

5:1–23 My son, attend unto my wisdom, . . . For the lips of a strange woman drop as an honeycomb, . . . Drink waters out of thine own cistern

This whole chapter has one topic: avoiding harlotry and adultery (Prov. 5:1–14) and retaining fidelity in proper, loving, marital relationships (Prov. 5:15–21). Some of the language is graphic, but not vulgar, in commending connubial life and denouncing illicit pleasures. As is usual in the wisdom literature, the poetry is beautiful in all of its wordplay.

6:1–5 if thou be surety for thy friend

The dangers in guaranteeing a loan or a promise for someone

else have led the speaker to suggest immediate and searching measures to make sure the risk is warranted.

6:6–11 Go to the ant, thou sluggard; consider her ways, and be wise

This famous passage commends industry, foresight, and preparation, with the busy ant as exemplar. Somehow one smiles even while accepting its advice and reading the poetic ascent to the climax in the last three verses.

6:12–15 A naughty person

There is wry humor in the characterization of the "naughty person"; he is "a good-for-nothing," according to the Hebrew term used; his perverseness (Prov. 6:12a) is implemented by expressions, gestures, and motions calculated to disarm, deceive, drive wedges of doubt, and sow discord. For all this he is to be punished.

6:16–19 These six things doth the Lord hate: yea, seven are an abomination unto him

Seven is a number that symbolizes completeness; this list covers most abominable attitudes and acts, including pride, lying, murder, malicious thought, eagerness for evil, false testimony, and raising dissension. These generate most of the ills of society.

6:20–35 My son, keep thy father's commandment, and forsake not the law of thy mother

The safeguard against social and moral evils as well as the sin and crime of adultery is obedience to the commandments of the father and the instructive guidance (Heb., torah) of the mother. The parents are the first to discipline the child by the "lamp" of the commandments, the "light" of the law, and the reproofs of discipline; but they will be effective only if the immature keep them in mind constantly, as a guide in the walks of life, a guard during sleep, and counsel in planning (Prov. 6:20–24).

This lesson goes from the abstract and general to the specific and anecdotal: the safeguards are "to keep thee from" hazards such as the "woman of evil" and "the smoothness of tongue of the [female] alien" (Prov. 6:24, translation mine). The warnings are not against females in general; they are specifically against whoredom. Stealing may be understandable and is remediable; but adultery affects "precious life," displays a lack of understanding, damages the soul with a wound and dishonor, and may beget the violence of vengeance.

7:1–27 My son, keep my words . . . That they may keep thee from the strange woman

The father next presents a dramatic anecdote by which he seeks to forewarn the naive "simple ones" and the uninitiated, who are "void of understanding." The commandments and the law should be as precious as the pupil of the eye. Wisdom and understanding should be cherished as a sister or kinswoman would be in order to keep one from women of infidel intents and ways. The example of what happens to a youth if he remains "void of understanding" is easy to understand and to believe. See the footnotes and references for more on unfamiliar words or idioms. Contemplate the poetry of such passages as Proverbs 7:9, 22, 23, and 27.

8:1–36 Doth not wisdom cry? and understanding put forth her voice? . . . Unto you, O men, I call; and my voice is to the sons of man

Anyone who understands that the Son of God was in the beginning with the Father will perceive that wisdom is identified with the Son of God (Prov. 8:22–36; cf. TG, "Jesus Christ, Creator"). This passage also certifies wisdom as a divine attribute. The trio of understanding, wisdom, and righteousness has been emphasized through the centuries by classical Judaism.

This chapter should be studied as a whole (and all fn.).

9:1–18 Wisdom hath builded her house, . . . she crieth upon the highest places of the city, Whoso is simple, let him turn in hither

Wisdom is personified as a gracious hostess inviting the "simple" to "forsake the foolish" and to gain "understanding"

(Prov. 9:1–6). A few aphorisms contrast the responses of the scorner or foolish with those of the humble and wise. Reverence, "the fear of the Lord," is the attitude out of which wisdom can spring and flourish.

A contrasting hostess, personified as a foolish woman, entices the simple and offers them not wisdom but forbidden indulgences (Prov. 9:17). The rewards of foolishness are death and hell, whereas the rewards of wisdom are life and understanding. The first segment of the book of Proverbs ends here.

10:1–32 The proverbs of Solomon

The central collection of Proverbs begins here, and with only a slight change of literary structures (beginning at Prov. 22:17), continues to the end of chapter 24. It is noteworthy that the first of these couplets in antithetical parallelism treats matters of the home—the joys that come from righteous children contrasted to the burdens caused by the rebellious or foolish. The joys extend outward, represented by the father, who is more in public life than the mother; but the burdens weigh heavily within the home, which is the mother's chief domain.

11:1–31 A false balance is abomination to the Lord: but a just weight is his delight

The first proverb of the chapter does not necessarily characterize the chapter, except in its emphasizing an attribute of all biblical morality: it begins with God, not with the experiences and observations of man. It makes the point that the Lord cares about such matters as honesty in a person's behavior. Notice the broad scope of these lessons on morality in the number of different topics covered by these thirty-one verses.

12:1–28 Whoso loveth instruction loveth knowledge: but he that hateth reproof is brutish

Intelligence, truth, honesty, justice, and mercy in dealings with man and beasts are commended by these proverbs. See in the footnotes how many topics these verses cover.

13:1–25 A wise son heareth his father's instruction: but a scorner heareth not rebuke

The essential family concerns of parental instruction and children's response are emphasized in Proverbs 13:1, 13, 18, 24.

Literary art and beauty may be found in such verses as 12 and 14; the enigmatic, in such verses as 7 and 25.

14:1–35 Every wise woman buildeth her house: but the foolish plucketh it down with her hands

This chapter begins with the virtue of wisdom at home and ends with the value of righteousness and wisdom in the nation. In between is the promise of "strong confidence" and a place of refuge for all who revere the Lord. A broad spectrum of wise virtues is recommended.

15:1–33 A soft answer turneth away wrath: but grievous words stir up anger

Several proverbs about peaceful and profitable communication are noteworthy, such as Proverbs 15:2, 4, 10, 12, 14, 18, 22, 28, 31, and 32.

An enigmatic proverb (Prov. 15:11) attests that since even "hell and destruction" (Heb., *sheol* and *abaddon*) are not hidden from the Lord, surely the hearts of men are not hidden from him.

16:1–33 The preparations of the heart in man, and the answer of the tongue, is from the Lord

In Hebrew, this proverb contains two complete clauses: "To man belong the meditations of the heart; but from the Lord come the utterances of the tongue" (translation mine). Anyone who has felt inspiration during a lesson, sermon, or blessing will understand how such collaboration of the mind and spirit works.

Many gems may be found in Proverbs 16; see especially verses 6, 7, 18, 20, 24, and 32. No one at any one time could appreciate all of the good ones; but each will be found to be good for someone or some situation at some time.

17:1–28 Better is a dry morsel, and quietness therewith, than an house full of sacrifices with strife

Again the first proverb of a chapter pertains to home life. The point is that the simplest fare in a humble home where love and peace abide is more wholesome than a sumptuous meal of meat in a home full of strife. The last phrase, translated literally from the Hebrew, may be rendered "than a house full of sacrifices of strife." To understand the phrase, one must know that flesh was not common fare. It was used for sacrifices on holy days and for food on festive occasions. When used in the home, it was like a kind of sacrifice, and if the spirit of the home was one of conflict and contention, discord and dissention, the sumptuous meal would be, ironically, "sacrifices with strife."

Other proverbs in this chapter also pertain to home management and a good atmosphere; see in particular Proverbs 17:2, 6, 9, 17, 19 through 22, and 25. But of course those may be applied otherwise also, and many others are good for both home and community.

18:1–24 Through desire a man, having separated himself, seeketh and intermeddleth with all wisdom

This proverb is so concise in Hebrew as to be cryptic. It can mean that out of lust one secludes himself and there rationalizes and violates the dictates of wisdom. It is one of those kernels of wisdom that can have many applications according to one's understanding and experience.

The proverb quoted above relates to isolation, but others inculcating communication may be complementary to it (Prov. 18:6–8, 13, 19, 21, 23–24) as well as having other applications.

Proverbs 18:5, 9, 10, 12, and 22 are also gems.

19:1–29 Better is the poor that walketh in his integrity, than he that is perverse in his lips, and is a fool

Typically in the book of the Proverbs, there is praise for integrity, knowledge, wisdom, discretion, prudence, obedience to law, compassion, reverence, and justice; and rebuke for ignorance, foolishness, perfidy, slothfulness, and contemptuousness. Being poor is no shame if it is not the result of slothfulness; and being rich is no honor if riches come only by inheritance— and worse than dishonor if acquired by injustice.

Who would deny that a prudent wife is a blessing from the Lord? (Prov. 18:22; 19:14).

20:1–30 Wine is a mocker, strong drink is raging: and whosoever is deceived thereby is not wise

Intoxication makes one a scorner and a brawler and is, of course, condemned. So also is the provoker, sluggard, braggart, cheater, deceiver, talebearer, and the disobedient to parents. Again commended are such virtues as peacemaking, fairness, good works, knowledge, and trust in the Lord.

21:1–31 The king's heart is in the hand of the Lord, as the rivers of water: he turneth it whithersoever he will

The proverb in verse 2 of Proverbs 21 complements the one in verse 1, for it deals with the Lord's cognizance of what is in a man's heart and what is best for humankind; the third proverb, about administering justice acceptable to the Lord, is related to both. With help from the footnotes, verse 4 may be understood thus: "Haughty eyes, and a proud heart—the cultivating of wickedness—is sin" (Prov. 21:4*a, c*).

Among the remaining proverbs concerning the usual virtues and vices are two more pertaining to home life; verses 9 and 19 are quite hyperbolic about a contentious spouse. Humor is rare in scripture, but these verses display it. There are also other teachings on a variety of matters, such as hypocrisy in worship (Prov. 21:27).

22:1–29 A good name is rather to be chosen than great riches, and loving favour rather than silver and gold

Some of the best-known proverbs of all are given in Proverbs 22. One, of course, is about the value of a good reputation and the virtue of "loving favor." Another concerns educating children early for good behavior all their lives (Prov. 22:6); and yet another recommends a "rod of correction" against foolishness (Prov. 22:15).

A number of verses deal with types of rich and poor (Prov. 22:2, 4, 7, 22–23).

Warnings against sexual aberrations are common in Proverbs (as in Prov. 22:14). Prostitutes are called "strange women," because their ways were not the ways of righteous Israelites but the ways of strangers to the covenant.

The two-part proverbs end with Proverbs 22:16. Longer aphorisms begin at verse 17 with three verses on hearkening to the wise; others, one to three verses in length, deal with refraining from defrauding the poor, emulating an "angry man," guaranteeing others' debts, or removing property landmarks, and being diligent is urged as a great virtue. These rules and sayings continue to the end of chapter 24.

23:1–35 When thou sittest to eat with a ruler—

Some fourteen different topics are treated in the thirty-five verses of Proverbs 23. Warnings against striving to be like the ruler or the rich occupy the first section. Many common topics of the book of Proverbs are treated, including warnings against those having an "evil eye," against dealing with the foolish, against taking advantage of the fatherless, against permissive raising of children, and against excessive drinking of wine. The joy of raising righteous children is a positive statement. Then warnings against participation in prostitution are repeated. A longer preachment against alcoholic indulgence ends the chapter.

24:1–34 Be not envious against evil men

The topic of Proverbs 24:1, refraining from envying the wicked, is bolstered by related topics in verses 8, 19, 20, 24, and 25. A number of familiar admonitions include a counterpart to the Golden Rule, reproach of the slothful or lazy, and disparagement of sleeping on the job (cf. Prov. 6:9–11).

The last verse of this chapter ends the second segment of the book of the Proverbs.

25:1–28 These are also proverbs of Solomon, which the men of Hezekiah king of Judah copied out

The third segment of the book of Proverbs begins with chapter 25 and continues to the end of chapter 29. These chapters contain more of the paired phrases properly called proverbs.

Two "men of Hezekiah" involved in writing projects were "Shebna the scribe, and Joah the son of Asaph the recorder" (2 Kgs. 18:18, 37; 19:2); however, the copying of a selection of proverbs of Solomon is not mentioned. King Hezekiah was himself a man of letters, as evidenced in his poem of gratitude to the Lord for his recovery from a near-fatal illness (Isa. 38:9–20).

Some rules for kings are given in Proverbs 25:1 through 7. A series of items follow on privately settling problems with neighbors and other items involving communication. Many are clever, picturesque, and poignant in their uses of similes and metaphors.

26:1–28 As snow in summer, and as rain in harvest, so Honour is not seemly for a fool

A fool (Heb., *ksil*) is one uninformed or uneducable in moral judgment and proper behavior, and a dozen proverbs consider what to do and what not to do with such a person (Prov. 26:1–12). The rest reproach the lazy, the practical joker, the tale-bearer, the deceiver, and the flatterer.

27:1–27 Boast not thyself of to morrow; for thou knowest not what a day may bring forth

As usual, the first verse of Proverbs 27 is a single proverb that does not represent the subject matter of the whole chapter, for it contains a miscellaneous collection of observations and advice. Most of the proverbs are easily understandable, but some, such as verse 10, do need scrutiny. That verse seems to recommend depending upon a nearby friend rather than on a distant relative when calamity strikes. Another verse recommends no empathy for one so foolish as to be surety for a stranger or for a strange woman; and still another proverb about a contentious woman is recorded here (Prov. 27:15 and fn. *a–b*). One proverb compares reflection of a face in water to reflections, heart to heart, between friends. Another uses irony and hyperbole to admonish disciplining the eyes. And one returns to the hopelessness of reforming "foolish" people. At the close are a few observations on the reliability of the prudent life on a farm.

28:1–28 The wicked flee when no man pursueth: but the righteous are bold as a lion

The first verse of Proverbs 28 is a dramatic statement of the worth of a clear conscience. Many other proverbs in this chapter are readily understandable, but several are enigmatic.

Rulers who violate their land and their trust and any who lack understanding are frequently replaced—and there are many of them; but individuals of understanding and knowledge enjoy stability and longevity (Prov. 28:2, 16, 18).

One proverb about ill-gotten wealth being passed on to righteous charities is problematical; it seldom happens (Prov. 28:8).

"To have respect of persons" (Prov. 28:21) is an idiom meaning to treat people unequally for personal reasons; the second clause suggests that one who will do so can be bribed. "An evil eye" is an eye for evil; a "bountiful eye" is an eye for good (Prov. 28:22; cf. 22:9).

29:1–27 He, that being often reproved hardeneth his neck, shall suddenly be destroyed, and that without remedy

Naturally, he who resists correction and never repents will come to destruction in this world or the next; and without repentance, such a person is without forgiveness.

Like the other chapters of this section of the book of Proverbs, there are many topics and quite a number of problem passages in chapter 29. In verse 4, the word *gifts* may be read as *bribes*. The meaning in English of another problem verse is clearer in Hebrew, which can be read, "Men of blood [or violent men] hate the wholesome; and as for the upright [man], they seek his soul" (Prov. 29:10, translation mine). Retranslation may also help in verse 13: "If the poor and the deceitful meet each other, the Lord will enlighten the eyes of both"; in other words, each will discover someone in worse condition than he is himself. The word *servant* may be understood as *slave* in verse 19; the point is that out of resentment, a slave will not respond to verbal correction.

Verses 2 and 18 are two well-known truths that apply to our political and religious life.

Thus ends the second segment of the book of Proverbs, and each of the next two chapters is a section by itself.

30:1–33 The words of Agur the son of Jakeh, even the prophecy

None of the people whose names are given in the title of Proverbs 30 are now known. The *prophecy* of Agur is more literally translated from the Hebrew as *burden,* which means "a message lifted up"; it is not necessarily a revelation from God. The introduction disclaims any worldly wisdom to give answers only God can give but also testifies that God's words are pure truth, a safeguard to them who trust him, and should be accepted unaltered. Note in verse 4 a possible reference to God and his Son, rare in the Old Testament.

In a humble prayer the author asked that he never become vain, that he be neither too poor nor too rich but have proper nourishment, and that he keep a good relationship with the Lord, becoming neither haughty nor desperate and sinful.

Early in the author's teachings are described four classes of undesirable people who are, unfortunately, quite common in any generation, including ours (Prov. 30:11–14). Next are listed four insatiable things, along with the parasite called the horseleach; the point seems to be that some needs and demands in this world are unending (Prov. 30:15–16). The judgment of one who sees with such perversion as to mock his father and despise obedience to his mother will be exploited by moral scavengers, who care as little for their victim as do ravens or young eagles; it is a subtle metaphor (Prov. 30:17). Four marvels of nature may be a humorous commentary on courtship (Prov. 30:18–19).

Then one as insatiable, perverted, and incomprehensible as the nine just illustrated is identified: an adulterer who denies any wickedness.

Next are named four things that are disquieting on the earth.

This is another passage that is humorous but true! (Prov. 30:21–23).

Four little creatures, each with some surprising power or attribute, are described in the next quatrain; doubtless the point is that power is not determined by size (Prov. 30:24–28). In some cases the author used cumulative rhetoric, "three . . . , yea four"; here he applied that figure to the grace in movement and invincibility of a lion, a hound, a ram, and a king (Prov. 30:29–31).

A final curious quatrain has two admonitions—to repent of pride and evil thoughts—and two examples of agitation, with a warning not to raise wrath lest it bring strife (Prov. 30:32–33).

Thus ends the "prophecy" of Agur.

31:1–31 The words of king Lemuel, the prophecy that his mother taught him

Proverbs 31 is the fifth and last section of the book of Proverbs. Neither its author nor his mother is known in scripture. The Hebrew word rendered *prophecy* here is the same as in the foregoing chapter.

In the first part of Proverbs 31, Lemuel's mother rhetorically asked three times what she should advise her son and then proceeded to warn against harlotry, intoxication, and injustice for the "dumb" (those who cannot speak in their own defense) as well as the poor and needy (Prov. 31:2–9).

One of the best-known passages in all of the book of Proverbs is this mother's description of desirable virtues and capabilities of a good wife. Indeed, it appears in the course of the list that there would be little left for the husband and father to do. In any case, this passage commends the capabilities and energies of an intelligent, caring, and reverent woman and to urge that they be recognized. The Hebrew word rendered *virtuous* here is *khayil,* "to be firm, strong, efficient" (Prov. 31:10).

Few of the activities listed are part of a homemaker's work in developed countries today, but they may be taken as representing the creative and administrative work women do. Indeed, they typify many cultures in which most of the food production, preparation, and serving is done by women while bearing and rearing the young, for whom they must also provide clothing and shelter.

So ends this collection of wisdom literature called Proverbs. Its contents include some prophetic and inspiring teachings and many rules and admonitions that if followed can engender a good life.

ECCLESIASTES

The book of Ecclesiastes is a report of a man's lifelong search for something enduring in this world "under the sun," where most things seemed to him transitory, evanescent, and ephemeral. One may be inclined to agree with some of his observations about what is "in vain" and what has lasting value; but it is evident that he lacked knowledge of the divine plan of redemption and eternal life and erred sometimes as a result.

The first two chapters introduce "the Preacher" and his problem; they report his observations on what he found transient and what of enduring worth. Then he declared that though there is a time for everything, many things are done out of time and place, and much injustice exists. The report continues in the same vein, after a few proverb-like admonitions, reporting some common frustrations and inequities of life. A short section discusses wisdom and a certain grace engendered thereby. The last chapters present the author's parting advice to the young, with his surprise summation of "the whole duty of man" and his solid conclusion about the ultimate justice of God.

There are many analyses and interpretations of Ecclesiastes, but one might as well study it out for oneself, checking the cross-references to related scriptures, and seeking the Spirit to perceive the truth and applicability of its teachings (BD, "Ecclesiastes").

COMMENTARY

1:1 The words of the Preacher, the son of David, king in Jerusalem

Preacher is used to translate *koheleth*, whose root *kahal* means "to gather, convoke, or call together." *Ecclesiastes* is a Greek word meaning "assemblyman." Why the author of these lifetime experiments so identified himself is not known. Neither is it known whether the author really was Solomon, or whether he merely chose and discussed experiences and values typical in a life like that of Solomon. Perhaps who he was does not matter, for he can represent a person of any era; he lived in our world, and for the worldly, much is still the same today as it was then.

1:2–11 all is vanity. What profit hath a man of all his labour which he taketh under the sun?

The word *vanity* means, essentially, "emptiness, uselessness, transitoriness" (Eccl. 1:2*b*); it translates a Hebrew word *hevel,* which means "a mere breath, a puff, a whiff, that which is here and gone." It is used in that sense in other scripture (Job 7:16; Prov. 13:11; 21:6; Ps. 39:6). It appears many times in Ecclesiastes.

In his opening statement, the Preacher observed that many things and processes tend to be transient but repetitive in this mortal world, the world "under the sun" (Eccl. 1:9).

1:12–18 I gave my heart to seek and search out by wisdom concerning all things that are done under heaven

Further introducing himself and his findings are his initial evaluations, made according to his "wisdom." His most gloomy views are not mere "pessimism"; he was apparently trying to be realistic while observing the whole spectrum of human activity, but his observations were mostly frustrating to himself (Eccl. 1:13*b*, 14*b*).

2:1–11 I said in mine heart, Go to now, I will prove thee with mirth, therefore enjoy pleasure

Next the Preacher reported his adventures in seeking satisfaction from wealth, beauty, and sensuality; but these too were temporary. He was looking for lasting values, things that would endure (Eccl. 2:18).

2:12–23 And I turned myself to behold wisdom, and madness, and folly

Among such abstractions as wisdom, madness, and folly, he found some were superior to others; but at that point he had to ask what remains after the death of either the fool or the wise. He decided that neither wisdom nor wealth would be of any ultimate worth to a mortal person. Here his lack of information about life after death and the perpetuation of knowledge and wisdom, and the fruits thereof, is evident. It is evident again later that the author, in his early life, was speaking only about values in the mortal world; he perceived simply that there is not any perpetuation of these intangibles in the grave—in the dead body. Later he realized that there are eternal values (Eccl. 9:10; 12:7, 13–14).

2:24–26 There is nothing better for a man, than that he should eat and drink, and that he should . . . enjoy good in his labour. This also I saw, that it was from the hand of God

The Preacher could at this point report one positive finding: one who labors can eat and drink and have enjoyment from his toil; and if he pleases God, God will give him wisdom, knowledge, and joy. On the other hand, the sinner works and accumulates wealth but with no satisfaction, for he leaves his material gains to people who survive. That, as he said, is as useless as "feeding on wind" (Eccl. 2:26; cf. 1:14*b*).

3:1–8 To every thing there is a season, and a time to every purpose under the heaven

It is not certain whether the Preacher's concept of "a time to every purpose under heaven" implies a fixed, determined, set time, as if predestined, or a proper and propitious time or season based on cause-and-effect sequences in nature. His idea that there is a time or season for everything may have been derived from his observations of the cyclical alternation in birth and death, hurting and healing, building up and breaking down, laughing and weeping (Eccl. 1:2–10; cf. 2 Ne. 2:11). The opposites are indeed there so that we may learn to discern between good and evil and choose intelligently. It would be a gross distortion to think that God created some as villains to perpetrate killing, hatred, or warfare; such deeds are done by people who, for their own reasons, choose to do them.

3:9–15 What profit hath he that worketh in that wherein he laboureth?

The Preacher's concept of the reward of work is largely positive. The translation of one item distorts the answers to questions he asked, and a plainer rendition is possible (Eccl. 3:9–11*b*). The Hebrew word *ha'olam* is better translated by the phrase "the eternal," as it is elsewhere in the Old Testament, or by the phrase "for ever," as it is in Ecclesiastes 3:14. Only in Mishnaic and modern Hebrew has a connotation of "the world" been attributed to *ha'olam*. Furthermore, the phrase "so that" should be rendered "without which" (Eccl. 3:11*b*).

The Preacher, in the course of his observations and meditations, had realized that there is much beauty in life that humankind can appreciate only by the spark of the eternal within, which inspires the heart of mortals. His positive identification of something worthwhile in the joy of work, nourishment, and rest reiterates what he had begun to see before. That view was enhanced by perceiving it as God's gift; for what God does "shall be for ever," and He is concerned about what man does (Eccl. 3:12–15; cf. 2:24).

3:16–22 moreover I saw under the sun the place of judgment

The Preacher observed that in this world "under the sun" there is much miscarriage of justice and also that where there should be righteousness is much iniquity. But he knew that God will bring all to His judgment. The things of this world will end in death for beast and mankind, because all bodies must return to the dust. Concerning their respective spirits, he simply asked, "Who knows whether the spirit of man goes upward and the spirit of the beast downward?" (Eccl. 3:18–21, translation mine). At this point in his life's study, the Preacher did not know much about life after death. Recall that in the Book of Mormon, Alma did not learn about "the state of the soul between death and the resurrection" from either the plates of brass or other past revelations; he learned of it through prayer to God and a direct answer through an angel (Alma 40:9–14).

4:1–7 So I returned, and considered all the oppressions

The oppressed "had no comforter"; workers were envied for their gain; and the "fool" who did no work hastened his own death by failing to provide. All of this was so frustrating that the Preacher observed that the dead are probably better off than the living—and the unborn better off still (Eccl. 4:3; cf. Job 3:11–13; 10:18–19). He was back to his original feeling that everything in mortality is in vain.

4:8–12 There is one alone . . . Two are better than one

One alone, with no child or brother, was seen to labor in vain, and that appeared to be "sore travail" (Eccl. 4:8 and fn.b). But two working together, sustaining and helping each other and keeping each other warm, was more tolerable.

4:13–16 Better is the poor and wise child than an old and foolish king, who will no more be admonished

A poor child, wise enough to be admonished still, has more potential than a king who is old and unteachable; for even if the poor be put in prison, he may be wise enough to be admonished and eventually rise up to reign. But the "old and foolish king, who will no more be admonished," may well lose his hereditary throne. That there is such instability generation after generation was still to the Preacher a "vexation of spirit" (Eccl. 4:15–16; cf. 1:14).

5:1–8 Keep thy foot when thou goest to the house of God, and be more ready to hear

On a more positive note, the Preacher still felt that reverence

for God and keeping covenants was better (and safer) than unfaithfulness, lest God be angry. He perceived that though leaders
of a province oppress the poor and pervert judgment and justice,
there is a higher judge. He implied that God is aware, and either
some higher earthly judges or God himself will restore justice.

*5:9–17 the profit of the earth is for all: the king himself is served by
the field*

The statement about resources introduces a section of
proverbs and axioms concerning silver, goods, abundance, and
riches; but all of them are lost at death: "naked shall he return to
go as he came." This also was frustrating, because all that a man
suffered counted for nothing.

*5:18–20 it is good and comely for one to eat and to drink, and to
enjoy the good of all his labour*

Again the Preacher concluded that to enjoy the fruits of honest
labor, with peaceful sleep thereafter, is "the gift of God." By
means of it "God answereth him in the joy of his heart" (Eccl.
5:19–20; cf 2:10, 24; 3:22).

*6:1–12 If a man beget an hundred children, and live many years,
. . . and his soul be not filled with good, . . . I say, that an untimely
birth is better*

The Preacher was convinced that it was not what a man's life
produced or his progeny that counted but the filling of his soul
with good; but he was not yet ready to identify what is really
good or what will remain after death.

*7:1–10 A good name is better than precious ointment; and the day
of death than the day of one's birth*

This strange couplet, containing a moral truth and a pessimistic assumption, is the first of another set of proverbs and
maxims. They commend soberness and even sorrow over laughter, rebuke by the wise, the end rather than the beginning,

patience over anger, and a warning against the common assumption that "the former days were better."

7:11–22 Wisdom is good with an inheritance: and by it there is profit to them that see the sun

Starting off with two aphorisms in appreciation of wisdom, this segment presents a variety of other admonishments and observations. What God has made can't be changed, so one should enjoy days of prosperity before the inevitable days of adversity, for no one knows what the future will bring. Like Job, the Preacher perceived that the righteous sometimes suffer while the wicked prosper, but he recommended a middle course, to be neither too righteous nor too wise, nor yet overly wicked or foolish (Eccl. 7:15–17).

All in all, said the Preacher, fear God and use wisdom; no one on earth is completely just, doing good and sinning not. And do not listen to everything lest you hear something said against you—remember what you have said at times against others (Eccl. 7:18–22).

7:23–29 All this have I proved by wisdom: I said, I will be wise; but it was far from me

With a review of his life's quest and a tentative report of partial failure, the Preacher observed with discouragement a woman's seductiveness and the victims of it (though he that pleases God could escape). He concluded that only one man in a thousand could he commend for righteousness, and no women. His gloomy conclusion was that God had made man upright, but man's many "inventions" had spoiled God's intent.

8:1–17 I counsel thee to keep the king's commandment, and that in regard of the oath of God

Again, the Preacher commended reverence and obedience. His admonitions are good regarding retaining the presence of God and avoiding evil. He warned that no man has power to retain his spirit or the power to stave off death; and though the sinner does evil and thinks he will get by, the Preacher was still confident that the future would deal better with the reverent before God than with the wicked and irreverent, despite common injustices in this world. So once again he commended living happily, enjoying the fruits of labor that God has given, though even a wise man cannot understand with his mortal mind all the works of God (Eccl. 8:17a–b).

9:1–18 For all this I considered in my heart even to declare all this, that the righteous, and the wise, and their works, are in the hand of God

So, the Preacher still knew of much injustice "under the sun" and nothing of justice, reward, punishment, or any further work, in or after death. Yet he felt that a humble living person could do more than an heroic dead one, a change from his previous view (Eccl. 9:4; cf. 4:2). Hence he again recommended enjoying life's everyday rewards of labor and the joys of love at home; he also recognized some value in keeping clean and well groomed (Eccl. 9:7–10). He was still frustrated when the swift did not win the race nor the strong win the battle, and he observed that men may be caught by snares like fish or birds. Furthermore, though a poor but wise man save a city, yet no one will remember him; still, it seemed that wisdom is better than might and the weapons of war (Eccl. 9:11–18).

10:1–20 Dead flies cause the ointment of the apothecary to send forth a stinking savour: so doth a little folly him that is in reputation for wisdom and honour

Knowing that an apothecary was a perfumer (Eccl. 10:1a) helps make this simile meaningful; the little dead flies and the little folly are parallels, and so are their devastating effects.

The Preacher felt that a wise man's "heart" (the seat of understanding) is at his right hand (ready for use), whereas the foolish man's capacity for understanding is not readily available ("at his left").

A few more proverbs are provided on wisdom versus folly, resisting foolish but imperious rulers, mischievous and malicious deeds, the woe of childish and self-indulgent rulers and the danger of voicing any complaint about them, the dangers of sloth, and, perhaps ironically, the power of money. A kind of negative Golden Rule concludes the chapter.

11:1–10 Cast thy bread upon the waters: for thou shalt find it after many days

Even though the recipient of your charity be unknown to you, be generous in giving—"to seven, and also to eight" (Eccl. 11:2) means going beyond the norm—and be hopeful that someone will be charitable to you in future, unforeseen times of need. Perhaps his observation that when clouds form it rains and where a tree falls it lies is a kind of persuasion to live in charitable ways, suggesting that certain laws of cause and effect are constant.

He warns about being too cautious or hesitant (Eccl. 11:4).

He left a masterpiece about the miracle of birth as an illustration of God's inscrutable good works around and within us (Eccl. 11:5).

A few more proverbs are offered on industriousness, accepting joys of the light but enduring the days of darkness—knowing that all things here are transitory—enjoying life in youth, and not harboring sorrows, keeping in mind both that youth is transitory ("vanity") and that there is immanent and imminent judgment with accountability to God (Eccl. 11:6–10).

12:1–14 Remember now thy Creator in the days of thy youth

A bit of poetry continues the counsel to youth to be cognizant of the divine source of all good while enjoyment is still possible—while the "light" of opportunity is not yet darkened and physical and emotional capacities not yet impaired—long before the "silver cord" of divine sustenance be loosed and the "golden bowl," "pitcher," and "wheel" of corporeal, mortal capacities (for perception, conception, and action) be broken (Eccl. 12:1–6).

The surprise in this last chapter is this: at this point in his lifelong quest for what endures, it was revealed to the Preacher that the "spirit" lives on and does return to God when the mortal body returns to its constituent "dust" (Eccl. 12:7). A survey of his lifelong observations of transitoriness in mortal life equipped him to make his knowledge and advice available to others in suitable words (Eccl. 12:8–10). Wise words can become "goads" to urge people on and "nails" to secure certain truths, "which are given from one shepherd" (the Lord, no doubt). So the young are urged to study, though there be no end of books and much study be "weariness of the flesh" (Eccl. 12:11–12).

Then, to his primary revelation that life endures in the spirit, was added the concluding revelation to the Preacher: work in the body is not all vanity; the works of everyone shall be brought to judgment and identified as good or evil; therefore the Preacher's final admonition to his son was a basic principle: "Fear God, and keep his commandments," for they are a complete guide for every one for good living (Eccl. 12:13–14).

For some students of Ecclesiastes, "the conclusion of the whole matter" is not logically a conclusion the Preacher could have reached from the experiences reported, given his pessimistic attitude about life. That view is not necessarily so, as may be seen by a review the Preacher's positive observations and admonitions. They tell of the value of wisdom over foolishness, of reverence, of doing good, enjoying the fruits of honest labors, God's gifts of wisdom and knowledge, timely industriousness, divine inspiration, the beauty of God's creations and the eternity thereof, the dependability of God's justice, proper worship (including sacrifice), fidelity, man's filling his soul with good, soberness, restraint, patience, the dependability of God's rewards, the potentials for good in life, cleanliness and good grooming, enjoyment of good home life, righteousness in government, generosity in giving to the needy, appreciation for God's creative hand in the miracles of procreation, light versus darkness, the joys of youth, and the opportunities to partake of them (Eccl. 2:13, 24, 26; 3:2, 11–14, 17; 5:1–7, 18; 6:3; 7:1–11; 8:2, 12; 9:4, 8–9; 10:16–17; 11:1–10; 12:1–7). Is that not adequate evidence of the Preacher's faith in God, appreciation of His ways, and conviction that good in life is possible through Him?

Probably anyone who has experienced lifelong progress in developing an understanding of the virtues of life, or anyone who has seen the miracle of conversion, can also perceive realism in the Preacher's report of his lifetime of searching. Thus, in spite of his early errors and insufficient information, it is possible for the reader to appreciate his progress and commend the consistency of his final conclusions.

SONG OF SOLOMON

The "song of songs" is composed as a poetic chronicle of love. It is good that among all the writings of "the people of the book" who wrote volumes on the laws of God, religious history, wisdom literature, and prophecy, this one small opus on love was preserved. Romantic love is a vital facet of life.

Like many other Hebrew writings, the Song of Solomon has been seen as symbolic, suggesting other truths of earth and eternity by the events it relates; probably that is why it has been preserved throughout the ages in both Jewish and Christian scriptures. But it is also worthwhile to enjoy its beauty as romantic literature, complementary to the other great types of the literature of Israel.

Although in the English translation this book is known as the Song of Solomon, its Hebrew title, *Shir ha-Shirim,* means "Song of Songs." That phrase, idiomatically, can mean "the best of songs." Tradition holds that King Solomon wrote this book in his youth, the Proverbs in his prime, and Ecclesiastes in his old age. It may be so; in any case, his is a character and a type in this romantic "triangle."

This book has been identified as "not inspired writings" in the usual scriptural sense (BD, "Song of Solomon"). That identification negates a role for it as inspired symbolism representing the love of the Lord for Israel, or for the Church, but it does not negate or depreciate its value as romantic prose and poetry from a very literate people. As such it has long been popular with Jewish people, rating high, along with the books of Esther and the Psalms, for festive occasions.

The narrative content has been variously dissected into dialogues between a maiden or bride with other maidens and dialogues with a lover. There are monologues addressed to other shepherds, and conversations between the lovers as bride and bridegroom. A few suggestions are provided in this commentary to help the reader discover the participants in the dialogues; but any reader may make different analyses or syntheses of these dramatic situations.

COMMENTARY

1:1– 4 the king hath brought me into his chambers

The young woman, who has been taken to be one of the king's maidens, yearns for her shepherd lover.

1:5– 6 I am black, but comely, O ye daughters of Jerusalem

She apologetically explains to the other maidens her darkly suntanned skin but does not feel she is unattractive. *Black* can mean "dark colored" in Hebrew, just as *white* can mean "light colored" (Song. 5:10; Lam. 4:7; John 4:35).

1:7– 8 Tell me, O thou whom my soul loveth, . . . where thou makest thy flock to rest

She yearns to know where her true lover and his flocks may be, speaking as if he were somewhere within range of her voice. The other young women suggest she track them down.

1:9–17 I have compared thee, O my love

Either she has escaped and found him or remembers and relates a former rendezvous on a bed of green amongst the cedars and fir trees, and contrasts it with the stilted situation of the king at his table (Song. 1:12).

2:1–17 I am the rose of Sharon. . . . As the apple tree . . . so is my beloved among the sons

She continues to describe their idyllic tryst to the "daughters of Jerusalem," relating in poetic lines his words when he came to get her. Note the beauty of the description of spring's approach (Song. 2:10–13). They hope that they will be secure and that nothing will destroy their happiness (Song. 2:14–17).

3:1–5 I sought him

She tells of having wished for her lover, seeking for him in the city and out, and having found him eventually to take him to her mother's house, perhaps in preparation for their marriage.

3:6–11 Who is this that cometh out of the wilderness

This passage may be either her memory of the arrival of King Solomon, who took her "into his chambers" (Song. 1:4), or her sublimation of the arrival of her true lover for the wedding.

4:1–5:1 Behold, thou art fair, my love

The bridegroom tells her how he sees her beauty and urges her to go with him from the high and remote places, perhaps symbolic of her former inaccessibility (Song. 4:8). He addresses her with all tenderness and affection, using metaphors from nature to describe his feelings for her. She invites him, and he responds (Song. 4:16; 5:1).

5:2–6:3 I sleep, but my heart waketh

She relates either a dream or her memory of her former yearning and searching for her lover. The events are dreamlike in her frustrations, her questions, and the maidens' responses (Song. 5:4–7, 8–9; and 6:1–2). But after all she knows that she and her love belong to each other (Song. 6:2–3).

6:4–10 Thou art beautiful, O my love

Again her lover praises her wondrous beauty.

Note in Song of Solomon 6:6 and 10 the descriptive words "fair as the moon . . . " They are used three times in that form or with little variation in the Doctrine and Covenants to describe the newly organized Church in the latter days (D&C 5:14; 105:31; 109:73).

6:11–7:13 I went down into the garden . . . Return, return, O Shulamite

The young woman has gone to the garden to look for fruits and flowers, and before she is aware, she is again beset with invitations and praises from her intended bridegroom. She responds with invitations and promises of love (Song. 7:10–13).

8:1– 4 O that thou wert as my brother . . . I would lead thee, and bring thee into my mother's house, who would instruct me

She wishes to marry her lover, that their love might be without reproach and without interruption.

8:5– 7 Set me as a seal upon thine heart, as a seal upon thine arm: for love is strong as death

As the couple walk back from the orchards and woods, they are observed by the villagers, and as they pass scenes of her birth (Song. 8:5), she vows that she desires everlasting covenants with him (Song. 8:6–7). The Hebrew indicates by the gender of the pronouns whether a male or female is addressed.

8:8–12 We have a little sister . . . what shall we do for our sister in the day when she shall be spoken for?

The bride recalls how in her childhood her brothers were protective of her, and with satisfaction she states that in her maturity she has kept chaste (Song. 8:8–10); King Solomon's rich vineyards and his thousand (wives?) were no match for her pastoral garden home: "My vineyard, which is mine, is before me" (Song. 8:12; regarding Solomon's thousand wives, 1 Kgs. 11:3).

8:13–14 Thou that dwellest in the gardens, the companions hearken to thy voice: cause me to hear it

Her true love calls to her in her vineyard and gardens and she responds, urging him to hasten to her.

So ends this sometimes enigmatic romance. It expresses things felt universally enough that many are intrigued with it, but no one is quite sure how to interpret all of it. Those who have made of it a type of the love of the Lord for his people (Jewish or Christian) also have difficulty in interpreting all its scenes and activities. The chapter headnotes and running heads in older printings of the Bible indicate some such interpretations.

ISAIAH

In the treasury of Hebrew writings is a wide variety of prophetic teachings with great moral and spiritual value. Isaiah's contributions are high among them, for they were valid for his times, for our times, and for the future. The book of Isaiah contains reprimands for evil, appeals for repentance, promises of forgiveness for those who do repent, and warnings to those who do not. In Hebrew, about three-fourths of the book is in poetic form.

Isaiah prophesied about the virgin mother and birth of the Savior, about his suffering for all and his making redemption available to all, and about his future reign of peace. Isaiah's prophecies emphasize the duty of Israel and of all true believers to prepare for Christ's reign and foretell the grandeur and glory of it. The Savior himself said: "Great are the words of Isaiah. For surely he spake as touching all things concerning my people" (3 Ne. 23:1–2).

Isaiah wrote also some historical chronicles of his times (2 Chr. 26:22) and, so far as we know, recorded his own prophetic revelations. The revelations are arranged somewhat according to subject, as follows:

Chapters 1 through 12 pertain mostly to Isaiah's times and nation; however, he often extended his scope from the immediate to the intermediate and then on to ultimate matters. This integration of past, present, and future is typical of the "manner of prophesying among the Jews" of which Nephi spoke; he said it was hard for his people to understand—and it may be harder still for us (2 Ne. 25:1). The center position in these chapters, Isaiah 6, is the report of Isaiah's call to be a prophet, which was extended to him in a vision of the Lord.

Chapters 13 through 23 are prophetic "burdens," or warnings, mostly to nations that affected Israel. Some are addressed to Israel and Judah. Much significant doctrine is found even in the prophecies to other nations.

Chapters 24 through 35 contain prophecies that are mostly concerned with the latter days.

Chapters 36 through 39 are historical, showing the prophet at work in his times (cf. 2 Kgs. 18–20). These chapters may be part of the chronicles he wrote (2 Chr. 26:22).

Chapters 40 through 49 are mostly concerned with the redemption of Israel and others through the ministry of the Lord as Savior.

Chapters 50 through 59 contrast the wickedness and fall of Israel with the suffering of the Redeemer and his comforting good tidings of salvation for all mankind.

Chapters 60 through 66 tell of the future glory of Zion, the new heaven and the new earth, after the destruction of wickedness.

Abundant cross-references and other helpful information may be found in the footnotes to the book of Isaiah.

COMMENTARY

1:1– 4 The vision of Isaiah . . . concerning Judah and Jerusalem . . . I have nourished and brought up children, and they have rebelled against me

Visions were frequently the source of Isaiah's information.

Though the information here was addressed primarily to "Judah and Jerusalem," Isaiah invited the attention of all who would hearken in heaven and earth. That is typical, for messages arising out of immediate situations often have future applications.

The "children" who had "gone away backward" were Israelites; they were the people chosen to teach the true religion to others but who learned and practiced others' idolatry instead.

1:5–9 Why should ye be stricken any more? ye will revolt more and more

The prophet described Israel as a body wounded, unsound from head to foot and sick at heart. The healing messages of the Lord had not been taken to heart and consistently applied.

Evidently the military attacks by Assyria were those that Isaiah predicted here (Isa. 1:7–9 and fn.; for historical details on the attacks, see Isa. 36–37; 2 Kgs. 17–20).

1:10–20 Hear the word of the Lord, ye rulers of Sodom; give ear unto the law of our God, ye people of Gomorrah

Isaiah called the leaders of Israel "rulers of Sodom" and their followers "people of Gomorrah," thus characterizing their sensual practices, false worship, and violence. The remedy would be cleansing by repentance. The promises of forgiveness and blessings were amazingly generous; the warnings were clear and vigorous about the grievous results of choosing the wrong alternatives (Isa. 1:16–18 and fn.; cf. D&C 19:15–20).

1:21–31 How is the faithful city become an harlot!

In poetic verses the prophet lamented Jerusalem's condition and added warnings, promises, and more warnings from the Lord. They are applicable to anyone in any time with similar ills. Note the phrase in Isaiah 1:26 echoed in our hymn, "The Spirit of God" (*Hymns* [Salt Lake City: The Church of Jesus Christ of Latter-day Saints, 1985], no. 2).

2:1 The word that Isaiah the son of Amoz saw

The Hebrew word *davar,* translated here as *word,* can also be translated *message.* The Hebrew word *khazah,* translated here as *saw,* indicates that Isaiah received this message also from the Lord in a vision (cf. Isa. 1:1).

2:2–4 And it shall come to pass in the last days, that the mountain of the Lord's house shall be established in the top of the mountains

This prophecy would be fulfilled when the true religion had

been restored, so that the chosen people could return to the true faith. That done, Abraham's mission would be resumed and peoples from all nations converted. The faithful would gather to the "mountain of the Lord's house" in Zion and to the restored Jerusalem to learn his ways and walk in his paths (Isa. 2:2–3; on two holy cities, Isa. 64:10; D&C 84:1–4; 133:9–13, 21–24; 3 Ne. 21:21–26; Ether 13:4–11; BD, "Zion"; TG, "Jerusalem, New"; "Zion").

The Lord shall rule, judge, and correct his peoples, and peaceful activities shall eliminate war at last.

2:5–22 O house of Jacob, come ye, and let us walk in the light of the Lord

This kindly appeal precedes another reminder of the reasons why the Lord would forsake his people, but that is only when they apostatize and turn to idols for guidance and for pleasure. All who refuse his loving appeal will want to hide themselves and bury their idols when "the day of the Lord" descends upon all the world (Isa. 2:6–21; note in 16*a* incidental evidence that the Book of Mormon had the complete original text from the plates of brass). The final admonition applies to those who refuse his invitation (cf. Isa. 2:22*b*, 5).

3:1–16 For, behold, the Lord, the Lord of hosts, doth take away from Jerusalem and from Judah the stay . . . of bread, and . . . water

In the time of Isaiah, the Lord was about to allow the invading Assyrians to destroy Israel's material security. The northern ten tribes were indeed conquered and taken away in the middle period of Isaiah's ministry (ca. 722 B.C.); however, one king of Judah hearkened to the Lord's warnings through the prophet Isaiah. As a result, though the people of Jerusalem suffered considerably during an Assyrian siege, the city was spared for another century, until it fell to the Babylonians.

When all capable leaders are decimated in a crisis, inept leaders take over; and then such moral and political problems develop that potentially capable people are reluctant to take office. Wicked leaders, who oppress their people and fail to defend them, will be held responsible by the Lord.

3:16– 4:1 the Lord saith, Because the daughters of Zion are haughty, and walk with stretched forth necks and wanton eyes . . . the Lord will smite . . . the daughters of Zion

Some, who are vanity-faddists and wanton women instead of being true "daughters of Zion," will contribute to Zion's downfall and be shamed and rejected. Yet when all vain things are taken away, and their men have fallen by the sword in siege, the surviving women will clamor for the security of marriage.

4:2– 6 In that day shall the branch of the Lord be beautiful and glorious

Then will come the day of the Lord, terrible for the wicked but great for others of the true "branch of the Lord" in the newly established Zion and the newly cleansed Jerusalem. They will be in the presence of the Lord, who will bring peace and security.

5:1– 7 My wellbeloved hath a vineyard in a very fruitful hill

In this parable, Israel is the vineyard of the Lord; abandonment of the vineyard symbolizes the scattering of Israel. Poetic assonance and parallelism of the Hebrew of the last two lines could be imitated in English thus:

> He looked for justice, but behold, jostling;
> for the righteous, but behold, the riotous.

5:8–25 Woe unto them that

In calling Israel to repent, Isaiah warned of the results that would follow various types of self-indulgence and perversion. They include greed, drunkenness, willful ignorance, habitual sin and doubt, perversion, self-righteousness, and corruption. Such modes of life naturally cause oppression, captivity, damnation, unfaithfulness, distorted values, and ultimately, self-destruction.

But though the anger of the Lord is kindled, the hope for the repentance and the return of the sinners is extended: "His hand is stretched out still" (for the meaning of that symbol, see Isa. 9:12; Jacob 5:47; 6:4. Some commentators believe it means his anger continues).

5:26–30 And he will lift up an ensign to the nations

There are many implications in the latter-day lifting of the gospel "ensign" to the nations to gather the righteous into the fold of the Lord. There will be miraculous migrations and divine help for the righteous in the end of times.

6:1–8 In the year that king Uzziah died I saw . . . the Lord

The word *also* was left out of the quotation from Isaiah 6:1, above, because no word requiring that translation appears in the Hebrew account.

Isaiah's vision and call were about 740 B.C., for we know that King Uzziah reigned 790 through 739 B.C. (2 Kgs. 15:1–7; 2 Chr. 26; BD, "Chronology," p. 638). Isaiah experienced the rare privilege of seeing the Lord (TG, "God, Privilege of Seeing"; "Jesus Christ, Appearances, Antemortal"). It was doubtless this visitation to which Nephi referred in his testimony that Isaiah had seen the Lord (2 Ne.11:2).

The *seraphim,* in covering their faces and feet, symbolized reverence (BD, "Seraphim"). Isaiah, conscious of his faults and those of his people, was overwhelmed. The symbolic cleansing by a live coal from the heavenly altar must have relieved Isaiah of guilt feelings, so that when he heard the divine request for a messenger he volunteered to serve. Recall that neither Enoch nor Moses responded so willingly when they were called (Moses 6:31; Ex. 4:10–14.)

6:9–13 And he said, Go, and tell this people, Hear ye indeed, but understand not; and see ye indeed, but perceive not

It was to a hardhearted and reprobate people that Isaiah would preach repentance on his mission (Isa. 6:9–10; Matt. 13:13–16). If Isaiah understood that his appeals for repentance would make the people only more obdurate, his pathetic cry, "Lord, how long?" was natural. The Lord's reply would not have given him much hope for success in his mission, but the people of Israel could not go to their destruction without a chance to repent. On that point, the prophet Amos, who lived a little earlier than Isaiah, pronounced: "Surely the Lord God will do nothing, but he revealeth his secret unto his servants the prophets" (Amos 3:7).

Note the potential for some of the holy seed of true believers to be perpetuated into the last days (Isa. 6:13*a–b*).

7:1–16 in the days of Ahaz the son of Jotham, the son of Uzziah, king of Judah, that Rezin the king of Syria, and Pekah . . . king of Israel, went up toward Jerusalem to war against it

Syria and Israel attacked Jerusalem when the grandson of King Uzziah ruled five or six years after Isaiah's call (BD, "Chronology," p. 638, for King Ahaz of Judah and King Pekah of Israel). The book of Isaiah gives more historical details than do the books of Kings and Chronicles about Syria and Ephraim combining against Assyria and trying to force Judah to join their alliance (Isa. 7:1*b–d*).

It is poignant to visualize the prophet and his little son going outside the walled city to meet the worried King Ahaz at the city's vital water supply (Isa. 7:3*a–c*). The prophet went to give the king some assurances and warnings; but the king would not believe that Syria and Ephraim (northern Israel) would be "broken." Ironically, King Ahaz, who was not known for faith or fidelity, piously refused the prophet's offer of a token, or symbol, to assure him that the prophet's message was truly from the Lord.

It was in that setting that the prophecy of the virgin birth of Immanuel was given by Isaiah (Isa. 7:14*a–e*). Doubtless the prophecy had little meaning or comfort for Ahaz, but for more than seven centuries it gave myriads of others comfort and hope, awaiting the day of Immanuel's first advent (related prophecies follow in Isa. 8–9).

7:17–25 The Lord shall bring upon thee, and upon thy people . . . the king of Assyria

Judah was at that time a bone of contention between the big power of the north and east (Assyria) and that of the south and west (Egypt). Of those, Assyria would give Judah the close shave as a "razor that is hired" (Isa. 7:20). The Lord did in fact let Assyria be the "rod of [his] anger" (Isa. 10). Isaiah foresaw that as a result of Assyria's scourge, Israel would become a land whose cities and economy were destroyed by war and plunder, so that only a few country folk could survive, too few to cultivate the vineyards and combat the weeds (see fn. for alternate translations).

8:1–4 she conceived, and bare a son. Then said the Lord to me, Call his name Maher-shalal-hash-baz

Isaiah had told King Ahaz that the threat from Syria and Ephraim (Israel) would pass and the child Immanuel would be born in Judah as part of the country's future destiny (Isa. 7:14–16). Then the promise of relief from attack was made more immediate by the Lord's assurance that before a son yet to be born to Isaiah and his wife could learn to say *avi* (daddy) and *immi* (mommy), both Damascus of Syria and Samaria of Israel would be conquered by Assyria. The name of this baby was a token of Assyria's attack on northern Israel (Isa. 8:1*d*).

8:5–18 Forasmuch as this people refuseth the waters of Shiloah . . . behold, the Lord bringeth up upon them the waters of the river, . . . even the king of Assyria

The "waters of Shiloah" had long been Jerusalem's water supply (2 Sam. 5:8 and commentary). Water flowed to Shiloah from the spring Gihon, which represented the Lord's providence, whereas the "waters of the river," the Euphrates, represented the forces of Assyria. King Ahaz did not follow the prophet's advice, so Judah was invaded and Jerusalem besieged. It was not conquered, however, thanks to the stronger faith and better behavior of the next king, Hezekiah, son of Ahaz. Jerusalem was saved by the Lord, as promised by the "stretching out of his wings" over the land of *Immanuel*. Nevertheless, the country was almost overwhelmed by Assyrian forces, reaching nearly to "the neck" (Isa. 8:8, 10; Isa. 36–37).

Because the Lord would save Judah, the prophet advised against a confederacy with other nations for security; the king and people should make the Lord their "sanctuary." Isaiah knew, however, that the Lord as Savior in those times, as also later during the Lord's life on earth, would be "a stone of stumbling," upon whom many unbelievers would "stumble, and fall, and be broken, and be snared, and be taken" (Isa. 8:14–15).

Neither the king nor the people would accept the testimony given to the Lord's disciples, nor would they understand the "signs" and wonders provided through Isaiah. The names of Isaiah and his sons symbolize the scattering and gathering of Israel and the salvation of the Lord (Isa. 8:18*a*).

8:19–22 And when they shall say unto you, Seek unto them that have familiar spirits, . . . should not a people seek unto their God?

The main point of this passage is that turning to any sort of spiritualism, such as turning to the dead on behalf of the living, is forbidden. People of faith should turn "to the law and to the testimony," which are the scriptures. If other sources do not agree, "it is because there is no light in them."

They of Israel who had ceased to seek the true God were about to pass into the bondage their king had led them to. Trouble, darkness, and the dimness of anguish lay ahead.

9:1–7 in Galilee of the nations. The people that walked in darkness have seen a great light . . . For unto us a child is born

The "dimness of anguish" and the "darkness" of exile and oppression (Isa. 8:22) are again mentioned, merging prophecies of affliction in exile with prophecies of later oppressions to come to northern Israelite lands, including Galilee. There the afflicted people would begin to see the "great light" of the life and teaching of the Messiah. If they could accept him and his way fully, then the yoke, burden, staff, and rod of oppression could be broken. All the paraphernalia of battle will eventually be done away by the cleansing fire of his kingdom (Isa. 9:5*a–b*).

Although the Child was not accepted in his first advent with all his potentials to heal, to save, and to rule, the increase of his government and the extension of his peace would continue to go forward by the zeal of the Lord of hosts until in his second advent all will be fulfilled (Isa. 9:1–7 and fn.).

9:8–10:4 The Lord sent a word into Jacob, and it hath lighted upon Israel. And all the people shall know, even Ephraim and the in-habitant of Samaria

Events that befell northern Israel (2 Kgs. 17) during the life and ministry of Isaiah were reviewed by the prophet. He knew that if the people of the northern kingdom—sometimes called by the name of the birthright tribe, Ephraim—had at any time hearkened and repented, the Lord's hand was "stretched out still" to help them (cf. Isa. 5:25 and commentary; Isa. 5:17, 21; 9:12*d;* 10:4; Jacob 6:4).

10:5–19 O Assyrian, the rod of mine anger . . . I will send him against an hypocritical nation

As anticipated in Isaiah 7:17–25, Isaiah explained why the Lord let Assyria be his tool, withdrawing his hand of protection from Israel and letting Assyria take the people of that kingdom. Isaiah also predicted that the Assyrians would suffer the effects of their own wickedness and corruption and fall prey to another powerful nation—a prophecy that was fulfilled a century later.

10:20–23 The remnant shall return . . . unto the mighty God

Prophecies of the ancient scattering of Israel are often accompanied by prophecies of their later return to the true God and then to the heritage foretold for true Israel (Isa. 10:20–23 and fn.).

10:24–34 O my people that dwellest in Zion, be not afraid of the Assyrian . . . For yet a very little while, and the indignation shall cease, and mine anger in their destruction

The son and heir of King Ahaz was the good King Hezekiah.

He accepted Isaiah's prophetic guidance, and most of Judah was saved from Assyria's siege (Kgs. 18–20; Isa. 36–38).

The approach of the Assyrians toward Jerusalem is sketched in dramatic poetry (Isa. 10:28–32). Then the destruction of the Assyrian hordes is described in metaphors (Isa. 10:33–34).

11:1–9 And there shall come forth a rod out of the stem of Jesse, and a Branch shall grow out of his roots

Because Jesse was the father of King David and his descendants were the kings of Judah, of whose lineage Jesus would be born, it is clear who this "Branch" is. Jesus *is* the Lord, Jehovah; hence the wisdom, understanding, counsel, might, knowledge, and reverence of the Lord reside in him. Jeremiah and other prophets also knew this "Branch" (cf. Jer. 23:5 and fn.). Matthew saw the residence of Jesus in Nazareth as symbolic, for *Nazareth* is derived from the Hebrew word meaning "branch" (Matt. 2:23). Modern revelation also confirms that Jesus was the one anticipated (Isa. 11:1–5; D&C 113:1–2). His righteous reign on earth, bringing justice and peace to man and beast, will be established in his second coming (Isa. 11:4–9; TG, "Jesus Christ, Millennial Reign").

11:10–16 the Lord shall set his hand again the second time to recover the remnant of his people

When the "Gentiles" see the gospel ensign and realize the nature of the Lord's kingdom, they will desire to be a part of it (Isa. 11:10). And when the Lord does restore priesthood power and set his hand again to gather Israel, there will be a reconciliation between Judah and Ephraim. Great movements of people and land masses will prepare the world for His reign (Isa. 11:10–16 and fn.).

12:1–6 Behold, God is my salvation; I will trust, and not be afraid; for the Lord Jehovah is my strength and my song; he also is become my salvation

This poetic song of praise and thanksgiving is to the Lord, the author of our salvation (Isa. 12:2a; cf. Ex. 15:2; Ps. 118:14).

The "water out of the wells of salvation" is a symbol also used in Jeremiah 2:13 and John 4:7–14. It is life-giving "water" of new birth unto salvation and atonement.

It would be a privilege to be among the choirs singing praises to the Lord in that day of salvation.

13:1–22 The burden of Babylon, which Isaiah the son of Amoz did see

Burden is used several times in Isaiah's prophetic addresses to several of Israel's neighboring nations and to Jerusalem itself in the next dozen chapters. It is used to translate the Hebrew *massa,* meaning "something lifted up" against the wicked, with a call for their repentance. While addressed to nations known in history, the messages have symbolic meanings also for peoples having like faults in later times.

This burden is addressed to Babylon, an ancient nation thriving first in patriarchal times but arising again after Isaiah's time (BD, "Chronology"; "Assyria and Babylonia"; "Babylon or Babel"; TG, "Babylon"). Isaiah's warning to King Hezekiah about Babylon as a future threat to Judah is recorded later (Isa. 39). Details of what Babylon eventually did to Judah are found in several places (2 Kgs. 24–25; and in the books of Jeremiah, Ezekiel, Daniel, and Habakkuk).

The first part of Isaiah's prophecy applies more to the destruction of the latter-day "Babylon," or the wicked world (Isa. 13:1–15 and fn.). The ancient nation of Babylon is more specifically and clearly addressed in the remaining verses. The suffering of children and women is not to be seen as the will of the Lord but is foreseen as part of the blood and horror of worldly strife. The Medes and Persians fulfilled this prophecy (ca. 539–538 B.C.).

14:1–3 For the Lord will have mercy on Jacob, and will yet choose Israel, and set them in their own land: and the strangers shall be joined with them

The prophecy of the gathering of Israel and the conversion of other peoples is resumed (cf. Isa. 11:10–16). Words about making some peoples "servants" and "captives" and establishing "rule" over them may be understood in a spiritual sense (Isa. 14:1–3 and fn.).

14:4–23 thou shalt take up this proverb against the king of Babylon, and say, How hath the oppressor ceased!

A dramatic description prophesied the Babylonian king's demise (Isa. 14:4–11). Then he was addressed metaphorically as if he were a paradigm of "Lucifer, son of the morning," whose origin in the Council in Heaven is depicted (Isa. 14:12–13 and fn.). A taunt-song reflects the joy of earth to be rid of this "king of Babylon" and depicts scorn by his peers in hell (Isa. 14:16–23).

14:24–32 The Lord of hosts hath sworn, saying, . . . I will break the Assyrian in my land . . . Rejoice not thou, whole Palestina

A short message of reassurance during the Assyrian siege begins a reiteration of earlier prophecies, all of which were fulfilled in Isaiah's lifetime (Isa. 14:24–28; 7:17–25; 10:5–19). They also have latter-day applications, however, as does the ensuing one on the doom of the Philistines (Isa. 14:29–32). They anticipate the kingdom of God replacing the nations.

15:1–9; 16:1–14 The burden of Moab

Israel's neighbors, the cousin-peoples east of the Dead Sea, were generally opposed to Israel from the time of Moses on. Nonetheless, Ruth came from Moab, and King David was descended from her and Boaz. The burden against Moab is not a total condemnation; empathy is expressed, with a lament for Moab's destiny (Isa. 15).

Isaiah suggested that Moab appeal to Judah to provide a refuge for the Moabite outcasts, with the merciful and just king on the throne of David (Isa. 16:1–5). But the idea was rejected by Jewish leaders as unwarranted, leaving Moab to mourn. The prophet felt sorry for the Moabites, however, and wrote another poignant lament (Isa. 16:6–14).

17:1–11 The burden of Damascus. . . . The fortress also shall cease from Ephraim

The first two verses of the burden against Damascus predict the Assyrian conquest of Syria, whose capital was Damascus; but

Syria's ally, northern Israel, is the main subject of this burden (Isa. 17:3a). Syria had been thought of as a "fortress" for the protection of Israel, but in vain. Israel would be devastated but not destroyed; a few people would remain, like the few gleaning grapes or olives left after the harvest. And why was Israel to suffer the invasion? Because the Israelites had forgotten the God of their salvation, the rock of their strength (Isa. 17:4–11).

17:12–14 Woe to the multitude of many people . . . and to the rushing of nations

Isaiah promised once again that invading multitudes, who would be permitted to punish Israel, would in time suffer the rebuke of God (Isa. 17:12a).

18:1–7 Woe to the land . . . which is beyond the rivers of Ethiopia: That sendeth ambassadors by the sea

The first word of Isaiah 18 would be better translated *Hail* than *Woe* (v. 1a). Any land "beyond" Ethiopia would be for biblical people a land very far away. The message the prophet sent back with the "ambassadors" seems reassuring. An "ensign" will be hoisted when the time comes for the Lord to take action to decimate the enemy. Thereafter, the people "scattered and peeled" will send a present "to the place of the name of the Lord of hosts, the mount Zion" (Isa. 18:2, 7).

Early Latter-day Saint interpretations applied the imagery of this prophecy to missionaries going from the western hemisphere to the scattered tribes of Israel. The Book of Mormon contains related prophecies that help apply it to that action or to messengers taking the gospel to the latter-day remnant of Lehi's descendants (Isa. 18:7a–b).

Translators have had many difficulties with this short chapter, and their translations differ considerably.

19:1–25 The burden of Egypt

Egypt also was in danger from the Assyrian empire; this burden may warn either of a threat of the same period when Israel

515

and Judah suffered invasion (670–660 B.C.) or of attacks by later empires. Civil strife in Egypt and agricultural and other problems arising from dependence on the annual floods of the Nile were foretold.

The prophecy reaches down to ultimate developments "in that day" when Judah is restored and has become a formidable power, and the language and religion of Israel will be spread into Egypt (Isa. 19:16–22). Miraculously the old enemies will be converted, and Assyria, Israel, and Egypt will be blessed by the Lord (Isa. 19:23–25). That will indeed be the great day of the Lord, when the burden to Egypt has become a major oracle about the Lord's plans for the earth when all peoples shall be governed by him and peace shall reign.

20:1– 6 In the year that Tartan came unto Ashdod, . . . the Lord said, . . . So shall the king of Assyria lead away the Egyptians prisoners, and the Ethiopians captives

This brief prophecy concerning an event that occurred in Isaiah's lifetime adds detail to the burden of Egypt (Isa. 20:1*a–b;* 19:1–15).

When King Sargon of Assyria sent his military leader, Tartan, to take the former Philistine city of Ashdod, Isaiah dressed like a slave for three years to warn Israel that if Egypt and Ethiopia were unable to defend themselves against Assyrian enslavement, they certainly could not help protect Judah (Isa. 20:2*a,* 5*a*). Within ten years Assyria indeed invaded Judah and besieged Jerusalem. Isaiah gave a detailed account later of how King Hezekiah of Judah did indeed depend upon the Lord and not upon "this bruised reed, even upon Egypt" (2 Kgs. 18:21; Isa. 20:6).

21:1–10 The burden of the desert of the sea

Babylon was addressed in this prophecy, though it was given for the benefit of Judah (Isa. 21:1*a*). Two centuries after Isaiah's time, this burden was fulfilled when Babylon was conquered by the Medes and Persians ("Elam") under Cyrus (Isa. 21:2*b*). Its fulfillment was good news for the Jews then in Babylonian captivity, for under the Persian kings they were permitted to return. Isaiah was dismayed at the cataclysm, but when the main message was given that Babylon would fall and her idolatry be destroyed, he addressed the future Jewish exiles with relief and joy (Isa. 21:10*a*).

This prophecy pertains in the latter days to the destruction of the wicked world, also called Babylon (Isa. 21:9*a*).

21:11–12 The burden of Dumah

It is interesting, but not surprising, that messengers from various lands sought out a Jewish prophet concerning their fate in those troublous times.

21:13–17 The burden upon Arabia

Arabian caravans, suffering from such invading empire-building forces as the Assyrians and later the Babylonians, made their way through forests (thickets) rather than along the regular trade routes, and compassionate towns such as Tema "prevented" (came before) them with food and water. Some of those desert towns would also be destroyed by invaders, especially if control of trade routes could be established thereby.

22:1–25 The burden of the valley of vision

Jerusalem is the "valley of vision," the source of these burdens. The largest of the valleys in Jerusalem, the Kidron, is sometimes called "the valley of vision" (Isa. 22:1*a*).

The prophet was distressed by revelry in the city when there were inadequate preparations for siege (Isa. 22:2–10 and fn.). Their preparations for saving water from the important spring in a "ditch" or pool would not be as vital for them as trust in the Lord, the "maker" of the spring (Isa. 22:11*a–b*). Isaiah urged the people to repent of indulgence and neglect. He made an example of a government official, Shebna, who was preparing a sepulchre, warning that he would likely die in exile.

Isaiah made a symbol of Shebna's replacement, Eliakim. His name means "God shall cause to arise," anticipating the Savior, who holds the "key of the house of David" but was fastened "as a nail in a sure place" until the burden of the Atonement was complete. Upon Him rests "all the glory of his father's house." Isaiah recommended depending on Him for everlasting security (Isa. 22:20–25 and fn.).

Gethsemane is in the Kidron valley, that "valley of vision."

23:1–18 The burden of Tyre

Despite their prosperity and power, Tyre and Sidon will also be made desolate for a time. Overconfident because they had never been conquered, they would be overcome and cease to be centers of trade. They were to lie waste for seventy years, about the life span of a man. Ultimately, Tyre's return and prosperity in lasting things would depend, as with all God's children, on consecration to the Lord (Isa. 23:18a).

24:1–23 Behold, the Lord maketh the earth empty, and maketh it waste

At the end, all the wicked world will be affected. Reasons for the end will include haughtiness, transgression, changing of ordinances, and breaking of eternal covenants. Instead of blessings, curses and confusion will prevail. The righteous ones saved will be like the gleaning grapes and olives left when the harvest is over. They will be grateful to be spared and sing praises to God.

The prophet lamented, as he occasionally did in seeing such evil and its destructive results (Isa. 24:16–19 and fn.). But he also saw that those in the spirit prison, after many days, would be visited (Isa. 24:22a–c; D&C 138:29–33). The Lord of hosts would finally reign in glory before the elders in both Mount Zion and in Jerusalem (Isa. 24:23a–c).

25:1–12 O Lord, thou art my God; I will exalt thee, I will praise thy name; for thou hast done wonderful things

A psalm of praise and thanksgiving follows the lament of the previous chapter. It is fine Hebrew poetry (as is about three-fourths of Isaiah's writings), employing rhetorical forms like those used in the book of Psalms. Respect by the strong and gratitude by the humble are proclaimed, and a great feast of the saved is anticipated (Isa. 25:1–6; D&C 27:5–14; 58:8–11; and all fn.). The "vail that is spread over all nations" will be removed, so all may know about the Lord's action. The first resurrection will be concluded, and the saved will "be glad and rejoice in his salvation" (Isa. 25:7–9). Adversaries such as Moab shall be brought down, their power and pride destroyed.

26:1–21 In that day shall this song be sung in the land of Judah; . . . Open ye the gates, that the righteous nation which keepeth the truth may enter in

This grand song of thanks and praise for redemption credits the Lord not only with bringing about resurrection but with initiating it in raising His dead body (Isa. 26:19 and fn.; Isa. 25:8–9). These are some of the best Old Testament statements on the resurrection of the dead. Enjoy the beauty and truth in many of the poetic couplets in this prophecy (e.g., Isa. 26:3–4, 7, 12, 19–20).

On "Lord Jehovah," see Isaiah 12:2a.

27:1–13 In that day the Lord . . . shall punish leviathan the piercing serpent, even leviathan that crooked serpent; and he shall slay the dragon that is in the sea

In the beginning, the Creators had to command and control unorganized, chaotic elements to organize an earth and its environs as a suitable abode for the children of God. The forces of chaos are sometimes poetically symbolized as the great powers in and of the seas, and even as sea monsters. A like event symbolically foretold here is the binding of Satan, who is the opponent of all of God's creative work (Isa. 27:1a–e; 1 Ne. 22:26; D&C 43:31).

Isaiah's song of redemption is about Israel as a vineyard that at last resumes bearing fruit for the Lord (Isa. 27:2–6 and fn.; cf. Isa. 5:1–6; Hosea 10:1).

Israel's unproductive days of wickedness and punishment are recalled in another song (Isa. 27:7–11). Then the prophet returned to anticipating the last days when the Lord will harvest the fruit (the redeemed) from Mesopotamia to Egypt. Israel will be gathered from lands of exile when the great *shophar* signal is sounded. All peoples will then worship in the temple at Jerusalem (Isa. 27:12–13 and fn.).

28:1–29 Woe to the crown of pride, to the drunkards of Ephraim, whose glorious beauty is a fading flower . . . hear the word of the Lord, ye scornful men . . . in Jerusalem

Ephraim was the tribe of Jeroboam, first king of the northern ten tribes of Israel after they separated from Judah, and Ephraim was often the name used for that northern Israelite nation (recall that Ephraim was the birthright tribe; Gen. 49:22–26; 1 Chr. 5:1–2). Most of the kings of northern Israel were apostates, and some were openly idolatrous. Isaiah here reproached Ephraim (northern Israel) for pride and drunkenness. He used poetic imagery to contrast their potential beauty and productive capacity to their actual performance—a "fading flower" and "hasty fruit."

"In that day" in Old Testament prophecy often means "in the day of the Lord." Sometimes the phrase is used, as here, without an evident antecedent, but the reader recognizes by context that it refers to the day of restoration, when a gathered remnant will be blessed by the Lord and will finally prosper (Isa. 28:2–6).

Israel's apostasy and degradation included indulging in alcohol and rejecting the prophets. The people had been taught from infancy, a step at a time, but by contrast they were to be instructed in exile with another language because they had not listened to their own. Ironically, their childhood instruction had been counterproductive, resulting only in rebellion and ending with their being taken captive (Isa. 28:9–13 and fn.).

The prophet turned next to Jerusalem and Judah, to warn that southern Israelite kingdom of false covenants they had made for protection and to decry false confidence in those covenants for safety against the Assyrian threat. The Lord revealed to Judah that the cornerstone of Zion was, and would be, in Jerusalem. For the time being, the plots that would destroy them would be abated and immediate exile avoided (Isa. 28:14–22 and cross-references).

A final parable compares the relationship of God and his people with that of a farmer and his crops. Both know how, what, and when to plant and harvest, and both use the proper instruments to thresh their different grains (Isa. 28:23–29).

29:1–24 Woe to Ariel, to Ariel, the city where David dwelt!

This great prophetic warning begins with Isaiah's vision of the siege of Jerusalem; however, it has a more infinite aspect, with elements applicable to a later "marvellous work and a wonder" to be done by the Lord. Nephi, writing about one hundred fifty years after the time of Isaiah in another hemisphere, saw that elements of this great prophecy would be fulfilled in the downfall of his own people centuries later. He foresaw the burial of the Nephite records, followed by their divinely directed retrieval and translation by an "unlearned" but inspired prophet of the latter days. That translation and publication would lead to the restoration of the true doctrines and covenants of God and the establishment of his Church for the benefit of all—the Gentiles and Jews, the spiritually deaf and blind, and all humble people who will hear and see (Isa. 29:1*a*; 2 Ne. 26–29).

30:1–33 Woe to the rebellious children, saith the Lord, that take counsel, but not of me; . . . That walk to go down into Egypt, and have not asked at my mouth

The immediate crisis addressed by this prophecy was still the Assyrian threat, which caused some politicians and people to look toward the other powerful nation of the time, Egypt, for help and defense. The prophet's admonition was to trust in the Lord, be still, hearken to the true seers and prophets, repent, and be confident; then blessings would follow. The unbelieving and rebellious, who rejected these admonitions, were severely reprimanded.

Again the prophet's vision of immediate events has applications to latter-day events, including the return of Israel to God and the establishment of His kingdom on earth.

31:1–9 Woe to them that go down to Egypt for help

A warning was given to those who trusted in Egypt and in

forces of the "flesh" rather than in the powers of God and the Spirit. A simile depicts the Lord's concern (Isa. 31:5). The anticipated fall of the Assyrians can be taken as symbolic of the ultimate triumph over evil by the power of the Lord (Isa. 31:6–9 and fn.).

32:1–20 Behold, a king shall reign in righteousness

Earthly kings should reign in righteousness, provide security, solve problems, and discern the churl from the charitable, but such an ideal government will come only with the true, anointed King (Isa. 32:1–8 and fn.). Meanwhile, the heedless (represented this time by the "women that are at ease") must repent lest their lands be desolated, palaces and forts abandoned, and all be taken into exile (Isa. 32:9–14). Only when revelations from heaven resume and works of righteousness and peace prevail are people to be gathered to their rightful places again, to be blessed by God's providence (Isa. 32:15–20).

33:1–24 Woe to thee that spoilest, and thou wast not spoiled

A forecast of doom was addressed to the Assyrian siege armies again, and the prophet prayed for Israel's salvation; then Assyria's destruction was prophesied (Isa. 33:1–4; 10:5–19; fulfillment is recorded in Isa. 37:35–38).

Anticipation of the reign of the Lord is the main substance of the rest of the chapter, beginning with a review of times of suffering and want and continuing with a surprising picture of the cleansing by fire that will precede the Lord's reign. Who can survive such fire and indeed "dwell with everlasting burnings"? Only the righteous can do so (Isa. 33:5–15 and fn.; Mal. 4:1). The chapter closes with a beautiful picture of the millennial reign of the Lord from Jerusalem and Zion (Isa. 33:16–24).

34:1–17 the indignation of the Lord is upon all nations, and his fury upon all their armies

The end of the wicked world is the subject of this vision (footnoted cross-references lead to other prophetic pictures of this scene, and translation notes explain some idioms). Idumea

(Edom) is a metaphor for the wicked world (Isa. 34:6; D&C 1:13). The symbol of the sword of the Lord, all bloody, may not be a pleasant one, but the idea of a violent end to violence, blood, and horror is often prophetically conveyed (Isa. 34:5–10). The desolated earth before a renewal and the reign of peace ends the vision (Isa. 34:11–17).

35:1–10 The wilderness and the solitary place shall be glad . . . the desert shall rejoice, and blossom as the rose

The earth is renewed to enjoy its paradisiacal glory (see the cross-references to other prophetic visions of this happy state). Note the glorious promises to the earth; to the weak and feeble; to the blind, deaf, and lame; to the thirsty ground; and to the ransomed who shall return to the Lord and come to Zion.

36–39 Now it came to pass in the fourteenth year of king Hezekiah, that Sennacherib king of Assyria came up against all the defenced cities of Judah

Isaiah's historical chapters repeat, with a few differences, reports in the historical books of the Old Testament: 2 Kings 18:13–37 corresponds with Isaiah 36; 2 Kings 19, with Isaiah 37; 2 Kings 20:1–11, with Isaiah 38; and 2 Kings 20:12–19, with Isaiah 39 (see the commentary on those passages).

Two verses in 2 Kings 18 (vv. 15–16) about Hezekiah's delivering precious metals from the palace and temple to Assyria are not repeated in Isaiah. Four verses in 2 Kings 20 (vv. 8–11) about King Hezekiah asking Isaiah (and Isaiah asking the Lord) what sign would assure Hezekiah that he would recover from his illness are not repeated in Isaiah; however, a voluntary sign is reported in Isaiah.

On the other hand, something is added in the Isaiah account: King Hezekiah's psalm of thanks and praise to the Lord for saving him after he had considered in deep sorrow the prospect of coming to the end of his life. He was grateful for his added fifteen years (Isa. 38:9–20; that item is not recorded in 2 Kgs. 20).

40:1–8 Comfort ye, comfort ye my people . . . her warfare is accomplished, that her iniquity is pardoned

Jerusalem's restoration near the end of time is anticipated in this announcement heralding comfort to come when mortal struggles and suffering for past sins are at last over. Cataclysmic changes heralded by a voice in the wilderness will prepare for earth's renewal and the Messiah's coming in glory; "and all flesh shall see it together." Mortal flesh will pass, but things eternal will go on (Isa. 40:6–8; 1 Pet. 1:18–25 regarding the Messiah-Redeemer who makes it possible). Words from this passage in Isaiah are used in Handel's *Messiah* and in Brahms's *German Requiem.*

40:9–31 O Zion, that bringest good tidings, . . . the Lord God will come

"The Lord God" is *Adonai JHVH* in the Hebrew text, that is, "My Lord Jehovah." Though many of Judah do not yet know it, the Lord is the Messiah and someday will say "Behold your God." He will reign, feed his flock, gather the lambs, and tenderly care for all (Isa. 40:9–11). Not at all like idols created by man, the Lord is the all-knowing and all-powerful Creator (Isa. 40:12–27). He is eternal and never fails; he can give power to the faint; they who hope for him and live his laws shall "run, and not be weary; . . . walk, and not faint" (Isa. 40:28–31 and fn.).

41:1–29 let the people renew their strength: let them come near; then let them speak: let us come near together to judgment

As the return under Cyrus would be directed by the Lord, so shall the future gathering of Israel be divinely directed (Isa. 41:1–7; 44:28 and 45:1). Israel in the latter days shall fulfill its mission (Isa. 41:8–10; "How Firm a Foundation," *Hymns,* no. 85, v. 3). The Lord will aid in the latter-day gathering and the earth will be made productive and beautiful. Former "gods" are impotent to know or act, but the Lord is omnipotent (Isa. 41:11–29).

42:1– 4 Behold my servant, whom I uphold; mine elect, in whom my soul delighteth; I have put my spirit upon him: he shall bring forth judgment to the Gentiles

This servant is Jesus the Messiah, servant of the Father (as Matthew correctly recognized; Isa. 42:1*a*). Aspects of His work in both the first and the second advent were foretold in these verses. Be aware, however, that Isaiah sometimes calls Israel the "servant" of the Lord.

42:5–25 Thus saith God the Lord, . . . I the Lord have called thee, . . . and give thee for a covenant of the people, for a light of the Gentiles

The speaker here is "God the Lord" (Heb., *Ha-El JHVH,* meaning, "the God Jehovah"). The work that he will do, and calls his people to help him do, is to bring light to the other nations (the "Gentiles") and also to the spirit world, making the saving covenants available to all (Isa. 42:5–7 and fn.).

The prophet exulted with a song of praise and awe as he envisioned the might of the Lord in destroying decadence and disease, to create new ways and works on earth (Isa. 42:8–18).

The prophet lamented, with a song of reproach, about the past failings of the Lord's servant-people, Israel. Because of their failings, the Lord let them be taken into exile and awaited their return unto him (Isa. 42:19–25; JST Isa. 42:19–23).

43:1–28 But now thus saith the Lord that created thee, O Jacob, and he that formed thee, O Israel, Fear not, for I have redeemed thee

The Creator is also the Redeemer and Savior. He will gather latter-day Israel to resume the mission of Abraham and Israel to enlighten the "blind people that have eyes, and the deaf that have ears" in all nations. Those who respond and truly serve the Lord become his "witnesses" (Isa. 43:1–10 and fn.). The Lord (that is, Jehovah) is the only Savior, the Redeemer, the Holy One, the Creator, and King; he will make new ways for peace and end old wars (Isa. 43:11–17).

This vision ends with a fervent call from the Lord to his people to forsake and forget their former sinful ways, fulfill their covenant duties, be relieved of their suffering, and rejoice that the Lord will blot out transgressions for all who turn to him and communicate with him. They can become "justified" (Isa. 43:18–28).

44:1–27 Yet now hear, O Jacob my servant; and Israel, whom I have chosen

These synonymous clauses are a poetic couplet introducing another of Isaiah's prophetic delineations of the mission of the faithful for the Lord. He created them, called them, and will prosper them. Their converts will take upon themselves the name of Israel and also become the Lord's people. He identifies himself by names and titles: King of Israel, Redeemer, the Lord of Hosts, the First and the Last, and God. He is the revealer of things to come, and his covenant peoples are his witnesses (Isa. 44:1–8).

By contrast, idols and they who manufacture them are ridiculous; the shaper of a wooden idol profits more from the part of the wood he burns to warm himself and cook his food than from the part he makes into a wooden god (Isa. 44:9–20 and fn.).

The miracles of the forgiveness of sins and the restoration of "decayed places" by the Redeemer are dramatically promised (Isa. 44:21–26).

44:28– 45:4 That saith of Cyrus, He is my shepherd

Isaiah foretold a dramatic event to come—which it did in about two hundred years, ca. 539 B.C.—when a king named Cyrus would be raised up to shepherd the Lord's people (Judah) back from Babylonian captivity to Jerusalem and would facilitate the rebuilding of the city and the temple (2 Chr. 36:22–23; Ezra 1:1–4; and commentary). The "higher critics" of the Bible commonly reject this as a prophecy by Isaiah because he lived centuries before Cyrus, who is called by name here; but our belief in divine foreknowledge allows us to accept Isaiah's authorship.

45:5–25 I am the Lord, and there is none else, there is no God beside me

In this theological revelation, Isaiah declared a number of the Lord's creative and redemptive works. Like the Father, the Son is uniquely God, and there is no other in his role (Isa. 45:5–6).

Light and darkness, peace and evil, in a poetic couplet, illustrate both ends of the spectrum of things permitted to exist under the divine system. That spectrum allows exercise of individual agency, because it permits "an opposition in all things" (2 Ne. 2:11). Moral evil is, of course, not created by God (Isa. 45:7*b*), but he did create a system wherein it is allowed to be present, just as Satan is permitted to be among humankind.

When punishment or suffering comes upon people under the Lord's hand, they call their sufferings "bad"—and they are, compared to the good they could have had if they had qualified for blessings.

Atheism was shown by the prophet to be illogical—as if a clay pot were to question the potter and deny the work of his hands or children were to deny that parents begot and bore them (Isa. 45:9–10).

More reviews of the works of the Lord include another declaration about the mission of Cyrus (Isa. 44:13 and fn.). Unlike idols, the Lord is not commonly seen, but he is "the Savior," who saves "with an everlasting salvation." Worshippers of visible idols shall be ashamed and confounded (Isa. 45:11–17).

The prophet testified that the Lord, the God who created the heavens and who formed the earth, is not secretive, but straightforward and righteous (Isa. 45:18–19).

In conclusion, our Savior and God invites the gathered of Israel and "all the ends of the earth" (Isa. 45:22) to look unto him and be saved. Eventually, every knee shall bow and every tongue covenant with him (Isa. 45:20–25 and abundant fn.).

46:1–13 Bel boweth down, Nebo stoopeth, their idols were upon the beasts . . . To whom will ye liken me, and make me equal

Here is another scathing rebuke of idolatry; though modern

"idols" may look different, they are in essence the same as the ancient ones. Because the true God has borne his people from the beginning, they greatly offend him by lavishing adoration and adornment upon idols, which indeed bear nothing, but they themselves have to be borne. "To whom will ye liken me, and make me equal" (v. 5) is a challenge to which any nomination would be absurd; then the Lord states again the absurdity of making idols to worship. Isaiah urged people to be firmly faithful, remembering the true God's deeds and words, which are dependable, authoritative, helpful, and corrective. The Lord invites all to trust in his salvation.

A strange metaphor was added to what had been revealed about Cyrus of Persia, who would let the Jews return (Isa. 46:11*a*; 44:28; 45:1).

47:1–15 Come down, and sit in the dust, O virgin daughter of Babylon, sit on the ground: there is no throne

Although in Isaiah's time Babylon had been suppressed by Assyria and neo-Babylonia would not rise for about a hundred years (ca. 625 B.C.), this prophetic chapter by Isaiah anticipated its downfall yet another century later (ca. 539 B.C.), after having held Judah captive for a time (Isa. 47:1–6 and fn.). This whole word-picture may also be read as a prototype for destruction of the wicked world at the end of time, for Babylon is sometimes so used in the scriptures (BD, "Babylon").

48:1–22 Hear ye this, O house of Jacob, which are called by the name of Israel, and are come forth out of the waters of Judah

The people of Israel, either by birth or baptism, who are not faithful to their covenants or have not hearkened to prophetic warnings, if they are not summarily cut off, shall be refined "in the furnace of affliction" (Isa. 48:3–11, 1*a*, 2*b*). Part of that affliction would be in Babylon, where Israel would be exiled because they did not hearken to their Redeemer. The Lord would have power to deal with Babylon and redeem Israel when they had hearkened to his commandments. Had they done so sooner, peace would have flowed for them as a river and their numbers been as the sands of the sea (Isa. 48:12–19).

The prophecy ends with an invitation for Judah's future and for ours, "Go ye forth of Babylon" (Isa. 48:20; D&C 133:14). A reminder is added about the saving power of the Lord, demonstrated in the Exodus; and another reminder affirms that there is no peace unto the wicked (Isa. 48:20–22 and fn.).

49:1–26 Listen, O isles, unto me; and hearken, ye people, from far; The Lord hath called me from the womb; . . . And he hath made my mouth like a sharp sword

In this somewhat complicated review (involving concepts from Isa. 40–48), Isaiah declares his own call and mission and Israel's mission. The mission of Israel is the dominant subject, but the Messiah who comes *through* Israel is the primal "light to the Gentiles" and the source of "salvation unto the end of the earth" (Isa. 49:1–6; 1 Ne. 21; D&C 86:8–11).

It is again declared that the Lord, the Redeemer of Israel, had chosen Israel and would help them as a covenant people to redeem even the prisoners in the spirit prison. For the great work to be done, Israel would be saved and preserved and in the end gathered from all directions (Isa. 49:7–12, 9*a*). Great rejoicing is to accompany that gathering, and all shall know the Lord has not forgotten his covenant promises. Mention of the signs engraven in the Lord's hands may be an allusion to an event Zechariah foresaw in the second coming of the Messiah, when some shall say, "What are these wounds in thine hands?" (Zech. 13:6; Isa. 49:13–17; D&C 45:48–54).

The remainder of the review tells of the great numbers of the restored of Israel. The Lord promises them help from other nations through their "kings" and "queens." A rhetorical question is posed about whether the "lawful" captives of "the mighty" can be delivered during the gathering; impossible as it would be for mortal deliverers, yet the Lord indeed promises deliverance. All shall know he is Savior and Redeemer, while the "mighty" destroy each other (Isa. 49:18–26).

50:1–11 Thus saith the Lord, Where is the bill of your mother's divorcement, . . . Wherefore, when I came, was there no man?

The Lord, through the prophet Isaiah, challenges His people to answer why they act as if they have been divorced from God or sold by Him—indeed, why they sell themselves for iniquitous pleasures. Why have they not responded when He called? In view of all He has done, do they yet think He has no power to redeem? (Isa. 50:1–3). Isaiah reviewed his prophetic credentials—his inspiration as a spokesman, his receptivity. He envisioned the future persecution and torture of the Savior and the things He would suffer and endure for mankind. It strengthened the prophet's confidence that the Lord would help, defend, and justify him, whereas his condemners would wax old and be consumed (Isa. 50:4–9).

The prophet, speaking for "the Lord God," invited all who fear the Lord and obey His servant, to trust Him, even if they were still in darkness. The alternative is to walk by the light of their own fire, their own little "sparks"; but if they do, they will "lie down in sorrow" (Isa. 50:10–11; 2:5).

51:1–23 Hearken to me, ye that follow after righteousness, ye that seek the Lord: . . . Look unto Abraham . . . and unto Sarah

A message of comfort and reassurance is given to all the seed of Abraham to anticipate true Zion, renewal of the Eden-like glory of earth, righteous rule, salvation, and an end to reproach and revilings at the end of the wicked world (Isa. 51:1–8 and fn.). The same faithful people are invited to "awake, put on strength." It means that they should resume functioning in the power of the true priesthood in the last days (Isa. 51:9; D&C 113:8 concerning Isa. 52:1). That priesthood, which is the power of God, is the same power that overcame chaos in the creation of the world, parted the waters for Moses and Israel, and shall accomplish the latter-day gathering of Israel. The Lord gives assurance that he will comfort his people, destroy the oppressors, loose the captives, put words in the mouth of his people, and lay the foundations of Zion; then Jerusalem can awaken and arise (Isa. 51:9–17).

At a time when there is none to guide the people of Jerusalem during the gathering and the conflict, "two sons" shall arise and prophesy; though smitten, they are redeemed, and former oppressors shall be oppressed at last (Isa. 51:18–23; 2 Ne. 8:19–20; Rev. 11:3–12; D&C 77:15).

52:1–12 Awake, awake; put on thy strength, O Zion; put on thy beautiful garments, O Jerusalem, . . . loose thyself from the bands of thy neck

Repeating the summons to the latter-day heirs of the mission of Abraham, the prophet Isaiah spoke for the Lord in urging the chosen people of the end of time in Jerusalem to do better than the redeemed Israelites of the exodus from Egypt who eventually suffered the Assyrian captivity. Those gathered in the last days must eliminate hypocrisy and blasphemy and function truly as the Lord's messengers (Isa. 52:1–6; 51:9; D&C 113:7–10).

Then "How beautiful upon the mountains are the feet of him that bringeth good tidings" (v. 7) of the gospel of peace and salvation. The latter-day messengers help the Lord to establish Zion, redeem Jerusalem, and make the power of the Lord dominant in all the world (Isa. 52:7–10). They are urged to go out on their missions, being clean, as those "that bear the vessels of the Lord," and God will go with them (Isa. 52:11–12*b*).

52:13–53:12 Behold, my servant . . . shall be exalted and extolled, and be very high . . . his visage was so marred more than any man . . . He is despised and rejected of men

In this passage lies the heart of the message of Isaiah and of all the prophets (Mosiah 13:33). There should be no problem in identifying this Servant of God. He is our divine Redeemer—he who was both humble and mighty, persecuted and honored. He was stricken and rejected, but he still perfected our salvation and atonement. Many commentators recognize this as a prophecy about the Messiah; though not all who read it recognize Jesus of Nazareth as the Messiah, they will when they see the wounds in his hands (Isa. 52:13–15; Zech. 13:6; D&C 45:52).

Appreciation of this great prophecy can be enhanced by study of the version of it, and the commentary on it, in the Book of Mormon and other scriptures (Isa. 53:1–3 and fn.; Mosiah 13:33–35; 14:1–12; 15:1–31).

Because the Lord is the Savior, what may be meant by the phrases "the Lord hath laid on him the iniquity of us all," "it pleased the Lord to bruise him," and "the pleasure of the Lord shall prosper in his hand"? Remember that the Firstborn Son of God volunteered in the Council in Heaven to become the Savior (Moses 4:2; Abr. 3:27; TG, "Jesus Christ, Messiah"; "Jesus Christ, Jehovah"). He was "pleased" to lay upon *himself* our sins and let *himself* be persecuted and bruised; his pleasure (the joy of the redemption of all humankind) shall indeed prosper by his hand (cf. Mosiah 15:5–8). Consider what he was willing to suffer (1 Ne. 19:9–10). Thus, he "poured out his soul unto death: . . . and he bare the sin of many" (Isa. 53:4–12 and fn.).

54:1–17 Sing, O barren, thou that didst not bear; . . . for more are the children of the desolate than the children of the married wife, saith the Lord

Israel was sometimes compared by the prophets to a wayward and estranged wife. Here Israel is promised that in spite of "the shame of [her] youth" and "the reproach of [her] widowhood," her Maker and Husband is also her Redeemer, and He will gather her in (Isa. 54:1–5; Hosea 2).

The children of the erstwhile "desolate" will be more numerous in the latter days than the children of the former "married wife" (covenant people) in the early history of Israel. Therefore the "tent" of Israel will have to be enlarged, its fabric extended, its cords lengthened, and its stakes strengthened in the latter days (Isa. 54:2; D&C 82:14; TG, "Stake"). Even as there will never be another flood like the "waters of Noah," so the Lord's people will never be scattered and lost again. The ultimate picture is of millennial peace and beauty (Isa. 54:6–14).

The Lord created all and controls all, including the "waster to destroy" and the weapons formed against his people; by him they will be condemned to destruction at last (Isa. 54:15–17).

55:1–13 Ho, every one that thirsteth, come ye to the waters, and he that hath no money; come ye, buy, and eat; yea, come, buy wine and milk without money and without price

This short poetic prophecy is about salvation and redemption. The opening words are an invitation to everyone who has spiritual desires to come unto the Lord and receive the blessings of sacrifice and sustenance ("wine" and "milk"). In contrast, it disparages spending labor and means on nonessential things.

The poetic metaphor "sure mercies of David" (Heb., lit., "the established loving kindnesses of David") is a synonymous parallel with the "everlasting covenant." "David" here is he who is given "for a witness to the people, a leader and commander to the people": he is the Messiah, the Christ. That he provides all the blessings he has freely promised is evident (Isa. 55:1–4 and fn.).

The mission of Abraham and Israel will be fulfilled when peoples of all nations come unto the Lord, the Holy One of Israel. All are admonished to seek him "while he may be found"—while they are still spiritually sensitive enough recognize him. The way to come to him is to repent, believing that he will pardon, and covenant with him (Isa. 55:5–7). If such generous promises of salvation and loving kindness seem too good to be true, it is because our thoughts are not like God's thoughts nor our ways like his ways. His are higher than ours, but his words will as surely bear fruit as will the soil watered by the rain—and his words will not evaporate (Isa. 55:8–11).

Some lovely aspects of life in the renewed, righteous earth conclude the prophecy (Isa. 55:12–13).

56:1–8 Thus saith the Lord, Keep ye judgment, and do justice: for my salvation is near to come

A topic broached above is further developed in this segment, with blessings promised to old and young who live justly and keep the Sabbath, including converts and those who had been excluded (such as the eunuch; BD, "Eunuch"). "Even them will I bring to my holy mountain, and make them joyful in my house of prayer"; for that house, the temple, "shall be called a house of prayer for all people," including "outcasts." Thus the mission of the chosen people will be fulfilled when they have borne "this ministry and priesthood unto all nations" and "all the families of the earth [are] blessed" (Isa. 55:5; 56:3–8; Abr. 2:9, 11).

56:9–57:12 All ye beasts of the field, come to devour . . . His watchmen are blind: they are all ignorant, they are all dumb dogs, . . . Yea, they are greedy dogs

Turning from the lovely anticipations of the future world of fulfillment and peace, Isaiah abruptly pronounced a scathing rebuke upon Israel's careless, ineffective, and selfish leaders, whose failings and faithlessness had caused the righteous to perish with their only comfort being that they were thus taken away from further evils to come (Isa. 56:9–12; 57:1–2). The rebuke could have been addressed to such leaders as the last kings and leaders of northern Israel (cf. 2 Kgs. 15–17). Their evils included sorcery, adultery, rudeness, falsehood, idolatry, sexual aberrations, necromancy, and refusal to repent. Their "righteousness" and "works" were not adequate to save them (Isa. 57:3–12).

57:13–21 but he that putteth his trust in me shall possess the land, and shall inherit my holy mountain

In contrast to the wicked leaders, who will cry in vain to their idols for deliverance, leaders and people trusting in the Lord can ask for the stumbling blocks to be removed and the way of return prepared. The true God who dwells "in the high and holy place" will hear those of "a contrite and humble spirit"; he will return to heal them and gather them. They shall finally hear his blessed words, "Peace, peace to him that is far off, and to him that is near." The wicked, however, shall remain filthy and have no peace (Isa. 57:13–21; 48:22).

58:1–14 Cry aloud . . . shew my people their transgression . . . they seek me daily, and delight to know my ways

To questions about performing such ordinances as fasting and then failing to feel any spiritual results, the prophet's answer from the Lord explained that the fasting was perfunctory, for they had not lived as their ordinances had pledged them to. Fasting should increase charity in the heart and charitable deeds in the community. Real blessings, both spiritual and material, will flow from sincerely fasting and giving fast offerings (Isa. 58:9–12). Even such a simple virtue as sincere Sabbath keeping is a sign that all covenants are held sacred, and the way of life that results therefrom will be rewarded (Isa. 58:13–14; Ex. 31:12–17; D&C 59:9–24).

59:1–21 Behold, the Lord's hand is not shortened, that it cannot save; . . . But your iniquities have separated between you and your God, and your sins have hid his face from you

Sin had separated the people of the Lord from him: "*your sins* have hid *his face* from *you*" (Isa. 59:2, emphasis added). There had been too much bloodshed, lying, injustice, vanity, plots and webs, eagerness for evil, and haste to violence (Isa. 59:1–8).

Misery and insecurity had resulted from that separation; fair judgment and justice were lacking (Isa. 59:9–15). But the Lord feels compassion for humankind and has provided salvation; he intercedes and defends and will recompense; and as the Redeemer, he will come to Zion. At last his people will act in accordance with his covenant and become his faithful messengers (Isa. 59:16–21 and fn.).

60:1–22 Arise, shine; for thy light is come, and the glory of the Lord is risen upon thee. For, behold, the darkness shall cover the earth, . . . but the Lord shall arise upon thee

True Israelites will fulfill their missions by letting their light illuminate life for others (Isa. 60:1–3).

In the gathering of Israel to Zion, many converted peoples of other nations ("Gentiles") will participate, helping Israelite people come home "as the doves to their windows" (these words were quoted by Orson Hyde in his dedication of the Holy Land). "Sons of strangers" and of former oppressors will help in rebuilding and reclaiming the land (Isa. 60:4–14).

Under the Lord as Savior and Redeemer, Zion will reach "eternal excellency" (v. 15), and precious things from many nations shall adorn her. Violence will cease, and Zion's walls shall be salvation and praise of righteousness. The Lord shall be her light, and her people shall gain their eternal inheritances, multiply, and be blessed abundantly (Isa. 60:15–22).

61:1–11 The Spirit of the Lord God is upon me; because the Lord hath anointed me to preach good tidings

As the chapter heading states, Isaiah spoke messianically to announce the beginning of the Messiah's redemptive work on earth. The words that open this chapter were quoted by Jesus in his hometown of Nazareth, and the people were told he would fulfill this prophecy (Isa. 61:1–2 and fn.; Luke 4:18–19; 3 Ne. 22; 23:1).

The themes of restoration of the previous two chapters are continued with further messages about the rebuilding and the establishment of Zion. Moses' prophecy that Israel would become "a kingdom of priests, and an holy nation" is finally to be fulfilled (Ex. 19:6; Isa. 61:3–6).

Reversing the disinheritance status of the years of exile, Israel will at last inherit a birthright ("double") portion, and the mission of the seed of Abraham will finally be fulfilled.

A song of rejoicing ends this prophecy (Isa. 61:7–11 and fn.).

62:1–12 And the Gentiles shall see thy righteousness, and all kings thy glory

The prophecies of restoration continue, and Isaiah was ardent in prophesying about this subject. Israel of the future shall have a "new name"; new titles will characterize her restored status (Isa. 62:1–5 and fn.).

The Lord will appoint prophets as watchmen on the walls of Jerusalem to watch for the coming of the Lord—proclaiming salvation and bringing his redeemed with him. Jerusalem shall be called, "Sought out, A city not forsaken" (Isa. 62:6–12).

63:1–19 Who is this that cometh from Edom, with dyed garments from Bozrah? . . . I that speak in righteousness, mighty to save

As the footnotes and cross-references to other scriptures

(including the Doctrine and Covenants) show, the meaning of this passage is that the Savior will come again, having overcome such enemies as sin and death. The metaphor is of sin and death as people whose blood stained the Redeemer's garments. In fact, when he ransomed us from sin and death, his garments were stained with his own blood (Isa. 63:1–6 and fn.; Luke 22:44; D&C 19:18; John 19:34).

Isaiah declared the Lord's loving kindnesses and His great goodness in His service also as temporal Savior in redeeming Israel of old from afflictions in bondage and in the wilderness. Even though they rebelled and vexed the Spirit sent to be their guide in the days of Moses, yet the Lord "put his holy Spirit within" Moses and made him their shepherd to lead them through wilderness and sea and down into the valley to rest in the promised land (Isa. 63:10–14).

Then the prophet addressed a direct supplication to the Lord as "our father," as one who cares for the people of Israel even more than did their earthly forefathers, Abraham and Israel. The prophet inquired for the people: "Why hast thou made us to err" (corrected in JST; Isa. 63:17*a*). By erring, Israel lost His protection, so that invaders could take over their inheritance and tread down the sanctuary. The prophet pleaded for salvation from the invaders and redemption for those who bear His name (Isa. 63:15–19).

64:1–12 Oh that thou wouldest rend the heavens, that thou wouldest come down . . . to make thy name known to thine adversaries, that the nations may tremble at thy presence!

The supplications are continued (from 63:16–19) in a yearning prayer for the Lord to establish his beautiful kingdom for all who believe in and look for him (Isa. 63:16–19; 64:1–4).

Unworthy, unclean, and unfaithful though decadent Israel was, yet the prophet pleaded for them with the Lord as their Father and as the divine Potter in whose hands they are the clay (Isa. 64:5–8).

Then the vision shifted from the times of Israel's decadence to the last days when the "holy cities are a wilderness, Zion is a wilderness, Jerusalem a desolation" awaiting the restoration and establishment of the Lord's kingdom on earth (Isa. 64:9–12). Note the reference to two "holy cities"—Zion and Jerusalem (Isa. 64:10; TG, "Jerusalem, New"; "Zion"; BD, "Zion").

65:1–16 I am sought of them that asked not for me; I am found of them that sought me not: . . . I have spread out my hands all the day unto a rebellious people, which walketh in a way that was not good, after their own thoughts

Responding to Isaiah's previous supplications, the Lord indicated that he had always been available, but only in distress had his people turned to him; they had not sought him or heeded his outstretched hands. His erring people had dealt in "abominable things" and yet said to others "I am holier than thou." They had been offensive, iniquitous idolaters and would be recompensed for their wickedness (Isa. 65:6–7).

Nevertheless, the Lord knows there is always some good juice in a cluster of grapes, for which reason they may be saved. There were some good seeds in Jacob (Israel) and Judah, and they would yet qualify for an inheritance. Sharon, on the western slopes, and Achor, in the eastern valley of Jordan (where trouble arose in Joshua's time), shall become peaceful pastures in the time of restoration (Isa. 65:8–10; on Achor, see Josh. 7:24; Hosea 2:14–15).

All will not be blessed, however. They who forsake the Lord will leave their names for a curse. They will be differentiated from the true servants who seek the blessings of the true God and are true to their covenants (Isa. 65:11–16).

65:17–25 For, behold, I create new heavens and a new earth: and the former shall not be remembered, nor come to mind

The epoch-making change when the kingdom of God is fully established on earth has been foreseen by prophets of many periods of history, but nowhere is the picture more appealing than here in the details of family life, freedom from sorrow and bereavement, and divinely blessed life, labor, and peace among all living things on earth (Isa. 65:17c–e).

66:1–24 Hear the word of the Lord, ye that tremble at his word; your brethren that hated you . . . shall be ashamed

This chapter has seemed to many to be anticlimactic, following as it does the lovely vision of the new heavens and the new earth. But it does deal with the advent of that splendid state, even though it emphasizes the destruction of evil that will precede it. The old rituals, so often hypocritically performed, will be done away, and they who have only such worship to their credit shall suffer the consequences (Isa. 66:1–4 and fn.).

The righteous with joy will see the Lord appear; but they who hate righteousness will be ashamed. The new Jerusalem and the the new Zion will be born "in one day," and they who take part in them will rejoice. Peace will flow on like a river, and the Lord will comfort his people (Isa. 66:5–14 and fn.).

"The Lord will come with fire," purifying the earth of all idolatrous peoples. Then they who accept the Lord will be gathered from "all nations and tongues." Those who do not know him will be provided a sign (or ensign), and missionaries will declare his glory among all those Gentiles. Israel's gathering will be completed, the priesthood will again be established, and worship of the Lord by all will begin (Isa. 66:15–23).

The book ends with a sobering scene of the destruction of the wicked who have not repented and accepted the Lord (Isa. 66:24).

The Savior himself quoted some of Isaiah's prophecies, and he recommended that we study them (3 Ne. 23:1–2). It is rewarding and instructive for us to do that—reading the whole book to get the whole perspective and then pondering on each topic. As the Lord said, "Great are the words of Isaiah."

JEREMIAH

Jeremiah began to prophesy to the nation of Judah about a hundred and ten years after Isaiah began prophesying to Judah and northern Israel. Jeremiah's call from the Lord came to him near the middle of the reign of the last good and righteous man to reign in Judah, King Josiah, in the thirteenth year of his reign (Jer. 1:2; ca. 626 B.C.). When the righteous King Josiah was killed in battle against Pharaoh Necho in the valley of Megiddo, Jeremiah was one of those who lamented him (2 Chr. 35:20–37). Well might he have done so, for the last righteous king and religious reformer was gone and bitter days were ahead (BD, "Jeremiah").

Jeremiah lived on through the lives of the last four kings, and into the time of the Babylonian exile because the captain of the guard of the Babylonians loosed him from the chains with which he had been bound when Jerusalem was taken and allowed him to choose whether to go with the Jewish captives to Babylon or to remain with Gedaliah and the people left in Judah to till the land (Jer. 39:11–14; 40:1–6). He chose to stay with the remnant of Judah. After Gedaliah was assassinated by a royalist (Jer. 41–42), the prophet advised the remnant Jews to abide in Judah and not go to Egypt, as some wanted to do. They rejected the advice, refusing to believe it was really from the Lord, and went to Egypt, taking Jeremiah with them. There he prophesied that Babylon would also conquer Egypt (Jer. 43; 46). He prophesied that the Jewish remnant there would perish not only because they had rejected the Lord's word but because many believed they had been better off when they worshipped "the queen of heaven" (Jer. 44:17–19). They turned again to worshipping idols in Egypt (Jer. 44:8, 15, 23). Only a small number would survive and escape back to Judah to bear witness of Jeremiah's words (Jer. 44:28–30).

The fate of the prophet thereafter is not known, though legends in the British Isles have asserted that he and the daughters of Zedekiah (Jer. 41:10; 43:6) migrated there from Egypt. It is further said that those daughters married there, and their lineage is still shown in certain royal genealogies.

COMMENTARY

1:1–3 The words of Jeremiah the son of Hilkiah, of the priests that were in Anathoth in the land of Benjamin: To whom the word of the Lord came

Jeremiah, like Ezekiel, was a priest (Jer. 1:1; Ezek. 1:3). Anathoth was one of thirteen cities appointed by Joshua for the priests of Aaron among the forty-eight cities designated for the Levites (Josh. 21:18; BD, "Levites"; "Priests"; "Aaronic Priesthood").

The span of the reigns of kings mentioned would point to a mission of forty years for Jeremiah (ca. 626–586 B.C.; Jer. 1:2–3); how long he lived before and after that period is not told.

1:4–19 Then the word of the Lord came unto me, saying, Before I formed thee in the belly I knew thee; and before thou camest forth out of the womb I sanctified thee, and I ordained thee a prophet unto the nations

This passage is one of the few clear revelations about foreordination in the scriptures. It tells of Jeremiah's being sanctified for special service and ordained to be a prophet in his premortal life—in the spirit world, for it happened before his body was even formed (Jer. 1:5 and fn.). Nevertheless, like Moses and Enoch before him, Jeremiah felt inadequate for his calling (Jer. 1:6a). The Lord assured him he would be able to go where divinely sent and speak what he would be commanded to speak, but he must not be afraid. The Lord touched Jeremiah's mouth and assigned him six difficult tasks as a reformer (Jer. 1:6–10 and fn.).

As a reminder that the Lord would fulfill Jeremiah's prophecies, the almond tree was given as a symbol; the Hebrew letters of its name (*shqd*) are the same letters as the word for "be alert, wakeful"; thus whenever Jeremiah saw that tree (which is the earliest tree to bloom in Israel), he would be reminded of the promise that the Lord would be attentive to his prophecies and fulfill his words (Jer. 1:11–12; BD, "Almond").

As a symbol of the main threat of invasion at the time, the Lord showed the prophet a cooking pot, facing north. Babylon, with the nations already conquered and pressed into her service, would come from the upper Euphrates valley and attack Judah from the north, by way of Damascus. Jeremiah was to warn of invasion and remind Judah that the only way to safety was through repentance and prayer to the Lord (Jer. 1:13–16).

The prophet was challenged to be bold and was promised the Lord's protection though he be set against kings, princes, priests, and people, and they against him; for they would not be allowed to "prevail" (Jer. 1:17–19). As noted later, however, he was not shielded from opposition and persecution.

2:1–37 Israel was holiness unto the Lord. . . . What iniquity have your fathers found in me, that they are gone far from me

Israel had been quite well prepared in Joshua's time to enter the promised land and become a "kingdom of priests, and an holy nation" as the Lord and Moses had intended (Ex. 19:4–6; Josh. 1). But in the nine hundred years thereafter, their spiritual condition had been up and down many times. During Hezekiah's reign and Isaiah's ministry, northern Israel was conquered and exiled; Judah, however, hearkened to the king and the prophet and was saved by the Lord from Assyria's siege (2 Kgs. 17–20).

The "fathers" mentioned in this prophecy may have been those of the long, idolatrous reign of Hezekiah's son Manasseh and grandson Amon (ca. 697–640 B.C.; 2 Kgs. 21; cf. Jer. 15:4). Many of the evils Jeremiah condemned and fought against throughout his mission were the religious and social sins made common in that fifty-seven year period. The reforms of King Josiah no doubt had some good effects; but just as good character grows like a tree and evil multiplies like weeds, so did Judah slip back into evil ways after Josiah's death.

In his opening charge, the prophet Jeremiah reprimanded Judah for forgetting past blessings and for failing to turn to the Lord for future blessings needed. Negligent priests and false prophets were partly to blame, but so were the people.

Jeremiah ridiculed idolatry and chided Judah for having "changed their gods." In this matter they had been more fickle than the idol-worshipping people who clung to their "gods." His metaphor equated the true God and his blessings to a spring of living waters and idolatry to a cistern (a container for water storage)—indeed, a broken cistern. A spring ("fountain") produces water, but a cistern can only give out what has been put in, and a broken cistern would lose even that (Jer. 2:11–13).

He ridiculed Judah's turning to decadent Egypt or to Assyria for help. Had the Israelites forgotten the Lord's defense of them during all the centuries past? Had they forgotten his planting them in the promised land, expecting them to bear fruit? Could they ever wash sin away with harsh cleansers, turn from idolatry and from indulging their sensual urges, cease from enjoying carnal things? Evidently not, for they showed love of strangers' ways and said "after them will I go" (Jer. 2:14–25).

He ridiculed the Israelites' considering wood or stone as fathers or creators and challenged the people to turn to those wooden or stone "gods" for help. He pleaded with them to repent, turn to the Lord, and not contend with Him. Yet, though they suffered, they would not return.

With a metaphor likening idolatry to adultery, Jeremiah ended this discourse by calling attention to Israel's perfidy as the Lord's bride. He showed evidence of their infidelity and their denial of guilt. Their hope of aid from Egypt or Assyria against Babylon was fruitless; they would go out of their lands as exiles, with their hands bound over their heads (Jer. 2:31–37).

3:1–11 thou hast played the harlot with many lovers; yet return again to me, saith the Lord

Although a husband seldom returns to a divorced wife, yet if Judah repented and called upon God, He would take her back. The Lord would not retain his anger forever, even though she had "spoken and done evil things" (Jer. 3:1–5). In a sense, northern Israel was less blameworthy than "her treacherous sister Judah," for Judah had the example of Israel's apostasy and exile as a warning. Even in King Josiah's reforms, Judah had not turned to the Lord sincerely but only superficially.

3:12–25 Go and proclaim these words toward the north, and say, Return, thou backsliding Israel, saith the Lord; . . . and I will take you one of a city, and two of a family, and I will bring you to Zion

The Lord turned the prophet's attention from his failing nation to the future Israel, proclaiming in the direction of northern Israel's exile an invitation to return through repentance. Although but "one of a city, and two of a family" responded, "Zion" would commence to be built (Jer. 3:12–14). *Family* can mean the extended family, or clan, and thus be a very large unit; it is often used in that way (e.g., Jer. 1:15; 8:3; 25:9).

In the future Zion, the Lord's shepherds ("pastors") will do what Israel's leaders anciently should have done, but the ark of the covenant and worship procedures associated with it will not be revived. All nations will be gathered unto the Lord, and thus the mission of Abraham will be fulfilled. Judah and the ten tribes of Israel will again be united, and all will worship the Father forever. In anticipation and yearning for that day, Jeremiah again lamented the apostasy ("as a wife treacherously departeth from her husband"), heard her voice of weeping, and declared that salvation is only through the Lord. He even spoke for Israel a confession of error, disobedience, and shame (Jer. 3:20–25).

4:1–18 If thou wilt return, O Israel, saith the Lord, return unto me

The prophet's appeal for repentance and renewal of covenants continued. People must recultivate their minds and cease sowing "among thorns"; using another metaphor, Jeremiah urged them to circumcise their hearts, symbolizing a cleansing and recommitment. The alternative was to assemble defenses, for the destroyer was on his way and defenders would faint before him. Under that option the prophet spoke with irony about the Lord's promises of peace to earlier Israel, for surely the invader would be like a dry wind from the east, which destroys. Once again the prophet pleaded for repentance from the ways and doings that had procured such destruction for them.

4:19–31 I am pained at my very heart; . . . Destruction upon destruction is cried; . . . I beheld the earth, and, lo, it was without form, and void; and the heavens, and they had no light

Jeremiah saw the decline and fall of Judah as a vision of the end of the world, a return to chaos as it was before the earth was organized (Jer. 4:23a–b). But the Lord assured him this would not yet be "a full end." In the closing verses, the prophet related his vision of ultimate destruction to the immediate ills and their results. The people of Jerusalem would be fleeing before the Babylonian invader and crying out in agony like a woman in travail, because of violence and bloodshed; but death, not life, would come of it.

5:1–31 Run ye to and fro through the streets of Jerusalem, and see now, and know, . . . if there be any that executeth judgment, that seeketh the truth; and I will pardon it

The Lord's challenge to Jeremiah to find a righteous person in Jerusalem resembles the impossibility faced by Abraham over Sodom thirteen centuries before, when he hoped to save Lot's family, pleading with the Lord to save that city if even ten righteous people could be found in it (Jer. 5:1*a*). The Lord, in mercy, did save Lot and some of his family; and in Jerusalem of the time of Jeremiah and Lehi, He guided a few righteous souls to safety, but because too few could be found to preserve the city, Jerusalem would be destroyed (Jer. 5:1, 7, 10–11, 19–21, 25–27; cf. 1 Ne. 1:4–7, 18–20). In Jerusalem of Jeremiah's day, negligent judges ignored injustices, false prophets mollified the people, and priests took authority by their own hand—and the people liked it so.

6:1–30 this is the city to be visited; she is wholly oppression in the midst of her. As a fountain casteth out her waters, so she casteth out her wickedness: violence and spoil is heard in her

The theme of chapter 6, stated in verses 6 and 7, introduces a multifaceted condemnation of Jerusalem and Judah. First, the people of Benjamin were addressed; they lived in the suburbs of Jerusalem and in areas toward the northwest, west, and southwest.

In the face of the great destroyer coming from the north, Jerusalem would be as "a comely and delicate woman." A brief symbolic dialogue characterized the invasion, and decrees were issued against Jerusalem because of her evils. The thoroughness of the gleaning was depicted. Those most blameworthy in causing, or in failing to halt, the decay were again identified as the false prophets and priests who reassured the people of "peace, peace; when there [was] no peace." And these were "not at all ashamed" (Jer. 6:1–15).

The people were also blamed for refusing to stand in the old ways and to seek good ways; they rejected the watchmen who did arise to warn them. So unto all was the punishment of Jerusalem. Offerings would not stop it, and escape from the great invading nation coming out of the north country would be impossible.

Finally, the Lord urged His errant people to lament, for though the prophet had been set as a tower to warn and a fortress to defend them, the fire of the smelter of His chastisement had not purified them; they were as rejected silver, and so the Lord must reject them.

7:1–16 Thus saith the Lord . . . Amend your ways and your doings, and I will cause you to dwell in this place

The variety of appeals and declamations following one upon another in Jeremiah's book make it evident that it is a collection of his speeches from time to time and place to place during the years of his ministry. There was no one time and place when he could once and for all present the charges against his decadent people, call them to repentance, and proffer them God's merciful desires to take them back. He had to warn them of the terrible alternatives, and he tried again and again.

This time, the prophet was asked to "stand in the gate of the Lord's house" and proclaim his message to temple worshippers to amend their ways and doings and become just. They could not assume that by going to the temple and making perfunctory sacrifices in it, they could be excused from repenting. They must learn to do good and cease to do evil. They must not make the temple "a den of robbers" and hope to hide in it, thinking it would not be destroyed. They should remember that the tabernacle at Shiloh had not saved Israel from the Philistines but was destroyed for Israel's wickedness. If the people would not change, Judah would be cast out, just as Ephraim (northern Israel) had been cast out (Jer. 7:1–15, 12*a*).

7:17–28 Seest thou not what they do in the cities of Judah and in the streets of Jerusalem?

The Lord called the prophet's attention to the people's worship of the "queen of heaven" and to their continuing failure to perform the proper sacrificial ordinances. Hence they must feel the outpouring of His anger.

7:29–34 O Jerusalem, . . . take up a lamentation . . . for the children of Judah have done evil in my sight

Jeremiah urgently appealed for repentance from Judah's gross apostasy and idolatry in offering their sons and daughters in human sacrifice at Tophet, in the valley of Hinnom southeast of Jerusalem. The Lord had never required human sacrifice. For this evil Judah would be destroyed as if by predators. If the Lord withdrew from them, all joy and mirth would cease and the land would be desolate.

8:1–22 bring out the bones . . . out of their graves: And they shall spread them before the sun, and the moon, and all the host of heaven, whom they have loved . . . and whom they have worshipped

The dire predictions of the previous chapter continue. Even

the dead will be dishonored by the invaders, and that dishonor will not be ameliorated by the idol gods they have worshipped. For the survivors, death will be more to be desired than life.

The Lord asked why this people of Jerusalem were perpetually backsliding. A man who falls may rise, and one who turns away may return; why would not the wicked repent? Birds know the season to return home; why not people? Why do not the wise and learned in the law know what they must do? They must lose their homeland because false priests and prophets take the dangers lightly, saying "Peace, peace; when there is no peace." Such have not done their duty and "shall be cast down" (Jer. 8:1–12; cf. 6:14).

Lacking justification to save them, the Lord would "consume them." The leaderless people would seek refuge in vain. They had unrealistically looked for peace and health, though the Lord had told them how near the trouble was. The prophet was pained at heart because it was so, for he knew they could have turned to the Lord before the harvest was past and the summer ended—before it was too late to repent. The Lord and the prophet were grieved because of them; they had not used the healing balm of repentance, and their leaders had not been physicians concerned with helping them recover their spiritual health.

9:1–26 Oh that my head were waters, and mine eyes a fountain of tears, that I might weep day and night for the slain of the daughter of my people

Speaking for himself and for the Lord, the prophet uttered an elegiac lament; tears were inadequate to express the tragedy of it all. The lies, mistrust, slander, and deceit should not have prevailed among this people; but they did prevail, and none repented. Idolatry flourished, and bitter experiences would come when the people would be exiled. Because the Lord and the prophet could not persuade the people to repent, the mourners were summoned, for death would come into their windows, even into palaces, destroying children and young men in the houses and in the streets and also in the fields.

None of that terror was what the Lord wanted, but it had

come in spite of Him; hence He desired that none would glory in wisdom, might, or riches but only in learning that His way is to "exercise lovingkindness, judgment, and righteousness"; in such things He delights. But what became of Judah is what will become of all the wicked world at last.

10:1–25 the customs of the people are vain: for one cutteth a tree out of the forest. . . . They deck it with silver and with gold; they fasten it with nails . . . that it move not

"Learn not the way of the heathen" the prophets from Moses on had preached; but such idolatrous vain-glory as the decorated tree (or idol) here described always attracts worshippers. It was amazing to Jeremiah, as it is to us, that speechless and powerless idols can replace the living God in the hearts of human beings. The contrast between the true God who "is the living God, and an everlasting king" and the "gods that have not made the heavens and the earth" should have decided that contest in all the ages past, but even to the present it has not done so. Therefore, because of vanity and mockery, people lose their heritage (Jer. 10:1–18).

The prophet lamented the loss of homes and people, the failure of leaders, and the imminent invasion. He uttered for the land a supplication for guidance, correction, justice—and hoped that at last the Lord's wrath would turn upon the heathen.

11:1–23 The word that came to Jeremiah from the Lord, saying, Hear ye the words of this covenant

In contrast to the previous castigations, calls for repentance, and forecasts of calamity, the prophet reminded Israel of the Lord's covenants and promises and His help in bringing them out of Egypt unto the land of their inheritance, a land "flowing with milk and honey." He reminded them also of prophetic admonitions and warnings since then in their land, so often ignored by the people. He told them the Lord had revealed to him their "conspiracy" of evil and intent to turn back to the idolatrous ways of their forefathers, and he disclosed the evils that would come upon them as a result of their idolatrous worship. Prayers for them and temple worship by them would be futile. They had been the Lord's "beloved" and his "green olive tree," but because they had neither reciprocated nor produced, they would be destroyed.

The prophet told of a plot against him, revealed to him by the Lord. He had been "like a lamb or an ox that is brought to the slaughter" without knowing that the people of his own home city, Anathoth, had planned to kill him. He left vengeance to the Lord, who promised that they who had forbidden him to prophesy, lest he die by their hand, would themselves die by the sword and by famine in Anathoth in "the year of their visitation" (Jer. 11:18–23). Compare Jesus' words about His rejection in Nazareth (Matt. 13:54–58).

12:1–17 Wherefore doth the way of the wicked prosper? Wherefore are all they happy that deal very treacherously?

Jeremiah's guarded question about the apparent material prosperity of the wicked is not an uncommon question, even among prophets (Jer. 12:1–4; cf. Job 24; Ps. 35:17–28; Hab. 1:2–4: D&C 121:1–6; 122:5–9). The answer is not comforting: in this world of agency for every soul, some will find ways to get gain unjustly. But if one is dismayed by the small things, he may not survive the deeper and the larger problems. The prophet's disturbed feeling about the prosperity of the wicked was transcended by the Lord's sorrow over the prevalence of wickedness among His people and especially among their leaders. Their wickedness made it necessary to let the "spoilers" come upon the land. Yet again, the Lord gave assurance of ultimate justice, including removal of the oppressors and restoration of repentant people to their heritage. Any others who will covenant in His name may "be built in the midst" of His people.

13:1–27 Take the girdle . . . go to Euphrates, and hide it there in a hole of the rock. . . . it came to pass after many days that the Lord said unto me, Arise, go to Euphrates, and take the girdle from thence, . . . and, behold, the girdle was marred, it was profitable for nothing

Euphrates, which is used here to translate the Hebrew *Prath,* was possibly a city of that name north of Jeremiah's home, but the name could symbolize the great Euphrates valley, nearly three hundred miles away, where Judah would be in bondage for many years. The symbolism of the demonstration is clear.

With another metaphor, the Lord decried the existing social and religious decadence of Judah and warned the people, king, and queen to humble themselves and repent lest they suffer.

If the prophet and those who heard him wondered why destruction could not be avoided, the reply was that repentance and change for the better is as difficult as changing the color of a man's skin or a leopard's spots.

14:1–22 The word of the Lord that came to Jeremiah concerning the dearth

A cyclical drought must have been particularly severe at some time during Jeremiah's ministry, for this chapter records his supplicating "the hope of Israel, the saviour thereof" for relief. It reports the Lord's negative response because of the people's unworthiness.

One cause of the people's ambivalence had been false prophets who prophesied comforting lies in the name of the Lord, although he had "sent them not." The Lord assured Jeremiah that such prophets would themselves be consumed by famine and the sword along with their followers, but their destruction was also a cause for the Lord to mourn and lament.

Apparently there were some yet in Jerusalem who listened to the messages of the Lord and the true prophet, for they sought the Lord's forgiveness and salvation from drought and famine— for they knew no power among the gentiles could save them.

15:1–9 Then said the Lord unto me, Though Moses and Samuel stood before me, yet my mind could not be toward this people

Responding to the supplications of the prophet and some of the people of Jerusalem that they might be spared, the Lord told the prophet that regardless of the appeals—even if joined by such former prophets as Moses and Samuel—Judah could not thereby be saved. Both Moses and Samuel had in their times gained a reprieve for their people (Ex. 32:30–35; 1 Sam. 7), but their people had repented; few—if any—were genuinely repentant in Jeremiah's time. Seeking blessings through the merits of renowned leaders is justifiable only for humble, worthy people.

Part of the blame belonged to wicked King Manasseh for having reversed the reforms of his father, Hezekiah. The people's responsibility lay in their having gone backwards in their way of life; that is, instead of teaching others, they had learned and lived the ways of the people among whom they dwelt (Jer. 15:1–6; cf. Isa. 1:4; 2 Kgs. 21; and commentary). As a result, they would be fanned like grain at threshing time and carried away as useless chaff is carried away by the wind. Many would be widowed, and sadly, as always, widowed mothers would suffer from the terrors of military actions.

15:10–21 Woe is me, my mother, that thou hast borne me a man of strife and a man of contention

The prophecy about the widowed mothers seems to have led the prophet to lament his own mother's having borne him to see such suffering and to suffer persecution himself at the hands of those whom he had tried to save. The Lord assured him the enemy (Babylon) would treat him better than his own people had, though for others the "iron and the steel" of that invader would not be soft. His people's substance and treasure would become spoil, and they would pass into unknown lands. That warning is phrased as if it pertained to the prophet's own substance and treasure, but that meaning is corroborated nowhere else. The Hebrew of the passage is difficult, and so the translation is debatable.

So depressed was Jeremiah that he seems to have retired for a time from the work. He sought more comfort from the Lord, reviewed his efforts and its negative results, and spoke of his "perpetual" pain. The Lord had promised him protection when he called him as a prophet, and he frankly wondered whether the promise would be fulfilled. To this the Lord responded that if he would return to his work and separate "the precious from the vile" in his thoughts and spirit, he would continue as the Lord's prophet and would be sustained as he had been promised (cf. Jer. 1:17–20).

16:1–13 The word of the Lord came also unto me, saying, Thou shalt not take thee a wife, neither shalt thou have sons or daughters in this place

Another sacrifice was required of Jeremiah: he would live and work alone, without a wife for a companion or children for comfort in the future. In so doing, he would emphasize the warning that many sons and daughters, wives and mothers, would "die of grievous deaths," with none to lament or bury them when the invader came. He might have had a family and they could have received supernatural protection, but that kind of charmed life is seldom provided for prophets (Jer. 16:1–4; cf. TG, "Suffering"; "Prophets, Rejection of").

A horrible picture of death, decay, bereavement, and despair had to be communicated to the people. If the people asked why such horrible events should come, the prophet was to recite their guilt and that of their forefathers and give them the ultimatum.

16:14–21 it shall no more be said, The Lord liveth, that brought up the children of Israel out of the land of Egypt; But, the Lord liveth, that brought up the children of Israel from the land of the north, and from all the lands whither he had driven them

Yet glorious hopes for the future were extended to Judah by the Lord through Jeremiah. Seldom are dire prophetic predictions given and a hopeless picture left without the future hope also being extended. That gives hope to those who believe and testifies to those who doubt that the Lord's program for earth will eventually be implemented.

"The land of the north" was the unspecified area to which the departing exiles went. It became a name for the lands of the lost tribes, and modern revelation so uses it; nevertheless, prophecies make it clear that Israel will be gathered from east, west, north, and south, and from islands of the sea (TG, "Israel, Gathering of"; D&C 133:18–30, esp. v. 26). The gathering, one by one, by "fishers" and "hunters" searching the mountains, hills, and holes in the rocks (Jer. 16:16 and fn. *a*) is the mode of operation for missionaries of the latter-day restored Church.

The conversions of "Gentiles" as well as the blood of Israel will bring fulfillment of the mission of Abraham's seed (Jer. 16:19–21; TG, "Abrahamic Covenant").

17:1–11 The sin of Judah is written with a pen of iron, and with the point of a diamond: it is graven upon the table of their heart, and upon the horns of your altars

Instruments for engraving on metal had metaphorically engraved the hard hearts and the altars of apostate Israel, and because they continued their idolatry, they were losing their land and spiritual heritage (Jer. 17:1–4; on the craft of engraving, see 1 Ne. 3:3; BD, "Engraving").

Trusting in man, or the arm of flesh, rather than trusting in God brought no safety or salvation. Trust in the Lord, or faith in him, is the way to obtain hope, blessings, sustenance, and inner peace. Symbolic language conveys that assurance (Jer. 17:5–11; TG, "Trust Not in the Arm of Flesh").

17:12–18 O Lord, the hope of Israel, all that forsake thee shall be ashamed . . . Heal me, O Lord, and I shall be healed; save me, and I shall be saved

This lovely prayer by Jeremiah is filled with good thoughts and expressions useful to any in praying and worshipping the Lord.

17:19–27 Thus saith the Lord; Take heed to yourselves, and bear no burden on the sabbath day

An admonition on keeping the Sabbath day holy—fidelity to which commandment indicates fidelity to the Lord and his law— is like the teachings of Isaiah and of modern prophets. Naturally, the results of desecrating the Sabbath are also noted (Isa. 58:13–14; D&C 59:9–24; TG, "Sabbath").

18:1–17 Arise, and go down to the potter's house, and there I will cause thee to hear my words

The metaphor likening the potter's shaping pliable clay to the

Lord's trying to shape His people is simple and vivid; the correlative fact is implicit that pottery, once dried and fired, cannot be reshaped. This denunciation of Israel is resumed in the next chapter (Jer. 18:6–12; 19:11; cf. Isa. 45:9). The symbolism of forsaking the pure waters from on high is also vivid (Jer. 18:14–15; cf. 2:13; TG, "Living Water"). The warning of exile and scattering is plain.

18:18–23 Then said they, Come, and let us devise devices against Jeremiah

The reasons for rejecting the prophet Jeremiah were the usual ones: his teachings were different from those of the priests, "wise" men, and popular "prophets." Jeremiah's bitter reactions may have been intensified by the threats and oppression under which he lived (Jer. 18:19ff.; cf. 20; 26; 37; 44; 1 Ne. 1:4, 13, 18–20).

19:1–15 Thus saith the Lord, Go and get a potter's earthen bottle, and take of the ancients of the people, and of the ancients of the priests; And go forth unto the valley of the son of Hinnom

The pottery jug is breakable, for it is no longer pliable clay. The valley of Hinnom was the place where idolatrous altars and images had long been established, and the worst of Israel's apostate practices were enacted there. It was also a place for dumping refuse, sometimes called Tophet (BD, "Hinnom, valley of"; "Gehenna"; "Topheth").

Jeremiah took with him certain elders to hear his condemnation of human sacrifice, a horror never to be resorted to, much less used in worship of the Lord (Jer. 19:1–7, 5*a*). The prophet made dire predictions of parallel horrors to develop under siege and broke the pottery jug as a sign that neither it nor the idolater could be reshaped, hence they would be broken and cast away. Grim predictions of starvation, death, and conflagration followed; and history shows that all those horrors came with the Babylonian invasion. Why did the Lord not prevent it? He could not do so and preserve principles of agency and law in His world. With their agency, the people had "hardened their necks, that they might not hear [his] words" (Jer. 19:8–15).

20:1–18 Then Pashur smote Jeremiah the prophet, and put him in the stocks that were in the high gate of Benjamin, which was by the house of the Lord

A senior officer at the temple was brazen enough to "smite" the prophet, confine him in a device that holds the body in a distorted position, and keep him there overnight in a public place—all because of his prophecies. Undaunted, Jeremiah renamed him "terror all around"; the name *Pashur* appears to have meant something like "prosperity all around"—quite the opposite of his new name (Jer. 20:3*a*). He prophesied Pashur would suffer terror with the exiles and die in Babylon; the royal house would fare no better (Jer. 20:4–6).

Jeremiah's integrity held throughout the rejection and physical abuse he suffered, but he was not happy in his lonely and stressful calling. He had been reluctant to undertake it but had been persuaded by the Lord to do so (Jer. 20:7*a;* cf. 1:17–19). He felt that he had aroused only reproach and derision, yet his convictions were so strong that he could not forbear preaching repentance. In response he heard plotting and "fear on every side" (the same words in Hebrew as the new name he gave Pashur); and people watched for a reason to take revenge on him (Jer. 20:8–10). On the other hand, he was confident that the Lord would defend him and avenge his suffering; therefore, he praised and thanked the Lord, even though he lamented at times as Job had (Jer. 20:11–18; cf. Job 3:3–4).

This masterpiece in the biblical prophetic literature displays pressures and afflictions experienced by a prophet.

21:1–14 The word which came unto Jeremiah from the Lord, when king Zedekiah sent unto him Pashur the son of Melchiah . . . saying, Enquire, I pray thee, of the Lord for us; for Nebuchadrezzar king of Babylon maketh war against us

This account seems a surprising change from the narrative of the preceding chapter, but this Pashur is of a different family. Furthermore, it will be seen later that the king of Judah really wanted information from the prophet but was afraid to let his court know about it (cf. Jer. 37).

The king's receptiveness was not seen by the prophet as repentance unto salvation, however, and the message from the Lord was that He would "fight against" the king and deliver him and his people into the hand of the invaders. The only way to save their lives at this juncture was to surrender to the Chaldeans (Babylonians) and not try to resist.

The last part of this prophecy was addressed to the royal house and to Jerusalem, though the metaphors are unusual; the "inhabitant of the valley" and the "rock of the plain" may have symbolized both the lowly and the high and mighty. The admonition to the government to do justice and deliver the oppressed was the same message as usual—and so were the consequences if the leaders would not heed the admonishment (Jer. 21:11–14).

22:1–30 Hear the word of the Lord, O king of Judah

Amplification of a previous message to the "house of David" is provided in a review of prophetic warnings to three kings of Judah who succeeded King Josiah and reigned in sequence before Zedekiah (Jer. 22:2–9; cf. 21:11–14). A prophecy to Shallum (or Jehoahaz, son of Josiah) had warned that death was to be desired rather than exile, but he was gone and could never return. Next is the warning that had been given to Jehoiakim, second heir to the good King Josiah. He was reprimanded for a life of opulence and failure to do justice in a time of need, and his ignoble end was predicted (Jer. 22:13–19; cf. Jer. 36). Last is the prophecy about the third king after Josiah, who was not a son but a grandson called Coniah, Jeconiah, and Jehoiachin. He was young and inept and mercifully was not killed but was taken alive to Babylon, where he lived many years. He was even elevated later to be a kind of leader in exile. The prophet said there was no way to save him or his kingdom in his time and lamented him as "childless" because no son of his would reign in Jerusalem. Nonetheless, his lineage would be preserved and become the ancestry of Joseph and Mary the mother of Jesus (Jer. 22:20–30;

52:31–34 cf. 2 Kgs. 24:8–16; 1 Chr. 3:17–24; Matt. 1:11–12; TG, "Jesus Christ, Davidic Descent of").

The fourth and last king of Judah was Josiah's son Zedekiah.

He was placed on the throne after young King Jehoiachin was exiled, but his reign is not covered by this chapter.

23:1– 40 Woe be unto the pastors that destroy and scatter the sheep of my pasture! saith the Lord

After the first declaration of woe to the bad shepherds of Jeremiah's times, the Lord promised a future restoration with good shepherds and a righteous Branch of the royal line as King. The prophet titled him *JHVH Tzidkenu,* "Jehovah is our righteousness," and promised restoration of both parts of Israel as a kingdom of peace and safety. This will be the kingdom of the Lord. So phenomenal will the last gathering and restoration be that the deliverance from Egypt under Moses will be eclipsed as the lost tribes gather from the north country and elsewhere (Jer. 23:1–8).

Jeremiah lamented his own times, in which false prophets and priests fostered such wickedness, adultery, lies, and collaboration in evil as had flourished in Sodom and Gomorrah. False prophets promised "peace," but they and the people faced destruction. If they had really taught the Lord's words, they could have saved the people. The Lord is a God near at hand, and He knows what people and prophets do, both false and true.

True prophets will give to the people "wheat," not "chaff," but the Lord's words from them can be like a fire to burn or a hammer to break. False prophets get messages from each other and claim the Lord spoke them. They have dreams *not* from God and cause people to err by reason of them.

If anyone asked the true prophet, "What is the burden of the Lord?" he would reply with warnings against their wickedness. No other priests, prophets, or people were to present any other "burden" and pretend it was from the Lord (Jer. 23:34–40; *burdens* are messages of doom "lifted up" against a people).

24:1–10 The Lord shewed me, and, behold, two baskets of figs were set before the temple of the Lord, after that Nebuchadrezzar king of Babylon had carried away captive Jeconiah

The time of this message was about 598 B.C., which was about two years after Lehi's group escaped from Jerusalem and ten years after King Jehoahaz was killed and Daniel and his friends were taken to Babylon. During that time Jehoahaz's brother Jehoiakim, the father of Jehoiachin, had also been dethroned and killed and young Jehoiachin (Jeconiah) installed. Within the year of the prophecy recorded here, Jehoiachin and yet another group were taken to Babylon, so this prophecy was addressed to the people left in Jerusalem. Those people may have felt that they were good enough to have been spared, but in truth they were likely not good enough to be carried off, for the Babylonian leaders took away the best people of a nation—those with the capacity to organize and to produce. That practice reduced the power of a captive nation and gave the captors more valuable servants (see Dan. 1 and commentary). Thus the vision of two contrasting baskets of figs: the first taken were the best; those remaining were not to feel superior or secure, because they also would go out in time (Jer. 24:8–10).

25:1–38 The word that came to Jeremiah . . . in the fourth year of Jehoiakim . . . , the first year of Nebuchadrezzar king of Babylon

The date of this revelation would be 604 B.C. (BD, "Chronology," p. 639), an ominous year for Judah and for all nations in the path of the Babylonian empire. Note that the prophecies of Jeremiah have not been arranged chronologically; this revelation was received before the preceding four from Zedekiah's time.

The difference between the more familiar *Nebuchadnezzar* and the variant *Nebuchadrezzar* is in the transliteration of the Babylonian name *Nabu-kudur-usur* (BD, "Nebuchadnezzar").

Although the rise of Nebuchadnezzar was threatening, the prophet had little hope that the people of Judah would hearken to his warning because they had not done so during the preceding twenty-three years of his ministry. Indeed, all the prophets of the Lord were sent well in advance of events ("rising early and sending them") to warn the people, but the people had refused to heed his words.

Jeremiah prophesied precisely that Judah and other lands would be subjected to Babylonia for "seventy years" (Jer. 25:8–14); that period ended at the time Cyrus of the Medes and the Persians overthrew Babylon, ca. 536 B.C.). The prophet's vision was then extended to the terrors of the universal reign of wickedness among all nations in the last days. He addressed all nations then known, listing them from south and west to north and east; *Sheshach* was a code name for Babel. The "city which is called by my name" was the city of the temple, Jerusalem; and from thence the destruction would proceed to all nations (Jer. 25:15–29; cf. D&C 112:25–26).

In keeping with his justice and mercy, the Lord will "plead with all flesh" to repent before destruction comes; but it will be universal. The "shepherds," or leaders of the nations, shall "howl" in desperation, with no place to turn or to flee when the power of the Lord cleanses the earth (Jer. 25:30–38).

26:1–24 In the beginning of the reign of Jehoiakim . . . came this word from the Lord, saying . . . Stand in the court of the Lord's house, and speak unto all the cities of Judah, which come to worship in the Lord's house, all the words that I command thee

The first of twenty historical chapters that relate many of the prophet's experiences and the persecution he suffered as he continued his mission, chapter 26 dates to five years before the previous chapter, being "in the beginning of the reign of Jehoiakim," or 609 B.C. Jeremiah delivered this message from the Lord on the temple grounds, so that the worshippers might repent and be saved. If they would not do so, they might know that they would be overcome and the temple itself destroyed, as was the tabernacle at Shiloh in Eli's time (Jer. 26:6a; BD, "Shiloh"). Again false "priests and the prophets" led the people in objecting to the true prophet, and they actually sought his life; the "princes" of Judah listened as Jeremiah stated his message and made his appeal. With astounding insight, they defended him (Jer. 26:10–19a).

The king had put one prophet to death for such prophesying

(see Jer. 26:20*a*, on the similar danger to Lehi, another prophet of this same time); however, Ahikam, son of Shaphan the scribe of the days of good King Josiah, successfully defended and saved Jeremiah (Jer. 26:20–23*a*, 24*a*).

27:1–22 In the beginning of the reign of Jehoiakim . . . came this word unto Jeremiah from the Lord, saying . . . Make thee bonds and yokes, and put them upon thy neck

Symbolic "bonds and yokes" were to be prepared by the prophet about eleven years before Zedekiah's time and sent to the neighboring nations with the warning that the Lord was permitting Babylon as His "servant" to dominate them for a time (Jer. 27:6–8). The false "prophets" who promised them safety, or said the vessels taken earlier from the temple would soon be returned, were not to be trusted. The way for Zedekiah of Judah to survive was to submit to Babylon. Otherwise, the temple would be destroyed and its vessels, font, and pillars taken away (Jer. 27:9–22; cf. 39; 2 Kgs. 25).

28:1–17 in the beginning of the reign of Zedekiah . . . in the fourth year . . . Hananiah the son of Azur the prophet . . . spake unto me in the house of the Lord, . . . I have broken the yoke of the king of Babylon

The dramatic exchange between the true prophet and a false one happened at a time when Judah and other nations were considering rebelling against Babylon, who had already invaded them twice, once in 609 B.C. and again in 598. Note the false hopes of Hananiah, the restrained reply by Jeremiah, the dramatic breaking of Jeremiah's symbolic yoke by Hananiah, and then the hard and forthright declaration of Jeremiah. The outcome was conclusive; Hananiah died as Jeremiah had prophesied.

29:1–32 the words of the letter that Jeremiah the prophet sent from Jerusalem unto the . . . elders which were carried away captives, and to the priests, . . . prophets, . . . and . . . people . . . carried away captive from Jerusalem

As will be noted in other prophetic books of the time, the

Lord did not neglect those in captivity in Babylon: Daniel and Ezekiel were there, and Jeremiah also communicated with the captives. This conciliatory letter was addressed to the exiles, including King Jeconiah and many leading citizens, who were taken to Babylon in 598 B.C. It was sent along with the messengers of Zedekiah to the king of Babylon. It recommended that the captive peoples maintain positive attitudes and actions. It warned against false prophets and predictions, and it promised a return after seventy years. Meanwhile, the exiles would be nourished by the word of the Lord and by "thoughts of peace, and not of evil" (Jer. 29:8–12). A promise (familiar as an aria in Felix Mendelssohn's *Elijah*) states that any who seek the Lord with all their hearts shall surely find him; indeed, he will gather them.

The prophet warned the people, both at home and in exile, to beware of prophets and priests who were not of the Lord. People still in Jerusalem who were deceived by them would soon find themselves under siege. These had suggested that Jeremiah be put in stocks for telling the people that their captivity would be long and for urging them to seek normal ways of life in Babylon. Jeremiah gave them a revelation from the Lord against false prophets and against false priests (Jer. 29:15; 20–32).

30:1–24 The word that came to Jeremiah from the Lord, saying, . . . Write thee all the words that I have spoken unto thee in a book. For lo, the days come, saith the Lord, that I will bring again the captivity of my people Israel and Judah, . . . and I will cause them to return to the land that I gave to their fathers, and they shall possess it

We have such ancient prophetic books as the book of Jeremiah because the Lord commanded that they be written; in them are recorded prophecies for the latter days so that the people who had sinned and were exiled would know that their latter-day descendants would fulfill the mission of Abraham and Israel and that the Lord's purposes would be accomplished.

Jeremiah spoke of Israel and Judah as if they were two peoples, because they had been two nations since the division of the kingdom after Solomon's reign on through the loss of the ten tribes and the captivity of Judah and they would be separate until the latter-day gathering.

The times of "trembling, of fear, and not of peace" before the day of deliverance are in the latter days. The time of peace and salvation is to come in the messianic kingdom. Humankind could not cure their own ills, and Israel's idol gods, far from being any help to anyone, had been a major cause of their rejection. Their sorrows would be incurable but for the Lord; He will heal and restore the outcasts whom people denigrate, scoffing at their "Zion."

"I will bring again the captivity" means, "I will return the captives." The city of Jerusalem, its dwellings, and citadel shall be restored. A lovely picture of joy and thanksgiving in those times is given when all shall have a renewed relationship with the Lord. It is contrasted with an opposite picture of the fate of the wicked in the latter days.

31:1– 40 At the same time, saith the Lord, will I be the God of all the families of Israel, and they shall be my people

This statement, which ends the previous chapter in the Hebrew scriptures (to avoid its ending with negative predictions), expresses the theme of chapter 31. It anticipates divine loving kindness, the gathering of Israel and Judah, the establishment of Zion, the restoration of spiritual fruitfulness, and the establishment of a new covenant. Pure joy in the restoration of Zion is symbolized by the virgins, the young men, and the old—all singing and dancing. Abundant sacrifices in thanksgiving respond to goodness from the Lord.

The next section harks back to the tragic times of the apostasy and loss of the northern ten tribes. "Ramah" is a point south of Jerusalem, looking toward Bethlehem; it is still called *Ramat Rachel* ("height of Rachel"), in memory of the death of Rachel, wife of Jacob, because she bore her last baby near that point and died. The original concept of her mourning for her children arose from the captivity of the ten tribes (whose leader was the birthright tribe of Ephraim, son of Joseph, son of Rachel and Jacob). This prophecy ends with anticipation of their return. Matthew adapted the words to characterize the lamentation in nearby Bethlehem after the slaughter of the innocents by Herod (Jer. 31:15–17; Matt. 2:1–2, 16–18).

Following Ephraim's "bemoaning himself," the prophet indicated that the Lord is aware of both their sorrow and their repentance and will speed the return of Ephraim and the others. The righteousness of those latter-day generations of Israel shall exceed that of the former who departed.

Judah too appeared in the prophet's vision of the return. With an anticipation of the new place of the true government and temple of God, the prophet "awoke" from the vision that must indeed have been sweet to him.

Then Jeremiah recorded the Lord's promises to "sow" Judah and Israel again with people and animals. At last the prophet could enjoy the other part of his mission—"to build, and to plant." The adage that the children suffer for the parents' deeds will no longer be heard; all will know that they are accountable only for their own sins.

The new covenant of the latter days will not be a set of standards imposed externally but an internal set, with individuals' minds and hearts committed to right and justice.

In conclusion, the prophet foresaw the establishment of the kingdom of God on earth for a time of peace forever, and ordinances of the new covenant will remain like the ordained motions of sun, moon, and stars.

32:1– 44 The word that came to Jeremiah from the Lord in the tenth year of Zedekiah king of Judah, which was the eighteenth year of Nebuchadnezzar. For then the king of Babylon's army besieged Jerusalem

Significant incidents occurred in the life of the prophet at the beginning of Babylon's last siege of Jerusalem (ca. 587–586 B.C.; Jer. 37). Jeremiah had been remanded to "the court of the prison" for continually predicting Judah's inevitable overthrow by Babylon unless the king and people repented. A cousin of Jeremiah asked him to redeem some property of his family in Anathoth. After asking the Lord about it, Jeremiah did so as a symbolic act, signifying that though the Lord had said Judah would be captured, yet "houses and fields and vineyards shall be possessed again in this land" (Jer. 32:1–15).

With many avowals of faith that the Lord could do anything, the prophet asked for reassurance, and the word of the Lord came again, reaffirming that indeed nothing is "too hard" for the Lord. Though He would give Judah into the hands of the Chaldeans (Babylonians), He would bring them back to be His people again, and He would be their God. Then fields shall indeed be bought again, as symbolized by Jeremiah's act. The whole land shall be inhabited and productive at last.

33:1–26 Moreover the word of the Lord came unto Jeremiah the second time, while he was yet shut up in the court of the prison, saying, . . . I will cause the captivity of Judah and the captivity of Israel to return, and will build them, as at the first

Some words from Jeremiah while in prison, and some from an earlier prophecy, seem to have inspired part of the third verse of the latter-day hymn "How Firm a Foundation" (*Hymns* [Salt Lake City: The Church of Jesus Christ of Latter-day Saints, 1985], no. 85; Jer. 30:10–11; 33:7).

The theme of restoration continues, promising the gathering of Judah and Israel and their establishment as a unified, righteous kingdom at last, with a divine "Branch" descended from David as King to "execute judgment and righteousness" (Jer. 33:7–18). The promise of these actions is as sure as the sequences of day and night and the order of the heavens and earth.

34:1–22 The word which came unto Jeremiah from the Lord, when Nebuchadnezzar . . . and all his army, and all the kingdoms of the earth of his dominion, and all the people, fought against Jerusalem, and against all the cities thereof

These are prophetic words and political actions from the last days of Jerusalem, 588 to 586 B.C. Jeremiah gave the king one more warning and promise as the siege was being prepared against his fortress cities—Jerusalem, Lachish, and Azekah. The king and people were by that time fearful enough that they made a token repentance, freeing their fellow Hebrews who were in bondage to them, as the law of Moses required. Society had become polarized into the rich and the poor. If a poor family could not pay their rent and taxes, part or all of the family could be taken into servitude for the debt.

Then Jerusalem had a little respite from the siege when Babylon heard that Egypt was sending an army to oppose their further advance. It may have been this respite that permitted the rich and powerful in Jerusalem to void their repentant acts and take their servants back (Jer. 34:1–16; 37:5; Ex. 21:1–6; Deut. 15:7–15). Consequently, a more stringent prophecy was issued by the Lord through the prophet, who declared, ironically, "Behold, I proclaim a liberty for you": they would have liberty from serving the Lord and would go "to the sword, to the pestilence, and to the famine." Alluding to the covenant of Abraham under which they should have been living, the Lord declared that His protection of them was voided; Judah would be "a desolation without an inhabitant" (Jer. 34:16–22, 18a–b).

35:1–19 The word which came unto Jeremiah from the Lord in the days of Jehoiakim . . . saying, Go unto the house of the Rechabites, and speak unto them

This revelation came much earlier than those preceding (see Jer. 27, which records a revelation from Jehoiakim's time).

The Rechabites, here presented as an example for Judah, were descendants of Hobab, the brother-in-law of Moses. He served as a guide to Israel in the wilderness, and his people were given an inheritance in the promised land with Israel. The Druze people of Lebanon, Syria, and Israel have traditions connecting them back to those ancient people (Jer. 35:2a; BD, "Kenites").

The Rechabites' exemplary behavior was their obedience to the teachings of the law and of their forefathers. They would not drink wine, even wine offered them in the temple. They had abandoned their traditional tents and come to Jerusalem because of the Babylonian threat; but on account of their integrity, they were given a prophetic promise of preservation.

In contrast, neither northern Israel nor Judah had kept the law, nor had they hearkened to the prophetic messages from the

Lord. They had therefore forfeited divine protection and were doomed to exile in Babylon.

36:1–32 in the fourth year of Jehoiakim . . . this word came unto Jeremiah from the Lord, saying, Take thee a roll of a book, and write therein all the words that I have spoken unto thee against Israel, and against Judah, and against all the nations, . . . from the days of Josiah, even unto this day

This event is also from an earlier time. The fourth year of Jehoiakim would have been about 605 B.C. This chapter provides an example of the way Jeremiah's revelations and historical sketches were written and preserved (TG, "Scriptures, Writing of"; "Scriptures, Preservation of"; BD, "Canon). It tells that the prophet used the services of a scribe and indicates the materials used; it also shows the period covered by his writings to this point—about twenty-three years (Jer. 1:1–2; 36:1–2, 18). It tells the purposes of the prophetic writing and shows Jeremiah's situation as he dictated the revelations. It records the response of the servants and princes and the response of the king. Finally, it shows how the copies of revelations destroyed by the king were restored through the prophet.

37:1–21 And Zedekiah the king sent Jehucal . . . and Zephaniah . . . to the prophet Jeremiah, saying, Pray now unto the Lord our God for us

This incident and prophetic warning came in the days of King Zedekiah, at a time of a break in the Babylonian siege (ca. 588 B.C.; Jer. 35:1–5; 34:10–11). It seems surprising that the king would finally ask the prophet to pray in behalf of Judah; it is possible that he hoped the Babylonians would be beaten by the Egyptians and the temporary lifting of the siege would become permanent. Neither Judah nor the king was worthy of such a blessing, however, and the answer from the Lord was another condemnation and message of doom.

When the prophet sought a little respite out of the city, he was apprehended, accused of deserting to the enemy, flogged, and imprisoned. Oddly enough, when the king heard of the incident "many days" later, he sent for the prophet and secretly asked again for the word of the Lord. Even though the word was still that he would be overthrown by Babylon, he granted the prophet's request that he not be returned to the dungeon. Jeremiah remained in protective custody (with food provided) in "the court of the prison," where he was involved in events discussed in earlier chapters (Jer. 37:11–21; 32:1–2; 33:1).

38:1–28 Therefore the princes said unto the king, We beseech thee, let this man be put to death: for thus he weakeneth the hands of the men of war that remain in this city

Because Jeremiah continued to assert that the Lord would not save Jerusalem and Judah from Babylon and that anyone who wanted to survive must surrender, the leaders insisted that he be put to death. This time King Zedekiah yielded to his evil counselors, and Jeremiah was put in a pit, possibly a cistern, with no water but only some residual sludge in the bottom.

The faith and courage of the Ethiopian *Ebed-melech* (which means "the king's servant"), is noteworthy, and his practical way of rescuing the prophet admirable. Miraculously, the king allowed the rescue, which must be attributed to divine intervention.

The pitiable king's last consultation with the prophet drew from him the same divine edict: unworthy of protection, he could only surrender. The promise was merciful, for he could thereby live and the city would not be burnt, but the king had no faith in that promise. He feared Jewish defectors among the Babylonians, despite the prophet's reassurances. The interview did end with a plan being made that would keep the prophet out of the hands of his adversaries until the city fell.

39:1–18; 40:1–6 In the ninth year of Zedekiah . . . came Nebuchadrezzar . . . against Jerusalem, . . . And in the eleventh year . . . the city was broken up

The commentary on another account of this event (2 Kgs. 25) gives some details of the tragic devastation of Judah and Jerusalem and demolition of the great temple there—the temple of Solomon, which had been there some four hundred fifty years.

Note again the fate of the leaders and of the king's family. In contrast to their fate, note that the poor, who had often been taken into servitude by the leaders and rich land owners, were given "the vineyards and the fields" by the Babylonian captain of the guard (Jer. 34:8–11; 39:1–10, 6*b*; 41:10; 43:6). The Babylonians treated the prophet well, as had been promised (Jer. 15:11); further details are given in Jeremiah 41.

Gedaliah, who was appointed by the Babylonians to rule over the Jews remaining in the land, was the son of the same Ahikam who had defended the prophet earlier (Jer. 39:11–14; 26:24; 40:2–5).

An earlier prophecy to Ebed-melech, promising him deliverance, is mentioned (Jer. 39:15–18).

The "testimony" of Nebuzaradan is noteworthy, as is his consideration for the prophet (Jer. 40:1–6).

40:7–16; 41:1–18 Then they came to Gedaliah

Gedaliah was accepted as the leader of the remnant of Judah, and he was fair and conciliatory; the Lord must have brought about his appointment by Nebuzaradan. Even Jews who had taken refuge in neighboring nations to avoid captivity gathered to him. Indeed, when told that an enemy had arisen to destroy him, Gedaliah was such a good and trusting man that he would not believe it (Jer. 40:14–16).

The wicked prevailed, however; with a false show of friendship, Elishama "of the seed royal," with some princes, ate with Gedaliah and then rose up to slay him. All who were with him, and even some who were coming to worship at the ruins of the house of the Lord, were ruthlessly slain.

Nothing is known of the pit "which Asa the king had made," though it may have been part of that good king's defenses of Jerusalem (1 Kgs. 15:21–23). Whatever it was, it gave the assassins time to escape detection for a while. The royalist Ishmael even seized the surviving daughters of King Zedekiah but did not harm them (Jer. 41:10*a*). The true friends of Gedaliah were unable to catch the killers, but they did rescue those who had been taken captive. It is understandable but unfortunate that the survivors chose to go to Egypt for refuge (Jer. 41:11–18; 42).

42:1–22 pray for us unto the Lord thy God, even for all this remnant . . . That the Lord thy God may shew us the way wherein we may walk, and the thing that we must do

Johanan and Jezaniah, who had been faithful friends to Gedaliah, appeared to be humble, faithful, and receptive to divine guidance when they asked counsel of the Lord through the prophet; but Jeremiah knew their minds and asked for their promise that they would do what the Lord directed. They said, perhaps intentionally, "pray to the Lord thy God," but he countered, "I will pray unto the Lord your God" (Jer. 42:1–6).

The counsel came that they should not take refuge in Egypt but trust the Lord's promises of safety and mercy in Judah and strongly warned against their plan to flee. The Lord and the prophet knew that Johanan and Jezaniah had not sincerely asked for advice but merely desired consent or confirmation in doing what they had decided to do (Jer. 42:20). The prophet told them that they would die if they pursued their willful way.

43:1–13 Then spake Azariah . . . and Johanan . . . and all the proud men, saying unto Jeremiah, Thou speakest falsely: the Lord our God hath not sent thee to say, Go not into Egypt

Refusing to heed the revelation, the leaders and people chose to go to Egypt. They blamed the prophet's scribe, Baruch, for instigating Jeremiah's opposition to the move. Surprisingly, the prophet and his scribe were taken along by the refugees, as were "the king's daughters." They stopped at Tahpanhes, a fortified border town on an eastern branch of the Nile in the delta (Jer. 43:1–7, 6a). Though the translation is not certain about the meaning of the stones to be hidden outside the entry to the royal house there, Jeremiah's prophecy was essentially about Babylon's coming conquest. Egypt's armies, idols, and people would all suffer the invasion of Nebuchadnezzar (Jer. 43:8–13).

44:1–30 The word that came to Jeremiah concerning all the Jews which dwell in the land of Egypt

There were four places in which Jews already dwelt in Egypt; evidently many refugees had fled there before the little group that included Jeremiah. The revelation to them about their faults and sins is similar to a review of evils in Israel written a century and a quarter earlier, at the time of the fall of the northern ten tribes. It is evident that these exiles had not been faithful, were not humbled by their circumstances, and still refused to observe the divine laws (Jer. 44:2–14; cf. 2 Kgs. 17:6–23).

Far from being repentant, the spokesmen among them in Egypt were quite defiant and justified their wives in worshipping "the queen of heaven." They claimed that even in Jerusalem they had had more food when they sacrificed to her.

The prophet responded with a stinging reprimand of them and their forefathers for their idolatry and their perfidious justification of it. He essentially affirmed their excommunication from God and his goodness. Only a small remnant would return to testify of their fate. The prophet gave them, as a certification of his word, a prophecy that Pharaoh Hophra would be conquered by Nebuchadnezzar as Zedekiah had been (Jer. 44:20–30).

45:1–5 The word that Jeremiah the prophet spake unto Baruch

The prophet's faithful friend and scribe, who was also taken into Egypt by the Jewish refugees (Jer. 43:6), lamented their situation there. What "great things" he had hoped for himself is not clear, but the Lord had told him he would come through all trials with his life as his trophy (Jer. 45:3, 5; cf. D&C 9:3–6).

46:1–28 The word of the Lord which came to Jeremiah the prophet against the Gentiles

It was part of the mission of several of the prophets of Israel to warn and instruct other nations ("gentiles") as well. Indeed, it was a small beginning in their role as the seed of Abraham. Much more is yet to be done, for God is concerned with all nations, all peoples.

Jeremiah's messages to other nations are compiled in the next six chapters. In Hebrew, they are mostly in poetry. Some information pertinent to Israel is included within them.

The first message came about five years after King Josiah was killed in opposing the Egyptian armies passing through Israel to do battle against Assyria. It anticipated Egypt's later campaign against Nebuchadnezzar at Carchemish, about 605 B.C., prophesied Pharaoh Necho's defeat there, and anticipated the eventual fall of Egypt to Babylon (Jer. 46:1–12).

The second message may have been received after Jeremiah's arrival in Egypt, ca. 587 B.C. It anticipated Nebuchadnezzar's invasion of Egypt and was a message of doom foretelling the vanquishing of Egyptian forces and the captivity of many of its people: although they were numerous as the trees of a forest, they would be cut down. After a poetic portion on lower Egypt, one prose verse spoke of upper Egypt and another promised that Egypt would be inhabited again (Jer. 46:13–26).

The two closing verses of chapter 46 are a slightly revised repetition of a prophecy of the gathering and return of Israel after her correction and punishment (vv. 27–28; cf. Jer. 30:10–11).

47:1–7 The word of the Lord that came to Jeremiah the prophet against the Philistines

The date of this prophecy is not known. The anticipated destructive forces rising "up out of the north" as a flood were undoubtedly those of Nebuchadnezzar, which would also destroy the Philistine allies, Tyre and Zidon (Jer. 47:4; 25:22). Caphtor (Crete) was the place of origin of the Philistine people. Gaza and Ashkelon were two major Philistine cities along the coast of southern Israel.

48:1–47 Against Moab thus saith the Lord of hosts, the God of Israel; Woe unto Nebo! for it is spoiled

The prophetic prediction of the downfall of Moab is longer than the messages to any other neighboring nation; recall that Isaiah's prophecy concerning Moab was also long, occupying two chapters (Isa. 15–16), and several verses by Jeremiah are similar

(Jer. 48:1–47 and fn.). The prophecy includes a lament and some poetic phrases of pity, but it condemns Moab's idolatrous worship of the dread idol, Chemosh (Jer. 48:7, 13, 46). In addition to Nebo (the name of a deity, a mountain, and a city), many cities and places of Moab were appointed for destruction.

The Moabites were the descendants of Lot and one of his daughters (Gen. 19:37), but many other peoples had no doubt blended with them in the intervening thirteen hundred years. In the days of the judges, the family of the Israelites Elimelech and Naomi went to Moab to survive a famine. Later, their Moabite daughter-in-law, Ruth, accompanied Naomi back to Bethlehem and became an ancestress of David (Ruth 1:1–2; 4:17). Later still, when David was being pursued by King Saul, he sent his parents to the king of Moab for safety (1 Sam. 22:3–4). Though there were many other interactions through the years in which Moab and Judah were adversaries, some empathy for the Moabites was expressed by the prophets who pronounced doom upon them (Jer. 48:5–6, 9; 31–40; Isa. 15:1, 4–5; 16:1–5, 9–11).

At the close is a positive view for the latter days, as there was also in Isaiah's prophecy of doom for the Moabites (Jer. 48:47*a–b*).

49: 1– 6 Concerning the Ammonites, thus saith the Lord

Like the Moabites, the Ammonites were identified with the family of Lot, nephew of Abraham (Gen. 19:36–38). Their territory was part of what is now the nation of Jordan, whose capital, Amman, retains the ancient name *Ammon;* it is on the site of ancient Rabbah. Scholars have wondered why a non-Israelite people would be called "backsliding"—a term usually applied to apostasy in Israel; but it is possibly an allusion to their loss of the faith once held by their forefathers. After the prophet's condemnation and prediction of doom, a message of hope for return was given them (Jer. 49:6).

49: 7–22 Concerning Edom, thus saith the Lord

Edom was another neighbor and a related people, identified with Esau, brother of Jacob (Jer. 49:7*a;* BD, "Edom"). Their territory was south of Ammon and Moab, in the valley and on the tablelands south of the Dead Sea. Jeremiah's message is much like that of Obadiah, a contemporary of his, whose short book concerns Edom's doom. Jeremiah offered no comfort to Edom. In spite of her cliff-ringed fortress (possibly the area called Selah, or Petra, meaning "rock"), desolation was predicted for her cities. *Idumea* is derived from a Greek spelling of the Hebrew word usually rendered *Edom*. It was later used to symbolize "the wicked world" (BD, "Edom"; "Idumea"; "Selah").

49:23–39 Concerning Damascus . . . Kedar, . . . Hazor, . . . Elam

A short prophecy for three other neighboring peoples and one distant nation completes this chapter.

Damascus, capital of Syria, which had been conquered by Assyria just before the fall of northern Israel, elicited Jeremiah's pity. Part of this prophecy was expressed as if Syria's former inhabitants were speaking (Jer. 49:23–27). Kedar was part of Arabia; Hazor may have been also, although another city by the same name was north of Galilee. Nebuchadnezzar is identified as the destroyer of both (Jer. 49: 28–30, 28*a*).

Elam was in the south of the Median empire, near the Persian Gulf, and had little contact with Israel or Judah. The prophecy came early in the reign of Zedekiah and, like a few others, ended with a promise of a return of her scattered peoples in the latter days. There must be something symbolic about it and about setting up the Lord's throne in Elam, but that remains to be clarified (Jer. 49:34–39).

50:1–46 The word that the Lord spake against Babylon and against the land of the Chaldeans by Jeremiah the prophet

The land of Babylon, wicked though it was, had been allowed to be the instrument of the destruction of other wicked nations, much as Assyria had been a century and a quarter earlier. It is never implied that because these nations thus served as instruments of the Lord's punishment of others, their own wickedness was condoned. Like Isaiah's prophecies, this chapter clearly points out that truth. The instrument of Babylon's punishment was also a nation to the north: the Medes and the Persians. The return of

Judah from Babylon was clearly envisioned, and the gathering of Israel was prophesied. A brief interlude sings praises to the Redeemer of Israel.

Then the implements of Babylon's destruction are named: the sword, drought, and wild beasts would leave her as desolated as Sodom and Gomorrah. Her overthrow by the powerful people from the north (Persia) is described here almost as dramatically as it is in the book of Isaiah (Jer. 50:35–46; 51; Isa. 13–14).

51:1–64 Thus saith the Lord; Behold, I will raise up against Babylon, . . . a destroying wind

This long chapter continues the prophecy on the destruction of Babylon, told in even greater length here than in Isaiah.

The picture of the downfall of Babylon is clear. Some verses have implications for the ultimate destruction of the wicked world in general (e.g., Jer. 51:7–10).

The assembly of nations associated with "the kings of the Medes" were called anciently to do to Babylon what she had done to others. Those who could flee Babylon (or who can get out of the ways of the wicked world) were urged to do so.

A copy of this long prophecy was made to be sent with Seraiah, a brother of Jeremiah's faithful scribe, Baruch, to take into Babylon when Zedekiah was taken. There the prophecy was to be read, and then, with a stone attached, it was to be cast into the Euphrates, symbolizing the ultimate sinking of Babylon, never to rise again (Jer. 51:59–64).

52:1–32 it came to pass in the ninth year of his reign, in the tenth month, in the tenth day of the month, that Nebuchadrezzar . . . came . . . So the city was besieged unto the eleventh year of king Zedekiah

This review of the fall of Judah is more detailed than that in Kings (Jer. 39; 2 Kgs. 25; and commentary).

Faithful Jewish people still observe a fast on the ninth day of the month named *Ab* (in late July to early August) to commemorate the destruction of the first temple (and to remember also the destruction of the second temple).

Although the beautiful temple was broken up and the wood thereof burned, many sacred vessels were taken to Babylon, and preserved during the remaining fifty years of Babylon's continuance. Many of the vessels were returned under Cyrus and Darius, and the temple was rebuilt within seventy years (by 519 B.C.; Ezra 1:7–11; 8:24–30, 33–34).

More details, including dates and numbers of people, were given by Jeremiah about the three groups of exiles taken away by Nebuchadnezzar. Jeremiah, in the midst of all these events, may have known more about them than did the scribes of the books of Kings.

The account of the release of the former King Jehoiachin from prison after thirty-seven years and the status accorded him at the royal house in Babylon is repeated (Jer. 52:31–34: cf. 2 Kgs. 25:27–30).

So ends the book of the great prophet Jeremiah, but this is not the end of his words, for the five elegiac chapters of the Lamentations of Jeremiah follow.

LAMENTATIONS

The title "Lamentations" (Heb., *Kinoth*) came from the rabbis of long ago, but the name of this book in the Hebrew scriptures is simply the first word of the first verse, *Eikhah,* which means "how." That it was written by Jeremiah is also ancient tradition. The book of 2 Chronicles may allude to this collection of songs of lament; it is there recorded that Jeremiah lamented the death of good King Josiah and that "the singing men and the singing women" spoke thereafter of him in their laments, which became part of their ritual, being "written in the lamentations" (2 Chr. 35:25; cf. Lam. 4:20). In any case, this brief collection of five poems, or songs, of lament and prayers for relief must have been written after the fall of Jerusalem and Judah, a tragedy that the prophet Jeremiah had tried for more than forty years to prevent—and the trauma of which he had personally experienced. He doubtless could have been the author.

The first two chapters have twenty-two verses each, one for each letter of the Hebrew alphabet, with the first letter of the first word of each verse in its proper alphabetical sequence. Naturally, that pattern is lost in translation. The third chapter has three verses for each letter; therefore, sixty-six in all. The fourth chapter also has twenty-two verses, in alphabetical arrangement; but the twenty-two verses of the fifth chapter are not in the alphabetical pattern.

Part of the effect of alphabetic acrostic poetry is to convey the impression that the poem covers the whole spectrum of the feelings with which the poem is concerned. The first four chapters portray the sorrows of the prophet and the people for the tragedy in their community and in their lives. The last chapter reviews their suffering in a prayer for the people's return to the Lord and for his return to them.

COMMENTARY

1:1–11 How doth the city sit solitary, that was full of people

The prophet's lament for what had happened to the city of Jerusalem pertained to all of Judah, not to the capital alone.

Most of the expressions of regret, descriptions of suffering, and statements of the causes are understandable. Some are difficult to understand either in Hebrew or in English. Some are particularly poignant; one could be rendered: "Judah is in exile of affliction and much servitude" (Lam. 1:3, translation mine).

1:12–22 Is it nothing to you, all ye that pass by? behold, and see if there be any sorrow like unto my sorrow, which is done unto me, wherewith the Lord hath afflicted me in the day of his fierce anger

The prophet became a voice for the personified city, lamenting what had come upon her, describing her, confessing her faults, but praying that the oppressors would also be punished for their wickedness. An arioso in Handel's *Messiah* (no. 30, G. Schirmer ed.) was adapted from some of these words, letting the suffering of Judah foreshadow the suffering of our Redeemer (Lam. 1:12).

2:1–22 the Lord covered the daughter of Zion with a cloud

Lest it appear that the prophet blamed the Lord for the tragic events, it must be recalled that throughout his prophetic career, Jeremiah had warned Judah that imminent conquest by Babylon was no coincidence of history but a result of people's unworthiness of the blessings of the Lord; their sufferings would be due to the withdrawal of His hand (Lam. 2:3, 8, 18). All the verses in which the prophet credited the Lord with the destruction seem in harmony with his many warnings about what the Lord would let come upon vain, idolatrous, and carnal people. God did not specifically create wicked Babylon to invade Judah but did let him who rules by bloodshed and terror have dominion.

Symbolic expressions are abundant in this song of lament for Judah and Jerusalem. A frequent metaphor is "daughter of Zion," for example. It is often understood as a cognomen for Jerusalem; but "Zion" is a concept and an ideal, and a "daughter of Zion" should be one who is a product of that ideal. The "habitations of Jacob" is a phrase used to render a Hebrew term for shepherd dwellings; it implies not only the humble homes but also the shepherds' way of life. The "horn of Israel," which had been cut off, refers to the real power of Israel, the divine power in times of righteousness. The view of the Lord "like an enemy" and "as an enemy" were similes in shocking contrast to the view of him as the "wall of the daughter of Zion," for he had turned and "purposed to destroy" the wall of the daughter of Zion.

There is both irony and hyperbole in the enemy clapping their hands, hissing, and wagging their heads over the "daughter of Jerusalem" in ruins, in contrast to the scene in which they exulted with the former view of her as "the city that men call The perfection of beauty, The joy of the whole earth."

It would be impossible for anyone to point out all significant items in these poems; every reader who ponders them will find unique and impressive types and figures of speech that are full of meaning.

3:1– 66 I am the man that hath seen affliction by the rod of his wrath

Although written in the first person by the prophet, he voices most of this series of triple laments in behalf of the conquered people of Judah. True, the prophet had suffered woes of his own, but most statements do not describe his personal relationships with the Lord or his experiences at the Lord's hand. (A unit of thought in this poem often occupies three verses or some multiple of three.)

The prophet expressed for the people their new hope after

afflictions had humbled them. For them he also expressed a testimony of the Lord's control over all things, both good and evil. Then he voiced the people's resolution, "Let us search and try our ways, and turn again to the Lord" (Lam. 3:40–42).

He reviewed their suffering before the Lord and expressed his own sorrow over the situation. He recalled his own dire straits in the dungeon, sunk in the mire, and his prayer and rescue there (Lam. 3:55–57; cf. Jer. 38:6–13).

He may have written his closing lament in the camp of the refugees in Egypt, as he cries out for comfort (Lam. 3:58–66; Jer. 43–44).

4:1–22 How is the gold become dim! . . . The precious sons of Zion, comparable to fine gold, how are they esteemed as earthen pitchers . . . the daughter of my people is become cruel

This lamentation deals with causes as well as effects of the overthrow of Judah. The "precious sons of Zion" had been as fine gold but were now turned into earthen things. The mothers of children had lost their tender instincts. All the erstwhile covenant people, generalized under the term *Nazarites,* had been beautiful but were of a different look since the terrible siege. People who had died a quick death were thought to be better off. In an awful reprise of the hunger suffered by people under siege, cannibalism by mothers is cited (Lam. 4:10c; cf. 2 Kgs. 6:24–30 for such a horror earlier in Israel's history).

Only the withdrawal of the Lord's favor could have brought on Jerusalem's destruction; the "kings of the earth, and all the inhabitants of the world" would not have thought it possible to invade the city when the Lord was the defender of it.

The "sins of her prophets and the iniquities of her priests" were some of the causes of decay, for they had been blind to duty and were polluted with blood in their hypocrisy. Even the populace had ostracized them. The Lord did not regard them as prophets, and people respected priests and elders no more. (Translation problems exist in these verses, but that is probably the essence.)

Expectation of help from another nation (Egypt) was in vain;

she did not come, but even if she had, she could not have saved Judah from the might of Babylon. Life for the inhabitants left in the land was very precarious; they were hunted and persecuted. The last king of the line of David was gone (Lam. 4:20).

Edom had been granted some areas of Judah by Babylon as a reward for not joining Egypt against her (Lam. 4:21–22 and fn.; Obad. 1:11–14). This circumstance added to the miseries of the remnant of Judah still scattered through the country.

5:1–22 Remember, O Lord, what is come upon us: consider, and behold our reproach

Finally, in a ledger of lament with verses equal in number to all the letters of the alphabet but without acrostic arrangement, the prophet listed the woes that had befallen Judah. In the last two verses, the prophet prayed that the Lord would turn His people back to Him, vowing that they would indeed return and regain hope; but there was little hope while they were rejected.

"Assyrians" were people from *Ashshur* (a patriarchal name for part of Mesopotamia). The word was used here in disdain for the Babylonians, who were dominant there at the time.

In citing the sins of the fathers, the prophet implied that the evils of the time had not arisen in one generation but had developed over many. The miseries that resulted were numerous. Wild animals ("foxes") could walk over the ruins of the former city of Zion.

The prophet knew from his many prophecies that the Lord had not forsaken Judah and Israel "for ever," but for the time being, his generation of the chosen had lost their status with the Lord.

This book of lamentations has many gems of truth and beauty that could be read and applied with corrective benefit in these latter days.

EZEKIEL

The book of the prophet Ezekiel, from the different world of a prophet among the exiles in Babylon, covers some topics from a different perspective. In the midst of Babylon, he received some vital revelations about the faults of his people and of the future world, and he indicated ways to change to achieve better things for them and for the future kingdom of the Lord with a glorious temple in a peaceful world (BD, "Ezekiel").

COMMENTARY

1:1–3 Now to came to pass . . . as I was among the captives by the river of Chebar, that the heavens were opened, and I saw visions of God

The first vision of Ezekiel, in which he was called to become a prophet of the Lord, came in what was probably the "thirtieth year" of the reigning dynasty in Babylon. Nabopolassar, father of Nebuchadnezzar, started it in 625 B.C. (BD, "Chronology," p. 639); thus, 595 B.C. is a plausible date for the beginning of Ezekiel's mission.

The place was "by the river of Chebar" (Heb., *Nehar-kevar,* cognate with the Babylonian word for "great river," *Euphrates*). Excavations at Nippur, along that river, provide evidence that it may indeed have been the center of the ancient Jewish community in exile.

The vital event in Ezekiel's call as prophet was the opening of the heavens, providing him with "visions of God." Ezekiel, Jeremiah, and Isaiah all had distinctive revelations calling them to the work of the Lord and the awesome experience of being personally called of God to become prophets. Thus, at the time of his call and on several later occasions, the prophet felt "the hand of the Lord was there upon him."

Ezekiel, like Jeremiah, was of the priestly lineage; however, no indication is given that either of them officiated in Aaronic ordinances.

1:4–28 a great cloud, and a fire infolding itself, and a brightness was about it, and out of the midst thereof as the colour of amber . . . came the likeness of four living creatures

Thus begins Ezekiel's attempt to describe, in the inadequate words of this earth, the glories of a heavenly vision. The details of the heavenly chariot-throne are marvelous, but it must have been nearly impossible to describe. The account of Ezekiel's vision and divine visitation is much more complicated than Isaiah's general description, but they both saw the Lord. With words of reverence, Ezekiel testified, "upon the likeness of the throne was the likeness of the appearance of a man above upon it." He struggled with words to tell of the glory of that Being, surrounded, as it were, by "the appearance of fire." Using the spectrum of the rainbow as a simile for light and color, he testified, "This was the appearance of the likeness of the glory of the Lord. And when I saw it, I fell upon my face, and I heard a voice of one that spake" (Ezek. 1:26–28).

2:1–10 And he said unto me, Son of man, stand upon thy feet, and I will speak unto thee. And the spirit entered into me when he spake unto me. . . . And he said unto me, Son of man, I send thee to the children of Israel

Thus Ezekiel received the calling and authority to become a prophet—a spokesman for the Lord. He was consistently called "son of man" (Heb., *ben-adam,* "human") by the Lord, as if to emphasize that he was the human agent to transmit the divine messages. The phrase "son of man" occurs many times throughout this book and is nowhere else as prominent; however, in the New Testament, Jesus chose to call himself "Son of Man."

Ezekiel was called to teach some of the same people whom Jeremiah was teaching, so the demands he made and the warnings he gave were similar. The people in exile in Babylon should have been humbled by their experiencing the fulfillment of some of Jeremiah's prophetic warnings, but there is little indication of it.

The first half of Ezekiel's book contains messages that were addressed in part to people still in the land of Judah and in the city of Jerusalem who had not yet been taken captive. Some of them evidently thought they had been spared because they deserved to be (cf. Jer. 24 and commentary).

The new prophet was presented with a "roll of a book" to ingest as a symbol that he would get his information from the Lord and be His spokesman (Ezek. 2:9–10; Ezek. 3).

3:1–14 Moreover he said unto me, Son of man, eat that thou findest; eat this roll, and go speak unto the house of Israel

Ezekiel's mental and spiritual ingestion and digestion of the messages of the Lord were sweet to him; nevertheless, in the messages to the people, there would also be "lamentations, and mourning, and woe," and he was made aware that people would be not receptive but "impudent and hard-hearted." Therefore, like Jeremiah, he was made strong and fearless to stand against them. He was sent to speak to "them of the captivity"; and whether they would hearken or not, they would be without excuse, for a prophet had been sent to warn them (Ezek. 3:4–11; 2:5, 10; cf. Jer. 1:17–19).

At this point Ezekiel's first vision ended, and the Spirit conveyed him away from the divine presence. The chariot-throne with its wheels, as well as the beings and the "voice of a great rushing," were "behind" him for a time. Understandably, he left that divine Presence with reluctance (Heb., lit., "bitterness," which connotes "deep sorrow, distress"). Ezekiel responded and went, feeling the hand of the Lord upon him, for he did not resist the power and authority of the Lord (Ezek. 3:12–14).

3:15–21 Then I came to them of the captivity at Tel-abib, that dwell by the river of Chebar, . . . and remained there astonished among them seven days

In preparation for his second vision, Ezekiel was taken "to them of the captivity at Tel-abib, that dwell by the river of Chebar," and he "sat where they sat" for a week, silent and observing. Then the word of the Lord came again: "Son of man, I have made thee a watchman unto the house of Israel." As their watchman, if he gave them no warnings and they died in their wickedness, he would be responsible. If he warned and taught them but they refused to repent, they would die in their sins but he would be blameless. If a righteous man turned to evil and was not warned and instructed, the watchman would be blameworthy; but if the watchman helped him to remain honorable and good, both the person and the prophet would be saved. Thus ended the prophet's second charge (repeated with some amplifications later, in Ezek. 33). There was another break before his third revelation began.

3:22–27 And the hand of the Lord was there upon me; and he said unto me, Arise, go forth into the plain, and I will there talk with thee

Ezekiel was instructed to go out alone to an uninhabited place. There the glorious experiences of his first vision were repeated for him, and he prostrated himself in deep obeisance as his third vision began.

He was again raised up and filled with the Spirit, but he was warned that he was not to go out and begin preaching on his own initiative (cf. D&C 11:15–16). The people would naturally reject him as one of them; the Lord was not making him merely "a reprover" but His spokesman, to speak when inspired and commanded to do so and to deliver the messages of the Lord. There should then be no arguments; the people could either hear or forbear to hear; it would be the Lord and not the prophet whom they would be accepting or rejecting.

4:1–17 son of man, take thee a tile, and lay it before thee, and pourtray upon it the city, even Jerusalem

As a mode of communicating with his people, Ezekiel was to use symbolic objects, illustrations, and acts. Some of them are described in this and the next chapter. It was fitting that Ezekiel, who was called and instructed by spectacular visual revelations, was also to use visual aids to instruct the people (Ezek. 4:1–8).

A portrayal on a clay tablet and a small model demonstration were used to show the Babylonian siege of Jerusalem, which was to occur nearly ten years after Ezekiel's call. How these drawings were shown to the people is not told.

Next, the prophet was shown symbolically that he had to counter the rebelliousness Israel had shown for three hundred ninety years (from the division of the kingdom under Jeroboam until the Babylonian captivity); he was also to combat the rebelliousness the Jews had shown for forty years. Just how the prophet could symbolically lie on his left side for three hundred ninety days and on his right side for forty days is not clear.

Ezekiel's third demonstration was to prepare and eat a small amount of mixed-grain bread (about one-half pound) and a small amount of water (about one quart) each day for a period of time to symbolize the defiled and limited food they would eat in captivity. The polluted fuel for baking the bread was so repulsive that he objected and was given a less objectionable option. The message was that lack of proper food and drink was part of the price the people paid for infidelity.

5:1–17 And thou, son of man, take thee a sharp knife, . . . a barber's razor, and cause it to pass upon thine head and upon thy beard: then . . . divide the hair

A fourth demonstration of the fate of the exiled chosen people required the prophet to cut his hair and beard and divide the hair into three parts. One-third was to be burnt, one-third to be smitten with a sword, and one-third to be scattered. The symbolism is fairly evident: the hair of the head (chief adornment of a chief part of the body) represented Israel in her former status. Death by fire or the sword or exile from the homeland were the results of her iniquity.

The guilt of Israel was worse than that of other nations because of the advantages Israel had enjoyed in her divine calling with divine laws and prophetic guidance. Even if she had done exactly what other nations did, she was more blameworthy, because others had not been taught as she had.

6:1–14 Son of man, set thy face toward the mountains of Israel, and prophesy against them

The phrase "mountains of Israel" can have a dual meaning as the "high places" where idolatrous worship had taken place and as a representation of the high and mighty leaders of Israel. The term *Israel* rather than *Judah* indicates that all of Israel had been guilty of the idolatry here denounced; Judah was the part of Israel that remained identifiable at the time.

It was starkly symbolic that where the bones of animals sacrificed to idols had been strewn, the bones of the slain idolaters would lie. But a hope-filled future view was also shown with reference to all Israel, a scattered remnant of whom would be among all the nations. Eventually they would remember the Lord and remember the anguish he had suffered by Israel's infidelity. That remembrance could bring resumption of their mission, for a future restoration was promised.

Once more there was a review of Israel's guilt and punishment, at which the prophet was to express dismay: "Smite with thine hand, and stamp with thy foot, and say, Alas for all the evil abominations of the house of Israel" (Ezek. 6:11–14).

7:1–27 Also, thou son of man, thus saith the Lord God unto the land of Israel; An end, the end is come upon the four corners of the land

Ezekiel did not write in measured lines of poetry as did Isaiah, Jeremiah, and others of the prophets, but he certainly employed structured, emphatic prose in effectively crafted phrases, such as those about the end and the evils which had come. Contrasted, but related, is his declaration about the coming of the morning, the day, and the time of trouble.

"The rod hath blossomed" recalls the rod of Aaron, which blossomed in the wilderness to certify his priesthood leadership after the mutiny of Korah (Ezek. 7:10; Num. 16; 17:5–8); but the contrasting line in the time of the exile was "pride hath budded." The result of budding pride was that "violence is risen up into a rod of wickedness." That is poetic language, regardless of meter or strophe (Ezek. 4:2–12).

Resuming the consequences of evil, the prophet listed the follies of commerce in view of imminent invasion, the futility of fleeing, and the paradoxical worthlessness of priceless things. Even the precious, sacred things of the temple were "for a prey" (Ezek. 7:12–22).

Whether the prophet was to "make a chain" to symbolize the sequences he was uttering or his utterance was the "chain," he indeed spoke of the sequence of crime, violence, destruction, mischief, rumor, and lack of direction. The "vision of the prophet," "the law," and the "counsel from the ancients" would not be available to people always. The guilty leaders would suffer "according to their deserts" and come to know the justice of the Lord (Ezek. 7:23–27).

8:1–18 the spirit lifted me up between the earth and the heaven, and brought me in the visions of God to Jerusalem

This vision came a year and two months after Ezekiel's first vision and allowed him to perceive the flagrant idol worship right in the temple at Jerusalem. He saw again the Being he had seen in his first vision, felt again the divine hand, and beheld again the glory he had beheld during his call by being transported in the spirit to Jerusalem (Ezek. 8:1–4 and fn.).

He was shown idols and idolatrous worship at the north gate and in secret chambers (with elders participating); he saw also at the door of the north gate that women supplicated a nature god and eastward in front of the temple men worshipped the sun god while turning their backs on the temple. With a now unknown obscene gesture involving a branch and the nose, they spurned the Lord. It is evident that virtually everyone had turned to other gods for help, knowing that the living God was against them (Ezek. 8:5–18).

9:1–11 And the glory of the God of Israel was gone up from the cherub . . . to the threshold of the house

Next, in a vision of the temple, Ezekiel saw the beginning of the withdrawal of the glory of the Lord from the now desecrated place (cf. Ezek. 10). The coming death of the remnant in Jerusalem, except the few marked to be spared, was symbolized as if accomplished by angels of death; in fact it was brought about within five years by the army of Nebuchadnezzar. The few righteous "marked" for divine protection included, at that time, such men as Jeremiah, Ebed-melech, and the faithful scribe, Baruch (Jer 39:11–18; 45; and commentary). The symbolic marking of those to be saved has future prophetic ramifications (Ezek. 9:4*a;* Rev. 7).

10:1–22 Then the glory of the Lord departed from off the threshold of the house

Verse 18 summarizes the theme of chapter 10. When the Spirit of the Lord has departed from a temple, it becomes a common house; thus the once glorious building was destined for destruction. The dread drama had spiritually begun before.

The vision Ezekiel had seen in his first vision reappeared, and fire from the heavenly altar was taken to be scattered over the city. The awesome withdrawal of divine Glory continued, as the cherubim, symbols of God's omniscience and omnipotence, departed when the Glory of God departed.

11:1–16 Son of man, these are the men that devise mischief, and give wicked counsel in this city

Yet, before his vision of Jerusalem closed, the prophet was shown twenty-five of the chief leaders responsible for the rebellious attitude in that city; they were denying that any crisis was near and advising business as usual. The Lord's message about them was that their counsel would increase the number who would fall in the siege. Instead of the leaders being as the sacred flesh protected in a caldron, they would be taken out and subjected to just punishment (Ezek. 11:3, 9–11).

Even as Ezekiel had prophesied, one of the leaders, Pelatiah, died. The prophet wondered whether that instant punishment signaled the beginning of the end of the "remnant of Israel." The Lord replied that though they were cast off among the heathen and scattered "among the countries," yet he would remain "to them as a little sanctuary in the countries where they shall come" (Ezek. 11:13–16). That promise that some people would have a little sanctuary of faith in God in all lands was an important statement of an aspect of the mission of Abraham through the scattering of Israel.

11:17–25 Thus saith the Lord God; I will even gather you from the people, and assemble you out of the countries where ye have been scattered, and I will give you the land of Israel

As is usual in connection with prophecies of the scattering and exile of Israel, the Lord renewed his promise of the latter-day gathering. It must have given some comfort to the faithful to know that the plans of the Lord would not be thwarted and in time would be fulfilled. For faithful people who know the prophecies in the last days, it is reassuring still.

Some important corollary promises were added: the former abominations in idolatrous worship will exist no more, for the people will be of "one heart"; a "new spirit within" will be given. The unreceptive attitude called "the stony heart" will be replaced by a receptive and sensitive "heart of flesh." True worship of the true God will then resume.

This marvelous vision of Ezekiel concluded when the cherubim and the wheeled throne-chariot bearing the Glory of the Lord moved up and away from the midst of the city, to hover for a time over the mount (of Olives) east of the city and then depart. Then the Spirit returned the prophet to Chaldea to those in captivity, and he related to them the marvelous vision.

12:1–28 Son of man, thou dwellest in the midst of a rebellious house, which have eyes to see, and see not; they have ears to hear, and hear not: for they are a rebellious house

There must have been a lingering resentment among the first

exiles, knowing that they had been taken captive and others had not, for a saying had arisen: "The days are prolonged, and every vision faileth." The many prophetic predictions of the complete fall of Jerusalem had seemed never to be fulfilled. After all, ten years and more had passed since the exile to Babylon of the captives of Jehoiachin's time. Therefore, for the people who had not seen or heard or who perhaps had simply not believed, Ezekiel was instructed to dramatize the refugees' future situation by packing a few belongings, digging through a wall, crawling through the hole in the wall, hiding his face, and slipping away through the twilight with his belongings on his shoulders. In the morning, when the people asked what he was doing, the prophet was to explain that as he had done, so would the people and "the prince" (Zedekiah) have to do. Zedekiah would be taken to the land of the Chaldeans (Babylon), yet never see it. Jeremiah reported the fulfillment of that prophecy; for the last thing that King Zedekiah saw was the execution of his sons, after which his eyes were put out and he was taken into captivity (Ezek. 12:3–13; Jer. 39:7; 52:11).

Another prophecy of the scattering of Israel "toward every wind" concluded this revelation to Ezekiel.

In yet another demonstration, Ezekiel was to eat food and drink water furtively, with evident anxiety, to show the captives in Babylon how it would soon be among the people back home. Then he was to tell them plainly that it was wrong for them to keep saying that the days passed and the prophecies and visions were never fulfilled; moreover, the vain and "flattering" false prophecies, claiming that all would be well back home, would cease. True messages from the Lord were to be taken seriously and would be fulfilled.

13:1–23 Son of man, prophesy against the prophets of Israel that prophesy, and say thou unto them that prophesy out of their own hearts, Hear ye the word of the Lord

The prophetic message to the false "prophets of Israel" was "Woe unto the foolish prophets, that follow their own spirit and have seen nothing!" Like a wily fox that dashes here and there to protect itself, the false prophet neither stands in the breach to warn the people nor does he prepare a defense to help them stand in the day of trial. He prophesies in lies, claiming that the Lord has instructed him when He has not. The sinister effect was that such prophets assured the people of "peace; and there was no peace"; thus any "walls" they built up against danger were subject to crumbling. For those reasons, the true prophets had to try to break down the false security thus established.

Ezekiel also had to counter some magical arts practiced by daughters of the chosen people. Apparently, one of the objects of such arts was the procurement of a little food, saving lives that should not be saved, and letting people die who should not die. All such activities would also end in the coming disaster (Ezek. 13:17–23 and fn.).

14:1–11 Then came certain of the elders of Israel unto me, . . . And the word of the Lord came unto me, saying, Son of man, these men have set up their idols in their heart

Ezekiel not only had false prophets to deal with but also elders that were unfaithful to their divine responsibilities of leadership. In the patriarchal system of government, they were the leaders of the families and clans. But far from preserving the faith of the fathers, these apostate elders were idolatrous at heart, given to magic and mystics, and willing to accept guidance from such sources rather than from the Lord. The Lord was not willing to be supplicated by such people except on condition of their repenting and returning to him.

14:12–23 Son of man, when the land sinneth against me by trespassing grievously, then will I stretch out mine hand upon it, and will break the staff of the bread thereof, and will send famine upon it, and will cut off man and beast from it

Continuing the theme of his refusal to accept the supplications of the apostate elders except upon repentance, the Lord asserted that the status of the one praying does not persuade him to bless those for whom the prayer is said; rather, the faith and needs of those seeking the blessing influences him. Noah was righteous but could save his people from the deluge only if they hearkened and repented (Gen. 6:5, 11–13; Moses 8:16–30). Job was righteous, but other factors were involved, and because of them, his prayers did not keep the catastrophes from coming. Daniel was famous for his fidelity to the Lord right in the court of the Babylonian kings and the first of the Medo-Persian rulers, but his prayer for his own people went up unto the Lord only after they had been humbled and prepared for seventy years to return to their homeland (Dan. 9).

In short, four examples were offered of cases wherein the Lord would bless people with salvation only on condition of worthiness. Then hopes for the future were declared.

15:1–8 Therefore thus saith the Lord God; As the vine tree among the trees of the forest, which I have given to the fire for fuel, so will I give the inhabitants of Jerusalem

That is the essence of this short chapter, but there is also an unstated implication that Israel should have been a *fruitful* vine, not merely a "vine tree among the trees of the forest"; such a vine has no value for fruit or wood but only for fuel.

16:1–63 Son of man, cause Jerusalem to know her abominations, And say, Thus saith the Lord God unto Jerusalem; Thy birth and thy nativity is of the land of Canaan; thy father was an Amorite, and thy mother an Hittite

This long chapter is not about the biological genealogy of Israel but about the sources of her apostate spiritual life. As Isaiah earlier had said, the Israelites had "gone away backward"; they should have taught others about the true God and his ways but instead they had learned the ways of the Canaanites, Amorites, and Hittites who lived before them in the land. They had adopted their gods and supplicated them for help (Ezek. 1:1–3; Isa. 1:4; Jer. 44:15–19; TG, "Israel, Mission of").

By means of a long allegory about Israel as a foundling baby girl, cleansed and brought up to marriageable age by the Lord, adorned and blessed but in time patently unfaithful as a bride, the prophet again demonstrated why Israel had been carried into exile.

Judah had behaved like her sister Samaria (northern Israel) and her "sister" Sodom before. Indeed, because Judah had the examples of Sodom and Samaria before her, she would be more severely punished for sinning knowingly. Nevertheless, the constant hope of redemption was offered for the time when Judah would remember, repent, and realign herself with other repentant "sisters" (Ezek. 16:60–63).

17:1–24 A great eagle . . . came unto Lebanon, and took the highest branch of the cedar. He cropped off the top of his young twigs, and carried it into a land of traffick; he set it in a city of merchants. He took also of the seed of the land, and planted it in a fruitful field . . . by great waters

This "riddle" or "parable" clearly symbolizes several facets of the exile of Judah, beginning with young King Jehoiachin in Babylon (Ezek. 17:3–6). The next great wave of exiles, under Zedekiah, was also described and the interpretation of the parable given (Ezek. 17:7–20). A third group of exiles involved taking one "of the highest branch of the high cedar," even "from the top of his young twigs a tender one." The Lord proposed to "plant it upon an high mountain and eminent; in the mountain of the height of Israel will I plant it" (Ezek. 17:22–23, 22a–b). Consider the possibility that Zedekiah's son Mulek and his company, who came to the western hemisphere, may have been this group.

18:1–32 What mean ye, that ye use this proverb concerning the land of Israel, saying, The fathers have eaten sour grapes, and the children's teeth are set on edge? . . . ye shall not have occasion any more to use this proverb in Israel

This revelation corrected a misunderstanding of a phrase in the Decalog about "visiting the iniquity of the fathers upon the children unto the third and fourth generation of them that hate me" (Ex. 20:5–6). It also confirmed another teaching of the Lord through Moses that "the fathers shall not be put to death for the children, neither shall the children be put to death for the fathers:

every man shall be put to death for his own sin" (Deut. 24:16). While it is true that the sins of parents may affect children—may cause them to suffer and may lead them also to sin—yet the Lord will not impose punishment on children on behalf of fathers or forefathers.

He made clear to Ezekiel through a series of examples that a man who is just and does what is lawful and right "shall surely live" (that is, be protected or saved). A son who is the opposite, who breaks all the commandments and does no good "shall surely die; his blood shall be upon him." A son of the wicked who rejects wickedness and does good "shall not die for the iniquity of his father, he shall surely live," though his wicked father "die in his iniquity."

Thus the clarification to the question "doth not the son bear the iniquity of the father?" The sinner is punished, the righteous rewarded, and neither for the other. As used here, "to live" is to be blessed, whereas "to die" is to be punished. In eternal terms, to live is to be blessed in the presence of God and to die is to be shut out of his presence. The Lord's reasons are vital: he has no pleasure at all that the wicked should die but desires that they should repent and live (Ezek. 18:23).

Then two other cases were propounded: if a righteous man changes and becomes wicked, his former righteousness will not protect him from punishment, even though people may think that unfair; but if a wicked man repents and does what is lawful and right, "he shall save his soul alive" (Ezek. 18:27–28). Obviously the way a person develops and what he becomes is the criterion for judgment. The important admonition is to seek a new heart and a new spirit (Ezek. 18:31).

19:1–14 a lamentation for the princes of Israel

This very brief lament (compared to Jeremiah's whole book of lamentations) is for the last "young lions" of the royal house of Judah and for the nation of Judah. The metaphor of the lion may be derived from the patriarchal blessing bestowed by Jacob upon the head of Judah (Gen. 49:8–12). The "mother" of the lions, in the manner of speaking here, was the nation Judah.

The first king was Jehoahaz, who was removed by Egypt after the last good king, Josiah, was killed in battle at Megiddo by Pharaoh Necho (Ezek. 19:3–4 and fn.). The other young lions are summarized in one, because all were killed, taken to Babylon, or both. They were Jehoiakim, killed; his son, Jehoiachin, taken to Babylon but left alive; Zedekiah, half brother of Jehoiakim, blinded, taken to Babylon, and killed (Ezek. 19:5–9 and fn.).

The "mother" was at first like a fruitful vine, but she became "exalted" and "the east wind [Babylon] dried up her fruit," plucked her up, and planted her in the wilderness of exile. The "fire" that went out of "a rod of her branches" was the rebellious Zedekiah, who refused to hearken to the advice of Jeremiah and brought on the devastating siege by Nebuchadnezzar (Ezek. 19:10–14 and fn.).

One fact lamented was that no more earthly kings of the line would ever rule. Ezekiel knew of the divine King of David's line who would yet rule, but he treated that topic in another place.

20:1– 49 certain of the elders of Israel came to enquire of the Lord . . . son of man, wilt thou judge them? cause them to know the abominations of their fathers

This long revelation on the scattering of Israel and the reasons for it is also about Israel's repentance and return to the Lord and the establishment of a new covenant. A short addendum addressed the process of the downfall of Judah in Ezekiel's time.

Regarding the Lord's reluctance to hear the prayers of those "elders of Israel," recall a previous attempt spoken of in Ezekiel 14.

This chapter reviews Israel's opportunities and failings since the deliverance from Egypt; it mentions the covenants and commandments revealed in the wilderness, which the Israelites often failed to keep but by which they were eventually established; it reviews their opportunities and failings in the promised land; it reiterates the Lord's intent to gather and restore Israel; and it promises his counting them into the fold again ("cause you to pass under the rod") so that they might come again "into the bond of the covenant"; it clarifies the purging of the righteous from among the rebels; and finally it promises acceptance of, and blessings to, those free from "wicked ways" and "corrupt doings."

This prophecy was given "in the seventh year" (Ezek. 20:1) of the captivity of the group of which Ezekiel was a member, several years before the last siege of Jerusalem; hence, these last verses were addressed "toward the south" (Ezek. 20:46), to Judah, warning about the fire that would consume her.

The prophet complained that the people rejected his revelations because they were in "parables," or figurative language.

21:1–32 Son of man, set thy face toward Jerusalem, and drop thy word toward the holy places, and prophesy against the land of Israel

The prophecy against Judah was continued in this chapter; in fact, in the Hebrew scriptures the five preceding verses are the first part of this chapter.

It was hard for the people to believe that the Lord would let "the holy places" ever be destroyed (Ezek. 21:2; Jer. 7:1–16). But He let them know that Babylon's swords and fire would be as the sword of the Lord drawn from its sheath to destroy them; wherefore, all ought to fear and tremble, knowing there would be no escape from that which was coming.

With many complicated poetic figures, Ezekiel elaborated the concept of the sword being sharpened and polished, ready to fall upon the people, both small and great, both in Judah and in Ammon; and the "wicked prince" (King Zedekiah; Ezek. 21:25–26) would lose his crown and diadem. The throne of Israel would be "overturned"—vacated completely—"until he come whose right it is; and I will give it him." This is clearly a messianic promise (Ezek. 21:27a–c; Gen. 49:10c).

The king of the Ammonites, who were included in this devastating prophecy against Judah, had conspired with Ishmael, who slew Gedaliah, the good man appointed to rule over the remnant of Judah left behind. It was prophesied that Ammon also would suffer at the hand of Babylon (Jer. 40:14–16; 41:1–15; Ezek. 21:20, 28–32).

22:1–31 Now, thou son of man, . . . wilt thou judge the bloody city?
yea, thou shalt shew her all her abominations

Another inventory of Judah's sins and violent crimes should
surely have let the exiles in Babylon with Ezekiel know why their
homeland had been invaded and why it would be destroyed.
Whether some of those prophecies were somehow sent back to
Jerusalem as final warnings is not known, but it does seem likely.

In the first segment Ezekiel listed bloodshed, idolatry, rule by
violence, dishonoring parents, oppressing foreigners, desecration
of the holy things and the Sabbath, violence by perfidy, lewdness,
violation of privacy, adultery and incest, bribery, usury, and ex-
tortion (Ezek. 22:3–12).

In the second segment, the Lord demonstrated dismay at all
the dishonest gain and bloodshed committed by the leaders and
people and warned of the results thereof, which were fast approaching. The people would be scattered, and their only inheritance would be what was within themselves. They were as an
amalgam of metals and would have to be purified by the smelter
of suffering (Ezek. 22:18–22).

In the third segment, the word of the Lord through Ezekiel
specifically condemned the land not cleansed, for the popular
prophets were false, priests failed their duty, princes shed blood
for gain and power, and the "prophets" confirmed them in their
acts. The people, too, turned to oppression and robbery, taking
advantage of the poor, the needy, and the foreigner. No wonder
there was not a righteous man found for whose sake the nation
could be spared (Ezek. 22:23–31).

23:1– 49 Son of man, there were two women, the daughters of one
mother: . . . the names of them were Aholah the elder, and
Aholibah her sister: and they were mine, and they bare sons and
daughters. . . . Samaria is Aholah, and Jerusalem [is] Aholibah

This long allegory of the two sisters, Israel and Judah, daughters of the same mother (that is, united Israel), delineates
the moral and religious decline and downfall of the first sister

(northern Israel); and then with amazement observes the same moral and religious decline and downfall of the second sister (Judah).

The prophet knew by revelation and history that Israel never did rid herself of the idolatrous and immoral practices learned from the Egyptian culture. Another fact not made as explicit by other prophets is that the idolatrous practices, the ritual immorality, personal debauchery, modes of dress, and pompous finery of powerful Assyria had been eagerly adopted by Israelites *before* Assyria conquered them. The nation of Israel had been attacked because their last king refused to pay the tribute levied by the Assyrian rulers, but they were conquered because the Lord could not help them when they had refused to turn to him.

Similarly, the younger sister, Judah, adopted practices of vanity, idolatry, and immorality from the Babylonians and suffered invasion and eventual captivity because of that wickedness; the triggering incident was Judah's leaders refusing to pay the tribute and be subject to the overlordship of the Babylonian rulers.

Aholah ("her tent") stands for the dwelling place or people of northern Israel; and *Aholibah* ("my tent is in her") stands for Judah, in whose capital city, Jerusalem, the house of God stood. Judah's greater sin lay in her failure to learn from Israel's experiences and her failure to use the temple sanctuary properly or even to protect it from abuse.

A most heinous combination of these evil elements was idolatrous, ritual adultery resulting in illegitimate children, who were then sacrificed to an idol (Ezek. 23:37; 2 Kgs. 16:3).

The chapter ends with the familiar warning of captivity and the end of pleasure through sinful practices (Ezek. 23:45–49).

24:1–14 in the ninth year, in the tenth month, in the tenth day of the month, . . . even of this same day: the king of Babylon set himself against Jerusalem this same day

After many prophetic warnings, Ezekiel was told to symbolically announce, by a "parable" (a symbol) of a pot with meat in it, the Babylonian conquest of Jerusalem. Tevet is the tenth month, which corresponds on modern calendars to late December and early January; the tenth day of Tevet is remembered by a fast. In the pot, choice meat with the bones was first to be boiled and then burned to powder and the pot melted. The pot represented Jerusalem and its once choice inhabitants who were destroyed in and with their city by the Babylonian siege; it was "purified" by fire. It must have been a terrifying message for the exiles that day.

24:15–27 Also the word of the Lord came unto me, saying, Son of man, behold, I take away from thee the desire of thine eyes with a stroke: yet neither shalt thou mourn nor weep . . . So I spake unto the people in the morning: and at even my wife died; and I did in the morning as I was commanded

The terrible news to the prophet and people was emphasized for Ezekiel and symbolized for the people by the prophet's personal loss—the sudden death of his beloved wife, "the desire of [his] eyes." His restriction from carrying on the usual mourning in dress, demeanor, or ceremony was to teach the people that in their irretrievable losses they should not lament the past but go on with hope into the future.

25:1–17 The word of the Lord . . . against the Ammonites, . . . Moab and Seir, . . . Edom . . . [and] the Philistines

The indictments and the warnings for Judah and Jerusalem were finished. In this revelation about their nearest neighbors, the prophet began his series of prophecies about other nations, which make up eight chapters.

As in the chapters of Jeremiah and Isaiah addressed to other nations, the nations that were nearest Israel were addressed first and those who invaded from afar, next. Some of the smaller prophetic books, such as Amos, have similar lists; the smallest books, such as Obadiah and Nahum, address one foreign nation each.

As observed before, the Ammonite king and people had exulted in Judah's downfall, participated in looting, and had aided and abetted the plot that destroyed the good governor Gedaliah after the exile of most of the people of Judah. The fulfillment of the prophet's forecast of Ammon's downfall came soon thereafter (Ezek. 25:2–7; cf. 21:20, 28–32; and commentary).

The other related peoples, Moab and Seir (Edom), were similar to Ammon in their history of depredations against Israel and were somewhat involved in taking advantage of the downfall of Judah. None of them survived the invasions of the series of empire builders that began with Assyria and continued with Babylon.

Israel's old nemesis, the Philistines of the coastal plains of Israel, had been vanquished in turn by Saul, David, and Solomon; but survivors had remained as thorns in Israel's side. Having risen against the Israelites at every opportunity, they were castigated by Ezekiel. The name *Cherethim* reflects their origin in Crete.

26:1–21 Son of man, because that Tyrus hath said against Jerusalem, Aha, . . . I shall be replenished, now she is laid waste

Somewhat unaccountably, a long reprimand of Tyre and Sidon was delivered by the prophet (Ezek. 26–28). From the times of David and Solomon, mutually profitable commercial relationships had existed between those Phoenician ports and Israel, and there had been no threats or invasions by them. Perhaps the revelations were given in part as a warning to them of the fate that awaited them in the face of the Babylonian imperialism. Ezekiel's message to and about them is, in part, a lamentation.

No sympathy for Jerusalem and Judah, as a former trading partner, was evident in Tyre; and it is somewhat surprising that she would see Judah as a fallen competitor, because Israel was never a notable sea power.

In any case, Nebuchadrezzar (as the Babylonian king's name is sometimes rendered) would come in from the north and east and proceed toward the coastal and island strongholds. Other islands and "princes of the sea" would be dismayed at the siege (which lasted thirteen years). They would lament that imperial forces could conquer such a strong city. The complete ruin that Ezekiel foresaw was not accomplished by Babylon but came about by the hands of others during the centuries following.

27:1–36 Now, thou son of man, take up a lamentation for Tyrus

The prophet perceived and vividly described the "multitude of the wares" involved; his lists of trading items and trading partners is impressive (Ezek. 27:2–25 and fn.).

The seafaring men and those dependent upon them would naturally be the most affected and have cause to lament. Other seafaring peoples would "hiss" (Heb., lit., "whistle" in amazement, not, as in English, in disdain) at Tyre's downfall.

28:1–26 Son of man, say unto the prince of Tyrus, Thus saith the Lord God Because thine heart is lifted up, and thou hast said, I am a God, I sit in the seat of God, in the midst of the seas; yet thou art a man, and not God

As the prophet's message to Tyre continued, a chief reason for her downfall was declared: it was pride, reaching unto blasphemy. The ironic statement "thou art wiser than Daniel" (Dan. 28:3) may be understood in light of the young prophet Daniel's status at court in Babylon, where Nebuchadnezzar himself is quoted as saying to Daniel, "no secret troubleth thee" (Dan. 4:9; cf. 2:46–48). The intent was to humble the "prince" (king) of Tyre.

The lamentation upon him has an air of irony also, with references to his "wisdom" and perfection of "beauty." He had been, metaphorically speaking, "in Eden the garden of God," and hyperbole is used to describe him. Thus, with a multitude of charges against his pride and opulence, he was condemned (Ezek. 28:6–19).

Tyre's sister city, Zidon, of lesser grandeur, was sentenced to violence and pestilence (Ezek. 28:20–23).

Then, almost as an appendix to the three chapters, a brief prophecy of the restoration, gathering, and ultimate blessing of Israel was given. In context here, it has the feeling of the peace and calm that follow a storm.

29:1–21 Son of man, set thy face against Pharaoh king of Egypt, and prophesy against him, and against all Egypt

With this charge began messages of doom and lamentations for Egypt, occupying four chapters.

The first indictment is a double one: Egypt's Pharaoh (no doubt Hophra) had been as guilty as Tyre's king in claiming godly powers (Ezek. 29:2–9; Jer. 44:30). For all his vaunted power he had proved an undependable ally to Judah. The language of this charge is appropriate to Egypt, as that of Tyre was to it. The Pharaoh was called by the metaphor "dragon" (Heb., *tannin,* probably a "water monster" such as the crocodile); his capture and death and those of his people were portrayed by similar metaphors.

Warnings repeated without figures of speech indicated devastation along the entire length of the land (Ezek. 29:10*a*); but a promise of some return in forty years and resumption of national life at a lower standard was given. Israel should not trust in Egypt but in the Lord.

Some seventeen years later (according to Ezek. 29:1, 17), the prophet indicated Egypt became a prize as compensation to Babylon in lieu of Tyre, which, according to some evidence, was besieged for thirteen years without success.

Lastly, a brief prophecy was again given of Israel's restoration. The prophet used a phrase common in Egyptian rituals in behalf of the dead, assuring resumption of life: "I will give thee the opening of the mouth."

30:1–26 The word of the Lord came again unto me, saying . . . the sword shall come upon Egypt

Prophecies of the doom of Egypt and her idols continue. Some neighbors who "uphold Egypt" were also warned (Ezek. 30:5–6, 9). This segment contains a detailed list of shrine cities and their idols, all of which would suffer from the invasion of Nebuchadnezzar. A general picture of the captivity and scattering of the Egyptians was drawn.

31:1–18 Son of man, speak unto Pharaoh king of Egypt, and to his multitude; Whom art thou like in thy greatness?

Although this revelation continued the reprimand of Egypt, only the introductory and concluding verses directly address the Pharaoh and his land; the rest constitute an elaborate simile, recalling the last king of Assyria and his land in their decline and fall, likening it unto Egypt.

Thus the Assyrian king (Sennacherib; cf. Isa. 36–37) "was a cedar in Lebanon" (v. 3) with many branches, great height, and great strength; and many birds (other nations) were within his boughs. In hyperbolic metaphors, he exceeded "the cedars in the garden of God" (v. 8) who envied him (Ezek. 31:3–9).

Briefly the Pharaoh was addressed in second person, because he had also lifted himself up; and then in third person the description of Sennacherib continues concerning his pride, his fall, and his death. The nations he had subdued were shaken; left without leaders or viable ways to survive, many perished, and the remnant went to the next empire builder. Thereupon, the Pharaoh was again asked who he thought he was like "among the trees of Eden"; and he was relegated to the same end as the Assyrians (Ezek. 31:10–18).

32:1–32 in the twelfth month, in the first day, . . . the word of the Lord came unto me, saying, Son of man, take up a lamentation for Pharaoh king of Egypt

All of these revelations concerning Egypt came at about the time of the Babylonian siege of Jerusalem; this one was after its fall, perhaps 584 B.C. It is a song of doom, not a lament with any pity for Egypt. The beginning of it should be retranslated thus:

> Like a young lion of nations thou didst make thyself;
> But thou art like a monster (crocodile) in the seas.

It is curious that the Hebrew word translated as *dragon* in Ezekiel 29:3 has here been translated *whale*. It is an ancient and mysterious word and is rendered according to context.

In this metaphorical warning, Pharaoh as a great sea creature and his people as fish would be taken with a net and left to die and decay in strange fields and rivers; many peoples who saw their destruction would be amazed (Ezek. 32:2–10). A plainspoken warning of Babylon's conquest of Egypt followed. "The daughters of the nations" would lament "for Egypt, and for all her multitude" (Ezek. 32:11–16).

Fifteen days later, the prophet was told by the Lord to bewail not only the demise of the Egyptians but also their relegation to the nether world where they would be with such nations as Assyria, Elam, Meshech, Tubal, Edom, Zidon, and others "uncircumcised" with whom Pharaoh and his slain multitude would have to "be comforted" (Ezek. 32:17–32).

33:1–10 So thou, O son of man, I have set thee a watchman unto the house of Israel

After eight chapters about neighboring nations, this one returns to the prophet's messages to Israel.

The first message reviews the heavy responsibility of Ezekiel as a watchman appointed by the Lord (Ezek. 33:2–9; cf. 3:17–21). It continues with a reiteration of answers to the question of how there was hope for humankind if their sins and transgressions remained upon them. Hope arises because the Lord takes pleasure not in punishing the guilty but in their repenting and qualifying to "live." But again the righteous are warned that by turning to sin they can lose their status. The Lord is concerned with what they have become, and mere man should not declare him inequitable (Ezek. 33:11–20; 18:20–32).

33:21–29 one that had escaped out of Jerusalem came unto me, saying, The city is smitten

This message is dated three years after the final siege began; upon hearing it, the prophet was again overwhelmed (Ezek. 33:21–22; 24:1–2, 27).

The people of the captivity were complaining that because the land was promised to their ancestor for his seed, they, his many descendants, should have it. The answer was as always: they had sinned in their infidelity and depended upon their own might to defend them while living in sin, and the land was desolated.

33:30–33 Also, thou son of man, the children of thy people still are talking against thee by the walls and in the doors

Finally, in this review chapter, the prophet was reassured by the Lord. Though his people talked against him, heard his words but would not do them, showed "much love" but acted contrarily, listened as if to a "lovely song of one that hath a pleasant voice" but obeyed not—yet when all his words about the desolation of the homeland came to pass, they would know a prophet had been among them.

34:1–31 Woe be to the shepherds of Israel that do feed themselves! should not the shepherds feed the flocks? . . . I will feed my flock, and I will cause them to lie down, saith the Lord God

The Israelite leaders were given this classic statement about bad shepherds versus the Good Shepherd. The bad leaders had profited by their position and status and had failed to teach and keep their people worthy for the Lord's protection; therefore, the flock was scattered, and those shepherds were held culpable (Ezek. 34:2–10).

The Lord, as the Good Shepherd, will search for his sheep and seek them out, gather them, and feed them in good pastures on the high mountains of Israel. He will restore them, give them security, and heal them. He will judge the flocks and discern the bad from the good—those who use well the good pasture and those who tread it under foot and foul the deep waters (Ezek. 34:11–19*a*).

And as for the leaders who made some fat and some lean, thrust some aside and cared not for the sick, and brought about the scattering of Israel—they would all be replaced with true shepherds, servants of the Lord: "I the Lord will be their God, and my servant David a prince among them; I the Lord have spoken it" (Ezek. 34:20–24*a–d*).

Restoration of "a covenant of peace" was also promised, along with fruitfulness, security, and providential productivity (Ezek. 34:29*a*).

Ultimately, the flock is the Lord's, the pasture is his, and he is the true Shepherd (Ezek. 34:25–31; recall 34:15).

35:1–15 Thus saith the Lord GOD; Behold, O mount Seir, I am against thee, . . . and all Idumea, even all of it . . . shall know that I am the Lord

Thus begins and ends this revelation that is seemingly out of place (as one of those against neighboring nations, Ezek. 25–32). It is a message of doom to ancient Edom (also called by the name of its mountains, Seir; and in the last verse by an equivalent to Edom, "Idumea"). Edom had been an inveterate enemy of Israel, and after the Babylonian siege she had hoped to take over the territory of northern Israel and Judah. Hence Edom was condemned to disappear (Ezek. 35:9–15; cf. 25:12–14).

Because of its enmity against Israel throughout the generations, Edom, or Idumea, became symbolic of the wicked world (D&C 1:36; BD, "Edom"; "Idumea"). Hence, the last verse of this prophecy makes the whole chapter a fitting sequel to the revelation on the coming of the Good Shepherd; for the commencement of his peaceful reign brings an end to the wicked world ("Idumea"), and all shall know the Lord (Ezek. 34; 35:15).

36:1–38 thou son of man, prophesy unto the mountains of Israel, and say, Ye mountains of Israel, hear the word of the Lord

This revelation, in turn, is a sequel to the two chapters above, being a preview of latter-day Israel making the name of the Lord known to "the heathen," even to "flocks of men." Observing that "the enemy" had long enough taken the land for themselves, and that Israel would have borne derision and the shame of the heathen long enough, the Lord promised that the days of prey and derision would pass (Ezek. 36:1–7).

The waste places of Israel are to be fruitful again and thrive. The land that has for years devoured peoples shall sustain the people Israel (Ezek. 36:8–15).

As for the people of his time, the prophet reminded them that they were in exile because they defiled the promised land and profaned the Lord's name. Yet because of his name (and the covenant promises made in his name), he will work with later generations and bring them back in covenant relationships (Ezek. 36:16–24).

The cleansing preparation for making the covenants anew will be a ceremonial washing, after which "a new heart" and "a new spirit" will govern their walks and ways (Ezek. 36:16–24). With all uncleanness done away, the people and land will become fruitful and productive; indeed a "garden of Eden" state (paradisiacal glory) will result. These restoration phenomena and the future work of the Lord's people will impress the unbelievers (Heb., lit., "heathen") and they shall also know the Lord (Ezek. 36:25–38).

37:1–14 The hand of the Lord was upon me, and carried me out in the spirit of the Lord, and set me down in the midst of the valley which was full of bones

Another restoration prophecy follows. Using the symbolism of the resurrection of dry bones, it bears a double meaning. The prophet did not know the dead bodies could be resurrected until the Lord told him (Ezek. 37:3). He described the reassembly and revivification processes, the reentry of the spirit and resumption of breathing; and then the double meaning was made clear: it represented both the reassembly of Israel and the resurrection of the body from the grave to house again the spirit.

37:15–28 Moreover, thou son of man, take thee one stick, and write upon it, For Judah, and for the children of Israel his companions: then take another stick, and write upon it, For Joseph, the stick of Ephraim, and for all the house of Israel his companions

Yet another restoration prophecy was given with a double meaning. This one involved two symbolic pieces of wood. Commonly translated *stick,* the Hebrew word used is *etz,* a generic word meaning "wood" (there are other words meaning "stick," "staff," "branch," or "scepter"). This was wood upon which it was possible to write. Babylonian writing tablets of wood have been found hinged together and faced with wax, with writing engraved on them. Two wooden tablets represent the scriptures from Judah (the Bible) and Joseph (the Book of Mormon) to "be one in mine hand" (Ezek. 37:15–19 and fn.). With the two labeled wooden tablets in hand, the prophet was to show his people that the children of Israel will be gathered from among the heathen to become one nation, with one king, never to be "divided into two kingdoms any more at all" (Ezek. 37:18–22).

United Israel will not turn to idols again, for the people will be cleansed to become the people of the Lord, with one King and Shepherd. His new "covenant of peace" with Israel "shall be an everlasting covenant." The Lord's sanctuary shall be "in the midst of them" and his "tabernacle also shall be with them." Then all other peoples (the "heathen") will understand why the Lord has consecrated Israel to his eternal service (Ezek. 37:23–28).

38:1–23 And the word of the Lord came unto me, saying, Son of man, set thy face against Gog, the land of Magog

After the gathering but before the kingdom of peace shall be established, one last mighty attack will be mounted against the Lord's potential kingdom. The attackers will come from all sides. Gog, "chief prince of Meshech and Tubal," is evidently of the Japhetic peoples of the Caucasus and northward, as are Gomer and the house of Togarmah (Gen. 10:2; BD, "Gog"). Persia comes from the east, Ethiopia the south, and Libya the west; thus, they may represent all nations (Ezek. 38:2–7; Zech. 14:1–3).

Ezekiel prophesied against these latter-day attackers. Speaking to Gog, the leader from the north, he foretold his mustering troops for service and plotting with "an evil thought" against undefended villages to take spoil and prey from the gathered of Israel. Merchant nations will take interest in the contraband (Ezek. 38:8–13).

But when all these forces come "out of the north parts" against Israel "as a cloud to cover the land," the Lord will be glorified, not Gog. Addressing Gog with a rhetorical question about His coming to fulfill prophecies, the Lord warns that His fury and fervor ("jealousy") will arise, and there will be earthquakes, swords, pestilence, and storms of rain, hail, fire, and brimstone against the invaders. They will find out that they have not attacked an undefended people but the people of the Lord (Ezek. 38:14–23).

39:1–29 Therefore, thou son of man, prophesy against Gog, and say, Thus saith the Lord God; Behold, I am against thee, O Gog, the chief prince of Meshech and Tubal. And I will turn thee back

The prophecy continues, foretelling destruction of the attacking forces, leaving only one-sixth of them alive. Their bodies will be carrion, and their homelands will be burned (Ezek. 39:2–7). Cleanup operations will take seven years and the burial of the remains of the armies seven months, even though scavenging birds and animals will have done their work (Ezek. 39:8–20). Then the unbelieving nations (the "heathen") will know that divine power and judgment are at work, and Israel will know the Lord again. All nations will know that only because of disobedience, sin, and iniquity will people suffer who have made covenants with the Lord (Ezek. 39:23–24). Then, after the justice of punishment is finished, the mercy of compassion will bring a restoration. The people will come to know by their experience that the Lord is God and that in righteousness he will not abandon them (Ezek. 39:25–29).

Note that this battle with Gog from the land of Magog is to be before the Millennium (cf. D&C 29:20–21). Another conflict will come after the Millennium, when "Satan shall be loosed out of his prison, And shall go out to deceive the nations which are in the four quarters of the earth, Gog and Magog, to gather them together to battle" (Rev. 20:7–8).

40:1– 49 in the fourteenth year after that the city was smitten, . . . the hand of the Lord was upon me, and brought me thither. . . . and, behold, there was a man, whose appearance was like the appearance of brass, with a line of flax in his hand, and a measuring reed; and he stood in the gate

Ezekiel's last great vision came in the twenty-fifth year of his residence among the captives in Babylon, the fourteenth year after Jerusalem was conquered and the temple destroyed. He was taken in vision to the future land of Israel, to the top of a very high mountain from which he could see "the frame of a city on the south." His angelic guide met him at the gate and conducted him to a great enclosure five hundred cubits square (as calculated from the measurements of the gates, the temple, the altar, and the spaces between. Ezek. 42:16–20 renders the measurement as five hundred "reeds" but that may be in error). The guide showed him the measurements of the outer gatehouses, porches, and chambers of the east, north, and south sides and the seven steps that led up to each gate. Then the guide showed him three inner gatehouses with their courts and chambers and the tables for preparation of sacrifices (Ezek. 40:2–43), the chambers for the singers and for the priests, the sons of Zadok (Ezek. 40:44–46), and the central court for the great altar that stood in front of the temple proper. Finally, the guide showed him the porch of the temple, its great posts and gates (Ezek. 40:48–49).

By correlation of these descriptions and those in the chapters that follow concerning the temple facilities and their uses, it is possible to sketch the ground plan and floor plan; such a sketch may be found in most Bible encyclopedias.

41:1–26 Afterward he brought me to the temple

Ezekiel's spiritual guide conducted him through the temple proper, showing him measurements of the door to the holy place, the walls, and the side chambers. These were in three stories, each being widened by rebatements as the wall went up (Ezek. 41:1–11). The guide showed the prophet a space west of the temple, the outer measurements of the temple, the windows, and decorations of cherubs and palm trees (Ezek. 41:12–21). Then he showed him the inner altar of incense, the table, doors, windows, and chambers (Ezek. 41:22–26).

42:1–20 Then he brought me forth into the utter court. . . . and over against the pavement which was for the utter court, was gallery against gallery in three stories

The guide showed Ezekiel the chambers north of the temple proper, but the description given is difficult to visualize. Evidently there were also chambers to the south of the temple. The priests' ceremonial and preparatory activities in those chambers were briefly indicated (Ezek. 42:1–14). The prophet was also shown dimensions of the outer walls. As indicated above, the outer walls were probably five hundred cubits on each side, even though they are here described as five hundred "reeds" (Ezek. 42:15–20; cf. Ezek. 40; and commentary).

43:1–27 Afterward he brought me to the gate . . . that looketh toward the east: And, behold, the glory of the God of Israel came from the way of the east

The high point of the final revelations to Ezekiel is described in this chapter and the next. He saw the return of the Glory of the Lord to the future temple in some of the same imagery he had seen in his call and in the departure of the Spirit of the Lord from the temple (Ezek. 43:1–6; 1:4–28; 3:22–23; 10; 11:23).

During this vision, the prophet was promised that the Lord will come to dwell in His house on earth forever, but the voice of the Lord reminded him about the inimical acts and attitudes of former Israelite kings, which had caused His Spirit to withdraw before. Ezekiel was told to communicate these things and teach Israel the modes of worship and the law of the future temple (Ezek. 43:6–12). After being told some specifications about the altar, he was taught the ordinances that the future priests, "the seed of Zadok," would conduct (Ezek. 43:13–27).

44:1–31 Then he brought me back the way of the gate . . . toward the east . . . Then said the Lord unto me; This gate shall be shut, . . . and no man shall enter in by it; because the Lord, the God of Israel, hath entered in by it. It is for the prince; . . . he shall sit in it to eat bread before the Lord; he shall enter by the way of the porch

The Lord explained that the east gate of the temple compound will be restricted to access by the Lord, who will meet there with the "prince," who will there "eat bread before the Lord" (Ezek. 44:1–3a). No further information was recorded about the future government, but it is described elsewhere (TG, "Kingdom of God, on Earth").

Ezekiel saw that "the glory of the Lord filled the house of the Lord" (Ezek. 44:4), and he fell upon his face in awe, whereupon the Lord again told him to remind the rebellious of Israel of their lack of reverence and obedience, which had separated them from Him in the past. No unworthy people will have temple privileges in the future, and only worthy priests will minister in it (Ezek. 44:5–16). The proper clothing and conduct of the ministering priesthood was then reviewed (Ezek. 44:17–31 and fn.). This was not the end of the great vision and revelation on the temple.

45:1–25 when ye shall divide by lot the land for inheritance, ye shall offer an oblation unto the Lord, an holy portion of the land

This chapter begins the description of the divisions of the Holy Land of the future. An immense rectangle is first specified, in the midst of which was a square like that previously described (in Ezek. 42:16–20) to be allocated for the temple. Allocations within the great rectangle were made for the priests, Levites, other Israelites, and for "the prince" (Ezek. 45:1–8; 48).

The rest of this chapter specifies future offerings by the "princes of Israel." Some are like former offerings, and some are new (Ezek. 45:9–25 and fn.).

46:1–24 Thus saith the Lord God; The gate of the inner court that looketh toward the east shall be shut the six working days; but on the sabbath it shall be opened, and in the day of the new moon it shall be opened. And the prince shall enter by the way of the porch . . . and shall stand by the post of the gate

Further specifications were given for the use of the eastern gate (Ezek. 46:1–3; cf. 43:4; 44:1–3). Apart from the way the "prince" will have access to the area, the people may enter by the north gate and leave by the south, or enter by the south and leave by the north. Offerings are specified for the prince and people (Ezek. 46:4–15). Regulations are given concerning inheritances for descendants of the prince and for the servants (Ezek. 46:16–18).

The divine guide conducted the prophet to the chambers of the priests and the place where trespass offerings and other offerings are to be boiled or baked (Ezek. 46:19–24).

47:1–23 Afterward he brought me again unto the door of the house; and, behold, waters issued out from under the threshold of the house eastward

The guide had yet more physical and spiritual marvels to teach the prophet. Water flowing from the right side of the temple by the altar into the valley (Kidron) toward the sea (Dead Sea) is to become an ever-greater river as it goes, bringing life along its course and healing (making fresh) the salty water of that sea.

Fish shall abound and trees bear fruit for food every month and leaves for healing. Similar revelations have been given to other prophets (Ezek. 47:1–12, 1*b;* note that Zechariah saw the healing waters go toward both the east and the west seas). The concept is evident that "living water" shall flow forth from the presence of the Messiah and indeed bring life and healing as it flows, renewing the whole world.

The remainder of the chapter sets out the boundaries of the future promised land and promises portions to all twelve tribes, with a brief note to indicate that Joseph's two tribes will help make up the twelve portions. It is made explicit in the next chapter (Ezek. 48) that the tribe of Levi has a special portion in connection with the temple area. The boundaries of the future promised land can be compared to those of the original by referring to the cross-references cited in the footnotes (Ezek. 47:13–21; Num. 34–35; Josh. 14–17).

Note the Mosaic laws regarding treatment of "strangers" (Ezek. 47:22–23).

48:1–35 Now these are the names of the tribes. From the north end to the coast

The north border is again identified; then an equal portion is prescribed for each of seven of the tribes (Ezek. 48:1–7; cf. 47:13–21). Further details are given about the large tracts for the temple, the priests and Levites, and the "prince." The portions for the remaining five tribes are then listed (Ezek. 48:8–29; cf. 45:1–8).

The city walls and gates are also described. The length of each side may be calculated (cf. Ezek. 40:5*c*). Compare those descriptions to the future city seen by John the Revelator (Ezek. 48:30–35; Rev. 21:12–27).

In the conclusion to his great vision, the prophet was told "the name of the city from that day shall be, The Lord is there" (Heb., *JHVH Shamah*) or, according to latter-day revelation, "the name of the city from that day shall be called, Holy; for the Lord shall be there" (JST Ezek. 48:35).

For this prophetic book by Ezekiel—about the end of the ancient Israelite kingdoms, the departure of the Spirit of the Lord from the first temple in Jerusalem, and the destruction of that temple—the last nine chapters fittingly detail the prophet's visions of a glorious future temple, to which the Lord will come to rule the world amidst peace and beauty at last.

DANIEL

Daniel was a prophet in the court of the conquerors of his people. The narratives in his book show how the help of the Lord was extended to bless His people in exile who had faith in Him and tried to be obedient to His divine laws. Daniel was one of them. He appears to have been an inspired, wise, and faithful young man who was saved along with his friends through their courage, faith, and integrity. Thereby they were also able to rise to positions of leadership. Later, as a mature prophet in the court of his captors, Daniel brought divine guidance to the Babylonian and Persian kings he served until he was more than eighty years old.

The predominantly narrative portions of his book (Dan. 1, 3, 5–6) have become the favorites of untold numbers of children and Bible students. They illustrate faithfulness, courage, and heroic steadfastness and demonstrate that God rewards such qualities and behavior.

The prophetic, sometimes called "apocalyptic," portions of the book of Daniel (Dan. 2, 4, 7–8, 10–12), record much information of value for the prophet's time, for centuries thereafter to the time of the Savior, and for the latter days of the earth's temporal existence. Daniel's visions pertained to the empires of Babylon, Persia, Macedonia, and their successors. He anticipated the return of Judah and the first coming of the Messiah, and he envisioned the latter-day struggles between the kingdoms of the world before their ultimate breakdown and replacement by the kingdom of

God. He foresaw the resurrection of the just and the unjust and received a brief glimpse of eternity (BD, "Daniel"; "Daniel, Book of").

The book of Daniel is not reckoned among the Prophets in the Jewish canon but is categorized in the Writings; however, it is placed among the Major Prophets in Christian Bibles.

In its original languages, the book of Daniel is peculiar in the Hebrew Bible: the first part (Dan. 1–2:3) is in Hebrew; the middle part (Dan. 2:4–7:28), in Aramaic, a language closely related to Hebrew; and the last part (Dan. 8:1–12:13), in Hebrew.

COMMENTARY

1:1–21 In the third year of the reign of Jehoiakim king of Judah came Nebuchadnezzar . . . And the Lord gave Jehoiakim . . . into his hand . . . And the king spake unto Ashpenaz . . . that he should bring certain of the children of Israel, and of the king's seed, and of the princes . . . to stand in the king's palace

Jehoiakim was made king by the Egyptian overlords after Josiah was killed at Megiddo and his son Jehoahaz proved unsatisfactory. When Nebuchadnezzar took areas Egypt had controlled, Jehoiakim "became his servant" for three years, but when he rebelled against Babylon, Nebuchadnezzar besieged Jerusalem, took hostages, and deposed him (Dan. 1:1–2; 2 Kgs. 24:1–6). If that happened in 606 B.C. (BD, "Chronology," p. 639), Nebuchadnezzar was probably serving under his father, for he became sole king of Babylon two years later (604 B.C.); precise dates of these events are difficult to certify, however.

The first vessels plundered from the temple were taken at this time, more were taken later, and virtually all that remained were taken in 586 B.C. when the temple was destroyed. Choice people of the land were also taken as prizes to Babylon. Daniel, with three of his friends, was among some of "the king's seed, and of the princes" taken, who had the qualities requested by the king (Dan. 1:1–4).

The names of the boys were fitting: *Daniel* means "my judge is God"; *Hananiah,* "gracious is the Lord"; *Mishael,* "who is what

God is?"; and *Azariah,* "my helper is the Lord." It is unfortunate that three of them are better known by the Babylonian names given them—Shadrach, Meshach, and Abed-nego. Daniel also received a Babylonian name, Belteshazzar, but it is seldom used in the text (Dan. 1:5–7).

They were good Jewish boys with great potential, and they were blessed for maintaining their proper way of life, being endowed with spiritual gifts that enhanced their native intelligence. After three years of preparation, they passed their tests before the king with performance "ten times better" than his masters of mystic arts (Dan. 1:8–20).

2:1– 49 in the second year of the reign of Nebuchadnezzar Nebuchadnezzar dreamed dreams, wherewith his spirit was troubled

The second year of Nebuchadnezzar's reign as king would have been 602 B.C., four years after Daniel and his friends were taken captive and one year after they passed their tests so impressively before him. Evidently the king wanted to be sure his official "Chaldeans," as masters of mystic arts, really possessed supernatural powers; for he demanded that they reveal to him a dream he had dreamt and also interpret it (Dan. 2:5*a*). It is at this point that the language of the account changes from Hebrew to Aramaic (called "Syriac" in Dan. 2:4).

When the king was convinced that his masters of the occult arts were indeed charlatans and decreed the doom of all such men in Babylon, that decree was taken also to Daniel and his companions, because of their special status. All they needed to meet the challenge was time, faith, and an answer to prayer. When Daniel received the needed revelation, he did not forget to give thanks and praise to God. In his prayer of thanks, he expressed valid concepts of God that are still valuable (Dan. 2:5–23).

When Daniel offered Nebuchadnezzar the desired information and interpretation, he graciously sought clemency for other "wise men of Babylon." He claimed no supernatural power and taught the king about the power of the true, living, and all-knowing God. Daniel humbly and truthfully declared that the secret was revealed not because of his own wisdom but because God had information for the king (Dan. 2:24–30*b*).

The great image in Nebuchadnezzar's vision, with head of fine gold and each descending body part of less and less valuable metal, was interpreted as a representation, at the top, of the great empire of Nebuchadnezzar and of successively lesser domains afterwards until a latter-day deterioration into incohesive, small nations and ethnic groups. Attempts to identify the states precisely have proven quite pointless, but the general trend of history is clear. The most significant symbol of all—the great stone rolling forth to break the image and fill the earth—is most easily recognizable and most important. It represents the kingdom of God, starting small and growing ever greater until the breakup of the kingdoms of this world. It was launched "without hands" (that is, by the power of God) and will roll on until it fills "the whole earth" (Dan. 2:31–45*a*).

Out of the king's experiences in the dream and interpretation from the Lord, he gained a concept of the living God, as Daniel had intended. Nebuchadnezzar did not "worship" Daniel but did homage out of awe and gratitude; he acknowledged the real "God of gods" (Dan. 2:46–49).

The status and power given Daniel and his friends as an honest reward naturally caused jealousy among other royal aides.

3:1–30 fall down and worship the golden image that Nebuchadnezzar the king hath set up

There is no clear connection between the events related at the end of chapter 2 and those at the beginning of chapter 3. It is plausible, in a world of polytheism, that the king could do obeisance to the true "God of gods, and a Lord of kings," as he had just done, and still require his people to worship his own grand idol. Obviously, he had not been completely converted to the new faith (Dan. 2:47; 3:1–7).

There were ominous consequences for the Hebrews appointed to high office in the accusations and hostile actions of the Chaldeans who fostered worship of the golden image and then accused the Jewish boys (Dan. 3:8–12). Where Daniel was, or why he was not affected by this test, is not reported. His three friends were certainly equal to the challenge, however. With integrity and courage, they expressed confidence that if God saw fit, he would save them; but even if not, they would still not serve other gods to save themselves. In their confidence they felt no need to be "careful" (v. 16) in the way they responded. Of course the rage of the earthly king at such effrontery was inevitable.

Nebuchadnezzar was astonished at seeing the three young men walking about in the superheated furnace accompanied by a divine being. The phrase "the Son of God" is used to translate the Aramaic *bar 'elahin,* which means, literally, "a son of the gods." Naturally the king had no acquaintance with the Son of God whom we worship, and he would certainly not have been qualified to see Him (TG, "God, Privilege of Seeing"). The Aramaic words mean "a divine being"; later the king called him an "angel" of the God of the Hebrews (Dan. 3:13–28).

It is amazing that the king humbled himself enough to acknowledge the act of God in saving these young Hebrew men, even if it meant overturning his own decree. It is also amazing that he made a new decree to protect them and their God in his kingdom thereafter. In consequence of these astonishing events it is therefore not surprising that he promoted the young men.

4:1–37 I thought it good to shew the signs and wonders that the high God hath wrought toward me

The purpose of this narrative chapter is stated in words from King Nebuchadnezzar himself (Dan. 4:1–3). This series of events, like the earlier one, began with a challenge in which all the king's masters of mystic power failed and Daniel succeeded. The king's command to "tell me the visions of my dream" has to be understood as a command to relate the dream part by part, each with its interpretation, for he had already told Daniel the whole dream (Dan. 4:4–18).

When Daniel heard the recital of the dream and realized its meaning, he was reluctant to tell its meaning to the king. He tried to prepare him by voicing a wish that it might apply rather to the king's enemies, for it was a warning from "the most High" that the king would fall from his high status, might, and dominion. For a pointed lesson, the dream also provided him a means of escape if he would repent and become upright and merciful.

When such repentance had not occurred in a year's time and the king vaunted his power, might, and majesty, his fall began. It is generally understood that the "seven times" he suffered was seven years. At last his mind was restored, and he did acknowledge the most high God as King of heaven, whose dominion is over all; he testified that God's works are true and His ways are just. The king was restored to his status and a degree of majesty.

5:1–31 Belshazzar the king made a great feast to a thousand of his lords, and . . . commanded to bring the golden and silver vessels which his father Nebuchadnezzar had taken out of the temple which was in Jerusalem; that the king, and his princes, his wives, and his concubines, might drink therein

About fifty years had passed from the time Daniel was taken to Babylon until Belshazzar became a coregent with Nabonidas in Babylon, and seventeen additional years had passed from then until the time of the events of this chapter, which led to the coming of Cyrus. The relationship of Belshazzar to Nebuchadnezzar was not simply that of son to father but as one of his successors (BD, "Belshazzar"; "Chronology," pp. 639–40).

The previous chapter showed the most high and living God as supreme; this one shows him in control at the fall of Babylon and the rise of the Medo-Persian empire (BD, "Media"; "Persia"). If Daniel was perhaps thirteen to fifteen years of age when taken to Babylon, he could have been in his early eighties at the time of the events told in this chapter. That may account for the queen (possibly the queen mother) coming forward to tell Belshazzar about Daniel's deeds and repute in the days of Nebuchadnezzar; she knew that Daniel could interpret the cryptic message written on the wall.

The spiritual qualifications of Daniel were somehow noted by the king, who observed, "The spirit of the gods is in thee." Although anyone literate could have read the four common Aramaic words written on the wall, it is not surprising that no one was able to understand their message. They were key words to the concepts to be revealed.

Daniel disdained any reward for interpreting the writing and frankly testified that it told what the true God was about to do, though the message must have been devastating to the king. The lesson was similar to the one Daniel had sought to teach Nebuchadnezzar about the need for humility and righteousness before God. But for Belshazzar, it was too late (Dan. 5:13–30 and fn.).

The precise identity of "Darius the Median" and his relationship politically with "Cyrus King of Persia" are not entirely clear (Dan. 5:31; cf. 6:28; 10:1; BD, "Cyrus"; "Darius"). Both Isaiah and Jeremiah prophesied of "the Medes" overcoming Babylon, and Daniel saw the conqueror as a Mede, perhaps under the auspices of Cyrus, who combined Media with Persia (Isa. 13:17–18; 21:2; Jer. 51:11, 28).

6:1–28 this Daniel was preferred above the presidents and princes . . . Then the presidents and princes sought to find occasion against Daniel

In this narrative chapter the lesson is like that of chapter 3: they who oppose the living and true God and persecute his servants will eventually suffer for it. In this account, as in the other, the retribution was swift.

They who contrived a flattering requirement on behalf of the king in this episode counted on the integrity of a true worshipper of God to entrap him (Dan. 6:4–13; cf. 3:8–12). In the case of the three friends versus Nebuchadnezzar, the king in a rage commanded them to be punished. In this account of Daniel and Darius, the king himself was entrapped and "was sore displeased with himself"; he even "laboured till the going down of the sun to deliver" Daniel. When the adversaries "assembled unto the king," the Aramaic indicates they *rushed* to him, showing their fear of failure (Dan. 6:14–17).

Daniel was as cool and deliberate in praying as his three friends had been in refusing to worship the image or excuse themselves before Nebuchadnezzar (Dan. 6:10; cf. 3:8–18). Daniel's courage no doubt increased the king's assurance that

Daniel's God would surely deliver him. Darius spent the night awake, fasting, and was evidently the first at the lions' den in the morning, calling to "Daniel, servant of the living God." Daniel's response and the king's rejoicing were appropriate, but the mass punishment of the wives and children of the adversaries along with them violated divine principles of justice (Dan. 6:18–24; Deut. 24:16; Ezek. 18:20).

The concluding edict about Daniel and the living God states good theological truths, as did the early assertion that the prime cause of Daniel's excellence was "because an excellent spirit was in him" (Dan. 6:3, 25–28).

7:1–28 In the first year of Belshazzar king of Babylon Daniel had a dream and visions of his head upon his bed

Daniel 7 is another of the apocalyptic chapters. The sequence of episodes in the book of Daniel is not chronological, for this incident occurred before the Medo-Persian conquest.

The events covered here are virtually the same as those in Nebuchadnezzar's dream, but they are represented with quite a different set of images (Dan. 7 and all fn.; cf. Dan. 2 and commentary). The curious beasts seem to signify some characteristics of the kingdoms of this world. The coming of the kingdom of the Messiah, given only two verses in Daniel 2, occupies more than two-thirds of this chapter (Dan. 2:44–45; 7:9–28 and cross-references).

The Aramaic portion of the book of Daniel ends here; the Hebrew is resumed in chapter 8.

8:1–27 In the third year of the reign of Belshazzar . . . I saw in a vision . . . a ram which had two horns: and the two horns were high

The rise of the Medo-Persian empire and the fall of it to Alexander the Great, king of "Grecia," or Macedonia, are the chief events in this chapter. Daniel's vision on these matters came near the time of the downfall of Babylon and anticipated the continuing cycles of empires, as the angel Gabriel explained, until "in the latter time . . . , when the transgressors are come to the full." Then

shall come the ultimate confrontation of "a king of fierce countenance" with the "Prince of princes" (the Messiah), an event "many
days" in the future (Dan. 8:15–26). The angel Gabriel was delegated to help Daniel understand the vision (BD, "Angels";
"Gabriel"). Angels are mentioned in about half of the books of the
Old Testament, but this is the first one mentioned by name.

Inasmuch as Daniel was transported in vision to "Shushan in
the palace," in the rising Persian empire, it is curious that he did
not at that time learn that a Persian king would release the Jewish
people to return to their homeland. That became the subject of
his thoughts and prayers, however, the account of which is given
in the next chapter.

*9:1–27 In the first year of Darius the son of Ahasuerus, of the seed
of the Medes . . . I Daniel understood by the books the number of
the years, whereof the word of the Lord came to Jeremiah the
prophet, that he would accomplish seventy years in the desolations
of Jerusalem*

The Darius of this chapter seems to be the same one named
earlier in the book of Daniel in the overthrow of Babylon (ca. 538
B.C.; Dan. 5:31; 6:1), but he and Ahasuerus cannot be the ones
mentioned in the books of Ezra and Esther (Ezra 4:5–6; Esther 1:1;
BD, "Chronology," p. 640).

Regarding the seventy years of exile, recall the history of the
end of it (Dan. 9:2*a;* Ezra 1:1; and commentary).

Confessing the sins of Israel, Daniel prayed in fasting and humility. He sought mercy and forgiveness for his people, admitting
the justice of the punishment. He recalled how the Lord had
brought Israel out of Egypt and prayed that the Jews might again
be brought to their promised land and city.

In response, the angel Gabriel was sent with great promises,
including the promise of "the Messiah the Prince," who was to
come at a mysteriously calculated time after the "commandment
to restore and to build Jerusalem" (Dan. 9:25). It is clear that
Daniel prophesied both the restoration of Judah and the coming
of the Savior. Furthermore, in one verse he concisely anticipated
the last week of Jesus' life, in which He fulfilled and concluded

the practices of sacrifice and oblation as they had been known and anticipated the times of apostasy and abominations until the consummation of all things (Dan. 9:27).

10:1–21 In the third year of Cyrus king of Persia a thing was revealed unto Daniel, . . . and the thing was true, but the time appointed was long

The final three chapters of the book of Daniel are a unit; they pertain to the remaining years of the Persian empire and the empires of Alexander and his successor, but they contain symbolism pertaining to all kingdoms of the world and their end at the coming of the Messiah.

The time of these three chapters was the third year of Cyrus, about 536 B.C. The prophet Daniel could then have been about eighty-five years of age. He set his heart to understand what would befall his people in the time to come; and in seeking for the information, he restricted his food and prayed in deep concern and solemnity for three weeks. The place was somewhere along the River Tigris. There were at first others with him, but when the vision opened, he alone saw it; the others all fled, much afraid.

In the first vision Daniel saw the Lord and was overwhelmed (Dan. 10:5–9; cf. Isa. 6; Ezek. 1–3; TG, "God, Privilege of Seeing"). A delegated messenger raised the prophet up, comforted him as "a man greatly beloved," and quieted his anxiety. He assured him that from the beginning of his humble supplication, God had heard his prayers; for some reason, the Lord withheld information about the future until Michael the archangel was sent to help Daniel understand what would befall his people "in the latter days." The prophet was again overcome until a messenger touched his lips, assuring him that he was accepted and greatly beloved; then the messenger touched him again and strengthened him.

As a preview, the angel reminded the prophet of his desire for foreknowledge and prepared to predict the wars to be suffered by Persia against whom Grecia (Macedonia) would arise. During this revelation Daniel was sustained by Michael (Dan. 10:10–21).

11:1– 45 And now will I shew thee the truth. Behold, there shall stand up yet three kings in Persia

After reminding Daniel that the Lord had confirmed and strengthened the first Medo-Persian king, the messenger revealed the future of Persia. The empire would end when a "mighty king" of "the realm of Grecia" arose (Dan. 11:1–4). History knows him as Alexander of Macedonia, or Alexander the Great; he is not identified by name in this scripture. Next, a Ptolemid king is introduced, not by name but as "the king of the south," and then a king of the line of Seleucids as "king of the north." The kings of the south were those based in Egypt and those of the north in Syria. (See BD, "Chronology," pp. 640–43, for the last of the Persian kings and the rise of Alexander. In parallel columns are listed the leaders in the history of Judah, Egypt, and Syria.) Enough details are given by Daniel to identify the dominant kings, their intrigues and battles, and their rises and falls. The effects of those competing powers upon the Jewish populace and their Hasmonean leaders (BD, "Maccabees") is also broached, as are the first incursions of Rome. Because of the intricacy, uncertainty, and sheer volume of those details, only a few identifications are attempted in this commentary.

The king of the north who would impose the worst suffering and indignities on the Jewish patriots was Antiochus Epiphanes, and his exploits are told. So terrible was he that his activities, described in the last half of the chapter, may also be taken as symbolic of the latter days of earth and the actions of an anti-Christ against the people of God (Dan. 11:16–45; BD, "Antiochus Epiphanes"). That application of these prophecies continues in the next chapter.

12:1–13 And at that time shall Michael stand up, the great prince which standeth for the children of thy people: and there shall be a time of trouble, such as never was . . . and at that time thy people shall be delivered

This chapter is best understood as a prophecy of the end of the wicked world, the deliverance of the righteous with the help of Michael, the resurrection of the just and the unjust, and the assignment of "they that be wise" to their kingdom of glory. Thus far were these matters revealed to Daniel, but "knowledge shall be increased" more completely in "the time of the end" (Dan. 12:1–9 and fn.). Then, in conclusion to his many revelations, the prophet Daniel again saw angels beside the river and the same Being whom he had seen earlier and before whom he was overwhelmed—no doubt, the Lord (cf. Dan. 10:5–9).

In Daniel's vision of the great events of the Resurrection, he perceived that some arise to undesirable status and some to everlasting life; they who are "purified and made white, and tried" may be those who will inherit celestial glory (Dan. 12:3, 10 and fn.; cf. Rev. 7:13–14).

The book of Daniel has served to instruct many through the centuries because of its numerous teachings by example and precept. We may have to await future revelations to gain a full understanding of some of its more apocalyptic prophecies.

HOSEA

Hosea was among the earliest of the writing prophets in the last centuries of northern Israel's history. His book is first among the twelve minor (meaning "small") prophetic books. Though they may be smaller in size, these books are not of minor importance; their doctrines are as true and their messages as vital as those of the major ("large") books. *Minor* describes the quantity rather than quality of prophetic content.

All of the prophets whose work is recorded in the Old Testament taught some of the same basic concepts, doctrines, warnings, and promises. Their teachings are in the books of Moses, the so-called historical books, and in the sixteen prophetic books. In particularly critical times, the Lord sent prophets to urge his chosen people to repent, return to spiritual and moral fidelity, and fulfill their covenants with God; to warn the Israelites and others of the consequences of failing to repent; to remind people that the Lord does not forsake them, though they sometimes forsake him; to let future generations of Israel and others know that if they are faithful to the true and living God, he will fulfill his covenant promises; and to let all people know of a brighter destiny for all humankind through the grace of the divine Redeemer. As Isaiah said, "Of the increase of his government and peace there shall be no end" (Isa. 9:7).

Prophets of God are spokesmen for God. Some of the writing prophets were called to warn the people during crisis times when

Israel was threatened by the Assyrians; others, when Judah was threatened by the Babylonians; two, at the time of the return of Judah to rebuild Jerusalem and the temple; and one, at the end of the Old Testament period. Nevertheless, despite the warnings the Lord sent to the people by his "servants the prophets . . . they would not hear, but hardened their necks, like to the neck of their fathers, that did not believe in the Lord their God" (2 Kgs. 17:12–14).

According to the opening of Hosea's book, he received and recorded his revelations during the time of the second King Jeroboam in Israel and of the kings Uzziah to Hezekiah in Judah. Those were the same kings of Judah during Isaiah's and Micah's ministry, but the part of Hosea's service during the reign of Jeroboam would have been earlier than the service of Isaiah and Micah. Both Amos and Jonah prophesied in the time of the second Jeroboam of Israel, so part of their ministry was contemporary with Hosea's. (For an overview of Hosea's life and work and a chart of his place among the other prophets and the kings of the Old Testament, see BD, "Hosea"; "Chronology," p. 638.)

Hosea has been called a "prophet of love" because he showed forth the Lord's love of His people in his teachings and in his feelings for Israel.

COMMENTARY

1:1–11 And the Lord said to Hosea, Go, take unto thee a wife of whoredoms and children of whoredoms: for the land hath committed great whoredom, departing from the Lord

After describing the setting of his ministry, Hosea described his call in symbolic terms. Whether the woman of unfaithfulness was that way when Hosea married her or became that way later is not stated, but Israel was certainly unstable religiously and morally when the Lord took her out of Egypt. She was faithful at times thereafter, but her faithfulness rose and fell throughout a long series of repenting and backsliding before her fall to conquering nations. Thus the strange, symbolic marriage of Hosea to Gomer represented the long, undulating covenant relationship of

Israel with the Lord. The woman's name, Gomer, means "one who finishes, one who ends," but whether that has anything to do with the end of northern Israel near the end of Hosea's life is not told.

The name of the first child of Hosea and Gomer was *Jezreel,* the name of the valley where King Jehu had put many people to death in violation of the Lord's law of justice (Hosea 1:4*a*). *Jezreel* means "God shall sow" or "scatter abroad." As a name for their first child, it doubtless alluded to the imminent overthrow and scattering of Israel, which came in 722 B.C., only about seventy years later. The name of the second child, *Lo-ruhamah,* or "not pitied," warned that the mercy of God would not rob justice to save northern Israel, though Judah still qualified to be saved. The name of the third, *Lo-ammi,* "not my people," is a lament over the broken covenant relationship. Then the prophecy immediately turned to the future gathering of both Israel and Judah and a happier time when "it shall be said unto them, Ye are the sons of the living God" (Hosea 1:10). Israel shall again be united and serve God under one King.

Thus were launched both the account of Hosea's symbolic marriage and family and the themes of his prophetic mission.

2:1–23 Say ye unto your brethren, Ammi; and to your sisters, Ruhamah. Plead with your mother, plead: for she is not my wife, neither am I her husband

The allegory of the prophet's marriage to an unfaithful wife and their family of symbolically named children continues in this chapter. The application of the allegory to the Lord and his covenant relationship with unfaithful Israel is made clear. The prophet and people were urged to remember the covenant of the Lord with his people *(Ammi);* then they could receive his mercy *(Ruhamah).* The prophet pleaded for Israel to put away whoredoms and adultery and return to the true God, the provider of all good. The alternative was to be stripped, shamed, abandoned, humiliated, and exiled.

The warning of dire conditions in captivity was intensified. There would be "thorns" of frustration, lifeless idols to supplicate for sustenance, no providence from the true God, and no recourse to comforting Sabbaths and feast days for the sustaining worship of the Lord.

The message turned to the loving offer of the Lord to guide Israel "into the wilderness," reminiscent of the escape from Egypt to the wilderness and then to the promised land. The *Achor* ("trouble") of Israel's former entry into the promised land will become a future "door of hope" (Heb., *Petah-tiqvah;* Hosea 2:15*a*). The Lord is to become the true Husband (not the "Baal") of Israel upon renewal of the covenant (Hosea 2:16*a*–*c*), and that renewal of the covenant is to last forever. Finally, only loving kindness, mercy, and faithfulness will characterize the relationship, and Israel will "know the Lord." In that day heaven and earth will respond to each other, and good things shall be created. The pathetic negative names will be reversed (Hosea 2:14–23 and fn.).

3:1–5 Then said the Lord unto me, Go yet, love a woman beloved of her friend, yet an adulteress. . . . So I bought her to me for fifteen pieces of silver, and for an homer of barley, and an half homer of barley

It seems evident that this was the same wife, Gomer, thus symbolizing the Lord's redeeming Israel. Hosea's paying half the price of a slave, plus an homer and a half of barley (perhaps equivalent to the other half of the price), may suggest partly the betrayal money paid to Judas Iscariot and partly the suffering of the Redeemer in his work of atonement (cf. Zech. 11:12). In order that mercy might not utterly rob justice, the redeemed wife was to repent and abide with the husband "many days" and not "play the harlot"; that would also symbolize Israel's repentance and return to "the Lord their God, and David their king; and shall fear the Lord and his goodness" (BD, "Fear").

4:1–19 the Lord hath a controversy with the inhabitants of the land, because there is no truth, nor mercy, nor knowledge of God in the land. By swearing, and lying, and killing, and stealing, and committing adultery, they break out, and blood toucheth blood

Herewith begins a series of prophetic teachings about the nature and results of Israel's sins in Hosea's time.

What a trilogy of deficiencies: no truth, mercy, nor knowledge of God! The result was the flourishing of all the evils well-known in their last days—and in ours. The prophet succinctly outlined the results of such a lack of true values in society. He spoke vehemently for the Lord against the related sins of idolatry and adultery.

Though Hosea was a prophet chiefly to northern Israel (sometimes called Israel and sometimes Ephraim), he had warning words also for Judah. Anyone who has tried to lead a calf or to keep a lone lamb in a large area can understand Hosea's similes here; certainly everyone can understand the prophet's castigation of the evils of both women and men. The leaders loved indulgence too well to change, though turmoil and disaster faced them.

5:1–15 Hear ye this, O priests; and hearken, ye house of Israel; and give ye ear, O house of the king . . . ye have been a snare on Mizpah, and a net spread upon Tabor

The priesthood and the government were blameworthy both in causing and in allowing moral decay. Mizpah was an important mountain in Judah; and Tabor, in Israel. They represent the places where the watchmen (leaders) should have been conscientiously watching for dangers. They had not done so but had instead continued their useless and sinful apostate sacrifices. All this was known to God and to them, but they would not change and return to God. So Ephraim (northern Israel) was on the way out. Meanwhile, warnings from high places in Judah and Benjamin (Gibea and Ramah) might help Judah, though Ephraim be desolated; but faulty leadership in both nations was fostering decay. One foolish thing that both nations had done to win respite was to appease the approaching invaders, and both would suffer for it (Hosea 5:13–14; cf. 2 Kgs. 15–25). Judah, however, repented during the onslaught of Assyria, under the guidance of the Lord through Isaiah, and that nation was spared for a century.

Sometimes even the Lord retreats from efforts to save recalcitrant people until their suffering humbles them and makes them more receptive.

6:1–11 Come, and let us return unto the Lord: for he hath torn, and he will heal

This gentle persuasion was coupled with promises of redemption. Note therein a symbolic prophecy of the first resurrection and attendant restorations through an allusion to the resurrection of the Savior after three days. But because his people would not respond to persuasion, the Lord spoke to them like an exasperated parent. He had tried to hew (shape) them by the prophets to know that such values as mercy and knowledge were what he wanted, not empty ritual offerings (Hosea 6:4–6; cf. 1 Sam. 15:22). Ever since Adam, many of His children had broken covenants and committed sins, and some of Israel's priests had been the worst offenders.

7:1–16 When I would have healed Israel, then the iniquity of Ephraim was discovered

A recitation of the ills of Ephraim and all northern Israel includes all the well-known evils—burning lust, inebriation, political corruption, unfulfilled duty. Like a half-baked cake (not adequately prepared) or like a "silly dove" (lacking understanding), Ephraim was easy prey for Assyria. Ephraim had invited dangerous alliances sometimes with Egypt, sometimes even with Assyria, so it was destined for destruction. They who turned to God only in desperation did so without heart and quickly returned to mischief; therefore they must go into captivity.

8:1–14 They have set up kings, but not by me . . . Thy calf, O Samaria, hath cast thee off

Of the eighteen kings of northern Israel since the division of the kingdom after Solomon's death, only two had any semblance of being "set up" by the Lord; most had taken the throne by the sword. The Levites and Aaronic priests had been immediately displaced by the first king Jeroboam and had fled to Judah. Little wonder that apostasy was rampant two hundred and thirty years after the division. The Lord had sent Elijah and Elisha and some of the "sons of the prophets" to serve northern Israel, but they had been able to accomplish precious little.

This revelation heralds the invader who was allowed to come upon a people who had transgressed their covenants and trespassed the law. Their self-made kings and manmade idols ("calf") had caused Israel to be cut off from the Lord (Hosea 8:1–6). Thus, because of many individual wrongs committed, a great national catastrophe, a "whirlwind" of invasion, was coming. The kings had tried to pacify Assyria with gifts and bribed other nations to no avail (Hosea 8:7–10 and fn.). They had worshipped in wrong ways, supplicated the wrong gods, and built unhallowed temples; therefore, they were on their way to bondage ("Egypt").

Judah was not without fault and would also be invaded but not taken captive at that time (Hosea 8:11–14).

9:1–17 Rejoice not, O Israel, for joy, as other people: for thou hast gone a whoring from thy God

The rebuke and chastisement of northern Israel continued. The people should expect no pleasures in the festivals of the harvest in "Egypt" (bondage) but would eat improper foods and dwell among "nettles" and "thorns" (Hosea 9:1–6). Eventually they would see that they had followed the wrong "prophets," just as they had in the early days at Gibeah and earlier at Baal-peor, though the Lord sought for the firstfruits of righteousness from them (Hosea 9:7–10 and fn.).

Because they brought up children with false ideas and wicked ways, the prophet prayed they might not beget, bear, nor rear children any more. Their wickedness "in Gilgal" may have been the lust for possessions exemplified by Achan, who kept valuable things at the fall of Jericho while Israel was encamped at Gilgal. Because of that misdeed, Israel failed in the siege at Ai (Josh. 5:10; 7:16–26). And because of more such wickedness, they would be smitten and scattered among the nations.

10:1–15 Israel is an empty vine, he bringeth forth fruit unto himself: according to the multitude of his fruit he hath increased the altars

In the vineyard of the Lord, the fruit of the Lord's people should be the good they bring into the lives of others, rather than each seeking "fruit unto himself" (Hosea 10:1c). Worshippers of the Lord should not be "divided" in their loyalties (Hosea 10:2a). Hence northern Israel would be exiles without a king. Like their ancestors who offered offerings to golden calves, they would be forsaken and fearful. *Bethel* means "house of God," but the Israelites had worshipped a calf-image there; so Hosea called it *Beth-aven*, "house of Sin" (Hosea 10:3–4, 5a, 8). The law of the harvest applied: as the first Assyrian invaders had done in Galilee ("Beth-arbel"), so Israel's sins at Beth-el would let invaders do to them, and their king would be cut off early (Hosea 10:6–15 and fn.).

In Gibeah, Israel had once nearly destroyed one tribe, Benjamin, because of sin; now all tribes but one would be destroyed for sinning ever since. Light work would not be found in captivity, but heavy toil (Hosea 10:9–11).

11:1–12 When Israel was a child, then I loved him, and called my son out of Egypt

As the chapter heading and the footnotes to the first verse indicate, the love of God in bringing young Israel out of Egypt became a symbol of his future bringing of the child Jesus back out of Egypt. The Lord had led Israel in the spirit of love when He gave young Jeroboam of Ephraim leadership of the ten tribes; but because of their apostasy since that beginning, their evils would take them back to bondage not in Egypt but in Assyria; they had been called to the most High but failed (Hosea 11:2–7; 1 Kgs. 11:28–36; 12:12–33; 13).

The love of God was shown in his lament, "How shall I give thee up, Ephraim"; he sorrowed to see them destroyed like the cities with Sodom and Gomorrah (Hosea 11:8a–b). He would not totally destroy "Ephraim," however, and in time the ten tribes will come to the Lord when he sends them a signal as strong as the roaring of a lion (Hosea 11:8–11).

In a brief summation, the Lord again chastened Ephraim but recognized some faithfulness in Judah.

12:1–14 Ephraim feedeth on wind, and followeth after the east wind

"Feeding on wind" symbolizes seeking and ingesting useless ideas and ways. The "east wind" is the dreaded *khamsin*, a desert wind bearing heat, dust, and destruction; here it symbolizes attempts to mollify the power of the east (Assyria), and Judah was not without fault in that regard. A symbolic overview of Israel's history follows.

At birth, Jacob's hand on Esau's heel was a sign that he would take his brother's place (Hosea 12:3*a*); when he wrestled with the angel and received the name Israel and when he covenanted at Bethel, he was blessed and gained good status with the Lord (Hosea 12:4–6 and fn.). On the other hand, Israel became an unfair "merchant," became rich, and turned from the Lord, who had brought the people out of bondage in Egypt and had given them the prophets. Northern Israel had turned to iniquity and vanity.

Jacob, as the patriarch, had worked for a wife in Syria (Haran) and been blessed; Israel as a nation had been saved from Egypt by the Lord through a prophet (Moses) and been blessed; but many times Ephraim and the rest of the ten tribes had provoked the Lord and had to bear their guilt.

13:1–16 When Ephraim spake trembling, he exalted himself in Israel; but when he offended in Baal, he died. . . . Yet I am the Lord thy God from the land of Egypt, and thou shalt know no god but me: for there is no saviour beside me

These statements point up the two major themes of the prophet Hosea: Israel, with Ephraim as her leader, began humbly and righteously, but her flagrant sins were causing the nation to go into bondage. Yet all was not lost forever; in the end they would know no other God and their Savior would triumph. The prophet summed up their sins and again stated the desires of the

Lord to save them. The Lord threatened punishment, using powerful symbols of predatory beasts that consume and destroy. He lamented the deterioration of the kingdom of Israel and renewed His promise to be their ultimate King. Finally, in one of the few Old Testament prophecies of the literal resurrection of the dead, Hosea promised ransom and redemption from the grave by the Lord (Hosea 13:14*a–c*).

The phrase "repentance shall be hid from mine eyes" should be part of the next verse. (Remember that versification is a modern modification of the ancient text.) Thus the final statement would be another lament that Israel's sins had been so prevalent that it was too late for repentance. Though once fruitful, Israel would be blasted by that "east wind" (Assyria) and would be desolated, "for she hath rebelled against her God" (Hosea 13:15–16 and fn.).

14:1–9 O Israel, return unto the Lord thy God; for thou hast fallen by thine iniquity. . . . I will heal their backsliding, I will love them freely

The final appeal by the prophet Hosea sought for Israel's repentance and return to true worship. He told Israel how to confess and worship the Lord; true prayer would be more acceptable than perfunctory sacrifice (the translation of verse 2 is inept). Israel should recognize that the power of Assyria and their horses and the power of the gods made by human hands were nothing. In the hands of the Lord, the fatherless can hope for salvation (Hosea 14:1–3).

In beautiful expressions the Lord promised through his prophet healing, love, and redemption. Then Hosea summed up the glorious future redemption of Israel under Ephraim's leadership. He challenged readers of his words to understand them through wisdom and prudence and to walk according to them, though "transgressors shall fall therein" (Hosea 14:4–9).

Hosea has been called a prophet of love, for in spite of all of Israel's sinning, he clearly conveyed to them the reluctance of the Lord to let them go, emphasizing His eagerness to redeem them.

JOEL

Joel's name proclaims that "Jehovah is God"; it is similar in meaning to Elijah's name: "My God is Jehovah." His father's name is given, *Pethuel* (perhaps meaning "opened of God"), but nothing more of his life or background is told.

The book of Joel mentions temple sacrifices and worship activities (Joel 1:9, 13–14, 16; 2:17, etc.), which may mean that he lived in Jerusalem and was familiar with the temple. Many have tried to deduce from the contents of the book when these revelations may have been given, but that is difficult to determine.

The value and importance of the revelations of Joel are not dependent, however, upon their historical derivation. They are clearly addressed to a people facing "the day of the Lord." A latter-day revelation indicates that one of his prophecies "was not yet fulfilled, but was soon to be" (JS–H 1:41; Joel 2:28–32). That being true, the series of destructive forces to be unleashed according to Joel's first chapter, as well as the wars of the second chapter, and the final judgment in the third, must all pertain to the last days (cf. Joel 1:1–3, 14–15).

After the phenomenal series of cataclysms anticipated in chapter 1, great conflicts between armies representing the Lord's people and the adversary are told in chapter 2, verses 1 through 27. The restoration of spiritual gifts, the appearance of "wonders in heaven," and the Lord's delivering Zion and Jerusalem are some of the great eschatological prophecies of Joel, recorded in chapter

2, verses 28 through 32; these five verses form a separate chapter in the Hebrew Bible. Chapter 3 tells of the judgment day to follow the restoration of Judah and Jerusalem, with a gathering of "all nations" to "the valley of Jehoshaphat" ("the valley of Jehovah's judgment"). The Lord will plead there for his people. The nations may prepare for war, but it will be to no avail, for they will be already in the final "valley of decision." That judgment day will be followed by restoration and renewal of the earth, and the Lord shall dwell in Zion.

COMMENTARY

1:1–20 Hear this, ye old men, and give ear, all ye inhabitants of the land. Hath this been in your days, or even in the days of your fathers?

A series of unprecedented cataclysms is symbolized by four future insect plagues, possibly representing repetitive wars, bloodshed, and terror in this world. The inebriate and careless caretakers of the vineyard will have double cause for lament (Joel 1:4–7, 4*a*). The bereaved, symbolized by a widowed young virgin, will lament the lack of food and drink for sacrifice and for sustenance (Joel 1:8–12). The priests and other religious leaders will be called upon to mourn and to sanctify a fast in preparation for a solemn assembly and the announcement of the imminent day of the Lord (Joel 1:13–15). Drought and famine, as precursors of the end, will be felt by all living things on earth (Joel 1:16–20).

2:1–32 Blow ye the trumpet in Zion, and sound an alarm in my holy mountain: let all the inhabitants of the land tremble: for the day of the Lord cometh, for it is nigh at hand

A mighty and apparently invulnerable army unlike any other symbolizes the forces of evil that invade and infiltrate everything before the day of the Lord. They are an irresistible force compared to warhorses, chariots, fire, mighty men, and forces of nature. They cannot be stopped; before them the earth quakes, the heavens tremble, and the sun, moon, and stars cease their shining.

This eschatological destroyer is later called the "northern army" (Joel 2:20).

But that mighty army is not an invulnerable force, for the Lord assembles his army for the day of the Lord. Who can abide it? They who repent and turn to the Lord and depend upon his grace, his mercy, and his compassion (Joel 2:11–14, 13*b, d,* 14*a*). In order that all who will hearken may hear in time, the herald trumpet in Zion is to call them to fasting and summon them to the solemn assembly. The priesthood leaders are to lead the prayers for protection and salvation—for a manifestion of the hand of the Lord. Then the Lord will show his zeal in behalf of the righteous; sustenance will be provided and the "northern army" of evil removed, driven, and slain. The earth will then be restored to its pristine glory and beauty.

A prophecy that began to be fulfilled on the day of Pentecost, and is being fulfilled more generally since the restoration of the gospel, will be totally fulfilled when "all flesh" will enjoy the gifts of the Spirit—old, young, male, female, servants, and handmaids (Joel 2:28–29; Acts 2:16–21; JS–H 1:41). Those phenomena presage cataclysmic wonders in the heavens and on earth, leading to the second coming of the Savior, the true day of the Lord. It will be the great day because there will be deliverance in Zion and in Jerusalem and among all the remnant called of the Lord who sincerely call upon his name.

3:1–21 For, behold, in those days, and in that time, when I shall bring again the captivity of Judah and Jerusalem, I will also gather all nations, and will bring them down into the valley of Jehoshaphat

After the great war of the good against the evil (Joel 2; cf. Ezek. 38–39; Zech. 14), all nations will be gathered into the valley of *Jehoshaphat* ("Jehovah judges"), where the Lord will judge them on behalf of the righteous oppressed of all the ages. With irony, the prophet Joel proclaimed that the gentiles (meaning peoples not yet converted to the Lord) could "prepare war" if they pleased and beat their "plowshares into swords" and boast in their strength. But it will not be a war they face: it will be the Lord's own judgment. It will be like harvest time for all those whose "wickedness is great" among the "multitudes in the valley of decision" (Joel 3:9–14). For them it will be a terrible, dark day, and the heavens and earth will shake, but the Lord will be the hope of His people. Then all shall know that Jehovah is God, "dwelling in Zion," and "then shall Jerusalem be holy," subject to no more invasions. The earth will be renewed, well-watered, and productive. Former nations shall exist no more, but the righteous who have been cleansed will belong to the kingdom of Zion (Joel 3:17–21).

The great message of the book of Joel is "whosoever shall call on the name of the Lord shall be delivered: for in mount Zion and in Jerusalem shall be deliverance, as the Lord hath said" (Joel 2:32). With all the terrible scenarios that lie ahead for the people of the world in the last days, it is comforting to know that there is something good to depend upon, toward which they who are humble and faithful may look with confidence.

AMOS

The book of the prophet Amos is the report of the mission of a farmer and shepherd from Judah, called to preach in the northern state of Israel in the time of "Jeroboam the son of Joash king of Israel" (Amos 1:1). He proclaimed to all Israel for the Lord, "You only have I known of all the families of the earth: therefore I will punish you for all your iniquities" (Amos 3:2); the principle is that where much has been given, much is required (cf. D&C 82:3). His nine chapters are one unit; perhaps they are the speech he delivered "at Bethel . . . the king's chapel" (Amos 7:10–13).

The prophet opened his record with a remarkable overview of inhumanity to fellow humans, as shown in five nations surrounding Israel (Amos 1:3–2:3). Then he chastised his own homeland of Judah for despising the law of the Lord (Amos 2:4–5). Finally, in great detail and biting vigor, he dealt with all the evils in northern Israel in particular and all Israel in general. He foretold Israel's being captured and scattered (Amos 2:6–9:10). Then at last he left a brief but beautiful preview of the great day of restoration in the last days (Amos 9:11–17).

In reprimanding Israel, Amos told why the Lord sends prophets (Amos 3:7). Later, in replying to the charge of the king's court priest, he gave an account of his own divine call to be a prophet and declared the purpose of it (Amos 7:10–17).

The time of Amos's mission "in the days of Uzziah king of

Judah, and in the days of Jeroboam . . . king of Israel" (Amos 1:1) was approximately 790 to 740 B.C., a little earlier than Isaiah's ministry and overlapping the first part of the mission of Hosea. How long he served is not now known. A good brief introduction to this prophet, his times, and his book is given in the Bible Dictionary ("Amos").

The book of Amos is acclaimed for its religious and humanitarian teachings and also for its literary excellence in Hebrew. A farmer and shepherd from a small town in Judah, Amos wrote as divine inspiration worked in and with his clear and active mind.

COMMENTARY

1:1–2 The words of Amos, who was among the herdmen of Tekoa, which he saw concerning Israel in the days of Uzziah king of Judah, and . . . Jeroboam the son of Joash king of Israel

Amos was evidently a common man of the land (Amos 7:14–15), called by the Lord about seventy years before northern Israel's exile. He warned the leaders and the people of imminent destruction and sought to save them, saying, "Seek good, and not evil, that ye may live" (Amos 5:14). The word *saw* in verse 1 is used to translate the Hebrew *chazah,* which denotes divine vision, not ordinary sight. The metaphor of a lion roaring in warning, "The Lord will roar from Zion, and utter his voice from Jerusalem" (v. 2), was also used by other prophets (Amos 1:2*a;* Joel 3:16). The temple in Jerusalem was a place for the Lord's communication with them. There is symbolism also in warnings going out from the mountain of the Lord's house in Judah, addressed to the high, beautiful, and productive Mount Carmel in northern Israel. The withering of Carmel's top represents the deterioration of the highest political and religious leaders of northern Israel who were the cause of many of her ills.

The earthquake mentioned by Amos and again by Zechariah (Amos 1:1*c*) two and one-half centuries later must have been a notable event in the days of King Uzziah.

1:3–15; 2:1–5 Thus saith the Lord; For three transgressions . . . and for four, I will not turn away the punishment thereof

Though the message of Amos was to northern Israel, he began by showing the Lord's concern with evils in nations all around. The formula "For three transgressions . . . and for four" (Amos 1:3) is a Hebrew way of saying they were full to overflowing with atrocities. Three symbolizes fullness, and four, excess. His introduction thus confirms that God is concerned with the evils of man's inhumanity to his fellowman everywhere. In Israel, this prophet who knew all the evils done by his neighbors may have seemed to be a prophet worth hearing—until he turned the condemnation upon the people of Israel themselves.

Note the merciless violence done, and the inevitable punishment to follow, in each nation named. They are Damascus, meaning Syria's leaders; Gaza and the other Philistine cities of Ashdod, Ashkelon, and Ekron; Tyre, which might imply all of Phoenicia; Edom, with its major cities Teman and Bozrah; Ammon, with its capital city Rabbah; and Moab, including "the palaces of Kerioth."

Then the prophet turned to his homeland, the southern Israelite kingdom of Judah. Those people and their king were more blameworthy than their neighbors, for they knew the law and the commandments of God but failed to keep them (Amos 2:4–5).

2:6–16 Thus saith the Lord; For three transgressions of Israel, and for four, I will not turn away the punishment thereof

The prophet began the reproof of northern Israel with the formula applied to the other six nations, but he continued to reprimand them—not in three or four verses but throughout most of the remaining chapters of the book. The enslavement of poor children, dispossession of the poor, immorality, ignoring compassionate principles and practices, and indulgence in confiscated wines were among the range of Israel's sins and crimes cited by the prophet (Amos 2:6–8).

Israel's ingratitude for the promised land after deliverance from bondage in Egypt was a general charge, introducing many others (Amos 2:9–10).

The calling of the Israelites, as heirs of the mission of Abraham, was to serve the Lord as dedicated messengers and exemplars before other nations (TG, "Abrahamic Covenant"; "Israel, Mission of"). That duty in service is symbolized here by the calling of Nazarites (people consecrated to the service of the Lord); but Israel was not giving consecrated service nor heeding the prophets, the spokesmen of the Lord. They had strayed far from being a dedicated people; indeed, they had violated true Nazarites and cast out the prophets. The result was that the Lord himself was oppressed and burdened by their wickedness and failure to serve Him. Therefore He would let them be punished (Amos 2:11–16, 11*a*).

3:1–15 Hear this word that the Lord hath spoken against you, O children of Israel, against the whole family which I brought up from the land of Egypt

Where much had been given, much was required; that principle was as logical as the laws of cause and effect—which the prophet illustrated by several examples (Amos 3:3–6). Yet the Lord will not take action without warning, and Amos was giving the warnings. Why would the people not hearken? (Amos 3:7–8, 7*a–d*).

With irony, the prophet invited the peoples of Ashdod (Philistines) and Egypt to assemble upon the mountains of Samaria, the capital of Israel, to see the tumult and oppression among the Lord's people, who "know not to do right" and "store up violence and robbery in their palaces" (Amos 3:9–10). Because of such sins and crimes in Israel, adversaries would surely be allowed to come into the land and plunder it. The remnants would be like a few bones and a piece of the ear of a lamb remaining after an attack by a lion. Of the luxurious trappings in their winter houses, summer houses, and "houses of ivory," only the corner of a bed or the leg of a Damascene couch would be left by the plunderers (as the Hebrew of v. 12 states). Idolatrous altars, such as the one built by the first King Jeroboam at Bethel, would be destroyed (Amos 3:11–15, 14*a–b;* 1 Kgs. 12:28–33).

4:1–13 Hear this word, ye kine of Bashan, that are in the mountain of Samaria, which oppress the poor, which crush the needy, which say to their masters, Bring, and let us drink

It is a lesson of history that when the women of any culture are as corrupt as the men, all is lost, for there is no one then to raise the children as a viable society. The prophet addressed the women of the upper classes in Israel as "cows of Bashan" (Amos 4:1*a*). Bashan was upper trans-Jordan pastureland, now called the Golan Heights, where cattle ate their fill and grew fat. The metaphor was a way of reprimanding women's self-indulgences. They and their "masters" (Heb., lit., "husbands") would be taken away as captives with "hooks" and "fishhooks." Indeed, an ancient bas-relief shows prisoners of war tethered in long, pitiful queues.

Scathing irony was in the prophet's words as he invited Israelites to continue their rituals of worship at idolatrous altars such as those at Bethel and Gilgal. Their reward would be famine—typified by "cleanness of teeth" and "want of bread"; for the Lord would send them drought and famine. Yet the Lord knew they would not repent and return to him—not by reason of famine, drought, crop diseases, nor pestilence. Therefore he gave them an ominous warning: "Prepare to meet thy God." The Lord, the Creator, knows even man's thoughts (Amos 4:12–13).

5:1–27 For thus saith the Lord unto the house of Israel, Seek ye me, and ye shall live

A lament over the fall of "the virgin of Israel" (Amos 5:2), followed by an invitation to return, opens this revelation. She, who had been sustained and defended by the Lord in former times when she was deserving, would not be defended in the coming invasion but must fall if she did not seek the Lord and live. Of cities that sent out a thousand to battle, a hundred would be left; of those that sent a hundred, ten would be left. Nevertheless, the prophet and the Lord never gave up hope of saving some of Israel; they repeatedly entreated Israel to seek the Lord, seek the Creator, seek good and not evil, hate evil, love good, and establish justice (Amos 5:4, 6, 8, 14, 15). The final appeal to foster justice and righteousness is poetically beautiful and religiously correct (Amos 5:24).

The Lord was cognizant of the people's rejection of the prophets, their oppression of the poor, their injustices, their hypocritical and token offerings, and their honoring of idols. Therefore, unless Israel repented, evil times were upon them. The "day of the Lord" would be a dark day for them, for they would go into captivity northward "beyond Damascus" (Amos 5:26–27).

6:1–14 Woe to them that are at ease in Zion, and trust in the mountain of Samaria

Zion often refers to Jerusalem, and Samaria was northern Israel's capital city. Woe was pronounced upon these erstwhile leaders because of their accelerating decadence; they were no better than Syrian or Philistine palaces. Those who were "at ease in Zion" assumed the day of reckoning would yet be far away and continued to enjoy luxurious, indulgent living, but they would be among the first in captivity (Amos 6:1–7).

Ironically the "excellency of Jacob" had turned into pride in palaces and possessions, which was, of course, abhorrent to the Lord. In the invasion, nine of ten people in a great house would die; survivors and relatives who came to dispose of the bodies would not dare to mention the name of the Lord any more because of the oppressor that had come to the land, terrorizing homes great and small (Amos 6:9–11).

It would be as illogical for the Lord to bless Israel in those times as for horses to run upon a rock or oxen to try to plow it; for the Israelites had rejoiced in idols and boasted in their own strength. Therefore, an invading nation (Assyria) would be raised up to afflict the land from its northern to its southern outposts (Amos 6:12–14).

7:1–9 Thus hath the Lord God shewed unto me; . . . grasshoppers . . . fire . . . a plumbline

Recorded here are three of five visions about impending destruction, which the prophet supplicated the Lord to hold back a while, hoping that the people might repent. The first vision was of a plague of grasshoppers that would destroy the second crop of grass to be mowed for hay, but the Lord did allow Israel time to repent (Amos 7:3*a*). The second was of a terrible fire that would destroy "Jacob," but the prophet prayed for time, which was granted (Amos 7:6*a*). In the third vision, the Lord was holding a plumbline, metaphorically to determine the uprightness of Israel. This time the verdict was that he would not grant any more time; the "high places" used for sinful worship since the days of Isaac and all other idolatrous "sanctuaries" would be laid waste, for the Lord would let the house of Jeroboam suffer the sword of the invaders (Amos 7:7–9).

7:10–17 Then Amaziah the priest of Bethel sent to Jeroboam king of Israel, saying, Amos hath conspired against thee

In this autobiographical segment, the prophet related his confrontation with Amaziah, a court "priest." Presumably it was over the prophet's frank statement that the Lord himself would "rise against" the king (cf. Amos 7:9, 11). Surprisingly, the king did not condemn Amos to death; and the priest commanded him to go back to his homeland of Judah to prophesy and make his living ("there eat bread") and not prophesy again in "the king's chapel, and . . . court" (Amos 7:13).

Amaziah's implication that Amos was a prophet like those of the priestcrafts of northern Israel, earning his "bread" by prophesying, aroused the resentment of the true prophet. He made it plain and clear that his work, his calling, and authority were from the Lord—not a profession. Instead of Amos's compliance, the court priest Amaziah received a prophecy in dire detail about himself and his family (Amos 7:14–17).

The account of the call of Amos shows who may be called on a mission by the Lord and by what authority a true missionary works.

8:1–14 And he said, Amos, what seest thou? And I said, A basket of summer fruit. Then said the Lord unto me, The end is come upon my people of Israel

An object was shown in this fourth vision (the first three are recorded in Amos 7:1–9), the name of which remind the prophet of the imminence of Israel's fall. Indeed, if the translation were slightly varied to "a basket of *fall* fruit; . . . the *fall* is come upon my people of Israel," the original wordplay in Hebrew would be preserved. The prophet foresaw more than the capture and scattering of the ten tribes of northern Israel, for he spoke of lamentation in the temple and "dead bodies in every place"; evidently, the fall of Judah (to come one hundred thirty years after northern Israel's exile) was included in Amos's general vision of the "fall" of the people Israel (Amos 8:1–3).

Reasons for the fall included all the wrongs Amos had so often denounced: oppression of the needy and the poor, merchants impatiently waiting through Sabbaths and festival days for resumption of commerce—and dishonest commerce at that, and rich people subjecting the poor and the debtors to involuntary servitude. A cataclysm of nature was anticipated: "I will cause the sun to go down at noon, and I will darken the earth in the clear day." Astronomers have long known that a total eclipse of the sun did occur on 15 June 763 B.C., which could have been in Amos's lifetime. The meaning of the prophecy may be extended, however, to anticipate the dark hours at midday at the death of the Savior and also to the remorse of some people, when they recognized that they had crucified the Lord (Amos 8:4–10, 9*b*, 10*c*; D&C 45:47–54; Zech. 12:10–12; Matt. 26:45).

The prophet then foresaw a long-range spiritual famine of "the word of the Lord." That famine continued from the last of the Old Testament prophets on, except for the period of the Savior's ministry, until the latter-day restoration. In Amos's application of this prophecy to his own times, he voiced a warning from the Lord that the spiritual thirst felt by the young people of the time was already at hand in Samaria, in Dan, the location of one of the golden calves of the first King Jeroboam (Amos 8:14*b*), and in Beer-sheba, known as a shrine for idolatrous worship in Amos's time.

9:1–15 I saw the Lord standing upon the altar: and he said, Smite the lintel of the door, . . . he that fleeth of them shall not flee away

This chapter records the fifth vision in the sequence. The context indicates it was given at the altar at Bethel, where the Lord symbolized destruction of the doorway so that none worshipping there could escape. Others in the community would be unable to hide anywhere, high or low (Amos 9:1–4). The land would be cursed and its dwellers would mourn, for Israel would become like the other nations around it (Amos 9:5–7).

In the future, however, the Lord will "sift" the Israelites who are scattered among all nations, to gather the good grain, not the least of which will "fall upon the earth" and be wasted, but the sinners shall perish (Amos 9:8–10). In that day, the Lord will restore the temple, and the remnants of the world ("Edom"), or the "heathen," who have been converted ("which are called by my name") shall live in his kingdom (Amos 9:11–12). The earth will be renewed and made productive, with harvest time running on into seed (planting) time. The descendants of the exiles of Israel will be gathered to "build the waste cities, and inhabit them," to plant vineyards and gardens, and enjoy the produce thereof. Peoples will be "planted" in their homelands, no more to be disinherited (Amos 9:13–15).

So ends the record of the prophetic teachings of Amos. At the last day his people will "hate the evil, and love the good, and establish judgment [justice] in the gate," and surely "the Lord God of hosts will be gracious" unto all (Amos 5:15).

OBADIAH

Nothing is known about Obadiah's background or mission but his name means "One serving Jehovah," which is appropriate for his calling. And all that is known of Obadiah's prophetic works is this short message from a vision of Edom's doom (BD, "Edom"; "Idumea"; "Obadiah"). The Edomites were the descendants of Esau, brother of Jacob, or Israel. Edom was virtually always an enemy to Israel and Judah, however, and as a result, the very name of Edom (or Idumea) came to symbolize "the world" (D&C 1:36; cf. Isa. 34:5a).

The particular occasion of Obadiah's prophecy was evidently the time of the Babylonian conquest of Judah. As with most of the prophecies to Israel, this one also extends far beyond the immediate, reaching to ultimate events in the earth's destiny. Much of what Obadiah prophesied can be found in other books of the Prophets, especially Jeremiah (see fn.), but there is one gem of information at the end that is unique (Obad. 1:21).

COMMENTARY

1:1–9 The vision of Obadiah. Thus saith the Lord God concerning Edom

Obadiah declared that he had heard "a rumor" (Heb., lit., "communication") from the Lord encouraging an attack upon Edom by other nations. Edom's location was in the Arabah, south of the Dead Sea, with abundant ravines, cliffs, and caves (as at

Petra). That terrain had given her a false sense of security. But she was about to be plundered more thoroughly than thieves could do, stripped more bare than harvesters in a vineyard would do, and utterly vanquished.

1:10–16 For thy violence against thy brother Jacob shame shall cover thee, and thou shalt be cut off for ever

In the prophet's view, the historical violence between the descendants of Edom and Jacob had been topped by the Edomites' willful participation in the Babylonian capture of Judah. The prophet mentioned their casting lots upon Jerusalem, jeering at the captives, exulting, plundering, and blocking the flight of refugees.

In the "day of the Lord" all "heathen" (people who will have chosen to remain out of the Lord's kingdom) will suffer according to their ways and deeds. In a dramatic characterization, Obadiah declared for the Lord that as they had "drunk upon my holy mountain," they and other "heathen" would "drink" themselves into oblivion.

1:17–21 But upon mount Zion shall be deliverance, and there shall be holiness

In contrast to those who have chosen to be out of the Kingdom, those within it shall inherit the earth after it is cleansed by fire (Obad. 1:18a; cf. Mal. 4:1–2). Israelite possessions in the former lands of Edom and Canaan are briefly outlined (cf. Ezek. 48).

The promise of "deliverance" in Obadiah 1:17 is enlarged upon in verse 21. Under the Spirit of holiness, "saviours" (Heb., moshi'im, "those bearing salvation") on Mount Zion will make deliverance available to all who are judged worthy (Obad. 1:21 and fn.). "Mount Zion" is the place of the temple, and so the ordinances of salvation there are implied. On the function of judging (Obad. 1:21c), allusion is made to the law that goes forth from Zion (cf. Isa. 2:3).

If only for the message of the last verse, this little book of prophecy would have been worthy of preservation through the ages.

JONAH

The book of Jonah is not so much a book of prophecy as it is a book about a prophet, but one experience of that prophet symbolizes the most important event in the history of the world since the fall of Adam.

The book tells of a prophet who was a reluctant missionary, sent to warn the Assyrian enemy. His call was not unique. Several of the prophetic books have messages to and about other nations: Amos, Isaiah, Jeremiah, Ezekiel, and Nahum. Furthermore, Ezekiel worked in Babylon, and Daniel prophetically advised some of the Babylonian and Medo-Persian kings. Jonah's origins were in Gath-hepher, three miles northeast of what would later be Nazareth. According to a note in the book of Kings, Jonah was a prophet in the time of King Jeroboam before being called on a foreign mission (2 Kgs. 14:25). The way he responded to the mission call and the way the Lord responded to him brought about the lessons for which this book is greatly valued.

The time was probably around 790 B.C. (BD, "Chronology," p. 638). That was halfway between the time of Assyrian empire builders such as Shalmaneser III (of the battle of Karkar, 853 B.C.) and the Assyrians who conquered Syria and Israel between 732 and 722 B.C., and threatened Judah in 701 B.C. This could have been in a time between periods of great power, when an Assyrian king was insecure enough to listen to a strange, foreign prophet and take his advice to avoid being overthrown (Jonah 3; BD, "Assyria"; "Jonah").

COMMENTARY

1:1–17 Now the word of the Lord came unto Jonah the son of Amittai, saying, Arise, go to Nineveh, that great city, and cry against it; for their wickedness is come up before me

The first lesson of the book of Jonah is in its first two verses: the God of Israel is concerned about nations other than Israel—even an enemy nation (BD, "Nineveh"). The idea of God's care for all is not unique to this book of scripture, but it is not generally understood even in the latter days. If Jonah understood it, he shrank from implementing it.

The second lesson is that no one can flee "from the presence of the Lord" (Jonah 1:3). Jonah probably knew that but tried anyway. When his attempt to get away to Tarshish (BD, "Tarshish") foundered in a storm and he was identified by lot as the one responsible, he identified his God as "the Lord, the God of heaven, which hath made the sea and the dry land" (Jonah 1:9). Why did he try to flee from the God of heaven and earth? He explained later that his action was based on "lying vanities" (Jonah 2:8).

The third lesson is that while the Lord may let one suffer for malfeasance, he will prepare a way whereby his banished may be saved (recall 2 Sam. 14:14). In the case of this runaway missionary, the Lord let him confess, repent, and manifest willingness to sacrifice himself to save those whom he had imposed upon. In so doing, he taught those sailors something about the Lord and those who believe in him, and the sailors worked and prayed to save him and themselves, apparently taking seriously what they had learned about the Lord (Jonah 1:10–16).

The way prepared for Jonah's rescue was a miracle. A "great fish" (as it is called in Hebrew) was "prepared" by the Lord to save him. But before Jonah was saved, he had to suffer a trauma in the fish "three days and three nights" and learn another lesson. It was that experience that Jesus cited as symbolic of his own death, the entombment of his body, and the initiation of resurrection for mankind (Jonah 1:17*a*).

2:1–10 Then Jonah prayed unto the Lord his God out of the fish's belly . . . out of the belly of hell cried I, and thou heardest my voice

Jonah declared that he prayed from the fish's belly, which for him was equivalent to the spirit world (Heb., *mibbetten she'ol*) when he had little hope to live. The prayer is not recorded, but Jonah's poetic psalm of thanks and praise to the Lord for hearing his prayer and saving him is. In form and substance it is fine poetry (Jonah 2:2–9). Fortunately the diction and parallel phrasing in English do preserve some of the poetry of the Hebrew original. Look for two or three parallel lines in each verse. Some of them are couplets of synonymous phrases, but most are "synthetic parallels," in which the second phrase or clause repeats a bit and adds to the first, and a third may likewise add to the second.

Jonah reported his prayer and the Lord's response, recalled his dire straits, cited his hopes, stated the impossibility of escape, and contrasted all that with his miraculous preservation; he told how desperation led to supplication and then to salvation; then he confessed his transitory false ideas ("lying vanities") that had led him to try to flee from the Lord's presence, and nearly led to the loss of any claim on the Lord's mercy (Jonah 2:8; cf. 1:3). He concluded with a promise to pay his vows gratefully and declared truly, "Salvation is of the Lord" (Jonah 2:9).

One quick prose line announces the denouement: the Lord spoke, and Jonah was delivered (Jonah 2:10). Economy of language characterizes this short book, and nowhere better than in this concluding verse of chapter 2.

3:1–10 And the word of the Lord came unto Jonah the second time, saying, Arise, go unto Nineveh, that great city, and preach unto it the preaching that I bid thee

Upon the repetition of his call, Jonah went a day's journey into the great city (Jonah 3:3–4, 3*a–b*).

The Lord's use of "preaching" to save people is noteworthy (Jonah 3:2, 5, and fn.). This book's terse record reports only the one essential warning Jonah preached; the response to it was indeed a miracle (Jonah 3:5–10, 9a, 10a, c–d). That repentant spirit in Nineveh was long gone before the Assyrian moves of the last thirty years of the century; but it is significant that because of Jonah's mission, the Assyrians did receive an opportunity to hear of and believe in the Lord; and for one shining moment in history they behaved accordingly.

4:1–11 But it displeased Jonah exceedingly, and he was very angry. . . . Then said the Lord, Doest thou well to be angry?

The last lesson learned by Jonah, and to be learned by anyone considering his record, arose out of his surprising reaction to the people's repentance (Jonah 4:1–4). Perhaps his lack of desire to preach in Nineveh lay in a lack of desire to save such a place, and perhaps it seemed enough simply to preach, "Yet forty days, and Nineveh shall be overthrown" (Jonah 3:4). Had he failed to perceive the Lord's real purpose in the mission? Was he indeed opposed to it, as shown by his remonstrance and complaint? (Jonah 4:2). Did he suffer wounded pride in having preached something that was not fulfilled? (Jonah 4:3). Perhaps so, for without repenting of his anger, he went out of the city to "see what would become of the city" (Jonah 4:4–5). The Lord provided a plant to supplement his shelter, but when the plant that had grown quickly perished suddenly (also by the hand of the Lord) and the sun and the east wind beat upon him—and nothing happened to the city—he was frustrated with his work and his life (Jonah 4:6–9).

Then came the final lesson: If Jonah saw value in a living plant and lamented its demise though he had neither planted nor created it (Jonah 4:6–10), could he not understand God's perception of value in a city full of people, including thousands of children who could not yet discern left from right (wrong from right) and also God's consideration for the many animals (Jonah 4:10–11)? It is like the lesson from Ezekiel on the Lord's desire concerning sinners: "Have I any pleasure at all that the wicked should die? saith the Lord God: and not that he should return from his ways, and live? . . . I have no pleasure in the death of him that dieth, saith the Lord God: wherefore turn yourselves, and live ye" (Ezek. 18:23, 32).

Such are the lessons from the experiences of Jonah and the Lord's dealings with and through him and with others, especially others who had not known the Lord.

The Lord himself made Jonah's suffering and activity in his "sheol," followed by his return to preach salvation in Nineveh, a type or symbol of the three days and three nights His body was in the tomb (Matt. 12:39–40; Luke 11:29–32).

MICAH

Micah was a prophet at the same time as Isaiah and part of the time of Hosea (BD, "Micah"). Isaiah and Micah gave similar prophecies on the rise of Zion in the latter days (Isa. 2:1–5; Micah 4:1–5), but Micah recorded some prophecies not found elsewhere. He foretold, for instance, the place of the anticipated birth of the Messiah (Micah 5:2). Some of his teachings are distinctive, too, such as his succinct summary of what the Lord requires of man: to do justly, love mercy, and walk humbly with him (Micah 6:6–8).

Little is known about Micah's place of origin as a "Morasthite." Two places with related names are mentioned in Micah's first chapter, "Moresheth-gath" and "Mareshah" (Micah 1:14–15). Both places are in the hill country about fifteen miles northwest of Hebron, near Lachish. Like Amos, Micah was evidently from a small town in Judah; but though we know that Amos preached in northern Israel, we do not know where Micah preached. His messages cover things "which he saw concerning Samaria and Jerusalem" (Micah 1:1) that also concern peoples of other times, including the latter days.

COMMENTARY

1:1–16 The word of the Lord that came to Micah the Morasthite in the days of Jotham, Ahaz, and Hezekiah, . . . which he saw concerning Samaria and Jerusalem

Except for the introductory statement, the whole prophetic

book is in good Hebrew poetry. That adds to its literary beauty but also contributes to obscurity in some passages.

Samaria was the capital of northern Israel and Jerusalem the capital of Judah; his salutation thus indicates that his book addresses both nations. Indeed, his announcement addresses everyone everywhere and commends the witness of the Lord to them— and against them. It is evident that Micah, as a spokesman for the Lord, intended his messages to be applied by anyone in the world experiencing such conditions of evil as he was about to describe and denounce in his own country.

That perspective continues in the general announcement that the Lord is coming down in ultimate judgment upon "the high places of the earth" (Micah 1:3). Like the melting of mountains and the splitting of valleys, he saw judgment poured down.

More immediately, because of the "transgression of Jacob" (meaning all Israel), judgment was coming to his land, and those most responsible for the people's transgressions were the leaders in Samaria and Jerusalem (Micah 1:5). The responsibility of the leaders for conditions in society is frequently expressed in the prophetic books.

The message to Samaria predicted total destruction of the city with its graven images, its merchandise in harlotry, and all the evils of both. Some of those evils had come also to Judah, even to Jerusalem (Micah 1:6–9).

Turning to Judah, Micah pronounced a series of dirges against cities, not all of which are now known. The dirges are expressed poetically in puns or other forms of wordplay, quite impossible to reproduce in translation but by using its name to typify its fate, these figures of speech imply that each place would suffer an end appropriate to the meaning of its name (Micah 1:10–16, 10*b*).

2:1–13 Woe to them that devise iniquity, and work evil upon their beds! when the morning is light, they practise it, because it is in the power of their hand

This prophecy also concerns all Israel, but more generally, it may apply to any leader or person who imposes suffering and injustice upon the poor and humble. A general application of

Micah's observation is that an evil mind thinks at night of evil deeds to do, and an evil one rises up in the light to do them. Examples of such deeds follow, and their results are depicted. The prophet foretold the regrets and complaints of evildoers, especially those who were Israel's leaders, when they lost their heritage and no one cast lots for redistributing it to them. Naturally, such people did not wish to hear such prophecies, so prophecy would cease—and so also would the opportunity to repent.

To the people's complaints, the prophet replied with challenges to the whole "house of Jacob," asking whether the Spirit of the Lord can be restricted or a limit placed on his actions. People should change their own ways and walk uprightly; thus, these prophetic words would accomplish some good (Micah 2:7).

The prophet told more of the people's evil ways, such as taking the clothes off the very backs of unsuspecting souls, leaving them like refugees, and taking homes away from women and children, denying them their heritage. They should repent of ways of life that could only destroy them.

True prophets they did not like, but lying prophets, telling of new indulgences in alcohol, they did like (Micah 2:6, 11).

The concluding prophecy of the chapter has been interpreted as a contrasting forecast of the gathering and the restoration of Israel, but it could also be a bitter warning that because of corruption, the Lord would lead the people of Israel (or let them be taken) out through the broken city walls and gates *into* captivity with their king.

3:1–12 Hear, I pray you, O heads of Jacob, and ye princes of the house of Israel; Is it not for you to know judgment?

Again addressing the leaders of Israel, the prophet characterized them as butchers and cannibals in their callous injustice to their own people. It was terribly shocking symbolism, but the prophet wanted them to know that because of their lack of justice in taking advantage of people, in their own time of need the Lord would "hide his face from them" and not listen to their pleas.

He turned again to the false prophets, who consumed what the people gave them and proclaimed "peace" unto them but

"prepared war" against any who would not give what they demanded. To such "prophets" the "night" was approaching in
which they would not know what to prophesy but be ashamed
and confounded; they certainly would not get any enlightenment
from God (Micah 3:5–7).

In contrast, the true prophet, who was full of the power of the
Spirit of the Lord, having judgment and might, proclaimed Israel's
sins and transgressions. He charged the leaders with miscarriage
of justice and equity: causing violence by taking profit from their
work (an evil called "priestcraft" in the Book of Mormon). Yet
they falsely claimed the protection of the Lord. In one withering
prophecy, he described their erstwhile "Zion" as plowed and
wrecked, with the temple mount looking like a wilderness.

*4:1–13 But in the last days it shall come to pass, that the mountain
of the house of the Lord shall be established in the top of the mountains, . . . and people shall flow unto it*

In contrast to the destruction prophesied for his times, Micah
foretold, as Isaiah had, the latter-day establishment of the house of
the Lord "in the top of the mountains" with people flowing unto it
from many nations to learn the ways and walk in the paths of the
God of Israel (Micah 4:1). His word and his law shall go forth from
the Zion in the mountains and from Jerusalem. "Strong nations"
(Micah 4:3) will be judged and rebuked, weapon makers will make
tools for farming, war will cease, peace will be in each home and
nation, and the only government will be that of the Lord. Because
these were events that the prophet Isaiah "saw concerning Judah
and Jerusalem," and Micah recorded almost the same words without saying they were revealed to him, it may be that Micah quoted
them from Isaiah (Micah 4:1–3 and fn.; Isa. 2:1–4; BD, "Zion").

Micah added statements, from the Lord, that people will have
their own homes and orchards and be true to the Lord, people
who have been afflicted or exiled will become a strong nation,
the Lord shall reign over them, and the kingdom "shall come to
the daughter of Jerusalem" (Micah 4:4–8).

Briefly, the prophet looked again at the pitiable Jerusalem of
his century. Except for one good king in Micah's own time

(Hezekiah) and one a century later (Josiah), there would be "no king in thee," and Judah would be taken captive to Babylon.

Again he considered the failed "Zion" of his times, with enemies looking greedily at her. He knew that they could not know the intent of the Lord for the future, and he wished for the great day when a future "daughter of Zion" shall "arise and thresh" and consecrate the harvest of peoples "unto the Lord of the whole earth" (Micah 4:9–13).

5:1–15 But thou, Bethlehem Ephratah, though thou be little among the thousands of Judah, yet out of thee shall he come forth unto me that is to be ruler in Israel; whose goings forth have been from of old, from everlasting

That passage states the theme of this chapter. Verse 1 belongs to the end of the previous chapter and the attack on Jerusalem there prophesied (Micah 4:11–5:1).

Micah prophesied the birth of our Savior. He was the only Old Testament prophet to name Bethlehem as the birthplace of the divine Messiah. It was, of course, the place of David's origin, and Isaiah referred to the Messiah as the "stem of Jesse" (Isa. 11:1). All the prophets knew he would be born of the royal line of Judah (TG, "Jesus Christ, Davidic Descent of"), which originated in Bethlehem. This divine Ruler's "goings forth," or origins, had been from the beginning, from days of eternity (TG, "Jesus Christ, Antemortal Existence of"). This prophecy was Micah's great "good news" for Israel and the world, but the immediate bad news was that the Israelites would be given up in their wickedness into the hands of conquerors and remain in exile until the messianic times.

The gospel hope was pronounced: the Messiah shall feed his flock and provide for their needs everywhere. He will do it "in the strength of the Lord," since he *is* the Lord. All the earth will know of his majesty, and he will maintain the peace when a latter-day "Assyrian" (adversary) attacks his people. He will have many leaders; "seven . . . and eight" is an idiom implying a complete roster, and more. They will "waste" (destroy) the enemy forces (Micah 5:4–6).

Then, in the time of peace, "Jacob" (or the chosen) will be a blessing to all peoples. "Israel," meaning the Messiah's latter-day people from whatever lineage they come, will be leaders in the midst of other peoples "as a lion among the beasts of the forest" (Micah 5:8)—invincible. They will vanquish all forms of evil. The struggle is told in terms of ancient wars, and one could wish it were told in more ideal descriptions of the triumph of truth, goodness, and peace over evil crafts, idolatrous practices, and destruction. The climax is that the Lord will at last be the true Ruler (Micah 5:7–15). The resurrected Lord cited these prophetic words to the Nephites and applied them to the overthrow of evil in the last days (3 Ne. 16:15; 21:12–18).

6:1–16 the Lord hath a controversy with his people, and he will plead with Israel

This message went back again to the situation existing in the prophet's own times. The Lord called to those on high and those at the foundations of the earth to be witnesses of what he had done to redeem his people and what they had done to provoke him, even as he brought them from bondage in Egypt and up to the promised land.

Then Micah posed some rhetorical questions about what the Lord really required of true followers: would it be burnt offerings, calves, great numbers of animals, great amounts of oil, even their firstborn children? After all those hyperbolic questions, his answer was one of pure peace and the essence of true religion: What is good in the eyes of the Lord? What is required by him? "To do justly, and to love mercy, and to walk humbly with thy God." That is a classic, succinct summary of good religion (Micah 6:6–8).

Immediately the prophet again challenged his people to hearken to the Lord's words; he urged them to be aware of the "rod" that the Lord had provided (Micah 6:9; 1 Ne. 11:25). Unrighteous gain, dishonest dealing, and violent and deceitful negotiations were among the common evils of the time. Therefore, the Lord would let his people be smitten with hunger, miscarriage, and death—and with failure of their crops (Micah 6:13–15). Because northern Israel had never forsaken all the ways of kings Omri and Ahab, and of Jezebel, they would be desolated, and they had to bear their reproach (Micah 6:16*a–c*).

7:1–20 Woe is me! for I am as when they have gathered the summer fruits, as the grapegleanings of the vintage: there is no cluster to eat. . . . The good man is perished out of the earth: and there is none upright among men

Somewhat in the manner later used by the prophet Jeremiah (cf. Lam. 3), Micah concluded his prophetic writings with words of lament about the Israelites. His words are straightforward and clear about the lack of goodness in Israelite society (Micah 7:2–4). His characterizations of family relationships indicate pathetic conditions. Under such situations, there is nowhere for a good person to turn for help but to God (Micah 7:5–7). Speaking for the people, however, he recommended that the enemies should not rejoice or consider Israel vanquished altogether, for under the Lord there is always hope for redemption. Continuing to speak for Israel, he also resolved to bear the just punishment until worthy of defense by the Lord; and he expressed hope for punishment of the injustices done by enemies (Micah 7:8–13).

The prophet prayed for the providential times of the Messiah to come. The "rod" here is the shepherd's staff with which the shepherd protects his flock. The prophet anticipated "marvellous things" the Lord would show the world. He anticipated the amazement of the nations in seeing the redemption of the Lord, falling down before Him in "fear" ("reverence"; Micah 7:14–17).

Micah uttered his own words of praise and gratitude for the Lord's mercy shown through His forgiveness and redemption, assuring the people of the Lord's compassion in subduing their iniquities and casting their sins into the sea (Micah 7:18–19). He closed his work with the assurance that the Lord will implement truth and loving kindness to "Jacob" and "Abraham" (the people of His covenant), according to His promises (Micah 7:20*a*–*b*).

This prophet's name is a short form of *Micayah,* a phrase asking "Who is like Jehovah?" Like the names of some of the other prophets and patriarchs, it is appropriate to the life's work of this man, who prophetically demonstrated in many ways that no one indeed is like Him, and everyone should strive to live His ways. No other power is like His power, and no king like this King.

NAHUM

Nahum gave his book the title "the burden of Nineveh," and its source of information, "the vision of Nahum the Elkoshite." *Burden* designates it as a message "lifted up" against Nineveh. *Vision* is used here to translate *chazon,* which denotes divine vision, not ordinary sight. *Nahum* means "full of comfort" and could relate to the comfort he brought to Judah in the knowledge of the end of the threat of Assyria. The meaning or location of Elkosh is not known, but tradition holds that ancient Capernaum was the home of this prophet; its Hebrew name, *Kephar-Nahum,* means "village of Nahum."

Nineveh was the capital city of Assyria, which had been a threat to Israel since at least 850 B.C. Assyria finally conquered and exiled northern Israel in 722 B.C. and threatened Judah until Sennacherib's forces were divinely decimated at the end of that century (2 Kgs. 19:20–37). Nahum may have lived about 642 B.C. (BD, "Chronology," p. 639).

Fulfillment of Nahum's prophecy came a short time after he gave it, about 614 to 606 B.C., when the mother city of Assyria, Asshur, was destroyed; then Nineveh, the capital city, fell; and finally the rest of the empire capitulated to Nabopolassar, king of the rising empire of Babylon (BD, "Chronology," p. 639).

Nahum was another poetic prophet; his language is picturesque and full of symbolism. In his first chapter, he wrote a partially acrostic poem to describe both the destructive might and the abundant goodness of the Lord. At the end of it, he foretold the end of wickedness and heralded the era of peace on earth in words similar to Isaiah's (cf. Isa 52:7). In his second chapter, Nahum graphically and dramatically described the invasion and overthrow of Nineveh; and in the third, he told why that destruction was deserved and decreed (BD, "Nahum").

COMMENTARY

1:1–15 The burden of Nineveh. The book of the vision of Nahum the Elkoshite

At first glance, it might appear that Nahum depicted only the destructive powers of the Lord in these fourteen verses; but he chose the symbolic third and seventh verses to characterize His patience, power, justice, and control of nature and then told of His goodness, helpfulness, and awareness of the faithful.

In the introduction to this prophecy of what the Lord would do to once-mighty Nineveh, the prophet told of the Lord's zeal (not His "jealousy"; recall Ex. 20:5) in destroying evil. He characterized the Lord's powers over nature, man, and armies. Those who imagine opposition to the Lord shall be vanquished. And though His people have been afflicted, they shall be afflicted no more when He reigns and breaks the yoke of the oppressors and enemies of righteousness. One Assyrian king who experienced something like this "burden" was Sennacherib, whose might was decimated by the Lord about a century before the fall of Nineveh (Nahum 1:11–14; cf. Isa. 36–37).

Nahum's vision of the herald of "good tidings" upon the mountains could have been a comfort to Jerusalem after the evil years of King Manasseh and before the rise of the Babylonian threat a few years later, but it is particularly applicable to humble believers in the latter days, who believe in the messengers who preach repentance and preparation for the Messiah (Nahum 1:15*a*).

2:1–13 He that dasheth in pieces is come up before thy face

These words were addressed to the Assyrians of Nineveh; they were ironically advised to prepare their defenses. It was true that "the excellency of Jacob," or Israel, had before been emptied out and marred at times, but the time had come for Nineveh to be emptied. The prophet continued, describing the Babylonian attackers, the agitated defense efforts in the besieged city, the opening of the sluice gates of the city moats, and perhaps the capture and exile of the queen, followed by the destruction and plunder of Nineveh. Finally, using metaphors of a lion pack, Nahum depicted the end of the terrible king and the end of his dynasty.

3:1–19 *Woe to the bloody city! it is all full of lies and robbery; the prey departeth not*

According to their own records, many of which have been unearthed and deciphered, as well as the biblical account, the Assyrian armies were violent, guilty of many atrocities. This chapter is a kind of taunt-song, reciting their vices and telling of equivalent violence to be wrought on Nineveh. No-amon and her allies had been overthrown by Assyrians half a century earlier (Nahum 3:8–10, 8*a*), but the time had come that Nineveh's defenders would be as dazed as the drunken. The strongholds would be like fig trees ready for harvest and the people in the midst of Nineveh as vulnerable as women. The gates would be opened and the bars burned. The prophet, in satirical phrases, told them they could prepare for siege but it would be in vain. Like the insects of a plague, her merchants, her crowned heads, and their armies had done their damage and would fly away.

Then, in a ten-stich (Hebrew) poetic epitaph, the prophet laid Nineveh's shepherds and nobles to rest, predicting applause for their downfall. Thus ends the burden of Nineveh.

Although it is a taunt-song, rejoicing over the vanquishing of an inveterate and violent enemy, this prophetic book teaches some religious truths: The Lord is patient, great, and just; he is good, dependable, and helpful; and the time is coming when all wickedness shall cease and He shall reign in peace (Nahum 1:3, 7, 15).

HABAKKUK

"The burden which Habakkuk the prophet did see" is somewhat like the "burdens" in the other prophetic books; they are typically pronouncements of doom upon peoples deserving punishment. This prophet saw (Heb., *chazah*, "envisioned") wickedness among his own people going unpunished while the righteous suffered. Then, in answer to his query about the justice of that, he was shown the Babylonians ("Chaldeans") being allowed to come in to administer the punishment. That compounded the problem, and again he remonstrated with the Lord.

The second chapter gives the Lord's terse reply, expressed in a couplet containing two principles of justice, followed by a pronouncement of woe upon a cross-section of all evildoers.

The third chapter is a psalm giving thanks to the Lord for righteous principles and for his powers to create, protect, and save. It ends with the prophet's promise to rejoice in the Lord no matter what may come, for He brings salvation.

Nothing is known about Habakkuk beyond what is given in his little book. His name, meaning "embraced," gives no clue. He seems to have lived after the fall of northern Israel and before the fall of Judah (BD, "Habakkuk").

COMMENTARY

1:1–17 the law is slacked, and judgment doth never go forth: for the wicked doth compass about the righteous; therefore wrong judgment proceedeth

Habakkuk was a prophet with a problem. It was one that many others, including the first prophet of our own dispensation, have shared: Why do the wicked seem to prosper while the righteous suffer in this life? (Hab. 1:2*a;* Job; Ps. 10). The answer is never obvious, for the cause is inherent in the principle and operation of agency among all children of God. Minds operating freely are allowed to choose evil or good and promulgate what they choose long enough to demonstrate what they have willed to become. Some choose to impose evils upon others, and that is allowed for a time.

Habakkuk's questions elicited the Lord's reply that the Chaldeans would soon come and the wicked of Judah would suffer at the hands of wicked Babylon. To that answer, the prophet managed a barely restrained reply, conceding to Deity the wisdom of eternity but protesting that his justice and purity were surely too great to allow that "the wicked devoureth the man that is more righteous than he." The prophet protested, "Thou . . . makest men as the fishes of the sea"; all would be caught in one net taken up by ignorant fishermen who would rejoice over their catch, sacrificing and burning incense to the very implements of their prosperity and continually repeating their undiscerning process.

2:1–20 I will stand upon my watch, and set me upon the tower, and will watch to see what he will say unto me, and what I shall answer when I am reproved

Habakkuk knew he had boldly questioned the Lord's ways, and he frankly expected reproof. Instead of reproof, however, he was taught a principle to be made plain for any to read and apply: the arrogant is not upright; the just lives by faith. The Hebrew word *amunah* means "strong faith, faithfulness, firmness." The

Lord's answer admonishes humility with the patience and trust to wait for justice; it will come in its time.

There was also an answer from the Lord about Babylon, personified perhaps as the king of Babylon, berated and condemned. The prophet had asked how long he must cry for justice, and the reply repeated the question "How long," implying "How long indeed!" He "that ladeth himself with thick clay" is one insulated against compassion or pity, as the oppressive Babylonian leaders had been. But the oppressed will not have to suffer forever, for someone will "rise up suddenly that shall bite" the oppressor or a remnant of the oppressed will eventually spoil him in turn (Hab. 2:5–8).

The revelation of woe to perpetrators of wickedness continued, denouncing all wrong principles and practices. It castigated greed and covetous actions, such as forcing enslaved people by violence to labor in wood and stone and in brick-kilns to build cities for a tyrant's transient glory. That will change when "the earth shall be filled with the knowledge of the glory of the Lord" (Hab. 2:9–14).

This sermon also condemned intoxicating a neighbor to use him immorally. There is no "glory" in that, but shame; and justice will cover such evildoers with their own filthiness. There was condemnation of the flagrant wasting of the forests and animals of Lebanon, as well as all the human violence committed there by Babylon's tyrant.

One more woe was uttered, condemning the costly, useless, and blasphemous business of idolatry. By contrast, the prophet characterized the sublimity of true worship: "the Lord is in his holy temple: let all the earth keep silence before him" (Hab. 2:20).

3:1–19 A prayer of Habakkuk the prophet

Habakkuk's prayer, like Job's after the Lord's responses to him, confessed humility and awe and a willingness to abide the Lord's management of things (cf. Job 40:3–5; 42:1–6). He recalled the Lord's manifestations during the Exodus and on into the conquest of the promised land (Hab. 3:3–16 and fn.).

The prophet testified that these revelations were a humbling and overwhelming experience. He pledged he would never doubt the Lord's management again; even though crops fail or herds perish, he averred: "Yet I will rejoice in the Lord, I will joy in the God of my salvation" (Hab. 3:18). Then he closed with words of praise and thanksgiving like the closing of a psalm:

> Jehovah, my Lord, is my power:
> he makes my feet like the antelope's,
> and to my exaltation he directs me.
> (Hab. 3:19, translation mine)

The vehicle of Habakkuk's message may be complicated, but the content of it is plain: if in this world injustices seem to predominate, have patience and humbly do what you can; then trust the overall management to the Lord's hands. While allowing agency to everyone, he will help those who trust him when they need help. He "is in his holy temple" and does not need suggestions to see that justice will be done.

ZEPHANIAH

Zephaniah was another prophet who warned Judah about impending invasion and exile, but his prophecies were expressed in terms that refer as much or more to the impending "day of the Lord" (Zeph. 1:7) in the last days. His time was in "the days of Josiah" (Zeph. 1:1), about 639 to 608 B.C. That was the period of the overthrow of Assyria and the rise of Babylon. King Josiah was a righteous king but the son and grandson of idolatrous and evil-doing kings. He was also a great-grandson of the righteous King Hezekiah. The prophet himself was a great-great-grandson of one Hizkiah (the same as *Hezekiah* in Hebrew), and it is entirely possible that he also was of the royal line.

Like much of the prophetic literature, Zephaniah's book is all in Hebrew poetry. Warnings and predictions of doom upon Jerusalem and Judah as well as similar messages for several other nations are expressed in terms relevant to the final destruction of the wicked world. The last chapter contains some particular condemnations of Judah's princes, false judges, and false prophets, but those are followed by anticipation of the time of restoration. The chapter concludes with a joyous heralding of the messianic time, when the Lord will be King (Zeph. 3; BD, "Zephaniah").

COMMENTARY

1:1–18 The word of the Lord which came unto Zephaniah . . . in the days of Josiah . . . king of Judah

The message contained in this revelation may well have come before King Josiah's great reform (2 Kgs. 22:8–23:25), but it seems also to anticipate the religious and moral degeneration that followed his death. Zephaniah condemned the rampant idolatry that would rise again and warned that "the day of the Lord is at hand" (Zeph. 1:7).

Punishment of "the princes, and the king's children" no doubt anticipated that members of the royal family would be taken to Babylon. That prophecy was fulfilled at the death of Josiah's son Jehoiakim and at the captivity of young King Jehoiachin, Josiah's grandson (2 Kgs. 24; Dan. 1:1–6).

Zephaniah also foretold the lament of survivors in Jerusalem. The pillage and plunder of the city would arouse yet more weeping and lament (Zeph. 1:8–13 and fn.). That "great day of the Lord," which was nigh unto the people of that time, prefigured the ultimate day of the Lord at the end of times. In neither event would silver, gold, or other worldly wealth avail anyone of salvation.

2:1–15 Gather yourselves together, yea, gather together, O nation not desired . . . Seek ye the Lord, all ye meek of the earth . . . seek righteousness

The word translated here as *nation* is the Hebrew *goi;* it is a generic word meaning "any or all people." Thus this chapter, which contains condemnations of various peoples other than Israel, begins with an invitation to people not before chosen ("desired") to respond to the call of Abraham and "seek . . . the Lord . . . seek righteousness, seek meekness" (Zeph. 2:3). It was an invitation little heeded before Babylon's invasion but one that will be heard and implemented in the days before the fall of spiritual Babylon.

Zephaniah then warned certain troublesome neighbors all around Judah of their woes to come. First were four city-states of the Philistines on the coastlands of the west and south. Next he addressed Judah's related peoples east and south in Ammon and Moab; their territories included the area of ancient Sodom and Gomorrah, and the prophet warned that their fate could be the same as the fate of those infamous places. Although "Ethiopians" (Heb., *Cushim*) were addressed, the nearer west-Arabians may have been intended (Zeph. 2:12*a*). Finally, the prophet addressed Assyria, to the north and east, which was to fall; he used words like those of Nahum's prophecies of Nineveh's doom.

3:1–7 Woe to her that is filthy and polluted, to the oppressing city!

Once more the prophet addressed Judah and Jerusalem, whose princes, judges, and false prophets had not accepted correction nor obeyed the Lord's messages. They had heeded, rather, their favorite "prophets," who were "light and treacherous persons" (Zeph. 3:4). Recall that these were also the years of Lehi's ministry in Jerusalem (1 Ne. 1:4, 13, 18–20).

The justice of the Lord would fall upon all unjust princes, judges, and prophets—and upon the nation. The Lord had given them assistance before, and he had corrected them before, all to no avail.

3:8–20 Therefore wait ye upon me, saith the Lord, . . . for all the earth shall be devoured with the fire of my jealousy

In conclusion, the prophet turned more specifically to the final cleansing of the earth by the fire of the Lord's zeal (the Hebrew word *qinati,* means, more accurately, "my zeal" rather than "my jealousy" with its bad connotations). Zephaniah prophesied of the gathering of the righteous thereafter and foretold a great contribution to peace and understanding on earth, when the Lord will restore "to the people a pure language, that they may all call upon the name of the Lord, to serve him with one consent." That unique prophecy from Zephaniah is one of great significance and worth; its fulfillment is greatly to be desired. The whole family of man has not been blessed with one *pure* language with which to communicate since Adam and the early patriarchs (Zeph. 3:8–9 and fn.; cf. Moses 6:5–6).

From the farthest reaches of the then-known world, the prophet foresaw worshippers of the Lord gathering. None shall be ashamed of their affiliation, and none shall be haughty because of it. The meek of the earth among the "afflicted and poor people . . . shall trust in the name of the Lord" (Zeph. 3:12; Matt. 5:5). Israel, no longer sinful, will dwell in safety among the peoples.

The prophet's final vision was a glorious one, showing the true Zion people rejoicing in the Lord, with no more enemies and unrighteous kings; "the king of Israel, even the Lord, is in the midst of thee: thou shalt not see evil any more." No more will they need to fear, and they who had sorrowed in exile will be gathered to a solemn assembly of the righteous, including the lame and the scattered remnant from all lands. All the Lord's people will be known and praised in every land; the days of captivity shall be at an end.

Zephaniah saw some special aspects of the great day of the Lord. Whatever the value of his prophetic teachings in the last days of Judah under kings of the line of David, their value can be greater still in the crisis times before the eternal Son of God, the Messiah, returns to reign.

HAGGAI

When the Babylonians had been overthrown by the Persians, about 539 B.C., and the humanitarian religious and political policies of Cyrus prevailed, the return of the people of Judah to rebuild Jerusalem and the temple became possible (Ezra; Isa. 44:28; 45:1–4; and commentary). Groups of the exiles returned, and when enough of them were back in Judah and had built homes or found shelter, the work of rebuilding the temple began. But it proceeded with difficulty, suffering from external and internal opposition.

The prophet Haggai recorded his efforts as an old man to arouse the people to work on the temple until its completion. The period involved was about 536 to 516 B.C., especially the last four of those years.

Haggai seems to have been one who remembered the first temple (Hag. 2:3), which had been built by Solomon about 1000 B.C. and destroyed by Babylonian invaders in 586 B.C. He must have been about eighty years old by the time of the ministry recorded here. The first revelation in his book, dated to the second year of Darius (that is, Darius Hystaspes; BD, "Chronology" p. 640), would have been about 520 B.C. The name *Haggai* means "my festivals," which is appropriate to his concern with the temple, the place of sacred worship festivals and ceremonies. Nothing more is known of his personal life.

COMMENTARY

1:1–15 In the second year of Darius the king, . . . came the word of the Lord by Haggai the prophet unto Zerubbabel . . . governor of Judah, and to Joshua the son of Josedech, the high priest

The "governor," Zerubbabel, was of the royal Davidic lineage (Hag. 1:1c). Haggai's first revelation on the governor's behalf came on the first day of the sixth month (*Elul,* in part of August and September). Joshua, whose name is spelled *Jeshua* in the books of Ezra and Nehemiah, was the son of the last high priest, who was taken captive to Babylon; his grandfather, Seriah, was slain by the Babylonians (2 Kgs. 25:18–21; 1 Chr. 6:14).

The return of the exiles had begun after the edict of Cyrus (ca. 538 B.C.; 2 Chr. 36:22–23). Upon their arrival, the people cleared the place of the former altar of the first temple, built a temporary altar, and made some efforts to begin the rebuilding, but many problems delayed it for eighteen years until this revelation in 520 B.C. (cf. Ezra 1:1–6:15).The prophets Haggai and Zechariah were called to expedite the work when Darius renewed the decree of Cyrus (Hag. 1:2–3; Ezra 6:1–14).

Haggai's first appeal focused on the people's motives. He reminded them that they had rebuilt houses for themselves, some of them fine (Hag. 1:4a), while the Lord's house had remained an open ruin. He informed them that the reason they were not prospering was that the Lord was not blessing them. The governor, the high priest, and the people responded positively to the call of the Lord through the prophet (Hag. 1:5–12).

A second revelation from the Lord assured them of his presence and his approval. He touched the spirit of the leaders and the people, "and they came and did work in the house of the Lord of hosts, their God," twenty-four days after the first revelation to Haggai (Hag. 1:1, 13–15).

2:1–9 In the seventh month, in the one and twentieth day of the month, came the word of the Lord by the prophet Haggai, saying, . . . Who is left among you that saw this house in her first glory? and how do you see it now? is it not in your eyes in comparison of it as nothing?

Nearly a month later (Hag. 2:1; cf. 1:15), enough work had been done for a preliminary evaluation to be made, and it was not good. Nevertheless, the word of the Lord was still encouraging to the leaders and the people; for they were promised that his Spirit would remain with them.

The prophet then opened up to them the distant view, telling of ultimate things, doubtless to help motivate them (Hag. 2:6–7 and fn.). The glory of the future temple would be greater even than the former temple had been, and even though they were not building that future temple, the prophet let them feel a relationship of their work to it (Hag. 2:6–9). This second temple, refurbished in the days of Herod, did become the temple to which Jesus Christ came, and a final replacement will be grander still (Ezek. 40–48).

2:10–19 In the four and twentieth day of the ninth month, in the second year of Darius, came the word of the Lord by Haggai the prophet, saying, . . . Ask now the priests concerning the law

About two months after the revelation about the glory of the future temple, in the ninth month (*Kislev,* in November-December) of the same year, the word of the Lord by Haggai the prophet requested the priests to clarify the laws about cleanliness. The essence was that a clean object touching an unclean one will not cleanse it, but an unclean object touching a clean one will defile it. That was a matter they needed to consider as they worked on the temple, for they needed to keep themselves worthy so as not to defile the holy place.

The prophet reminded the people again that though they had not had good crops in previous years nor in the current year until the time of the grape, fig, pomegranate, and olive harvests, yet the message from the Lord was, "From this day will I bless you."

December is the month of the all-important winter rains that saturate the soil enough to make the next season's crops, so that was a good time to get such a promise of blessings.

2:20–23 And again the word of the Lord came unto Haggai in the four and twentieth day of the month, saying, Speak to Zerubbabel, governor of Judah

On the same winter day as the revelation about cleanliness, Haggai received another revelation for Zerubbabel. Remember that he was of the royal Davidic line (Hag. 2:21; cf. 1:1c); it is evident in this revelation that he was made emblematic of the ultimate Davidic king, the Messiah, who shall come with the shaking of heaven and earth, the overthrowing of earthly kingdoms, and the destruction of warlike peoples by each other. The revelation was complimentary to Zerubbabel, and he was a "chosen" one in his time, but the Messiah at the end of that royal line shall be infinitely greater (Hag. 2:22–23 and fn.).

Thus ends the book of the prophet Haggai. A few important prophecies from the time of the commencement of the second temple and many more for the end of time are in the book of his contemporary prophet, Zechariah.

ZECHARIAH

Zechariah and Haggai were truly contemporaries. A comparison of the early chapters of their books shows that the first revelation to Zechariah was given within two months of the first revelation given to Haggai, and Zechariah's second revelation was received two months after Haggai's third. Ezra recorded that both prophets helped to stimulate and prosper the building of the second temple (Ezra 5:1; 6:14). The introductions to the books of Ezra and Haggai may therefore serve, in part, as an introduction to this book of Zechariah.

More prophecies from Zechariah than from Haggai have been preserved, and they cover a broader spectrum. The first eight chapters of Zechariah's book show the Lord's appeals to the newly returned exiles through visions concerning the restoration they were undertaking. These chapters deal with the problems, opportunities, and challenges of that restoration, especially in the rebuilding of the temple, often with ultimate, messianic implications included. Chapters 9 through 14 are replete with messianic prophecies, culminating in significant details about both the first and the second advent of the Messiah (BD, "Zechariah"). Some of these details are confirmed and reiterated or elucidated in latter-day revelations (e.g., D&C 45:48–53).

Zechariah was "the son of Iddo," who was of "the priests and the Levites that went up with Zerubbabel" in the return to Judah.

Like Ezekiel and Jeremiah, he was a prophet from a priestly lineage (Zech. 1:1; Neh. 12:1–4, 16).

COMMENTARY

1:1–6 Thus saith the Lord of hosts; Turn ye unto me, . . . and I will turn unto you. . . . Be ye not as your fathers, . . . they did not hear, nor hearken unto me, saith the Lord

Zechariah's first message to the former exiles, given between the first and second messages of Haggai during the early autumn, warned the people of Judah returning to their promised land, as the earlier prophets had warned their forefathers: "Turn ye now from your evil ways, and from your evil doings." Their forefathers had not heeded the warnings, but they learned that what the Lord had said he would do, he did (Zech. 1:6*a*).

1:7–21 the word of the Lord unto Zechariah, . . . saying, I saw by night, and behold a man riding upon a red horse, . . . and behind him were there red horses, speckled, and white

The messages of the Lord came to Zechariah in several visions using symbols, which an angel interpreted for the prophet. The first angels and horses represented God's messengers reporting in a valley of Jerusalem that, for a time, all the world was at peace. That may well have referred to the favorable conditions provided by the Persian empire for the peaceful reconstructive work in Judah (Zech. 1:7–11).

One angel asked the Lord when he would have mercy on Jerusalem and on the cities of Judah that had lain waste for seventy years. The Lord replied that he was indeed zealous for the building up of Jerusalem, Zion, the temple, and other cities of the land. He was displeased with the nations that had gone to terrible extremes in afflicting Israel, and he would help her recover (Zech. 1:14–17, 14*a*).

The nations that had "scattered Judah, Israel, and Jerusalem" were represented by four horns. Horns symbolize power, and four represented an excess of it used in the vanquishing of the last four kings of Judah. In contrast to the horns that push and hurt, the prophet next saw four craftsmen or artisans who would build and create, intimidating the "horns" of the surrounding nations who might be tempted to attack Judah again (Zech. 1:18–21 and fn.; for fulfillment, Neh. 4–7).

2:1–13 I lifted up mine eyes again, and looked, and behold a man with a measuring line . . . To measure Jerusalem

In the vision, the prophet asked the intent of a young man with a measuring line who was seeking to know the length and breadth of the future city of Jerusalem. The prophet's angelic guide interceded and he received assurance that Jerusalem would be much greater than a measured, walled city: it will be inhabited by a multitude. There will be no need for walls, for the Lord "will be unto her a wall of fire round about, and will be the glory in the midst of her" (Zech. 2:5). This vision doubtless comforted the people of the time, but it pertains even more to the future Zion, in which the Lord will dwell.

Latter-day events were presaged in the call summoning Israel "from the land of the north" and the invitation to future Zion to deliver herself from the last "Babylon," the wicked world (Zech. 2:6–7 and fn.). All who oppose that last gathering of Israel will be opposed by the Lord, and Zion will "sing and rejoice" at the presence of the Lord dwelling in the midst of her. Then the ancient Abrahamic mission will come to fruition, for "many nations shall be joined to the Lord in that day, and shall be my people." "All flesh" will be reverent when the Lord comes from his holy habitation and dwells upon earth (Zech. 2:8–13 and fn.).

3:1–10 And he shewed me Joshua the high priest standing before the angel of the Lord, and Satan standing at his right hand to resist him

Dramatic actions in this vision involving Satan, Joshua the high priest, and others told the prophet of the purification of the priesthood (and through them, the people of the land) for the coming of the Messiah—the "Branch."

Joshua the high priest, who appears in this vision, was no doubt the same who was involved in Haggai's first vision about two months earlier (Zech. 3:1; cf. Hag. 1:1). In Zechariah's vision, Joshua represented the priesthood leading the people newly returned from exile, who were still in their sins—without cleansing and consecration. Satan was taking advantage of the opportunity to "accuse" them as unworthy (Zech. 3:1*b*-*c*; Rev. 12:9–12 also shows Satan in the role of "accuser").

Knowing Satan's purpose, the angel of the Lord, speaking for the Lord himself, rebuked Satan before he leveled his charge. The angel excused the "filthy garments," because Joshua and the people had just been "plucked out of the fire" of Babylon and were worthy to be cleansed of their iniquities (Zech. 3:2–4). The prophet himself entered the drama and urged that a clean cap (Zech. 3:5*a*) be provided, and so they clothed Joshua with clean garments and put the clean cap upon his head. The angel of the Lord testified (not "protested"; Zech. 3:6) that if the priest and the people would walk in the ways of the Lord and keep their covenants, they would win a place among the angels (Zech. 3:7*c*). To Joshua and those whom he taught as "fellows" that sat before him—who were men of merit—the angel promised that God will bring forth His servant the Branch, the Messiah (Zech. 3:8*a*).

The "stone," which was "laid before Joshua" and had "seven eyes" and divine engraving, could symbolize an instrument prepared to reveal to the high priest what he needed to know to "remove the iniquity" of the land "in one day" (Zech. 3:9; cf. BD and TG, "Urim and Thummim"). Then the ideal era could begin, with every family well provided for and at peace under their own vine and fig tree (Zech. 3:10; Micah 4:4).

4:1–14 And the angel that talked with me came again, and waked me, . . . And said unto me, What seest thou? And I said, . . . a candlestick all of gold, with a bowl upon the top of it, and his seven lamps thereon, and seven pipes to the seven lamps, which are upon the top thereof: And two olive trees by it

The fifth vision to Zechariah, "as a man that is wakened out of his sleep," was also one with both immediate and ultimate significance. The "candlestick" was not a stick for a candle but the *menorah*, the seven-branched lamp of the tabernacle and temple (Zech.

683

4:2*a*). Doubtless such a lamp was made for the second temple, which was being built. The promise was given to Zerubbabel that he would overcome a "mountain" of problems and finally bring the capstone of the temple to its place (Zech. 4:7). His hands had helped lay the foundation and would finish it with the help of the priesthood—aided by the use of the stone with seven eyes (Zech. 4:9–10; cf. 3:9). His success, however, would be "not by might, nor by power, but by my spirit, saith the Lord of hosts." That statement has been a great and useful revelation applied by many latter-day leaders and should be a reminder to some in modern Israel.

This *menorah* was also symbolic. It had a bowl above it with two olive trees, one to the right and one to the left, which had two "branches" pouring oil through two golden pipes, apparently into the bowl, and thence into the seven pipes leading to the seven lamps (Zech. 4:2–3, 11–12). That could symbolize divine light, provided through prophets, to enlighten the temple worshippers. But there is additional significance in the angel's explanation that the two olive trees were not representative of prophets in general but of "the two anointed ones, that stand by the Lord of the whole earth." This revelation correlates with others in pointing to the two special prophets who will have a mission in Jerusalem of the last days. They will preach and will be slain there, but they will be raised up after three days, just before the blowing of the seventh trumpet, heralding the millennial reign (Zech. 4:11–14, 14*a*).

5:1–4 Then I . . . looked, and behold a flying roll

The sixth vision displayed a huge scroll, unrolled and bearing curses upon sins, such as "every one that stealeth" and "every one that sweareth" for they would be destroyed. The size of the scroll—fifteen feet by thirty—indicates the multitude of sins. This has significance especially for the last days.

5:5–11 Then the angel that talked with me went forth, and said unto me, Lift up now thine eyes. . . . And I said, What is it? And he said, This is an ephah that goeth forth. . . . And he said, This is wickedness

The seventh vision also pertained to wickedness being

removed from the earth. Apparently, the woman sitting in the midst of the *ephah*, or measure, with "their resemblance through all the earth" and with "a talent of lead" cast "upon the mouth thereof," symbolized the carrying away of wickedness back to "Shinar," or Babylon, which represents the wicked world, from which it came. The symbolism of the two women with wings of a stork (a migratory bird) could represent the grace of the Lord in removing sin back to its origins, thus stifling it.

6:1–8 And I turned, and lifted up mine eyes, and looked, and, behold, there came four chariots out from between two mountains

In the eighth and last vision of this series, Zechariah learned that the bearers of the Lord's power in all four directions of the earth brought indications that in the land of the north the pacifying was completed. No other information was revealed on this point.

6:9–15 And the word of the Lord came unto me, saying, Take of them of the captivity, . . . and go into the house of Josiah . . . Then take silver and gold, and make crowns, and set them upon the head of Joshua

Three men, bearing silver and gold offerings from former Babylonian areas, arrived. Two crowns were made from the precious metals—one for the high priest, Joshua, and possibly the other for Zerubbabel, governor, a descendant of David. The attention of Joshua was then directed to the future divine Branch, the Messiah, who will instigate the building of the final temple from whence he will rule (Zech. 6:12–13). Meanwhile, the crowns were to be kept in the second temple, whose construction was underway, as a memorial to those who brought the gifts from former Babylon. If the people continued obedient, more assistance would come from "far off" to help finish that temple.

7:1–14 in the fourth year of king Darius, that the word of the Lord came unto Zechariah . . . When they had sent . . . Sherezer and Regem-melech, and their men, to pray before the Lord

About two years after the prophet's first revelations came this revelation in response to the inquiries by a delegation who wanted to know about continuing the annual fasts in the fifth month to commemorate the destruction of the first temple and in the seventh month to commemorate the assassination of Gedaliah. The questions may have arisen because the return and the rebuilding of the city and temple were underway.

The first reply was a question about the former value of those fasts: "Did ye at all fast unto me, even to me?" Unless fasting were a function of worship, not merely a time of hunger followed by eating and drinking for their own satisfaction, its value was questionable.

The prophet suggested that they hearken to the word of the Lord sent by earlier prophets when Jerusalem and the other cities were inhabited and prosperous. The essential message was to "execute true judgment, and shew mercy and compassions every man to his brother: And oppress not the widow, nor the fatherless, the stranger, nor the poor," nor "imagine evil against his brother in your heart." Compare the Lord's teaching through Isaiah about the true purpose of fasting (Isa. 58:5–7). The former Israelites had refused to hearken and made their hearts adamant, which had brought "great wrath from the Lord of hosts." He had called but they would not hear; so when they cried, he would not hear and had let them be scattered—the ten tribes to Assyria, and Judah to Babylon.

8:1–23 Again the word of the Lord of hosts came to me

This revelation is a series of ten declarations by the Lord through the prophet Zechariah, each headed by "Thus saith the Lord."

The first and second declarations are about the Lord's return to Jerusalem with the Jews to rebuild after their exile in Babylon. That return symbolized the future time when "Jerusalem shall be called a city of truth; and the mountain of the Lord of hosts the holy mountain" (Zech. 8:3).

The third, fourth, and fifth declarations anticipated a time when people of all ages shall dwell in Jerusalem and the streets will be full of boys and girls playing; it will be marvelous in the eyes of both man and God. That is a prophecy applicable to the final gathering, when the people of Israel will again be the Lord's people and he "will be their God, in truth and in righteousness." That condition has not yet been reached in modern Israel, a largely secular state, for most of its people are not religious, but they sometimes point to evidences of this prophecy being fulfilled.

The sixth declaration reviewed again the days of the previous prophets, when there was no obedience and no peace. Then it addressed the more hopeful future situation when the Lord will help his people prosper, that they may cease to be "a curse among the heathen" and become "a blessing"; he urged them to be strong (Zech. 8:13).

The seventh contrasted the necessity to punish their fathers of apostate times with the Lord's wish to bless the returning exiles, if they will only speak truth, do justice in truth and peace, contemplate no evil, and love no falsity. This passage is a gem among Zechariah's teachings (Zech. 8:14–17).

The eighth declaration was, in a way, a response to the question about fasts: the fasts that commemorated former times of destruction were to be changed to feasts of joy and gladness, wherein people could "love the truth and peace" (Zech. 8:19; cf. 7:3).

The ninth anticipated a time when peoples from many cities will gather to pray; eventually, peoples of great nations will seek the Lord, coming to pray in Jerusalem (Zech. 8:20–22).

The tenth foresaw the fulfillment of the mission of Israel, when people of all languages and nations will follow the people of Judah—indeed, all Israel—in seeing that God is with them. Although it was not made clear here that this great conversion process was in preparation for the time of the Messiah, messianic concepts are present in most of Zechariah's revelations.

9:1–8 in the land of Hadrach, and Damascus shall be the rest thereof: when the eyes of . . . all the tribes of Israel, shall be toward the Lord

This short revelation is a "burden" to Syrian and Phoenician cities and to five Philistine cities, foretelling their destruction when Israel returns to the Lord.

9:9–17 Rejoice greatly, O daughter of Zion; . . . behold, thy King cometh unto thee: he is just, and having salvation; lowly, and riding upon an ass, and upon a colt the foal of an ass

Then the prophet turned to Judah and the first advent of the King (Messiah) in his triumphal entry (Zech. 9:9 and fn.). Zechariah also addressed Ephraim and all Israel of the last days concerning the establishment of the kingdom of the Lord "from sea even to sea, and from the river even to the ends of the earth" (Zech. 9:10 and fn.). He foresaw salvation from death, wrought by the shedding of the mortal blood of the Savior, and the release of all the dead from the spirit prison (Zech. 9:11–12 and fn.).

Returning to the theme of the establishment of the kingdom of the Lord in the last days, the prophet told in warlike language about Judah and Ephraim, as leaders of all Israel, overcoming all the world (Zech. 9:13–16 and fn.). Compare the language and theme of the latter-day hymn, "Hope of Israel" (*Hymns* [Salt Lake City: The Church of Jesus Christ of Latter-day Saints, 1985], no. 259).

In a final poetic stanza he spoke of the Lord's great goodness and beauty and the joy of the people. "New wine" is the phrase used to translate the Hebrew *tirosh yenovev,* which is fresh, unfermented grape juice.

10:1–12 And I will strengthen the house of Judah, and I will save the house of Joseph

The theme of chapter 10 is announced in verse 6. The prophet opened with a poetic verse about the renewed, verdant world, which he then contrasted with the "false dreams" of idolatrous "diviners" that had led the flocks of Israel astray. Because of such false shepherds, the Lord had to punish "the goats" for a time in exile, but Judah had been restored (Zech. 10:1–3). In a different metaphor, the prophet explained that out of Judah would come the Cornerstone—even He of the "nail" in a sure place, the Savior (Zech. 10:4a–b).

Then Zechariah returned to the missions of Judah and Joseph in the latter days, when they would be strengthened, saved, and restored. Those of Ephraim, the birthright son of Joseph, were scattered, for the Lord did "sow them among the people," but in time their descendants would be gathered out of exile ("Egypt" and "Assyria") and returned to their birthright lands (Zech. 10:7–10). Miraculous will be their gathering and their strengthening, and they shall walk in the name of the Lord.

11:1–17 And I took my staff, even Beauty, and cut it asunder, that I might break my covenant which I had made with all the people. . . . Then I cut asunder mine other staff, even Bands, that I might break the brotherhood between Judah and Israel

From the midst of this prophecy (Zech. 11:10, 14) came the metaphors of the Lord's rejection of those of the chosen people who had previously failed to keep their covenants with God and with each other.

The revelation opened with lamentations over the desolation of northern Israel, ranging from the southern mountains of Lebanon to the forests of Bashan and the valley of the Jordan. The prophet called for shepherds to "Feed the flock of the slaughter; Whose possessors slay them," for their former "shepherds pity them not." The time of restoration would come when the invading "inhabitants of the land" would no longer possess it.

The time would come to feed the poor of the flock again, the flock first guarded and guided by the staff "Beauty" (Heb., *no'am,* meaning "pleasantness"—as of love) and the staff "Bands" (Heb., *hovelim,* "bindings"—as of brotherhood). Previously the Lord had "cut off in one month" three shepherds—perhaps the last three kings of northern Israel or the last three of Judah, when the captivity and scattering began. At that time, because they had broken their covenant, the Lord broke (temporarily) the covenant of loving care he had made with them (the staff called "Beauty"; Zech. 11:10). When they were taken captive, they knew it was according to the word of the Lord.

Briefly the prophet saw a divine symbol. In vision he saw someone receive his "price" for betraying the Lord; it was the price of a slave, thirty pieces of silver. Symbolically, the Lord told the prophet to "cast it unto the potter," which he did "in the house of the Lord" (Zech. 11:13 and fn.).

Then the staff of "Bands" was broken, symbolizing the breaking of the bonds of brotherhood between remnant Judah and scattered Israel. Judah suffered thereafter under a "foolish shepherd," such as Herod the Great, and perhaps the tyrant idol-shepherds of lands where the people of Judah subsequently lived and suffered, foolish shepherds who cared not for the flocks (Zech. 11:15–17).

12:1–14 The burden of the word of the Lord for Israel . . . Behold, I will make Jerusalem a cup of trembling unto all the people round about, when they shall be in the siege both against Judah and against Jerusalem

Note in verse 1 the description of the dual nature of man, with an indwelling spirit (Zech. 12:1*b*).

Many problems have long prevailed in the interpretation of the prophecy recorded in Zechariah 12, but latter-day revelation and events are making the meaning clear. The twentieth century has already seen Jerusalem become "a cup of trembling" and "a burdensome stone" for some Middle Eastern nations and for the modern community of nations (Zech. 12:2–3). The time of the great siege is not as yet evident (Zech. 12:2–5). But Jerusalem will not be captured nor destroyed again, for the Lord shall defend it, and the attackers will be destroyed (Zech. 12:6–9*a–b*).

Then a spirit of grace and supplication for favor will come over Jerusalem and the rulers thereof, for the Lord has said, "They shall look upon me whom they have pierced" and mourn like the mourning for an only son, even the firstborn. The meaning and implications are clear enough, but latter-day revelations elaborate on them (Zech. 12:10–14 and fn.; D&C 45:45–56).

13:1–9 And one shall say unto him, What are these wounds in thine hands? Then he shall answer, Those with which I was wounded in the house of my friends

The central event of this prophecy is the identification of the martyred Redeemer (Zech. 13:6 and fn.; D&C 45:45–56). Preparatory to it, some will be converted to righteousness, and a baptismal place will be available for washing away their sins and uncleanness (Zech. 13:1*a*). Mistaken faith and modern idolatry will diminish, but many people will still reject the true prophets and prophecy, and no wonder, for many false prophets will be ashamed of their failure to know truth and deny their prophetic craft.

Some latter-day restorations of "plain and precious parts" make the transition to the next verse clear, telling who appeared with marks of wounds in hands and feet (Zech. 13:6; D&C 45:48–54).

It seems that Zechariah then saw a flashback to the strife between those who believed and those who did not believe in the Messiah at the time of his crucifixion and at the rise of his Church, when many were scattered, but a portion were tried and proved as gold. They became the Shepherd's people, and the Lord was their God. Those events may also presage events of the last days, before the Savior's reign of peace begins (Zech. 13:7–9).

14:1–21 Behold, the day of the Lord cometh, ...For I will gather all nations against Jerusalem to battle . . . Then shall the Lord go forth, and fight against those nations

This chapter begins with a reprise of the situation described in chapter 12. Here it is made plain that the city will suffer a siege and much violence before the Lord shall appear upon the Mount of Olives, be identified, and the foes of Jerusalem be vanquished (Zech. 14:1–4 and all fn.). It is evident that "plain and precious things" from here, along with those from 13:6 and 12:10, have been transmitted out of sequence; compare the sequence in Doctrine and Covenants 45:45–56, already cited.

The "valley" created may well become the valley of Jehovah's judgment (Zech. 14:5; cf. Joel 3:2, 14). The light of one day shall not be sufficient for that great event, so a day, a night, and a day without darkness will repeat a joyous phenomenon seen before in the western continent at the birth of the Messiah (Zech. 14:6–7; Hel. 14:3–7; 3 Ne. 1:13–19).

Another phenomenon, foretold by other prophets, was also foreseen by Zechariah: "living waters" from Jerusalem going to the seas (Zech. 14:8*a*–*b*).

A precious truth revealed to Zechariah is the plain statement that the Lord is the Messiah, the King over all the earth (Zech. 14:9*a*).

Land renewal will provide living space (Zech. 14:10–11).

Record of the plagues and battles before the kingdom of God is established seems to be out of place here, or perhaps it was another flashback (Zech. 14:12–15, 1–3; 12:2–8).

Finally, scenes of the peaceful city and world were revealed to the prophet. Converts from the nations that had come to fight will stay to "worship the King, the Lord of hosts" (Zech. 14:16*a*–*b*). Others who do not accept him must learn to do so or suffer the consequences.

All things, from the bells on the horses to the pots in the temple—even the cooking pots—will be dedicated to their functions in the kingdom of the Lord and inscribed with words that mean "sacred to the Lord" (Zech. 14:20–21).

"There shall be no more the Canaanite" (Zech. 14:21) is a metaphorical way of saying that in that future day, there will be no more unconsecrated people, for all who remain will have had the opportunity to become true members of the Lord's kingdom.

Great are the words of Zechariah, prophet of the former restoration at the time of the return from Babylon of old and prophet of the latter-day restoration at the time of the deliverance of all true believers from the Babylon of the wicked world and the commencement of the reign of the Messiah.

MALACHI

The name *Malachi* means "my errand-bearer" or "my messenger." It is such an appropriate label for a prophet that some have wondered whether it could be his title and not his name. It makes no difference, but it is quite common in the Old Testament for a proper name to have meaning related to the work of the one who bears it.

Neither the time and place of Malachi's work nor his origin and background are known. He was aware of priestly duties, and his first two chapters concern unacceptable offerings, unacceptable priests, and unacceptable behavior of the Lord's people. But those are all topics appropriate to many a prophet's mission and do not necessarily suggest his time as a prophet. It is commonly assumed that his work was after the time of Haggai and Zechariah, after the second temple had been built and some malpractices had again set in (BD, "Malachi").

Malachi's last two chapters anticipate a forerunner to the Savior; they also deal with tithes and offerings, the second advent of the Savior, and the restoration of priesthood power to seal on earth and in heaven blessings in eternal covenants. Indeed, the whole book of Malachi has much relevance for the latter days. Moroni, herald angel of the last dispensation, cited some prophecies by Malachi (JS–H 1:36–39), indicating that their fulfillment would come in this dispensation. There are many references to the book of Malachi in the Doctrine and Covenants.

Other ancient historical works, such as the books of the Maccabees from a later century, might well have been included in the Old Testament canon; but since they are not, the testimony of Malachi is its prophetic capstone.

COMMENTARY

1:1–14 I have loved you, saith the Lord. Yet ye say, Wherein hast thou loved us?

The mode of teaching characteristic of Malachi is to pose a question or make an assertion from the Lord and then give his diagnosis and prescription. In this case the Lord, through Malachi, invoked the well-known history—why Israel ("Jacob") had been blessed with many blessings whereas Edom had not. Those were the facts behind the shocking rhetoric, "I loved Jacob, And I hated Esau," attributed to the Lord. That treatment was based not upon favoritism for the individual but upon the principle that blessings result from obedience to God's laws. Jacob's blessings were pronounced upon him while he was still unworthy (as is true of many of us), and fulfillment of them came only when he fulfilled the law upon which they were based (BD, "Jacob"). Esau and Edom went another way. The Lord does not exalt people who live even on "the border of wickedness" (Mal. 1:4; TG, "Blessing"; "Obedience"). More specifically to the point, the prophet revealed that through the years the Lord was not content with Israel's rituals of worship. They did not honor God as either father or master, even offering "polluted bread" and blemished animals as sacrifices.

Malachi tried to teach the Israel of his time the reasonable principles of cause and effect, asking whether they thought God would be gracious to them simply because of who they were. Then he reasoned, when one opens or shuts a door, it is for a purpose; when one kindles a fire on the altar, it is for a reason; just so, one must have a sincere purpose in mind when offering sacrifices and do it righteously or the Lord will neither accept the offerings nor bless the worshipper.

The prophet tried to shock Israel with the future righteousness of converted people of other nations ("the Gentiles") in contrast to Israel's profaning his holy name by offering "contemptible" offerings, all the while protesting that worship was "a weariness." Among the heathen, said he, the name of the Lord would be more revered than by any Israelite who saved a good animal for himself and sacrificed a blemished one (Mal. 1:11–14). To do so was to show contempt for "the table of the Lord." In latter days comparable contempt could occur in the perfunctory paying of tithes and offerings, thoughtless sacrament worship, or unthinking performance of temple ordinances.

2:1–10 And now, O ye priests, this commandment is for you. If ye will not hear, and if ye will not lay it to heart, to give glory unto my name, saith the Lord of hosts, I will even send a curse upon you

The Lord had a covenant with Levi, a covenant for life, and a covenant of peace; but it required the Levites' reverent and dedicated performance of their duties. With the ideal priest, "the law of truth was in his mouth" and he was to act in peace and fairness, so that he might teach and turn many away from sin. He was to be knowledgeable, so that people could learn from his words as a spokesman for the Lord. But the priests had departed from such demeanor and duties, corrupting their covenant and causing many to stumble; therefore, priests had lost their reputation "before all the people" (Mal. 2:6–9).

In conclusion, the prophet taught excellent theology and ethics: we all have one father, even God, and are brothers and sisters; why then would we "deal treacherously" with each other, profaning the covenants that teach us good behavior? This passage is an Old Testament gem of religion and humanity (Mal. 2:10).

2:11–17 Judah hath dealt treacherously, and an abomination is committed in Israel and in Jerusalem; for Judah hath profaned the holiness of the Lord which he loved, and hath married the daughter of a strange god

The prophet began his lesson on fidelity and commitment by recalling treachery committed in Judah and Israel by those who had "profaned the holiness of the Lord" by marrying "the daughter of a strange god" by idolatry. He warned that the Lord will "cut off the man that doeth this, the master and the scholar." Weeping and covering the altar of the Lord with tears in false devotion to cover one's aberrations will not gain blessings.

Malachi spoke then of the covenant of Israel with God as if it were a covenant of marriage of a man with the wife of his youth, against whom he has dealt treacherously even though she is his companion and the wife of his covenant. The metaphor reflected both the infidelity of individual men and the apostasy of Israel. But the prophet illustrated the latter point more poignantly by details of the marriage covenant and commitment. The translation is difficult, but it could be rendered from the Hebrew thus: "And not one hath done so who had a remnant of the Spirit! For what one, seeking a godly seed, if ye take heed in your spirit, would deal treacherously with the wife of your youth?" (Mal. 2:15). Then he declared that the Lord himself "hateth putting away." The assertion that one guilty of infidelity "covereth violence with his garment" and the admonition to "take heed to your spirit, that ye deal not treacherously" are applicable in all latter-day marriages, and especially in temple marriages (Mal. 2:16).

It is a masterpiece of understatement to assert that one has "wearied the Lord" who says, "Every one that doeth evil is good in the sight of the Lord, and he delighteth in them; or, Where is the God of judgment?" (Mal. 2:17) To say so is to question the justice of God and question his caring—or even his existence.

3:1– 6 Behold, I will send my messenger, and he shall prepare the way before me: and the Lord, whom ye seek, shall suddenly come to his temple

As is evident from the many cross-references to the verses of this segment of Malachi's prophecies, a messenger prepared the way for the coming of the Lord in both his first advent and his anticipated second advent. But it is also evident that it will be in his second advent that the Messiah's coming will be as a refiner's fire, to "purify the sons of Levi, and purge them as gold and silver," so that they may function again at the altars and their offerings will be acceptable to the Lord (Mal. 3:3; D&C 13; 84:33–34; 124:39;

128:24). The Judgment before the Millennium will condemn sorcerers, adulterers, false swearers, and oppressors of hirelings, widows, and orphans. Only spiritually true sons of Jacob, the "seed of Abraham" either by birth or by conversion (Abr. 2:10) will not be consumed, for the Lord will not change his standards.

3:7–18 Even from the days of your fathers ye are gone away from mine ordinances, and have not kept them. Return unto me, and I will return unto you, saith the Lord of hosts

First among the exhibits of ways Israel had not kept the covenants was their "robbing" God of tithes and offerings. The method of teaching Malachi used should have shocked even the guilty. The generous promises, on the other hand, should have impressed them—and us—to repent and tithe honestly (Mal. 3:7–12).

The second charge was also serious: they had doubted God's justice because they had kept the ordinances and claimed to have walked soberly and humbly before the Lord, but they observed that the proud seem happy, the wicked prosper, and they that test God seem to get away with it (Mal. 3:13–15; cf. 2:17). For the truly humble and faithful among them, there was reassurance as they comforted each other, for the prophet taught them about a "book of remembrance" in which the deeds of the righteous are recorded. They shall be part of the Lord's royal treasure and be saved; the same Hebrew word rendered *jewels* here is also rendered *peculiar treasure* (cf. Ex. 19:5 and commentary). Thus, though injustices appear in this world, justice with due rewards and punishment will come later (Mal. 3:16–18 and fn.).

4:1–6 For, behold, the day cometh, that shall burn as an oven; and all the proud, yea, and all that do wickedly, shall be stubble: and the day that cometh shall burn them up

The topic of the last part of the foregoing chapter is continued with a terrible forecast of the fate of the wicked at the end of the wicked world (Mal. 4:1 and fn.).

When the Lord reigns on earth, all who revere and serve him will go forth under his watchful care. The "Sun of righteousness" is also written "Son of Righteousness"; but either way, it refers to the Savior (Mal. 4:2 and fn.).

The metaphor of treading down the wicked refers to the overcoming of all wickedness; the imagery comes from treading over the ashes of the wickedness that has been cleansed by fire (Mal. 4:3*a*). The way to qualify for salvation and triumph over wickedness, ultimately, is to keep the commandments, ordinances, and regulations; they help one steadily resist evil (Mal. 4:4*a*–*b*).

Elijah's latter-day mission is the ultimate extension of his earthlife mission: to turn hearts to God, to family, and to the promises made to the fathers (Mal. 4:5–6 and fn.; cf. 1 Kgs. 18:37). The description of Elijah's mission as given here (and in 3 Ne. 25:5–6) is understandable, but it was clarified by Moroni (JS–H 1:36–39; for fulfillment, see D&C 110:13–16). Through the gospel teachings and ordinances, the Lord will prepare a nucleus of true servants to help in teaching his gospel and in administering his kingdom now and when he comes. Then all who will listen will hear the gospel, and the earth will not be smitten with a curse of confusion and rebellion; rather, it will be renewed and restored to its paradisiacal glory.

Such are the prophecies of the last prophet of the Old Testament, who was also a herald of restorations in the last days, leading to the time when "the Lord, whom ye seek, shall suddenly come to his temple" (Mal. 3:1).

INDEX

Aaron: is appointed as spokesman,
89; is called of God, 91; holds up
Moses' hands, 102; holy garments
worn by, 115–16; fashions
golden calf, 119–20; complains of
Moses' marriage, 153; death of,
159

Aaronic priests: public consecration
of, 130; were not to care for dead
bodies, 138–39; Levites
appointed to assist, 147

Abel, 20–21

Abraham: introduction of, 35–36;
details about, in Pearl of Great
Price, 36; moves southward with
family and converts, 37; land
promised to, 37–38, 40; in Egypt,
38–39; divides land with Lot,
39–40; is identified as descendant
of Heber, 40–41; rescues Lot
from captivity, 41; meets kings,
including Melchizedek, 41–42;
asks Lord about promised seed,
42–43; revelations given to, 43,
45, 47; and Hagar, 44; receives
new name, 45; is promised a
son, 46–48; entertains three

messengers, 47–48; pleads for
Sodom, 48; makes covenant of
peace with Philistines, 50–51;
agrees to sacrifice Isaac, 51;
shows honesty in bargaining, 52;
and Keturah, 54; sons of, 54–55;
death of, 55; as "father of the
faithful," 55

Abrahamic covenant, 45–46;
circumcision as sign of, 46, 47,
50; is renewed with Isaac, 57;
involves sharing gospel, 58,
533–34, 682; is renewed with
Jacob, 60–61, 67; Israelites as
bearers of, 90; carried on by holy
people, 174; psalm recalling, 435.
See also Covenant

Abram. *See* Abraham

Absalom, 265–69

Accountability: age of, 46; preferring
slavery over, 154; involved in
agency, 187–88; for one's own
sins, 104–5, 185, 286, 594–95

Achan, 198

Acrostic poetry, 422, 424, 452,
455–60, 468, 577–78, 665

Adam: identified as Michael, 10;

170, 435, 533–34; Pharaoh
increases burdens of, 91–92;
compensation of, with Egyptian
valuables, 96, 98; leave Egypt,
98; God leads, with pillar of
cloud and fire, 99; are pursued
by Egyptians, 99; cross Red Sea,
99–100; murmuring of, 101, 152,
154; first battle of, 102; as
"peculiar treasure," 103; feared to
receive direct revelation, 104,
108; covenant to obey law of
Moses, 111–12; corrupt
themselves in Moses' absence,
119–20; census taken of, 145,
146, 161; complaints of, prevent
inheritance of promised land,
155; Moses reviews travels of,
168–69; trade with Tyre and
Sidon, 259, 279, 334; history of,
recounted in psalms, 439–40,
449–50, 465; wicked leaders of,
504, 505–6, 534
Issachar, 80, 191, 204

Jacob (Israel): birth of, 56; integrity
of, 56–57; Esau "sells" birthright
to, 57; Isaac confers birthright on,
59; is sent away to find wife, 60;
revelations received by, 61, 64;
works fourteen years for Rachel,
62; children of, 62, 68; leaves
Laban's employ, 63–64; seeks
peace with Esau, 64, 65–66;
wrestles for blessing and receives
new name, 65; settles in
promised land, 66; sons of,
avenge sister, 66–67; sons of, buy
grain in Egypt, 73–75; moves
family to Egypt, 75–77; gives
blessing to Pharaoh, 77; blesses
Joseph's sons, 78–79; prophesies

regarding sons, 79–81; death of,
81; burial of, 82
Jacob's well, 66, 208
Japheth, son of Noah, 32, 33
Jealousy, 59–60, 64, 69, 245–46
Jehovah, 9–10; terms referring to,
29; translation of name of, 88;
presence of, signified by cloud,
99, 125–26, 151, 282, 345; voice
of, Israel had heard, 170–71;
Jesus as, 512, 525
Jephthah, 218–19
Jeremiah, 540–51; foreordination of,
541; calling of, 541–42; people
plot to kill, 550, 560; leaves
ministry for a time, 552; is told
not to marry, 553; rejection of,
555; torture of, 556, 567–68;
confronts false prophet, 561;
communicates with exiles,
561–62; imprisonment of, 565,
567–68; scribe of, 567, 571, 575;
Babylonians' treatment of, 569;
prophecies of, to "other nations,"
572–75; as author of
Lamentations, 577
Jericho, siege of, 198
Jeroboam, 287–90
Jerusalem, 42; conquest of, 211;
becomes David's capital, 258–59,
421; ark is transported to,
260–61, 333–34; falls to Babylon,
363–64, 568–69; walls of, rebuilt,
377, 382; Assyrian siege of, 509,
517, 521; as valley of vision,
517–18; two prophets in, 531,
684; New, 538; pending
destruction of, 545; Babylonian
siege of, 564–66; prophet's
lament over, 578; measuring,
Zechariah's vision of, 682; Lord
to battle for, 691

Retribution, law of, 109, 141
Reuben, 68, 69, 73, 79; tribe of, 164, 190
Revelation: preparing to receive, 103, 187; direct, Israelites feared to receive, 104, 108; received through Urim and Thummim, 115–16; to multitude of Israel, 172; through visions, 503, 504
Reverence: removing shoes as sign of, 87; access to, 406; "fear" of Lord as, 471–72, 476; commendation of, 492–93; symbolized by seraphim, 507
River Jordan, Israel crosses, 196
Rivers: of Eden, 11; flowing from temple, 613–14
Rock: Moses strikes, to bring forth water, 158; as metaphor for Deity, 434
Rods representing tribes of Israel, 156, 588
Romantic love, 497–501
Rosh Hashanah, 163, 368, 379
Ruth, 224–29, 514

Sabbath: introduction of, 8–9; following Passover, 97; days especially designated as, 97, 140; manna not to be gathered on, 101; commandments regarding, 105, 110; year of, for land, 110, 141; as symbol of covenant, 118, 535; Nehemiah corrects violations of, 383; keeping, versus desecrating, 554
Sabbatical years, 179
Sacrifices: offered by Adam, 20; in similitude of Christ, 20–21, 127; offered by Noah, 30; procedures for, in law of Moses, 116–17; purpose of, 117–18, 128;

symbolic elements of, 128; proper offering of, 134, 694; of animals without blemish, 139; animals improperly saved for, 242–43; offered in Solomon's temple, 283; priests of Baal offered as, 307–8; human, 547, 555, 598; polluted, 694–95. *See also* Offerings
Salvation: yearning for, 418; hope of, 418–19, 429; as gift of Savior, 422, 445; way to, 533, 698; cannot be bought with gold, 673
Samaritans, 315–16, 366, 369, 377–78
Samson, 220–21
Samuel, books of, 230–31, 253, 254–55
Samuel: parents of, 231; birth and childhood of, 231–33; is called by Lord, 233–34; helps Israel defeat Philistines, 237; unrighteous sons of, 237; warns against having king in Israel, 237; anoints Saul as king, 238; teachings of, to Israel, 240; reproves Saul for disobedience, 242–43; anoints David king, 243; death of, 249
Sanctuary, instructions for building, 112–13
Sarah: as Abram's sister, 38–39, 49; and Hagar, 44; receives new name, 46; laughs at promise of son, 47–48; bears Isaac, 50; death of, 52
Satan: sought to destroy agency, 12; metaphorically called "serpent," 14, 16–17; tempts Adam and Eve in garden, 14; cursing of, 16; power to cast out, 16; Cain covenants with, 21; opposes God in heavenly council, 394; binding